MATHS IN ACTION

Intermediate 2
MATHEMATICS

D. Brown
R. Howat
G. Marra
E. Mullan
R. Murray
K. Nisbet
J. Thomson

First published in 1999 by:
Thomas Nelson and Sons Ltd

Reprinted in 2003 by:
Nelson Thornes Ltd
Delta Place
27 Bath Road
CHELTENHAM
GL53 7TH
United Kingdom

09 10 11 12 / 15 14 13

A catalogue record of this book is available from the British Library

ISBN 978 0 17 431494 3

Project Manager: Lesley Wiseman
Editor: Margaret Cameron

Page make-up by Upstream, London

Printed by Multivista Global Ltd

Contents

Preface

The purpose of this volume is to provide a comprehensive package of work, study and practice for the student attempting Intermediate 2 Mathematics.

It contains four units of work providing a course of study for Mathematics 1, Mathematics 2, Mathematics 3 and Applications of Mathematics.

All topics mentioned in the Arrangements documents are well covered.

It is assumed that the student has access to a scientific calculator. Whenever you use a calculator, an idea of the result expected should already have formed in your mind. *Estimate, calculate* and *check* are the buzzwords. You should be aware, of course, that there are many makes of scientific calculator and that variations of procedures exist. Selecting one calculator and sticking to it throughout the course is recommended.

Although you are primarily following the Intermediate 2 course to pass exams and gain qualifications, remember that maths can be fun. There is a lot more to the subject than the bare syllabus content. Look for mathematics everywhere. Graphics calculators and computers open many doors: the Internet is simply bulging with ideas.

A companion Resource book has also been written to supplement this volume. It contains a bank of material to assist in revision, homework and extension.

Some questions and exercises are deliberately more difficult than the rest, and these have a tint behind them. Some explanations are also tinted, and you only need to do this material if you are aiming for one of the higher grades.

1 Significant Figures

Reminder

Look at the examples to remind you of the rules for rounding numbers and writing numbers in standard form.

Example 1 Round 3.4156 and 3.4145 each to 2 decimal places.

Score out the digits you don't need. 3.41~~56~~ 3.41~~45~~

Look at the digit in the third decimal place.

If it is 5 or more then add 1 to the figure in the second decimal place. ↓ 3.4156 = 3.42 to 2 decimal places.

If it less than 5 then ignore it. 3.4145 = 3.41 to 2 decimal places.

Example 2 Write 653 and 0.0238 in standard form.

$653 = 6.53 \times 10^2$

$0.0238 = 2.38 \times 10^{-2}$

STARTING POINTS

1 Round the following numbers to 2 decimal places.
a 3.441 **b** 0.4676 **c** 81.255 **d** 79.050 **e** 0.016 **f** 0.008

2 Work out the following correct to 1 decimal place.
a 3.42×2.1 **b** $3.1 + 0.95$ **c** $17.3 \div 8.1$ **d** $1.005 - 0.41$ **e** $\sqrt{80}$ **f** 0.7^2

3 Jack Bean's annual salary is £25 000.
Calculate correct to 2 decimal places:
a his monthly income
b his weekly income.

4 A car uses 47 litres of petrol travelling 600 km.
Calculate correct to 2 decimal places:
a the petrol consumption in kilometres per litre
b the petrol consumption in litres per kilometre.

5 Express the following numbers in standard form.
a 341 **b** 7814 **c** 93 127 **d** 0.0271 **e** 0.0005

6 Write these numbers out in full.
a 3.94×10^3 **b** 8.1×10^5 **c** 6×10^1 **d** 1.10×10^{-1} **e** 6.69×10^{-3}

7 The radius of the Earth's orbit is 9.3×10^7 miles.
Calculate:
a the diameter
b the circumference of the orbit, giving your answers in standard form.

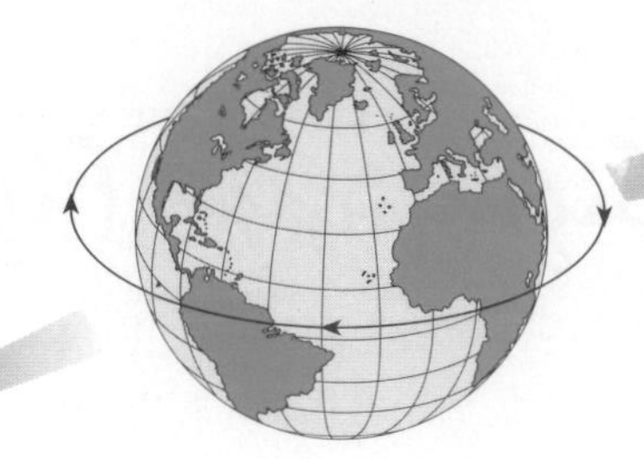

What are significant figures?

The dictionary defines the word 'significant' as 'having meaning'.
In mathematics a figure or digit in a number is significant if it gives an idea of:

(i) quantity
(ii) accuracy.

When zeros are only employed to position the decimal point then they are not significant.

Examples

607 cm has 3 significant figures.
60.7 cm has 3 significant figures.
6.07 cm has 3 significant figures.
0.607 cm has 3 significant figures (the first zero positions the decimal point).
607.0 cm has 4 significant figures (the last zero tells you that it is a more accurate measurement than 607 cm).
0.006 07 cm has 3 significant figures.

When dealing with whole numbers you need more information before you can tell if trailing zeros are significant.

Examples

3400 cm to the nearest 100 cm has 2 significant figures (think of it as 34 hundreds).
3400 cm to the nearest 10 cm has 3 significant figures (think of it as 340 tens).
3400 cm to the nearest centimetre has 4 significant figures (think of it as 3400 units).

'There are 360° in a complete turn.' There are 3 significant figures here.
'There are approximately 370 days in a year.' There are 2 significant figures here.

You can use the abbreviation 's.f.' for significant figures.

Scientists would normally express numbers like these in standard form to avoid mix-ups.

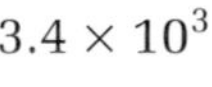

3.4×10^3 $\quad$ 3.60×10^2

3.40×10^3 $\quad$ 3.7×10^2

3.400×10^3

EXERCISE 1

1 How many significant figures are there in each of the following measurements?

a 3.4 cm	b 6.03 m	c 0.122 km	d 0.011 mm	e 0.10 cm
f 507.0 m	g 0.0009 cm	h 0.009 040 m	i 800.0 km	j 0.001 mm

2 Say how many significant figures there are in the numbers used in each sentence.

- a There are 500 pennies in £5.
- b There are approximately 90 days in winter.
- c To the nearest million miles the sun is 93 000 000 miles away.
- d The highest mountain in Asia is Everest at 8848 m.
- e The highest mountain in South America is Aconcagua at 6960.0 m.
- f The largest lake is Lake Superior, to the nearest 100 km^2 its area is 82 400 km^2.

3 Write down how many significant figures there are in each of these numbers. When it is impossible to tell without further information, then say so.

- a There were 36 000 people at the outdoor concert.
- b There are 36 500 days in a century, ignoring the extra days in leap years.
- c A jumble sale made £293.40 to the nearest penny.
- d There are 2800 books on science in the library.
- e There are 2100 minutes in 35 hours.
- f The postman delivers 700 letters a day.
- g A can of mineral water holds 440 ml, measured to the nearest millilitre.
- h If one more person attends then there will be 500 at the show.

4 Write down how many significant figures there are in each of these numbers.

a 36.0	b 2.00	c 5.005	d 954.0	e 70.3
f 50.050	g 1.010 10	h 180.0	i 0.639	j 0.52
k 0.1	l 0.0045	m 8.004	n 0.002 22	o 0.000 06
p 0.0101	q 0.0050	r 0.50	s 0.0070	t 0.0007

5 Round each of these numbers to: **(i)** 2 s.f. **(ii)** 3 s.f.

a 49 483	b 50 790	c 3456	d 245 790	e 7008
f 77.77	g 365.4	h 1.789	i 808.65	j 20.09

6 Round each of these to 1 s.f.

a 17.051	b 6.08	c 0.000 36	d 0.909
e 10.5	f 40.50	g 0.680	h 0.0300

7 Calculate each of the following, giving your answer correct to 3 s.f.

a $17 \div 9$	b $52 \div 23$	c $19 \div 6$	d $8 \div 3$
e $\pi \times 8$	f $\pi \times 12$	g $\pi \times 6.5$	h $\pi \times 3 \times 3$

8 The Northern Building Society requires borrowers to find 7% of the cost of a house themselves.
Calculate 7% of each of the following to 3 s.f.

a £125 000	b £97 420	c £217 400	d £399 945

9 You cannot expect to get answers which are more accurate than the data you use. When working with circles, people often use 3.14 as an approximation for π.

a Calculate the circumference of the following circles correct to 3 s.f. using $\pi = 3.14$.
  (i) diameter = 4.15 cm **(ii)** diameter = 56.2 cm **(iii)** radius = 125 mm

b Work these out again, this time using the π button on your calculator and correcting your answers to 3 s.f.

c Compare your answers and comment.

10 The measurements on these boxes have been given to 2 s.f.
So again you cannot expect answers with more.
Calculate the volume of each box correct to 2 s.f.

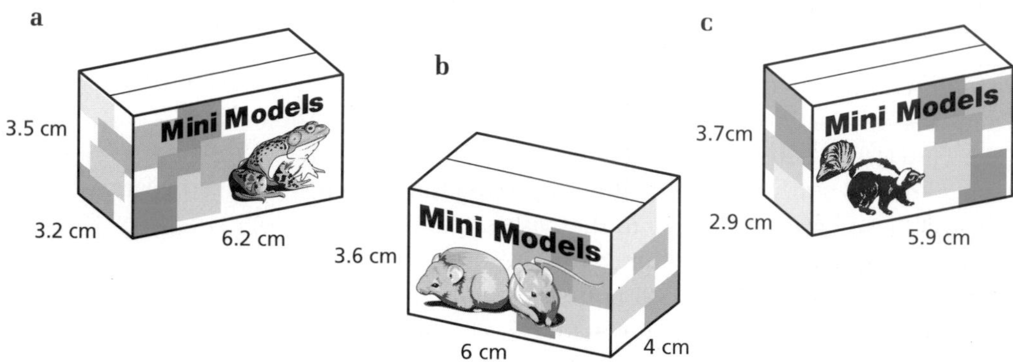

Significant figures on the calculator

Check how to make your calculator work in scientific notation, and how to get it to work to a fixed number of significant figures.

Example

   or perhaps    

will make it work in standard form to 3 s.f.

- If an answer is in the display at the time you make these button pushes, then it will be converted to standard form correct to 3 s.f.
- Any number typed in will be converted to standard form when the '=' button is pressed.

Warning

When the calculator works to 3 s.f., it still remembers all the figures.
It is not rounding at every step of the problem.
Do not round at every step. You will end up with a very inaccurate answer. Only round at the end of a problem.

EXERCISE 2

1 Convert each of the following numbers to standard form rounded to 2 s.f. by switching modes on your calculator.

a 495 **b** 3657 **c** 4009 **d** 798 **e** 0.412 **f** 0.004 67

2 Convert each of the following numbers to decimal form by switching modes on your calculator.

a 6.21×10^3 **b** 8.36×10^1 **c** 3.14×10^0 **d** 9×10^{-2} **e** 8.1×10^{-3} **f** 5.99×10^2

3 Perform each of these calculations while in scientific mode.
Convert to normal mode and give the answer correct to 3 s.f.

a A car salesman is paid 3% commission on all his sales.
How much is he paid when he sells a car worth:
(i) £8540 **(ii)** £12 500 **(iii)** £3459?

b Multiplying by 2.59 will convert square miles to square kilometres.
Convert the area of each island into square kilometres correct to 3 s.f.
(i) Area of Britain is 88 770 miles^2.
(ii) Area of Madagascar is 227 000 miles^2.
(iii) Area of Greenland is 840 000 miles^2.

c Bacteria in a lab increase in number by 18% each hour.
If there are 100 bacteria to start with, how many will there be after:
(i) 1 hour **(ii)** 2 hours **(iii)** 3 hours?

d Jupiter takes 9.8 hours to turn on its axis (a Jovian day).
It takes 11.86 years to go round the sun (a Jovian year).
(i) Convert 11.86 years to hours.
(ii) How many Jovian days are there in one Jovian year?

4 Value Added Tax (VAT) is to be added to each of the prices shown below.
It is calculated as 17.5% of the price.

a Calculate correct to 3 s.f. the VAT on:
(i) the computer system **(ii)** the disk drive **(iii)** the monitor.

b Calculate correct to 2 d.p. the VAT on:
(i) the computer system **(ii)** the disk drive **(iii)** the monitor.

c Which does it make more sense to use in this context, decimal places or significant figures?

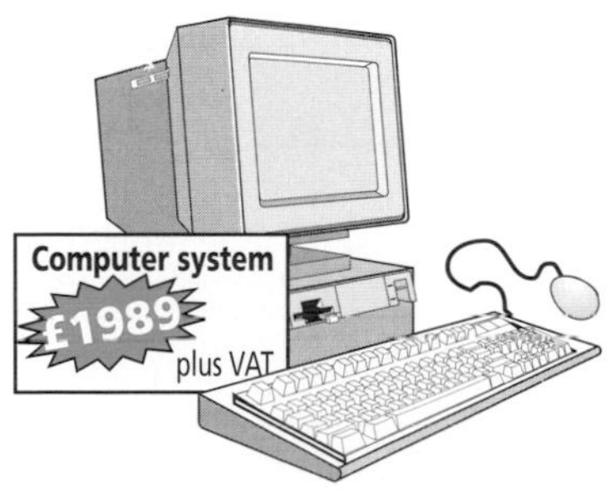

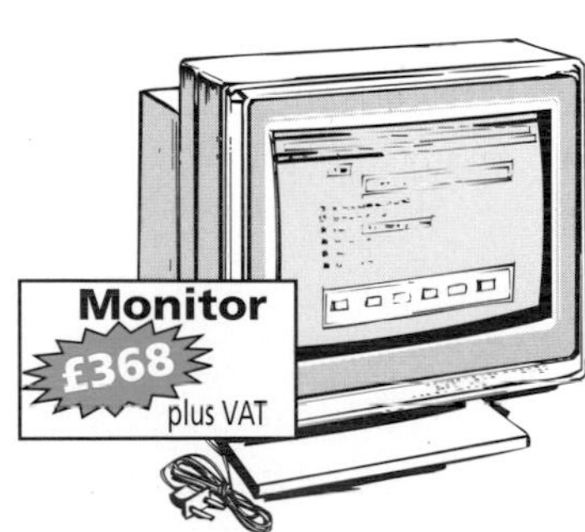

CHAPTER 1 REVIEW

1 State how many significant figures there are in each number.
a Michael paid exactly £10 for the CD.
b Margaret paid about £10 for the book.
c The path measured 10.00 m.
d The blink of an eye lasts 0.01 second.
e The thickness of a sheet of paper is 0.010 cm.

2 Round each of the following to 2 s.f.
a 354 **b** 2.398 **c** 0.144 **d** 0.0103

3 Calculate the following, giving your answer correct to 3 s.f.
a 3% of £2350 **b** 17.5% of £6000

4 Mars is in a circular orbit of radius 2.27×10^8 km.
Calculate, correct to 2 s.f.
a the diameter
b the circumference of its orbit.

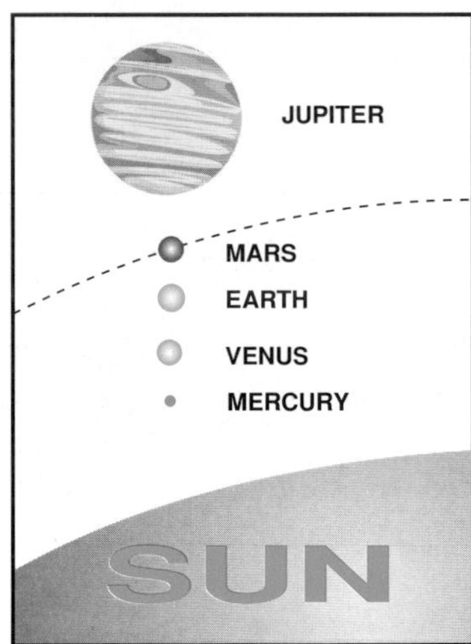

2 Calculations Involving Percentages

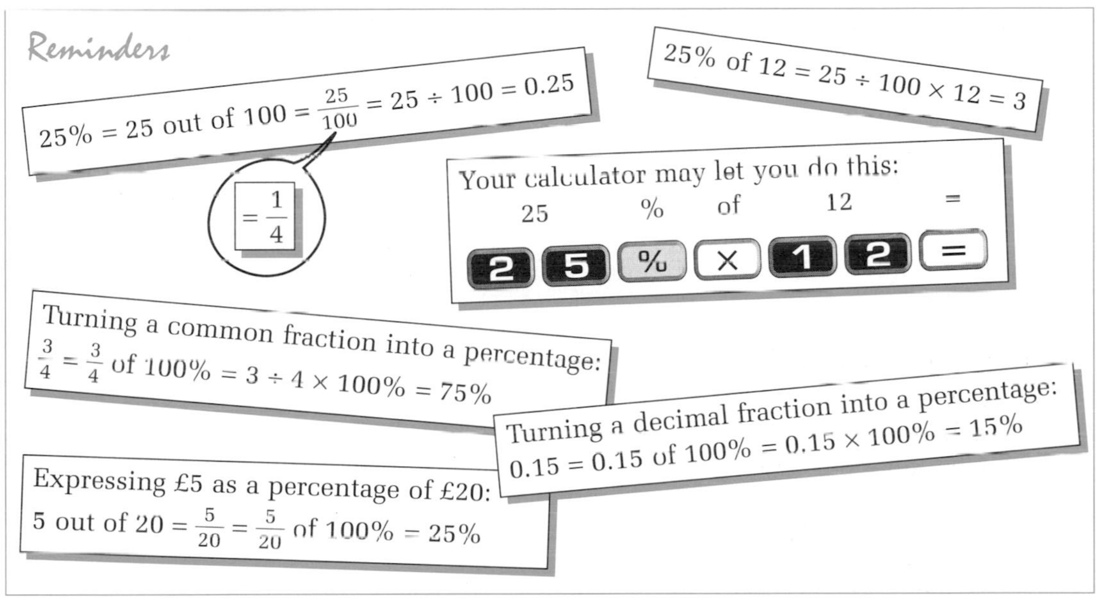

Reminders
25% = 25 out of 100 = $\frac{25}{100}$ = 25 ÷ 100 = 0.25
= $\frac{1}{4}$
25% of 12 = 25 ÷ 100 × 12 = 3
Your calculator may let you do this:
25 % of 12 =
2 5 % × 1 2 =
Turning a common fraction into a percentage:
$\frac{3}{4} = \frac{3}{4}$ of 100% = 3 ÷ 4 × 100% = 75%
Turning a decimal fraction into a percentage:
0.15 = 0.15 of 100% = 0.15 × 100% = 15%
Expressing £5 as a percentage of £20:
5 out of 20 = $\frac{5}{20} = \frac{5}{20}$ of 100% = 25%

STARTING POINTS

1 Calculate: **a** 50% of £25 **b** 75% of £40
c 8% of £26.50

2 Value Added Tax (VAT) is charged at 17.5%. Calculate the VAT to be paid on the guitar.

3 Which is the better mark, 21 out of 25 or 12 out of 15? Change each to a percentage to find out.

4 Calculate:
a 38% of £96.70, giving your answer to the nearest penny
b 44% of £78.32, giving your answer to the nearest pound
c 23% of £112, giving your answer to the nearest ten pence
d the VAT, at 17.5%, you would pay on a price of £68.45.

5 **a** Express an exam mark of 22 out of 40 as a percentage mark.
b Compasses bought for 70p each are sold at 80p. Calculate:
(i) the profit **(ii)** the profit as a percentage of the buying price, correct to the nearest whole number.

6 Calculate the actual cost when:
a a motorbike is listed at £3500 and there is a discount of 15%
b a pushbike is listed at £350 and there is an increase of 8%
c a car is listed at £5000 cash but you pay a 12% deposit and 10 instalments of £450.

Simple interest

Mary invests £400 in the Bank of Clyde for 3 years.
At the end of each year she receives 7% of the £400 in interest.
How much interest does Mary receive over the three years?

Interest each year = 7% of £400 = £28
Interest over 3 years = 3 × £28 = £84

Interest paid in this way is called **simple interest**.

EXERCISE 1

1 How much interest is obtained in one year from each of these investments in the Bank of Clyde?
a £1000 **b** £1200 **c** £650 **d** £2760

2 The following sums of money are borrowed from the Easy Loan Finance Company. The loan plus interest must be paid back after one year. Calculate the amount of money to be paid back at the end of the year on each of the following loans.
a £5000 **b** £3500 **c** £8500 **d** £16 500

The Easy Loan
Finance Company
Interest only
19% per annum

3 **(i)**

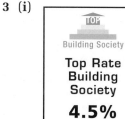

Building Society
Top Rate Building Society
4.5%
per annum

(ii)

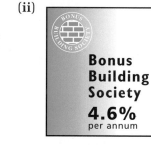

Bonus Building Society
4.6%
per annum

Calculate the total simple interest over two years from each building society if the investment is:
a £250 **b** £850
c £1750 **d** £3600.

4 **a** Calculate the interest paid out after one year by Bank of Forth on these investments.
(i) £6500 **(ii)** £14 800 **(iii)** £275 **(iv)** £820

Bank of Forth

Investment	Interest rate (p.a.)
£0 – £499	2.85%
£500 – £4999	3.15%
£5000 – £9999	3.65%
£10 000 – £25 000	4.25%

b Calculate the simple interest paid out by Bank of Forth for these investments.

Investment	£350	£9500	£17 000	£24 000
Investment period	1 year	6 months	2 months	9 months

5 The money invested to start with is called the **principal**.
Principal + Interest = Amount

Calculate the simple interest and amount for each of these investments.

a £550 invested for 4 years at 7% per annum
b £1450 invested for 3 years at 6.5% per annum
c £500 invested for 6 months at 5% per annum
d £2800 invested for 30 months at 5% per annum

Compound interest

Usually the interest is not a fixed quantity year after year. One year's interest becomes part of the next year's amount. Each year's interest is calculated on the amount at the start of that year. Interest calculated in this way is called **compound interest**.

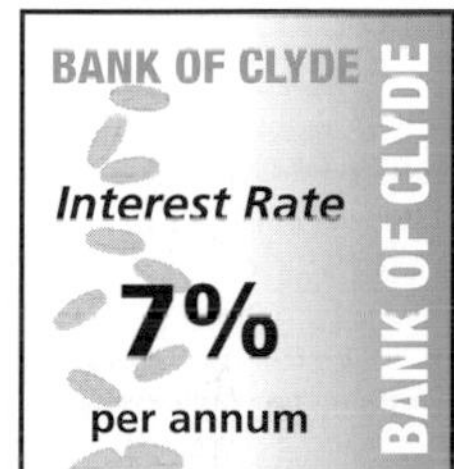

BANK OF CLYDE
Interest Rate
7%
per annum
BANK OF CLYDE

Example

Terry deposits £400 in the Bank of Clyde. He leaves it untouched for 3 years.
Calculate the compound interest and the amount of money he will have at the end of the 3 years.

Principal (i.e. money invested) = £400

Year 1: Interest = 7% of £400 = £28
Amount = £400 + £28 = £428

Year 2: Interest = 7% of £428 = £29.96
Amount = £428 + £29.96 = £457.96

Year 3: Interest = 7% of £457.96 = £32.06
Amount = £457.96 + £32.06 = £490.02

Compound interest after 3 years = Amount − Principal
= £490.02 − £400 = £90.02

Reminder
Have your calculator fixed to 2 decimal places for money.

Note that the compound interest for 3 years is £90.02.
The simple interest for 3 years is only 3 × £28 = £84.

EXERCISE 2

Reminder
'p.a.' means 'per annum'.

1 Calculate the compound interest on:

a £200 for 2 years at 5% p.a.
b £750 for 2 years at 4% p.a.
c £1250 for 2 years at 9% p.a.
d £850 for 2 years at 6% p. a.
e £1000 for 3 years at 5% p. a.
f £1500 for 3 years at 4% p.a.
g £1750 for 3 years at 6% p.a.
h £650 for 3 years at 5.5% p.a.
i £100 for 4 years at 5% p. a.
j £1600 for 4 years at 6% p.a.
k £3000 for 4 years at 8% p.a.
l £650 for 4 years at 10% p.a.

2 Jessica has £500. She hopes that by putting it in the right bank it will grow to £600. Which of the following schemes will *not* do the job?

a 4 years at 6% **b** 5 years at 4% **c** 3 years at 8% **d** 2 years at 5%

3 **a** Molly invests £1200 in the Tay Bank. Calculate the compound interest after 3 years.

b Compare your answer to the simple interest she would receive over 3 years at the same rate.

4

DON BUILDING SOCIETY

5% interest p.a.

How much better off would you be investing £800 for 3 years in the Don Building Society than in the Dee Building Society?

5 Barry borrowed £5000 from the Trusty Finance Company. He agreed to repay the loan plus interest in one payment after 3 years.

a Calculate the interest on Barry's loan.

b How much altogether would Barry have to pay back after 3 years?

TRUSTY FINANCE COMPANY

Loans from only 27% per annum

6 Calculate the compound interest on each of these investments.

Investment	£300	£1200	£1800	£2250	£4500	£10 000
Rate of interest	3%	6%	7.5%	5%	6.5%	4.25%
Time	2 years	3 years	3 years	4 years	2 years	3 years

7 The Ritchies invest £22 million of their lottery winnings at an annual rate of interest of 8.5%. How much is their investment worth after 3 years?

8 £23 000 is invested in the Bank of Ness. How much compound interest is earned in 3 years?

BANK OF NESS

6.9% interest p.a.

Challenge

Guess, check and improve!

Suppose a bank offers 6% interest. If you put enough in the bank you can live off the interest. How much money would you have to put in the bank if you wanted an annual income of £30 000?

Compound interest on the calculator

Example 1 £700 is invested at 9% per annum. This means that each year the amount is 109% of the previous year.

After 1 year the investment is worth 109% of £700 $= 1.09 \times 700$

After 2 years it is worth 109% of (109% of £700)

$= 1.09 \times (1.09 \times 700) \quad = (1.09)^2 \times 700$

After 3 years it is worth 109% of $(1.09)^2 \times 700$ $= (1.09)^3 \times 700$

After 10 years it is worth $(1.09)^{10} \times 700$

You can calculate these values using the x^y button on your calculator.

Note that the multiplier $x = 1.09 = (100 + 9) \div 100$

In general, $x = (100 + R) \div 100$, where R is the rate of interest.

Example 2 £600 is invested at 8% per annum.

a How much is in the bank after 6 years?

b What is the interest after 6 years?

The multiplier is $(100 + 8) \div 100 = 1.08$

a The amount after 6 years $= (1.08)^6 \times 600 =$ £952.12 to the nearest penny.

b The interest $= 952.12 - 600 =$ £352.12.

EXERCISE 3

1 Write down the multiplier when the interest rate is:

a 3% **b** 7% **c** 10% **d** 12% **e** 8% **f** 25% **g** 12.5%

2 Use the above method to calculate

(i) the value of the investment and hence (ii) the compound interest on:

a £1500 for 3 years at 4% p.a. **b** £1750 for 3 years at 6% p.a.

3 Calculate the compound interest on:

a £2650 invested for 5 years at 8% p.a.

b £1140 invested for 10 years at 12% p.a.

c £3850 invested for 8 years at 11% p.a.

4 Calculate the compound interest on:

a £950 invested for 4 years at 2.85% p.a.

b £1745 invested for 7 years at 3.16% p.a.

c £32 000 invested for 10 years at 4.95% p.a.

5 £6000 invested at 8% per annum | £8000 invested at 6% per annum

a Which is worth more after 10 years? **b** By how much?

6 In the story 'The Sleeper Awakes', H.G. Wells tells of a man who falls asleep in 1897 and wakes up in the year 2100. Mainly because of the compound interest on his savings, he finds himself the richest man on earth. How much would £1 be worth if it had been left in the bank at 10% for 203 years?

Appreciation and depreciation

The value of a house usually increases with time. Its value is said to **appreciate**.

Example 1

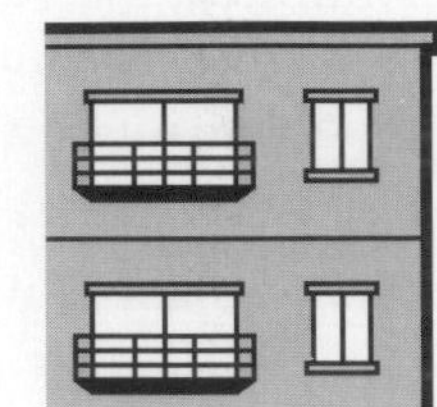

A flat bought for £30 000 in 1990 is sold in 1997 for £35 000.
Calculate the appreciation in the value of the flat as a percentage to 3 s.f.
Appreciation = £5000

Percentage appreciation = $\frac{5000}{30\,000} \times 100\% = 16.7\%$ to 3 s.f.

A car's value usually goes down each year.
Its value is said to **depreciate**.

Example 2

Toni and Tom bought a new car for £7500. In the first year its value depreciated by 20%, in the second by 15% and in the third by 10%.
Calculate the value of the car at the end of each year.
By the end of the first year, depreciation = 20% of £7500 = £1500.
Value = £7500 – £1500 = £6000
By the end of the second year, depreciation = 15% of £6000 = £900.
Value = £6000 – £900 = £5100
By the end of the third year, depreciation = 10% of £5100 = £510.
Value = £5100 – £510 = £4590

EXERCISE 4

1 A plot of land bought in 1996 for £12 000 has now appreciated in value by 14%.
What is its present value?

2 A caravan bought for £2300 in 1995 has depreciated in value by 7%.
What is its value today?

3 A painting was bought in 1992 for £850. By 1997 its value had appreciated by 35%.
What was the painting worth in 1997?

4 Sally buys a second-hand car for £4400. Its value depreciates by 10% over the first year and by 8% over the second year.
How much is Sally's car worth after the two years?

5 A student bought a flat for £33 000. Over the four years of the student's course the flat appreciated in value by 2%, 4%, 3% and 4.5%.
How much was the flat worth by the end of the course?

6 A diamond ring bought for £150 was sold two years later for £170.
Calculate the appreciation in its value as a percentage of the buying price.
(Give your answer correct to 3 s.f.)

7 A car bought for £2350 in 1994 had depreciated in value to £1550 by 1997. What is the depreciation as a percentage of the buying price? Give your answer to 3 s.f.

8 A cottage was bought for £57 000. Due to a lack of care and maintenance, it depreciated in value to £45 000.
Express the depreciation as a percentage rounded to 2 s.f.

9 Tim bought a computer three years ago for £1400. Each year since then it has depreciated by 15% of its value at the start of the year. (Its value at the end of a year is 85% of its value at the start of the year.)
How much is the computer now worth?

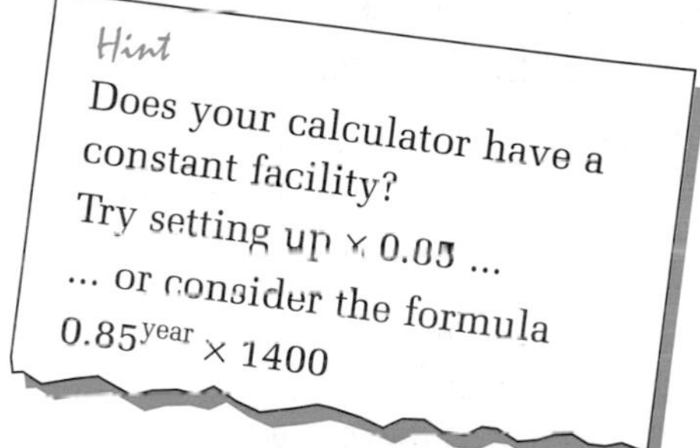

Hint
Does your calculator have a constant facility?
Try setting up × 0.85 ...
... or consider the formula
$0.85^{year} \times 1400$

10 A house which cost £43 000 four years ago appreciates in value each year by 1.5%. (Its value at the end of a year is 101.5% of its value at the start of the year.) Calculate the value of the house after four years.

11 A boat is worth £20 000. Its value depreciates by 9% each year. (Its value at the end of a year is only 91% of its value at the start of the year.)
a Calculate its value after: **(i)** 1 year **(ii)** 2 years **(iii)** 3 years.
b When will its value be less than half its original value?

12 A piano costs £3000. Its value depreciates by 18% each year.
a Calculate its value after: **(i)** 1 year **(ii)** 4 years.
b When does the value first go below £500?

13

The vintage car is worth £25 000. Its value appreciates by 3% each year. (Its value at the end of a year is 103% of its value at the start of the year.)
a Calculate its value after: **(i)** 1 year **(ii)** 3 years.
b When is it first worth more than £30 000?

14 An antique clock is worth £600. Its value appreciates by 10% each year. (Its value at the end of a year is 110% of its value at the start of the year.)
a Calculate its value after: **(i)** 1 year **(ii)** 5 years.
b When is it first worth more than £1000?

EXERCISE 5

1 a Gold bullion appreciated in value one week from 340.28 dollars an ounce to 347.64 dollars an ounce.
Express the appreciation as a percentage of its value at the start of the week.
Give your answer to 3 s.f.

b The following week gold bullion depreciated back to 340.28 dollars.
Express the depreciation as a percentage of its value *at the start of the week.*
Give your answer to 3 s.f.

2 Debbie bought a vase at a car boot sale for £30. She later discovered it was a Ming vase and she sold it for £9000.
Calculate the appreciation as a percentage of the price Debbie paid. Give your answer to 2 s.f.

3 a Carl bought a flat for £30 000. Its value depreciated by 2% in the first year and appreciated by 2% in the second year.
How much was the flat worth two years after Carl bought it?

b Hera's flat also cost £30 000. Its value appreciated by 2% in the first year and depreciated by 2% in the second year.
Calculate the value of Hera's flat after two years.

4 The MacDazzle Brooch was bought four years ago for £860. It has appreciated in value each year since then by 8%, 16%, 17.5% and 21%.
Calculate its present value.

5 Shares in the MacSpud Potato Crisp Company have appreciated each year over the last five years by 11% of their value at the start of the year. A single share could be bought five years ago for 86 pence.
How much is a share worth today?

6 Nicole bought a turbo-charged Flio car ten years ago for £40 000. During each of these ten years the car has depreciated by 10% of its value at the start of the year.
What is the present value of the car? (Give your answer to 2 s.f.)

7 Alamara has a house worth £100 000. The contents of the house are worth £100 000 also. While the value of the house appreciates at 8% per year the contents depreciate at the same rate.

a Work out the value of the house after: **(i)** 1 year **(ii)** 4 years **(iii)** 5 years.

b Work out the value of the contents after: **(i)** 1 year **(ii)** 4 years **(iii)** 5 years.

c The overall value initially is £200 000.
What is the overall value after: **(i)** 1 year **(ii)** 4 years **(iii)** 5 years?

d (i) What is the increase in overall value in the fifth year?

(ii) Express this increase as a percentage of the value at the start of the fifth year.

Inflation

The inflation rate is a measure of how much prices increase over the year. It is usually given as a percentage. This figure can then be used:

- to estimate new prices
- to compare with actual increases
- as a basis for wage increases or pension increases.

The following table gives approximate rates of inflation over a 12-year period.

Year	1985	1986	1987	1988	1989	1990	1991	1992	1993	1994	1995	1996
Rate %	6	5.5	5	8	7	10	5	4	2	1.5	2	3

Example 1

A CD cost £12 in 1995. If its cost increases in line with inflation, what is the 1996 cost of a CD?

1995 inflation rate = 2%

2% of £12 = £0.24

New cost = 12 + 0.24 = £12.24

Example 2

In 1992 a shop sold a power drill for £18. In 1993 the shop had repriced the drill at £20. Comment on the increase in price.

1992 inflation rate = 4%

4% of £18 = £0.72

Cost if in line with inflation = £18.72

Actual increase is well above the inflation rate.

Example 3

In 1994 a worker received a wage of £400 per week. What wage should he have the following year to keep in line with inflation?

1994 inflation rate = 1.5%

1.5% of £400 = £6

His 1995 wage should be £406.

EXERCISE 6

1 In the following assume that prices keep in line with inflation.

- **a** A bag cost £20 in 1985. What is its cost in 1986?
- **b** A car cost £3000 in 1990. What will it cost in 1991?
- **c** A home computer costs £1200 in 1993. What do you expect it to cost in 1994?

2 A house is valued at £40 000 in 1985. If its value keeps in line with inflation, what would you expect it to be worth in: **a** 1986 **b** 1987 **c** 1988 **d** 1989?

3 Peter works in a job where his wages are linked to the rate of inflation. In 1990 he earned £300 per week. Calculate his weekly wage in:

a 1991 **b** 1992 **c** 1994 **d** 1995.

4 The Smiths' summer electricity bill in 1989 came to £550. In 1990 they paid £590, having used roughly the same amount of electricity.
Work out the percentage increase. Comment on the increase.

5

A trip to Rome in 1988 cost £1200. Fairways Travel always keeps price increases in line with inflation.

a Calculate the cost of the trip in:
(i) 1989 (ii) 1990 (iii) 1991.

b Rivals Flyaway Tours charged £1300 in 1988. They increase prices at 3% below the inflation rate.
Calculate the cost of going to Rome with Flyaway in:
(i) 1989 (ii) 1990 (iii) 1991.

c In which year does Flyaway Tours first charge less than Fairways Travel for a trip to Rome?

6 Hamburger Harlequins sell fast food. In 1990 the ingredients for a hamburger cost £1. Hamburger Harlequins sell them for £2. The costs go up in line with inflation but Hamburger Harlequins always claim to increase their prices at 1% below the rate of inflation.

a Calculate the profit on one hamburger in: (i) 1990 (ii) 1991 (iii) 1992.

b When does the profit stop increasing?

7 Mr and Mrs Jeffry have a pension which is linked to inflation. This means their income should keep pace with price increases. In 1990 they received £170 per week.
What pension did they receive in 1996?

8 Because of necessary investment, the Midworld Water Company's charges increase at 2% over the rate of inflation in 1994, 1995 and 1996. Consider a £100 bill in 1994.

a Calculate the bill in:
(i) 1995 (ii) 1996 (iii) 1997.

b What would these prices be if they had grown in line with inflation?

9 Helen and Tommy were both earning £16 000 in 1991. Helen accepted a deal which linked her wages to the rate of inflation. Tommy accepted a pay rise of 11% for 1992 and no increase for 1993 and 1994.
Which person accepted the better deal?

10 Does falling inflation mean prices are getting cheaper?

Reversing the change

Example 1

After a 10% rise in prices a terraced cottage is worth £88 000.
What was it worth before the rise?

100% + 10% = 110%

£88 000 is 110% of the original price.

1% of original price = 88 000 ÷ 110 = £800

100% of original price = 100 × 800 = £80 000

Example 2

The value of a trombone depreciates by 15% . It is now worth £255.
How much was it worth before the depreciation?

100% − 15% = 85%

£255 is 85% of the original price.

1% of original price = 255 ÷ 85 = £3

100% of original price = 100 × 3 = £300

EXERCISE 7

1 A food processor is sold for £120 after its price is dropped by 20%.
What was its original cost?

2 The cost of a meal at a local restaurant has gone up by 8%.
What was the cost of a meal that is now priced at £12.96?

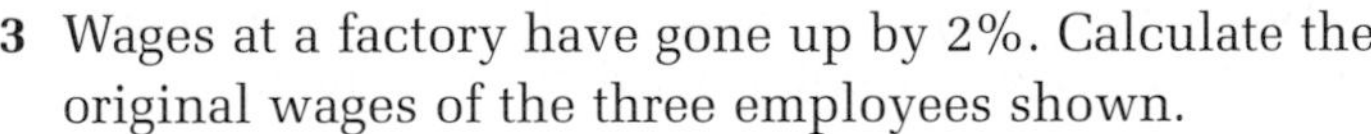

3 Wages at a factory have gone up by 2%. Calculate the original wages of the three employees shown.

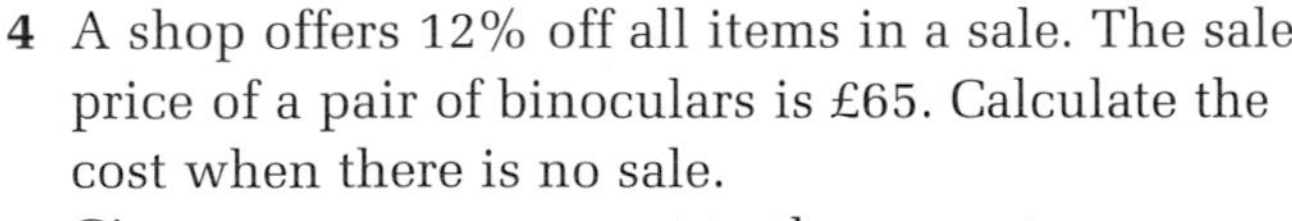

4 A shop offers 12% off all items in a sale. The sale price of a pair of binoculars is £65. Calculate the cost when there is no sale.
Give your answer correct to the nearest penny.

5 The value of a bungalow has appreciated by 6% in a year.
It is now valued at £180 000.
What, to the nearest pound, was its value last year?

6 The value of a computer depreciates by 18% in a year. It is now valued at £984.

a What was its value last year?

b The year before the rate of depreciation was 20%.
Calculate the value of the computer two years ago.

CHAPTER 2 REVIEW

1 Calculate the simple interest on £1500 invested at 4% per annum for:
   a 2 years   b 6 months.

2 An account is opened in the Tay Bank with a deposit of £1800.
   a Calculate the compound interest obtained after three years.
   b Calculate the amount of money in the account after three years.

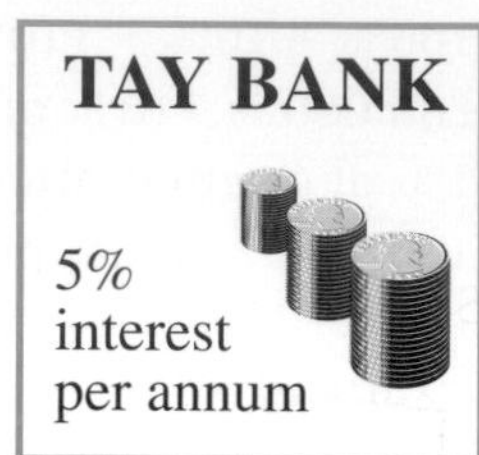

3 

Randolph borrows £2500 from the Squeaky Clean Finance Company. He promises to pay back the loan plus interest in one instalment after three years. Calculate the interest Randolph will pay on the loan.

4 Sal's motorbike cost her £1600 in 1995. It is now worth £1150.
Calculate the depreciation in value as a percentage, correct to 3 s.f.

5 The famous McGlumpher earrings were bought in 1990 for £7400 and sold in 1997 for £12 500.
Find the percentage appreciation in value to 3 s.f.

6 A Volkswagen Beetle car was bought new in 1970 for £655. By 1980 it had depreciated in value by 80%.
   a Calculate its 1980 value (to 2 s.f.).
   b By 1995 it had become a collector's item and had appreciated in value, from its original value, by 140%.
   Calculate its value in 1995 (to 2 s.f.).

7 A plot of land was bought three years ago for £21 500. It has appreciated each year by 2% of its value at the start of the year.
How much is the land worth today?

8 The table shows the inflation rate in various years.
   a The Cycle Shop sold a bike for £250 in 1990.
   It sold the same model in 1991 for £300. Is this increase in line with inflation?
   b In 1991 the railfare to get from Ayton to Beeton was £4.00.
   The rail company kept increases linked to inflation.
   Calculate the railfare in: (i) 1992 (ii) 1994.

Year	Rate (%)
1990	10
1991	5
1992	4
1993	2
1994	1.5

3 Volume of Solids

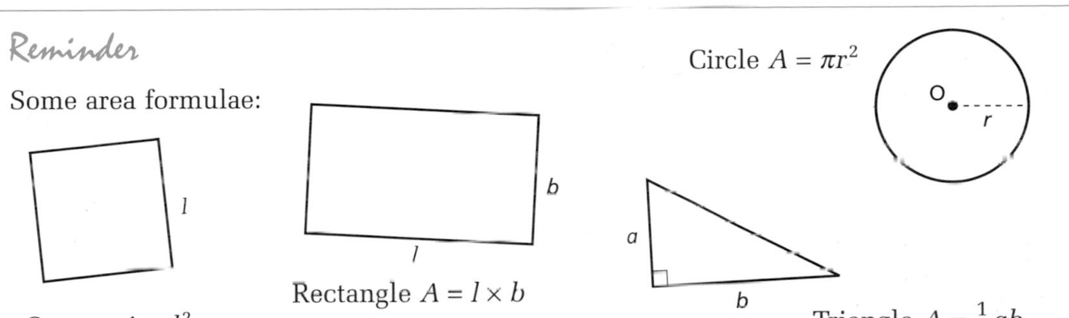

Reminder
Some area formulae:
l
Square $A = l^2$
b
l
Rectangle $A = l \times b$
Circle $A = \pi r^2$
O
r
a
b
Triangle $A = \frac{1}{2}ab$

STARTING POINTS

1 Calculate the area of each shape.

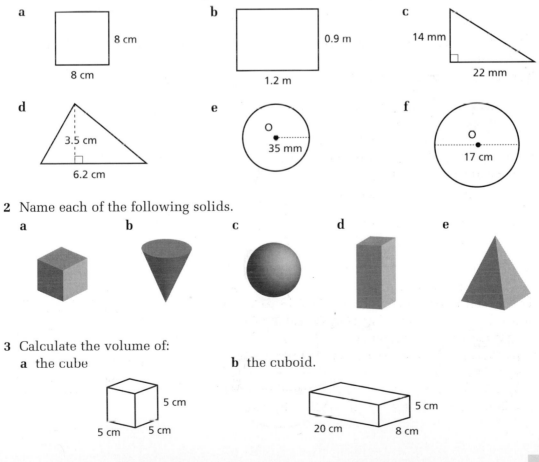

a

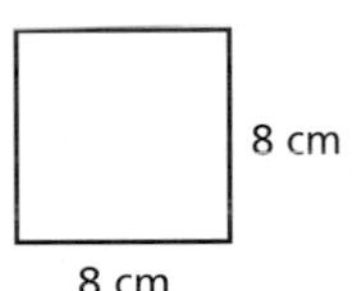

b

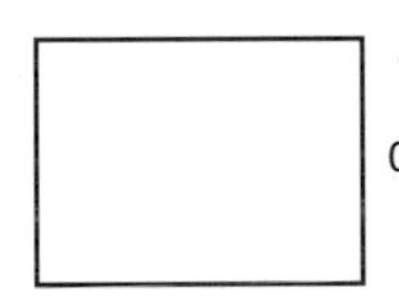

c

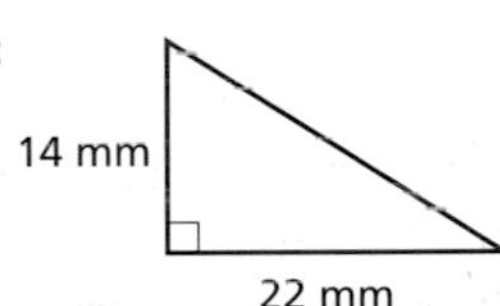

d

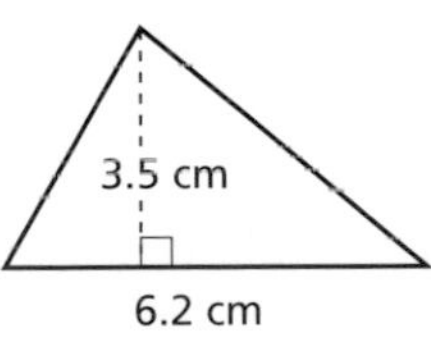

e

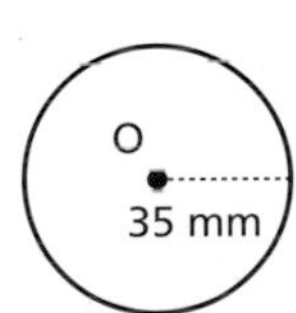

f

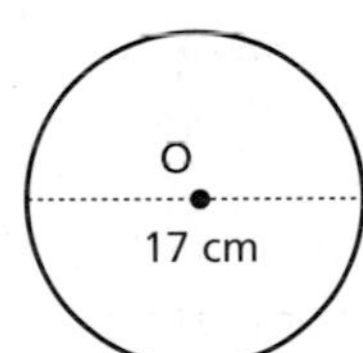

2 Name each of the following solids.

a

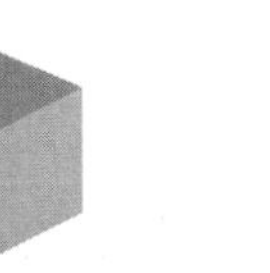

b

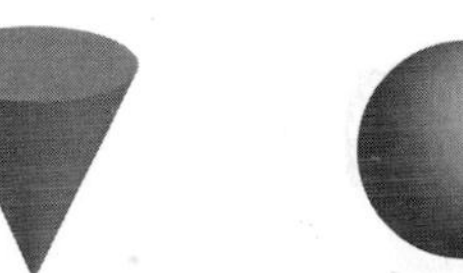

c

d

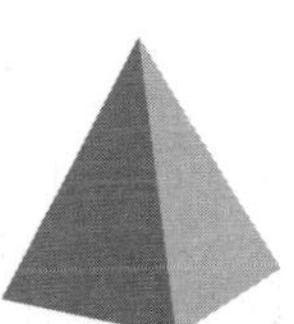

e

3 Calculate the volume of:

a the cube

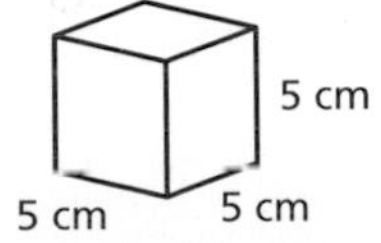

b the cuboid.

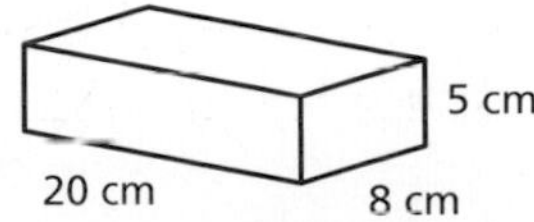

4 Round each of these to the number of significant figures given in brackets.
a 17.463 (3 s.f.) **b** 0.085 42 (2 s.f.) **c** 97 465 (3 s.f.)

5 Calculate: **a** $\frac{1}{3}$ of 14.7 **b** $\frac{4}{3}$ of 58.44 **c** 7.3^2 **d** 8.2^3

6 a If $M = 3ab$, calculate M when $a = 4.7$ and $b = 2.8$.
b If $T = 6y^2$, calculate T when $y = 5.5$.

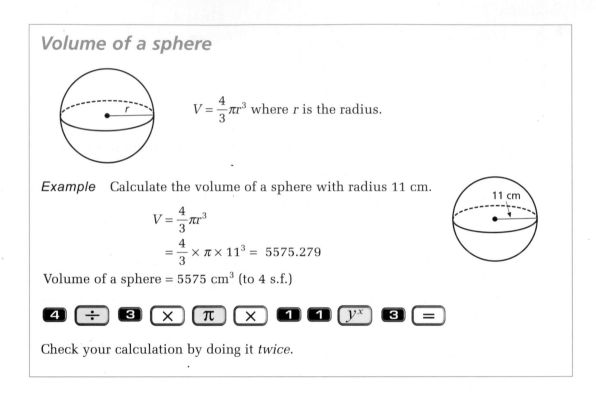

Volume of a sphere

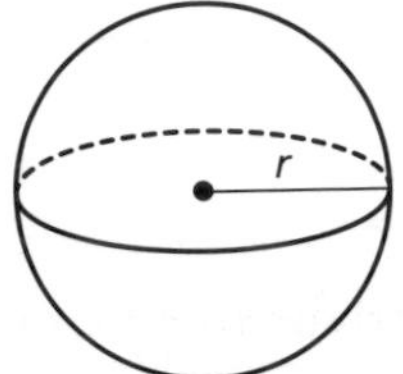

$V = \frac{4}{3}\pi r^3$ where r is the radius.

Example Calculate the volume of a sphere with radius 11 cm.

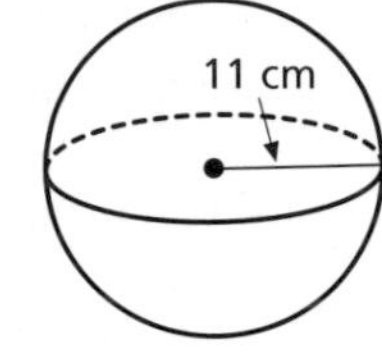

$$V = \frac{4}{3}\pi r^3$$
$$= \frac{4}{3} \times \pi \times 11^3 = 5575.279$$

Volume of a sphere = 5575 cm^3 (to 4 s.f.)

Check your calculation by doing it *twice*.

EXERCISE 1

Round your answers to 3 s.f. unless told otherwise.

1 Calculate the volume of spheres with:
a radius 6 cm **b** radius 23 mm
c radius 1.4 m **d** diameter 18 cm
e diameter 37.8 mm.

2 Calculate the volume of these spheres:

a

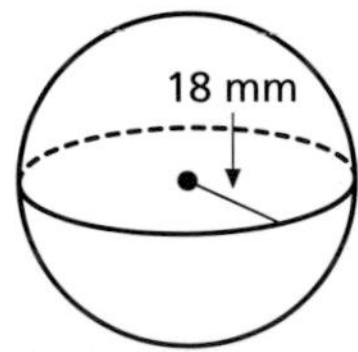

b

3 m

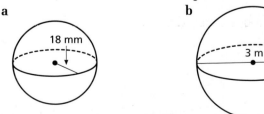

3 Beach balls come in three sizes.

Small Diameter	12 cm
Medium Diameter	22 cm
Large Diameter	30 cm

Calculate the volume of each ball.

4 A ball-bearing has a diameter of 8 mm.
a Calculate the volume of one bearing.
b What volume of metal is needed to make 100 of these ball-bearings?

5 A metal cuboid is to be melted down to make small metal balls.
The block measures 15 cm by 15 cm by 10 cm.
a Calculate the volume of metal available.
b Each metal ball is to have a radius of 0.3 cm.
Calculate the volume of one ball.
c How many balls can be made from the metal block?

6 A metal cube with sides of 8 cm has also to be melted down to make small metal balls.
Each ball is to have a radius of 0.4 cm.
Calculate how many metal balls can be made from the block.

7 A spherical globe has a diameter of 76 cm.
Calculate the volume of the globe.

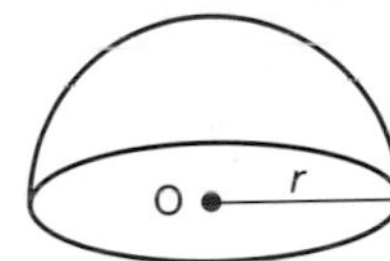

8 Half a sphere is called a **hemisphere**.
A glass paperweight is in the shape of a hemisphere.
The radius of the base is 6 cm.
Calculate the volume of the paperweight.

9

Each of these three mixing bowls is a hemisphere.
The small bowl has a diameter of 14 cm, the medium a diameter of 20 cm and the large a diameter of 26 cm.
Calculate the volume of liquid that each bowl would hold.

Volume of a cone

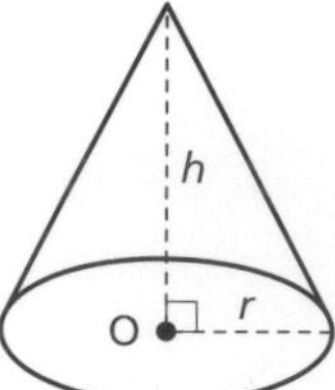

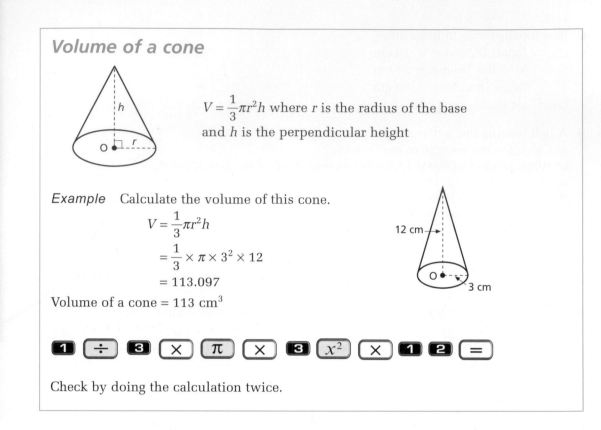

$V = \frac{1}{3}\pi r^2 h$ where r is the radius of the base and h is the perpendicular height

Example Calculate the volume of this cone.

$$V = \frac{1}{3}\pi r^2 h$$
$$= \frac{1}{3} \times \pi \times 3^2 \times 12$$
$$= 113.097$$

Volume of a cone = 113 cm^3

12 cm

O

3 cm

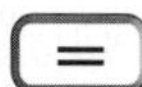

Check by doing the calculation twice.

EXERCISE 2

Round all your answers to 3 s.f. unless told otherwise.

1 Calculate the volume of cones with:

a radius 5 cm and height 11 cm
b radius 1.5 m and height 2 m
c diameter 26 mm and height 20 mm.

2 Calculate the volume of each of these cones:

a

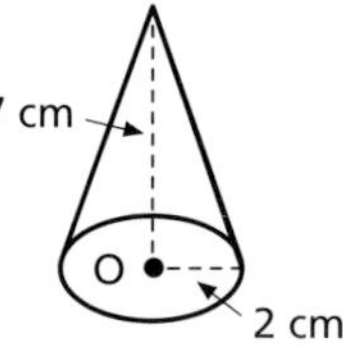

b

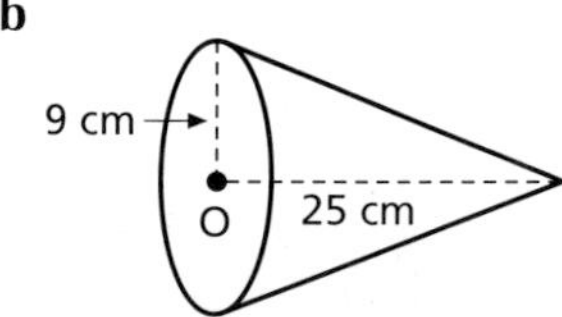

c

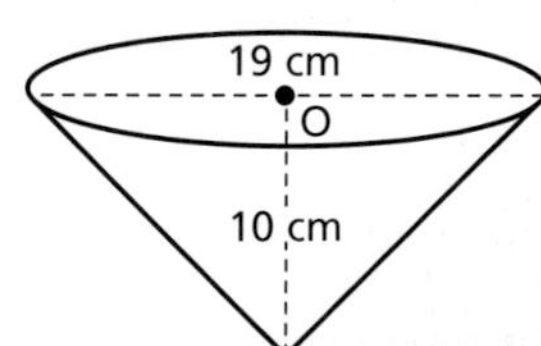

3 An ice-lolly is cone-shaped.
Its height is 14 cm and the radius of the end is 3 cm.
Calculate the volume of the ice-lolly.

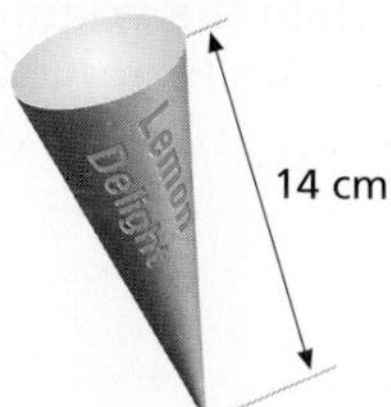

4 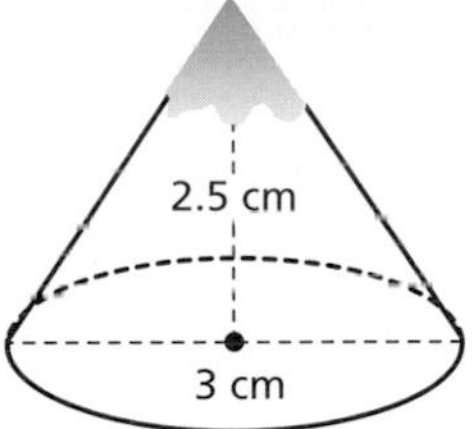

A sweet manufacturer makes a new variety of chocolates in the shape of cones.
Each chocolate is 2.5 cm high and the base has a diameter of 3 cm.
There are 12 chocolates in a box.
Calculate the volume of chocolate in the box.

5 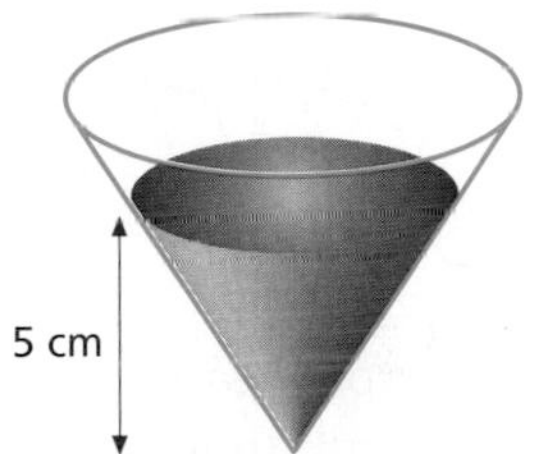

Waxed paper is folded to make a cone-shaped icing bag.
The depth of the icing is 5 cm.
The diameter of the top of the icing is 6 cm.
Calculate the volume of icing in the bag.

6 A conical hole is drilled from a solid metal cube whose edges are 10 cm long.
The hole has a depth of 9 cm.
The diameter of its opening is 7 cm.

a Calculate the volume of metal drilled out.
b Calculate the volume of metal left.

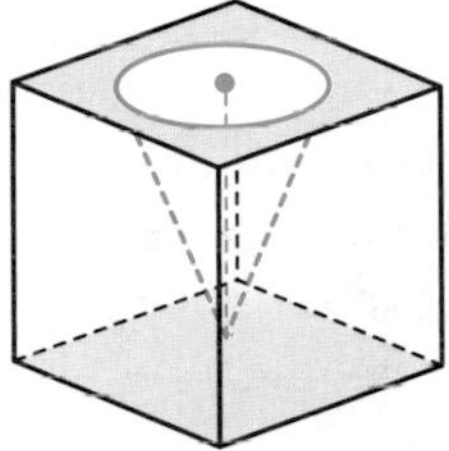

7 A local craftsman makes candles. His new range includes two conical candles.

a

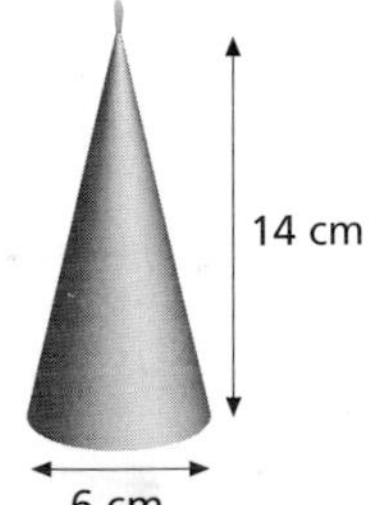

b

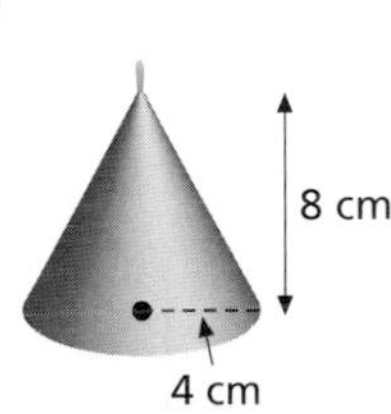

Which candle would require more candle wax to make?
(Show all your working.)

Prisms

A prism is a solid with a uniform cross-section. This means that no matter where it is sliced along its length the cross-section is exactly the same shape.
The prism takes its name from the shape of the cross-section.

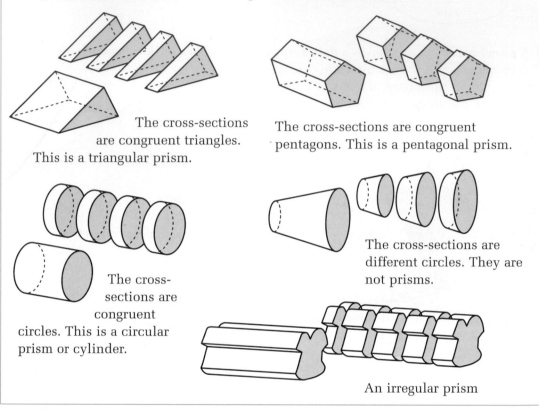

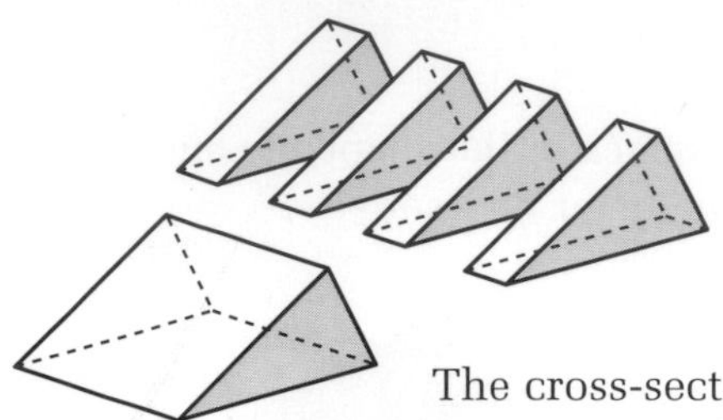

The cross-sections are congruent triangles. This is a triangular prism.

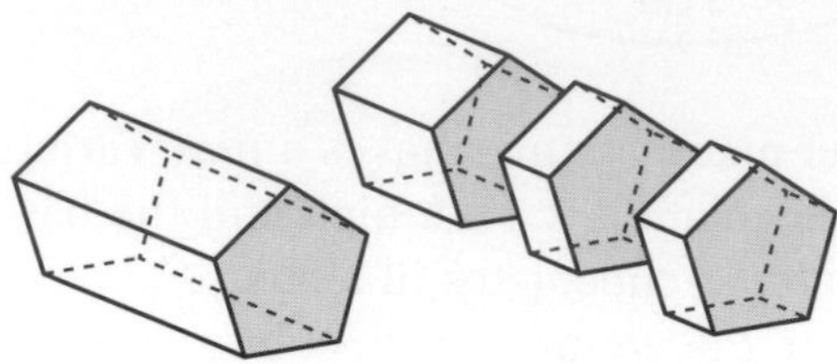

The cross-sections are congruent pentagons. This is a pentagonal prism.

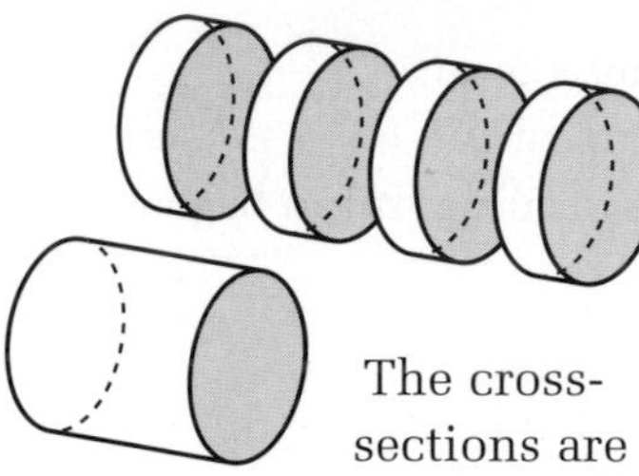

The cross-sections are congruent circles. This is a circular prism or cylinder.

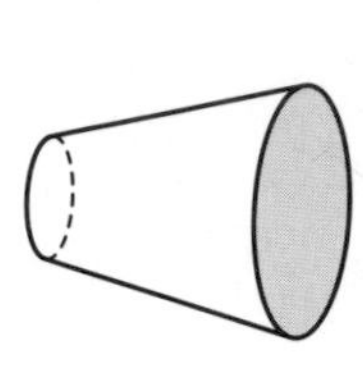

The cross-sections are different circles. They are not prisms.

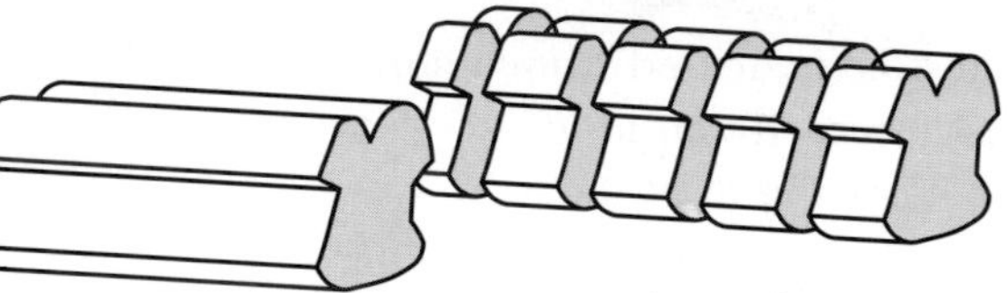

An irregular prism

EXERCISE 3

1 Name these shapes. If the shape is a prism try to identify the type of prism.

a 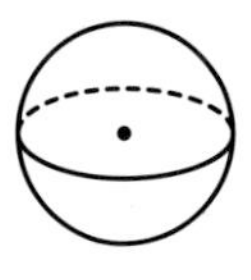

b 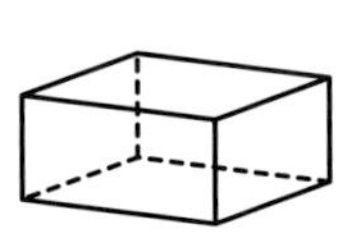

c 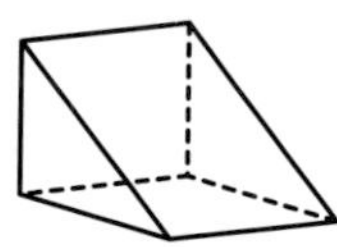

d 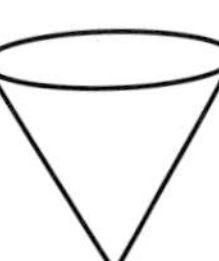

e 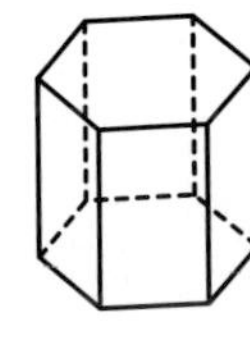

f 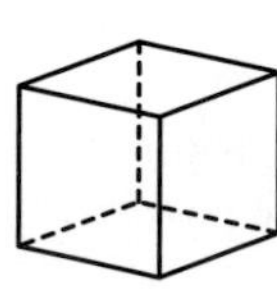

g 

h 

i 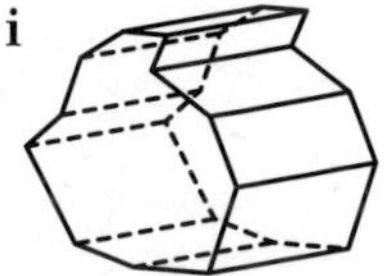

j 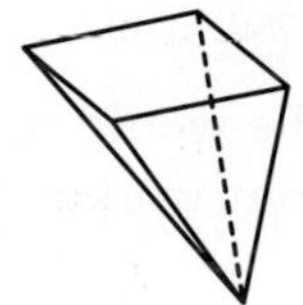

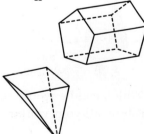

2 **a** Which solid could be described as a square prism?
b Is this the only answer? Explain.

Volume of a prism

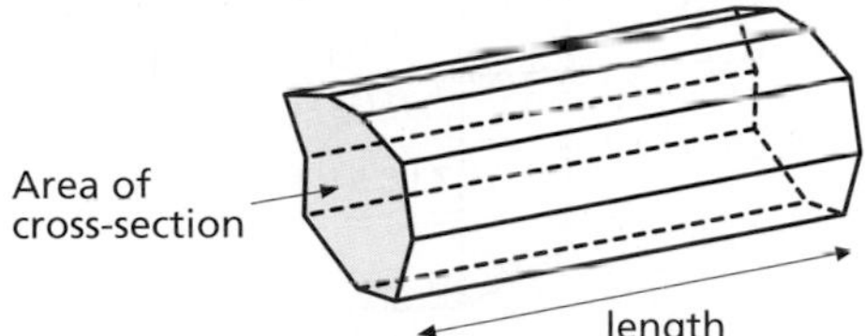

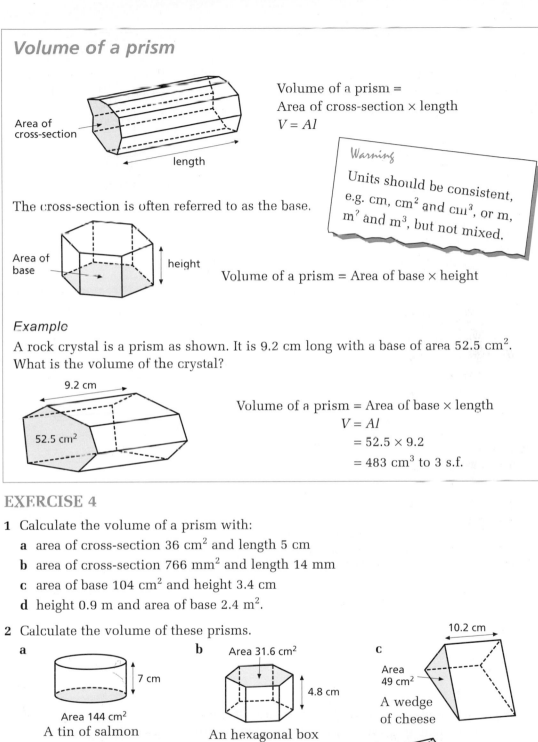

Volume of a prism =
Area of cross-section × length
$V = Al$

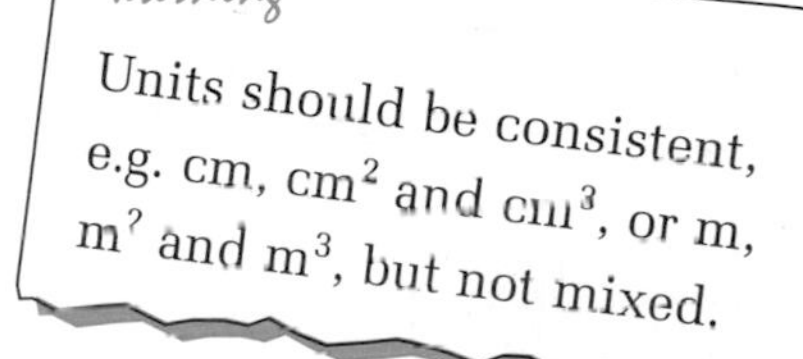

Warning
Units should be consistent, e.g. cm, cm² and cm³, or m, m² and m³, but not mixed.

The cross-section is often referred to as the base.

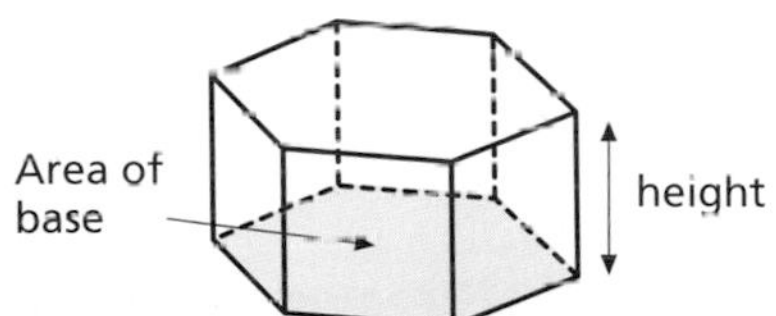

Volume of a prism = Area of base × height

Example

A rock crystal is a prism as shown. It is 9.2 cm long with a base of area 52.5 cm^2. What is the volume of the crystal?

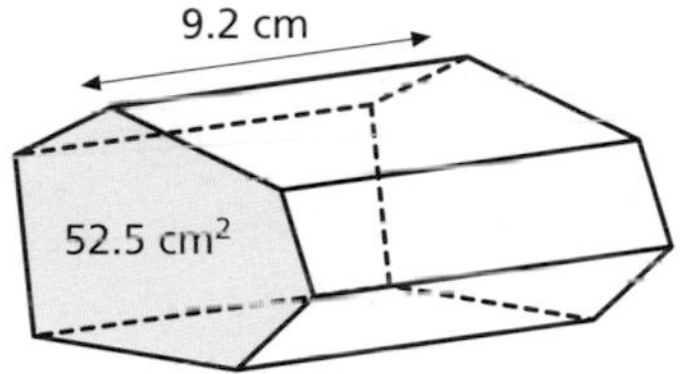

Volume of a prism = Area of base × length

$V = Al$

$= 52.5 \times 9.2$

$= 483$ cm^3 to 3 s.f.

EXERCISE 4

1 Calculate the volume of a prism with:

- **a** area of cross-section 36 cm^2 and length 5 cm
- **b** area of cross-section 766 mm^2 and length 14 mm
- **c** area of base 104 cm^2 and height 3.4 cm
- **d** height 0.9 m and area of base 2.4 m^2.

2 Calculate the volume of these prisms.

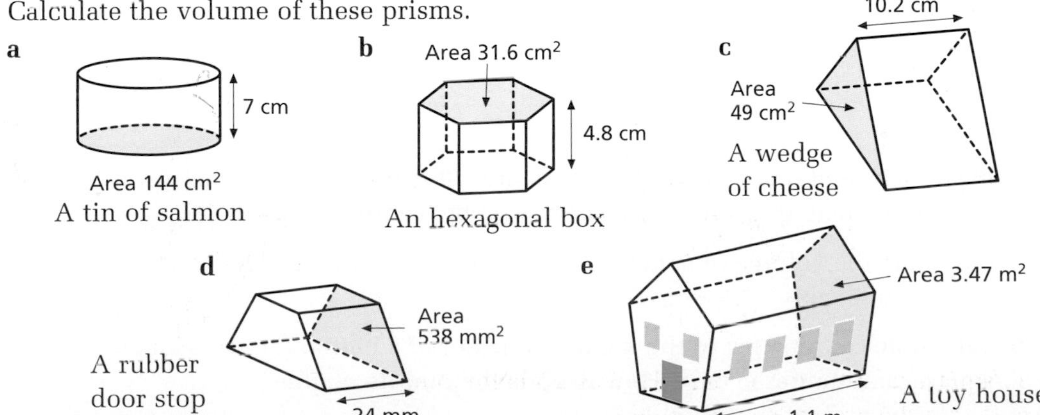

3 A tissue box is in the shape of a hexagonal prism.
The area of the base of the box is 96 cm^2 and its height is 11.5 cm.
Calculate the volume of the box.

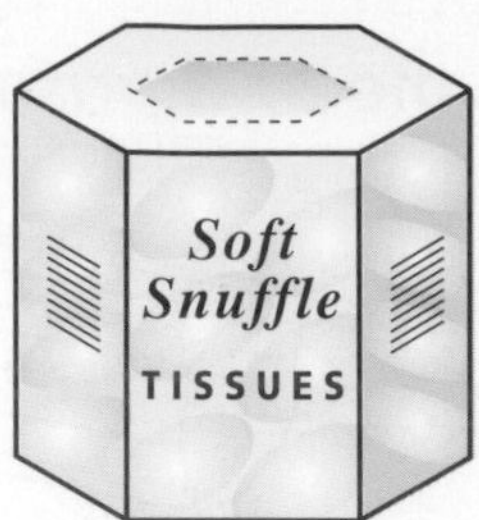

4 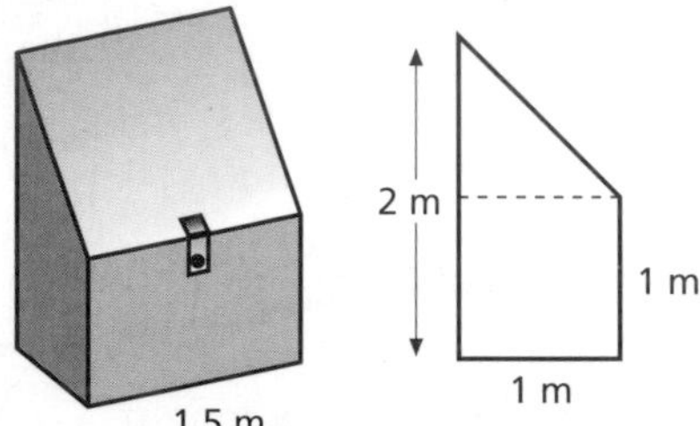

A coal bunker is shaped like a prism with trapezium ends.

a Calculate the area of an end.

b The coal bunker is 1.5 m long.
Calculate the volume of coal that the bunker would hold.

5 A wooden fence post is 180 cm high. It is shaped like a cylinder.
The radius of the top of the post is 4 cm. Calculate:

a the area of the top

b the volume of the post.

6 

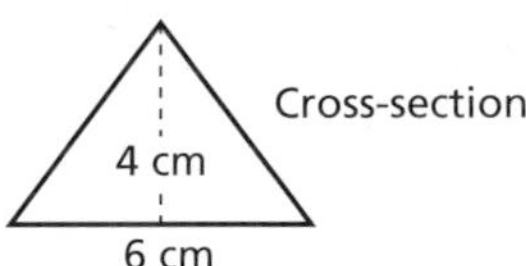

A Rocky Ridge Chocolate Bar is solid chocolate in the shape of a triangular prism. It is 24 cm long and has a cross-section as shown.
Calculate the volume of chocolate in the bar.

7 A swimming pool is shaped like a prism with a trapezium for a cross-section.
Its dimensions are as shown. Calculate:

a the area of the cross-section

b its volume.

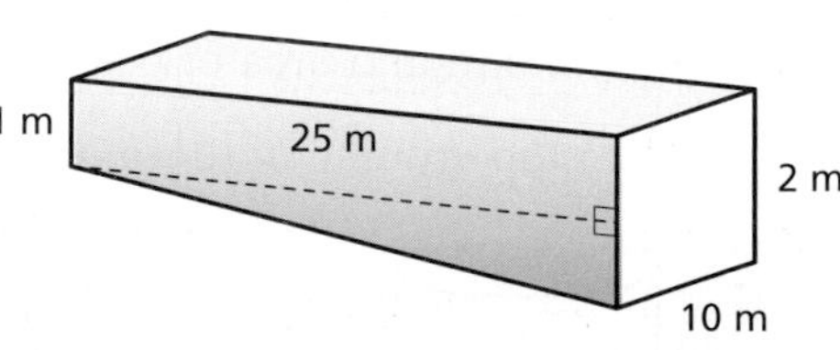

8 Pastry is rolled out evenly to cover an area of 226 square centimetres. It is 9 mm thick. Calculate the volume of pastry in cubic centimetres.

9 Calculate the volume of concrete needed to cover an area of 94 square metres to a depth of 6 cm.

10 128 cubic centimetres of thick glue spills out of a bottle. It covers an area of 320 square centimetres evenly. How deep is the puddle of glue?

Challenge

Investigate how much metal it takes to make a coin.

Example A cylinder (circular prism) has a radius of 3 cm and is 5 cm high. Calculate the volume of the cylinder.

Volume of prism = area of base × height

$V = \pi r^2 h$

$= \pi \times 3^2 \times 5$

$= 141.371\ 66$

$= 141\ \text{cm}^2$ (to 3 s.f.)

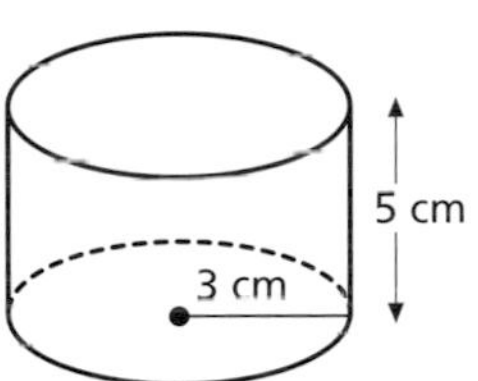

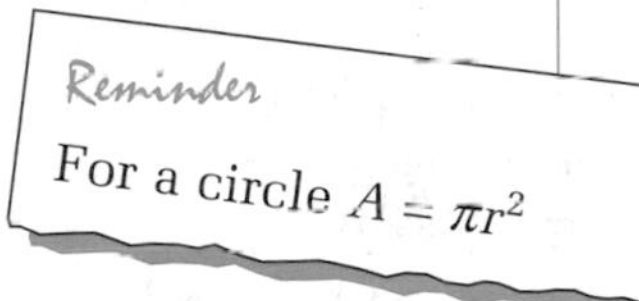

11 Calculate (to 3 s.f.) the volume of cylinders with:

a radius 6 cm and height 10 cm

b radius 17 mm and height 46 mm

c diameter 29 cm and height 23 cm.

12 Cans of soup come in three sizes, as shown.

a Calculate the volume of each can.

b If the small can is meant for one helping, how many helpings are in the large can?

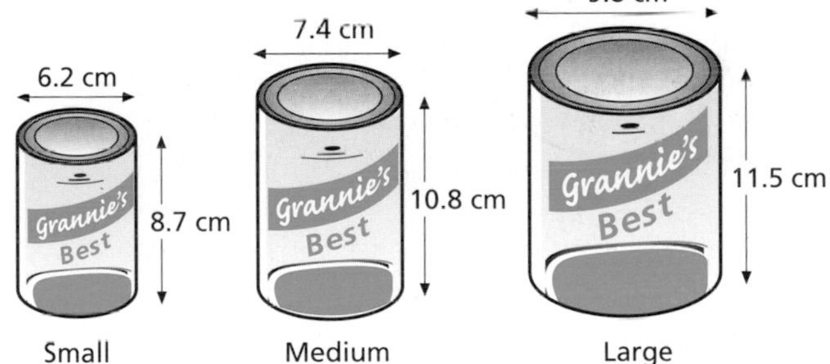

13 Glass fibres 100 m long are used for cable TV. Each fibre is a cylinder of radius 0.5 cm.

a How many centimetres are in 100 m?

b What volume of glass is in one fibre?

c The fibres are bound together in sevens to make a cable. What volume of glass is in 100 m of cable?

14 The roof space of a small factory is as shown. To estimate ventilation requirements, the volume must be calculated.

a What is the area of the shaded side?

b What is the volume of the roof space?

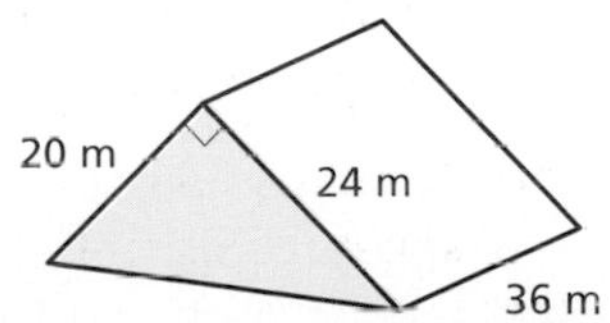

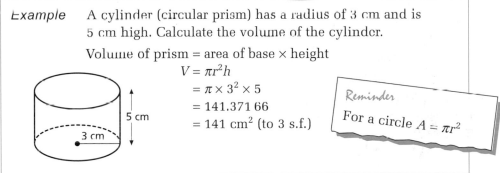

15 This gold ingot is a prism with a trapezium-shaped cross-section.

a What is the area of the cross-section?

b What is the volume of the ingot?

c One cubic centimetre of gold weighs 19.3 g. What is the weight of the ingot?

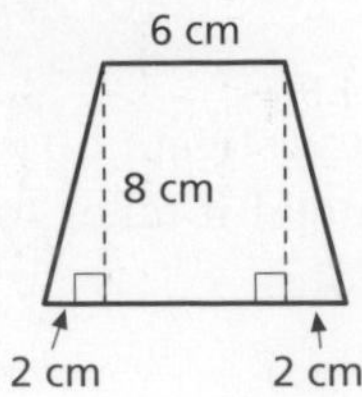

16

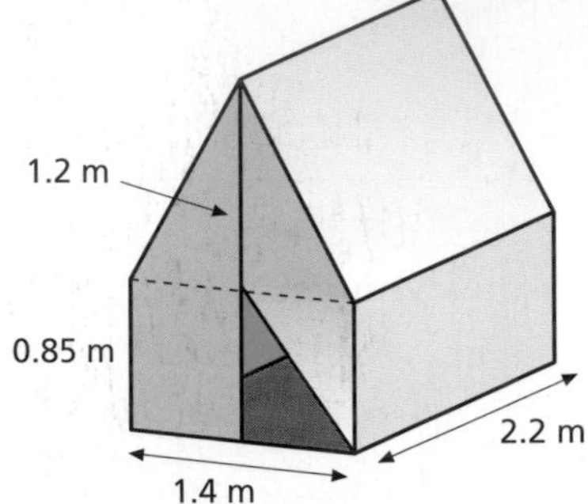

The roof of the tent is a triangular prism. The body of the tent is a cuboid.
Calculate the volume of the tent.

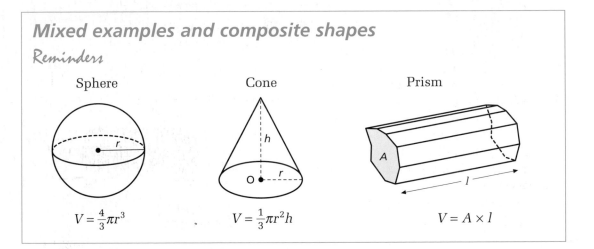

Mixed examples and composite shapes

Reminders

Sphere

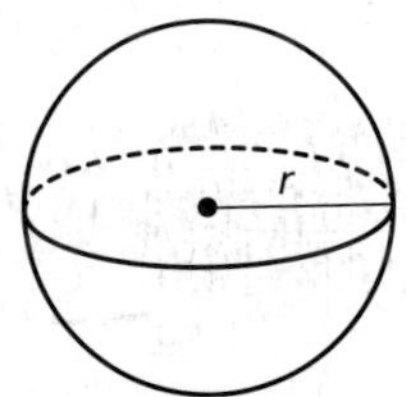

$V = \frac{4}{3}\pi r^3$

Cone

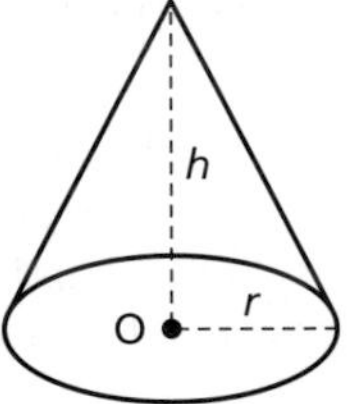

$V = \frac{1}{3}\pi r^2 h$

Prism

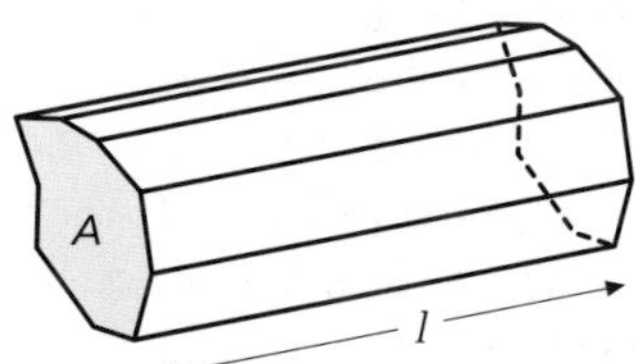

$V = A \times l$

EXERCISE 5

1 Use the formulae above to calculate the volume of these solids.

a

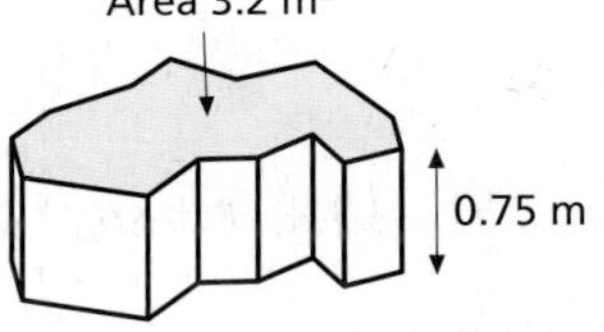

b

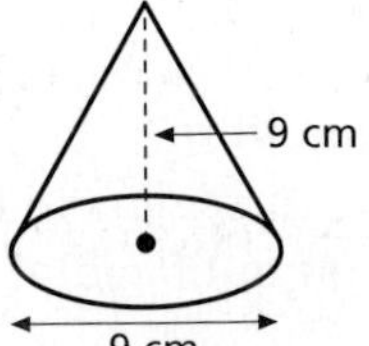

c

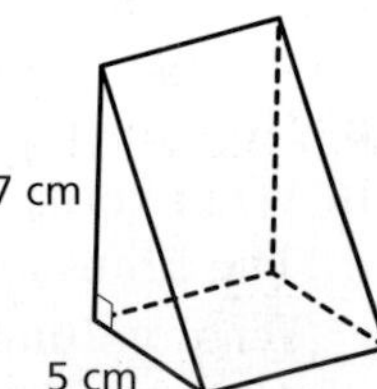

d

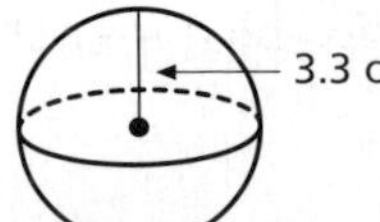

e

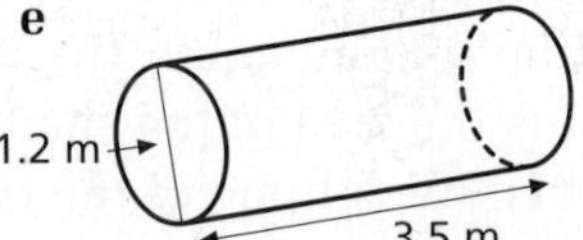

2

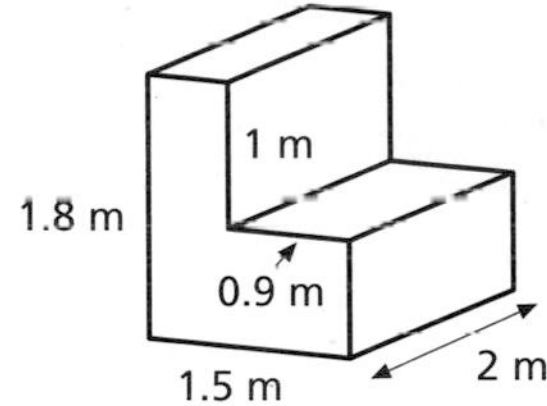

A park bench has been made in concrete.
Its dimensions are as shown.
Calculate the volume of concrete needed.

3 A primitive hut is cylindrical with a cone-shaped roof.
The cone is 2.4 m high.
The cylinder is 2 m high.
The hut has a diameter of 3 m.
Calculate the volume of space inside the hut.

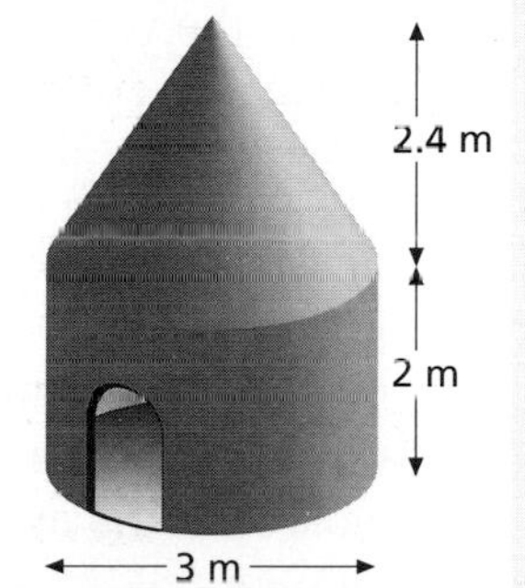

4

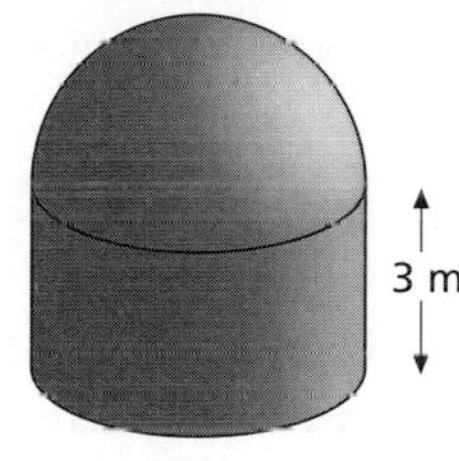

A silo is a cylinder with a hemisphere on top.
Its diameter is 5 m. Its walls are 3 m high.

a What is the radius of the hemisphere?
b What is the volume of the silo?

5 A capsule for medicine is a cylinder with a hemisphere at each end.
The pill is 10 mm long. It is 6 mm wide.

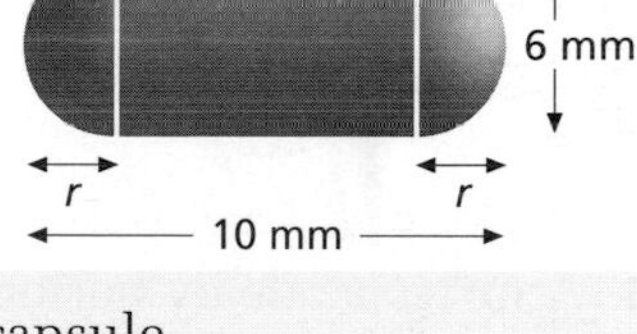

a State the size of:
(i) the diameter
(ii) the radius of each hemisphere.
b Work out the length of the cylinder.
c Calculate the volume of:
(i) both hemispheres (ii) the cylinder (iii) the capsule.

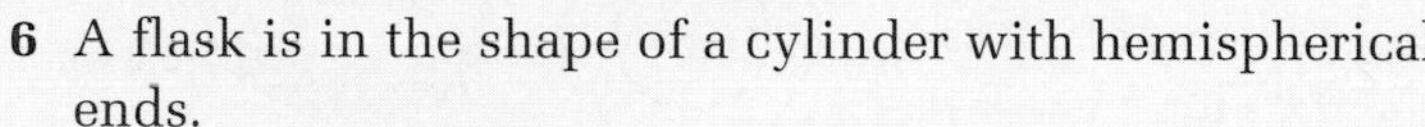

6 A flask is in the shape of a cylinder with hemispherical ends.

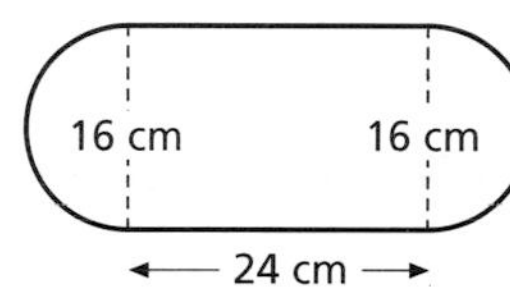

a Work out the radius of each hemisphere.
b Calculate the total volume of both hemispheres.
c Calculate the volume of the cylinder.
d Calculate the volume of liquid the flask will hold.

7

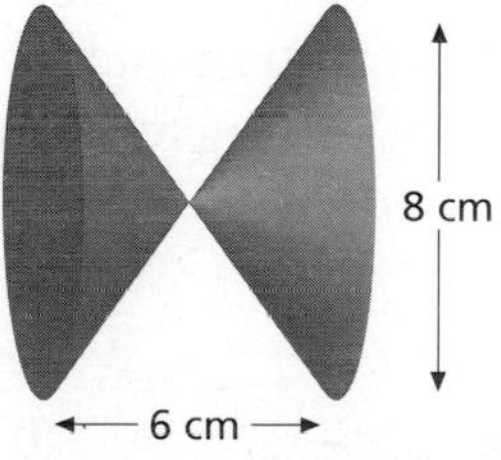

A children's toy is made of two identical cones as shown.

a What is the height of one cone?
b What volume of wood is needed to make the toy?

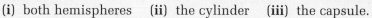

8

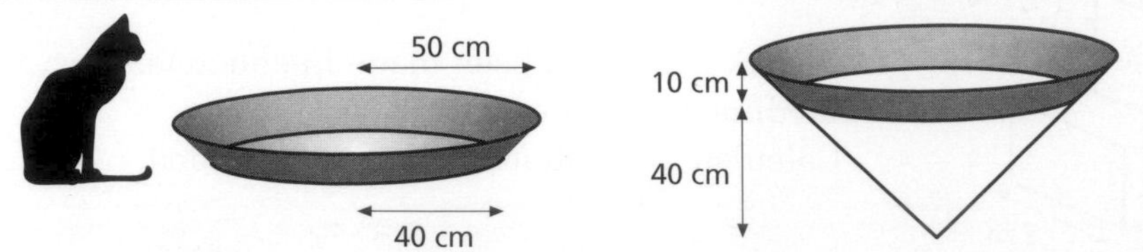

A cat's basket is a large cone with a smaller cone removed.
Calculate the volume of:

a the smaller cone **b** the larger cone **c** the basket.

9 A plastic pipe has an outer radius of 30 cm and an inner radius of 25 cm. Its overall length is 1000 cm. Calculate:

a the area of the outer circle
b the area of the inner circle
c the area of the cross-section of the pipe
d the volume of plastic needed to make the pipe.

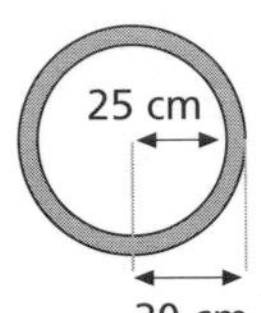

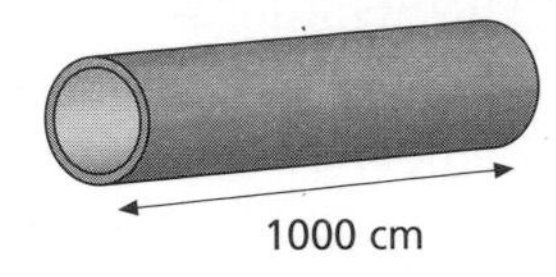

10

A diving bell is a hollow sphere.
The diameter of the inside is 2.5 m.
The diameter of the outside is 3 m.
Calculate:

a the volume of the inner sphere
b the volume of the outer sphere
c the volume of the material making the bell.

11 A nut is made by boring a hole through a hexagonal prism. This hexagon has an area of 10.4 cm^2. The hole has a radius of 1 cm. The thickness of the nut is 0.8 cm. What is the volume of metal in the finished nut?

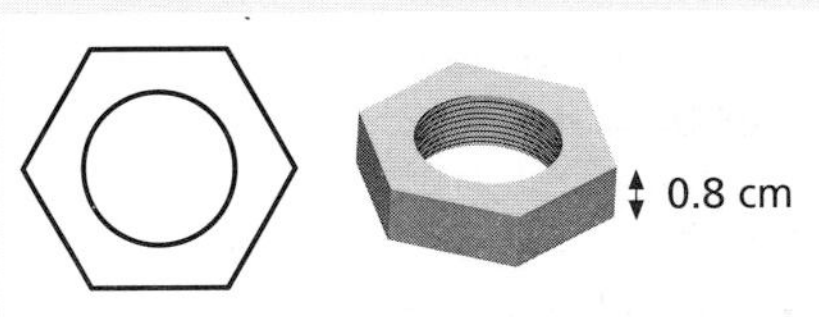

12

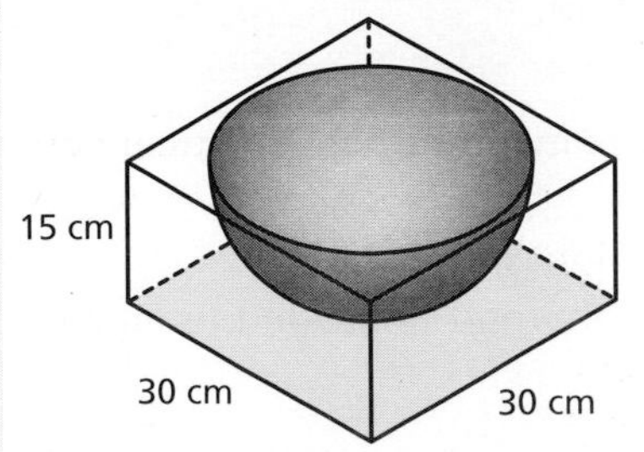

A basin is designed as shown. It is a hemisphere hollowed out of a cuboid. The cuboid is 15 cm × 30 cm × 30 cm. The hemisphere has a diameter of 28 cm. What is the volume of material making the basin?

CHAPTER 3 REVIEW

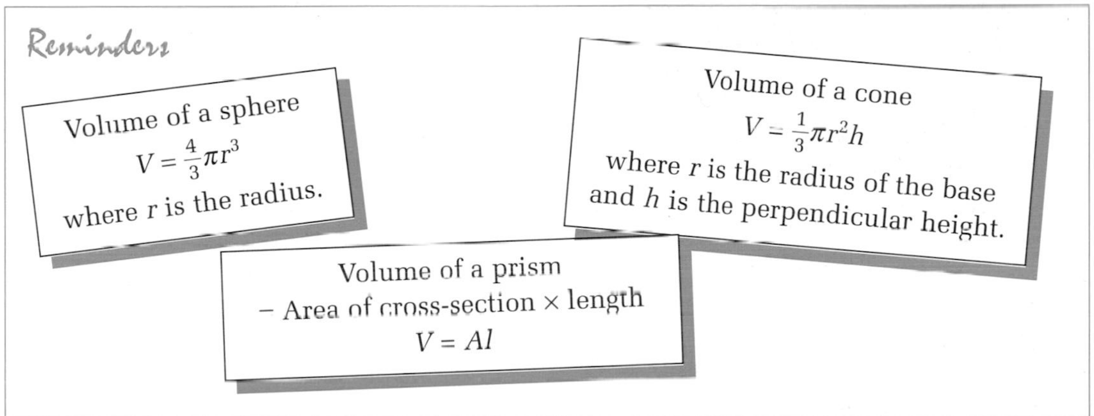

Reminders
Volume of a sphere
$V = \frac{4}{3}\pi r^3$
where r is the radius.
Volume of a cone
$V = \frac{1}{3}\pi r^2 h$
where r is the radius of the base
and h is the perpendicular height.
Volume of a prism
= Area of cross-section × length
$V = Al$

1 Calculate, correct to 3 s.f., the volume of:
  a a cone with radius 3.5 cm and height 6 cm
  b a prism with a cross-sectional area of 42 cm^2 and length 4.8 cm
  c a sphere with radius 5.3 cm.

2 Work out the volume of each of these solids.

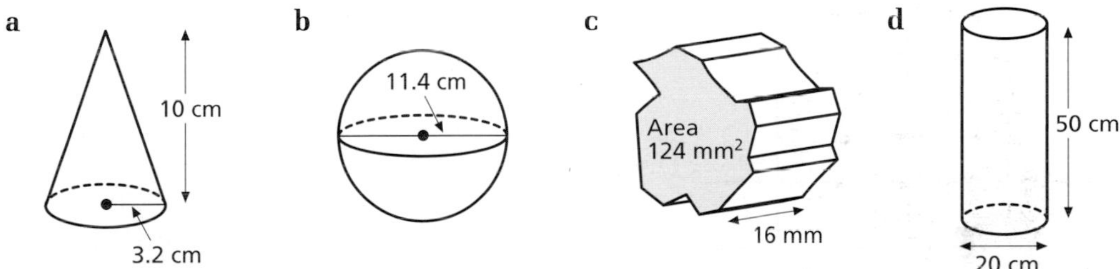

3 An oil drum has radius 32 cm and height 75 cm.
  Calculate the volume of oil it will hold.

4 A golf ball has a diameter of 4.2 cm.
  Calculate its volume correct to 3 s.f.

5

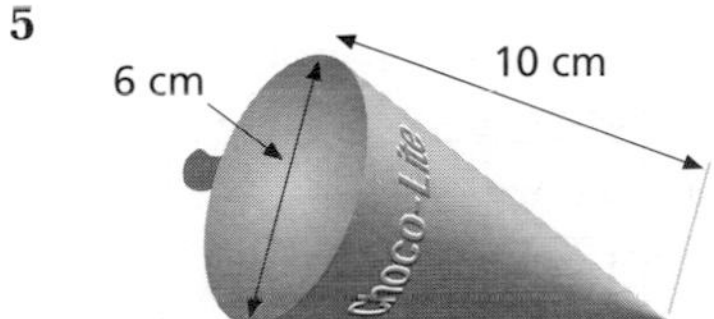

A paper cone is filled with chocolate ice-cream.
The cone is 10 cm deep and has a diameter of 6 cm.
How much ice-cream does the cone hold (to 1 d.p.)?

4 Linear Relationships

STARTING POINTS

1 Write down the coordinates of the points shown on the grid, for example A(5, 4).

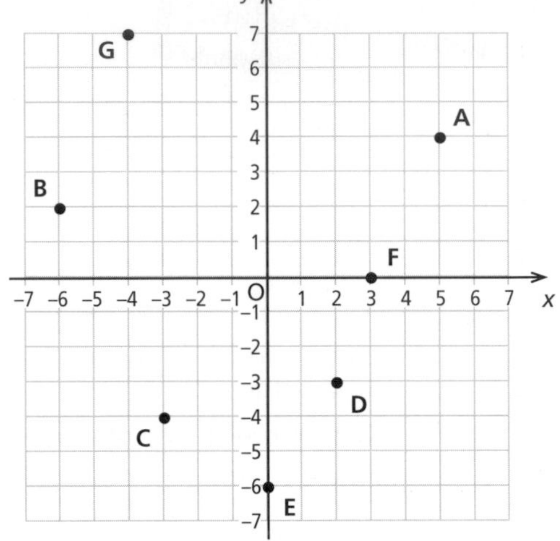

2 On a similar set of axes, plot and label these points.

a P(2, 4) **b** Q(−5, 6) **c** R(−1, −4)
d S(0, −3) **e** T(−1, 2) **f** U(−5, −3)
g V(2, 0) **h** W(5, 6) **i** X(−3, −4)

3

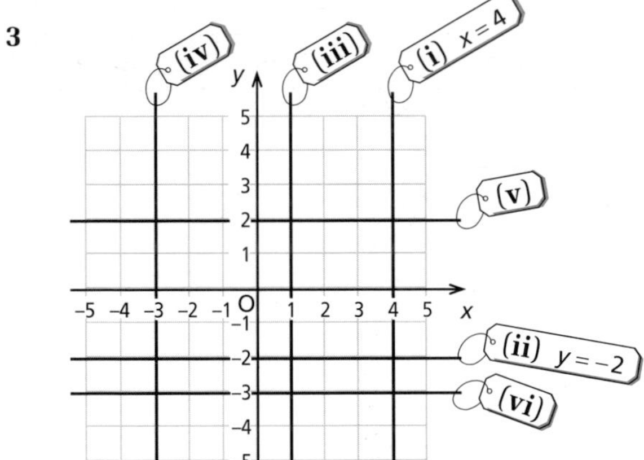

a The equation of line (**i**) is $x = 4$ and of line (**ii**) is $y = -2$.
Write down the equations of the lines (**iii**), (**iv**), (**v**) and (**vi**).

b Which two lines in the diagram does the point (1, −3) lie on?

c Which point lies on the lines $x = 4$ and $y = 2$?

d Which point lies on the lines $x = 1$ and $y = -6$?

4 Theatre tickets are £6 each. The total cost for a party of people going to the theatre can be worked out using the formula $y = 6x$, where y is the total cost in pounds and x is the number in the party.

a Copy and complete the table.

x	0	1	2	3	4	5	6
y	0	6					

b Why are there no negative values?

c Why are there no fractional values?

d Draw a graph of the situation by plotting the points (0, 0), (1, 6), etc.

e Why should the points not be joined in this graph?

5 a On the same diagram, draw graphs of each of the following equations. (Complete the tables first.)

$y = 3x$

x	−3	−2	−1	0	1	2	3
y	−9	−6					

$y = 2x$

x	−3	−2	−1	0	1	2	3
y	−6	−4					

b Which equation gives the steeper line?

6 a Copy and complete the table where $y = 2x + 4$.

x	−3	−2	−1	0	1	2	3
y	−2	0					

b Draw a graph of the table.

c Is the point (1, 5) above or below the line?

Drawing graphs

Reminder

To draw the graph of the straight line $y = 2x + 3$:

Step 1 Make a table.

x	−3	−2	−1	0	1	2	3
y	−3	−1	1	3	5	7	9

Step 2 Note the points from the table.
(−3, −3) (−2, −1) (−1, 1) (0, 3) (1, 5) (2, 7) (3, 9)

Step 3 Use suitable axes to plot the points, then draw and label the line.

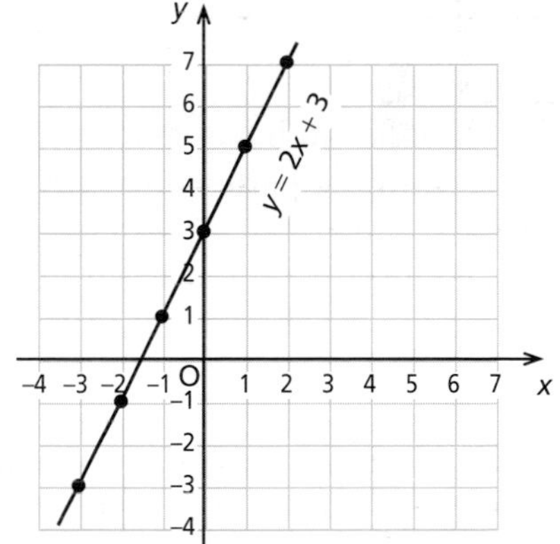

EXERCISE 1

1 a Copy and complete the table for $y = x - 1$.

b Use the values in the table to draw the graph of $y = x - 1$.

x	0	1	2
y	−1		

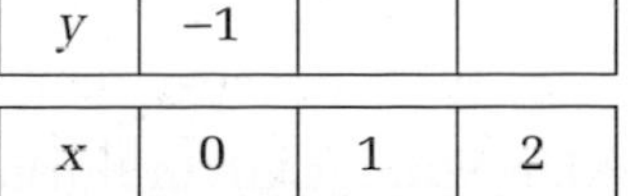

2 a Copy and complete the table for $y = -x$.

b Use the values in the table to draw the graph of $y = -x$.

x	0	1	2
y	0		

3 Draw graphs of the following straight lines.

a $y = x + 4$ **b** $y = -x + 1$ **c** $y = x - 2$ **d** $y = 3x + 2$ **e** $y = -2x$

4 Fishing on a lake costs £3 for a licence and £2 per hour.
This can be modelled by the equation $y = 2x + 3$ where x is the number of hours of fishing and y is the total cost in pounds.

a Make a table of values going from $x = 0$ to $x = 6$.

b Draw a graph of the table.

c Why do we say that the number of hours and the cost form a linear relationship?

5

1 2 3 4

A pattern of coins is being built up.

a Check that the patterns follow the formula $y = 2x - 1$ where x is the picture number and y is the number of coins in the picture.

b How many coins do you expect in the fifth picture?

c Copy and complete the table.

x	1	2	3	4	5	6	7
y	1	3	5	7			

d Plot the points on a grid.

e Why can we say that the number of coins and the picture number form a linear relationship?

f The points can be joined to stress this relationship. Why should we not read too much into the parts which lie between the plotted points?

6 A new battery in a torch has a life of 12 hours. The amount of life left in it can be calculated using the formula $y = 12 - x$ where x is the number of hours it has been used and y is the life left in hours.

a Copy and complete the table.

x	0	1	2	3	4	5
y	12					

b Draw a graph of the situation.

c The length of time used and the life left in a battery are in a linear relationship. How does the graph differ from the ones in questions **4** and **5**?

Many things are in linear relationships.
This makes it important to study the equation of the straight line.

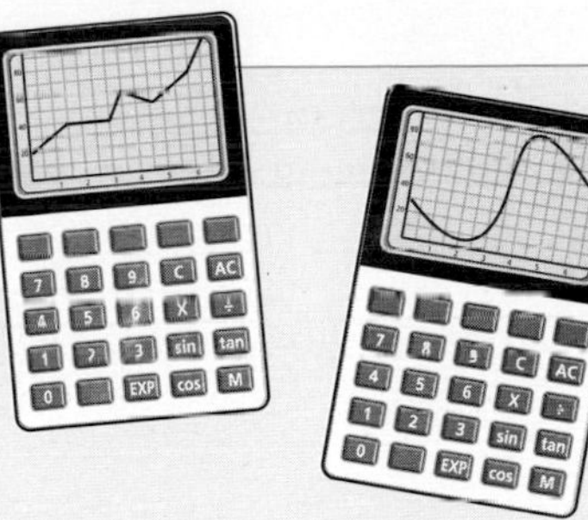

Challenge

Do this investigation if you have a Graph Drawing package. In each of the equations below, the number multiplying x is called the **coefficient** of x.

Task 1

Draw: $y = x$, $y = 2x$, $y = 3x$, $y = 4x$, $y = 5x$

Comment on how the slope of the line changes as the coefficient of x changes.

Task 2

Draw: $y = -x$, $y = -2x$, $y = -3x$, $y = -4x$, $y = -5x$

Comment on how the slope of the line changes as the coefficient of x changes.

Task 3

Draw: $y = x$, $y = \frac{1}{2}x$, $y = \frac{1}{3}x$, $y = \frac{1}{4}x$, $y = \frac{1}{5}x$

Comment on how the slope of the line changes as the coefficient of x changes.

Task 4

Draw: $y = x + 1$, $y = x + 2$, $y = x + 3$, $y = x + 4$, $y = x + 5$

What effect does changing the constant term have on the graph?

Task 5

By choosing suitable examples, investigate equations of the form $y = ax + b$ and say what effect changing **(i)** a **(ii)** b has on the graph.

The gradient

Reminder

The gradient of a slope $= \dfrac{\text{vertical change}}{\text{horizontal change}}$

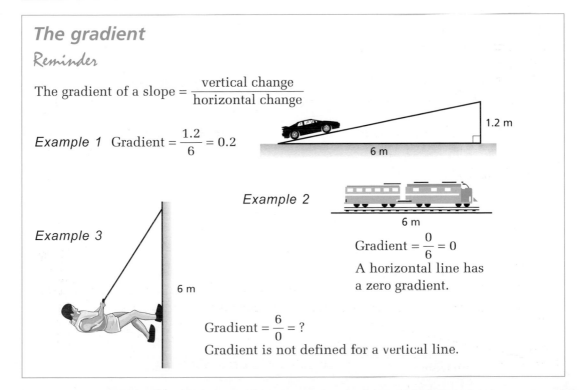

Example 1 Gradient $= \dfrac{1.2}{6} = 0.2$

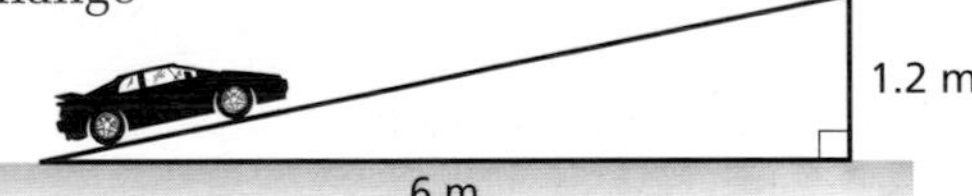

1.2 m

6 m

Example 2

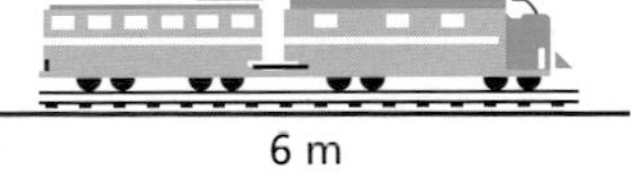

6 m

Gradient $= \dfrac{0}{6} = 0$

A horizontal line has a zero gradient.

Example 3

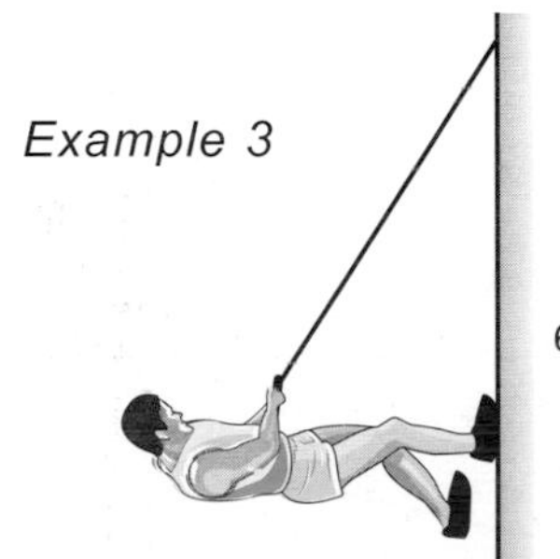

6 m

Gradient $= \dfrac{6}{0} = ?$

Gradient is not defined for a vertical line.

EXERCISE 2

1 Calculate the gradient of each sloping line.

a

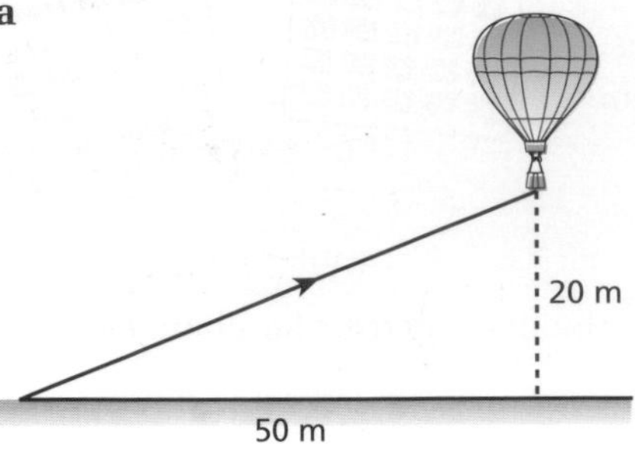

b

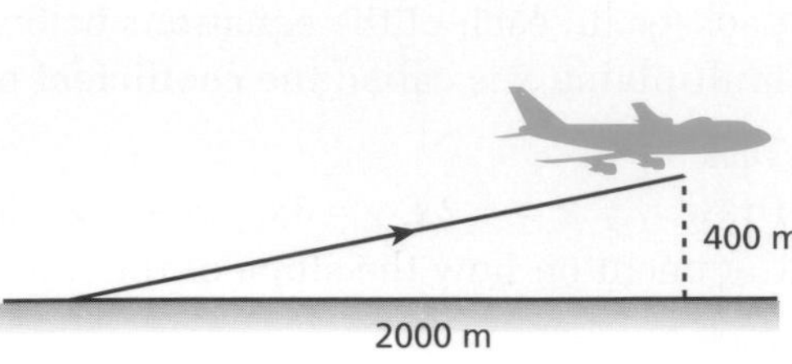

c

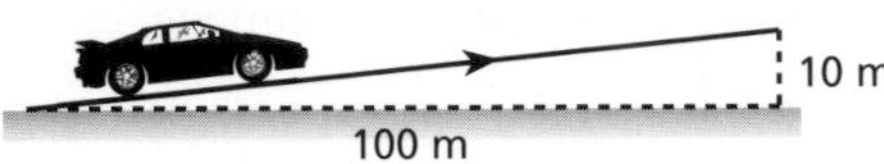

d

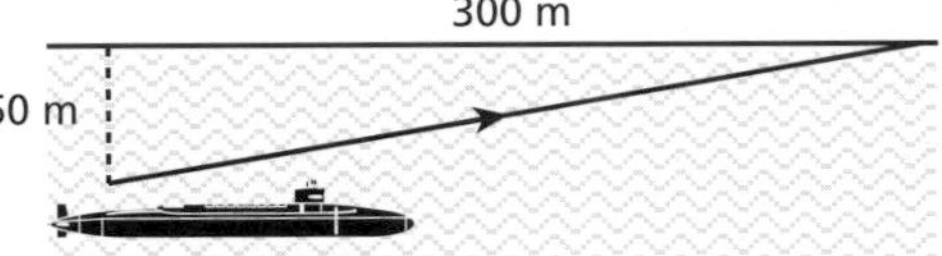

e

f

2 The regulations state that when digging a drainage trench the gradient of the trench must be between 0.1 and 0.2.
Which of these trenches are within regulation?

a

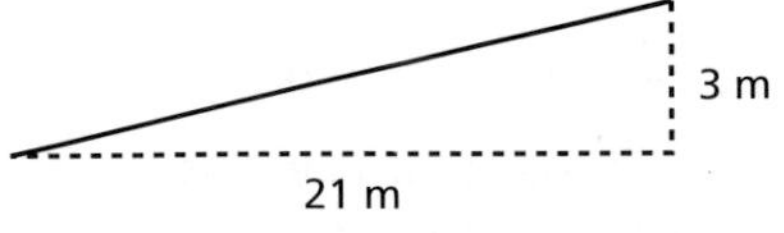

b

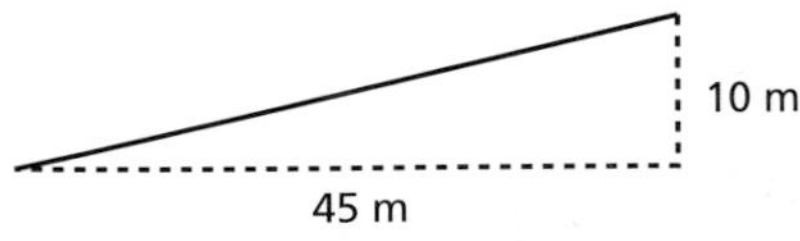

c

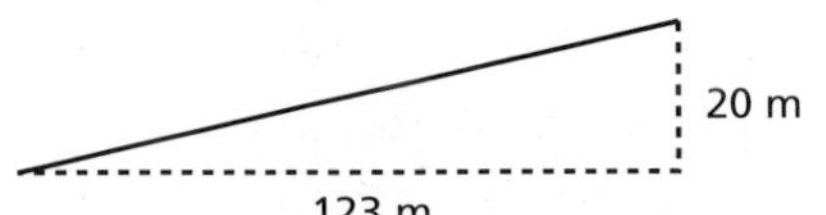

d

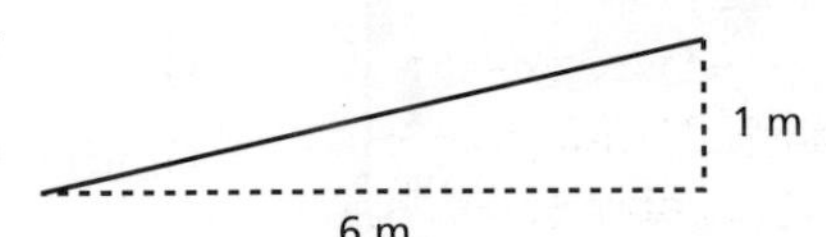

The gradient and coordinates

Finding the gradient of a straight line

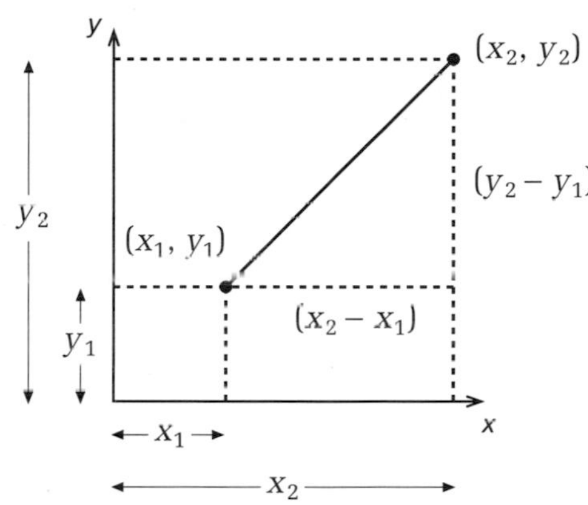

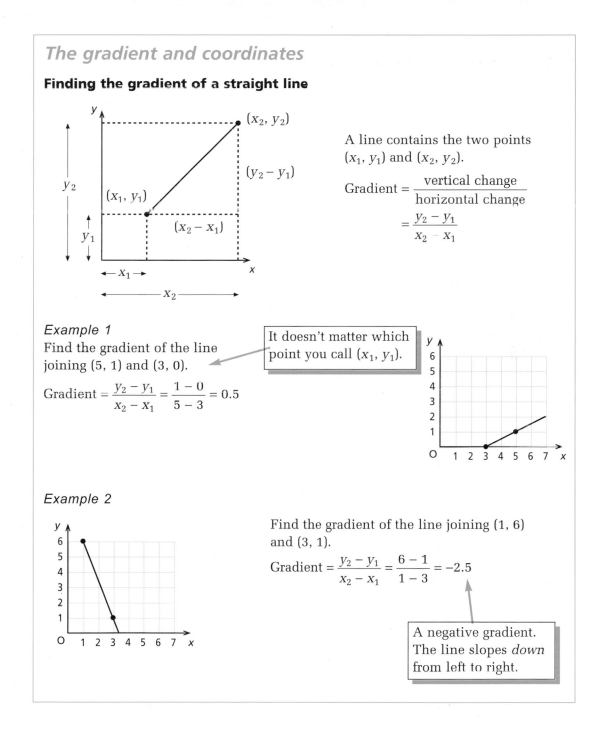

A line contains the two points (x_1, y_1) and (x_2, y_2).

$$\text{Gradient} = \frac{\text{vertical change}}{\text{horizontal change}} = \frac{y_2 - y_1}{x_2 - x_1}$$

Example 1

Find the gradient of the line joining (5, 1) and (3, 0).

It doesn't matter which point you call (x_1, y_1).

$$\text{Gradient} = \frac{y_2 - y_1}{x_2 - x_1} = \frac{1 - 0}{5 - 3} = 0.5$$

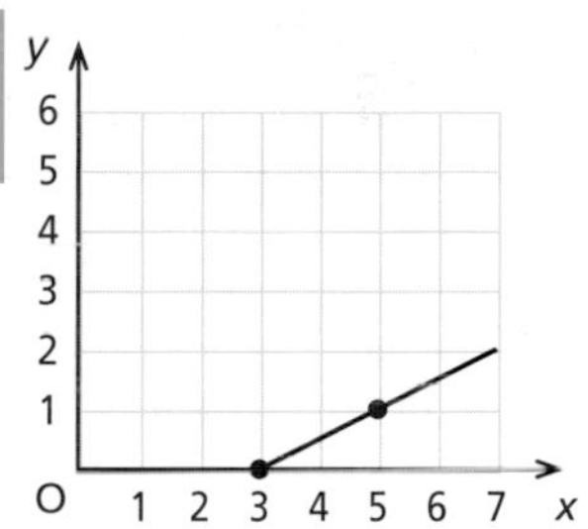

Example 2

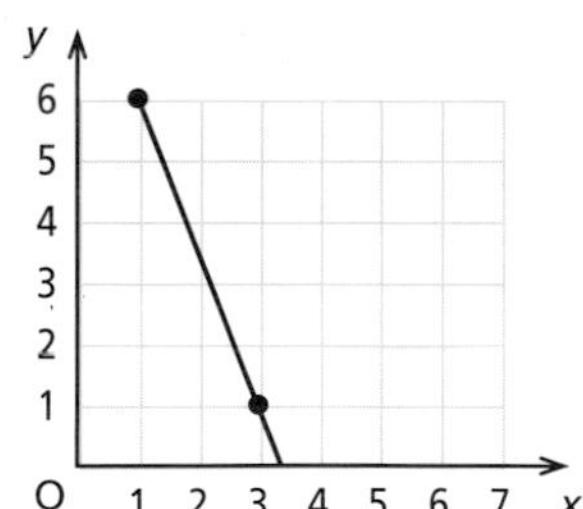

Find the gradient of the line joining (1, 6) and (3, 1).

$$\text{Gradient} = \frac{y_2 - y_1}{x_2 - x_1} = \frac{6 - 1}{1 - 3} = -2.5$$

A negative gradient. The line slopes *down* from left to right.

EXERCISE 3

1 Calculate the gradient of the line joining:

a (6, 1) and (8, 7)
b (1, 7) and (4, 16)
c (4, 4) and (14, 2)
d (8, 12) and (7, 18)
e (−1, 1) and (5, 13)
f (−2, −5) and (2, −7)
g (8, 2) and (4, −10)
h (−3, 4) and (−8, 4)

2 **a** State the coodinates of **(i)** A and **(ii)** B.
b Hence find the gradient of the line AB.

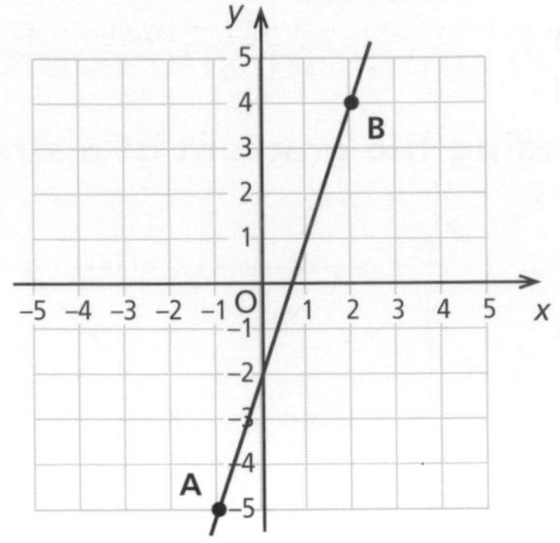

c In a similar fashion find the gradient of:
(i) CD **(ii)** EF **(iii)** GH **(iv)** IJ **(v)** KL **(vi)** MN.

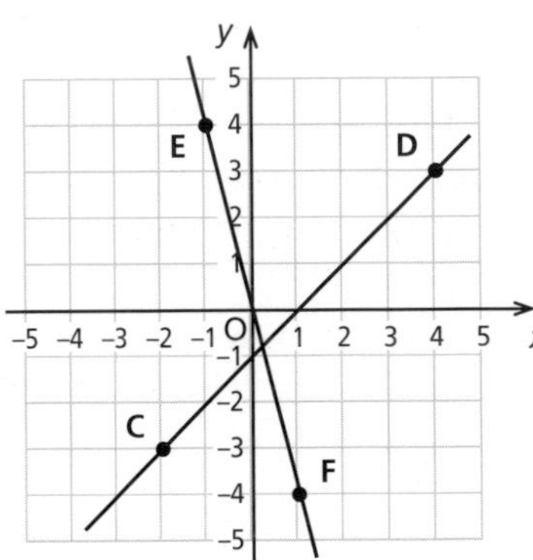

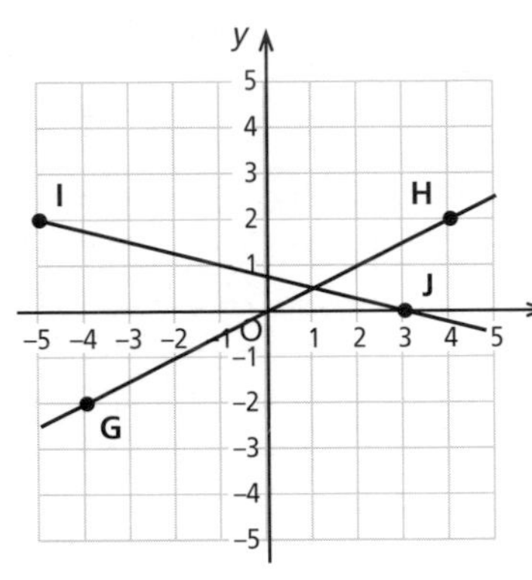

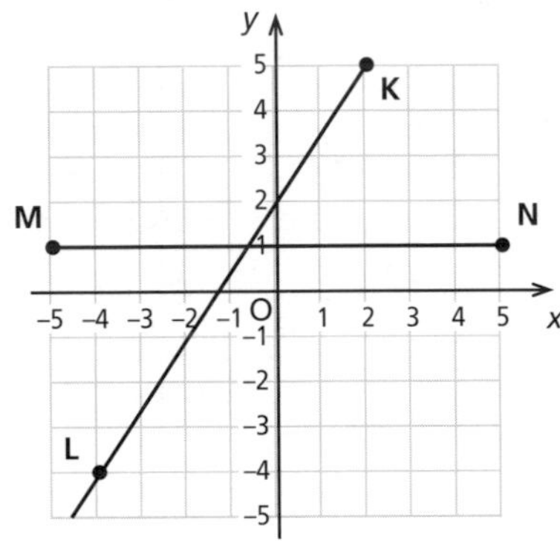

3 These lines are drawn in pairs.
a Give the coordinates of two points on each line.
b Find the gradient of each line.
c Comment on each pair of lines.
d What can be said about parallel lines?

(i)

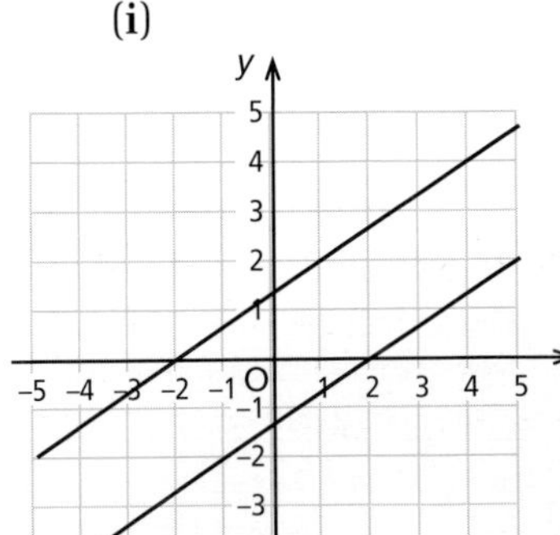

(ii)

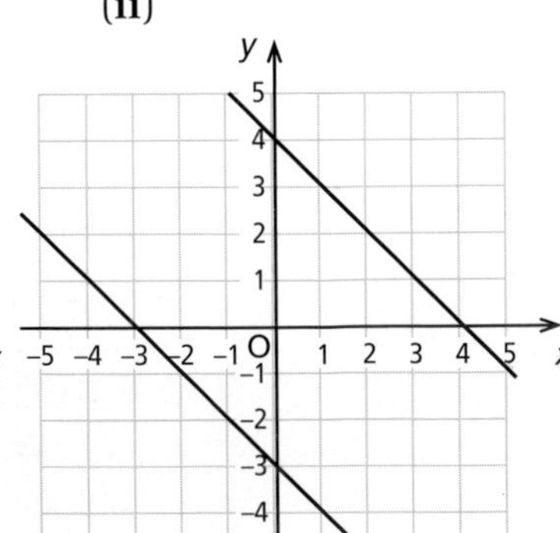

(iii)

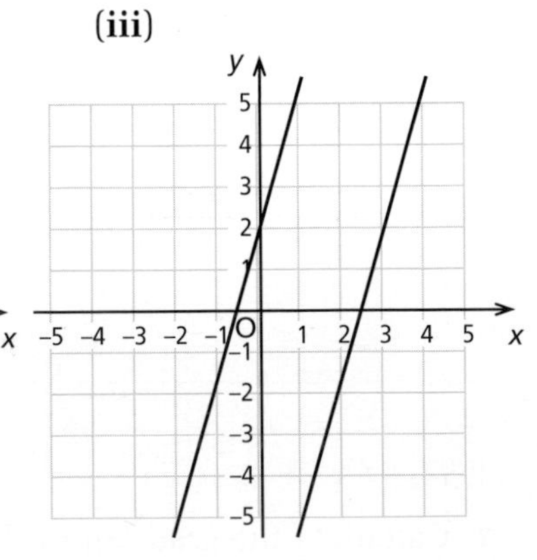

4 For each of the following equations:
(i) draw its line on a suitable grid **(ii)** work out its gradient.

a $y = 2x$ **b** $y = 3x + 1$ **c** $y = 0.5x$ **d** $y = x - 3$
e $y = 4x + 3$ **f** $y = -2x$ **g** $y = -0.5x$ **h** $y = -3x - 3$

5 By considering your answers to question **4**, state the gradient of a line with equation:

a $y = 10x + 1$ **b** $y = 25x - 2$

c $y = -13x + 3$ **d** $y = ax + b$

Hint

Parallel lines have the same gradient. The line $y = ax + b$ has a gradient equal to a.

6 Match up the lines in parallel pairs.

a $y = 8x + 1$ **b** $y = 0.5x - 2$ **c** $y = -4x + 3$ **d** $y = 7 - 6x$

e $y = 0.5x + 6$ **f** $y = 8x - 2$ **g** $y = -6x + 8$ **h** $y = -4x$

7

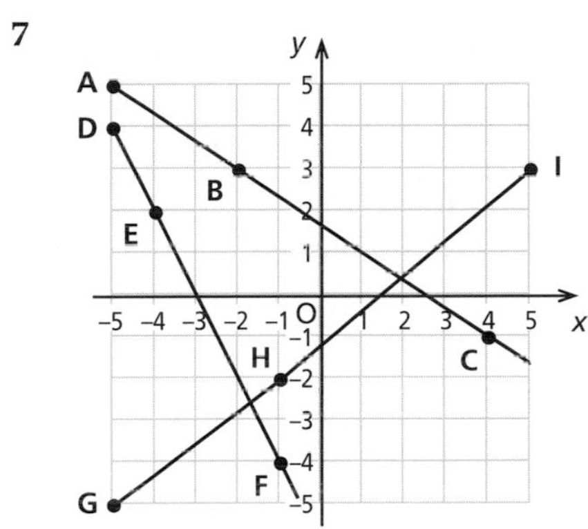

We want to know if ABC is a straight line or is there a bend at B?

a Write down the coordinates of A, B and C.

b Calculate the gradient of **(i)** AB **(ii)** BC.

c If the gradients are different then there is a bend at B.
If the gradients are the same then ABC is a straight line (because AB and BC are parallel and share a common point, B).
Is ABC a straight line?

d In a similar fashion decide if
(i) DEF **(ii)** GHI are straight lines.

In questions **8**, **9** and **10**, let the edge of each square represent 1 unit of measurement. The size of the unit differs from question to question.

8

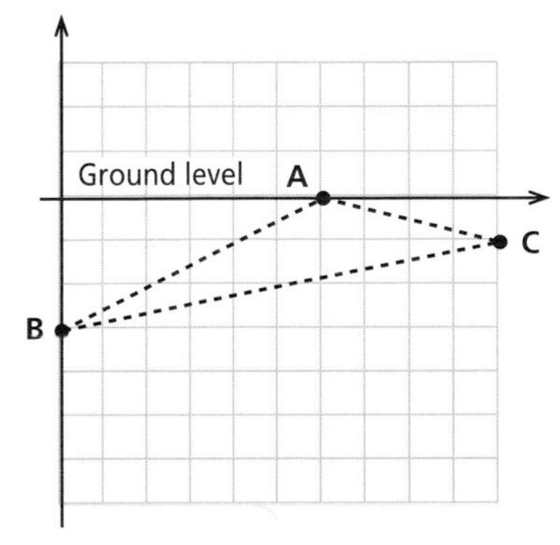

Engineers would like to run a drain from A to B. To meet regulations the gradient (ignoring sign) of any drain must lie between 0.1 and 0.3.

a Show that a drain running from A to B fails to meet regulations.

b The plan is to run a drain from A to C and then to B.
Show that each leg of the proposed drain meets with regulations.

9

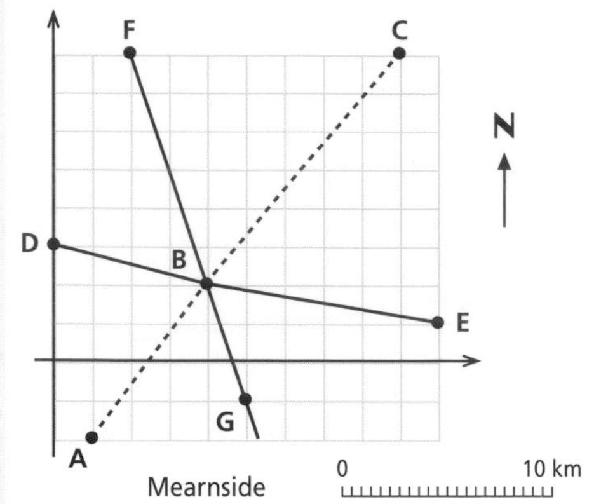

In the village of Mearnside there is a crossroads.
This has proved to be an accident blackspot.
The planners feel that accidents are occuring because, although the roads look straight, they are not.

a By comparing the gradients of AB and BC show that ABC is not a straight road.
b In a similar fashion decide if **(i)** DBE and **(ii)** FBG are straight.

10 For obvious reasons railtrack should be formed from parallel lines.
Overhead photos have been taken of two sections, as shown below.

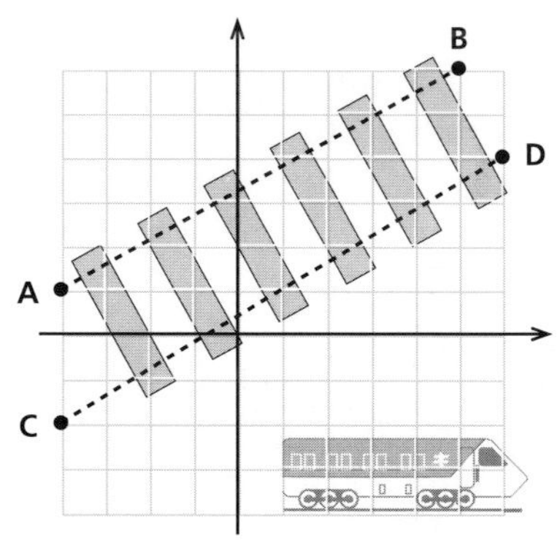

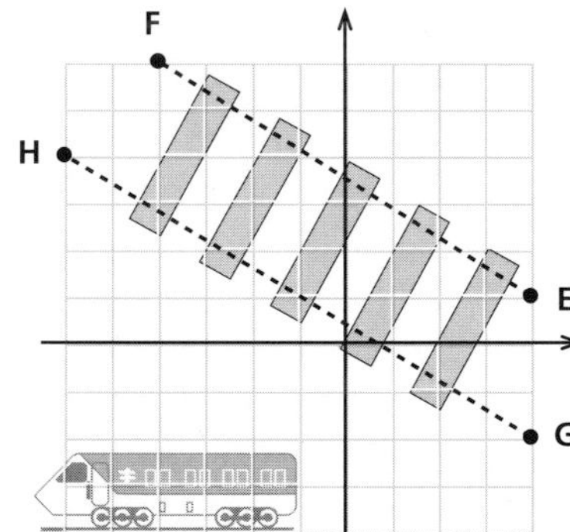

a By considering gradients decide:
(i) if AB is parallel to CD **(ii)** if EF is parallel to HG.
b If the rails are not parallel suggest an adjustment.

Challenge

The Highway Code describes how information about the gradients of hills is communicated to drivers.
Find out all you can about these signs.

The y-intercept

An equation of the form $y = ax + b$ produces a straight line when graphed.
a is the gradient of the line.
When $x = 0$ note that $y = a \times 0 + b$
or $y = b$
b is known as the y-intercept.
The line cuts the y axis at $(0, b)$.

Example 1

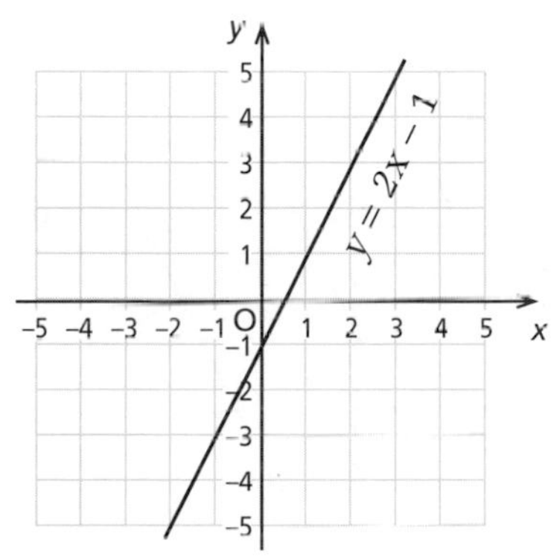

$y = 2x - 1$

Gradient is 2

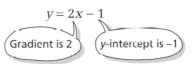

y-intercept is –1

Gradient is **positive**.
y-intercept is –1.
The line passes through the point (0, –1).

Example 2

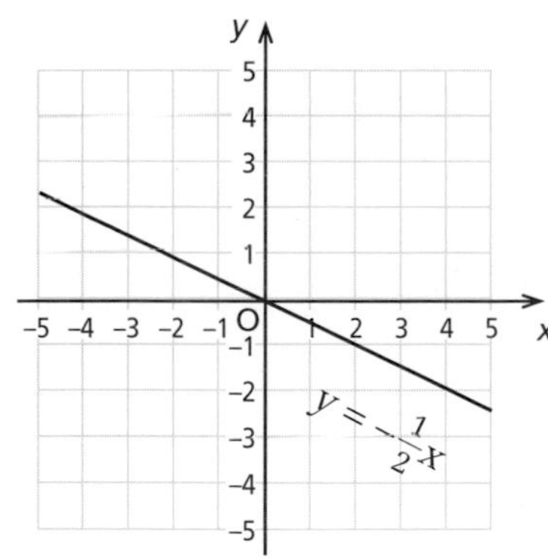

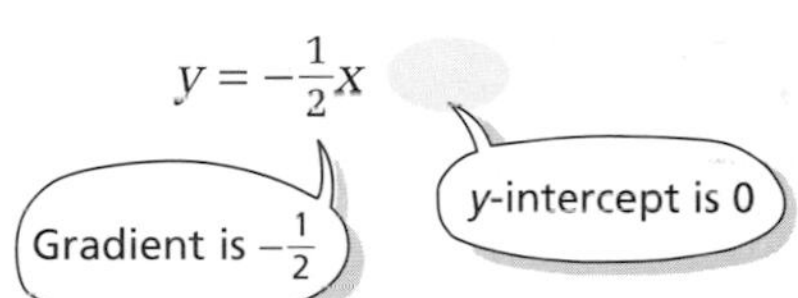

y-intercept is 0.
The line passes through the point (0, 0).

EXERCISE 4

1 Write down the gradient and y-intercept for each of these straight lines.

a $y = 2x + 5$ **b** $y = 3x - 2$ **c** $y = x - 2$
d $y = -3x + 1$ **e** $y = -x + 5$ **f** $y = 5x + 100$
g $y = -x$ **h** $y = \frac{2}{3}x - 1$ **i** $y = 3x$
j $y = 5$ **k** $y = 4 - x$ **l** $y = 3 - 2x$
m $y = 6 - 3x$ **n** $y = 1 - 7x$

2 For each line in the diagram,

(i) state the y-intercept

(ii) work out the gradient

(iii) write down the equation of the line in the form $y = ax + b$.

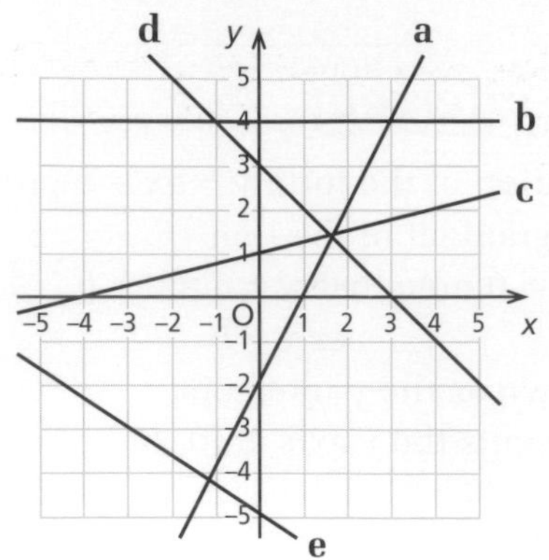

3 Match the equations to the correct lines.
(Look for the y-intercept, then the gradient.)

$y = -\frac{1}{2}x - 5$

$y = 6$

$x = -7$

$y = 2x$

$y = -\frac{1}{2}x + 8$

$y = 2x + 8$

$x = 2$

$y = -3$

$y = -\frac{1}{2}x - 1$

$y = 2x - 8$

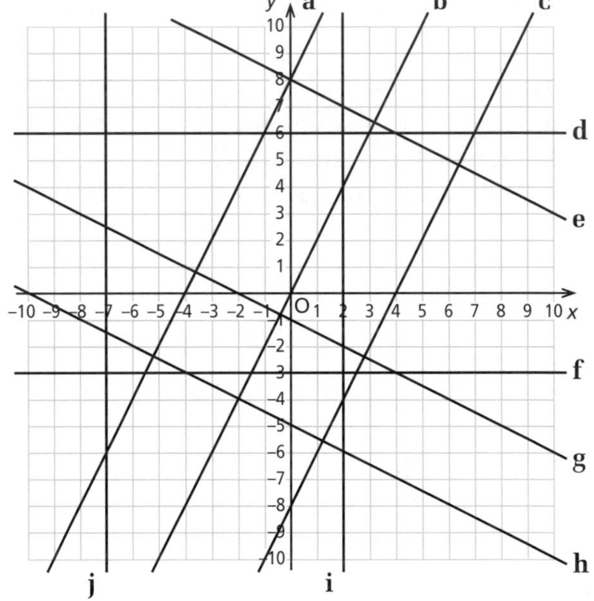

4

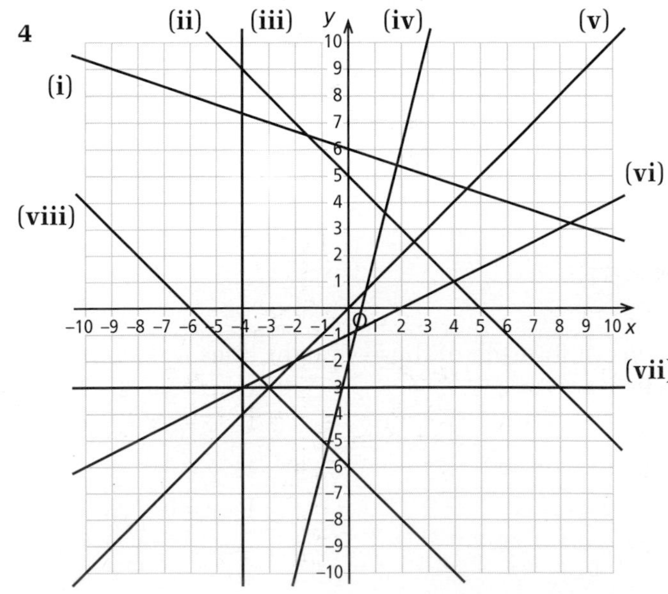

a Which of these lines have a positive gradient?

b Which line is parallel to the x axis?

c Which line is parallel to the y axis?

d Write down the gradient, y-intercept and equation for each line where possible.

5 Write down the equations of lines which have the following gradients and y-intercepts:

	Gradient	y-intercept
a	2	5
b	−4	0
c	$5\frac{1}{2}$	−1
d	$\frac{2}{3}$	2
e	0	3
f	−3	4

6 $y = 4x + 3$ is the equation of a straight line.
Write down the equations of three different lines which are parallel to $y = 4x + 3$.

7 The two lines in the diagram are parallel.
a Where does the line B cut the y axis?
b What is the gradient of line A?
c Write down the equation of line A.

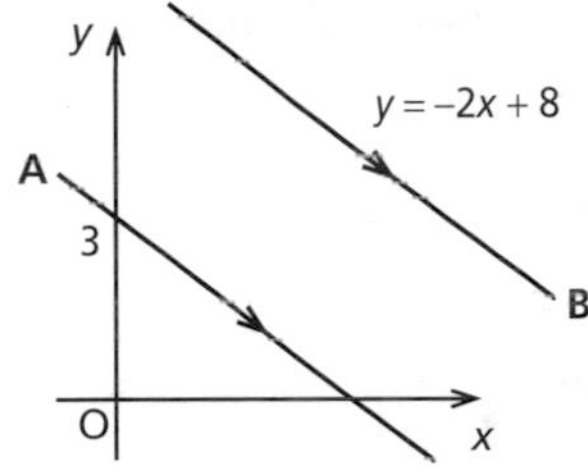

8 Use the clues to write down the equations of the lines **a**, **b**, **c** and **d**.

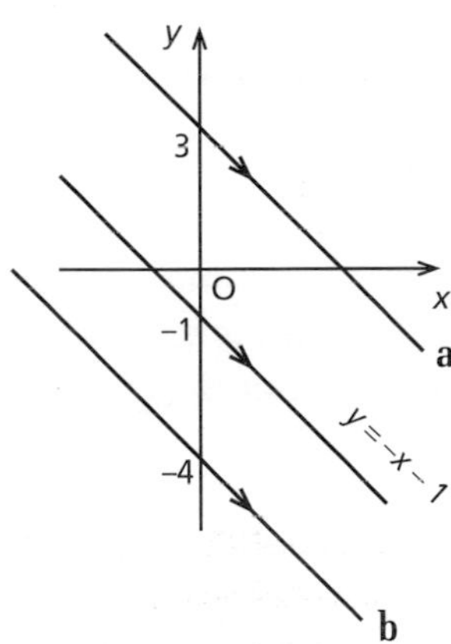

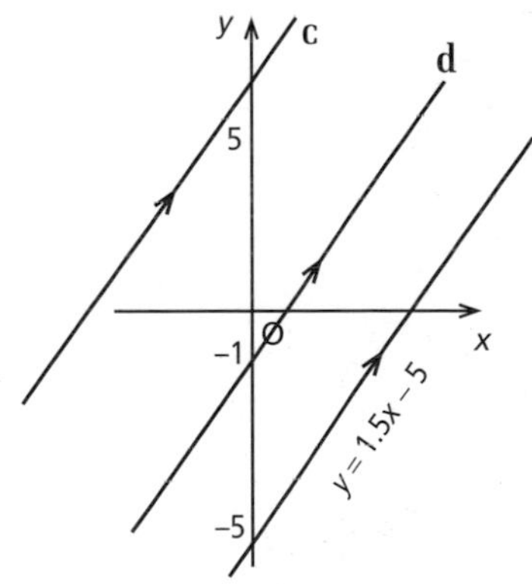

9 **a** Find the equations of the lines which form the perimeter of this quadrilateral.
b Name pairs of parallel lines.
c State the equation of each diagonal.
d What kind of shape is it?

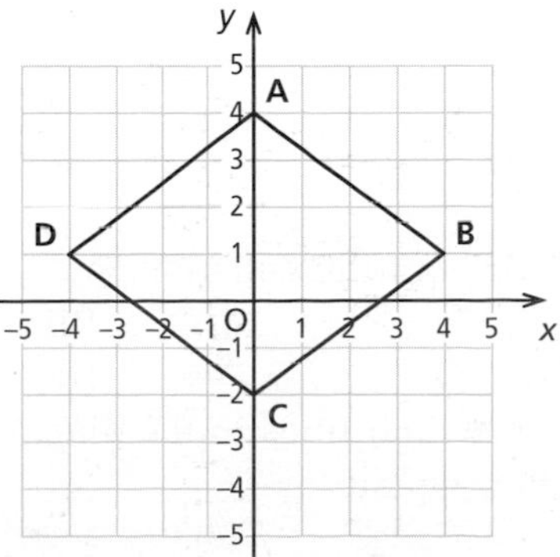

10

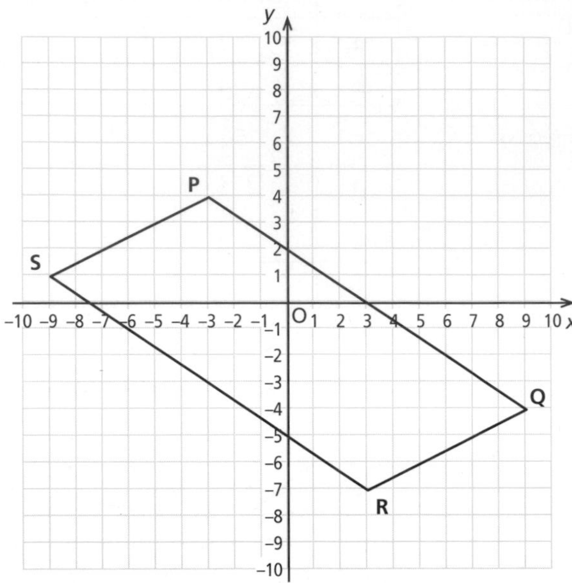

a What shape is drawn on the coordinate grid?

b Find the gradient of PQ.

c Which side has the same gradient as PQ?

d Write down the equations of PQ and SR.

e Calculate the gradient of SP.

f Which side has the same gradient as SP?

g What information would you need in order to write down the equation of SP?

11

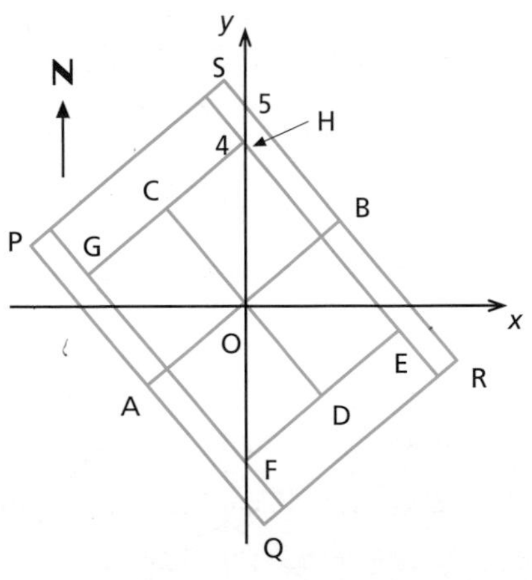

A planner is organising a tennis court on a plot of land.
He uses a computer design program.
You may assume that if lines look parallel then they are.
The court is symmetrical.
The equation of AB is $y = x$.
The equation of CD is $y = -x$.

a Work out the equations of:

(i) RS **(iii)** FE

(ii) PQ **(iv)** GH.

b For which lines in the diagram is there not enough information to work out their equations?

Other forms

Sometimes the equation of the straight line is disguised. It then has to be arranged into the form $y = ax + b$ to pick out the gradient and y-intercept.

Example $2x + 3y = 4$

$\Rightarrow 3y = -2x + 4$ $\qquad \Rightarrow y = -\frac{2}{3}x + \frac{4}{3}$

So $2x + 3y = 4$ is a straight line with gradient $-\frac{2}{3}$ and y-intercept $\frac{4}{3}$.

Just passing through

When a line passes through a point, the coordinates of the point fit the equation of the line.

Example 1
Does $y = 2x + 1$ pass through (1, 3)?

Note that $3 = 2 \times 1 + 1$, so the line *does* pass through the point.

Example 2
Does $y = 2x + 1$ pass through (3, 5)?

Note that $5 \neq 2 \times 3 + 1$, so the line *does not* pass through the point.

EXERCISE 5

1 Rearrange these equations in the form $y = ax + b$.
Find the gradient and y-intercept for each straight line.

a $y - 2x = 3$ **b** $2y - 3x = 1$ **c** $y - x + 3 = 0$ **d** $5y + 4x = 10$ **e** $2x - 2y = 5$
f $4x + y = 0$ **g** $2y - 4x = 14$ **h** $-2x + y = -5$ **i** $5y + 10 = 0$ **j** $12 - 2y = x$

2 Find the odd one out in each set of equations.

a $2x + 3y = 6$ $\quad \frac{2}{3}x + y = 2$ $\quad y = \frac{2}{3}x + 2$ $\quad y = -\frac{2}{3}x + 2$
b $4x + 5y = 10$ $\quad \frac{4}{5}x + y = 2$ $\quad y = -\frac{4}{5}x + 10$ $\quad y = -\frac{4}{5}x + 2$
c $x + 2y = 8$ $\quad \frac{1}{2}x + y = 2$ $\quad y = -\frac{1}{2}x + 2$ $\quad y + \frac{1}{2}x - 2 = 0$

3 A line is parallel to the line with equation $4x + 2y = 5$.
It passes through the point (0, 7).

a Work out its gradient. **b** Write down its equation.
c In a similar fashion find the following lines:
(i) parallel to $x + y = 0$; passes through (0, 2)
(ii) parallel to $x - y = 0$; passes through (0, –4)
(iii) parallel to $6x + 3y = 1$; passes through (0, 0)
(iv) parallel to $2x + 3y = 3$; passes through (0, 5).

4 Identify through which of the given points each line passes.

a line: $y = 3x + 2$; points (1, 5), (2, 7), (3, 11)
b line: $y = 5x - 3$; points (1, 2), (2, 7), (3, 11)
c line: $y = -x + 5$; points (1, 4), (2, 2), (3, 2)
d line: $y - 3x = 1$; points (1, 5), (2, 7), (3, 10)
e line: $y - 2x + 1 = 0$; points (1, 1), (2, 3), (3, 7)
f line: $3x - 2y = 2$; points (4, 5), (2, 2), (6, 7)

CHAPTER 4 REVIEW

1 It costs £10 to join a tennis club and £2 per game. The total cost in pounds can be calculated using the equation $y = 2x + 10$ where y is the cost in pounds and x is the number of games.

x	0	1	2	3	4	5
y	10	12				

a Copy and complete the table.
b Plot the points to illustrate the situation.
c Join the dots to highlight the linear relationship.
d Do the sections between the plotted points have any meaning?

2 **a** Copy and complete the table for $y = x + 2$.
b Use the values in the table to draw the graph of $y = x + 2$.

x	0	1	2
y	2		

3 Calculate the gradient in each picture.

a

b

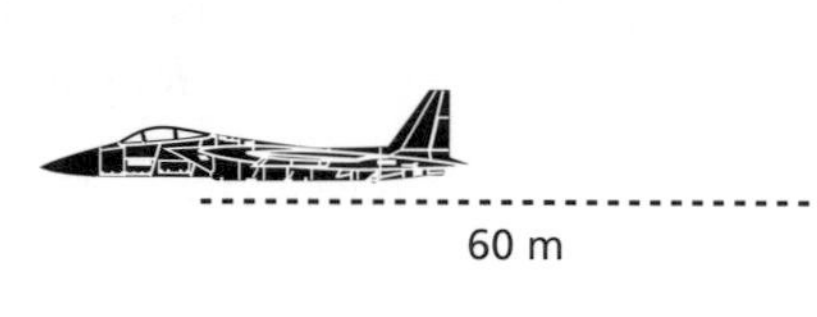

Horizontal flight

c

Vertical mast

4 Calculate the gradient of the line joining each pair of points.
a (1, 4), (6, 14) **b** (–2, 6), (8, 11) **c** (2, 4), (5, –2)

5 Graph these equations.
a $y = 2x - 1$ **b** $y = -x + 3$ **c** $y = 3x$

6 **a** Which of these equations pass through the origin?
b Which sets of lines are parallel?

$y = x + 1$ $y = 2x - 5$ $y = x$ $y = 2x + 3$
$y = 2x + 5$ $y = -2x$ $y = -0.5x + 10$

7 Write down the equation of the line:
a with gradient 2 and y-intercept –1 **b** with gradient 0 and y-intercept 3
c with gradient –3 and y-intercept 2

8 Work out the equation of each line.

a **b** **c**

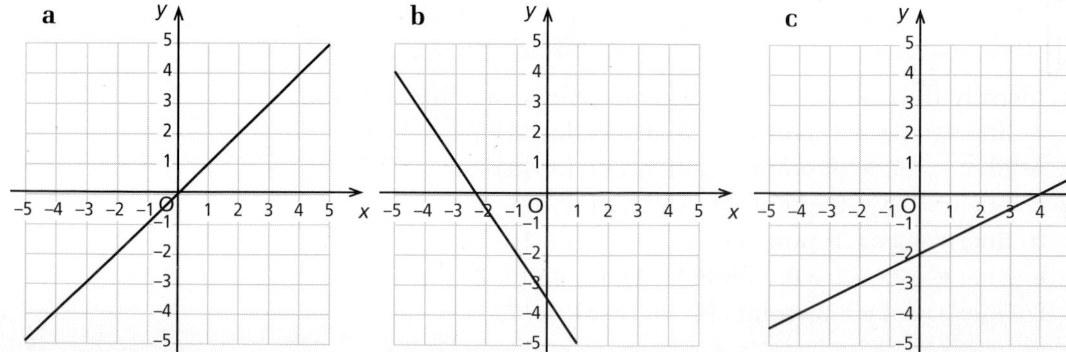

5 Algebraic Operations

STARTING POINTS

1 Simplify:

a $5y + 2y$ **b** $4x - x$ **c** $a \times a$ **d** $3m \times 2m$

e $5 \times 3x$ **f** $x^2 + 3x - x^2 + 2x$ **g** $y \times y^2$

2 Calculate (without a calculator):

a $-3 + 2$ **b** $-1 - 5$ **c** $4 - 7$ **d** $2 + (-5)$

e $2 \times (-3)$ **f** -2×3 **g** $(-3)^2$ **h** -3^2

i $-2 \times (-3)$ **j** $2 \times (-1)^2$ **k** $4 \div (-2)$ **l** $-3 \div (-6)$

3 Solve these equations:

a $x + 3 = 0$ **b** $2y - 1 = 0$ **c** $3x + 2 = 0$

Removing brackets

Examples

$$2(x - 3) = 2 \times x - 2 \times 3$$
$$= 2x - 6$$

$$5(2x + 7) = 5 \times 2x + 5 \times 7$$
$$= 10x + 35$$

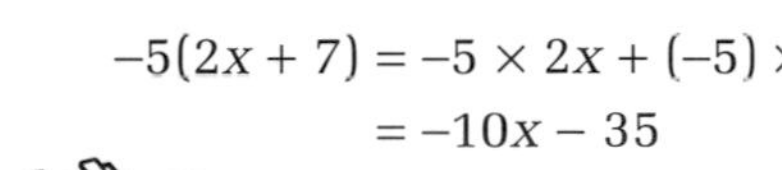

$$-5(2x + 7) = -5 \times 2x + (-5) \times 7$$
$$= -10x - 35$$

Reminder

Multiply each term within the bracket by the term outside the bracket.

(The cost of a film plus the cost of a set of prints) times 5 equals the cost of 5 films plus the cost of 5 sets of prints.

$$a(a + b) = a \times a + a \times b$$
$$= a^2 + ab$$

$$x(x - 5) = x \times x - x \times 5$$
$$= x^2 - 5x$$

$$y(2x - 3y) = y \times 2x - y \times 3y$$
$$= 2xy - 3y^2$$

EXERCISE 1

remember this shit

1 Remove the brackets:

a $2(x + 1)$ **b** $3(y - 2)$ **c** $5(x + y)$ **d** $6(5 - a)$
e $2(2 - t)$ **f** $3(a - b)$ **g** $10(2 - y)$ **h** $6(m - 3)$
i $7(n - 5)$ **j** $11(r - 1)$ **k** $2(3 + y)$ **l** $6(1 + t)$
m $4(a + b)$ **n** $3(6 - c)$ **o** $5(d - 10)$ **p** $10(y - 3)$
q $2(c + d)$ **r** $4(e - 12)$

2 7 times (the weight of a trailer plus the weight of the truck)
equals
7 times the weight of the trailer plus 7 times the weight of the truck.

In a similar fashion expand the following statements.

a 4 times (the cost of a sandwich plus the cost of a coffee) equals ...
b 8 times (the cost of a postcard plus the cost of a stamp) equals ...
c 12 times (the cost of the cola minus the discount) equals ...

3 Write the area of each rectangle (**i**) with and (**ii**) without brackets.
(All measurements are in centimetres.)

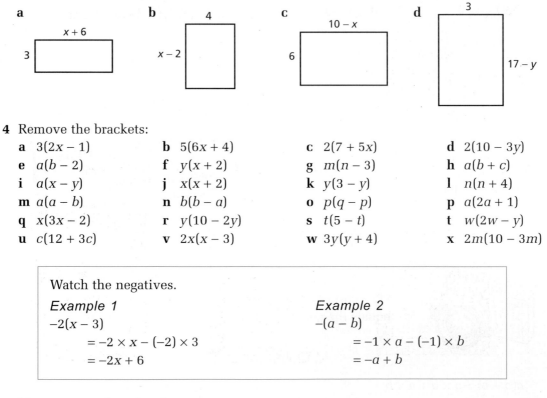

a
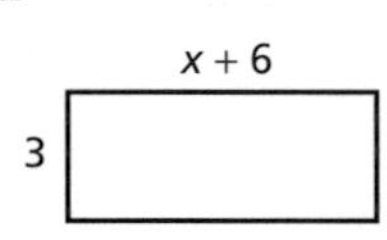

b
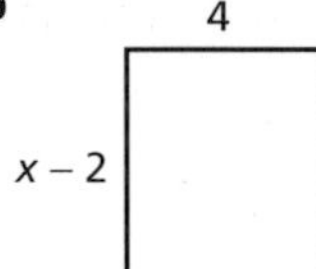

c
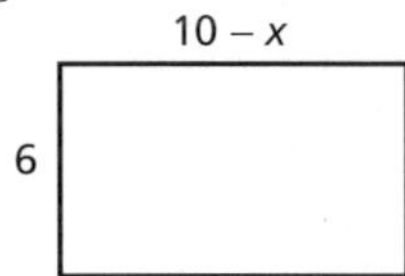

d
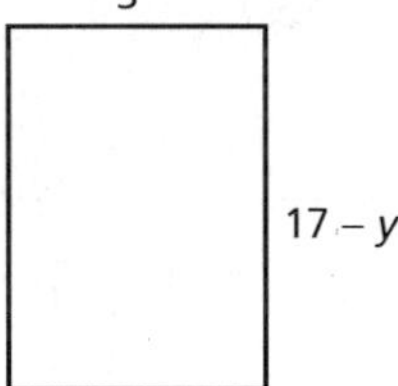

4 Remove the brackets:

a $3(2x - 1)$ **b** $5(6x + 4)$ **c** $2(7 + 5x)$ **d** $2(10 - 3y)$
e $a(b - 2)$ **f** $y(x + 2)$ **g** $m(n - 3)$ **h** $a(b + c)$
i $a(x - y)$ **j** $x(x + 2)$ **k** $y(3 - y)$ **l** $n(n + 4)$
m $a(a - b)$ **n** $b(b - a)$ **o** $p(q - p)$ **p** $a(2a + 1)$
q $x(3x - 2)$ **r** $y(10 - 2y)$ **s** $t(5 - t)$ **t** $w(2w - y)$
u $c(12 + 3c)$ **v** $2x(x - 3)$ **w** $3y(y + 4)$ **x** $2m(10 - 3m)$

> Watch the negatives.
>
> *Example 1*
> $-2(x - 3)$
> $= -2 \times x - (-2) \times 3$
> $= -2x + 6$
>
> *Example 2*
> $-(a - b)$
> $= -1 \times a - (-1) \times b$
> $= -a + b$

5 Now remove these brackets:

a $-2(x + 3)$ **b** $-3(y - 2)$ **c** $-5(5 - y)$ **d** $-2(6 - x)$
e $-(x + y)$ **f** $-(x - y)$ **g** $-4(y + x)$ **h** $-7(a - b)$
i $-x(x + 2)$ **j** $-p(2 - p)$ **k** $-l(l + m)$ **l** $-2x(4 - 3x)$
m $-a(2a - 3)$ **n** $-t(3t - 4m)$

Remove brackets before adding or subtracting.

Example 1

$8 + 2(x + 3)$
$= 8 + 2 \times x + 2 \times 3$
$= 8 + 2x + 6$
$= 14 + 2x$

Example 2

$4 - 3(x - 2)$
$= 4 - 3 \times x - (-3) \times 2$
$= 4 - 3x + 6$
$= 10 - 3x$

6 Simplify:

a $8 - 2(x + 3)$ **b** $4 - (2 - y)$ **c** $6 - 3(y - 2)$
d $2 + 6(x + 1)$ **e** $4 + 7(2 - x)$ **f** $3 - 2(2 - x)$
g $6(x - 2) - 3$ **h** $-2(x - 1) + 3$ **i** $x + 3(x - 2)$
j $y - (4 - y)$ **k** $2x - 3(x + 4)$ **l** $3y - 2(2 - 3y)$

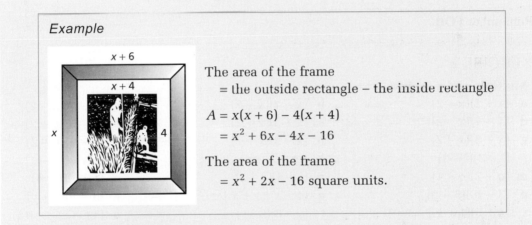

Example

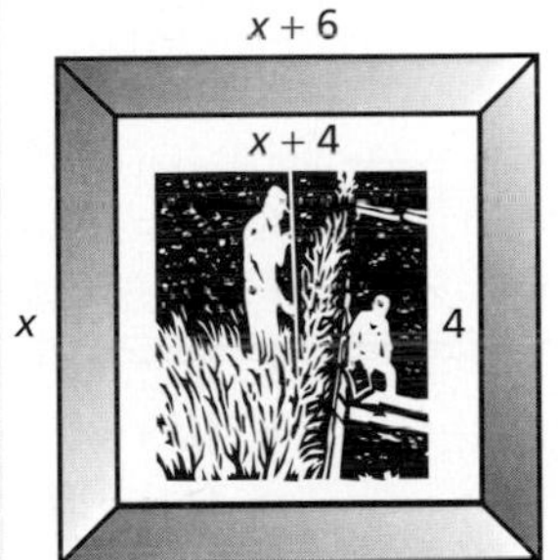

The area of the frame
$= $ the outside rectangle – the inside rectangle

$A = x(x + 6) - 4(x + 4)$
$= x^2 + 6x - 4x - 16$

The area of the frame
$= x^2 + 2x - 16$ square units.

7 In a similar fashion find the area of each of these frames.

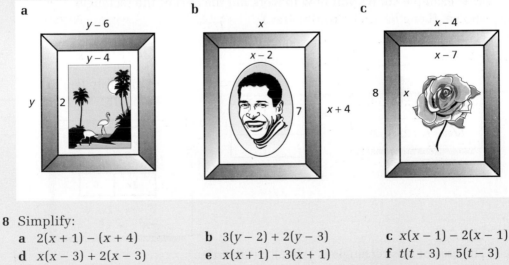

a

b

c

8 Simplify:

a $2(x + 1) - (x + 4)$ **b** $3(y - 2) + 2(y - 3)$ **c** $x(x - 1) - 2(x - 1)$
d $x(x - 3) + 2(x - 3)$ **e** $x(x + 1) - 3(x + 1)$ **f** $t(t - 3) - 5(t - 3)$
g $m(m + 3) - 5(m + 3)$ **h** $2x(x - 1) + 3(x - 1)$ **i** $x(3x - 2) - 5(3x - 2)$

Pairs of brackets

$$(a + b)(c + d) = a(c + d) + b(c + d)$$
$$= ac + ad + bc + bd$$

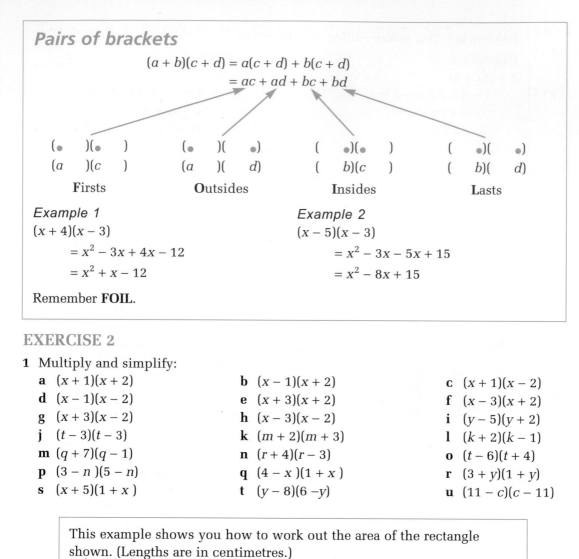

$(\bullet\quad)(\bullet\quad)$	$(\bullet\quad)(\quad\bullet)$	$(\quad\bullet)(\bullet\quad)$	$(\quad\bullet)(\quad\bullet)$
$(a\quad)(c\quad)$	$(a\quad)(\quad d)$	$(\quad b)(c\quad)$	$(\quad b)(\quad d)$
Firsts	**Outsides**	**Insides**	**Lasts**

Example 1

$(x + 4)(x - 3)$

$= x^2 - 3x + 4x - 12$

$= x^2 + x - 12$

Example 2

$(x - 5)(x - 3)$

$= x^2 - 3x - 5x + 15$

$= x^2 - 8x + 15$

Remember **FOIL.**

EXERCISE 2

1 Multiply and simplify:

a $(x + 1)(x + 2)$ **b** $(x - 1)(x + 2)$ **c** $(x + 1)(x - 2)$

d $(x - 1)(x - 2)$ **e** $(x + 3)(x + 2)$ **f** $(x - 3)(x + 2)$

g $(x + 3)(x - 2)$ **h** $(x - 3)(x - 2)$ **i** $(y - 5)(y + 2)$

j $(t - 3)(t - 3)$ **k** $(m + 2)(m + 3)$ **l** $(k + 2)(k - 1)$

m $(q + 7)(q - 1)$ **n** $(r + 4)(r - 3)$ **o** $(t - 6)(t + 4)$

p $(3 - n)(5 - n)$ **q** $(4 - x)(1 + x)$ **r** $(3 + y)(1 + y)$

s $(x + 5)(1 + x)$ **t** $(y - 8)(6 - y)$ **u** $(11 - c)(c - 11)$

This example shows you how to work out the area of the rectangle shown. (Lengths are in centimetres.)

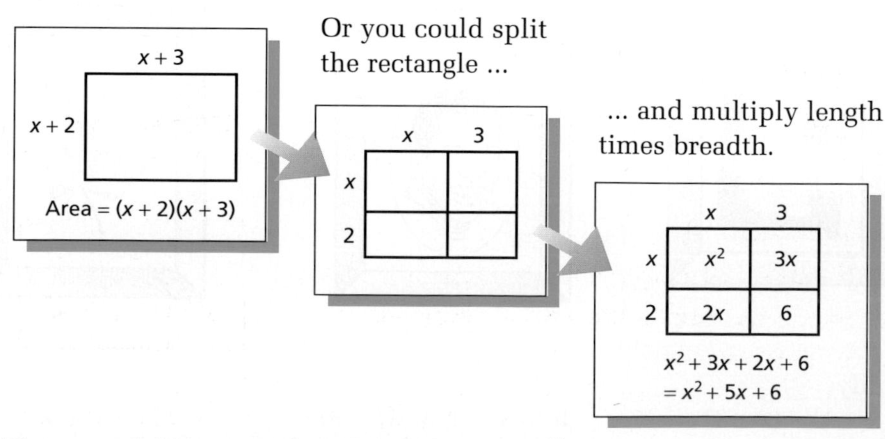

Area = (x + 2)(x + 3)
Or you could split the rectangle ...

... and multiply length times breadth.

x²

x² + 3x + 2x + 6
= x² + 5x + 6

The area of this rectangle is $(x + 2)(x + 3)$ cm^2.
It is also $x^2 + 5x + 6$ cm^2.

2 In a similar way, find the area of each of the following. (Lengths are in centimetres.)

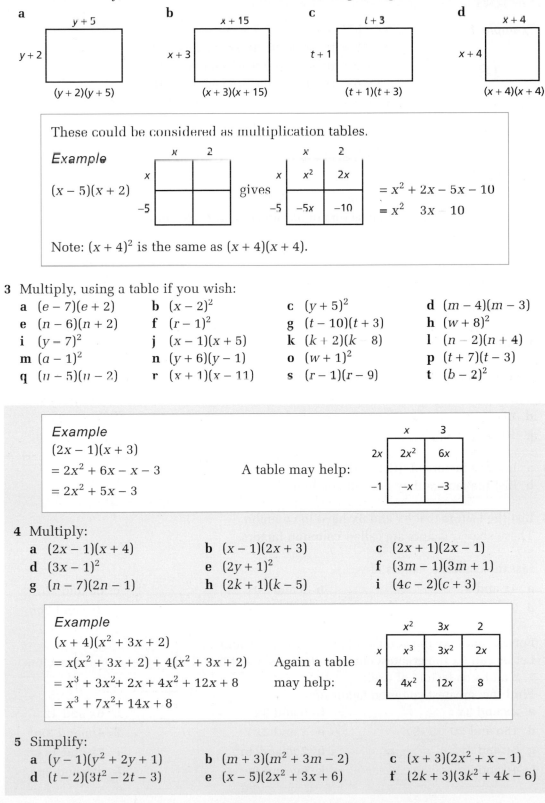

a

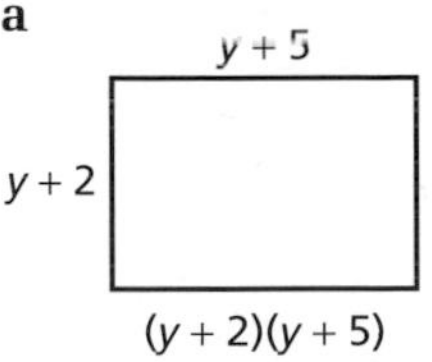

$(y + 2)(y + 5)$

b

$x + 15$

$x + 3$

$(x + 3)(x + 15)$

c

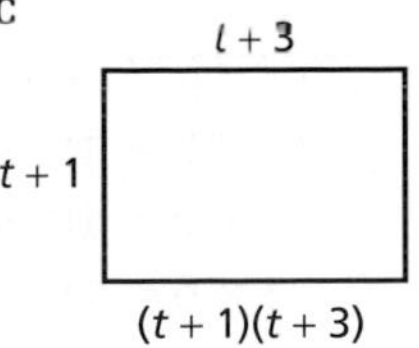

$(t + 1)(t + 3)$

d

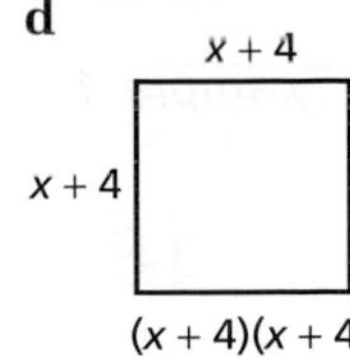

$(x + 4)(x + 4)$

These could be considered as multiplication tables.

Example

$(x - 5)(x + 2)$

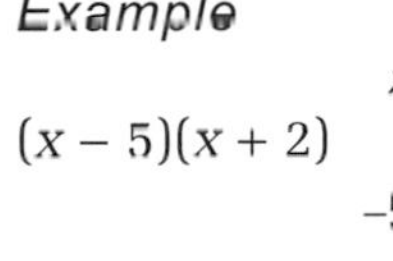

gives

	x	2
x	x^2	$2x$
−5	$-5x$	−10

$= x^2 + 2x - 5x - 10$

$= x^2 - 3x - 10$

Note: $(x + 4)^2$ is the same as $(x + 4)(x + 4)$.

3 Multiply, using a table if you wish:

a $(e - 7)(e + 2)$ **b** $(x - 2)^2$ **c** $(y + 5)^2$ **d** $(m - 4)(m - 3)$
e $(n - 6)(n + 2)$ **f** $(r - 1)^2$ **g** $(t - 10)(t + 3)$ **h** $(w + 8)^2$
i $(y - 7)^2$ **j** $(x - 1)(x + 5)$ **k** $(k + 2)(k - 8)$ **l** $(n - 2)(n + 4)$
m $(a - 1)^2$ **n** $(y + 6)(y - 1)$ **o** $(w + 1)^2$ **p** $(t + 7)(t - 3)$
q $(u - 5)(u - 2)$ **r** $(x + 1)(x - 11)$ **s** $(r - 1)(r - 9)$ **t** $(b - 2)^2$

Example

$(2x - 1)(x + 3)$

$= 2x^2 + 6x - x - 3$

$= 2x^2 + 5x - 3$

A table may help:

	x	3
$2x$	$2x^2$	$6x$
−1	$-x$	−3

4 Multiply:

a $(2x - 1)(x + 4)$ **b** $(x - 1)(2x + 3)$ **c** $(2x + 1)(2x - 1)$
d $(3x - 1)^2$ **e** $(2y + 1)^2$ **f** $(3m - 1)(3m + 1)$
g $(n - 7)(2n - 1)$ **h** $(2k + 1)(k - 5)$ **i** $(4c - 2)(c + 3)$

Example

$(x + 4)(x^2 + 3x + 2)$

$= x(x^2 + 3x + 2) + 4(x^2 + 3x + 2)$

$= x^3 + 3x^2 + 2x + 4x^2 + 12x + 8$

$= x^3 + 7x^2 + 14x + 8$

Again a table may help:

	x^2	$3x$	2
x	x^3	$3x^2$	$2x$
4	$4x^2$	$12x$	8

5 Simplify:

a $(y - 1)(y^2 + 2y + 1)$ **b** $(m + 3)(m^2 + 3m - 2)$ **c** $(x + 3)(2x^2 + x - 1)$
d $(t - 2)(3t^2 - 2t - 3)$ **e** $(x - 5)(2x^2 + 3x + 6)$ **f** $(2k + 3)(3k^2 + 4k - 6)$

Factors

Example 1

18

$1 \times 18 = 18$, so 1 and 18 are factors of 18.
$2 \times 9 = 18$, so 2 and 9 are factors of 18.
$3 \times 6 = 18$, so 3 and 6 are factors of 18.
The factors of 18 are 1, 2, 3, 6, 9 and 18.

Example 2

$5x^2$

$1 \times 5x^2 = 5x^2$, so 1 and $5x^2$ are factors of $5x^2$.
$5 \times x^2 = 5x^2$, so 5 and x^2 are factors of $5x^2$.
$5x \times x = 5x^2$, so $5x$ and x are factors of $5x^2$.
The factors of $5x^2$ are 1, 5, x, $5x$, x^2 and $5x^2$.

EXERCISE 3

1 Find all the factors of:
a 14 **b** 36 **c** 100 **d** 81 **e** $2x$ **f** $3y$ **g** ab
h $4x$ **i** $6x$ **j** y^2 **k** $2x^2$ **l** $3m^2$ **m** $15w$ **n** $7x^2$

2 Complete each of the following by writing the partner of the given factor:
a $6x^2 = 2x \times \ldots$ **b** $10xy = 2x \times \ldots$ **c** $3x^2 = x^2 \times \ldots$
d $21y^2 = 3y \times \ldots$ **e** $9x^2 = 3x \times \ldots$ **f** $4xy = 2y \times \ldots$
g $10ab = 5a \times \ldots$

3 **a** List the factors of **(i)** 12 **(ii)** 15.
b List the factors they have in common.

4 List the factors that $4x$ and $6x$ have in common.
These shared factors are called **common factors**.

5 List the common factors of:
a $4x$ and x^2 **b** 5 and $10x$ **c** ab and $2b$
d $3y$ and $2y^2$ **e** $4n$ and $8n$ **f** $2b^2$ and $3ab$

6 For $2x^2$ and $6xy$ the common factors are 1, 2, x and $2x$.
Let us call $2x$ the **greatest common factor** since it has all the other common factors 1, 2 and x as factors of itself.
Find the greatest common factor of:
a $2x$ and $3x$ **b** 6 and $3x$ **c** $6x$ and 12
d $15a$ and 20 **e** x and $2x^2$ **f** $4m$ and $2m^2$
g $6y$ and $3y^2$ **h** $2ab$ and $4a^2$ **i** $7k$ and $14k^2$
j $4c$ and $6c$ **k** $6w$ and $9w^2v$ **l** a^2b and $2ab$

Factorising

We factorise a number by rewriting it as a product, e.g $18 = 2 \times 9$.
It is said to be completely factorised when the factors cannot be further factorised, in this case

$$18 = 2 \times 3 \times 3$$

These are then called the **prime factors** of the number.
Note that 1 is not involved in prime factorisation since 1 is not a prime number.

Common factors

Example 1 Factorise $3x + 15$.

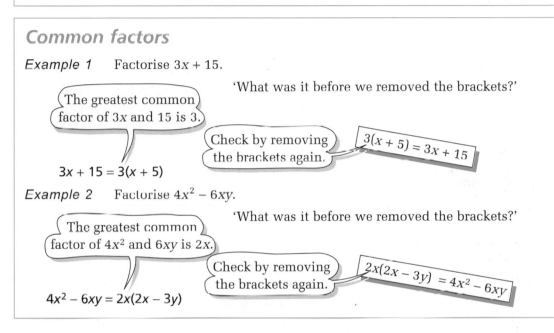

'What was it before we removed the brackets?'

The greatest common factor of $3x$ and 15 is 3.

Check by removing the brackets again.

$3(x + 5) = 3x + 15$

$3x + 15 = 3(x + 5)$

Example 2 Factorise $4x^2 - 6xy$.

'What was it before we removed the brackets?'

The greatest common factor of $4x^2$ and $6xy$ is $2x$.

Check by removing the brackets again.

$2x(2x - 3y) = 4x^2 - 6xy$

$4x^2 - 6xy = 2x(2x - 3y)$

EXERCISE 4

1 Factorise (by considering the greatest common factor):

a $3x + 6$ **b** $2x - 2$ **c** $4xy - 2x$ **d** $5x^2 - x$
e $6a - 3$ **f** $6a + 7a^2$ **g** $10x - 15$ **h** $y^2 - y$

2 Factorise:

a $3a - 3b$ **b** $2x^2 - x$ **c** $5y + y^2$ **d** $3ab + 2a$ **e** $9y - 15$
f $x^2 - 5x$ **g** $21m - 7$ **h** $4x + 8x^2$ **i** $x - 2x^2$ **j** $7c - 14$
k $5k^2 - 10k$ **l** $3m + 9m^2$ **m** $5ab + 10a$ **n** $6b - 8ab$ **o** $4qr + 6r$
p $3x^2 - 9xy$ **q** $16 - 8xy$ **r** $15y^2 - 3xy$ **s** $xy - 5y^2$ **t** $8ab + 24a^2$

3 In these the greatest common factors have not been taken outside the brackets. Finish the job and completely factorise the expressions.

a $4x^2 - 6x = x(4x - 6)$ **b** $3ab - 6a^2 = 3(ab - 2a^2)$ **c** $6y^2 - 12y = 2y(3y - 6)$
d $8 - 16m = 4(2 - 4m)$ **e** $12n^2 + 48n = 4n(3n + 12)$ **f** $6ab + 9ab^2 = 3b(2a + 3ab)$

4 Completely factorise:

a $x^3 - x^2$ **b** $5x^3 - 10x$ **c** $ab^2 + a^2b$
d $6a - 9b + 3$ **e** $2x^2 - 6x + 8$ **f** $12ab^2 - 6ab$

The difference of squares

Note that $(a - b)(a + b) = a^2 + ab - ab - b^2 = a^2 - b^2$.
We can reverse this to factorise expressions of the form $a^2 - b^2$.

$$\boldsymbol{a^2 - b^2 = (a - b)(a + b)}$$

Example 1

$10^2 - 5^2 = (10 - 5)(10 + 5)$
$= 15 \times 5$
$= 75$

Example 2

$y^2 - 16 = y^2 - 4^2$
$= (y - 4)(y + 4)$

Example 3

$81 - x^2 = 9^2 - x^2$
$= (9 - x)(9 + x)$

Example 4

$4y^2 - 16x^2 = (2y)^2 - (4x)^2$
$= (2y - 4x)(2y + 4x)$

EXERCISE 5

1 Express each of the following as the difference of two squares, e.g. $16 - 25x^2 = 4^2 - (5x)^2$.

a $4 - x^2$ **b** $9 - y^2$ **c** $49 - 4x^2$ **d** $1 - 16x^2$
e $x^2 - 25$ **f** $81x^2 - 25$ **g** $100x^2 - 121y^2$

2 Factorise by considering the difference of two squares:

a $y^2 - 9$ **b** $m^2 - 4$ **c** $n^2 - 1$ **d** $t^2 - 16$
e $9 - x^2$ **f** $49 - t^2$ **g** $64 - y^2$ **h** $m^2 - n^2$
i $p^2 - q^2$ **j** $d^2 - 81$ **k** $25 - e^2$ **l** $1 - x^2$
m $100 - y^2$ **n** $w^2 - x^2$ **o** $16 - f^2$ **p** $g^2 - 1$

Here are two more examples.

$4a^2 - 1 = (2a)^2 - 1^2$
$= (2a - 1)(2a + 1)$

$9x^2 - 16y^2 = (3x)^2 - (4y)^2$
$= (3x - 4y)(3x + 4y)$

3 Factorise:

a $4x^2 - 1$ **b** $9y^2 - 4$ **c** $a^2 - 4b^2$ **d** $4p^2 - q^2$
e $16 - 9r^2$ **f** $25 - 4x^2$ **g** $b^2 - 9c^2$ **h** $25w^2 - x^2$
i $64y^2 - 1$ **j** $25x^2 - 4$ **k** $4a^2 - 9b^2$ **l** $9x^2 - y^2$
m $9t^2 - 16$ **n** $4k^2 - 1$ **o** $81a^2 - 100b^2$ **p** $16e^2 - f^2$

Consider this example.

$2a^2 - 18 = 2(a^2 - 9)$ First remove the common factor,
$= 2(a^2 - 3^2)$ then use the difference of squares.
$= 2(a - 3)(a + 3)$

4 Factorise these in the same way:

a $6y^2 - 24$ **b** $8 - 2m^2$ **c** $3 - 3a^2$ **d** $2w^2 - 18$
e $20 - 5t^2$ **f** $8y^2 - 18$ **g** $3 - 12b^2$ **h** $27x^2 - 12$
i $7a^2 - 28$ **j** $16k^2 - 4$ **k** $45e^2 - 5f^2$ **l** $128x^2 - 2$

Factorising trinomials

Remember FOIL. $(x - 2)(x + 3) = x^2 + 3x - 2x - 6$
F O I L
$= x^2 + x - 6$

Trying to reverse this process means discovering how the middle term '+ x' can be obtained from the 'outsides' and 'insides'.
Here is a method for factorising $x^2 + x - 6$.

Step 1 Draw two sets of brackets. ( )( )

Step 2 Put in a possible pair of factors for the first term. $(x \quad)(x \quad)$

Step 3 Write down *all* the possibilities for the last term.
$(x + 6)(x - 1)$
$(x - 6)(x + 1)$
$(x + 3)(x - 2)$
$(x - 3)(x + 2)$

Step 4 For each possibility write down 'outsides' plus 'insides'.
Only one gives the middle term (+ x).
$(x + 6)(x - 1)$ gives a middle term $-1x + 6x = +5x$
$(x - 6)(x + 1)$ gives a middle term $+1x - 6x = -5x$
$(x + 3)(x - 2)$ gives a middle term $-2x + 3x = +x$ ✓
$(x - 3)(x + 2)$ gives a middle term $+2x - 3x = -x$

Step 5 Write down the successful result and check it by multiplying out.
$x^2 + x - 6 = (x + 3)(x - 2)$

Here is another example. Factorise $x^2 - 6x + 8$.
Looking for a middle term of $-6x$:
$(x - 8)(x - 1)$ gives a middle term $-1x - 8x = -9x$
$(x + 8)(x + 1)$ gives a middle term $+1x + 8x = +9x$
$(x - 4)(x - 2)$ gives a middle term $-2x - 4x = -6x$ ✓

$x^2 - 6x + 8 = (x - 4)(x - 2)$

EXERCISE 6

For questions **1** to **6** factorise each expression:

1 **a** $x^2 + 2x + 1$ **b** $y^2 + 3y + 2$ **c** $m^2 + 4m + 4$

2 **a** $t^2 + t - 2$ **b** $x^2 + x - 12$ **c** $y^2 + 3y - 10$

3 **a** $a^2 - a - 2$ **b** $w^2 - 2w - 8$ **c** $e^2 - 2e - 3$

4 **a** $b^2 - 4b + 4$ **b** $y^2 - 5y + 6$ **c** $y^2 - 4y + 3$

5 **a** $k^2 - 5k - 6$ **b** $x^2 + 8x + 15$ **c** $p^2 - 4p - 5$ **d** $x^2 - 11x + 18$
e $y^2 - 2y - 15$ **f** $n^2 + 7n - 8$ **g** $q^2 - 9q + 14$ **h** $x^2 + 8x + 12$
i $k^2 - 6k + 9$ **j** $x^2 - 3x - 4$ **k** $y^2 + y - 30$ **l** $a^2 - 9a + 20$
m $c^2 + 8c + 16$ **n** $e^2 - 8e + 15$ **o** $f^2 + 4f - 21$ **p** $x^2 - 6x - 7$
q $y^2 - 10y + 16$ **r** $x^2 + 9x - 10$ **s** $m^2 - 8m - 9$ **t** $k^2 + 9k + 18$
u $p^2 + 3p - 18$ **v** $x^2 + 2x - 8$ **w** $y^2 - 11y + 24$ **x** $m^2 - m - 12$

6 **a** $x^2 - x - 42$ **b** $y^2 - 13y + 40$ **c** $x^2 + 12x + 32$ **d** $t^2 + 2t - 24$
e $t^2 - 6t - 27$ **f** $k^2 - 12k + 20$ **g** $k^2 + 7k - 18$ **h** $x^2 - 14x + 40$
i $y^2 - 7y - 30$ **j** $x^2 + 11x + 28$ **k** $a^2 - 10a + 25$ **l** $b^2 + 12b + 36$
m $w^2 - 4w - 45$ **n** $x^2 + 4x - 60$ **o** $y^2 - 14y + 48$ **p** $k^2 - 2k - 35$

Some harder examples

Example 1

Factorise $3x^2 - x - 4$.

There is only one possibility for the first terms: $(3x \quad)(x \quad)$
There is more to consider about the last terms:
$(3x - 1)(x + 4)$ gives a middle term of $12x + (-1)x = 11x$
$(3x + 4)(x - 1)$ gives a middle term of $-3x + 4x = +x$
Only the sign is wrong, so switch signs and
$(3x - 4)(x + 1)$ gives a middle term of $3x + (-4)x = -x$
Check the factors by multiplying out.
$3x^2 - x - 4 = (3x - 4)(x + 1)$

Example 2

Factorise $8x^2 + 22x + 15$.

There are two possibilities for the first terms: $(8x \quad)(x \quad)$
or $(4x \quad)(2x \quad)$

There is more to consider about the last terms:
$(8x + 1)(x + 15)$ gives a middle term of $121x$
$(8x + 15)(x + 1)$ gives a middle term of $23x$
$(8x + 5)(x + 3)$ gives a middle term of $29x$
$(8x + 3)(x + 5)$ gives a middle term of $43x$

We have run out of possibilities so try $(4x\quad)(2x\quad)$

$(4x + 1)(2x + 15)$ gives a middle term of $62x$

$(4x + 15)(2x + 1)$ gives a middle term of $34x$

$(4x + 3)(2x + 5)$ gives a middle term of $26x$

$(4x + 5)(2x + 3)$ gives a middle term of $22x$ ✓

Check the factors by multiplying out.

$8x^2 + 22x + 15 = (4x + 5)(2x + 3)$

EXERCISE 7

Factorise in questions **1** and **2**.

1 **a** $2x^2 + 5x + 2$ **b** $2x^2 - 9x + 9$ **c** $2x^2 + x - 6$ **d** $2x^2 + 3x - 5$

e $3x^2 - x - 4$ **f** $3x^2 - 7x - 6$ **g** $2x^2 - 11x + 14$ **h** $4x^2 + 8x - 5$

i $3x^2 - 13x + 4$ **j** $3y^2 + 10y - 8$ **k** $3m^2 - 4m - 4$ **l** $6k^2 + 7k - 3$

m $2p^2 + 7p + 3$ **n** $5w^2 - 2w - 7$ **o** $3c^2 + 7c + 2$ **p** $2a^2 - 9a - 5$

q $8x^2 - 14x + 3$ **r** $7b^2 + 6b - 13$ **s** $3e^2 + 20e - 7$ **t** $3t^2 + 2t - 5$

u $2y^2 + y - 28$

2 **a** $12x^2 + 23x + 10$ **b** $12y^2 + 36y + 15$ **c** $9m^2 - 6m - 8$

d $4k^2 - 12k + 9$ **e** $10a^2 + 38a - 8$ **f** $6y^2 - 27y + 12$

Factorising priority

Step 1 Take any common factors and put them outside the brackets.

Step 2 Check for the difference of two squares.

Step 3 Factorise any quadratic expression left.

EXERCISE 8

Factorise:

1 $3x^2 - 12$ **2** $y^2 + 4y$ **3** $2x^2 + 16x + 32$

4 $5m^2 - 45$ **5** $3x^2 - 15x + 18$ **6** $3m^2 - 48$

7 $2x^2 + 14x + 24$ **8** $7x^2 - 7x - 14$ **9** $6n - 15$

10 $5a^2 - 20b^2$ **11** $5w^2 - 5$ **12** $4a^2 - 36$

13 $b^2 - 2b + 1$ **14** $162 - 2y^2$ **15** $36k^2 - 49$

16 $2m^3 - 8m$ **17** $5u^2 + 15u + 10$ **18** $2m^2 - 18n^2$

19 $a^2b^2 - 4b^2$ **20** $200y^2 - 2$ **21** $3 + 27x^2$

22 $3c^3 - 3c$ **23** $2x^2 - 2x - 144$ **24** $4a^2 + 6a - 10$

CHAPTER 5 REVIEW

1 Simplify:

a $2(3x - 1) + 2$ **b** $x(2 - x) + 3x$ **c** $1 - (x + 1)$
d $3(2x + 1) - 2(x - 1)$ **e** $x(x + 1) - x(x - 1)$

2 Multiply and simplify:

a $(m - 1)(m + 1)$ **b** $(x + 3)(x - 6)$ **c** $(p - 2)^2$
d $(2x - 1)(x + 3)$ **e** $(2t - 3)(2t - 4)$ **f** $(3y - 2)^2$

3 Factorise (removing the common factor):

a $2y - 8$ **b** $x^2 + x$ **c** $15m^2 - 3mn$

4 Factorise these expressions using the difference of squares:

a $e^2 - f^2$ **b** $16x^2 - 1$ **c** $81a^2 - 25b^2$

5 Factorise these quadratic expressions:

a $x^2 + 4x + 3$ **b** $y^2 - 5y + 6$ **c** $2a^2 + 5a - 3$

6 Factorise:

a $2 - 18x^2$ **b** $3x^2 - 18x + 15$ **c** $y^3 - y$

6 Circles

STARTING POINTS

1 Name the highlighted parts of the circle.

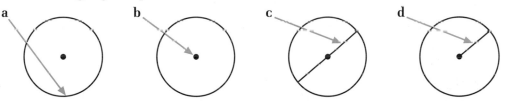

a **b** **c** **d**

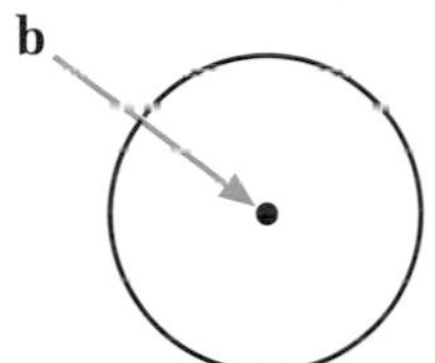

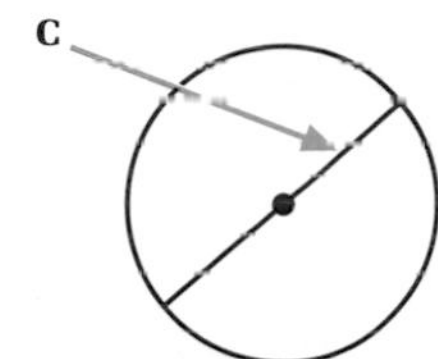

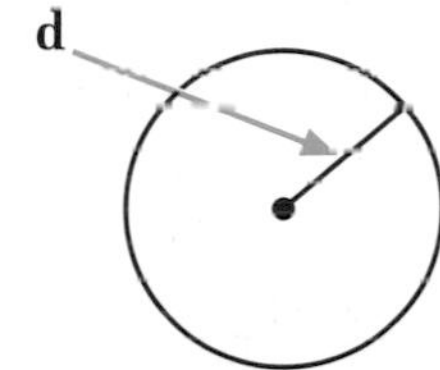

2 **a** A circle has a diameter of 20 cm. Calculate its radius.
b A circle has a radius of 4.6 m. Calculate its diameter.

In the following diagrams O is the centre of the circle.

3 Calculate the circumference of these circles (to 3 s.f.).

a

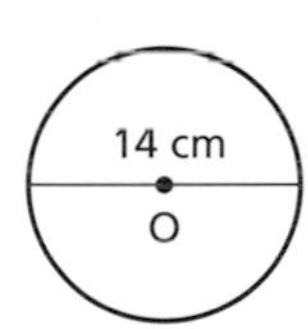

b

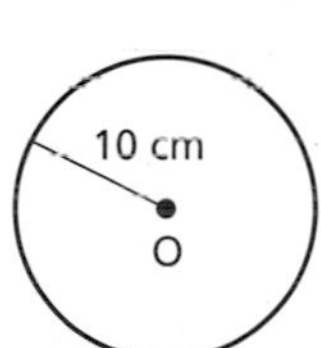

Reminder
$C = \pi d$

4 A ribbon fits round the edge of a circular Christmas cake. The cake has a diameter of 15 cm. Calculate the length of ribbon.

5 Calculate the area of these circles (to 3 s.f.).

a

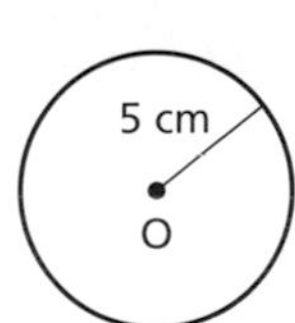

b

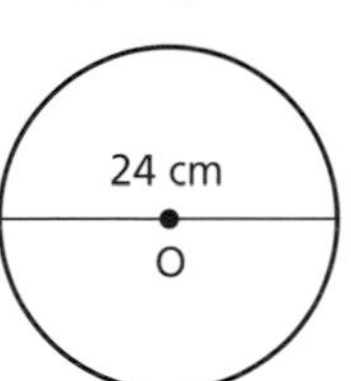

Reminder
$A = \pi r^2$

6 Find the area of a circular plate with radius 10 cm.

7

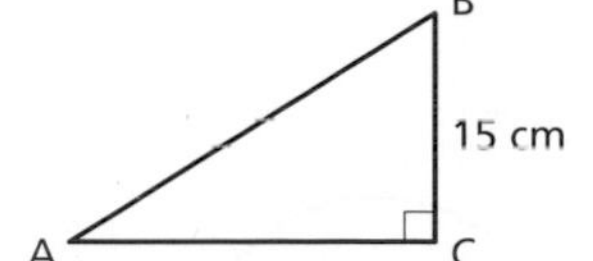

Use Pythagoras' Theorem to calculate the length of AB.

8 Use trigonometry to calculate the length of RQ.

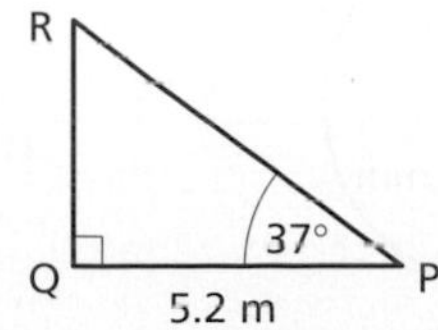

Length of an arc

The highlighted part of the circumference is called an **arc**.

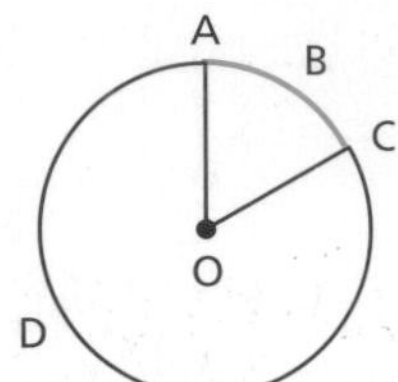

The minor arc ABC

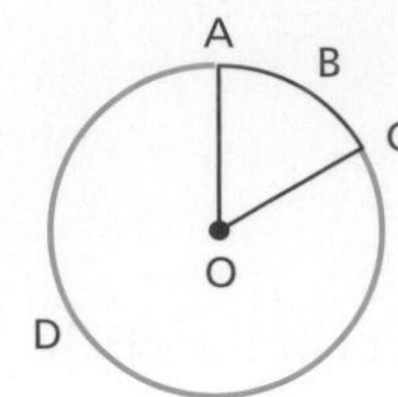

The major arc ADC

When the word minor or major is omitted, then we are generally referring to the minor arc AB when we say the arc AB.

Example 1 Calculate the length of arc PQR.

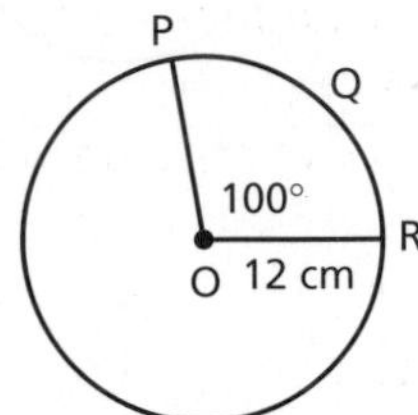

$C = \pi d = \pi \times 24 = 75.4$ (to 3 s.f.)

The circumference of the circle = 75.4 cm

Note that we are concerned with $\frac{100}{360}$ of the circle.

$\frac{100}{360} \times \pi d = 20.9$ (to 3 s.f.)

The length of the arc PQR = 20.9 cm (to 3 s.f.)

Example 2 Calculate the length of arc PTR.

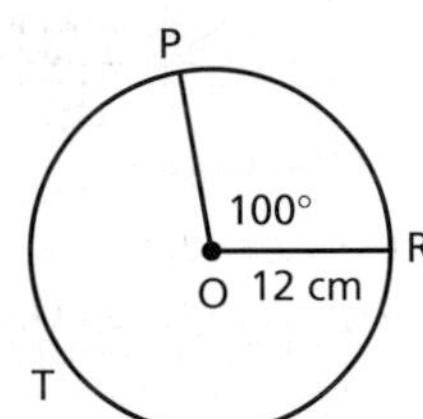

PTR is a major sector.

Note that we are concerned with $\frac{260}{360}$ of the circle.

$\frac{260}{360} \times \pi d = 54.5$ (to 3 s.f.)

The length of the arc PTR = 54.5 cm (to 3 s.f.)

EXERCISE 1

1 Calculate the length of each minor arc.

a

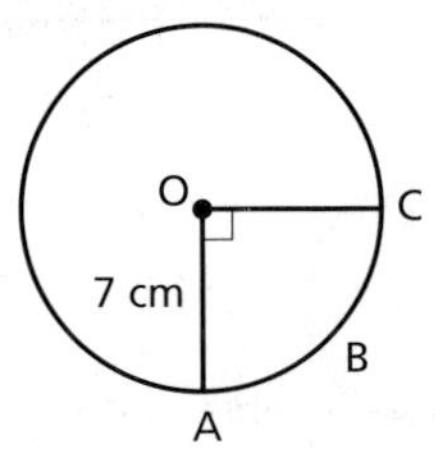

b

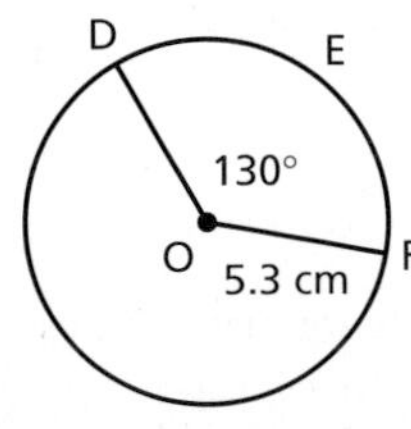

c

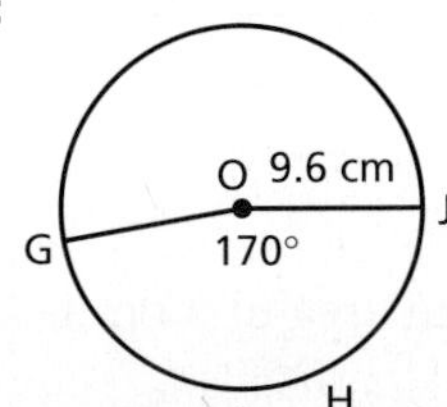

2 Calculate the length of each major arc.

a

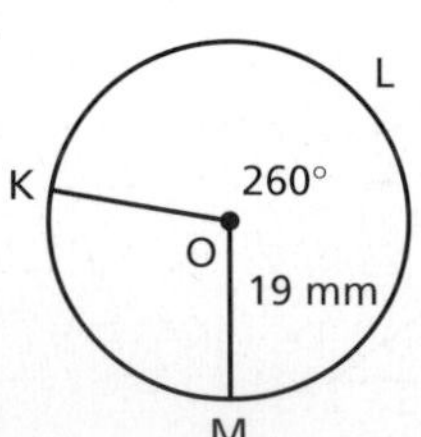

b

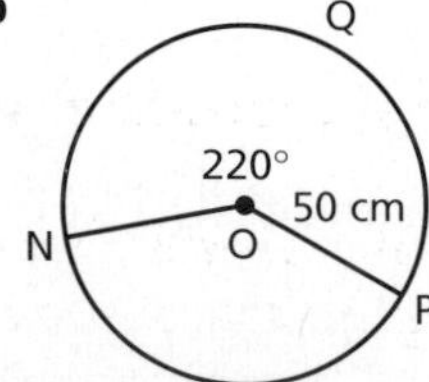

c

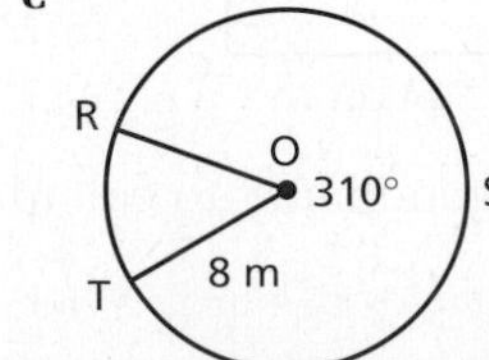

3 In the diagrams O is the centre of a circle. Calculate the length of each arc.

a

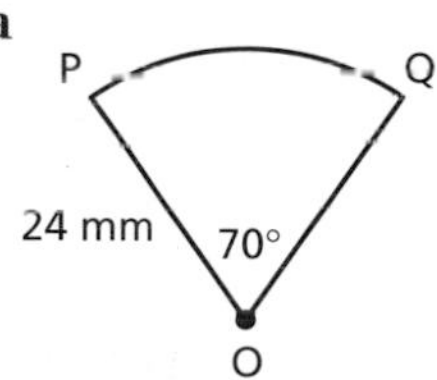

b

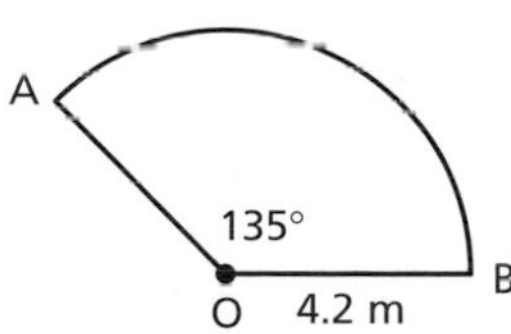

c

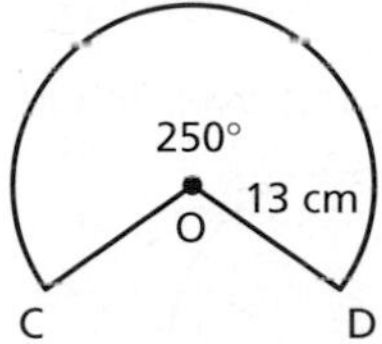

4 The arch of a bridge is in the shape of a semicircle with diameter 20 m.
Calculate the length of the curved arch of the bridge.

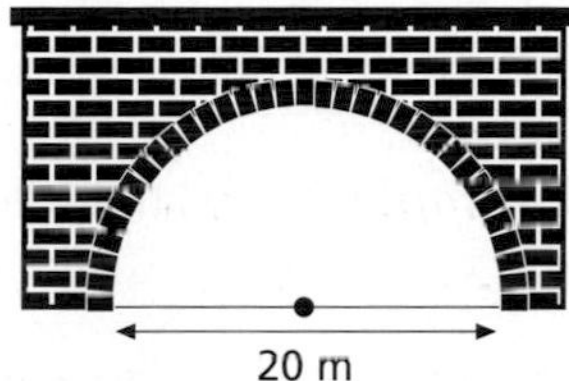

5

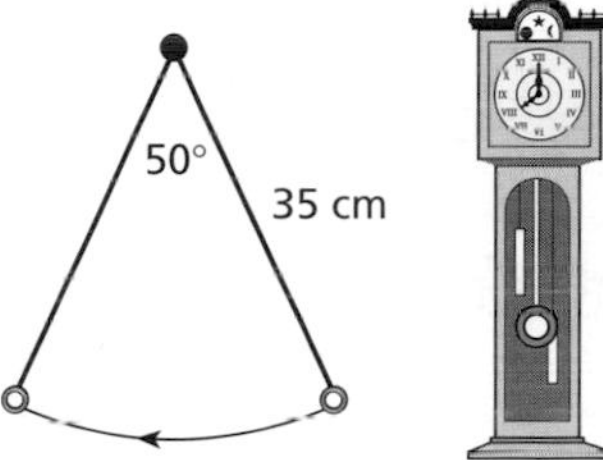

The pendulum on a clock is 35 cm long.
It swings through an angle of 50°.
Calculate the distance the end of the pendulum travels in one swing.

6 A windscreen wiper is 45 cm long. In one sweep the wiper swings through an angle of 115°. Calculate the distance the end of the wiper blade travels in one sweep.

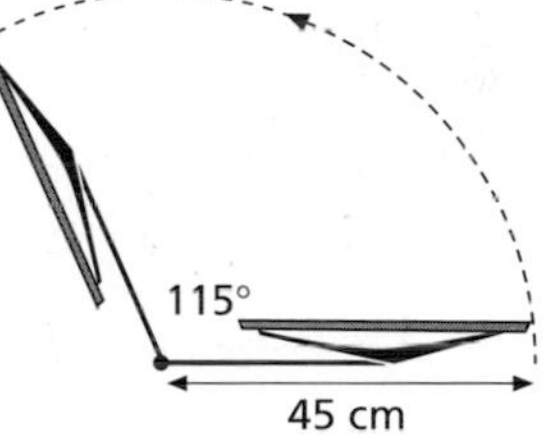

7

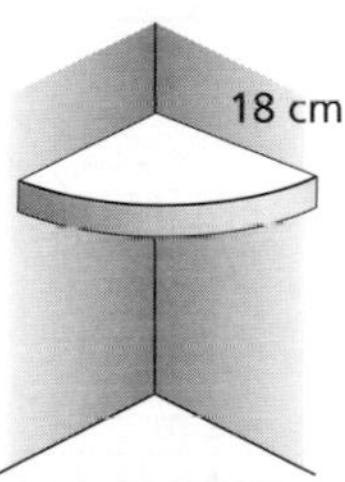

A shelf fits into the corner of a room.
It is in the shape of a quarter circle of radius 18 cm.
A strip of facing is being put on the curved edge of the shelf.
Calculate the length of facing needed.

8 A spade for cutting turf is in the shape of a sector of a circle.
The angle at the centre is 260° and the radius is 12 cm.
Calculate the length of the cutting edge of the spade.

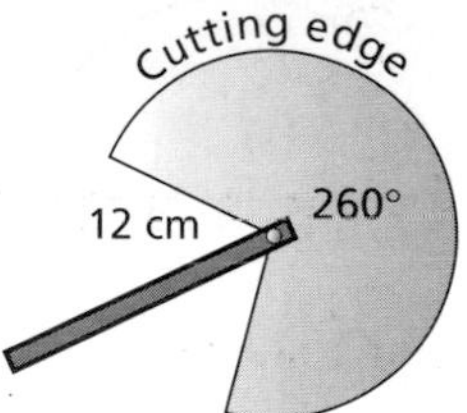

9 Architects renovating an abbey study the construction of a window.

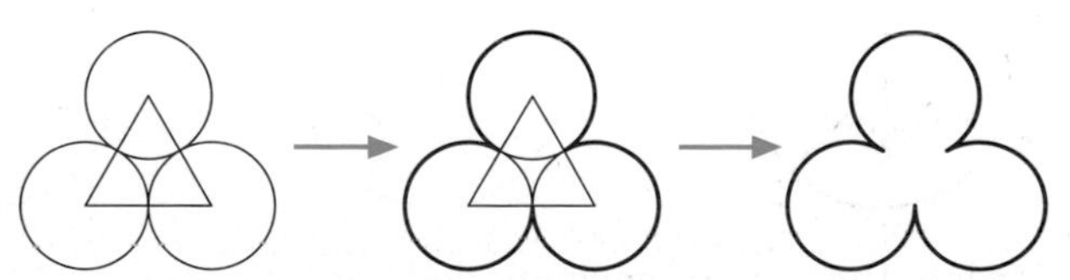

a Given that the triangle is equilateral with side 4 m, what is:

(i) the radius of one circle

(ii) the size of the angle at the centre of each of the major arcs?

b Calculate the perimeter of the window.

Area of a sector

The shaded area is called a **sector**.

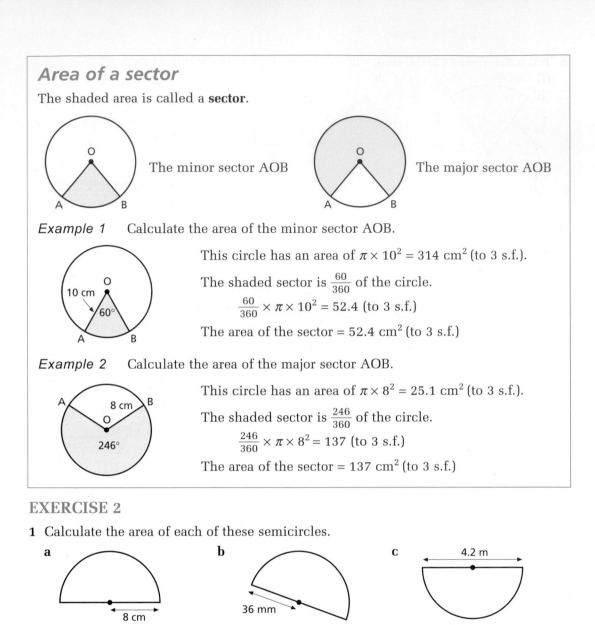

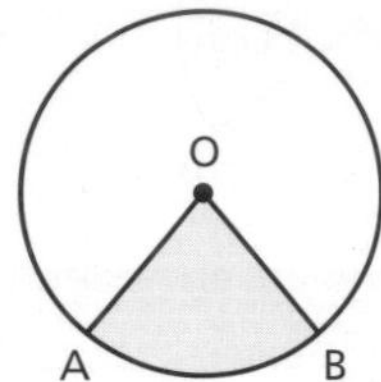

The minor sector AOB

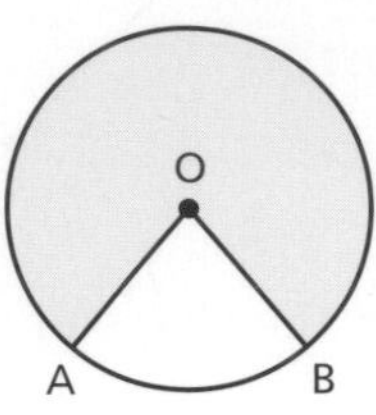

The major sector AOB

Example 1 Calculate the area of the minor sector AOB.

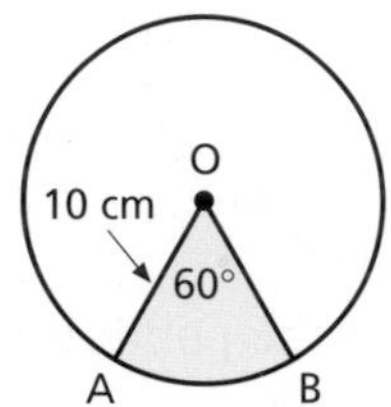

This circle has an area of $\pi \times 10^2 = 314$ cm^2 (to 3 s.f.).

The shaded sector is $\frac{60}{360}$ of the circle.

$$\frac{60}{360} \times \pi \times 10^2 = 52.4 \text{ (to 3 s.f.)}$$

The area of the sector = 52.4 cm^2 (to 3 s.f.)

Example 2 Calculate the area of the major sector AOB.

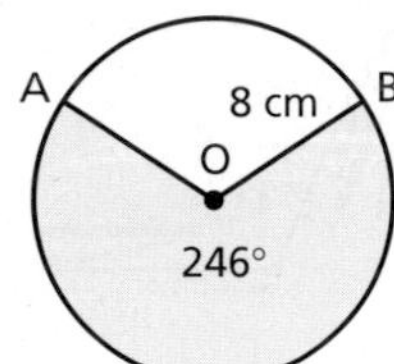

This circle has an area of $\pi \times 8^2 = 25.1$ cm^2 (to 3 s.f.).

The shaded sector is $\frac{246}{360}$ of the circle.

$$\frac{246}{360} \times \pi \times 8^2 = 137 \text{ (to 3 s.f.)}$$

The area of the sector = 137 cm^2 (to 3 s.f.)

EXERCISE 2

1 Calculate the area of each of these semicircles.

a

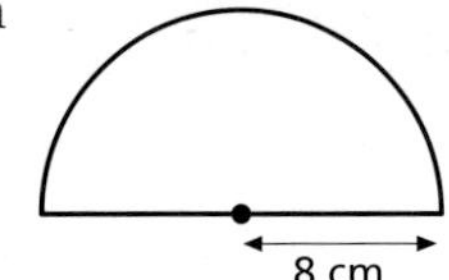

b

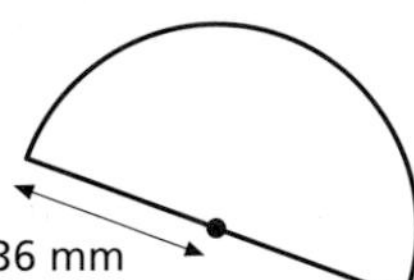

c

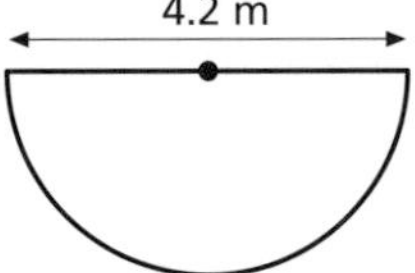

2 What fraction of circle is shaded in each diagram?

a

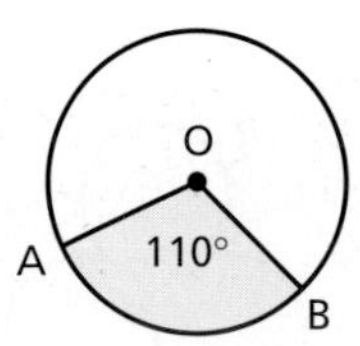

b

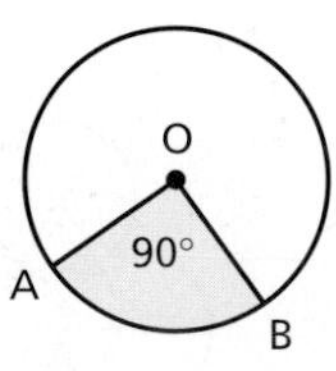

c

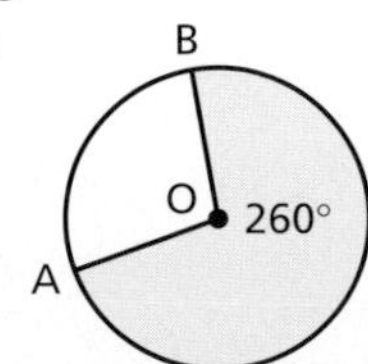

d

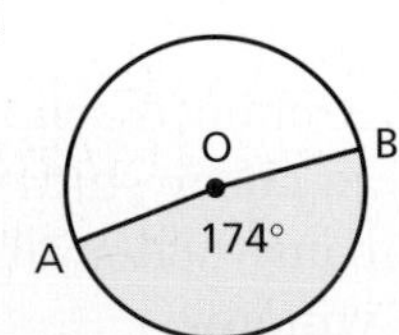

3 Calculate the area of each shaded sector.

a

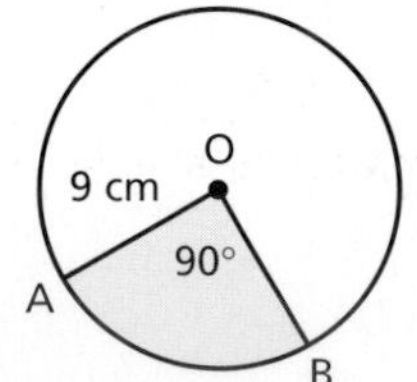

b

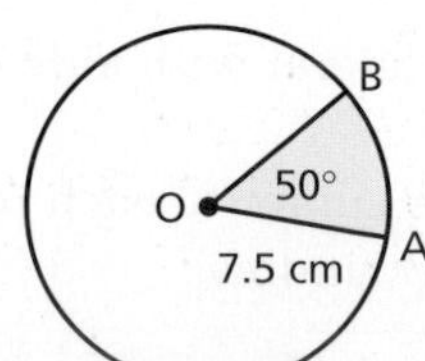

c

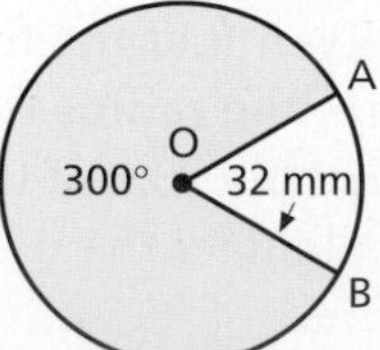

4 For each diagram:

(i) work out the angle at the centre of the shaded sector

(ii) calculate the shaded area.

a

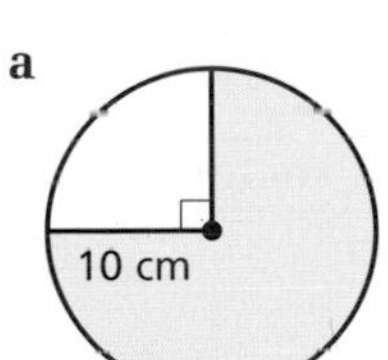

b

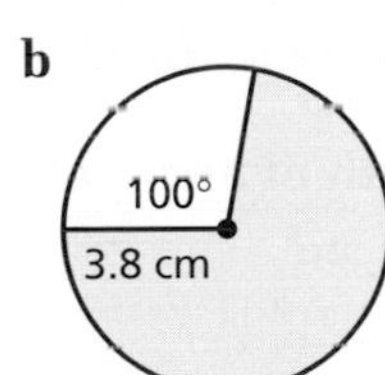

c

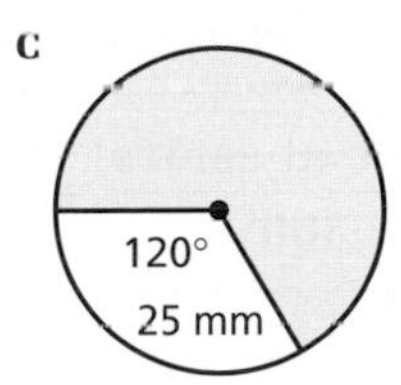

d

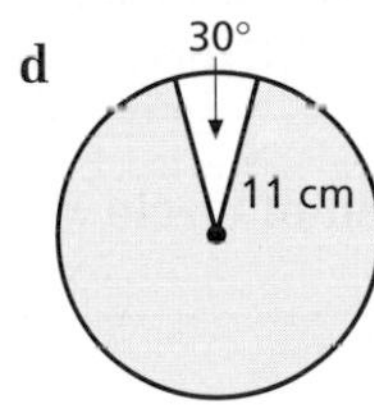

e

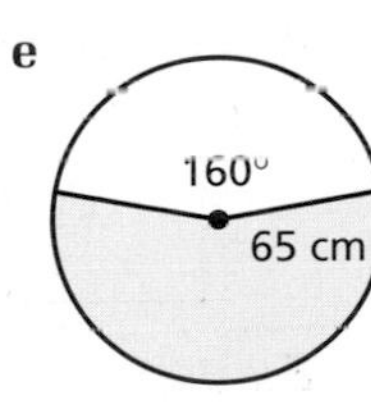

5 In each diagram O is the centre of a circle. Calculate the area of each sector.

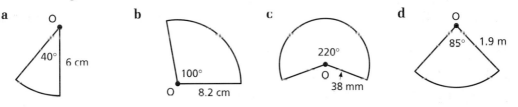

a

O

40°

6 cm

b

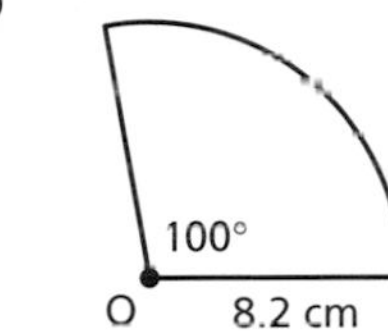

c

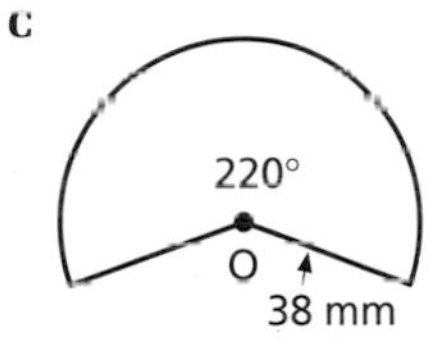

d

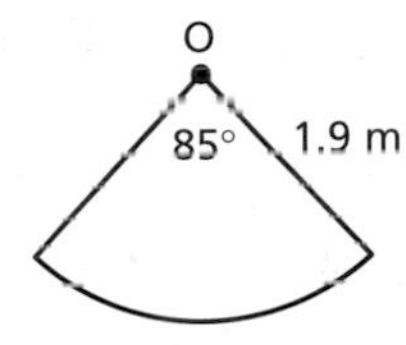

6 When a silk fan is opened it forms a sector of a circle with an angle of 160° at the centre. The distance from the centre to the edge of the fan is 18 cm. Calculate the area of the material in the fan.

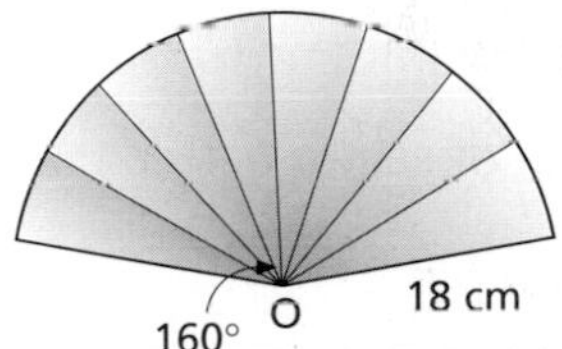

7 A cowl for a chimney is made from aluminium. A sector of a circle is cut out and shaped. The radius of the sector is 35 cm. Calculate the area of aluminium used.

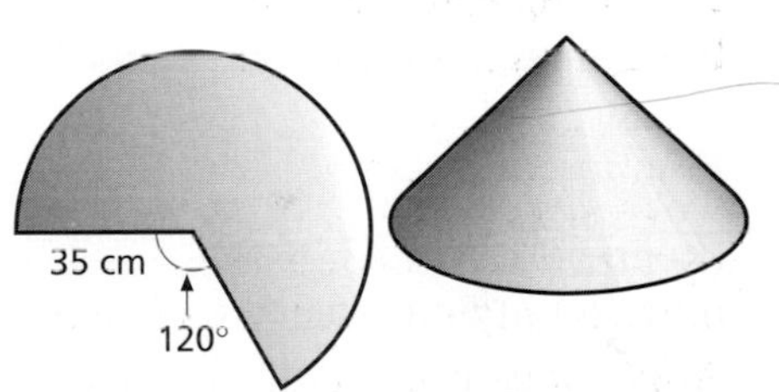

8 Eight identical cheese portions fit in a circular box. Each portion is a sector of a circle. The diameter of the box is 11 cm. Calculate the area of the top of one of the portions.

9 An ice-cream wafer is in the shape of a sector of a circle. The angle at the centre is 70°. The radius is 8 cm.

a Calculate the area of one side of a wafer.

b The manufacturers make a larger wafer. The angle at the centre is the same but the radius is 1 cm longer. What is the increase in area?

When we know what fraction a sector is of a circle, then we can easily calculate the various measurements within the sector.
So far this fraction has been found using the angle at the centre.
It can also be established using the length of arc or using the area.

$$\textbf{Fraction of circle} = \frac{\textbf{angle at centre}}{\textbf{360°}} = \frac{\textbf{length of arc}}{\pi d} = \frac{\textbf{area of sector}}{\pi r^2}$$

Example 1

If the length of the minor arc is 3 cm, calculate:

a the angle at the centre

b the area of the sector.

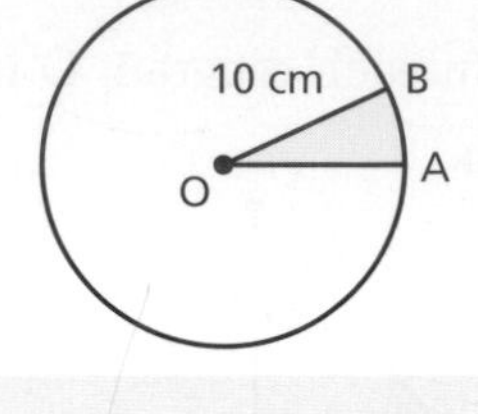

Fraction of circle $= \dfrac{3}{\pi \times d} = \dfrac{3}{\pi \times 20} = 0.047\,75$

(Keep at least 4 s.f. here. Never round too early.)

$0.047\,75$ of $360 = 0.0477 \times 360 = 17.2$ (to 3 s.f.)

Angle at centre $= 17.2°$ (to 3 s.f.)

$0.047\,75$ of $\pi \times 10^2 = 15.0$ (to 3 s.f.)

Area of sector $= 15.0\ \text{cm}^2$ (to 3 s.f.)

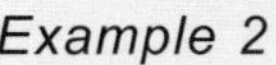

Example 2

If the area of the minor sector is 22 cm^2, calculate:

a the angle at the centre

b the length of the arc.

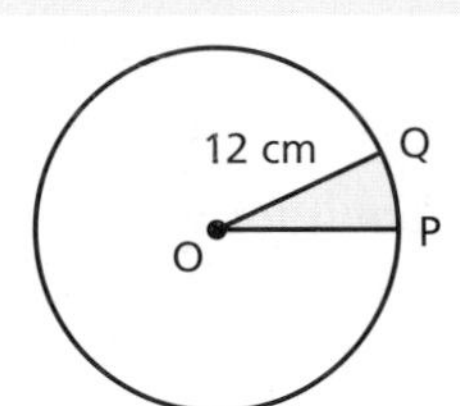

Fraction of circle $= \dfrac{22}{\pi r^2} = \dfrac{22}{\pi \times 144} = 0.048\,63$

(Keep at least 4 s.f. here.)

$0.048\,63$ of $360 = 0.048\,63 \times 360 = 17.5$ (to 3 s.f.)

Angle at centre $= 17.5°$ (to 3 s.f.)

$0.048\,63$ of $\pi \times 24 = 3.67$ (to 3 s.f.)

Length of arc $= 3.67$ cm (to 3 s.f.)

EXERCISE 3

1 a If the shaded area is 28.4 cm^2, calculate:

  (i) the angle at the centre

  (ii) the length of the arc.

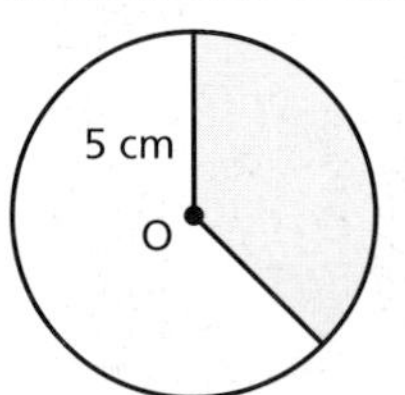

b

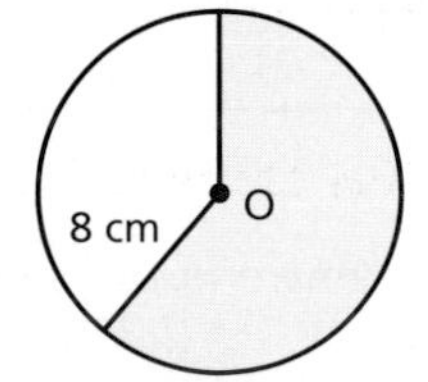

If the length of the arc is 32.1 cm, calculate:

  (i) the angle at the centre

  (ii) the area of the shaded sector.

c If the shaded area is 6.64 cm², calculate:
  (i) the angle at the centre
  (ii) the length of the arc.

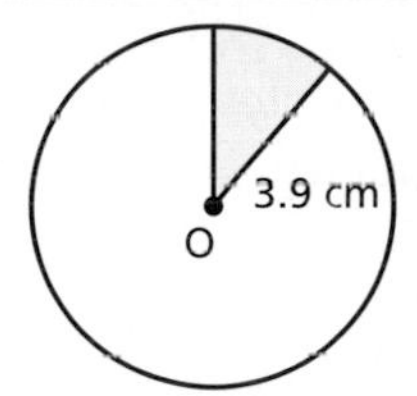

d

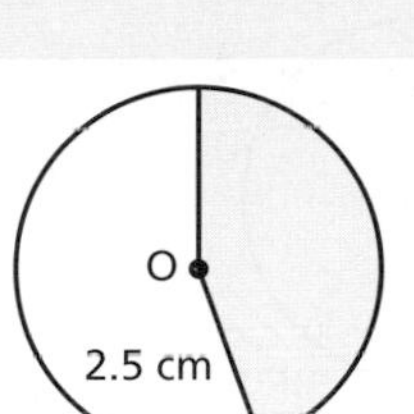

If the length of the arc is 6.33 cm, calculate:
  (i) the angle at the centre
  (ii) the area of the shaded sector.

2

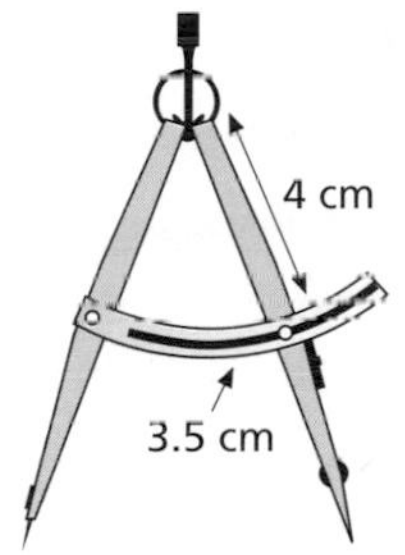

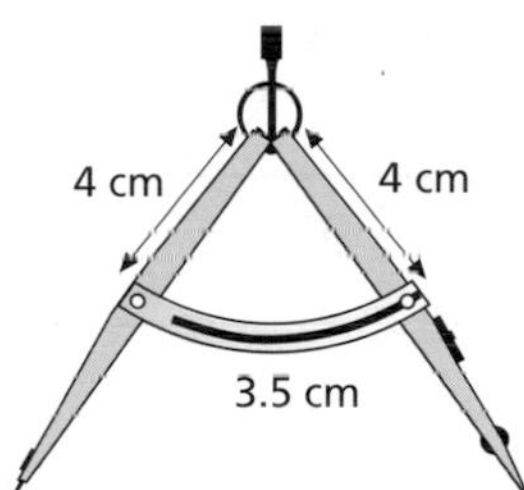

A pair of dividers has a curved metal strip 3.5 cm long. It is fixed 4 cm from the hinge.
Calculate the angle at the centre when the legs of the dividers are fully opened.

3 A church door is in the shape of a rectangle with an arc of a circle on top.
The radius of the circle is 1.6 m and the centre is as shown. The area of the sector is 1.57 m². Calculate:
  a the angle at the centre
  b the perimeter of the door.

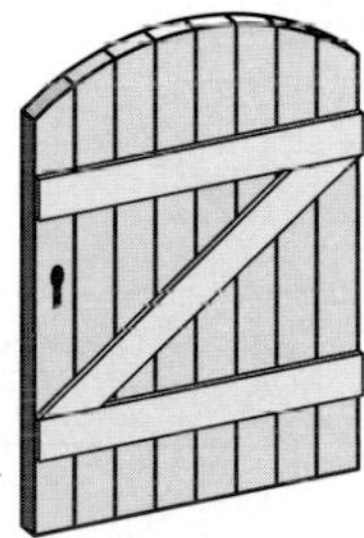

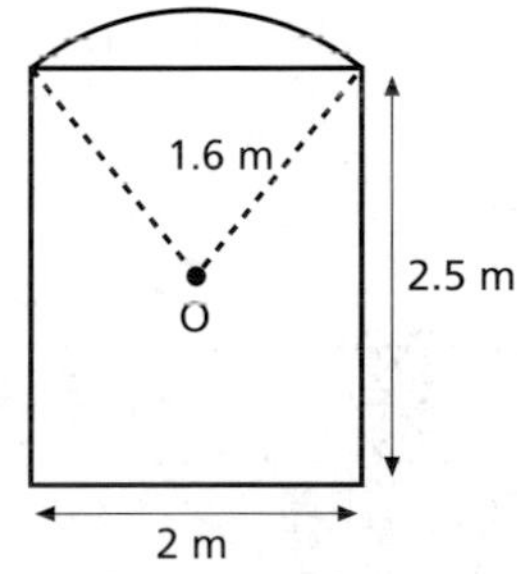

4

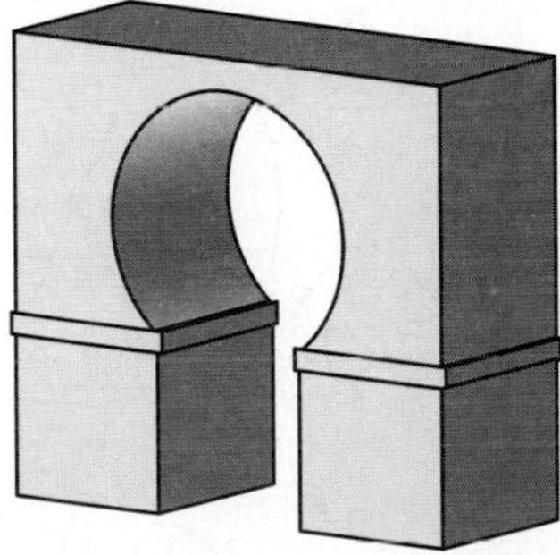

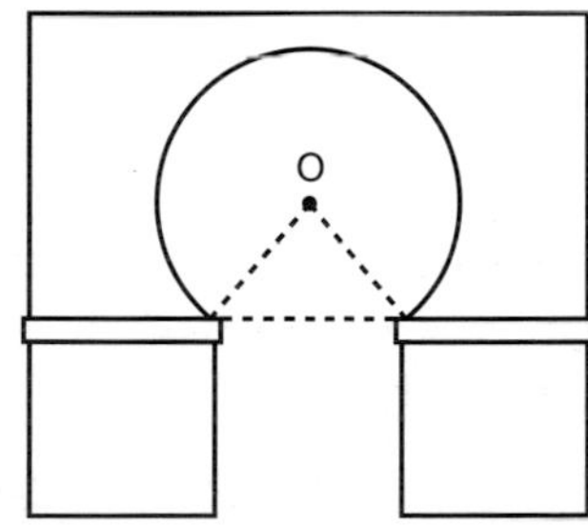

A Moorish arch is a major arc of a circle, as shown. The radius of the arch is 1.3 m. The length of the arc is 6.35 m. Calculate:
  a the angle at the centre of the major arc
  b the area of the major arc.

Symmetry in the circle

1 The diameter of a circle is an axis of symmetry.

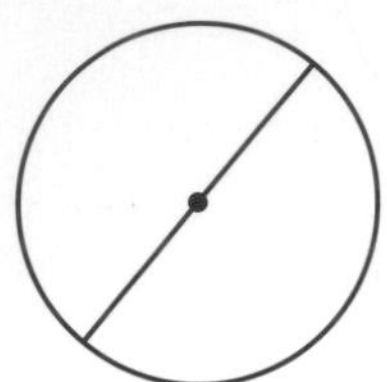

2 The centre of a circle is the centre of rotational symmetry.

3 Since the radii of a circle are equal, triangle AOB is isosceles.

OA = OB

∠OAB = ∠OBA

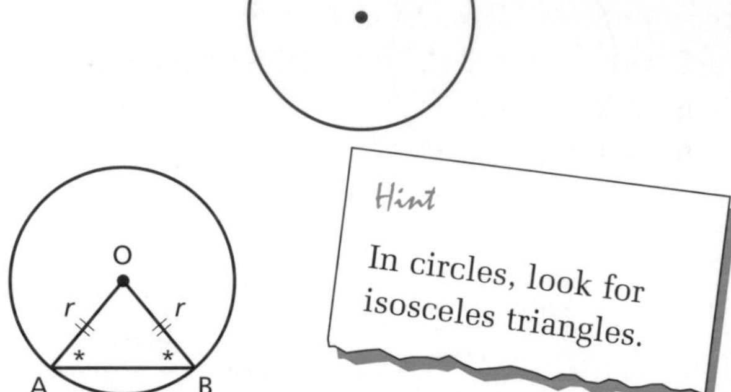

A line, such as AB, joining two points on the circumference of a circle is called a **chord**. A diameter is a special chord.

EXERCISE 4

In these circles, O is the centre of the circle. Calculate the size of each angle marked.

1

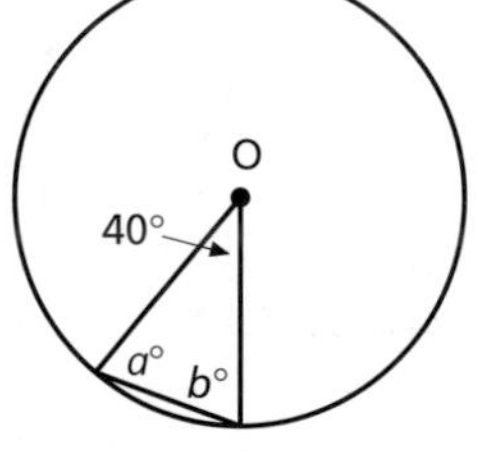

2

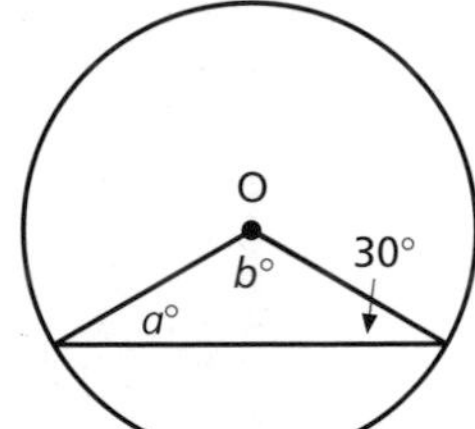

3

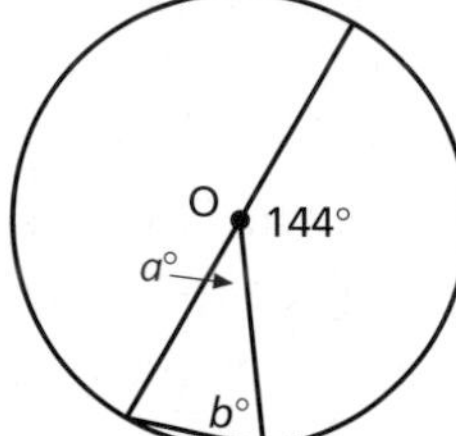

4

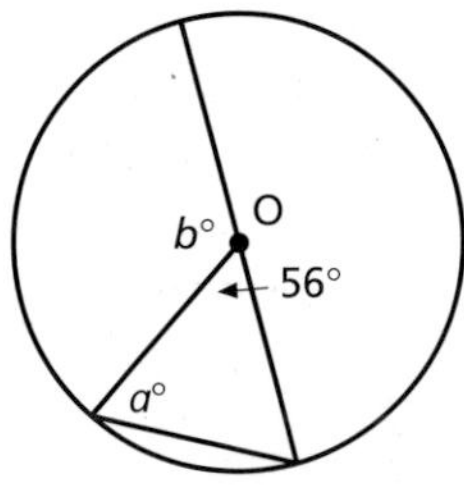

5

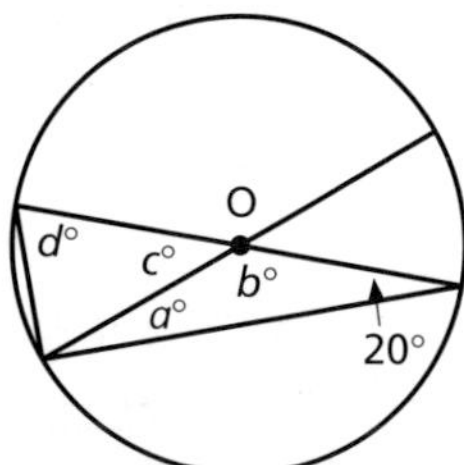

6

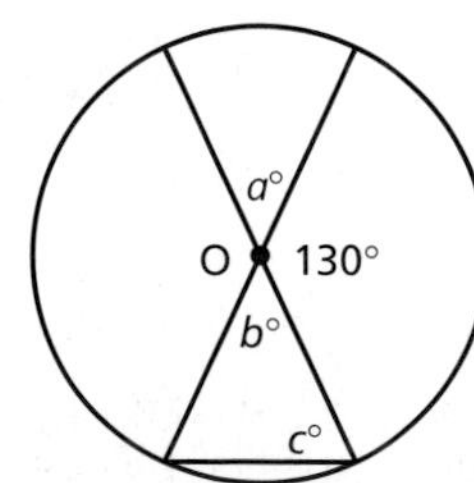

7

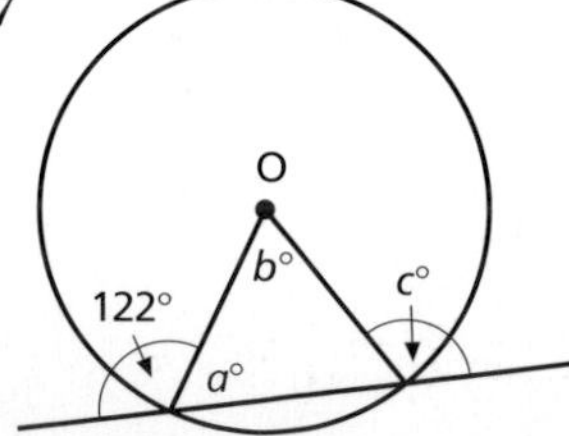

8

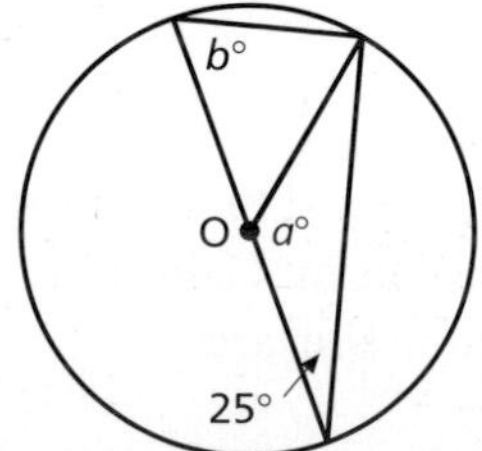

9

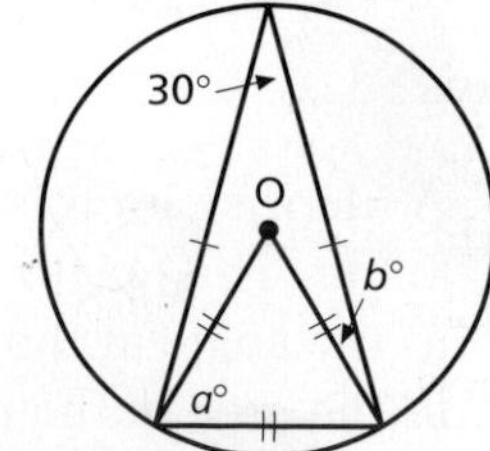

10 **a** Draw a large circle with centre O.
b Draw a chord AB.
c Pick a point on AB. Call it P.
Measure: **(i)** ∠APO **(ii)** AP **(iii)** PB **(iv)** OP.
d Repeat your measurements for several other positions of P. Make a table of your results.
e What do you notice about the size of ∠APO as the point P moves from A to B?
f Comment on the sizes of AP, PB and OP when ∠APO = 90°.
g Is this true for all chords in this circle? In any circle?
h Write down your conclusions.

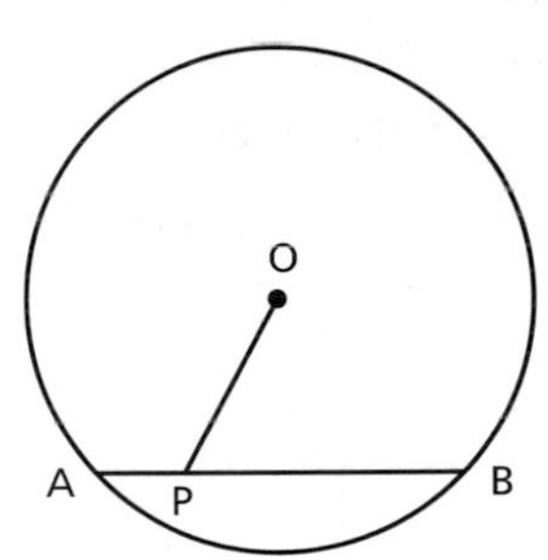

Symmetry and chords

Reminder

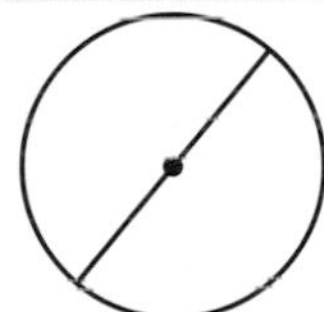

A diameter passes through the centre of the circle.

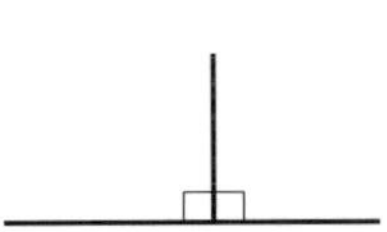

A perpendicular meets a line at right angles.

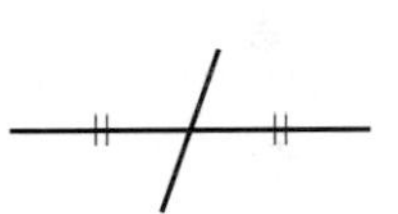

A bisector cuts a line in half.

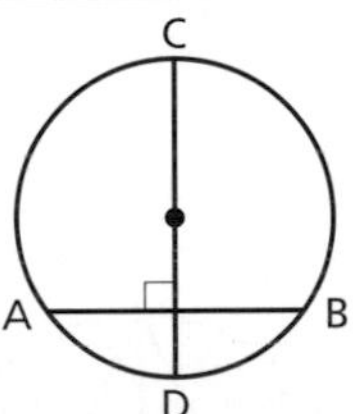

Given CD is a diameter and given CD is perpendicular to AB, then CD bisects AB.

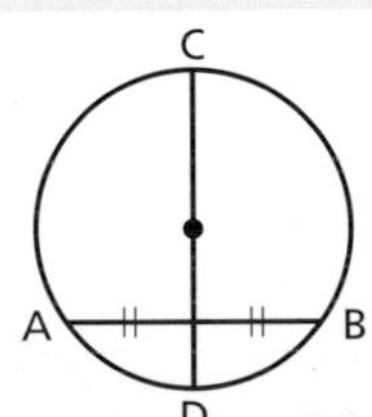

Given CD is a diameter and given CD bisects AB, then CD is perpendicular to AB.

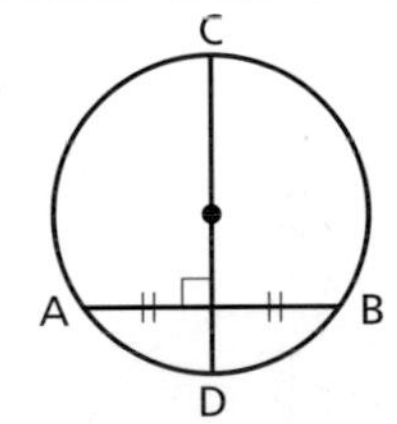

Given CD bisects AB and given CD is perpendicular to AB, then CD is a diameter.

Example A circle has a radius of 13 cm. A chord is 24 cm long. What is the perpendicular distance from the centre of the circle to the chord?

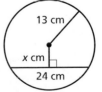

13 cm
x cm
24 cm

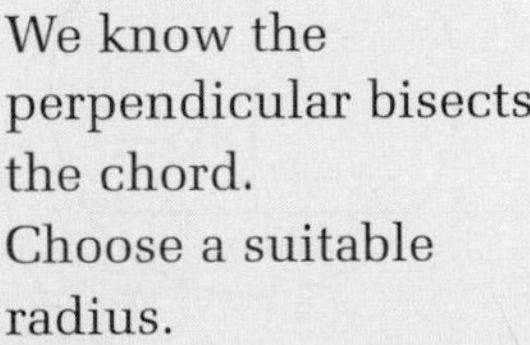

We know the perpendicular bisects the chord.
Choose a suitable radius.

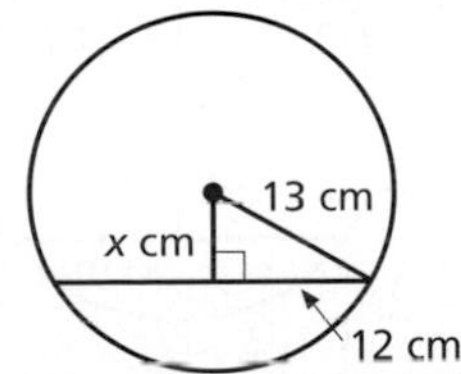

By Pythagoras,
$x^2 = 13^2 - 12^2$
$= 169 - 144 = 25$
$x = \sqrt{25} = 5$
The chord is 5 cm from the centre.

EXERCISE 5

Hint
With circles and chords look for right angles and suitable radii.

1 Find the sizes of the marked sides and angles.

a

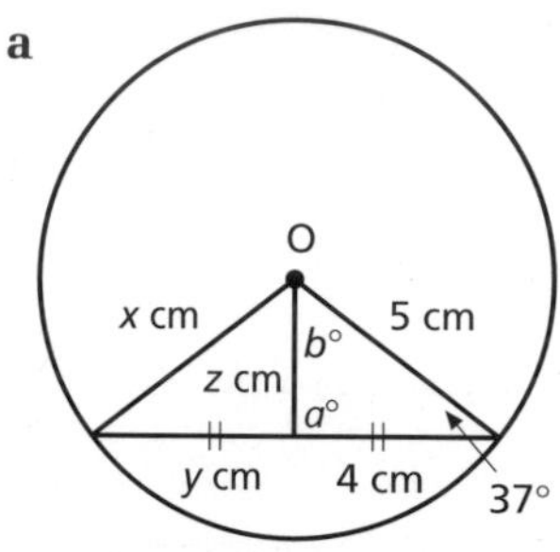

b

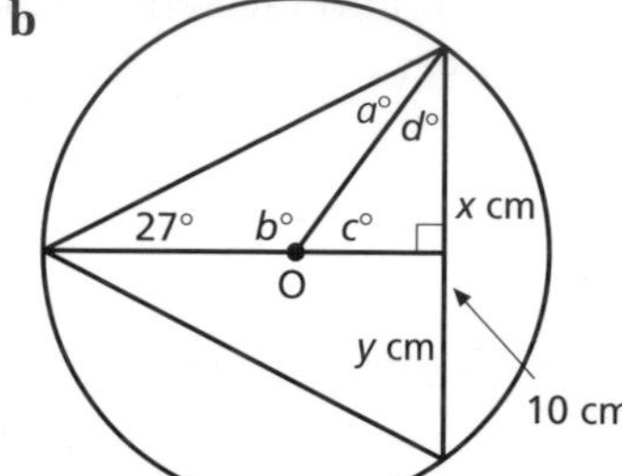

c

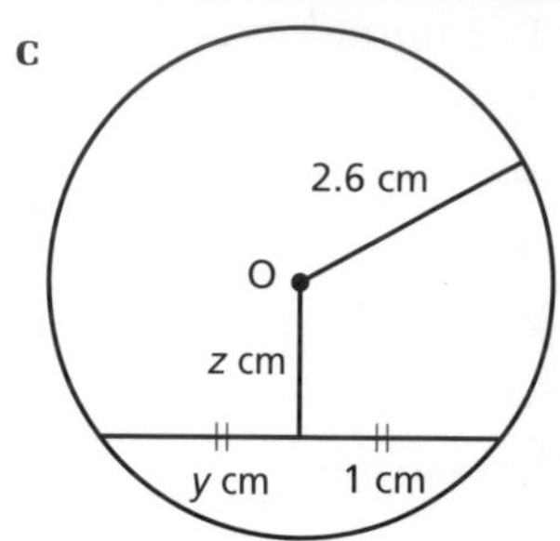

2 Chord PQ is 16 cm. OR bisects PQ.
The radius of the circle is 10 cm.

a What is the size of ∠ORQ?
b Calculate the length of OR.

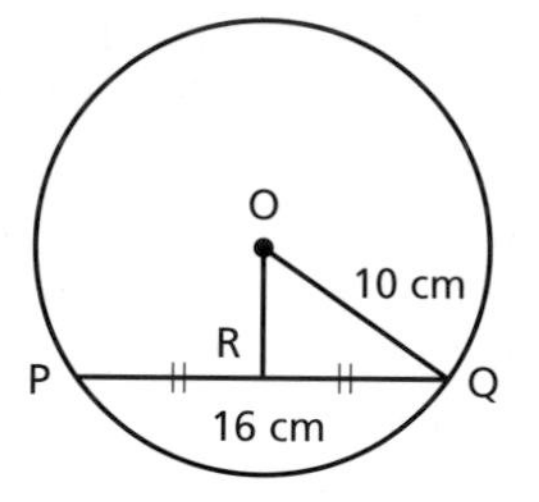

3 Calculate x in each case.

a

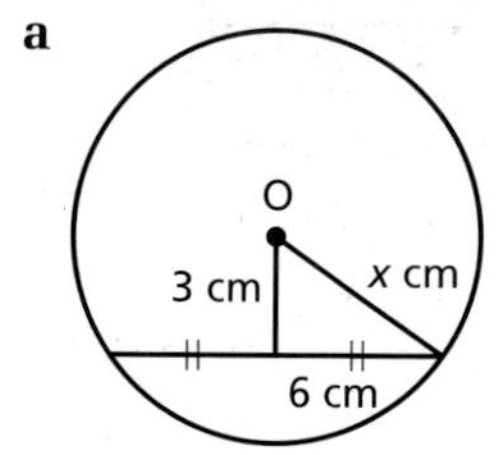

b

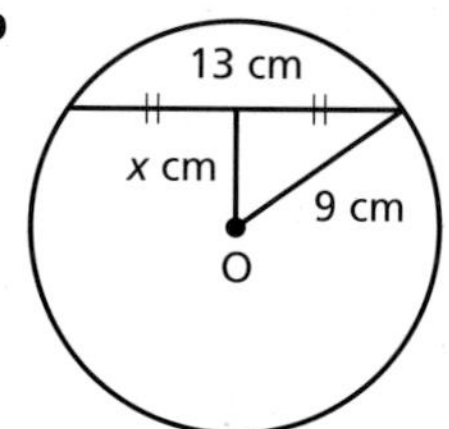

c

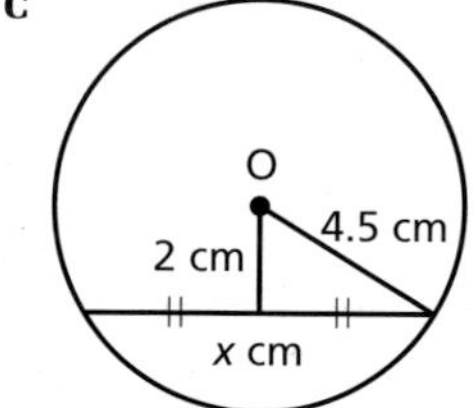

d

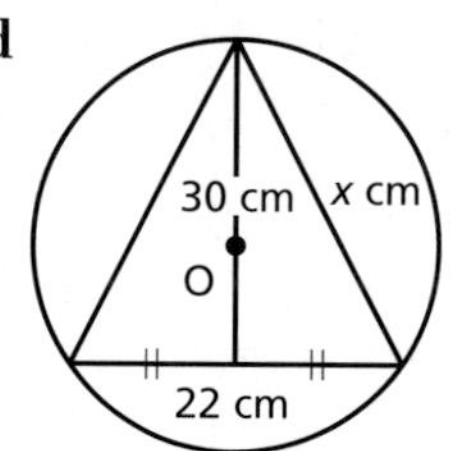

4 Redraw each diagram. Highlight a suitable right-angled triangle in each and then calculate x.

a

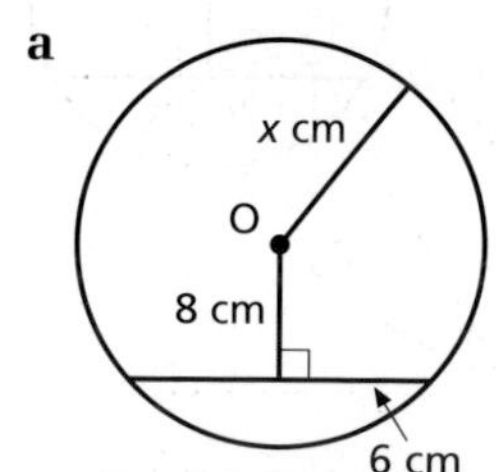

b

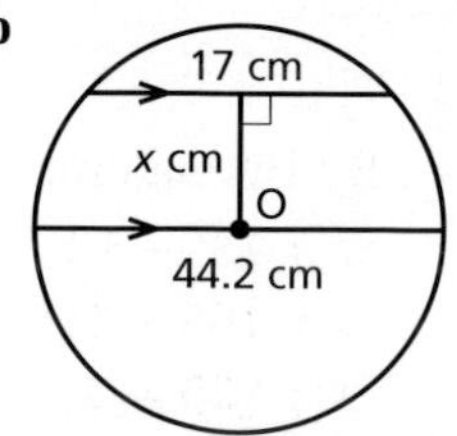

c

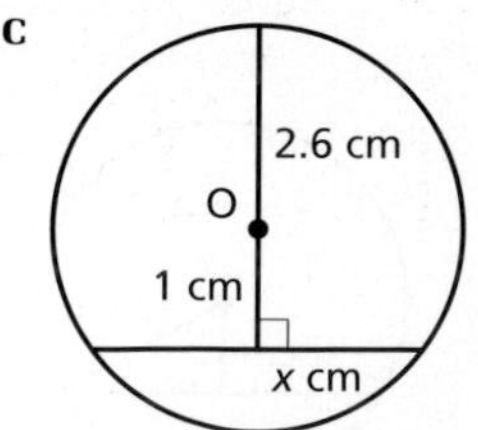

d

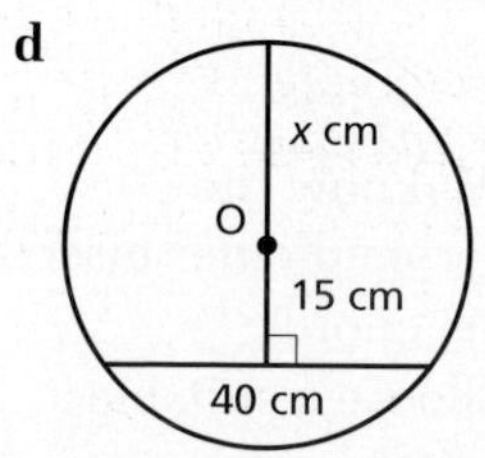

5

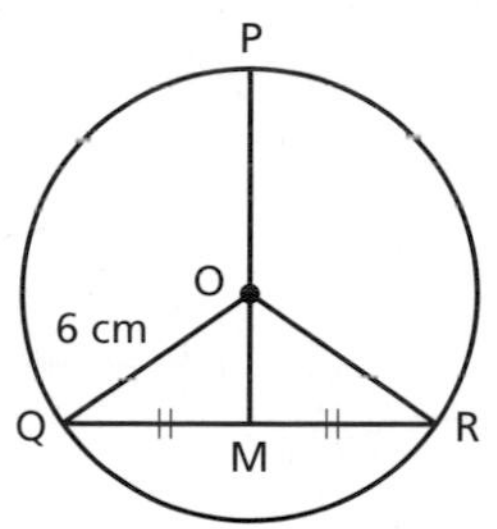

The radius of the circle is 6 cm long.
The length of chord QR is 7.8 cm.
M is the midpoint of QR.
Calculate the length of:

a OM **b** PM.

6

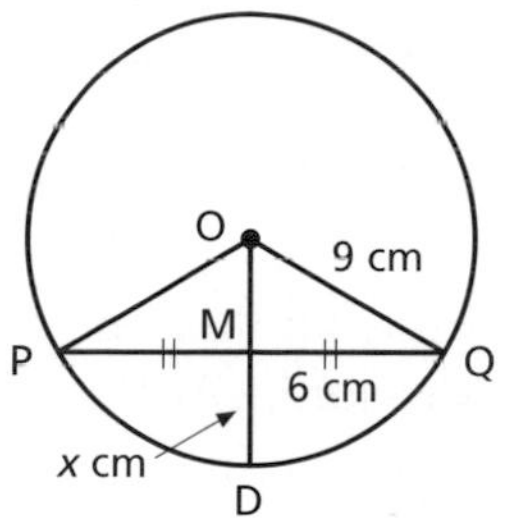

The radius of the circle is 9 cm long.
Chord PQ has a length of 12 cm.
M is the midpoint of PQ.
Calculate the length of:

a OM **b** MD.

7 The entrance to a tunnel is a circular arc of radius 5 m.
The width of the road is 7.6 m.
Calculate:

a the distance OM

b the height of the tunnel.

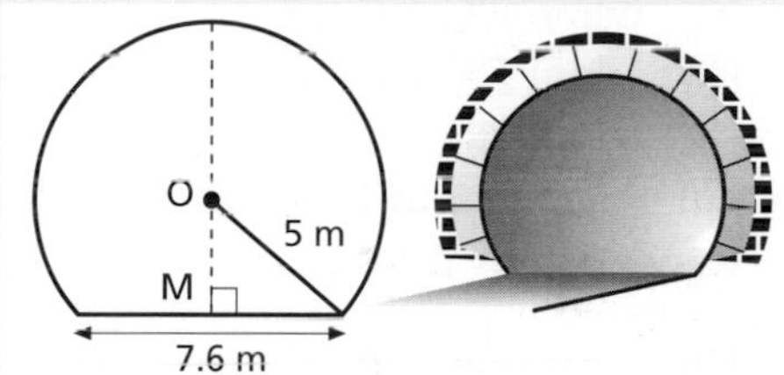

8 An oil tanker has a circular cross-section of diameter 4 m.
The surface of the oil is 2.8 m from the top of the tank.

a What is the height OM?

b What is the width of the surface of the oil?

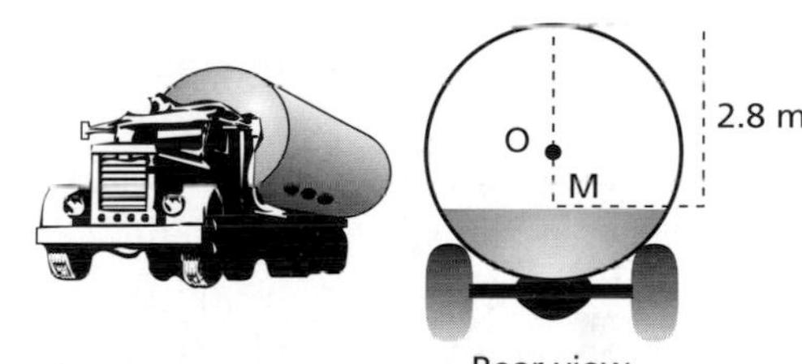

Rear view

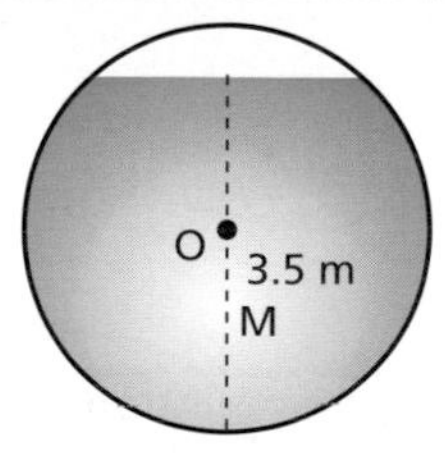

c The tanker is filled to a depth of 3.5 m.
What is the width of the surface now?

9 The design of a circular medallion is based on an equilateral triangle PQR.
The sides of the triangle are 3 cm long.
Calculate the radius of the circle.

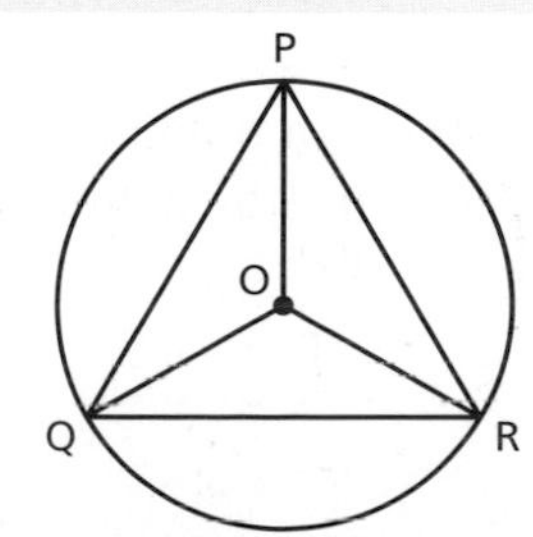

EXERCISE 6 (AN INVESTIGATION)

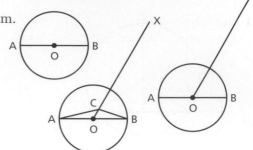

1 a Draw a circle with centre O and radius 6 cm.

b Draw a diameter AB.

c Draw a line OX, 10 cm long in any direction.

d Mark the point C on this line so that OC = 1 cm. Measure ∠ACB.

e Repeat this step, making OC = 2 cm, 3 cm, 4 cm, ... 10 cm.
Copy and complete the table.

OC (cm)	1	2	3	4	5	6	7	8	9	10
∠ACB										

f What do you notice about the size of the angle:
(**i**) when OC < 6 cm
(**ii**) when OC = 6 cm
(**iii**) when OC > 6 cm?

g Draw a different line OX 10 cm long.
Repeat steps **d** to **f**.

2 a Draw a circle with diameter AB.

b Pick a point C anywhere on the circumference.

c Draw the diameter CD.
What can be said about the lengths of AB and CD?

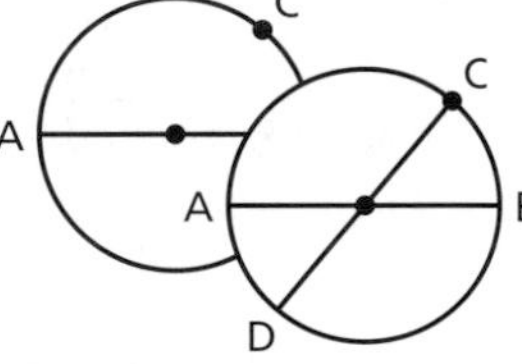

d Join A to C to B to D.
(**i**) What kind of quadrilateral is ACBD? Give a reason.
(**ii**) What is the size of the angle ∠ACB? Give a reason.

e The point C was any point on the circumference.
So what you found must be true for any point on the circumference.
The angle ACB is often called the angle in a semicircle for obvious reasons.
Copy and complete this sentence:

The angle in a semicircle = ...°.

Example

This circle has diameter AB = 13 cm. The chord AC = 12 cm.
How long is the chord BC?

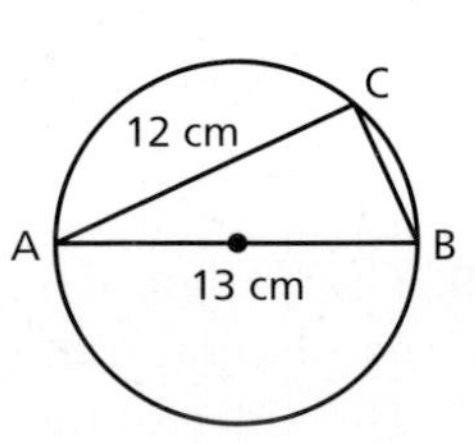

Since AB is a diameter then
∠ACB = 90° (the angle in a semicircle)

So, by Pythagoras: $CB^2 = 13^2 - 12^2$

$CB^2 = 169 - 144 = 25$

$CB = \sqrt{25} = 5$

CB is 5 cm long.

EXERCISE 7

1 In each diagram O is the centre of the circle and AB is a diameter. Copy each diagram and fill in the sizes of as many angles as possible.

a

b

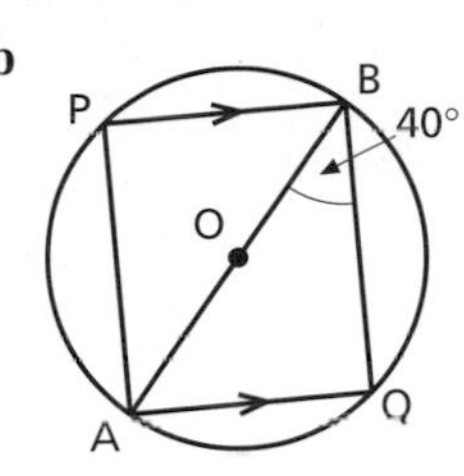

c

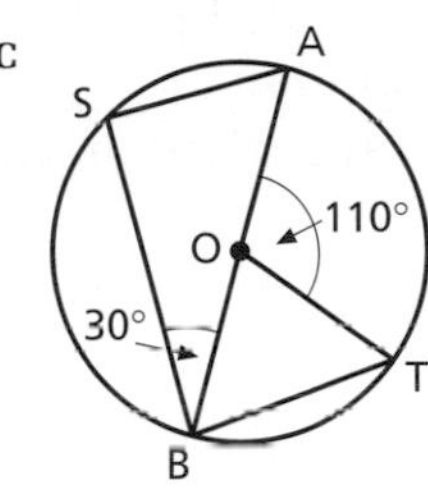

d

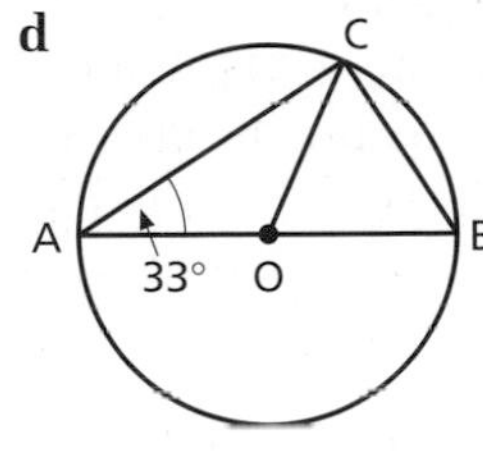

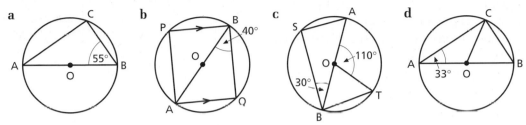

2 Use Pythagoras' Theorem to calculate:

a the chord AC

b the diameter of the circle

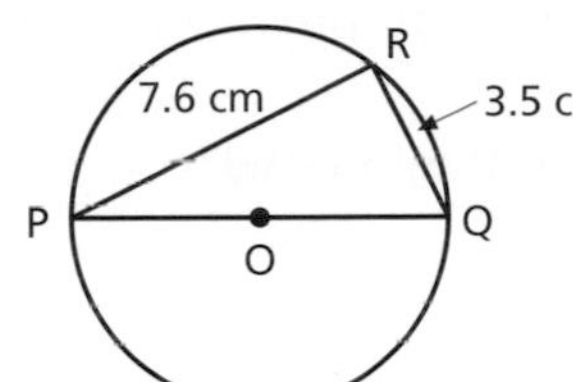

c the chord LN

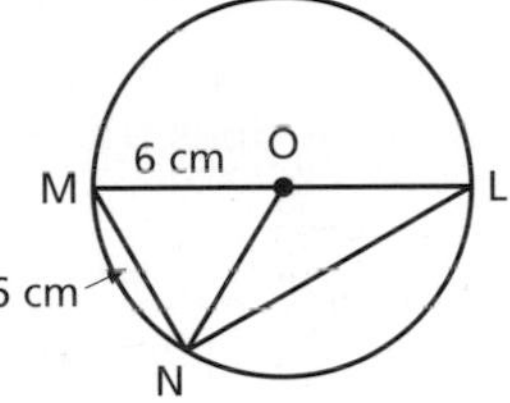

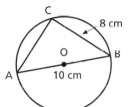

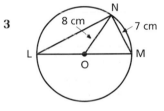

3 LM is the diameter of the circle. O is its centre.

a State the size of (i) OM (ii) LM.

b Calculate the value of LN.

4 The chord QR = 9 cm. OP = 6 cm. Calculate the length of:

a PR

b QP

c RS.

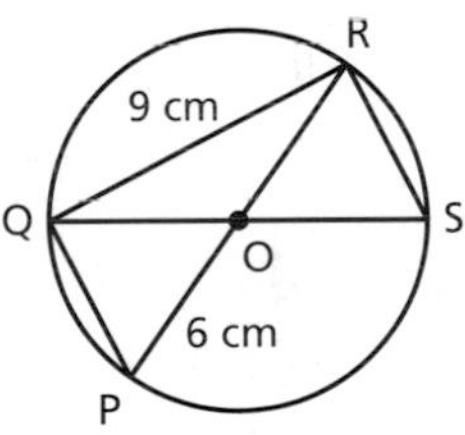

5 Identify the right angle then use trigonometry to calculate:

a ∠CDE

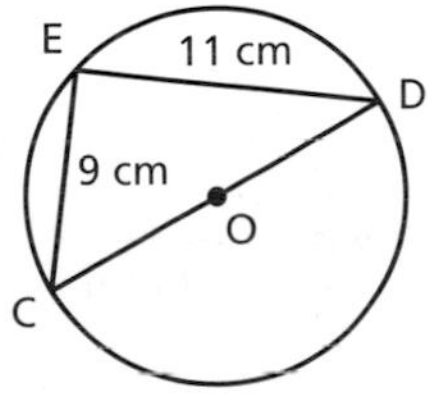

b the chord HF

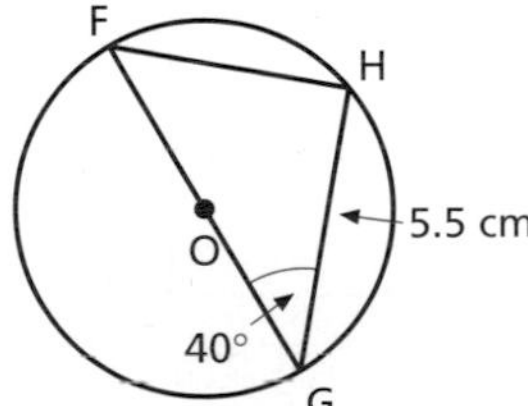

c ∠YXZ

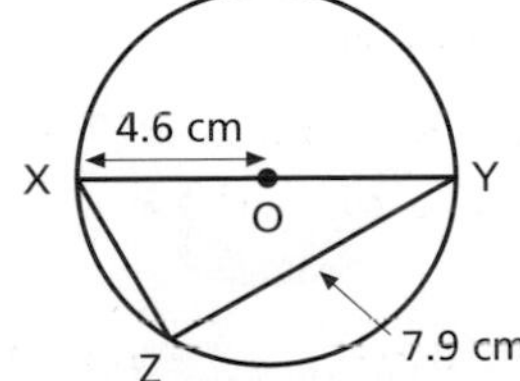

6 In the diagram, O is the centre of a circle of radius 6 cm. PQ is a diameter. Chord QR is 8 cm.

a Calculate the size of ∠QPR.

b Calculate the length of chord PR.

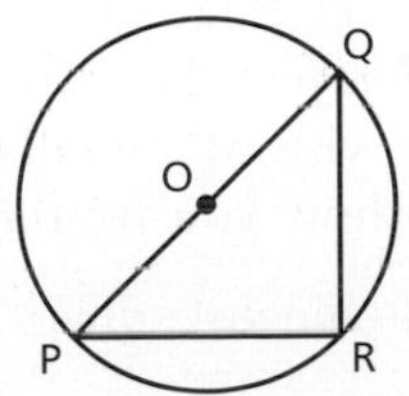

7 The body of a plane is circular in cross-section.
AB represents the floor. BC represents a wall.
AC is a diameter of the circle.

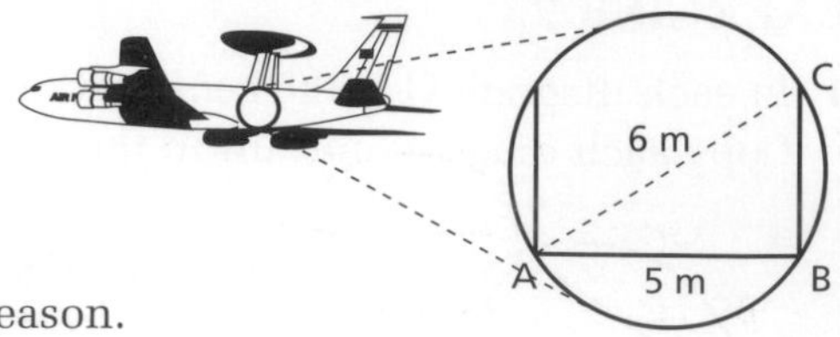

a Name a right angle in the diagram. Give a reason.
b How high is the wall BC?
c Calculate the size of ∠ACB.

8 If AB is a diameter then ∠ACB is 90°. True.
If ∠ACB is 90° then AB is a diameter. Also true.
a Use the converse of Pythagoras to prove ∠ACB is right-angled.
b What does this tell us about the line AB?

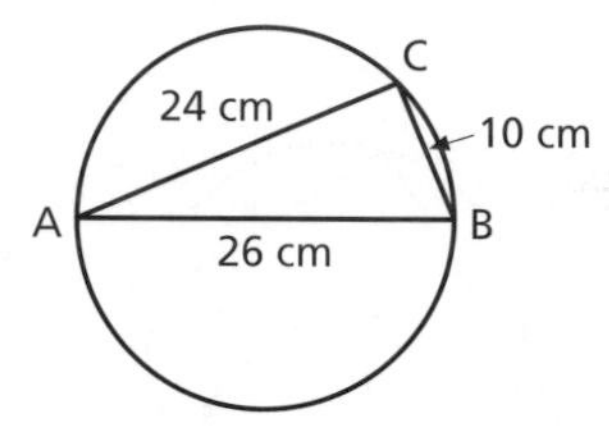

9 Prove, in each case, that AB is a diameter.

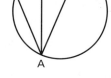

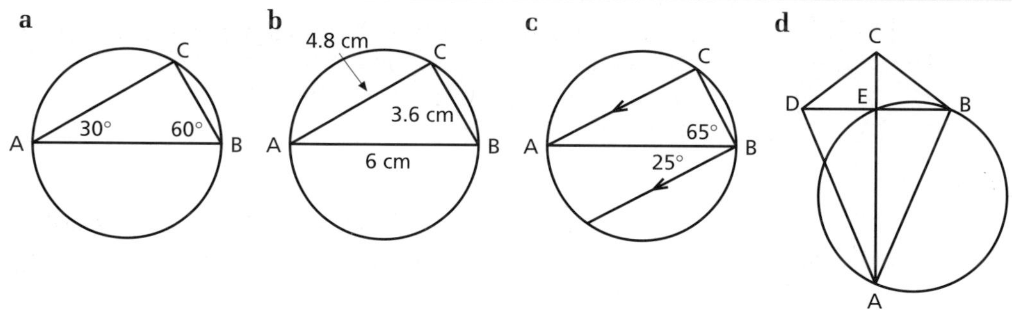

ABCD is a kite and E lies on the circumference of the circle.

10

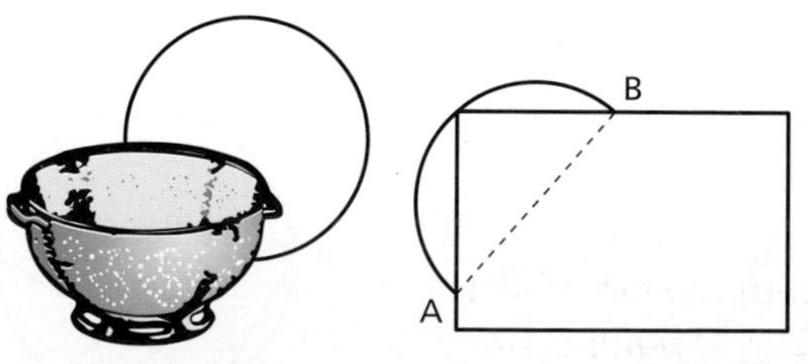

a Draw round a circular object.
b Put a rectangular sheet of paper on the circle so that a corner just touches the circumference. The circle just shows from under the paper at A and B. Explain why AB is a diameter.
c Explain how you would find the centre of the circle.

11 What is the biggest square you can draw inside a circle of diameter 10 cm?

Tangents

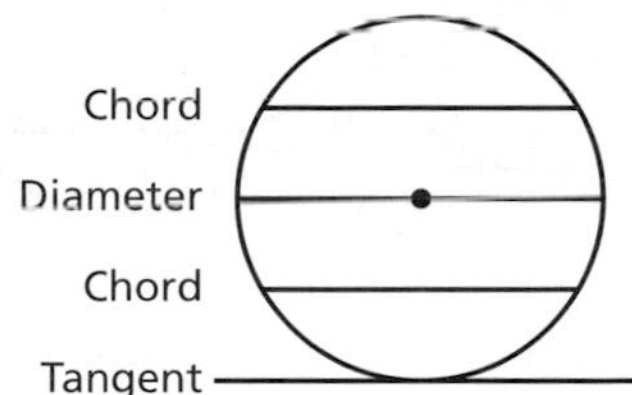

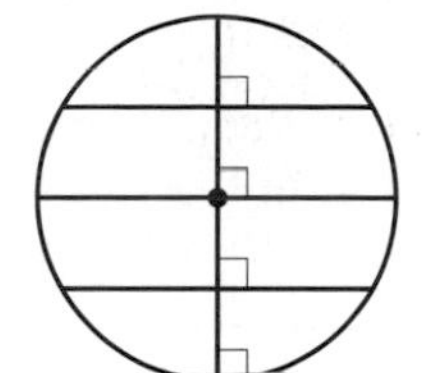

A **tangent** is a line which touches a circle at only one point.

The symmetry of the situation shows us that, at the point of contact, the tangent and radius are at right angles.

Example 1

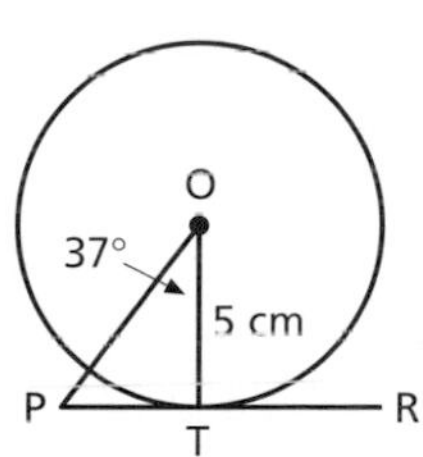

In the diagram, O is the centre of the circle.
OT is a radius of length 5 cm. PR is a tangent touching the circle at T. $\angle POT = 37°$. Calculate:

a the size of $\angle OPT$

b the distance PT.

$\angle OTP = 90°$ (angle between a tangent and a radius)

a $\angle OPT = 90° - 37° = 53°$

b $PT = 5 \tan 37 = 3.8$ cm (to 2 s.f.)

Example 2

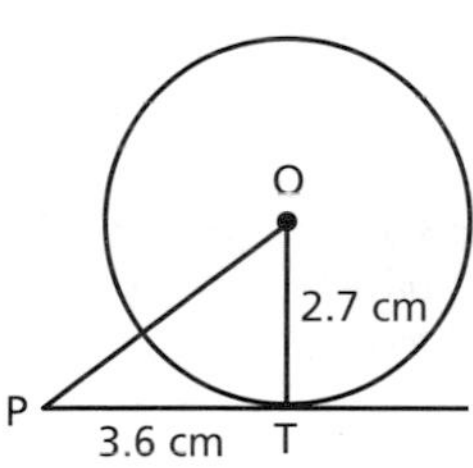

PT is a tangent to the circle centre O and radius OT. Given that PT = 3.6 cm and OT = 2.7 cm, find the length of OP.

$\angle OTP = 90°$ (angle between a tangent and a radius)

By Pythagoras: $OP^2 = 3.6^2 + 2.7^2$

$OP^2 = 20.25$

$OP = \sqrt{20.25} = 4.5$ cm

EXERCISE 8

1 In each diagram PT is a tangent touching the circle at T. Calculate the size of the angle marked $x°$ in each case.

a

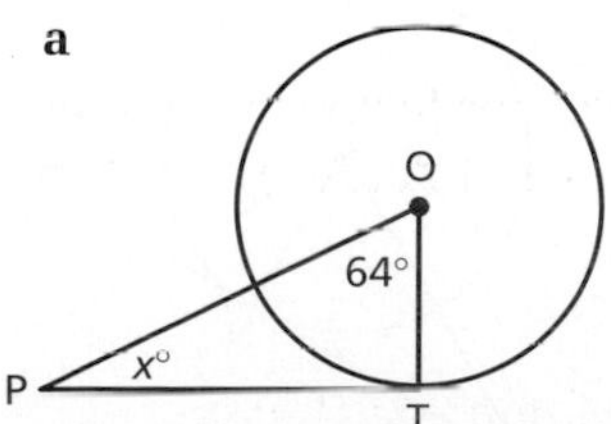

b

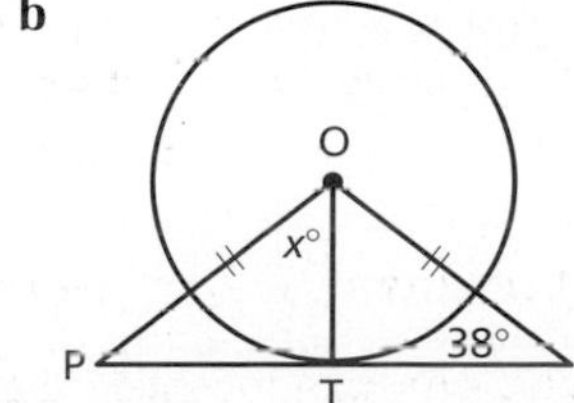

c

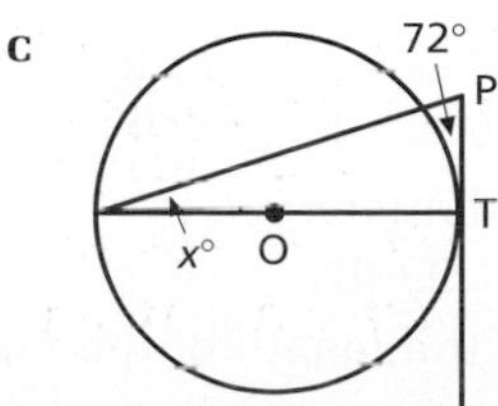

2 PQ is a tangent to the circle touching it at R.
Find the size of:
a ∠ORQ
b ∠ROQ
c ∠OPR.

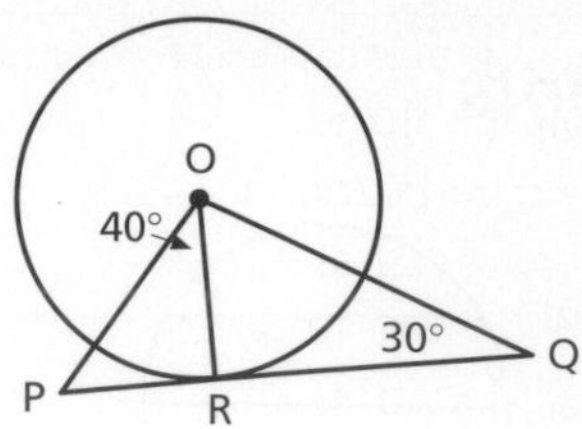

3

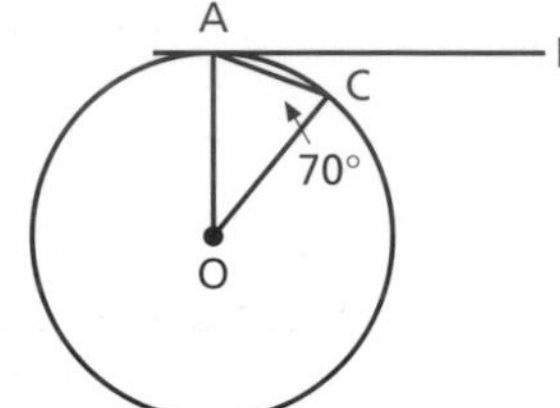

AB is a tangent to the circle touching the circle at A. Calculate the size of:
a ∠CAO
b ∠AOC
c ∠CAB.

4 LM is a tangent to the circle touching it at N.
Copy the diagram and fill in the sizes of as many angles as you can.

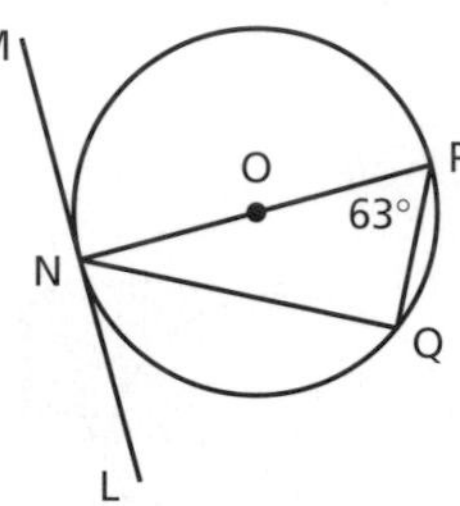

5

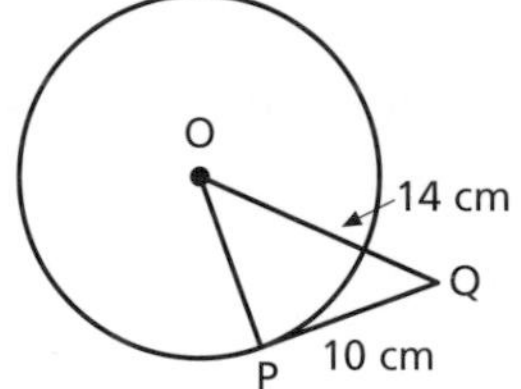

PQ is a tangent to the circle.
OQ = 14 cm. PQ = 10 cm.
Calculate the radius of the circle.

6 XY is a tangent to the circle. OY = 5 cm. XY = 7.5 cm.
Calculate:
a ∠OXY
b ∠XOY.

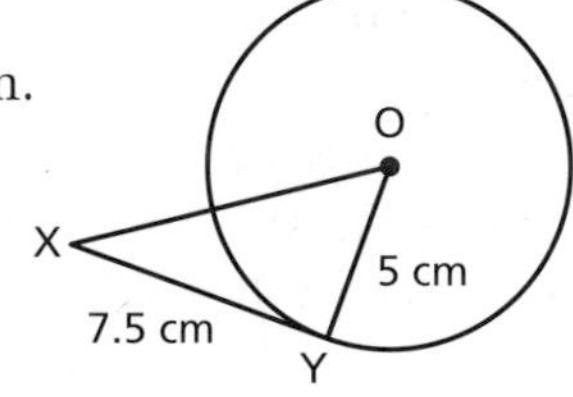

7

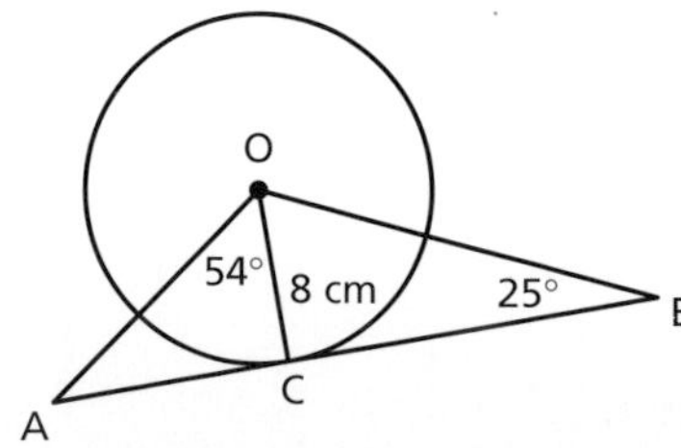

AC is a tangent to the circle.
The radius of the circle is 8 cm.
a Calculate the length of AC.
b Calculate the size of ∠COB.
c Calculate the length of CB.
d Find the length of AB.

8 LM is a tangent to the circle. ∠OLN = 29°. ∠LOM = 90°.
OM = 13 cm.
Calculate:
a ∠OMN
b the length of the radius ON.

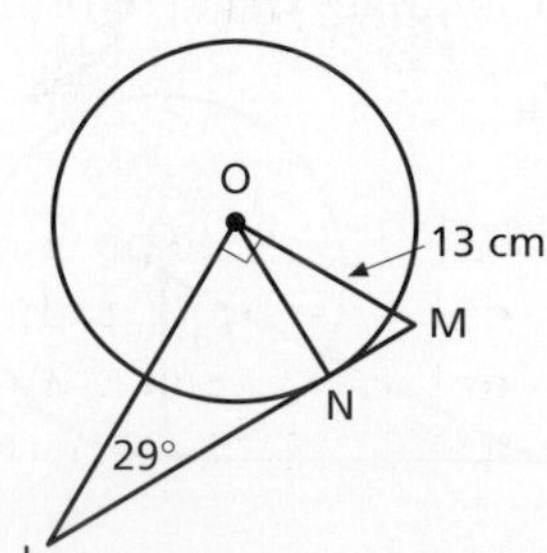

9 The diagram shows the coin slot for a vending machine.
It takes two coins at a time. The coins are 2.8 cm in diameter.
AE and AB are tangents to the circles representing the coins.
C and D are the centres of the circles.
Calculate:

a BC
b AE
c AC
d AD.

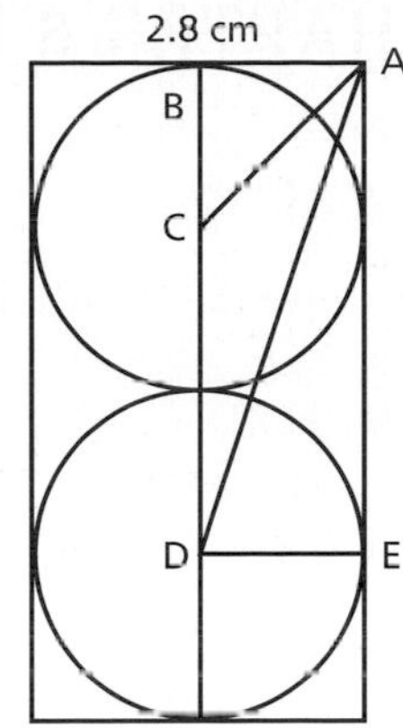

10

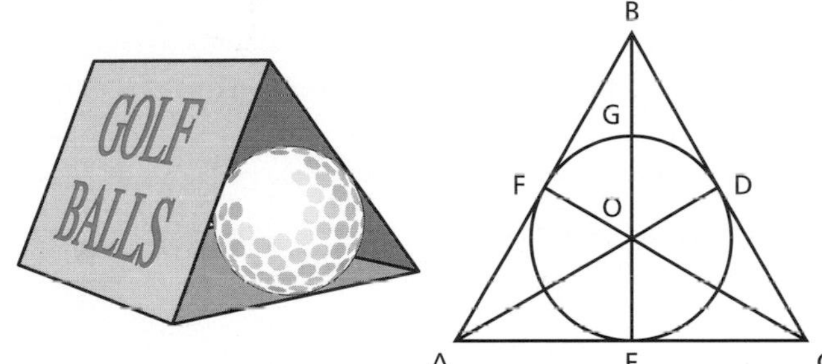

Golf balls with a radius of 3 cm are packed in a box with an equilateral triangle for a cross-section. In the diagram the circle represents the ball and AB, BC and CA are tangents to it.

a What is the size of ∠ABE?
b Work out the size of:
(i) OF (ii) OB (iii) BF (iv) AB (v) GB.

11

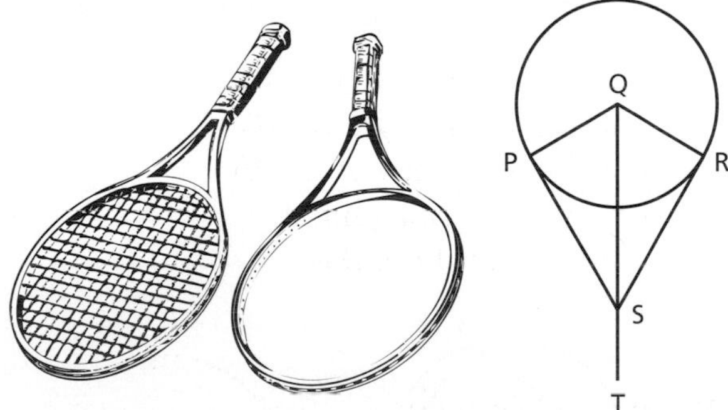

A company experiments with the design of a racquet. They base the design on a circle centre Q, radius 12 cm. Two struts, PS and RS, are tangents to the circle.

a If QS = 18 cm, what is the length of each strut?
b What is the size of ∠PSR?

CHAPTER 6 REVIEW

1 Name the highlighted features labelled:
a PQ
b AOB
c MN
d TR.

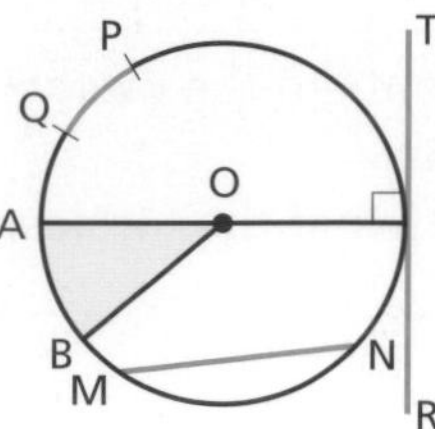

2

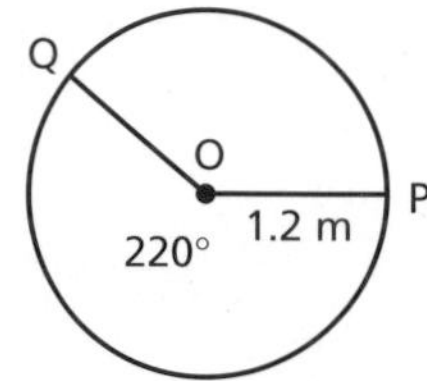

Calculate the length of the major arc PQ.

3 Calculate the perimeter of this sector.

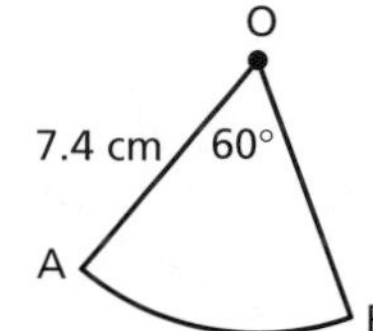

4

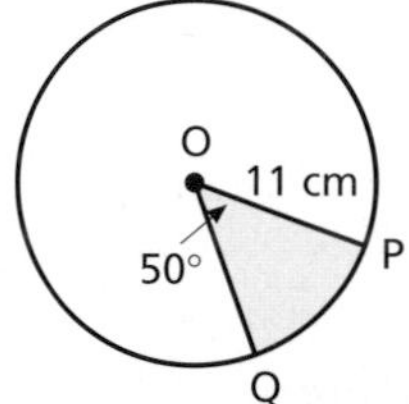

Calculate the area of the sector PQO.

5 Calculate the area of the sector AOB.

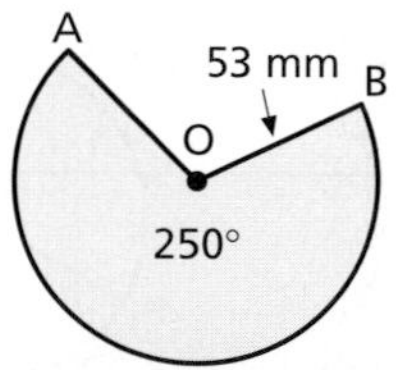

6 Calculate:
a the length of **(i)** OA **(ii)** AC
b the size of
(i) ∠OAD
(ii) ∠AOD
(iii) ∠ABC.

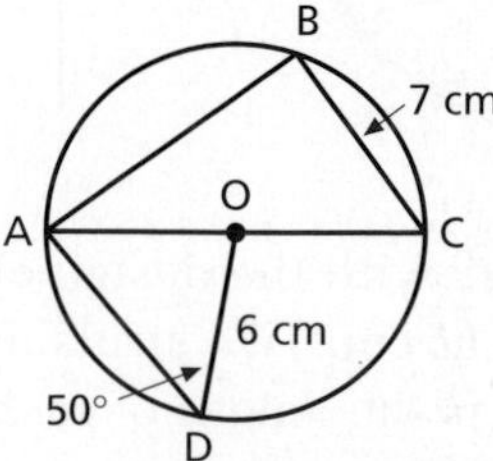

7 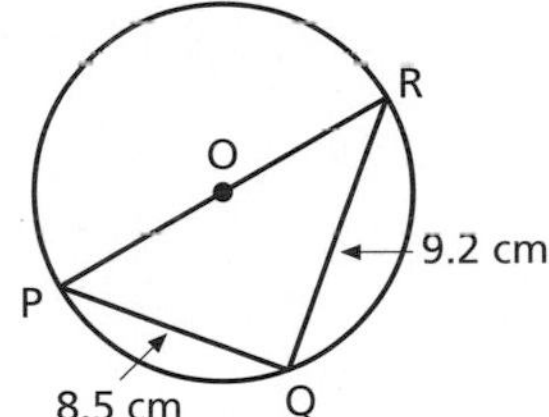

O is the centre of the circle.
PQ = 8.5 cm. QR = 9.2 cm.

a Calculate the radius of the circle.
b Calculate the size of ∠QPR.

8 AC is a tangent to the circle touching it at B.
Copy the diagram and fill in the sizes of as many angles as possible.

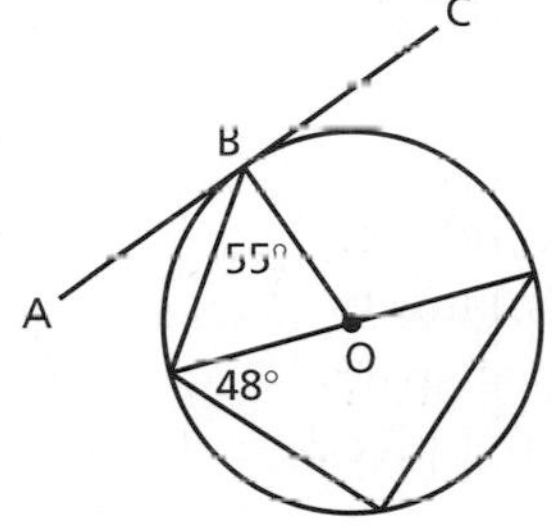

9 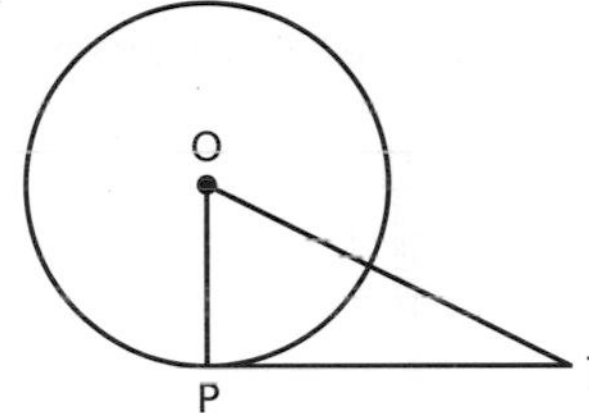

PT is a tangent to the circle with centre O and radius OP = 6 cm.
PT is 12 cm long.
Calculate the distance OT.

10 Calculate the sizes of the angles marked a, b and c.

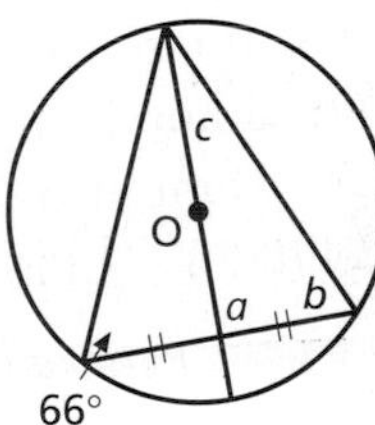

11 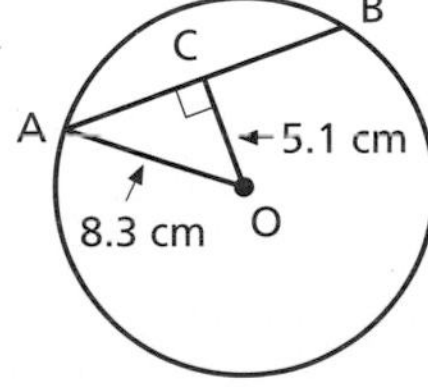

Calculate the length of the chord in the circle.

7 Revising Unit 1

Percentages

Reminder

Use FIX mode on your calculator to give your answers to 2 decimal places.

Simple interest
£350 is put in the bank, attracting simple interest at the rate of 5% per annum.
After 1 year:
5% of £350 = £17.50 interest
After 5 years:
5 × £17.50 = £87.50 interest
After 3 months:
$\frac{3}{12}$ × £17.50 = £4.38 interest (to nearest penny)

Compound interest
£350 is put in the bank, attracting compound interest at the rate of 5% per annum.
Each year the money grows by 105%.
After 1 year: amount in bank = £350 × 105% = £367.50
After 2 years: amount in bank = £367.50 × 105% = £385.88
After 3 years: amount in bank = £385.88 × 105% = £405.17
After 4 years: amount in bank = £405.17 × 105% = £425.43
After 5 years: amount in bank = £425.43 × 105% = £446.70
Interest = £446.70 − £350 = £96.70

Inflation: the rate at which costs increase.

Appreciation: when items increase in value.
Depreciation: when items decrease in value.

EXERCISE 1

1 Calculate the simple interest gained on:
  a £4000 invested for 1 year at 6% per annum
  b £600 invested for 6 months at 3% per annum
  c £50 invested for 9 months at 4% per annum.

2 Calculate the compound interest on:
  a £150 for 4 years at 3% per annum
  b £2000 for 36 months at 3% per annum

c £1750 for 2 years at 4% per annum
d £25 for 15 years at 3.2% per annum.

3 Mr and Mrs Morley invest £250 for their newborn baby. If they manage to achieve an average annual return on the money of 4% per annum, calculate the sum that will be available for their son on his eighteenth birthday.

4 A painting purchased for £1500 in 1992 is sold at auction in 1998 for £2350. Find the percentage appreciation in its value.

5 Mrs Gallacher retired in 1990 with an additional pension of £6500 per annum. This pension is automatically increased on 1st April each year by the rate of inflation for the previous year. Use the rates shown in the table to calculate her pension for the year beginning 1st April 1996.

Year	Rate of inflation
1990	10%
1991	5%
1992	4%
1993	2%
1994	1.5%
1995	2.2%

6 Gerry bought a brand new car in 1994 for £11 500. By 1997 it had depreciated by 38%. Calculate the car's trade-in value at this time.

7 The Prompt Prints Company spends £35 000 on new computer hardware. The value of the hardware depreciates by 26% each year. What value will it have in 3 years time?

8 The Proto Prints Company also spends £35 000 on new computer hardware. The value of their hardware depreciates by 18% each year.
a What value will it have in 3 years time?
b When will the value of the hardware fall below 50% of its original value?

9 Mrs Weir's vase was valued at £350 in 1993. The value has appreciated by 8% each year since then. Calculate its value in: a 1995 b 1998 c 2000.

10 When Angus was born his parents invested £500 for him at 5% per annum compound interest. How much will he have on his eighteenth birthday?

11 A car saleswoman receives a basic wage of £108 per week plus 1% commission on all sales. Calculate her total wage for the following weeks.

Week	Total sales
1	£7750
2	£2680
3	£15 755
4	£1235
5	£6555

12 A contractor requires 12 500 bricks to complete a new building. He needs to add an allowance of 8% extra for cutting and waste. How many bricks should he order?

13 A car component has a normal selling price of £5.85. A trade customer is given a discount of 12%. How much would he pay for the component?

Approximate rates of inflation

Year	1985	1986	1987	1988	1989	1990	1991	1992	1993	1994	1995	1996
Rate (%)	6	5.5	5	8	7	10	5	4	2	1.5	2	3

14 An early version of an electronic calculator was purchased in 1985 for £85. Calculate what it would cost in 1988 if prices had kept pace with inflation.

15 In 1990 Mrs Fortuna paid £280 for a new washing machine. If prices had increased at the rate of inflation what would she have paid in 1996 for an equivalent model?

16 Mr Chambers accepted a pension of £650 per month in 1990.
His pension is linked to inflation.
How much per month would he have received in 1996?

17 Mr Moras is quoted a price of £6550 for double glazing. He can choose to pay nothing for 12 months at a monthly interest rate of 2.6%.
Calculate what he will pay if he settles the account in full at the end of this time.

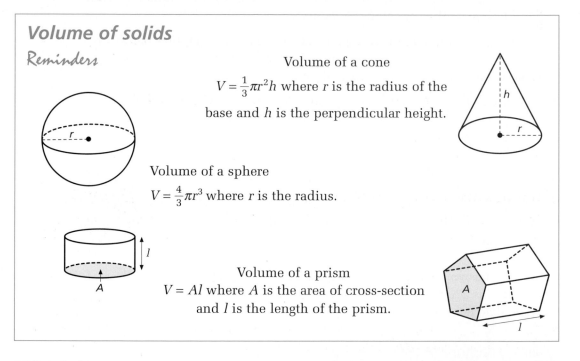

Volume of solids

Reminders

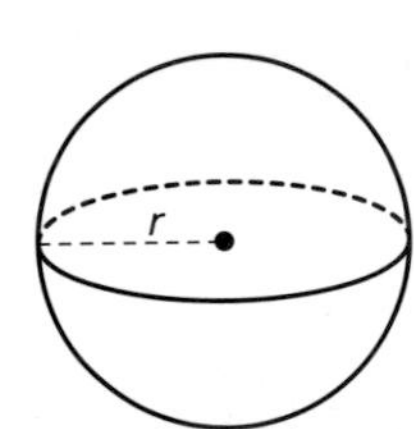

Volume of a cone

$V = \frac{1}{3}\pi r^2 h$ where r is the radius of the base and h is the perpendicular height.

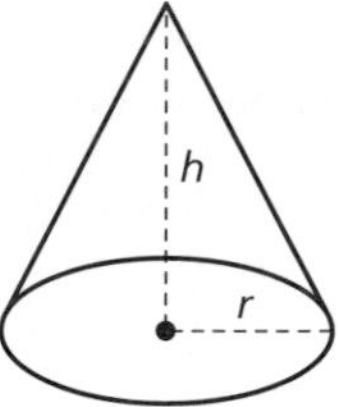

Volume of a sphere

$V = \frac{4}{3}\pi r^3$ where r is the radius.

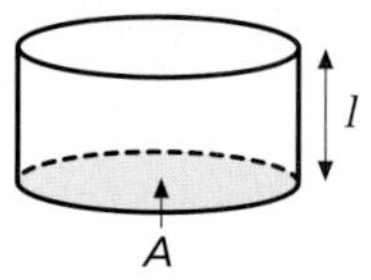

Volume of a prism

$V = Al$ where A is the area of cross-section and l is the length of the prism.

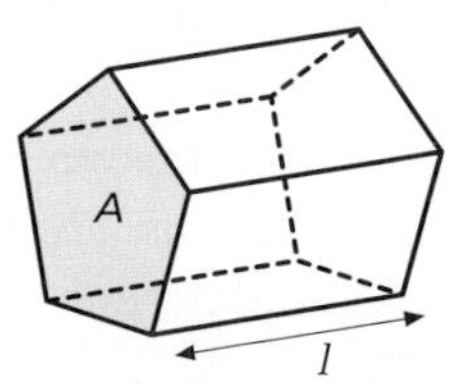

EXERCISE 2

1 Calculate the volume of each sphere.

a

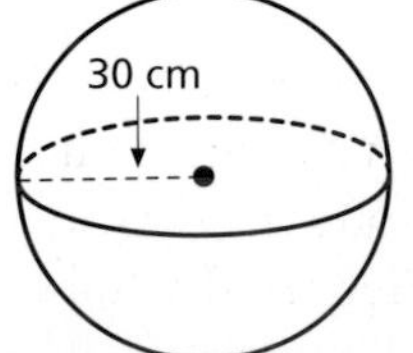

b

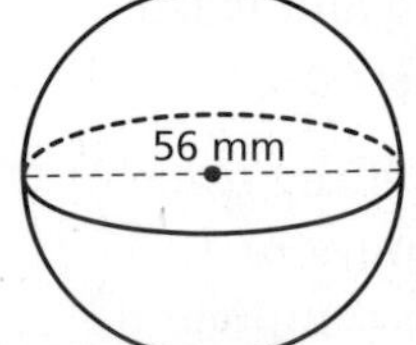

c

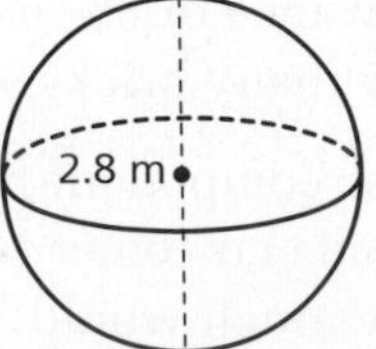

2 Calculate the volume of each cone.

a

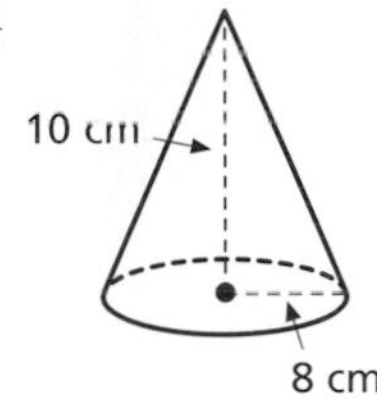

b

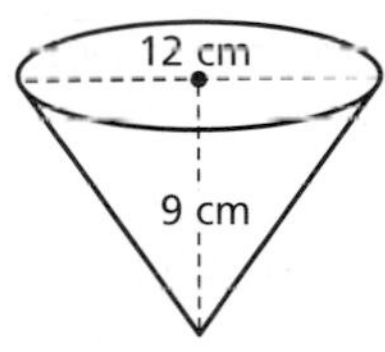

c

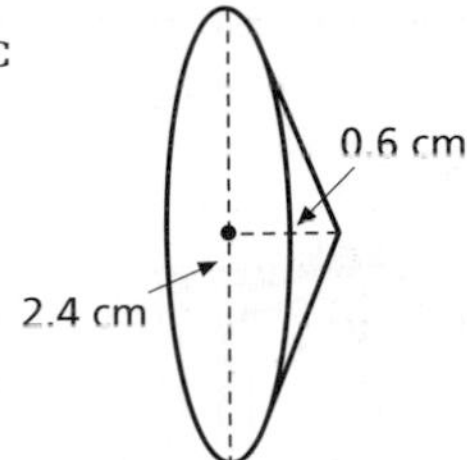

3 Calculate the volume of each prism.

a

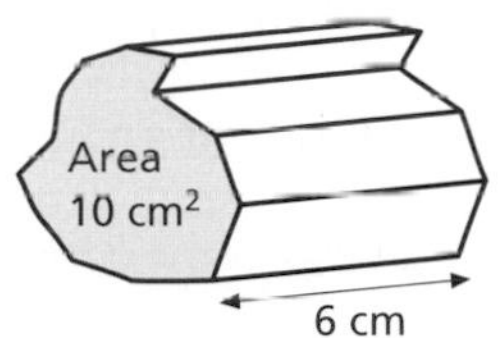

b

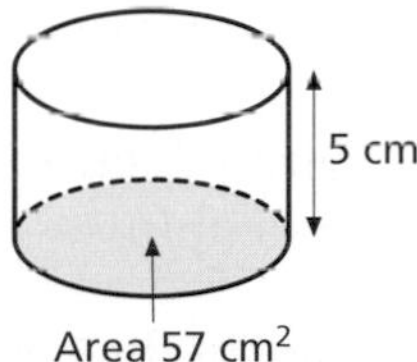

c

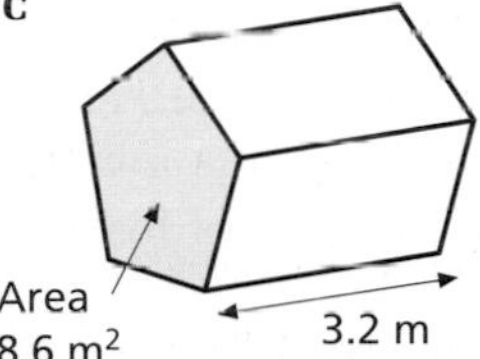

4 Calculate the volume of a cylinder with:

a radius 6 cm and height 12 cm

b radius 7 mm and height 12 mm

c diameter 1.2 m and height 2 m.

Area of circle = πr^2

5

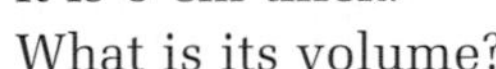

This clock is a prism.
The area of its front is 135 cm^2.
It is 10 cm deep.
Calculate its volume.

6 The pencil sharpener has a shavings collector which is a prism. The area of the face of the collector is 50 cm^2.
It is 5 cm thick.
What is its volume?

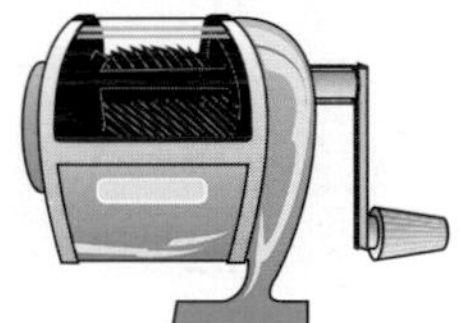

7 A pot has a spherical body. The radius of the sphere is 4 cm.
Calculate the volume of the body of the pot.

8 The glass is a conical container. The diameter of the mouth of the glass is 8 cm. The depth of the cone is 6 cm.
Calculate the capacity (volume) of the glass.

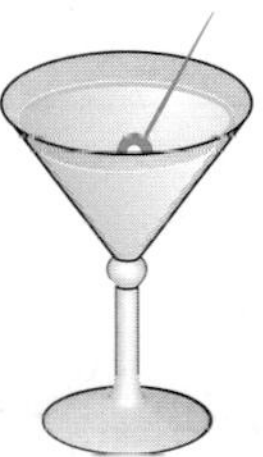

9

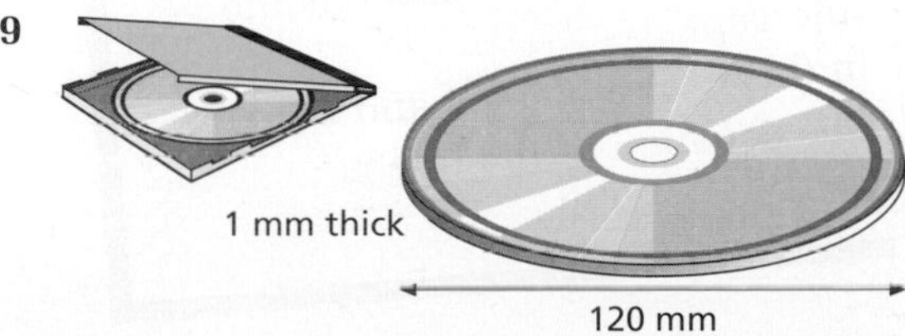

The CD is a cylinder which is 120 mm in diameter and only 1 mm thick. Calculate the volume of plastic needed to make the CD. (Ignore the hole in the middle.)

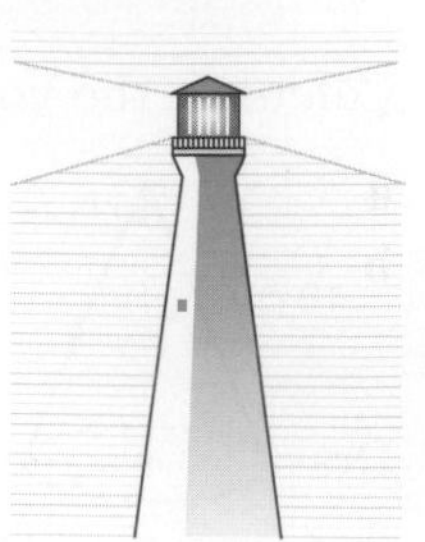

10 The lighthouse is basically a cone with base diameter 10 m and vertical height 80 m. Estimate its volume.

11

The butter churn is cylindrical. Its radius is 23 cm and its depth is 32 cm.

a Calculate its volume.

b When churning is complete only 30% of the volume remains as butter. What volume of butter would you expect from one batch?

12 The tea inside a teacup is a cylinder of diameter 9.6 cm with a depth of 10 cm. What volume of tea is needed for 12 cupfuls?

13 The asteroid Spiro is a perfect sphere of diameter 3500 km. Silicates make up 80% of its volume.

a Calculate its volume.

b How much of the asteroid is composed of silicates?

14 A tent is conical. Its height is 1.6 m. Its diameter is 2.8 m.

a Calculate its volume.

b The Jumbo tent is twice as high and has twice the diameter.

(i) Calculate its volume **(ii)** Comment on how much bigger it is.

Linear relationships

Reminders

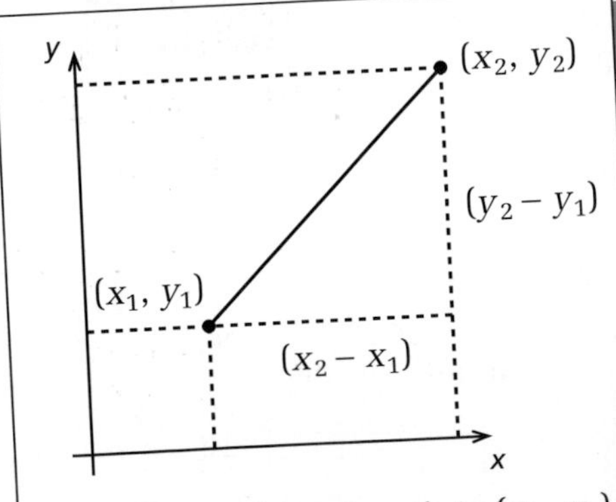

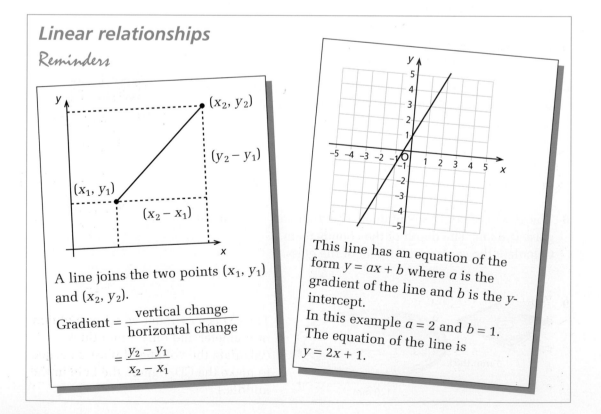

A line joins the two points (x_1, y_1) and (x_2, y_2).

$$\text{Gradient} = \frac{\text{vertical change}}{\text{horizontal change}}$$

$$= \frac{y_2 - y_1}{x_2 - x_1}$$

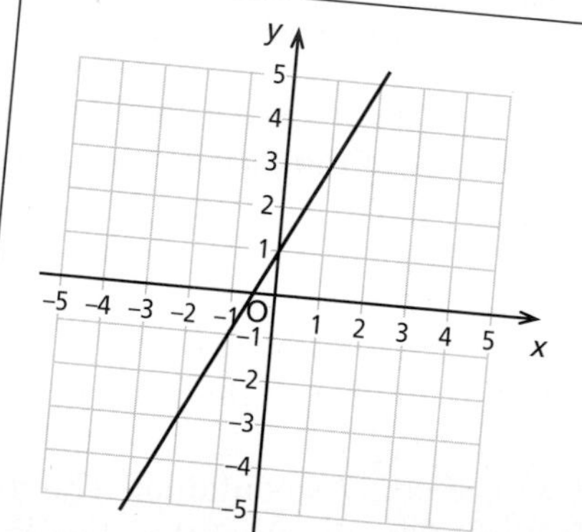

This line has an equation of the form $y = ax + b$ where a is the gradient of the line and b is the y-intercept.

In this example $a = 2$ and $b = 1$.

The equation of the line is $y = 2x + 1$.

EXERCISE 3

1 a Copy and complete the table for $y = 2x - 1$.

b Use the values in the table to draw the graph of $y = 2x - 1$.

x	0	1	2
y	−1		

2 Draw the graphs of the following straight lines.

a $y = x + 3$ **b** $y = -x + 1$ **c** $y = 3x - 5$ **d** $y = 4x - 2$ **e** $y = -2x$

3 Calculate the gradient of each sloping line.

a

b

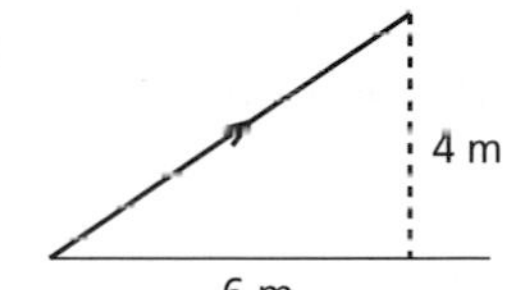

c

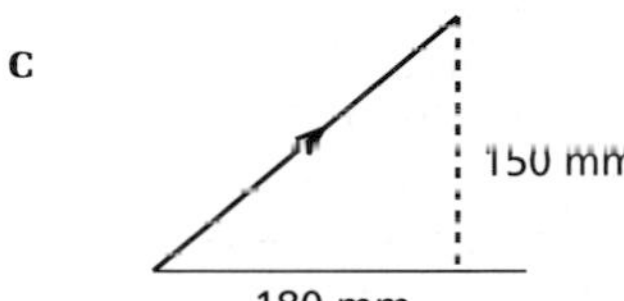

d

e

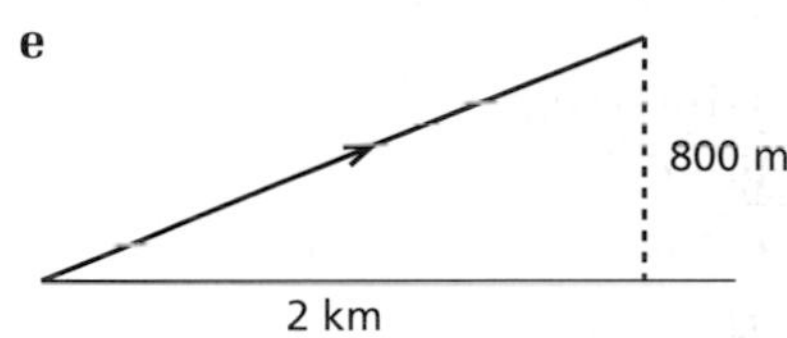

4 Calculate the gradient of the line joining:

a (3, 4) and (5, 8) **b** (−3, 1) and (6, −8) **c** (5, −2) and (3, 1)

d (0, 0) and (1, 2) **e** (−3, −1) and (2, 2) **f** (−4, 0) and (1, −5)

g (6, −6) and (−3, 3) **h** (4, 3) and (−1, 0)

5 Find the gradients of the lines.

a AB **b** CD **c** EF **d** GH **e** IJ **f** KL

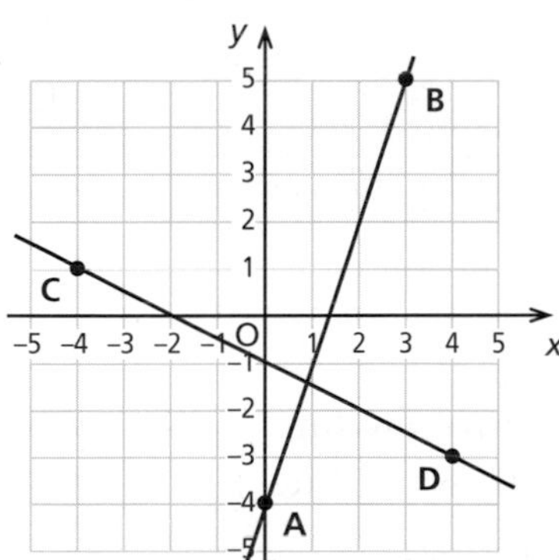

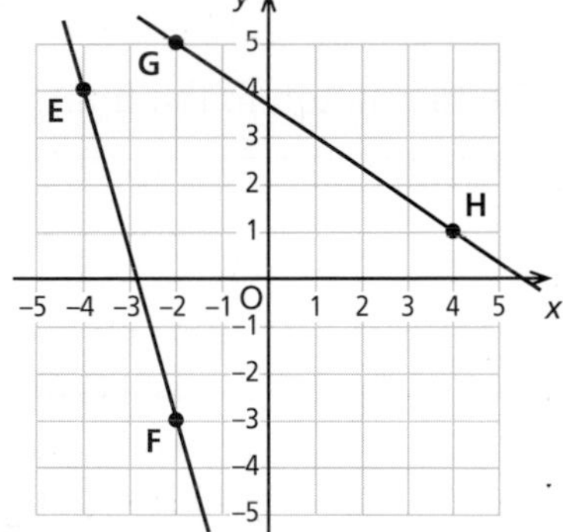

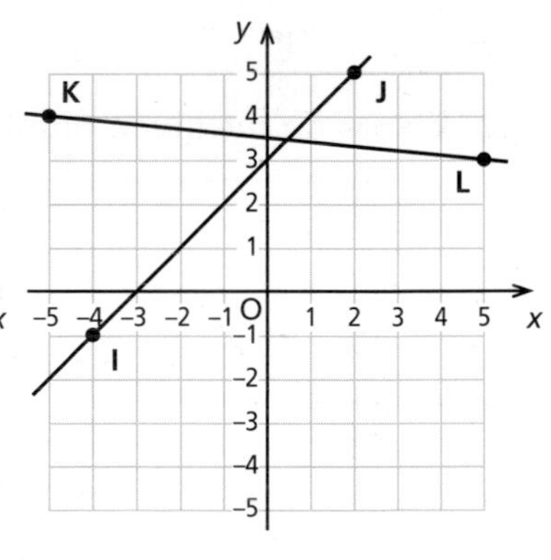

6 Write down the gradient of the following lines.

a $y = 2x - 3$ **b** $y = x + 2$ **c** $y = -4x - 5$ **d** $y = 0.3x + 10$ **e** $y = -x$

7 Parallel lines have equal gradients. Match up the lines in parallel pairs.

a $y = -2x + 100$ **b** $y = x - 3$ **c** $y = -6x + 1$ **d** $y = 5x - 1$

e $y = x + 8$ **f** $y = -6x + 100$ **g** $y = -2x$ **h** $y = 5x + 8$

8 **a** Calculate the gradient of:

(i) AB **(ii)** AC.

b Do A, B and C lie in a straight line? Justify your answer.

c Repeat these steps for the points P, Q and R.

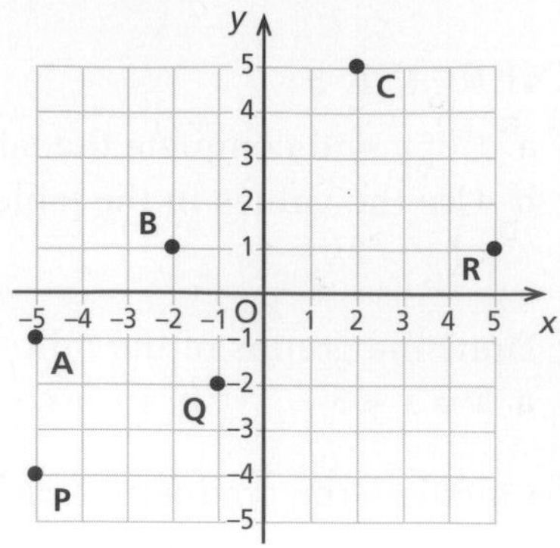

9 Write down the y-intercept for each of these straight lines.

a $y = -5x - 2$	**b** $y = x + 20$	**c** $y = -x$
d $y = 0.75x + 7.8$	**e** $y = -2x + 1000$	**f** $y = 7x - 12$
g $y = 4x + 3$	**h** $y = -12x + 15$	**i** $y = 5x + 0.1$

10 Find:

(i) the y-intercept

(ii) the gradient

(iii) the equation for each line.

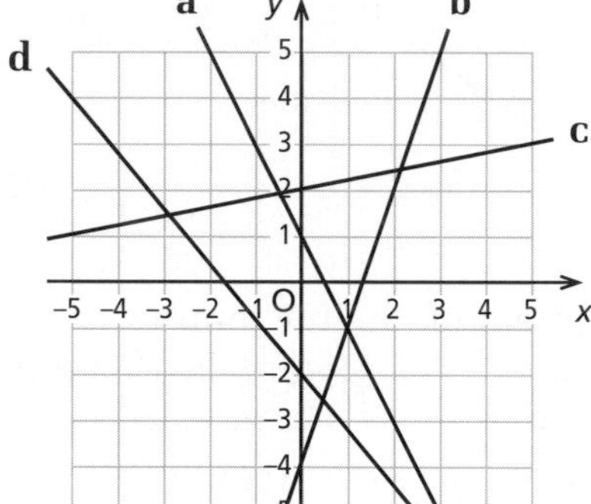

11 Find the gradient and y-intercept of the following straight lines.

a $y - 2x = 3$	**b** $y + 5x - 1 = 0$	**c** $2y = -4x + 10$	**d** $10y = 5x - 4$
e $x = y + 1$	**f** $2x = -3y$	**g** $-3x + 10y = 7$	**h** $3y = x$

12 Where do the given points lie in relation to the line?

> *Example*
>
> Take $y = 2x + 3$ and consider the points (3, 9), (1, 6) and (2, 4).
>
> (3, 9): $x = 3 \Rightarrow y = 2 \times 3 + 3 = 9$ (3, 9) is on the line.
>
> (1, 6): $x = 1 \Rightarrow y = 2 \times 1 + 3 = 5$ $6 > 5$ so (1, 6) is above the line.
>
> (2, 4): $x = 2 \Rightarrow y = 2 \times 2 + 3 = 7$ $4 < 7$ so (2, 4) is below the line.

	Line	Points
a	$y = 2x + 3$	(3, 9), (1, 6), (2, 4)
b	$y = -4x$	(1, −5), (0, 0), (−3, 12)
c	$y = -x - 1$	(2, −3), (−1, 0), (0, 2)
d	$y = 3x - 2$	(2, 3), (−1, −5), (0, 2)
e	$x + 3y = 0$	(3, −3), (6, −2), (0, 0)
f	$2x + 5y - 1 = 0$	(3, −1), (−8, 3), (0, 2)

13 **a** Find the equation of each of the lines shown.

b Are any of the lines parallel? Justify your answer.

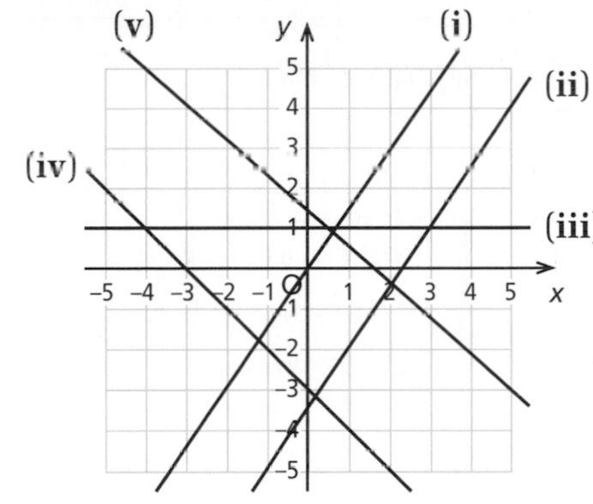

14

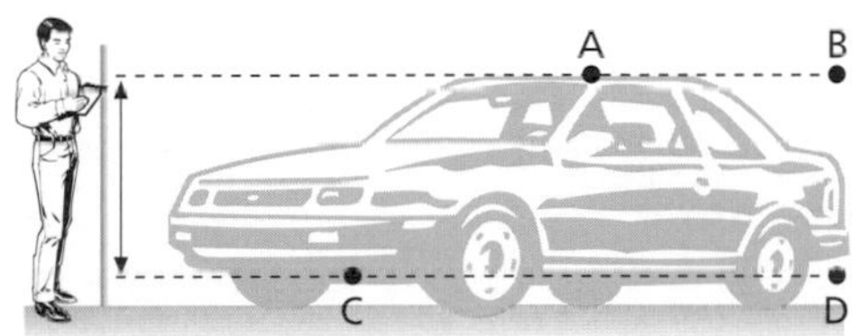

The 'trim' of a car is being measured. Relative to a certain set of axes, the points A, B and C are found to be A(12, 8), B(22, 9) and C(6, 2). For the car to be properly trimmed AB must be parallel to CD.

a Find the gradient of AB.

b Show that the car is not in trim when D is **(i)** (20, 3) **(ii)** (20, 4).

c Let D be the point (20, d). Find a value for d for which the car is in trim.

15 Relative to a suitable set of axes, the perspective view of an architect's sketch is as shown.

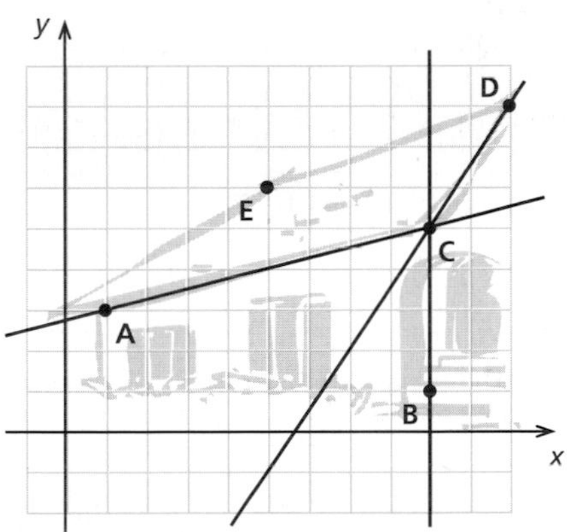

a State the coordinates of the points: **(i)** A **(ii)** B **(iii)** C **(iv)** D.

b Work out the equations of the leading edges of the drawing:
(i) AC **(ii)** BC **(iii)** DC.

c Is the line of the roof, ED, parallel to AC?

Algebraic operations

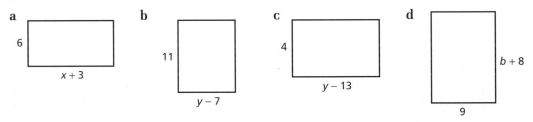

Reminders

$a(b + c)$
$= ab + ac$

$x(3x + 4)$
$= 3x^2 + 4x$

$4(3x - 5) - 3(2x - 1)$
$= 12x - 20 - 6x + 3$
$= 6x - 17$

$(x + 4)(x - 5)$
$= x(x - 5) + 4(x - 5)$
$= x^2 - 5x + 4x - 20$
$= x^2 - x - 20$

EXERCISE 4

1 Multiply out the brackets:

a $3(x + 2)$ **b** $2(y - 1)$ **c** $5(a - 1)$
d $7(p + 8)$ **e** $10(c - 1)$ **f** $8(x - 6)$

2 Write down the area of these rectangles two ways:
(i) with brackets **(ii)** without brackets.

a

6

$x + 3$

b

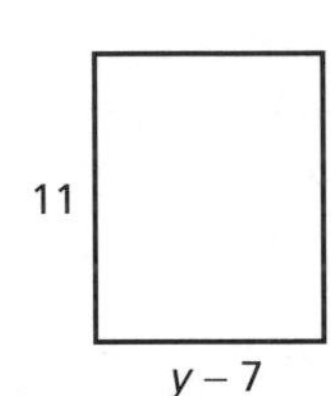

c

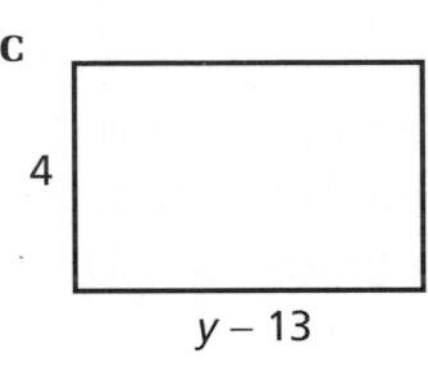

d

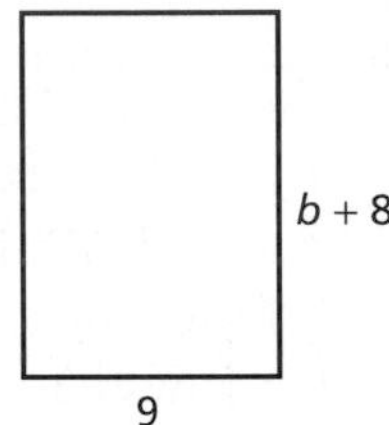

3 Multiply out the brackets:

a $3(2x + 5)$ **b** $4(5y - 2)$ **c** $4(6a - 8)$ **d** $2(9p + 3q)$
e $2(3d - 4e)$ **f** $5(4x - 6y)$ **g** $x(x + 3)$ **h** $y(4y + 2)$
i $x(5x - 2y)$ **j** $a(a + 2b)$ **k** $2c(4 - 3c)$ **l** $3x(6x + 2y)$
m $4a(8a - 2b)$ **n** $7x(3x + 4y)$ **o** $2x(4a - 3b)$ **p** $-2x(6 + 2x)$
q $-4c(2c - 2d)$ **r** $-4x(2x + 3y)$ **s** $-2x(4x - 3y)$ **t** $-3t(4t + 2)$
u $2f(2g - h)$ **v** $-4y(2y + 6)$ **w** $-x(x - 3y)$

Simplify in questions **4** to **7**.

4 **a** $3 + 4(a + 5)$ **b** $4 + 2(3m - 2)$ **c** $2 - 5(a - 7)$
d $-5(d + 5) + 2$ **e** $3 - (2a - 1)$ **f** $4 - 4(x - 4)$
g $1 + 3(a + 20)$ **h** $7 - 2(6p - 3)$ **i** $5 - (y - 7)$
j $x + 4(x + 9)$ **k** $10x - 3(3x - 7)$ **l** $5b - (3b - 7)$

5 **a** $2(x + 5) + 3(x - 6)$ **b** $3(x + 4) - 2(x - 1)$ **c** $6(a + 1) + 2(a - 2)$
d $x(x + 2) + 2(x - 1)$ **e** $4x(x + 5) - (3x - 2)$ **f** $5a(2a + 3) - 3(2a - 5)$
g $y(2y - 4) + 3(y - 3)$ **h** $4m(2m + 1) - (m + 4)$ **i** $6x(2x - 1) - 4(4x - 1)$
j $x(3x + 1) + 2x(x + 7)$ **k** $5b(3b - 2) - 2b(b + 12)$ **l** $-2x(x - 5) - 5(2x - 10)$

6 **a** $(x + 3)(x + 2)$ **b** $(x + 2)(x - 1)$ **c** $(a + 1)(a - 1)$
d $(x + 7)(x - 1)$ **e** $(a + 5)(a - 3)$ **f** $(p + 3)(p - 2)$
g $(t - 3)(t - 2)$ **h** $(r + 5)(r + 4)$ **i** $(s - 1)(s - 9)$
j $(k + 1)(k - 3)$ **k** $(g - 2)(g + 11)$ **l** $(j - 5)(j - 7)$

7 **a** $(a-4)(a+4)$ **b** $(x-1)^2$ **c** $(w+5)^2$
d $(y+5)(y-5)$ **e** $(s+2)(s-1)$ **f** $(x+3)^2$
g $(g-2)^2$ **h** $(k-2)(k+7)$ **i** $(m-6)(m-4)$
j $(p+1)(p-1)$ **k** $(f-2)^2$ **l** $(x-5)^2$

Example

$(x+3)(x+4)$

	x	4
x		
3		

	x	4
x	x^2	$4x$
3	$3x$	12

$= x^2 + 7x + 12$

8 The above illustrates how $(x+3)(x+4) = x^2 + 7x + 12$.
Draw similar diagrams to illustrate:
a $(x+2)(x+5) = x^2 + 7x + 10$ **b** $(x+4)(x+6) = x^2 + 10x + 24$.

9 Find the area of the following:

a

	x^2	$2x$	5
x			
2			

b

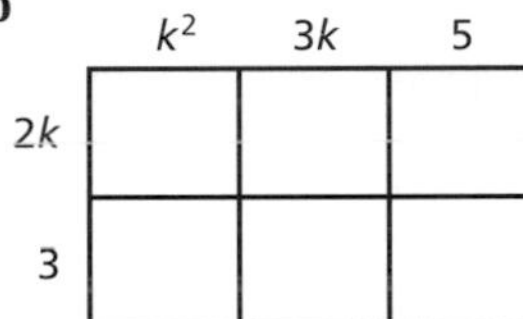

c

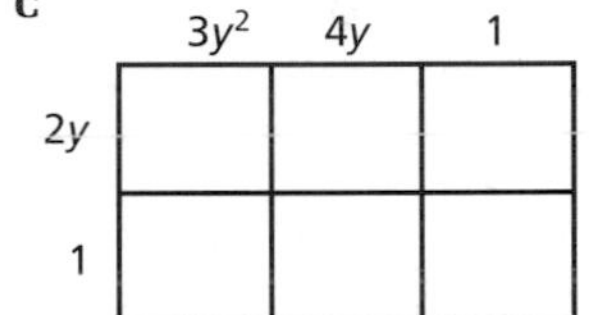

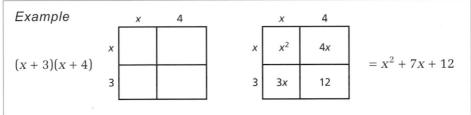

10 Simplify:
a $(x+2)(x^2+2x+3)$ **b** $(a+4)(a^2+a-1)$ **c** $(x-1)(x^2-3x-2)$
d $(p-8)(3x^2+x-2)$ **e** $(f+1)(2f^2-9f-4)$ **f** $(x-5)(3x^2-2x-1$

Reminders

Common factors

$3ab + 6b$
$= 3b(a+2)$

$4x^2 - 24x$
$= 4x(x-6)$

Difference of squares

$a^2 - b^2$
$= (a-b)(a+b)$

$4x^2 - 9y^2$
$= (2x)^2 - (3y)^2$
$= (2x-3y)(2x+3y)$

Trinomial expressions

To factorise $x^2 + 7x + 12$, we look for two numbers which multiply to make +12 and add to make +7.
The numbers are 3 and 4,
giving $(x+3)(x+4)$.

11 Factorise:

a $3t + 9$	**b** $4g + 2$	**c** $10a - 5$	**d** $4p - 8p^2$
e $2x + 2y$	**f** $6a + 2b$	**g** $3a + 3ab$	**h** $4r - 12s$
i $3xy + 9y$	**j** $15mn + 10n$	**k** $2c^2 - 6c$	**l** $12x^2 - 3xy^2$
m $11x + 3xy$	**n** $9ab + b^2$	**o** $16r^2 - 4rs$	**p** $24x^2y - 8xy^2$

12 Completely factorise:

a $3t + 9$	**b** $4g + 2$	**c** $10a - 5$	**d** $4p - 8p^2$
e $2x + 2y$	**f** $6a + 2b$	**g** $3a + 3ab$	**h** $4r - 12s$
i $3xy + 9y$	**j** $15mn + 10n$	**k** $2c^2 - 6c$	**l** $12x^2 - 3xy^2$
m $11x + 3xy$	**n** $9ab + b^2$	**o** $16r^2 - 4rs$	**p** $24x^2y - 8xy^2$
q $6t + 9t^3$	**r** $4x^3 - 2x^2$	**s** $10x^2 - 5x - 15$	**t** $2k - 8k^2 - 6$

13 Factorise by considering the difference of two squares:

a $x^2 - 4$	**b** $4x^2 - 1$	**c** $9y^2 - 25$	**d** $t^2 - 100$
e $36 - y^2$	**f** $49a^2 - b^2$	**g** $1 - 9a^2$	**h** $4p^2 - 25q^2$

14 Completely factorise:

a $3x^2 - 3$	**b** $8p^2 - 2$	**c** $18r^2 - 8s^2$	**d** $12x^2 - 27y^2$
e $72 - 2k^2$	**f** $6a^2 - 54b^2$	**g** $2 - 8b^2$	**h** $8c^2 - 50d^2$

Factorise in questions **15** to **17**.

15

a $x^2 + 3x + 2$	**b** $a^2 + 5a + 6$	**c** $v^2 + 7v + 12$
d $w^2 - 4w + 3$	**e** $s^2 - 8s + 12$	**f** $a^2 - 10a + 16$
g $x^2 - x - 12$	**h** $y^2 + y - 6$	**i** $m^2 - 2m - 15$
j $x^2 + 7x - 18$	**k** $g^2 - 9g + 20$	**l** $k^2 - 10k + 21$

16

a $6x - 9xy$	**b** $a^2 - b^2$	**c** $21x^2 + 7xy$
d $2w^2 - 2$	**e** $12a + 6b$	**f** $x^2 - 10x$
g $50x - 35x^2$	**h** $18y^2 + 3y$	**i** $20k^2 - 45$
j $12a - 15ab$	**k** $121 - x^2$	**l** $6x + 3y + 15z$
m $3x^2 - 12$	**n** $5r^2 + 15rs$	**o** $7x + 49y$
p $w^2 - 11w + 10$	**q** $p^2 + 5p + 4$	**r** $2x^2 - 6x + 4$

17

a $2x^2 + 7x + 3$	**b** $9x^2 - 9x - 4$	**c** $10x^2 + 9x + 2$
d $5x^2 + 13x + 6$	**e** $3x^2 + 5x + 2$	**f** $8x^2 - 26x + 15$
g $4x^2 - 15x + 9$	**h** $15x^2 - x - 2$	**i** $12x^2 - 8x - 15$
j $2x^2 - 15x + 18$	**k** $9x^2 - 18x + 8$	**l** $4x^2 + 8x + 3$

Circles

Reminders

To find **a** the length of an arc or **b** the area of a sector, you must first decide with what fraction of the circle you are dealing.

a We are dealing with $\frac{40}{360}$ of the circle.

The circumference of the circle $= 2 \times \pi \times 10 = 20\pi$

The length of the arc $= \frac{40}{360} \times 20\pi = 6.98$ cm (to 3 s.f.)

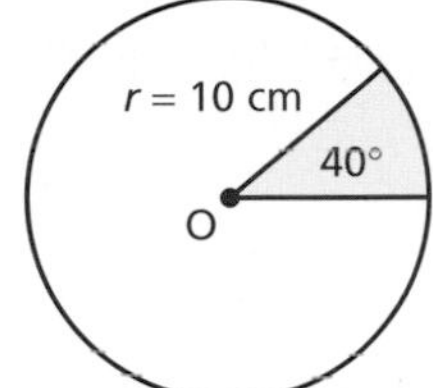

b The area of the circle $= \pi \times 10^2$

The area of the shaded sector $= \frac{40}{360} \times 100\pi = 34.9\ \text{cm}^2$ (to 3 s.f.)

EXERCISE 5

1 Calculate the length of the arc ABC in each diagram correct to 3 s.f.

a

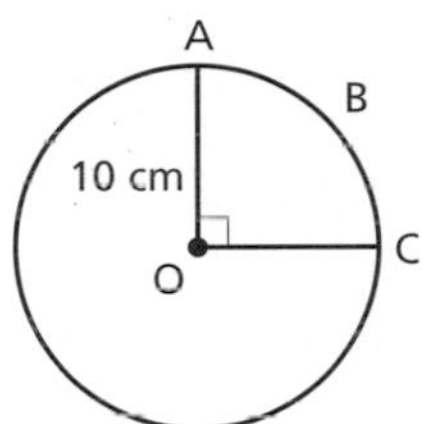

b

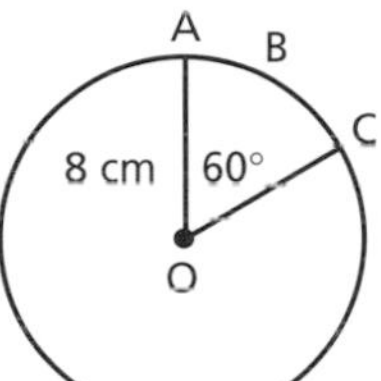

c

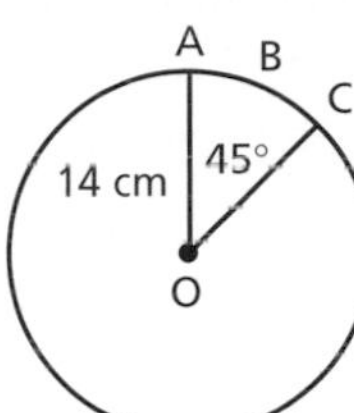

d

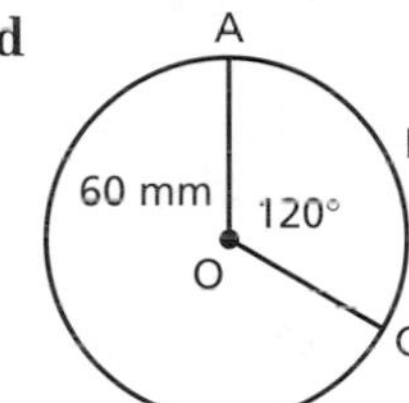

e

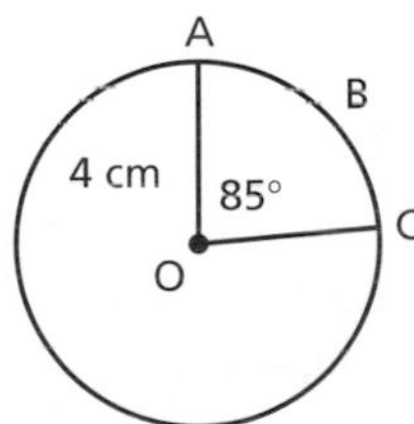

f

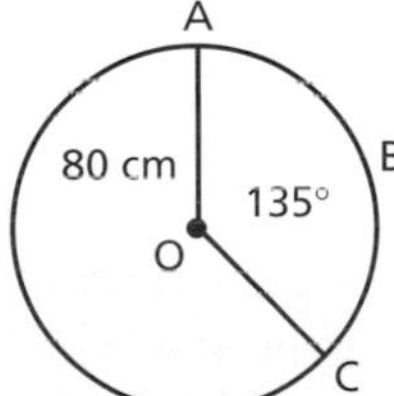

g

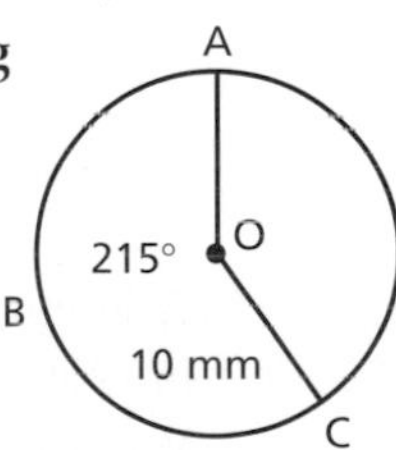

h

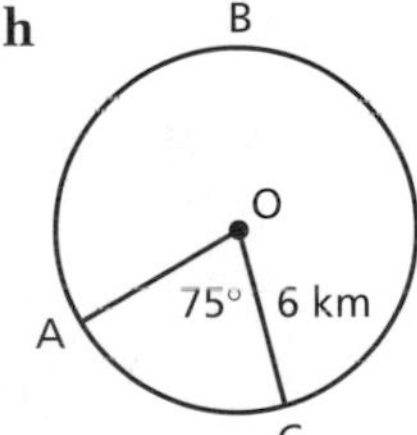

2 Calculate the area of each of these shaded sectors correct to 3 s.f.

a

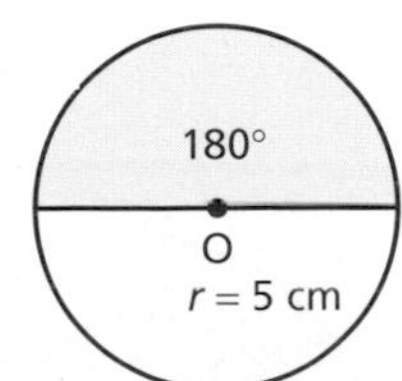

b

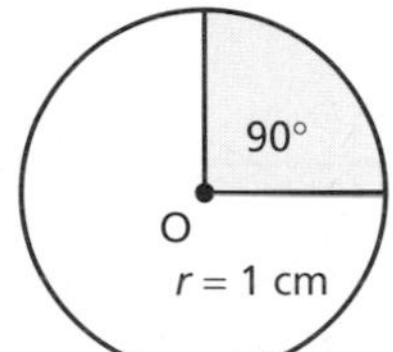

c

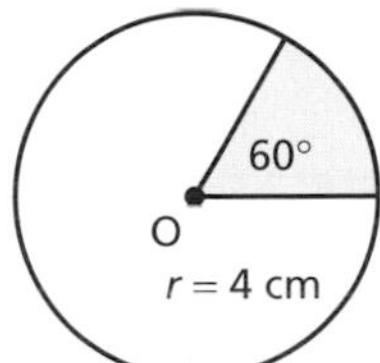

d

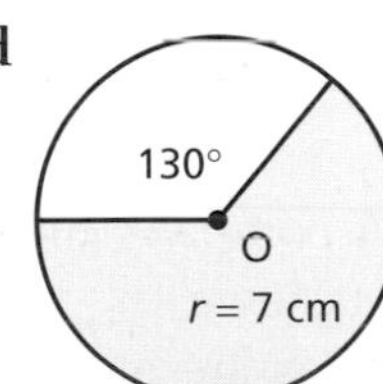

e

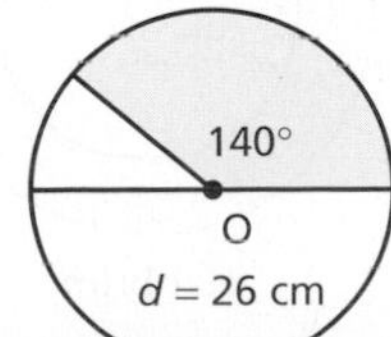

f

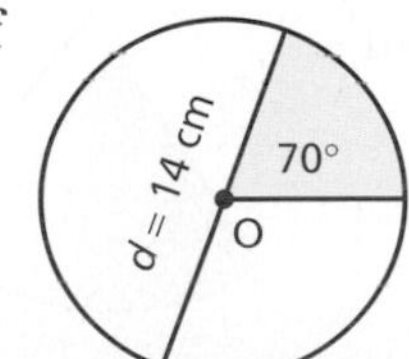

g

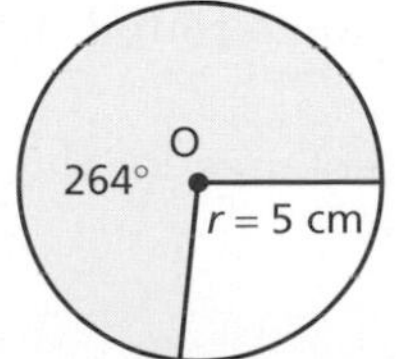

h

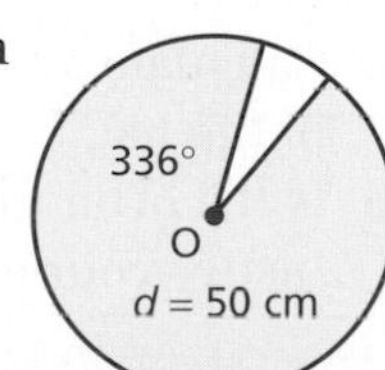

3 A traction engine has a special guard fitted to its wheel to minimise splashing.
The guard is the sector of a circle of radius 1.2 m.
The angle at the centre of the sector is 210°.
Calculate:

a the length of the arc on the guard

b the area of the guard.

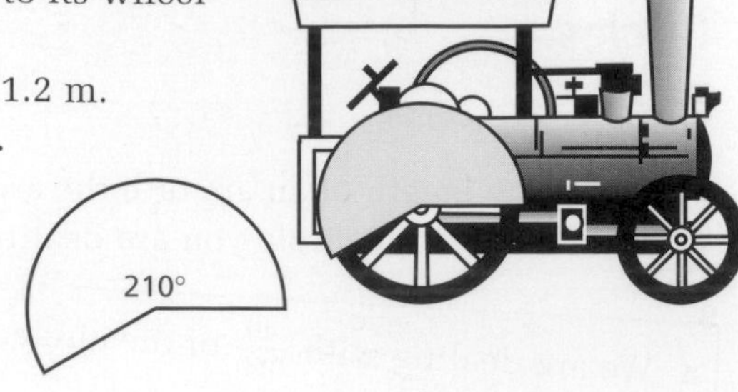

4

A
230°
18.4 m
B
C

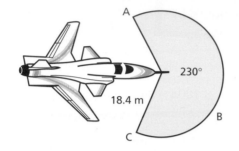

As it flies close to supersonic speeds the jet sets up a shock wave in front of it. This wave is an arc of a circle of radius 18.4 m.
The angle at the centre is 230°.
Calculate the total length of the shockwave, arc ABC.

5 The 50 pence piece is a curious shape. It is made up of sectors of circles. One such sector ABC has been highlighted.

a Calculate the area of the sector.

b Calculate:

(i) the length of the minor arc AB

(ii) the perimeter of the coin.

c The 20 pence piece is the same shape but BC = 2.2 cm.
How far will the coin roll in one turn?

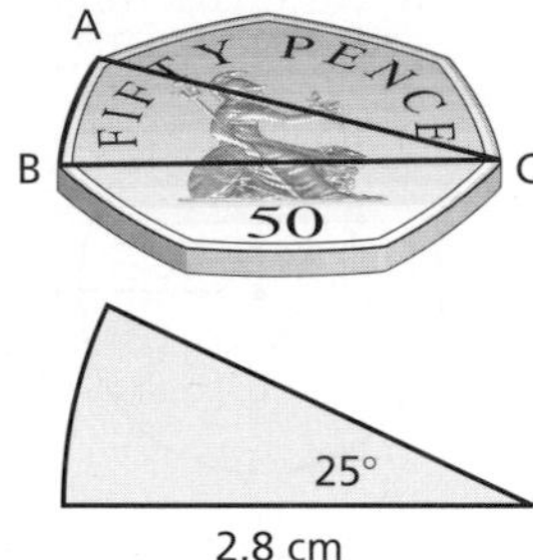

6

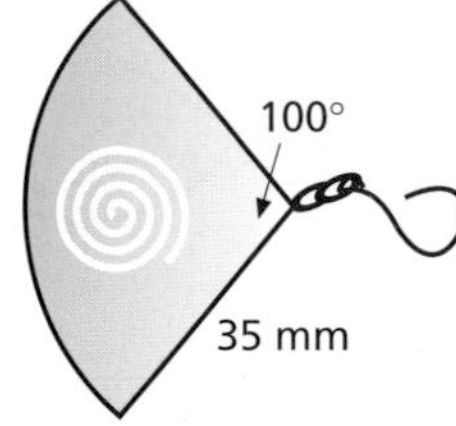

A jewellery designer intends to cut sectors of a circle from a sheet of silver to make earrings.
What is the area of one sector?

7 A company makes witches' hats for Hallowe'en.
They are made from sectors of circles as shown.

a Calculate x, the distance round the bottom of the hat.

b Is the brim the correct size for the hat?
Justify your answer.

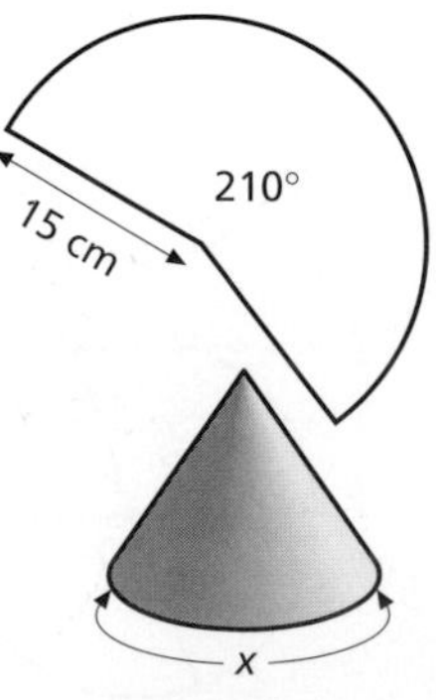

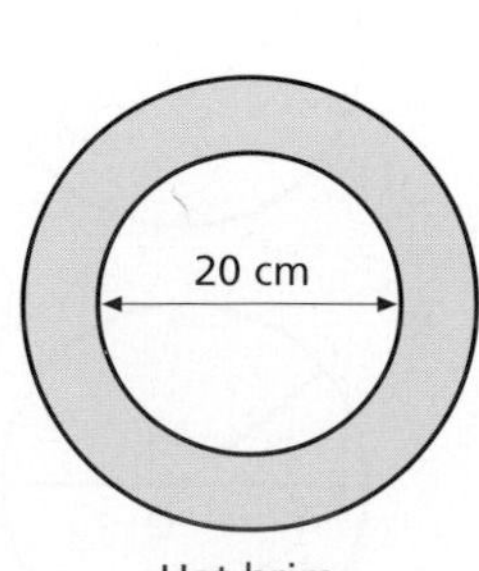

8 The area for a 'welly boot throwing' contest has to be marked out.
The area needed is a sector of a circle.
Calculate the total area required.

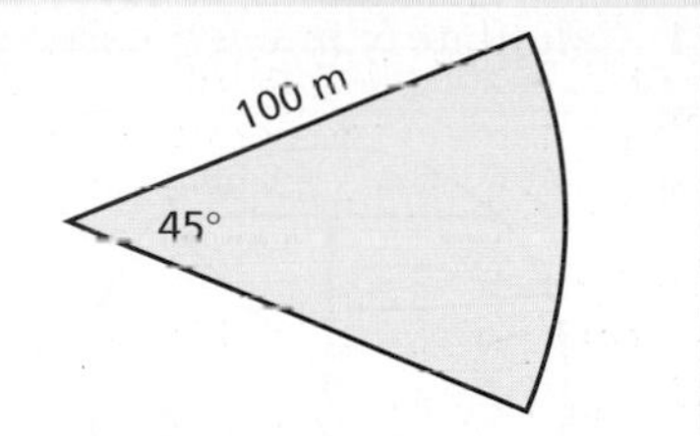

9

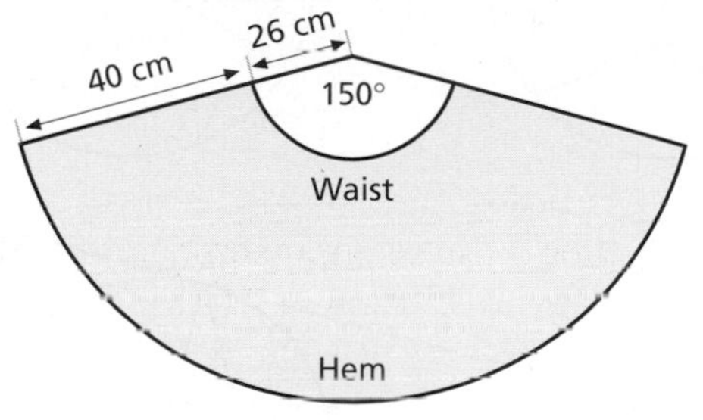

A skirt is made from a pattern based on a sector of a circle.
Calculate:

a the waist size of the skirt
b the length of the hem
c the area of material shaded.

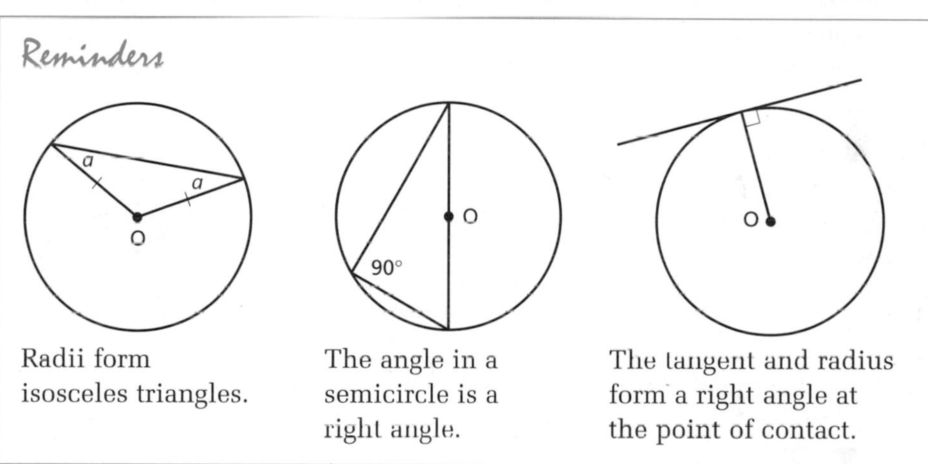

Radii form isosceles triangles.

The angle in a semicircle is a right angle.

The tangent and radius form a right angle at the point of contact.

10 Calculate the size of the unknown angles.

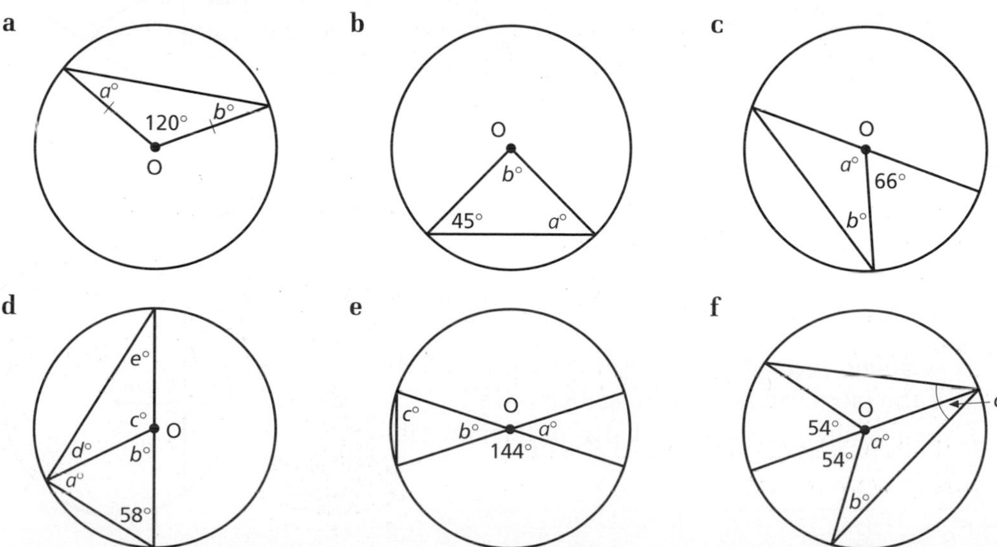

11 Calculate x in each case.

a

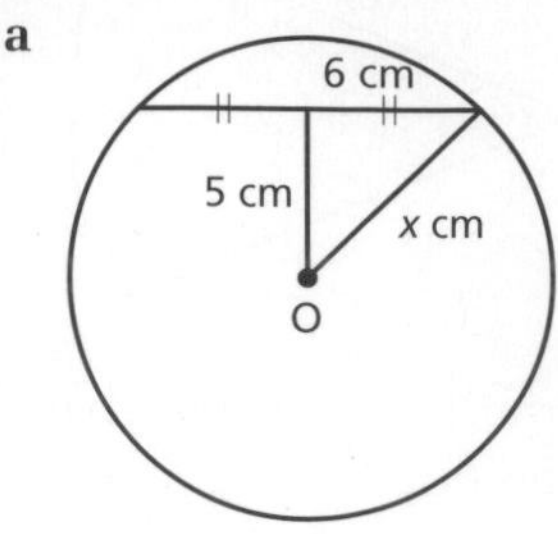

b

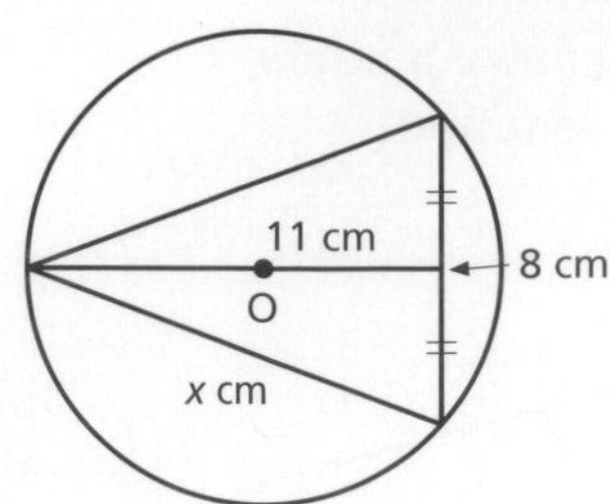

c

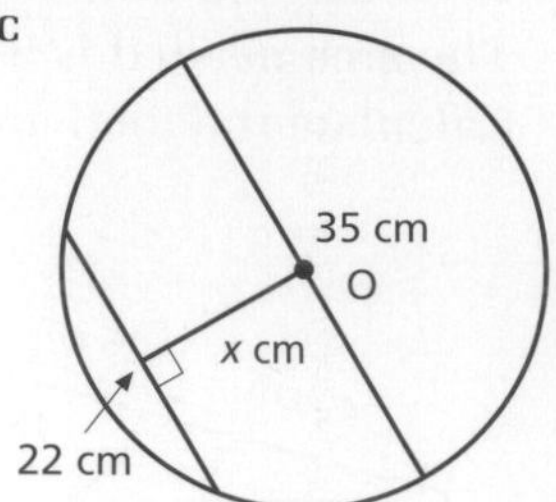

12 O is the centre of the circle.
From the diagram name the following:

a a radius
b a chord
c a tangent
d a diameter
e two right angles.

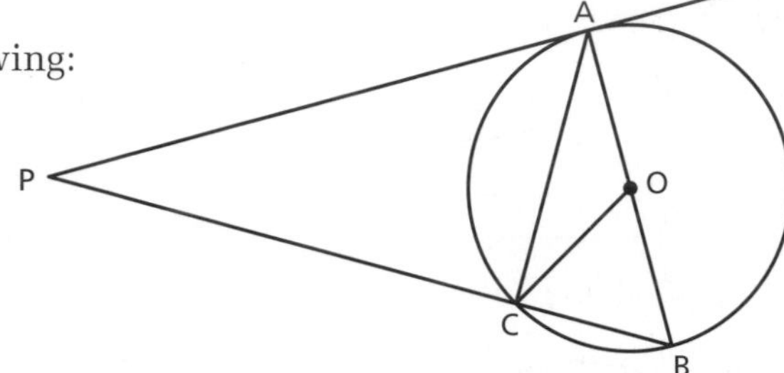

13

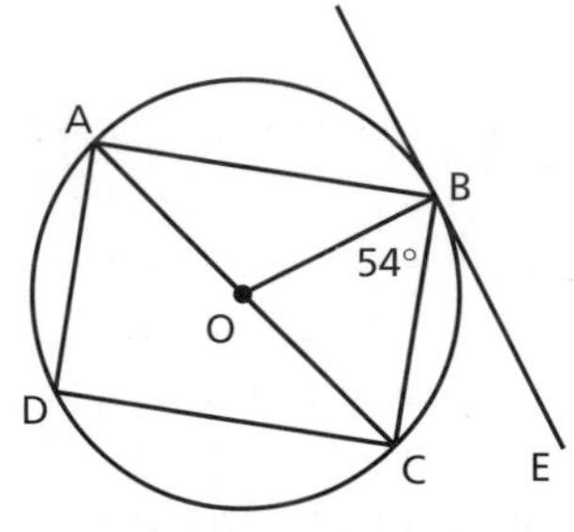

BE is a tangent to the circle.

a Name three right angles in this diagram.
b Calculate the size of:
(i) $\angle BOC$
(ii) $\angle BAC$
(iii) $\angle ACD$.

14 PS is a tangent touching the circle with centre X at Q and the circle with centre Y at R.
The circles are the same size. PX = SY = 18 cm.
Prove that QRYX is a rectangle and calculate its area.

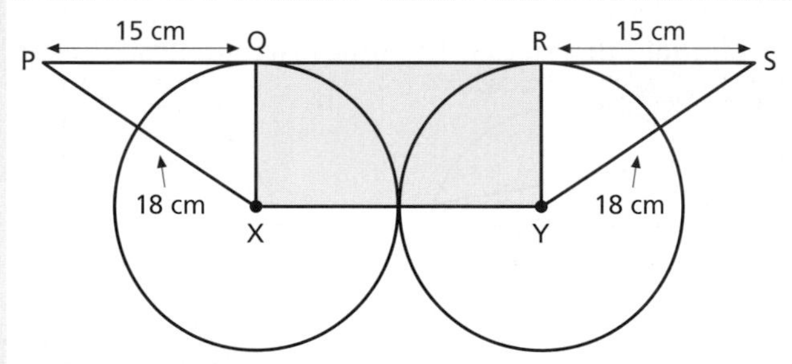

15 A circle with a radius of 1 m is to be used as a table top.
A segment, formed by a chord, is to be removed so that the table can be placed against a wall.
Calculate the perimeter and area of the new table top.

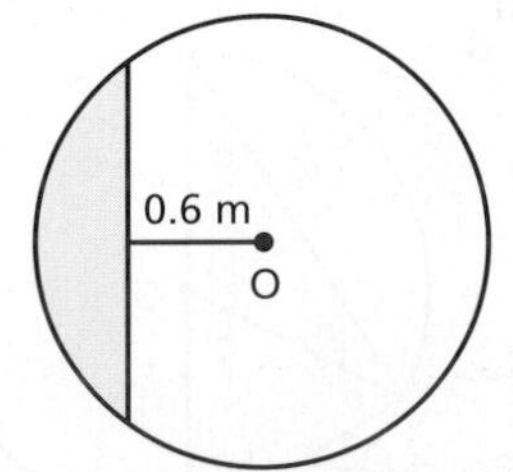

8 Trigonometry

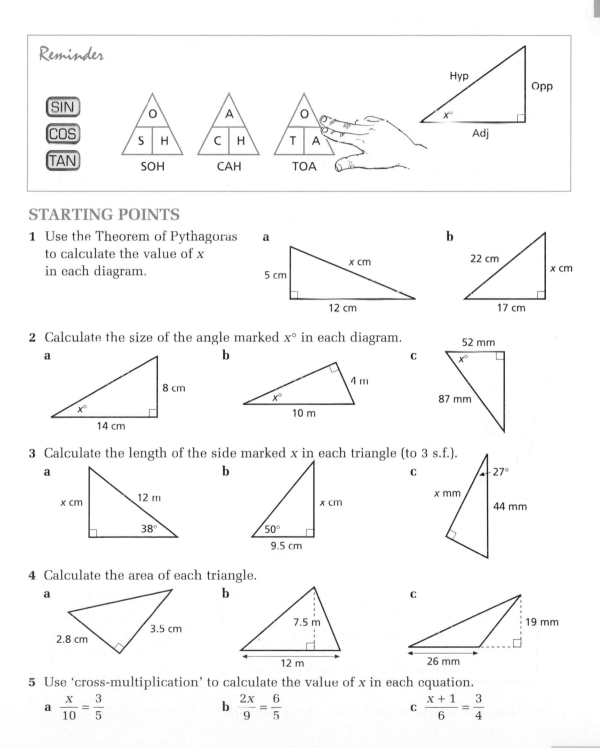

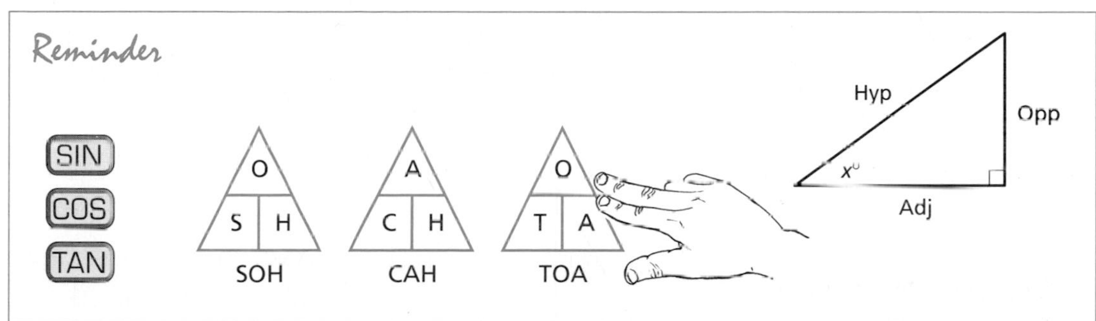

STARTING POINTS

1 Use the Theorem of Pythagoras to calculate the value of x in each diagram.

a
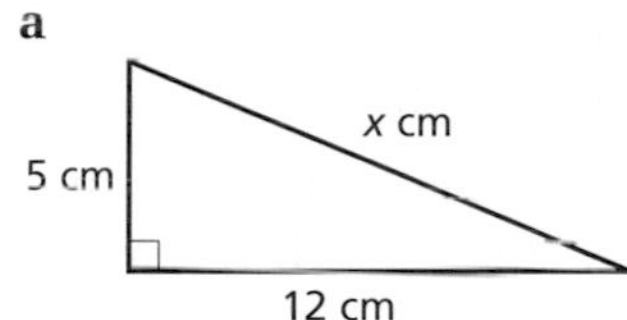

b
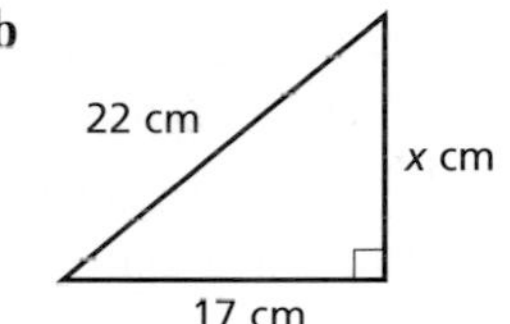

2 Calculate the size of the angle marked $x°$ in each diagram.

a
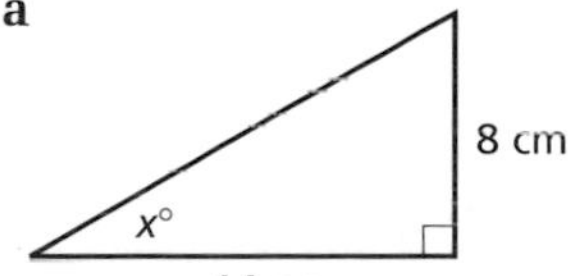

b
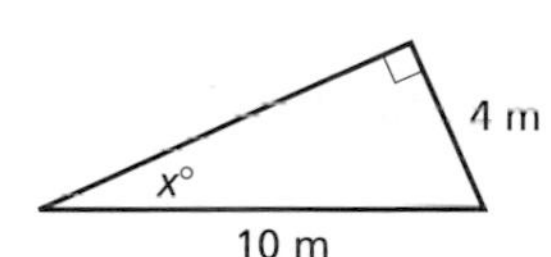

c
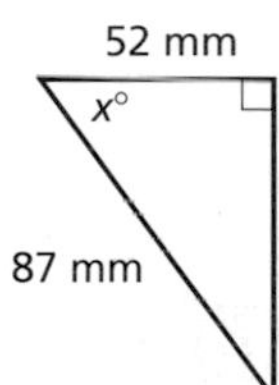

3 Calculate the length of the side marked x in each triangle (to 3 s.f.).

a
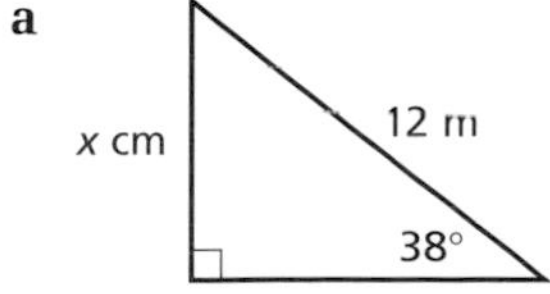

b
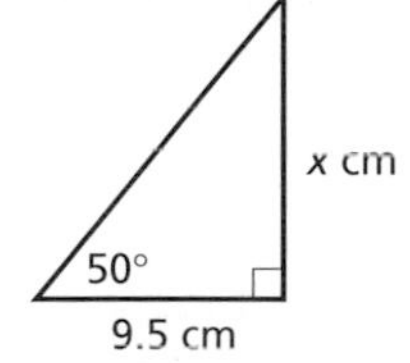

c
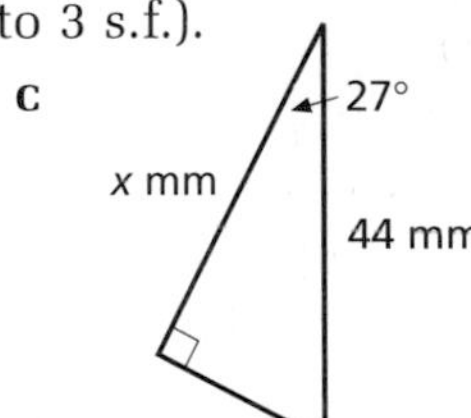

4 Calculate the area of each triangle.

a
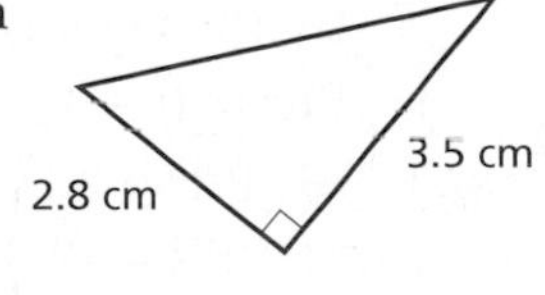

b
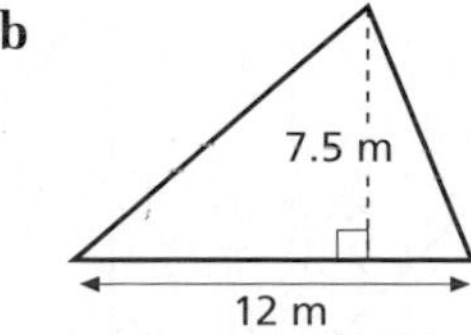

c
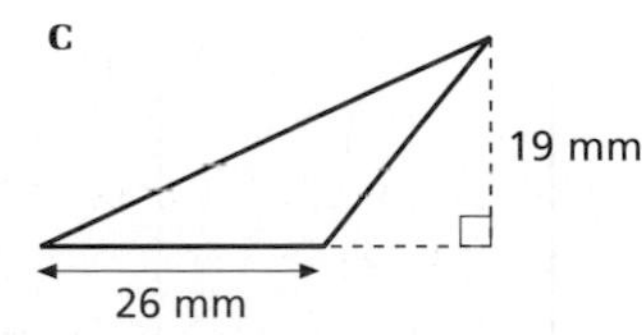

5 Use 'cross-multiplication' to calculate the value of x in each equation.

a $\frac{x}{10} = \frac{3}{5}$ b $\frac{2x}{9} = \frac{6}{5}$ c $\frac{x+1}{6} = \frac{3}{4}$

Exact values

Take an equilateral triangle with sides 2 units long.

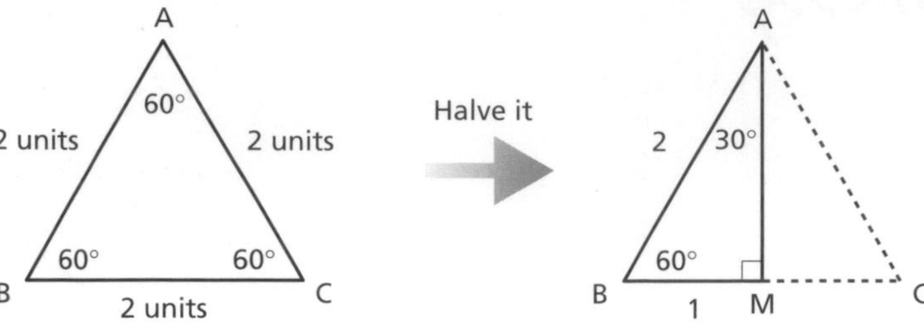

The triangle has angles of 30°, 60° and 90°.

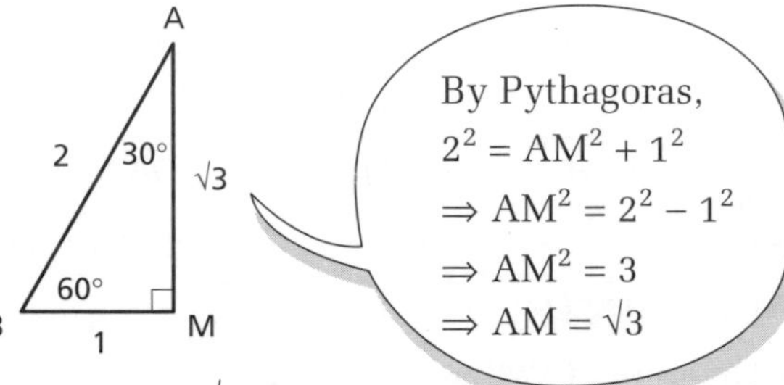

From the triangle we can see that $\sin 60° = \frac{\sqrt{3}}{2}$

Left in surd form it is known as the **exact** value of sin 60°.

When evaluated on the calculator and rounded this will give an approximate value.

EXERCISE 1

1 Write down the exact value of:

a sin 30° **b** cos 60° **c** tan 60°.

2 a Copy this table.

b Use triangle ABM to help you fill in columns **(ii)** and **(iv)**.

c Use your calculator to fill in columns **(i)** and **(v)**.

d What happens when you ask your calculator for tan 90°?

	(i)	**(ii)**	**(iii)**	**(iv)**	**(v)**
$x°$	0°	30°	45°	60°	90°
sin $x°$					
cos $x°$		$\frac{\sqrt{3}}{2}$			
tan $x°$					Not defined

3 Take a square of side 1 unit and halve it as shown.

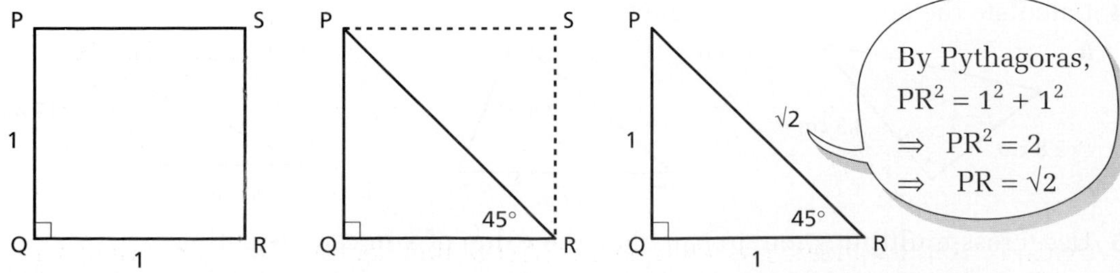

Use triangle PQR to help you fill in column **(iii)** in the table in question **2**.

Example

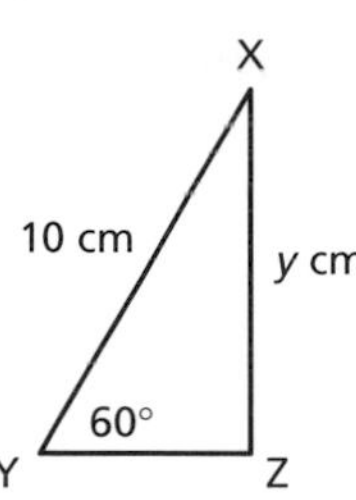

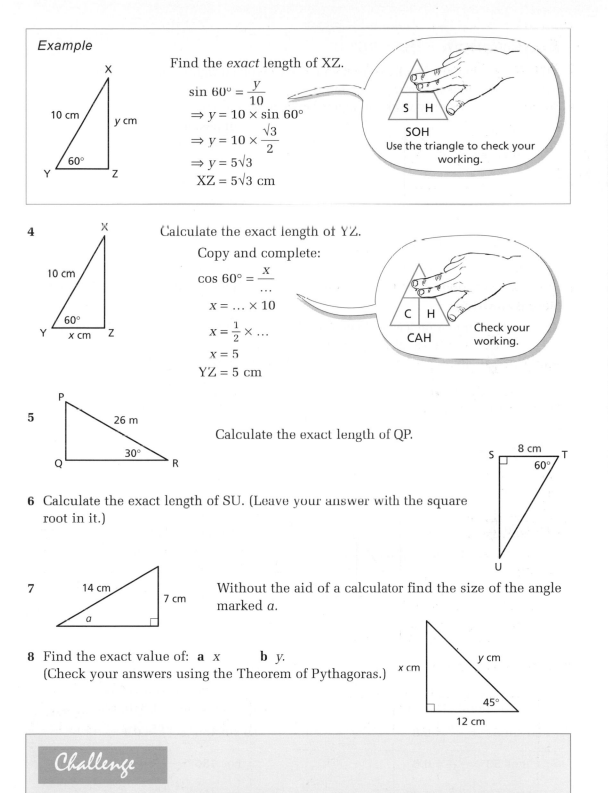

Find the *exact* length of XZ.

$\sin 60° = \frac{y}{10}$

$\Rightarrow y = 10 \times \sin 60°$

$\Rightarrow y = 10 \times \frac{\sqrt{3}}{2}$

$\Rightarrow y = 5\sqrt{3}$

$XZ = 5\sqrt{3}$ cm

S H
SOH
Use the triangle to check your working.

4

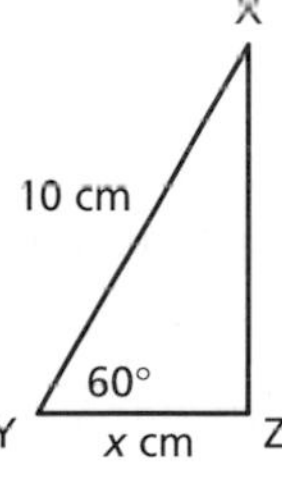

Calculate the exact length of YZ.

Copy and complete:

$\cos 60° = \frac{x}{\ldots}$

$x = \ldots \times 10$

$x = \frac{1}{2} \times \ldots$

$x = 5$

$YZ = 5$ cm

C H
CAH
Check your working.

5

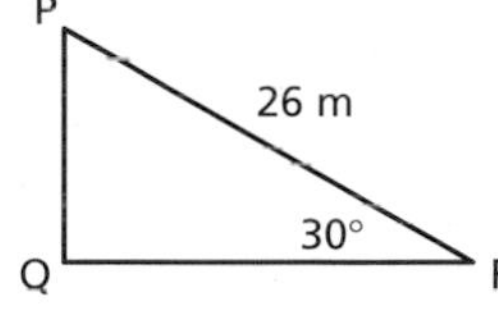

Calculate the exact length of QP.

S 8 cm T
60°
U

6 Calculate the exact length of SU. (Leave your answer with the square root in it.)

7

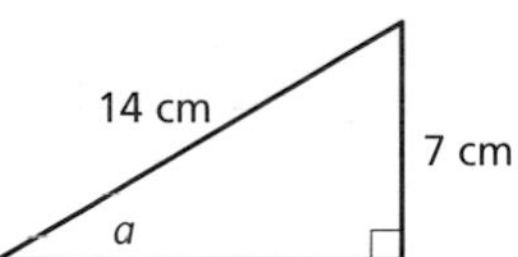

Without the aid of a calculator find the size of the angle marked *a*.

8 Find the exact value of: **a** x **b** y.
(Check your answers using the Theorem of Pythagoras.)

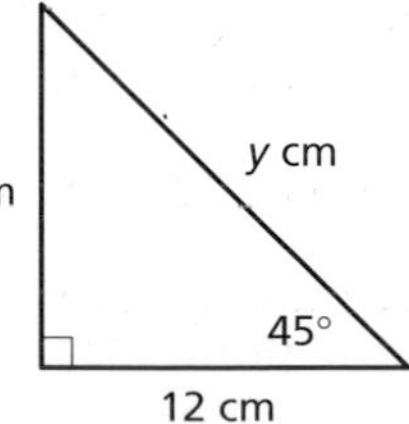

Challenge

Architects and engineers use **set squares**. What kinds are there? Get hold of some. Investigate their side lengths using the exact values that you have been studying.

Angles greater than 90°

All the trigonometry you have used so far has involved right-angled triangles.
All the definitions are for right-angled triangles.
So the definitions only work for angles between 0° and 90°.

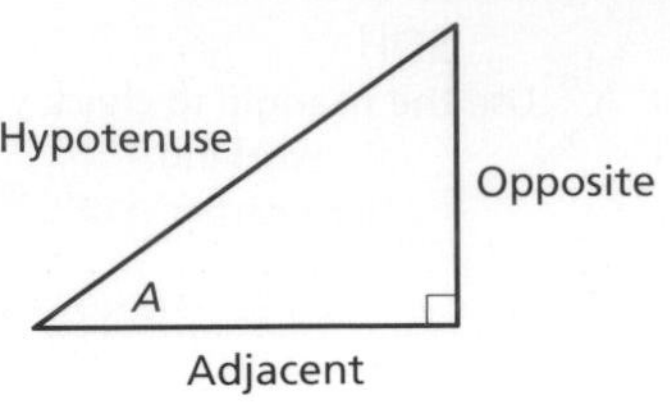

$$\sin A = \frac{\text{opposite}}{\text{hypotenuse}}$$

$$\cos A = \frac{\text{adjacent}}{\text{hypotenuse}}$$

$$\tan A = \frac{\text{opposite}}{\text{adjacent}}$$

Try this on your calculator: SIN 100°.

The calculator returns the value 0.985 (to 3 d.p.). It has been programmed with different definitions. How can the definitions be adapted for angles greater than 90°?

New definitions

This angle is drawn on a coordinate grid. It is measured anticlockwise with the x axis as one arm of the angle. A point P(x, y) is selected r units along the other arm. As the size of angle A increases, P traces out a circle radius OP.

$$\sin A = \frac{\text{opposite}}{\text{hypotenuse}}$$

$$\cos A = \frac{\text{adjacent}}{\text{hypotenuse}}$$

$$\tan A = \frac{\text{opposite}}{\text{adjacent}}$$

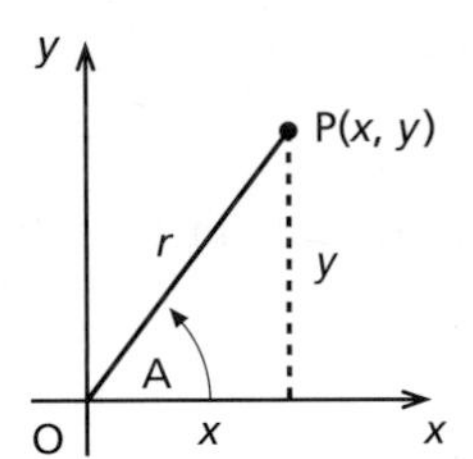

The new definitions are:

$$\sin A = \frac{y}{r}$$

$$\cos A = \frac{x}{r}$$

$$\tan A = \frac{y}{x}$$

Example 1

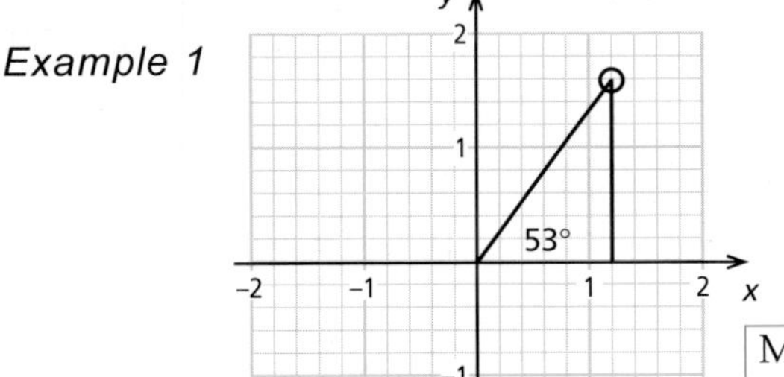

Example 2

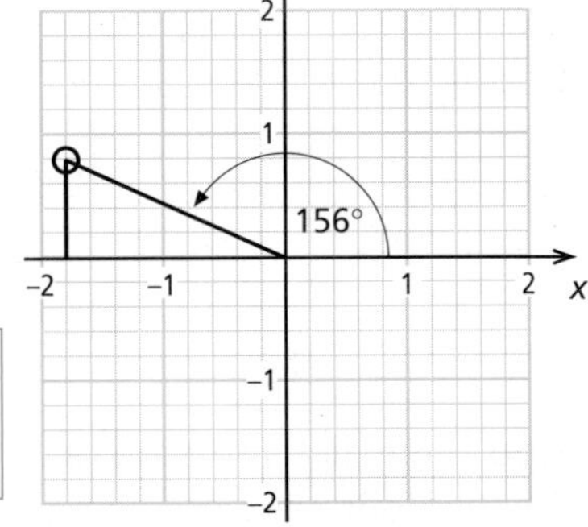

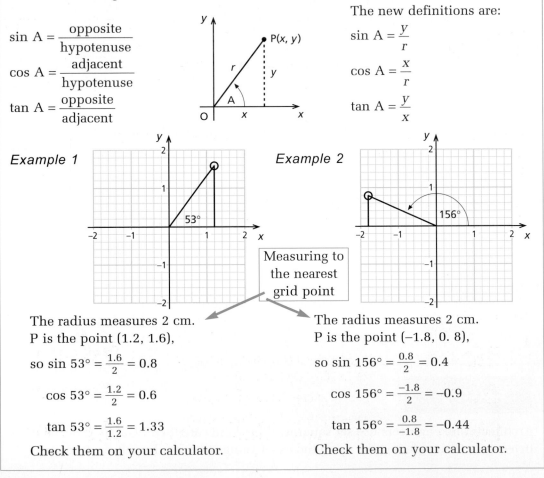

Measuring to the nearest grid point

The radius measures 2 cm.
P is the point (1.2, 1.6),

so $\sin 53° = \frac{1.6}{2} = 0.8$

$\cos 53° = \frac{1.2}{2} = 0.6$

$\tan 53° = \frac{1.6}{1.2} = 1.33$

Check them on your calculator.

The radius measures 2 cm.
P is the point (–1.8, 0. 8),

so $\sin 156° = \frac{0.8}{2} = 0.4$

$\cos 156° = \frac{-1.8}{2} = -0.9$

$\tan 156° = \frac{0.8}{-1.8} = -0.44$

Check them on your calculator.

EXERCISE 2

1 Use the grids to help you find the sine, cosine and tangent of the marked angle to 1 d.p. Check your answers using your calculator. Each radius is 2 cm long.

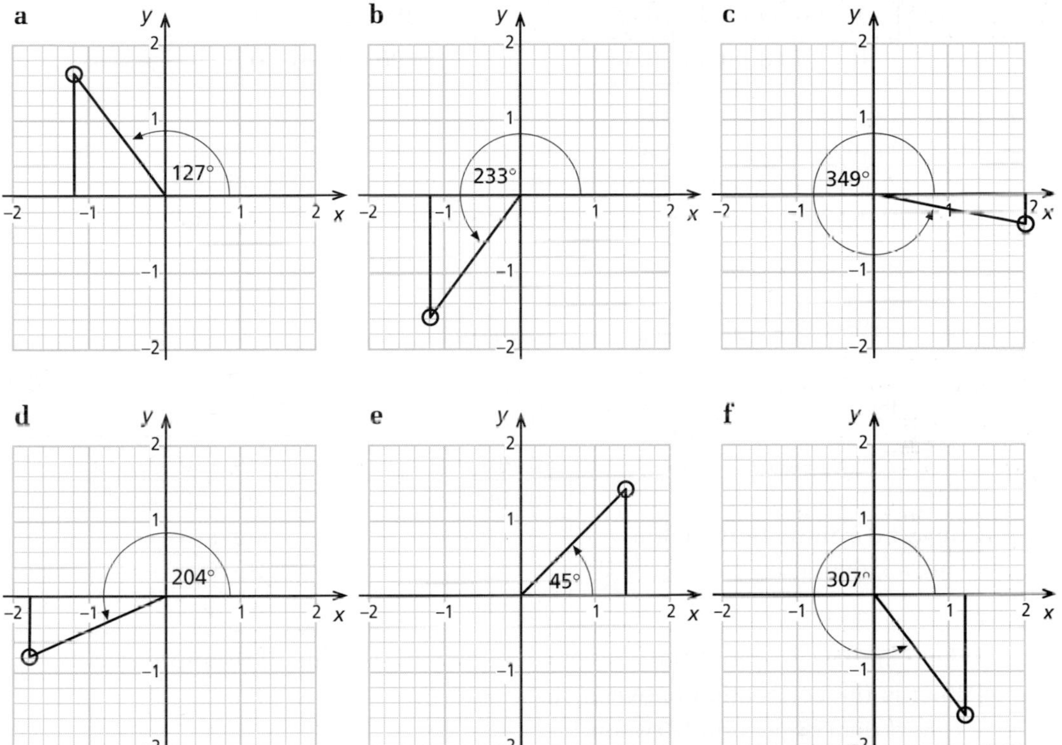

2 Draw a suitable diagram on graph paper to find the value, to 1 d.p., of:
a sin 100° **b** cos 200° **c** tan 300° **d** sin 320° **e** cos 340° **f** tan 210°.
Check your results on your calculator.

3 Use your calculator to work out, to 3 s.f., the value of:
a sin 125° **b** cos 200° **c** tan 194° **d** cos 310° **e** tan 295°.

Challenge

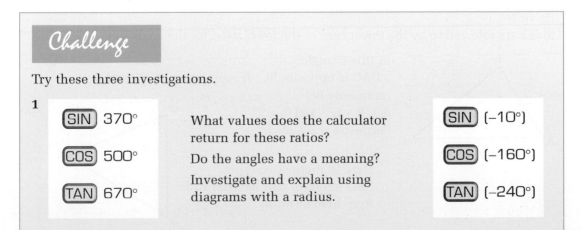

Try these three investigations.

1

SIN 370°

COS 500°

TAN 670°

What values does the calculator return for these ratios?

Do the angles have a meaning?

Investigate and explain using diagrams with a radius.

SIN (−10°)

COS (−160°)

TAN (−240°)

2

$x°$	0	10	20	30	…	340	350	360
$\sin x°$	0	0.17	0.34	0.50	…	–0.34	–0.17	0
$\cos x°$	1	0.99	0.94	0.8	…	0.94	0.99	1
$\tan x°$	0	0.18	0.36	0.58	…	–0.36	–0.18	0

a Copy and complete the table.
b Investigate the range of angles over which each of the ratios is positive/negative.
c Report on any patterns you might see in the numbers themselves.
Can you explain any of the patterns using diagrams with a radius?

3

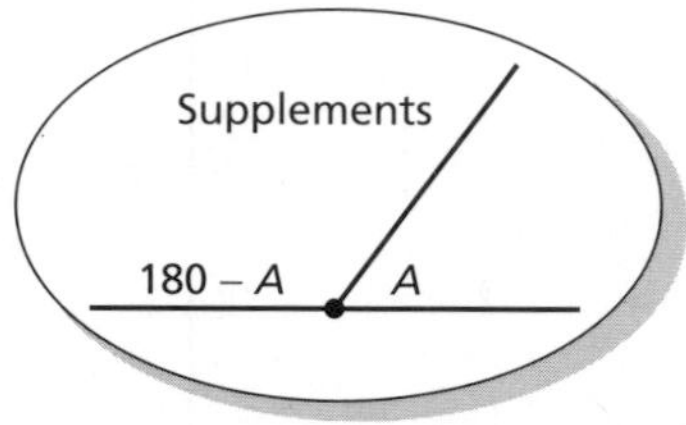

a Copy and complete the table using a calculator.

sin 40° =	sin 140° =
sin 60° =	sin 120° =
sin 10° =	sin 170° =
sin 30° =	sin 150° =
sin 180° =	sin 0° =

b What can be said about the sine of an angle and the sine of its supplement?
(What is the connection between $\sin x°$ and $\sin (180 - x)°$?)
c Explore the connection between:
(i) the cosine of an angle and the cosine of its supplement
(ii) the tangent of an angle and the tangent of its supplement.
d Draw an angle and its supplement on graph paper as before and compare coordinates.

Useful notation

When working with triangles, it is useful to refer to an angle by the capital letter at its vertex.
Sides are referred to by the lower case of the letter used for the angle opposite.

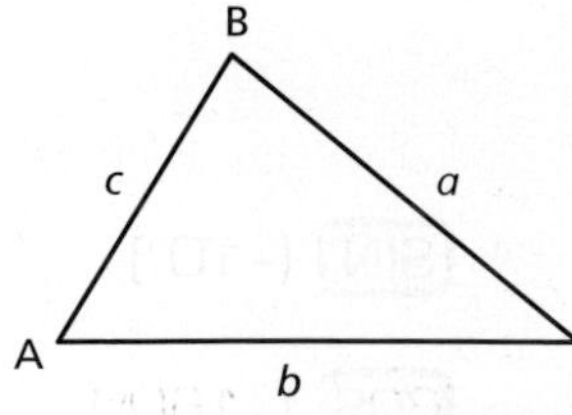

In this triangle:
∠BAC is opposite BC; A represents ∠BAC and a represents BC
A + B + C = 180
Perimeter = $a + b + c$.

Here is another example.
This notation will be used from here onwards.

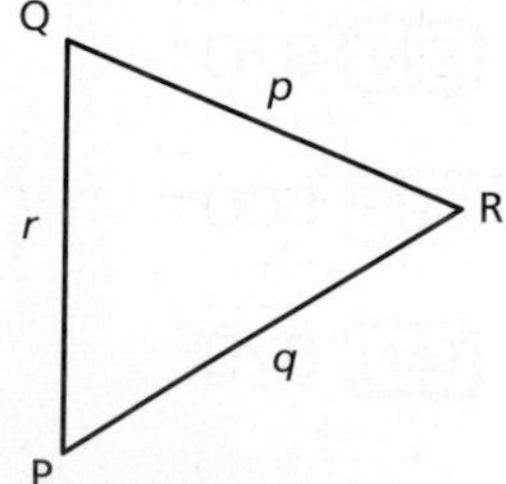

Area of a triangle

Example Calculate the area of triangle ABC.

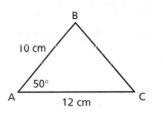

(i)

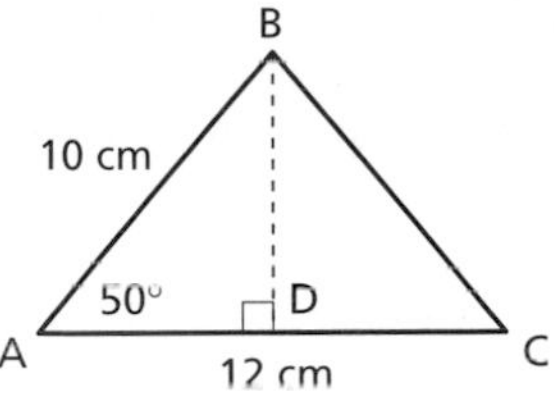

Draw a perpendicular from B to AC.

(ii) Calculate the height, BD.

In triangle ABD,

$\sin 50° = \frac{BD}{10}$

$\Rightarrow BD = \sin 50° \times 10$

$\Rightarrow BD = 7.66$ cm

(iii) Area of triangle $= \frac{1}{2}$ base × height

$= \frac{1}{2} \times AC \times BD$

$= \frac{1}{2} \times 12 \times 7.66$

Area = 46.0 cm^2 (to 3 s.f.)

EXERCISE 3

1 Use the above method to calculate the area of each triangle.

a

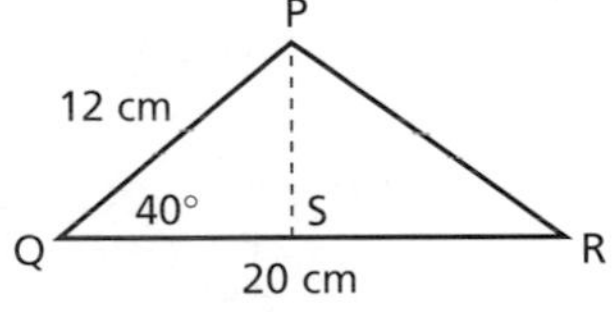

b

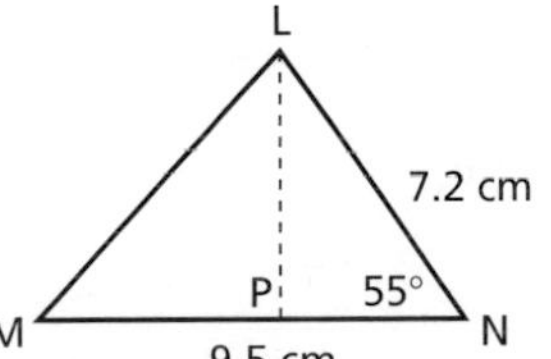

c

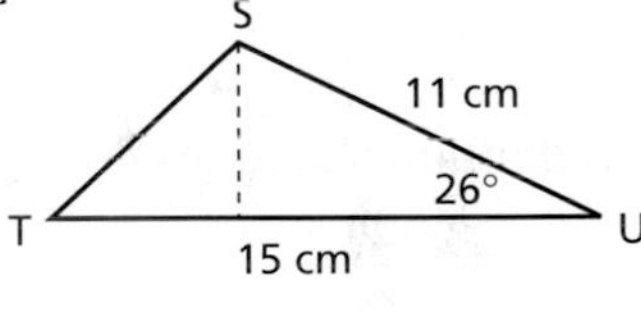

d

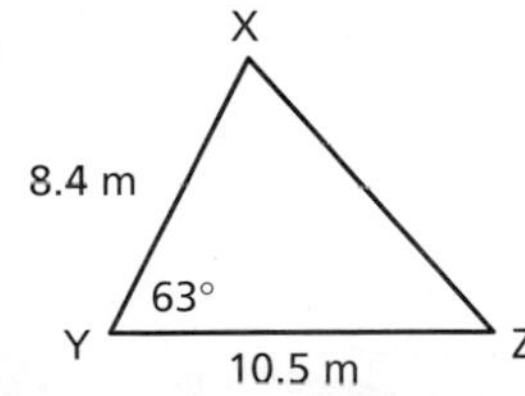

e

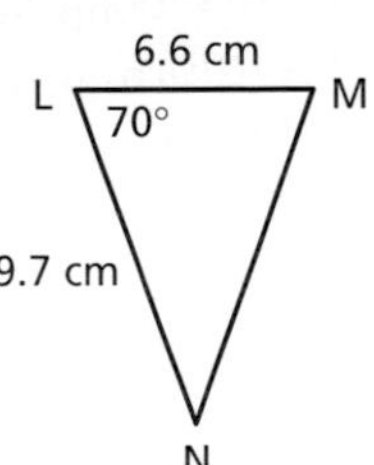

f

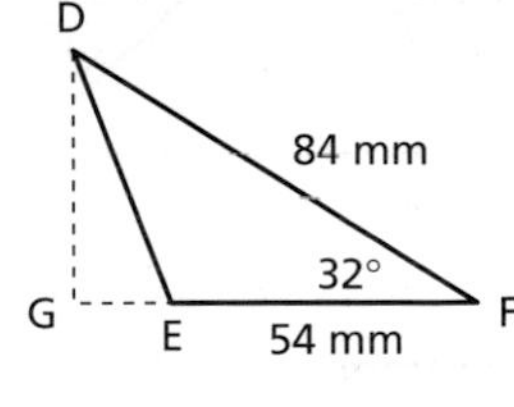

Challenge

Find three different expressions for the area of triangle ABC.

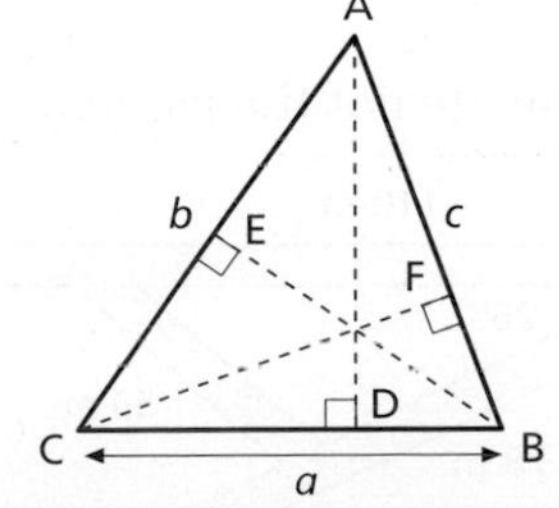

Using the formula

When two sides of a triangle and the angle between them are known, then the area can be worked out.

$$\text{Area} = \frac{1}{2}ab \sin C$$

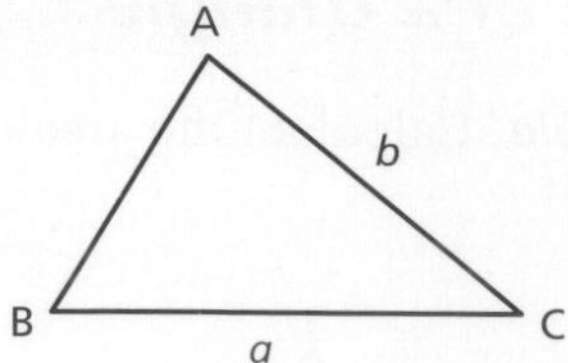

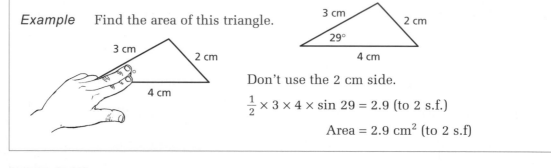

When deciding which sides to use in a triangle, cover up the angle. The side not touched is not used.

Example Find the area of this triangle.

3 cm 2 cm 29° 4 cm

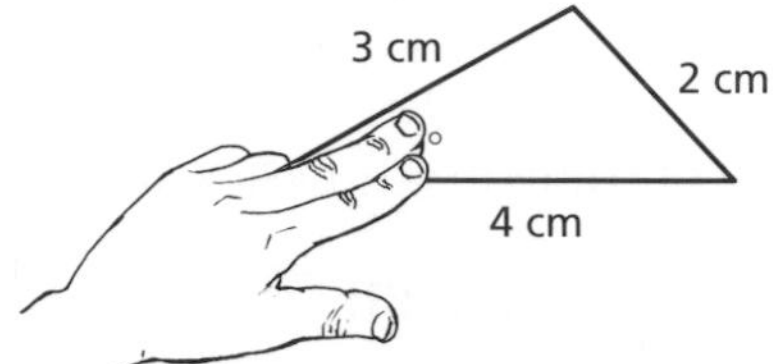

Don't use the 2 cm side.

$\frac{1}{2} \times 3 \times 4 \times \sin 29 = 2.9$ (to 2 s.f.)

Area = 2.9 cm^2 (to 2 s.f)

EXERCISE 4

1 Calculate the area of each triangle (to 3 s.f.).

a

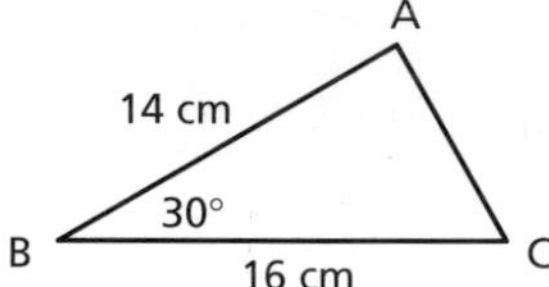

b

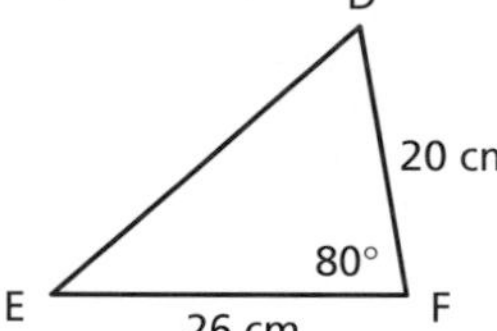

c

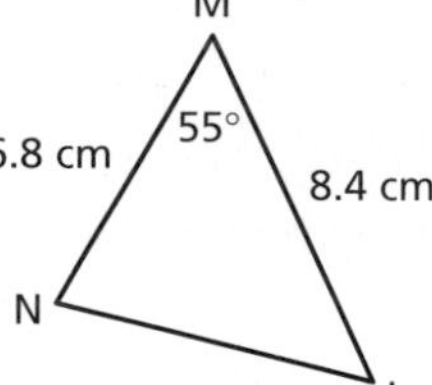

2 Calculate the area of triangle PQR.

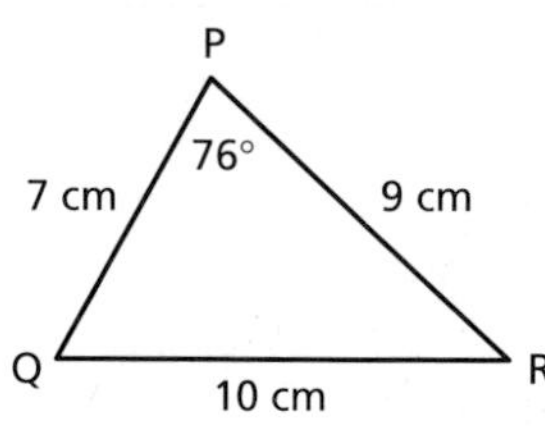

Hint

You have been given too much information. Which side do you not need?

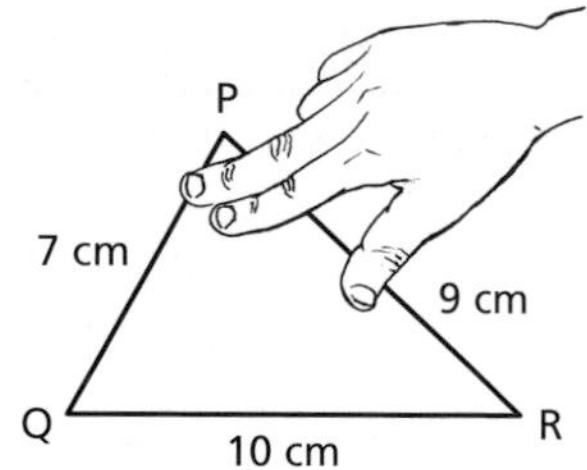

3 A cottage has a triangular garden. In order to work out how much fertiliser is needed, the area has to be calculated.
Work out the area of the garden.

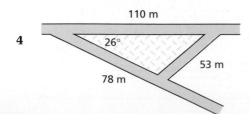

4 110 m 26° 53 m 78 m

The intersection of three roads leaves a triangular piece of ground in the middle. What is the area of this piece of ground?

5

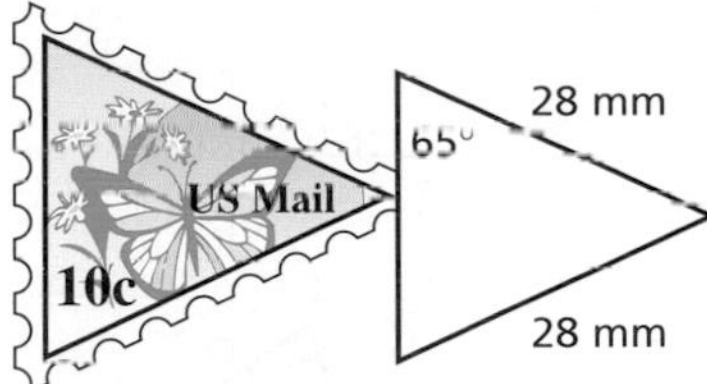

a Calculate the size of each angle in the triangular stamp.
b Calculate the area of the stamp.

6 An equilateral triangle, with sides 15 cm, is at the centre of the design on a cushion. Calculate the area of the triangle.

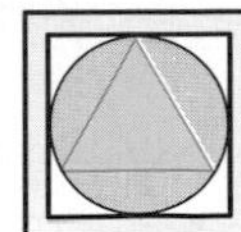

7

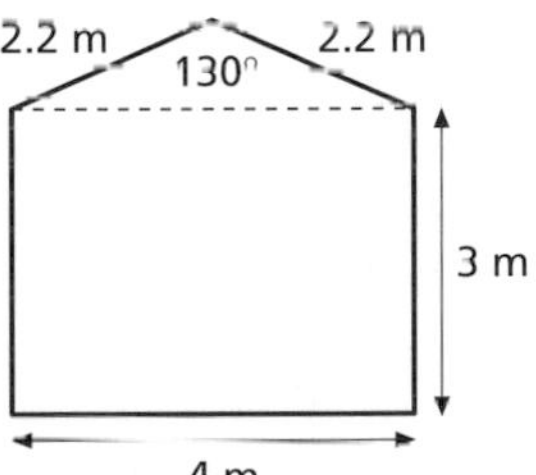

The gable end of a wooden shed is to be treated with weather sealer. In order to calculate how much to buy, the painter needs to know the area to be treated. Calculate the area of:

a the rectangular part
b the triangular part
c the complete gable end.

8 The diagram shows the dimensions of a children's playpark.
The diagonal shown measures 50 m.
Calculate the total area of the park.

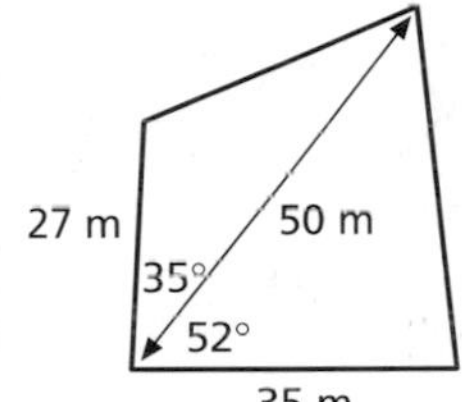

Finding the length of a side

Example Calculate the length of AC.

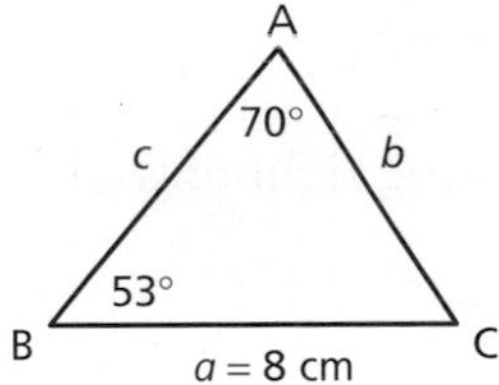

Step 1

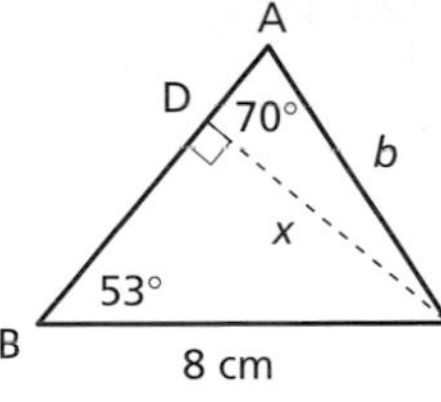

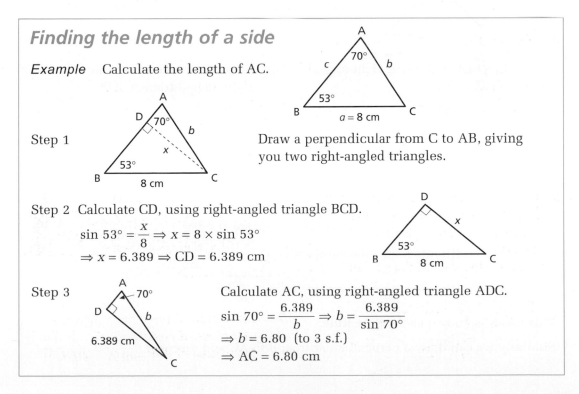

Draw a perpendicular from C to AB, giving you two right-angled triangles.

Step 2 Calculate CD, using right-angled triangle BCD.

$\sin 53° = \dfrac{x}{8} \Rightarrow x = 8 \times \sin 53°$

$\Rightarrow x = 6.389 \Rightarrow \text{CD} = 6.389 \text{ cm}$

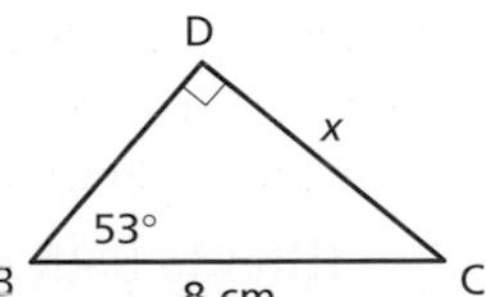

Step 3

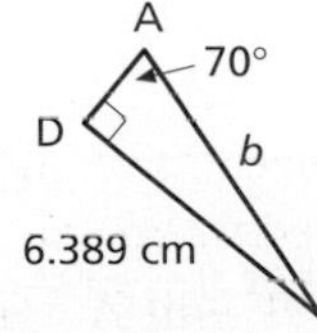

Calculate AC, using right-angled triangle ADC.

$\sin 70° = \dfrac{6.389}{b} \Rightarrow b = \dfrac{6.389}{\sin 70°}$

$\Rightarrow b = 6.80$ (to 3 s.f.)

$\Rightarrow \text{AC} = 6.80 \text{ cm}$

EXERCISE 5

1 Calculate the length of AC.

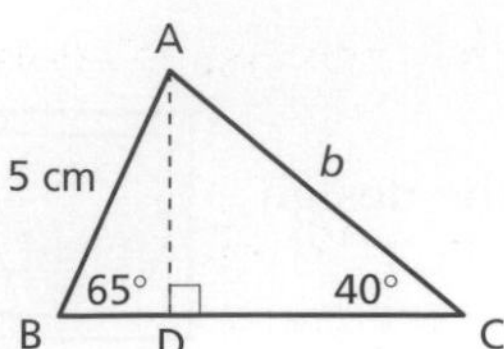

2 Calculate the length of QR.

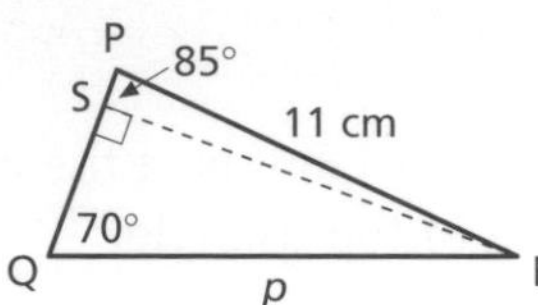

3 Calculate the length of LM.

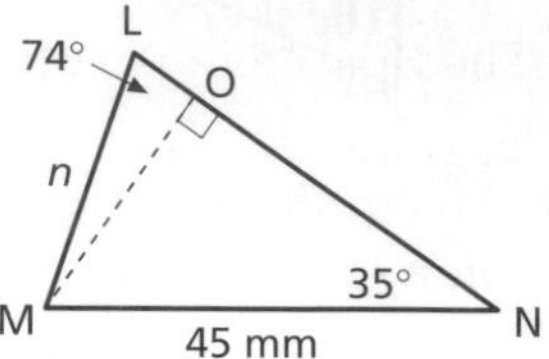

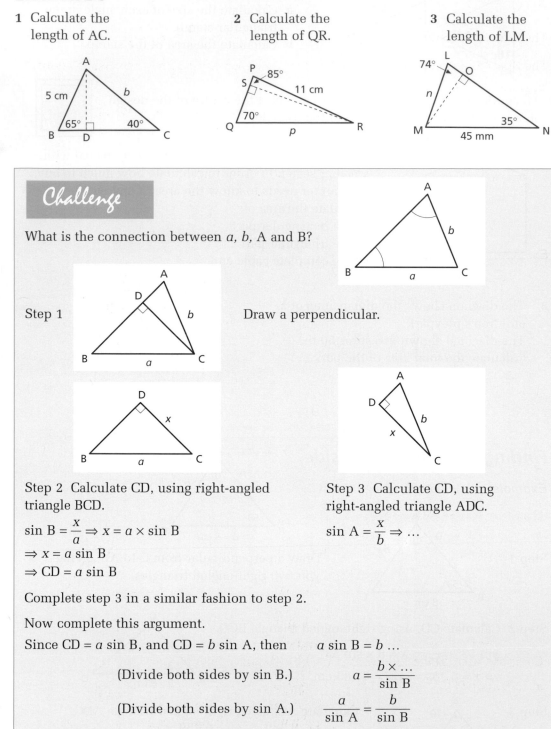

Challenge

What is the connection between a, b, A and B?

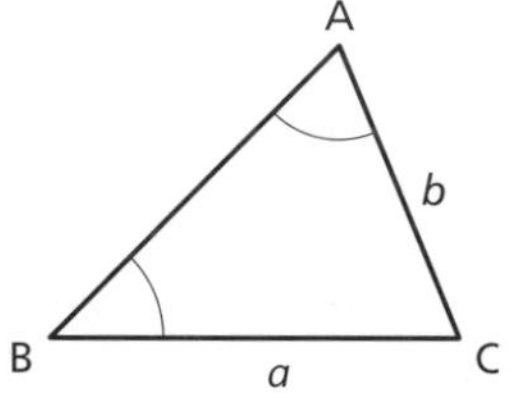

Step 1

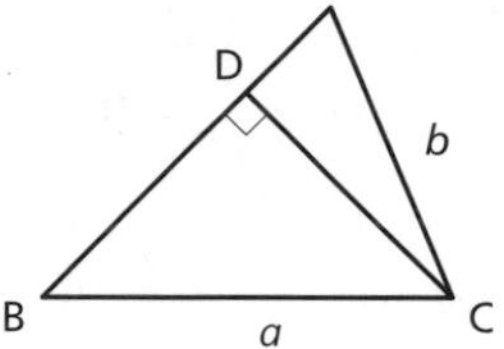

Draw a perpendicular.

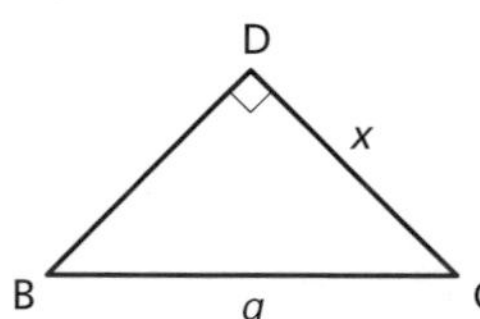

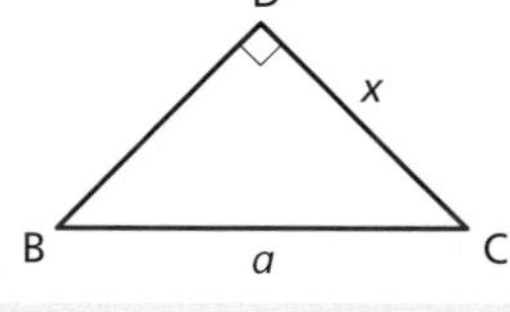

Step 2 Calculate CD, using right-angled triangle BCD.

$\sin B = \frac{x}{a} \Rightarrow x = a \times \sin B$

$\Rightarrow x = a \sin B$

$\Rightarrow CD = a \sin B$

Step 3 Calculate CD, using right-angled triangle ADC.

$\sin A = \frac{x}{b} \Rightarrow \ldots$

Complete step 3 in a similar fashion to step 2.

Now complete this argument.

Since CD = a sin B, and CD = b sin A, then $a \sin B = b \ldots$

(Divide both sides by sin B.) $a = \frac{b \times \ldots}{\sin B}$

(Divide both sides by sin A.) $\frac{a}{\sin A} = \frac{b}{\sin B}$

This result is known as the **Sine Rule**.

Similarly we can draw a perpendicular from B to AC and discover $\frac{a}{\sin A} = \frac{c}{\sin C}$

Finding a side

The **Sine Rule** states that in *any* triangle ABC: $\dfrac{a}{\sin A} = \dfrac{b}{\sin B} = \dfrac{c}{\sin C}$

The Sine Rule is very useful for solving triangles when a pair of opposites is known.

Example 1 Calculate the value of a.

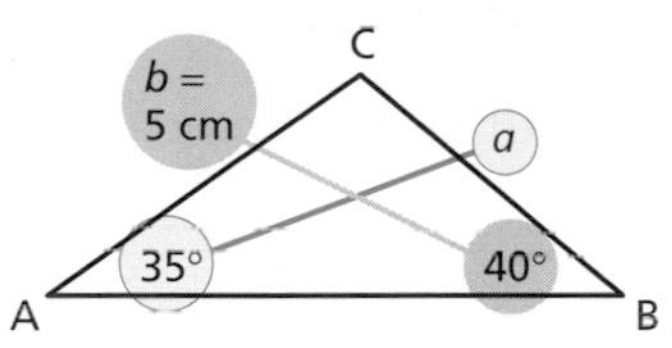

Here both b and B are known. We also know A.

$$\frac{a}{\sin A} = \frac{b}{\sin B}$$

$$\Rightarrow \frac{a}{\sin 35°} = \frac{5}{\sin 40°}$$

$$\Rightarrow a = \frac{5 \sin 35°}{\sin 40°}$$

$$\Rightarrow a = 4.46 \text{ cm (to 3 s.f.)}$$

Example: 2 Calculate the length of PR.

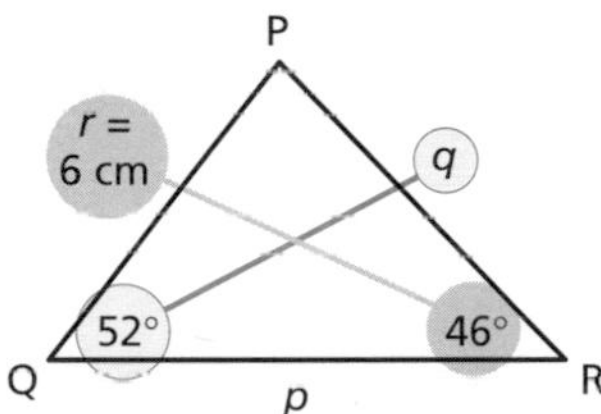

Using the Sine Rule: $\dfrac{p}{\sin P} = \dfrac{q}{\sin Q} \checkmark = \dfrac{r}{\sin R} \checkmark$

We know r and R. We also know Q.

$$\frac{q}{\sin Q} = \frac{r}{\sin R}$$

$$\frac{q}{\sin 52°} = \frac{6}{\sin 46°}$$

$$q = \frac{6 \times \sin 52°}{\sin 46°}$$

$$q = 6.5727$$

$$\text{PR} = 6.57 \text{ cm (to 3 s.f.)}$$

EXERCISE 6

1 Complete the Sine Rule for each triangle.

a

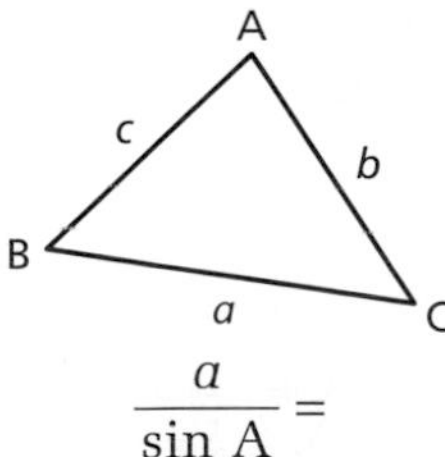

$\dfrac{a}{\sin A} =$

b

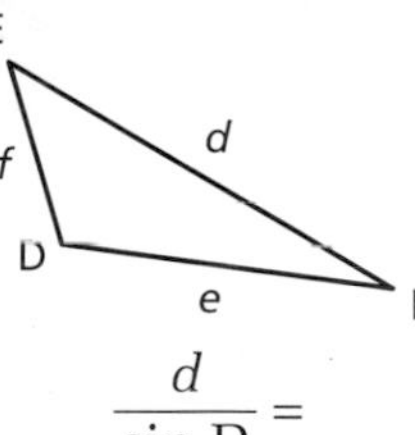

$\dfrac{d}{\sin D} =$

c

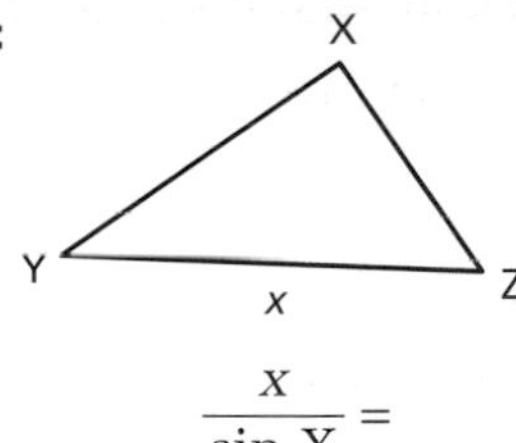

$\dfrac{x}{\sin X} =$

2 Complete each of the following to find the required length.

a Calculate PQ.

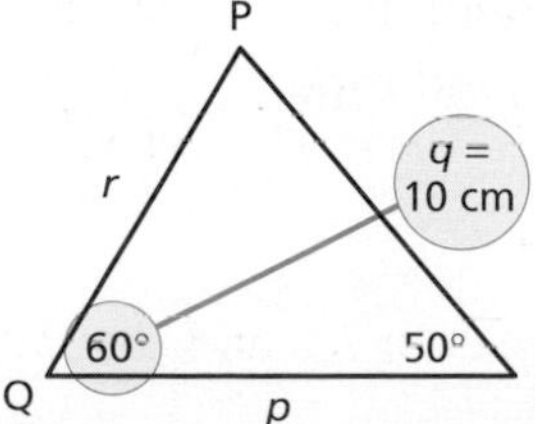

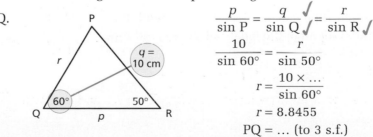

$$\frac{p}{\sin P} = \frac{q}{\sin Q} \checkmark = \frac{r}{\sin R} \checkmark$$

$$\frac{10}{\sin 60°} = \frac{r}{\sin 50°}$$

$$r = \frac{10 \times \ldots}{\sin 60°}$$

$$r = 8.8455$$

$$\text{PQ} = \ldots \text{ (to 3 s.f.)}$$

b Calculate DF.

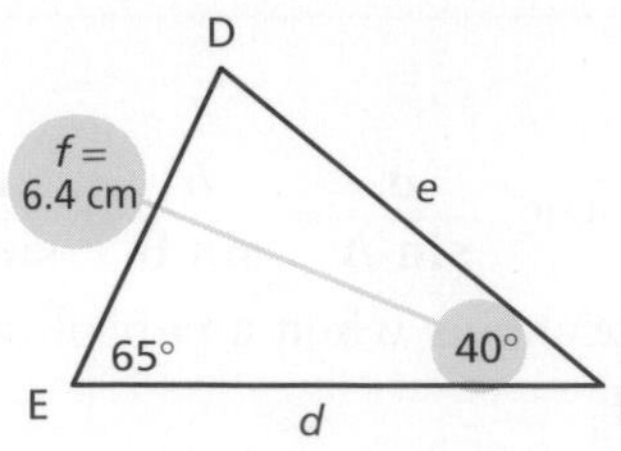

$$\frac{d}{\sin D} = \frac{\ldots}{\ldots} = \frac{\ldots}{\ldots}$$

$$\frac{e}{\sin 65°} = \frac{6.4}{\sin 40°}$$

$$e = \frac{\ldots \times \ldots}{\sin 40°}$$

$e = \ldots$

DF = … (to 3 s.f.)

3 Calculate the lengths of the sides marked *c, f, l* and *s*. Give your answers correct to 3 s.f.

a

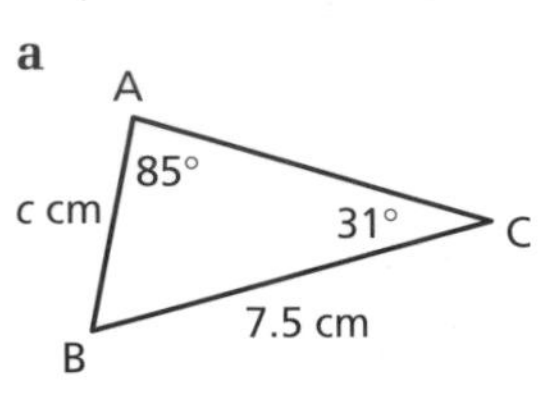

b

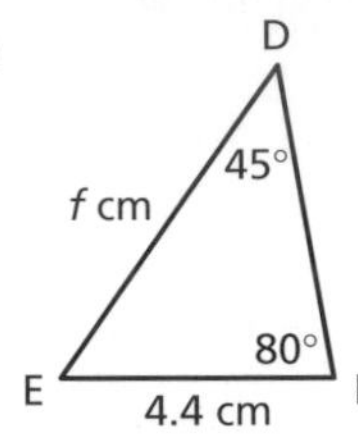

c

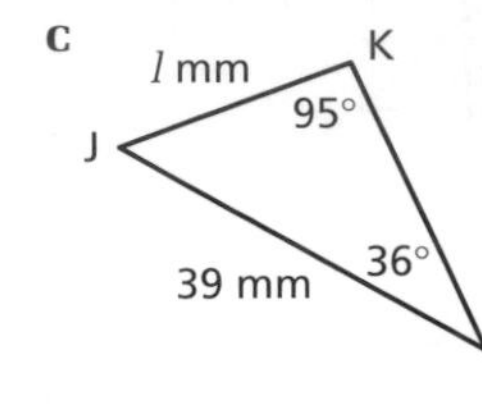

d

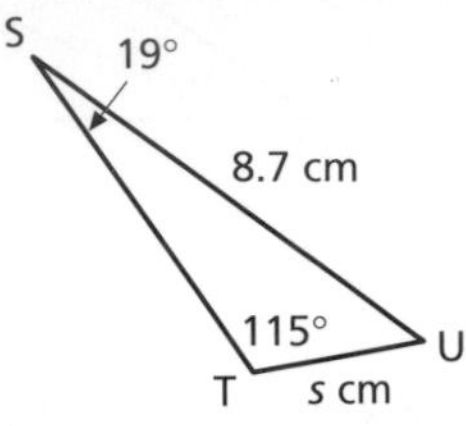

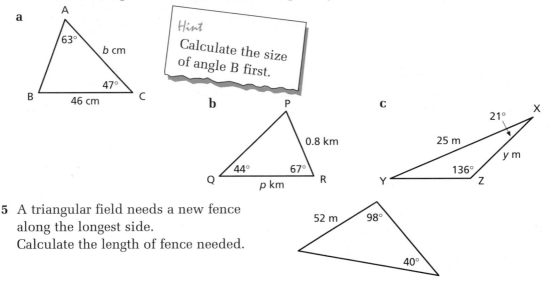

4 Calculate the lengths of the sides marked *b, p* and *y*.

a

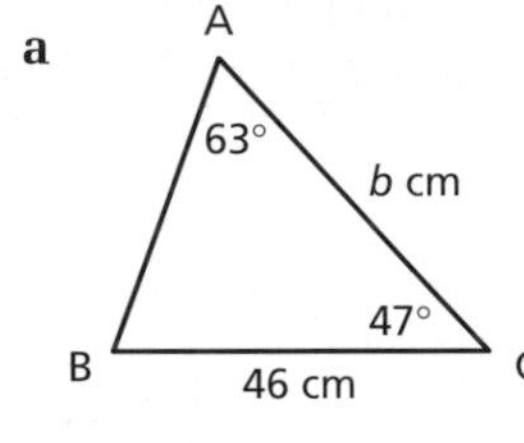

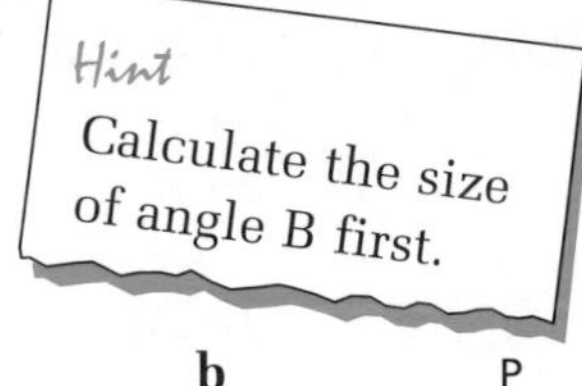

b

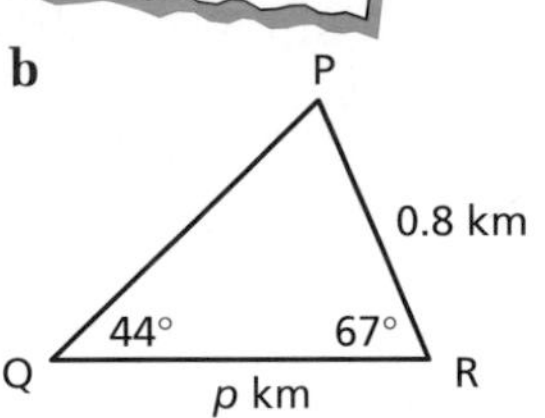

c

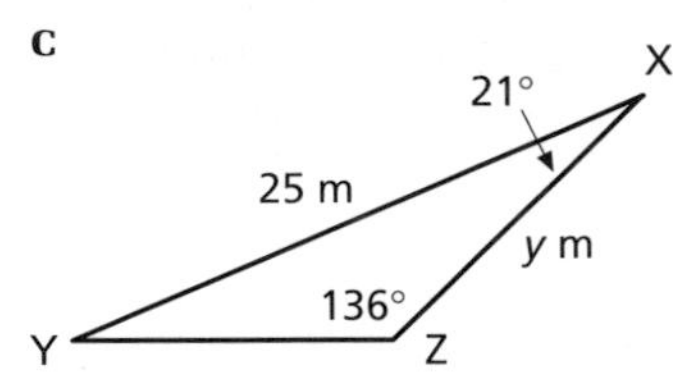

5 A triangular field needs a new fence along the longest side.
Calculate the length of fence needed.

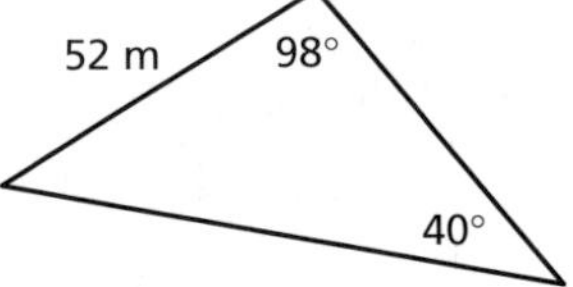

EXERCISE 7

1 a A hot-air balloon is tethered to the ground by two ropes.
The angle between the 25 m rope and the ground is 75°.
The other rope makes an angle of 70° with the ground. Calculate the length of the second rope (to 3 s.f.).

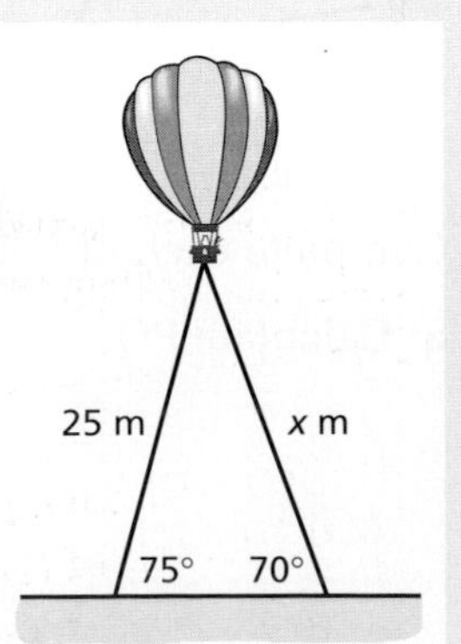

b A second balloon is tethered by two 30 m ropes. The angle between each rope and the ground is 80°.

(i) Calculate the angle between the two ropes.

(ii) Calculate the distance between the tethering points on the ground.

**2**

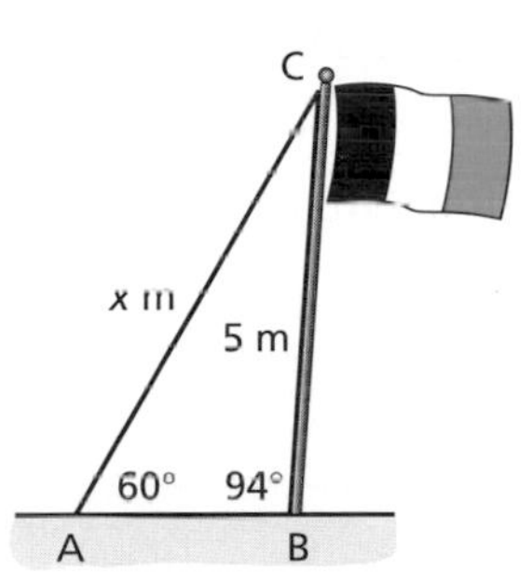

A 5 m flagpole is at an angle of 94° to the ground.

A rope is attached to the top of the pole and tethered to the ground at A.

a The rope makes an angle of 60° with the ground. How long is the rope?

b What is the distance between A and B?

c In order to make the pole vertical the rope is shortened. It is still fixed to the ground at A. How long will the rope need to be now?

3 An orienteering course is laid out as shown.

a Calculate the length of the second leg of the course.

b Calculate the length of the third leg.

c How long is the whole course?

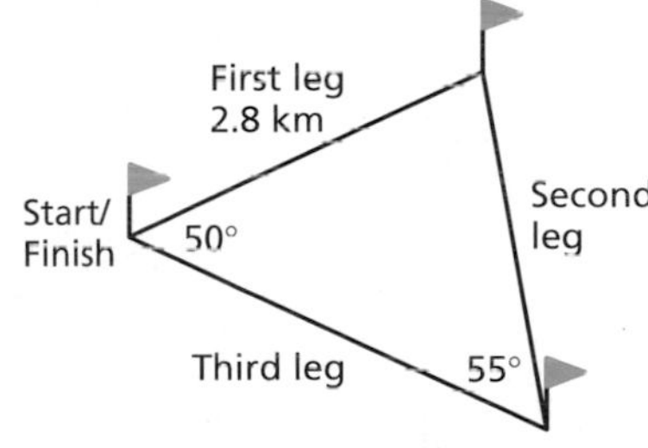

4

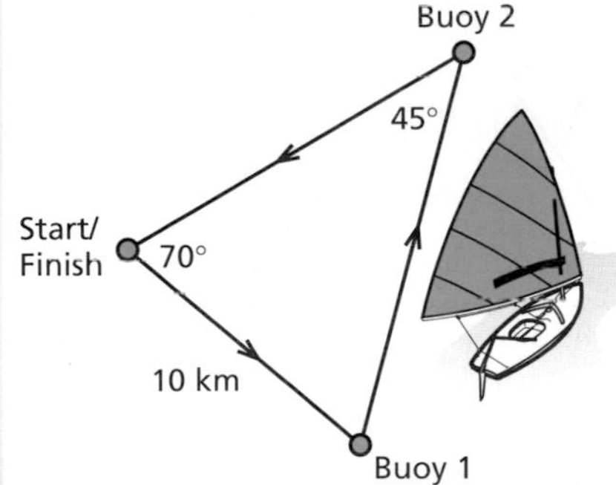

The course for a yacht race has three legs as shown. The first leg of the race is 10 km.

a Calculate the length of the race between buoy 1 and buoy 2.

b Calculate the total length of the race.

5 The diagram shows a plan for a car park. Calculate the perimeter of the car park.

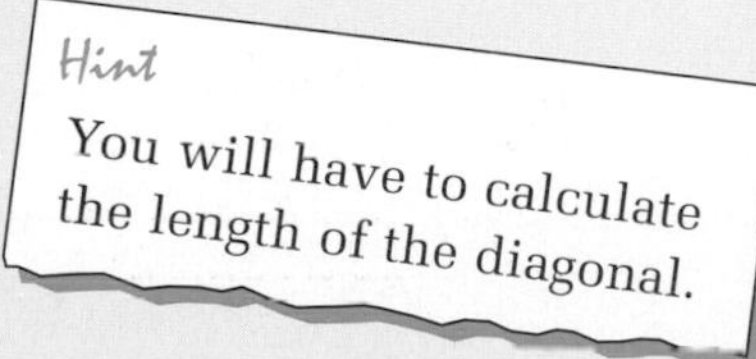
Hint

You will have to calculate the length of the diagonal.

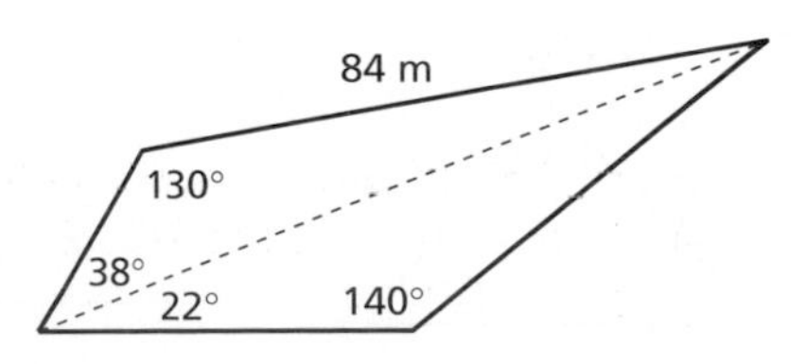

Finding an angle

Example Calculate angle A.

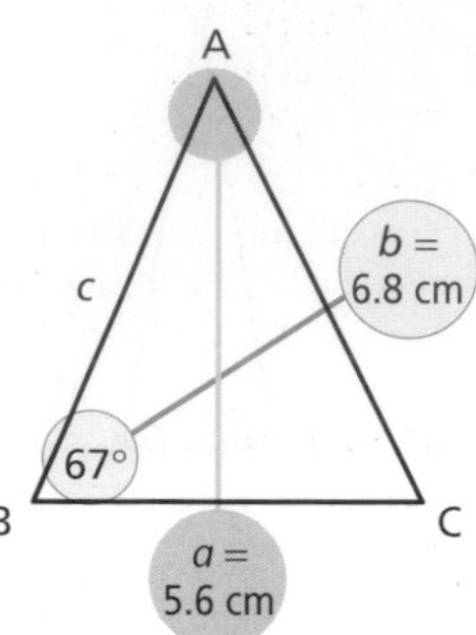

Check what you have. $\frac{a}{\sin A}$ ✓ $= \frac{b}{\sin B}$ ✓ $= \frac{c}{\sin C}$ ✓

$$\frac{a}{\sin A} = \frac{b}{\sin B}$$

$$\Rightarrow \frac{5.6}{\sin A} = \frac{4.8}{\sin 67°}$$ (Now cross-multiply.)

$$\Rightarrow \sin A = \frac{5.6 \times \sin 67°}{6.8}$$

$$\Rightarrow \sin A = 0.7580$$ (Remember not to round too early.)

$$\Rightarrow A = 49.293°$$

$$\Rightarrow A = 49.3° \text{ (to 3 s.f.)}$$

EXERCISE 8

1 Calculate the size of the marked angle in each triangle.

a

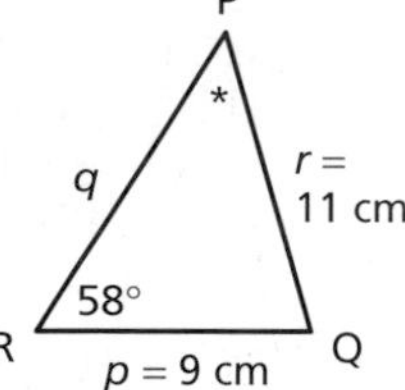

b

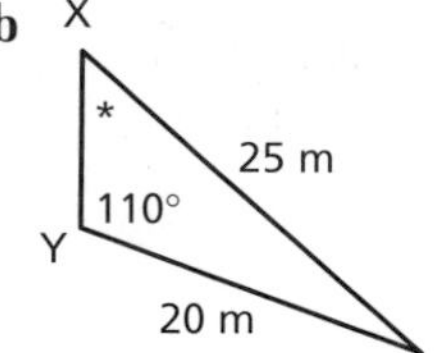

c

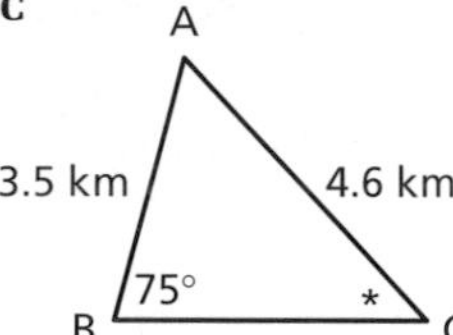

d

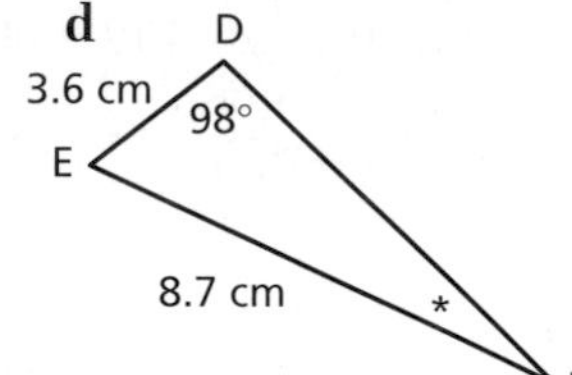

e

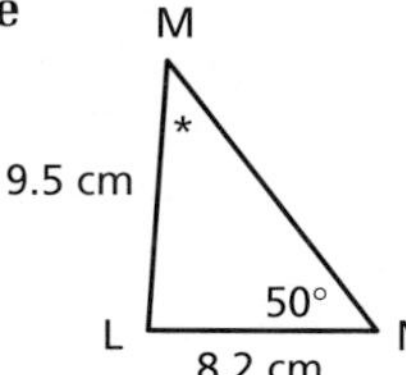

f

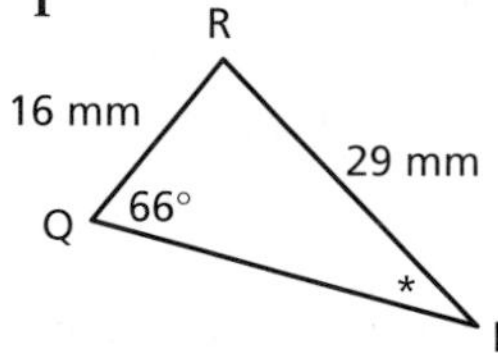

g

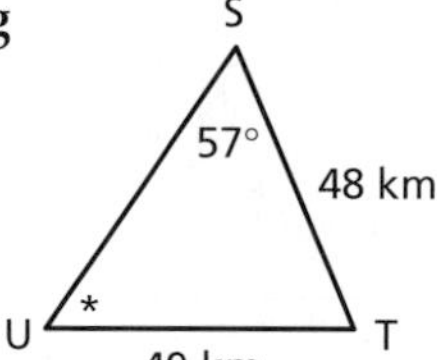

h

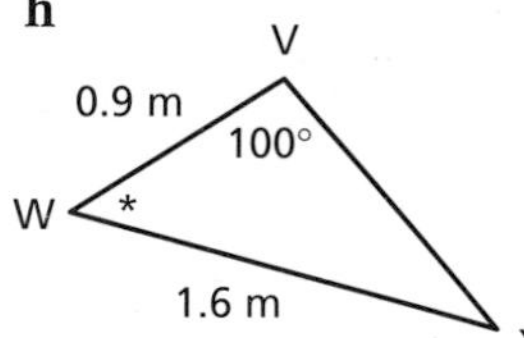

2 For each triangle calculate: **(i)** ∠C **(ii)** ∠B.

a

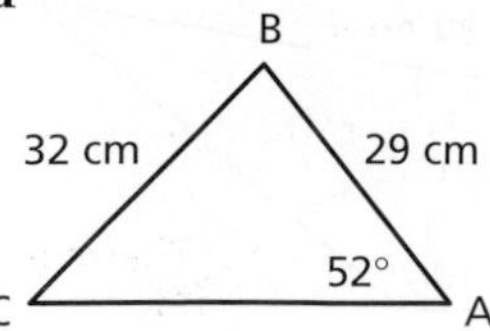

b

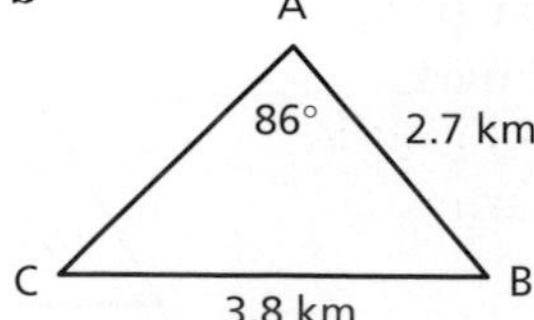

EXERCISE 9

1 A young tree is held in place by two wires.
Both wires are attached to the tree at the same point.
The 4.8 m wire makes an angle of 38° with the ground.
Calculate the angle the 4.1 m wire makes with the ground.

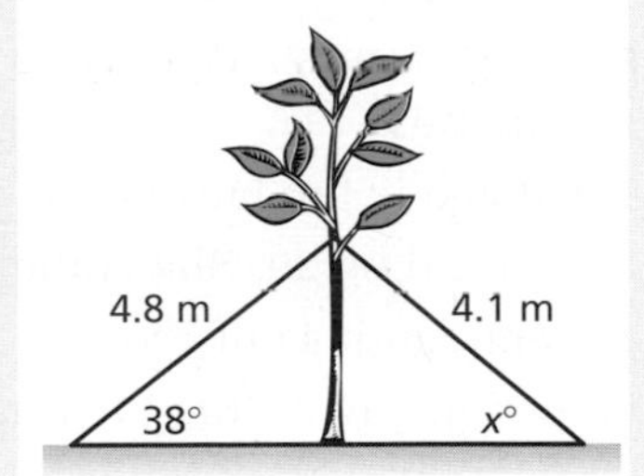

2

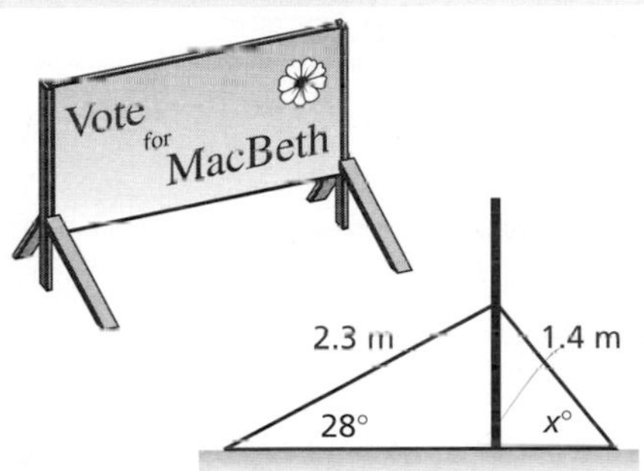

An advertising sign has two wooden supports.
The supports have been attached to the sign at the same height.
The longer support is 2.3 m long.
It makes an angle of 28° with the ground.
The shorter support is 1.4 m long.
What angle does it make with the ground?

3 A hot-air balloon is tethered to the ground by two ropes.
One rope has a length of 32 m and the other is 34 m.
The shorter rope makes an angle of 80° with the ground.
What angle does the longer rope make with the ground?

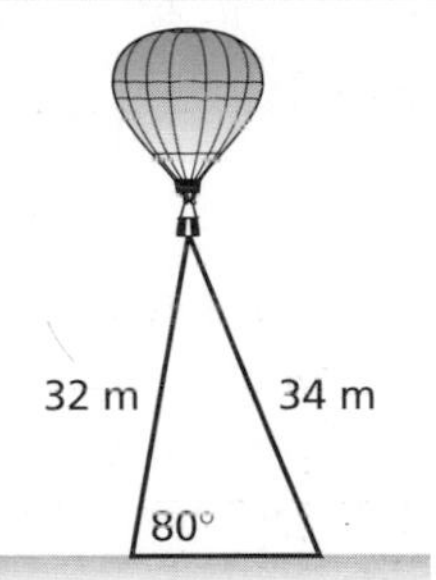

4

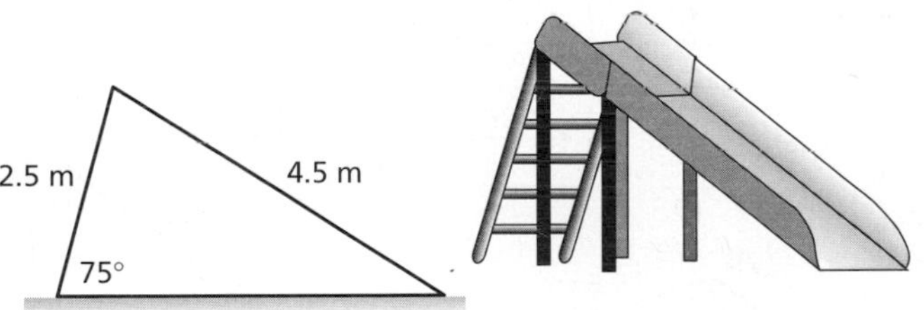

A playground chute has a 2.5 m ladder. The slide measures 4.5 m.
The ladder makes an angle of 75° with the ground.
Calculate the angle the slide makes with the ground.

5 Three oil rigs are situated in the North Sea.
Beaumont is 57 km north of Indio and is 66 km from Thermal.
Thermal is on a bearing of 070° from Indio.
Calculate the bearing of Thermal from Beaumont.

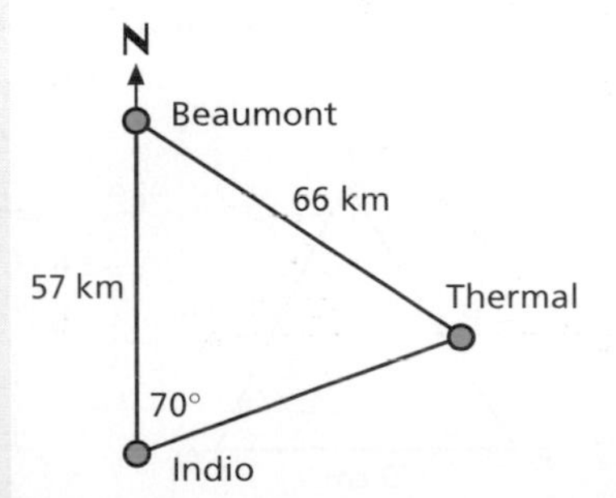

Ambiguous cases

If a question has more than one answer it is said to be ambiguous.
What age is the lady in the picture?
She could be 20. She could be 80.
An ambiguous question!
Questions involving the Sine Rule can also be ambiguous

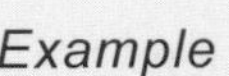
Example

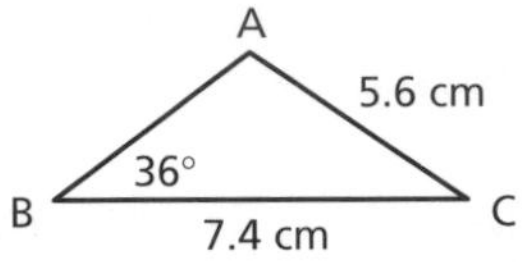

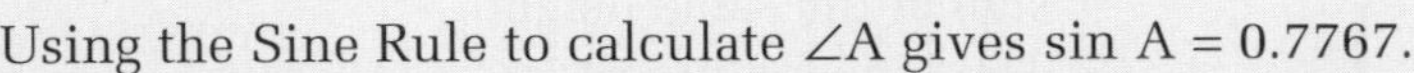
Using the Sine Rule to calculate ∠A gives sin A = 0.7767.

First answer: ∠A = 51.0° (using a calculator)
∠C = 180 − 51 − 36 = 93°

Check that the sine of both 51° and 129° is in fact 0.7767.

Second answer:
We know that sin A = sin (180 − A)°.
It may be that ∠A = (180 − 51.0)° = 129°
and ∠C = 180 − 129 − 36 = 15°.

So there are two possible triangles you could draw using the given information.

Draw a 7.4 cm line, BC.
Make a 36° angle, ∠ CBA.
Use compasses to draw an arc of radius 5.6 cm, centre C.
Note there are two possible places where A can be marked.

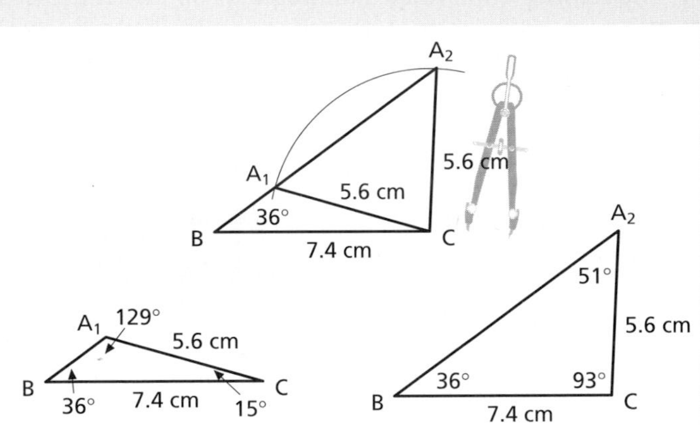

EXERCISE 10

1 Look back at question **1a** in Exercise 8. You found out that:

sin P = 0.6939
∠P = 43.9362
∠P = 43.9° (to 1 d.p.)

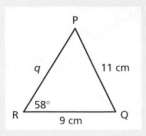

a Calculate another value for P, where sin P = 0.6939.

b Consider the value of Q.
Q = 180 − P − R
Explain why this value of P is *not* an acceptable solution for triangle PQR.

2 **a** **(i)** Calculate the size of ∠X.
(ii) Calculate ∠Z.
b **(i)** Calculate (180 – X)°.
(ii) Consider the corresponding value for Z.
(iii) Is this an acceptable solution?

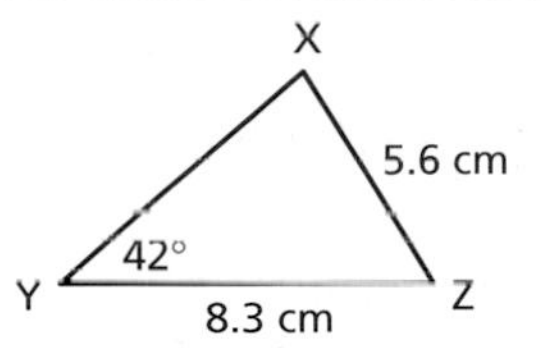

3 The sketches below are not accurately drawn. Solve each triangle completely. Be careful to include both possibilities when you have an ambiguous case. Make accurate drawings of the possible solutions.

a

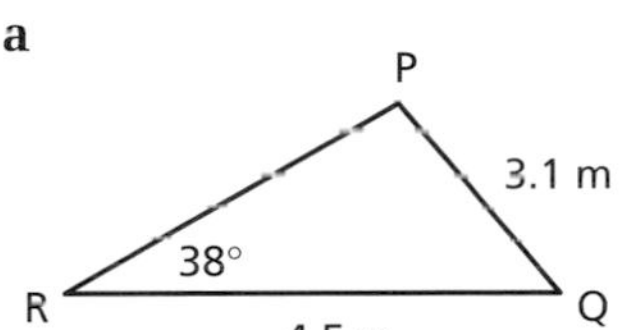

b

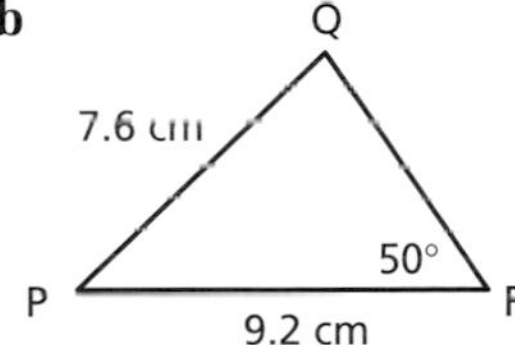

c

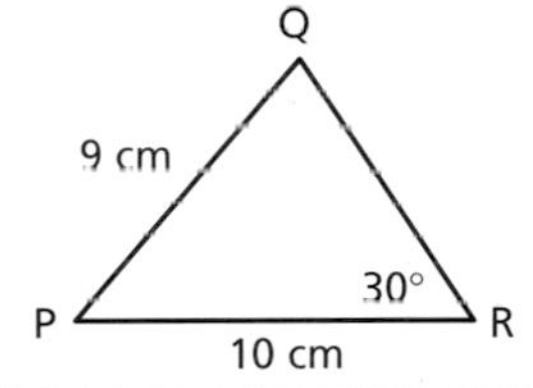

Challenge

An examiner is making up a question.
BC = 6 cm.
∠ABC = 40°.
He is about to assign a value to AC.

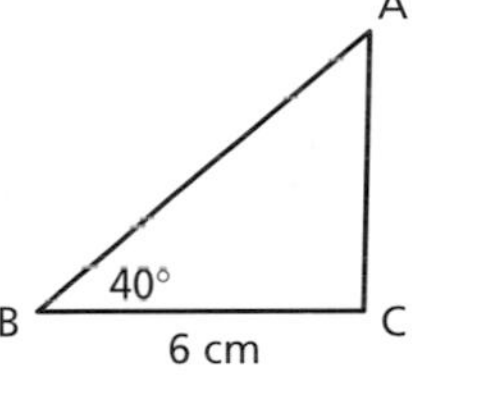

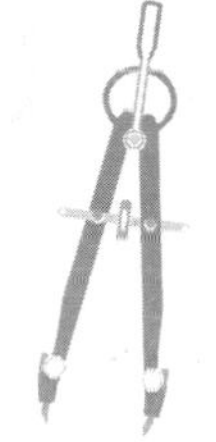

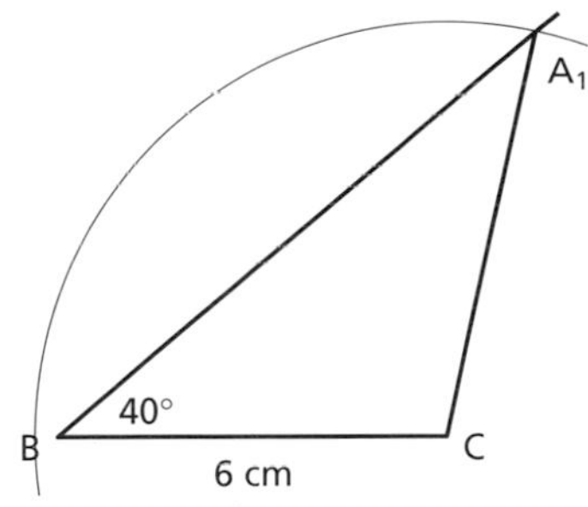

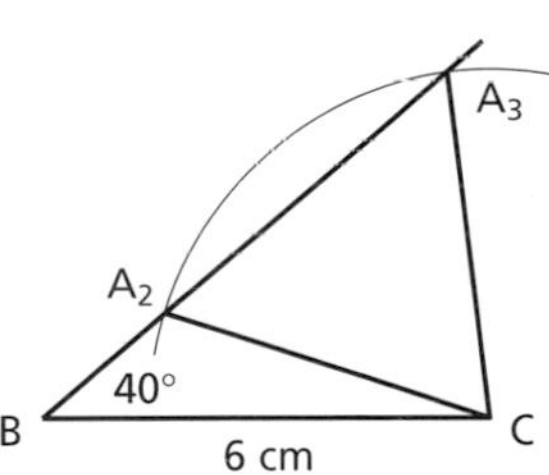

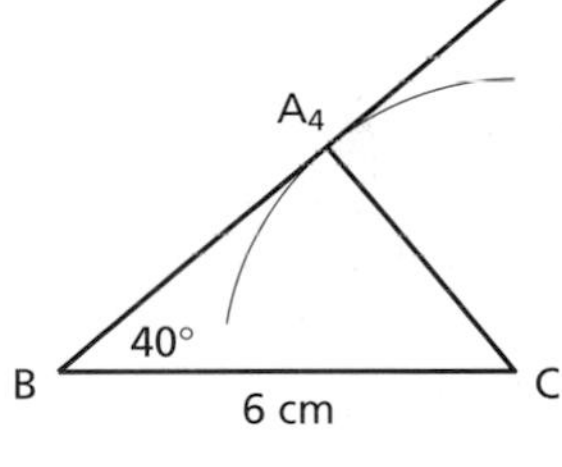

1 Investigate the different possible lengths of AC.
What lengths lead to:
a ambiguous cases
b one solution only
c no solutions (impossible triangles)?

2

If the angle you calculate is bigger than the given angle then the question is ambiguous!

Can you make sense of what is being said here?
Can you illustrate it?
Can you prove it?

The Cosine Rule

When two sides of a triangle and the angle between them are the given bits of information, then the Sine Rule is no use.
We can use another method to find the third side.

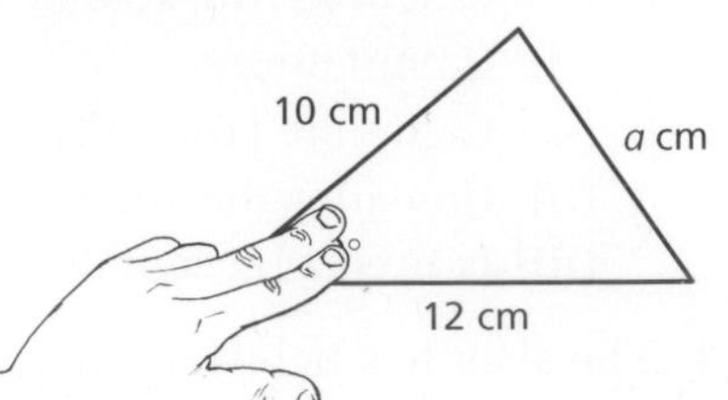

Example Calculate the length of BC.

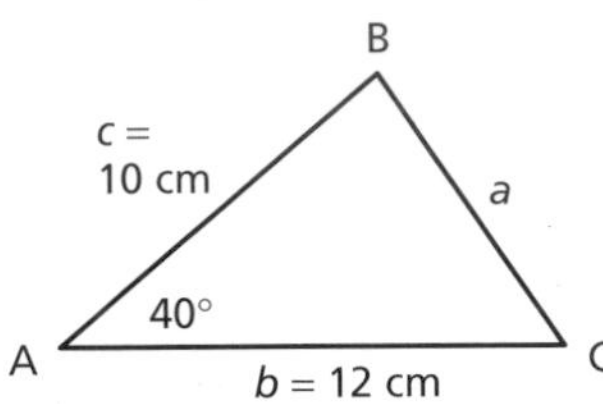

$$\frac{a}{\sin A} = \frac{b}{\sin B} = \frac{c}{\sin C}$$

We don't have a pair of opposites.
We can't use the Sine Rule.

Step 1 Drop a perpendicular from B to AC.

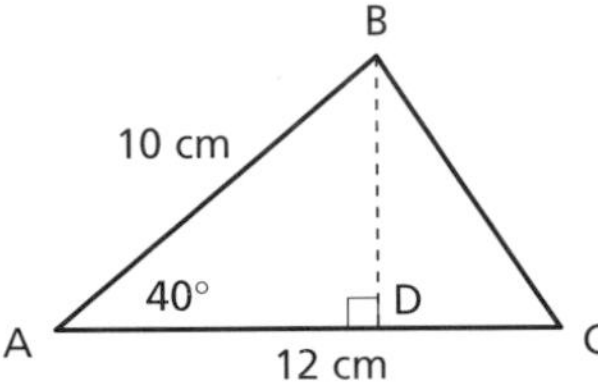

Step 2 In triangle BAD, calculate the length of BD and AD.

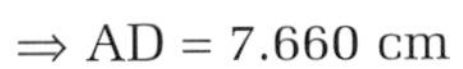

$\sin 40° = \frac{BD}{10}$

$\Rightarrow 10 \times \sin 40° = BD$

$\Rightarrow BD = 6.427$ cm

$\cos 40° = \frac{AD}{10}$

$\Rightarrow 10 \times \cos 40° = AD$

$\Rightarrow AD = 7.660$ cm

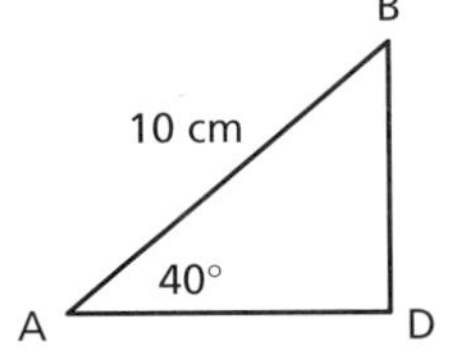

Step 3 Calculate DC.

$DC = 12 - AD = 12 - 7.66$

$DC = 4.34$ cm

Step 4 In triangle BCD, use Pythagoras' Theorem.

$BC^2 = BD^2 + DC^2 = 6.43^2 + 4.34^2$

$= 60.18$

$BC = \sqrt{60.18}$ cm

$BC = 7.76$ cm (to 3 s.f.)

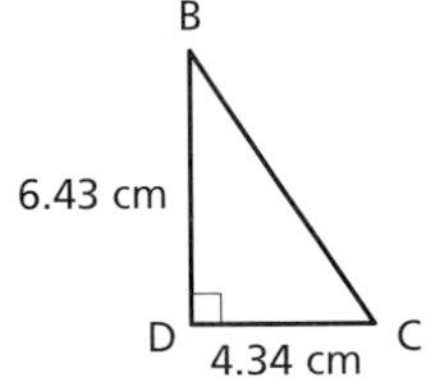

EXERCISE 11

Calculate the unknown side in each triangle by the method suggested above.
Round your answers to 3 s.f.

1

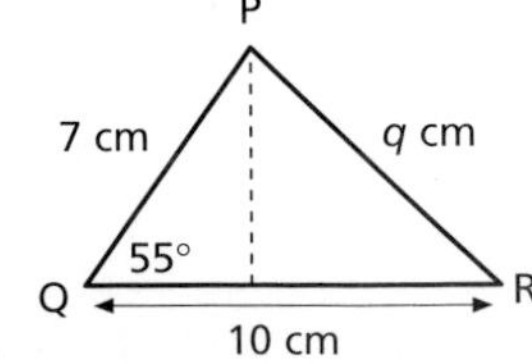

2

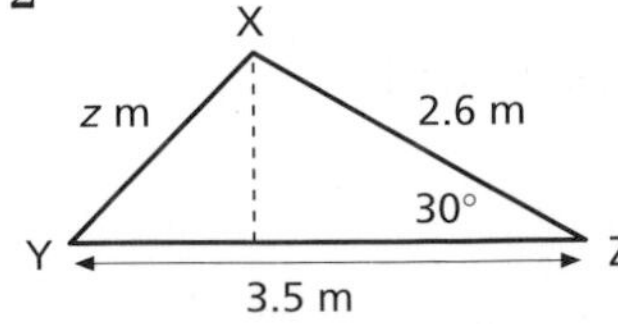

3

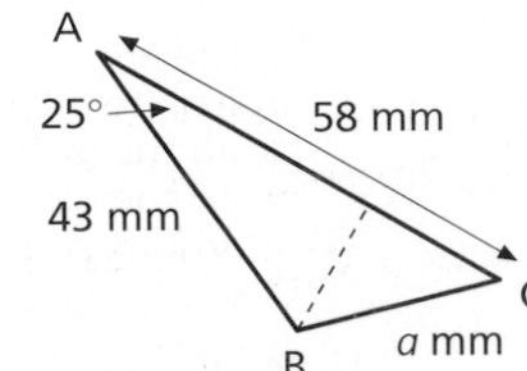

Challenge

> *Reminder*
> $\sin^2 A$ is another way of writing $(\sin A)^2$

1 a Use your calculator to find the value of $\sin^2 A + \cos^2 A$ when:
(i) $A = 30°$ (ii) $A = 86°$ (iii) $A = 1°$ (iv) $A = 129°$.

b Comment on your findings.

c Check your findings using a few more cases.

d By Pythagoras: $a^2 = b^2 + c^2$.
Dividing throughout by a^2 gives us:
$$\frac{a^2}{a^2} = \frac{b^2}{a^2} + \frac{c^2}{a^2}$$
Simplify this using the definitions of the trigonometric ratios.

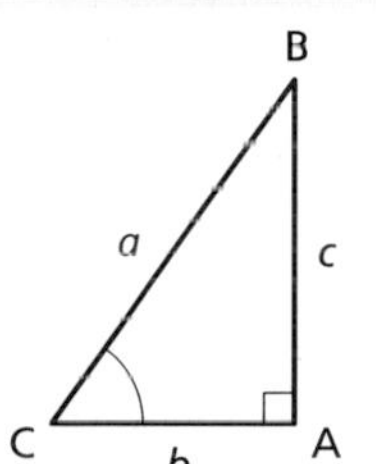

2 Follow this argument. In triangle BAD:

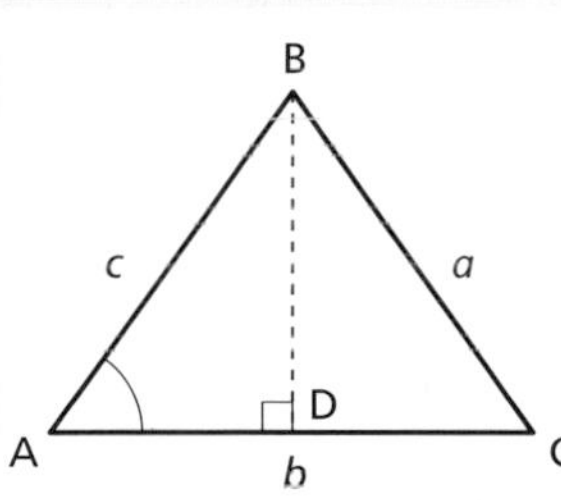

$\sin A = \dfrac{BD}{c}$

$\Rightarrow c \times \sin A = BD$

$\Rightarrow BD = c \sin A$

$\cos A = \dfrac{AD}{c}$

$\Rightarrow c \times \cos A = AD$

$\Rightarrow AD = c \cos A$

$DC = b - AD$

$\quad = b - c \cos A$

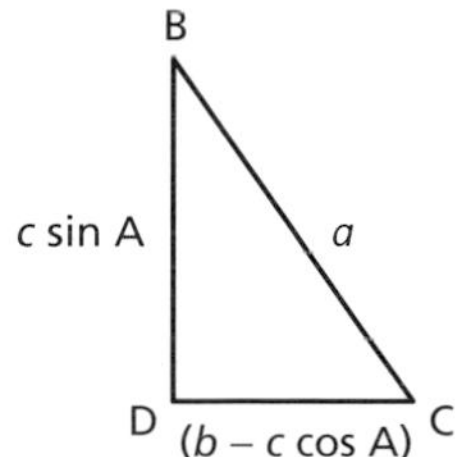

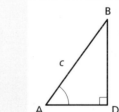

In triangle BDC, using Pythagoras' Theorem:

$BC^2 = DC^2 + BD^2$

$\Rightarrow a^2 = (b - c \cos A)^2 + (c \sin A)^2$

$\Rightarrow a^2 = b^2 - 2bc \cos A + c^2 \cos^2 A + c^2 \sin^2 A$

$\Rightarrow a^2 = b^2 - 2bc \cos A + c^2 (\sin^2 A + \cos^2 A)$

$\Rightarrow a^2 = b^2 + c^2 - 2bc \cos A$

This result is known as the **Cosine Rule**.
In any triangle ABC,
$a^2 = b^2 + c^2 - 2bc \cos A$

Using the Cosine Rule to find the length of a side

Whenever two sides of a triangle and the angle between them are known, the third side can be found using the Cosine Rule.

Example Calculate PQ.

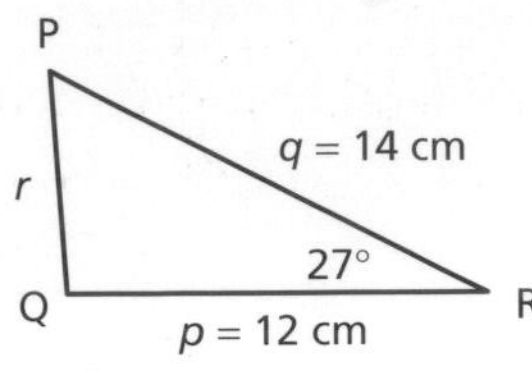

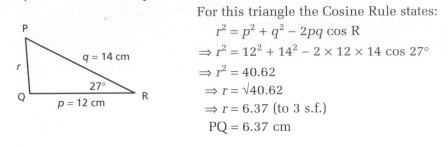

For this triangle the Cosine Rule states:

$r^2 = p^2 + q^2 - 2pq \cos R$

$\Rightarrow r^2 = 12^2 + 14^2 - 2 \times 12 \times 14 \cos 27°$

$\Rightarrow r^2 = 40.62$

$\Rightarrow r = \sqrt{40.62}$

$\Rightarrow r = 6.37$ (to 3 s.f.)

PQ = 6.37 cm

EXERCISE 12

1 Complete the Cosine Rule for each triangle.

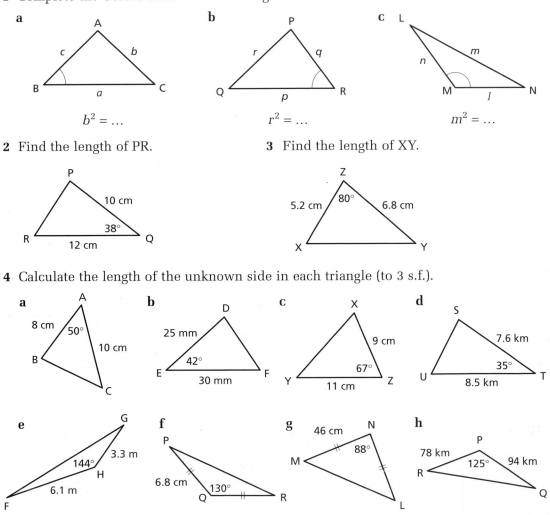

a

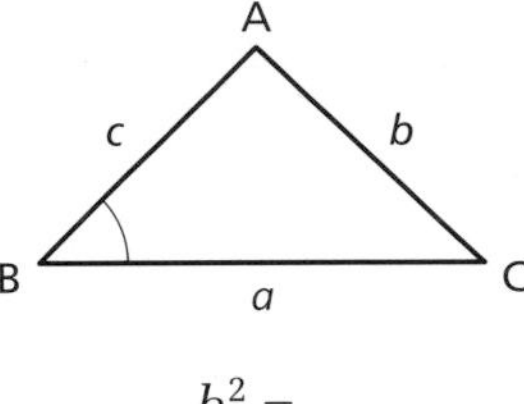

$b^2 = \ldots$

b

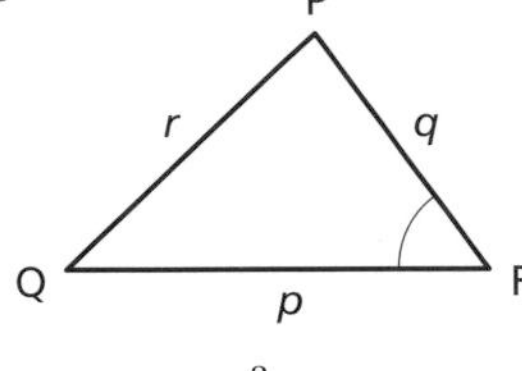

$r^2 = \ldots$

c

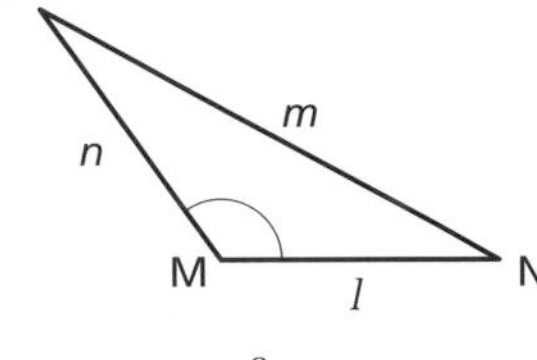

$m^2 = \ldots$

2 Find the length of PR.

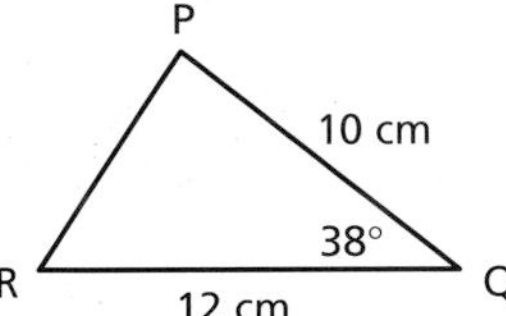

3 Find the length of XY.

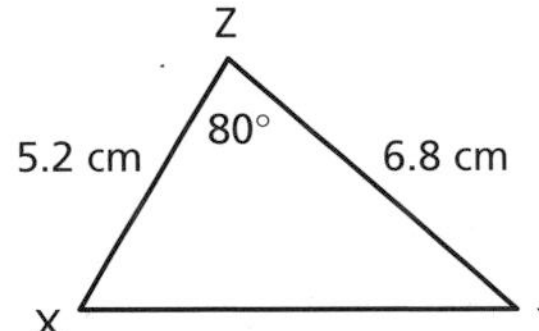

4 Calculate the length of the unknown side in each triangle (to 3 s.f.).

a

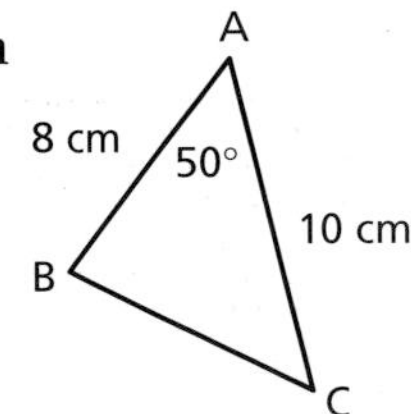

b

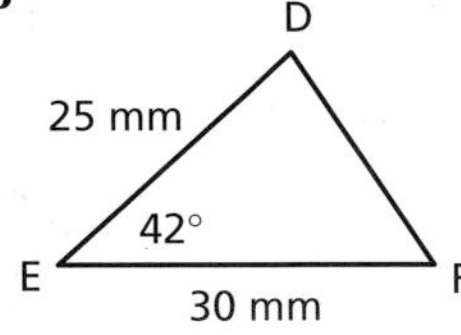

c

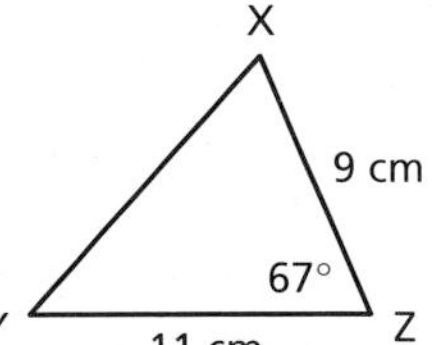

d

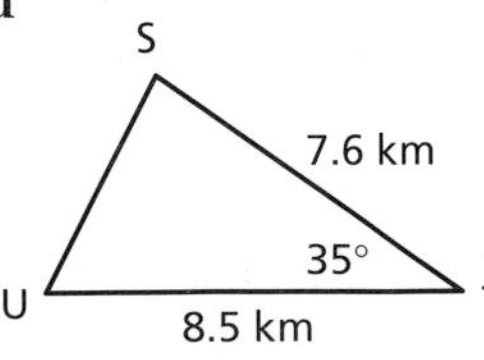

e

G, 3.3 m, 144°, H, 6.1 m, F

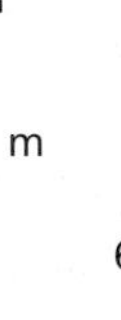

f

P, 6.8 cm, 130°, Q, R

g

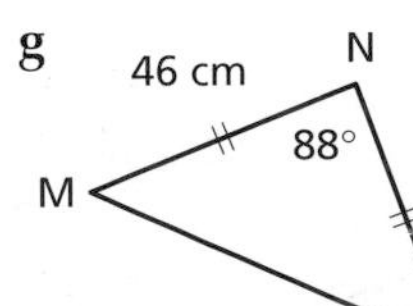

h

78 km, P, 125°, 94 km, R, Q

5 A triangular orchard has sides measuring 45 m and 40 m. The angle between these sides is 105°.

a Calculate the length of the third side.

b Hence calculate the perimeter of the orchard.

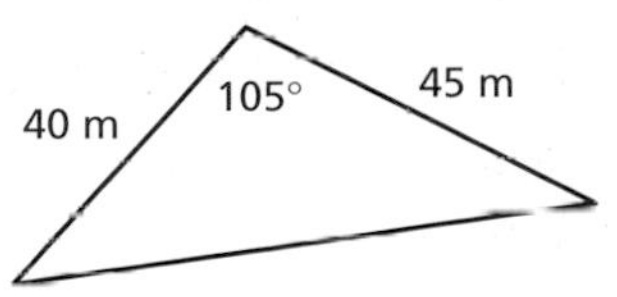

6

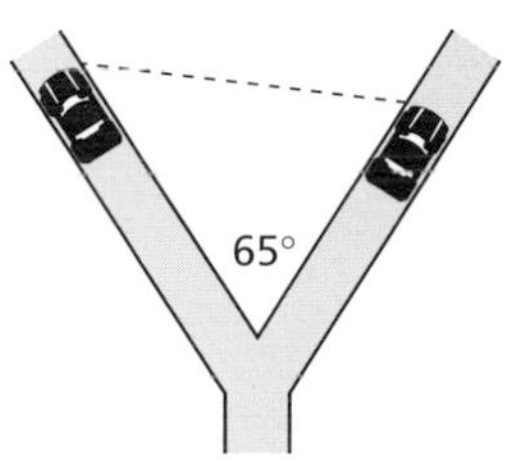

Two cars leave the same intersection at the same time. The roads are at an angle of 65° to each other. One car travels 360 m while the other travels 320 m. How far apart are the cars at the end of their journey?

7 The legs of a pair of dividers are each 12 cm long.

a The angle between the legs is 75°. How far apart are the points of the dividers?

b If the angle is reduced to 50°, how much closer will the legs be?

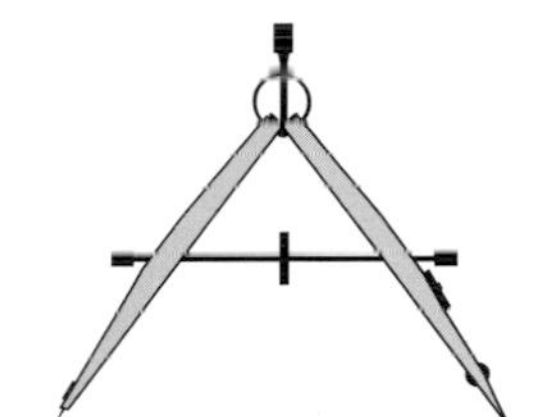

8 a A golfer is standing 4.2 m from a hole. He hits the ball 4.1 m but at an angle of 6° off-line. By how much has he missed the hole?

b His opponent is 3.8 m from the hole. His ball is hit 3.8 m but 7° off-line. How far is his ball from the hole?

c Which golfer's ball is closer to the hole?

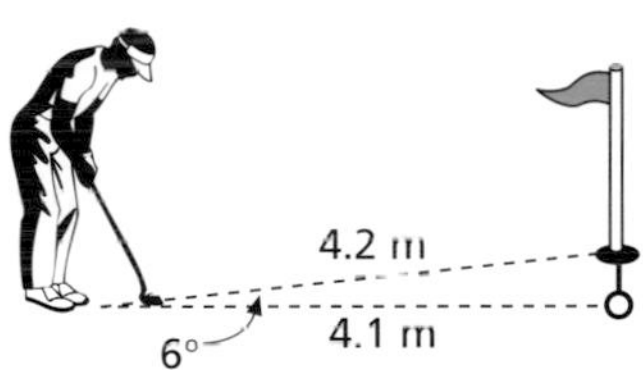

9 The Moon is 380 000 km from the Earth. A rocket is sent in a straight line to the Moon but is 1° off-line. How far from the Moon is it after 380 000 km?

10 A collapsable screen for drying clothes is held rigid by a triangular brace. The apex angle of the brace is 75°. Two of the sides of the triangle are 50 cm and 51 cm. What length is the horizontal part of the brace?

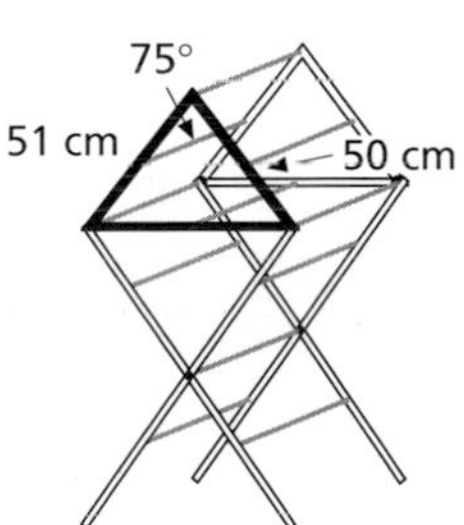

11 A signwriter makes very large tiles for a display.

a The 'V' has arms measuring 1 m each and the angle between the arms is 50°. How wide is the tile?

b Both arms of the 'X' are 1.2 m long. The arms cross over at the centre at an angle of 60°. Calculate the width of this tile.

12

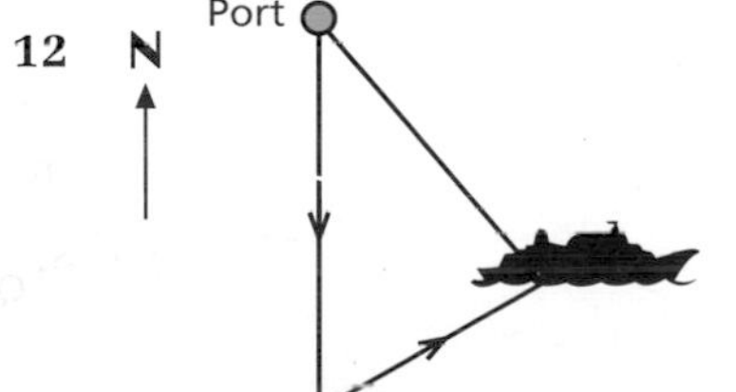

A ship sailed south from a port for a distance of 55 km. It then sailed on a bearing of 060° for 36 km. Calculate how far the ship is from the port.

UNIT 2 8 Trigonometry

Calculating an angle using the Cosine Rule

We can use the Cosine Rule to find an angle when we know all three sides.
We can make the calculation simpler by rearranging the formula.

$$a^2 = b^2 + c^2 - 2bc \cos A$$

$$\Rightarrow 2bc \cos A = b^2 + c^2 - a^2$$

$$\Rightarrow \cos A = \frac{b^2 + c^2 - a^2}{2bc}$$

Example Find the size of ∠A.

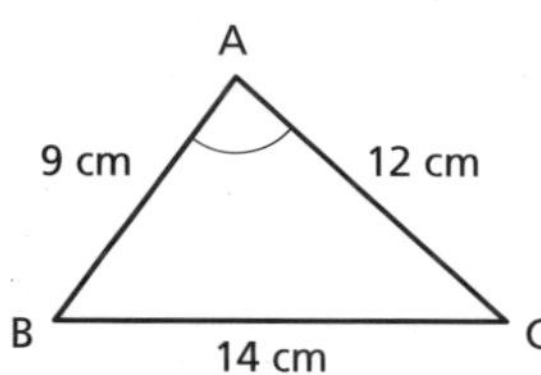

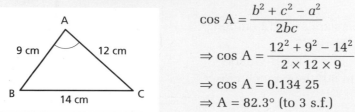

$$\cos A = \frac{b^2 + c^2 - a^2}{2bc}$$

$$\Rightarrow \cos A = \frac{12^2 + 9^2 - 14^2}{2 \times 12 \times 9}$$

$$\Rightarrow \cos A = 0.134\ 25$$

$$\Rightarrow A = 82.3° \text{ (to 3 s.f.)}$$

EXERCISE 13

1 Complete the Cosine Rule needed to calculate the marked angle.

a

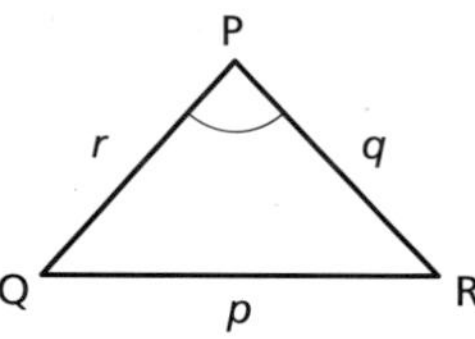

$\cos P = \frac{q^2 + \quad}{\quad}$

b

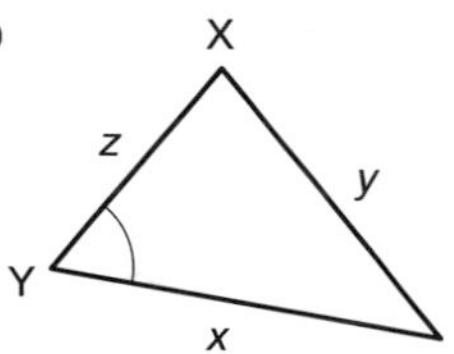

$\cos Y = \frac{x^2 + \quad}{\quad}$

c

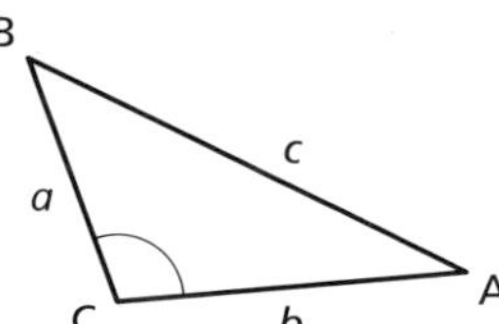

$\cos C = \frac{a^2 + \quad}{\quad}$

2 Calculate the size of the marked angle in each triangle.

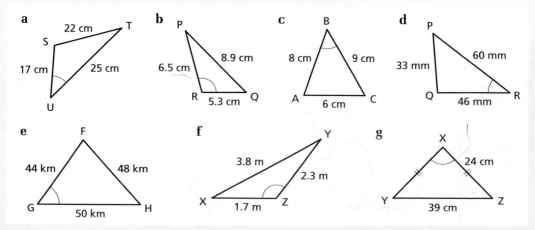

a

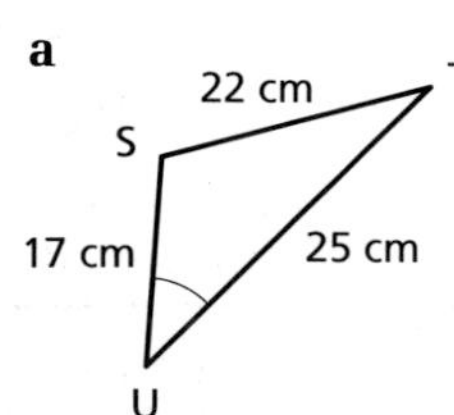

b

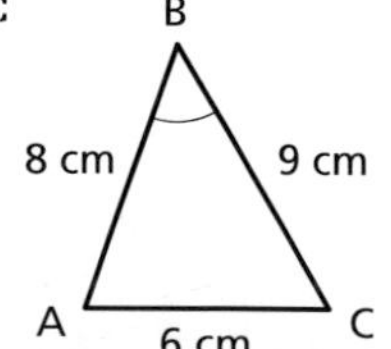

c

B
8 cm
9 cm
A
6 cm
C

d

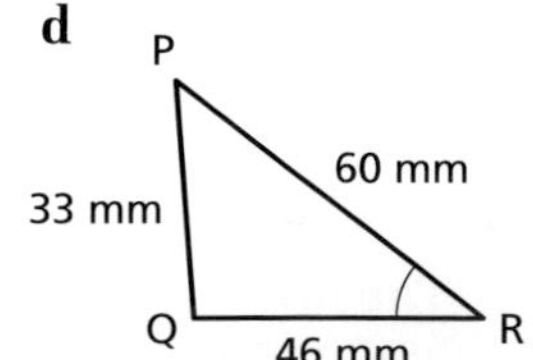

e

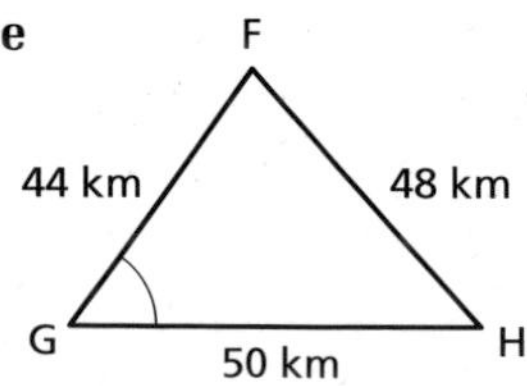

f

Y
3.8 m
2.3 m
X
1.7 m
Z

g

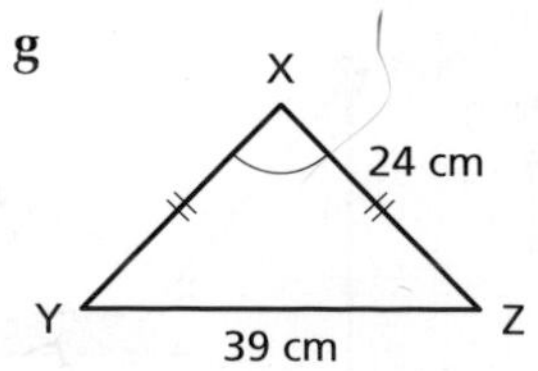

3 **a** Calculate the size of ∠Y.

b Explain why the numerator (top line) of the fraction in the Cosine Rule equals zero.

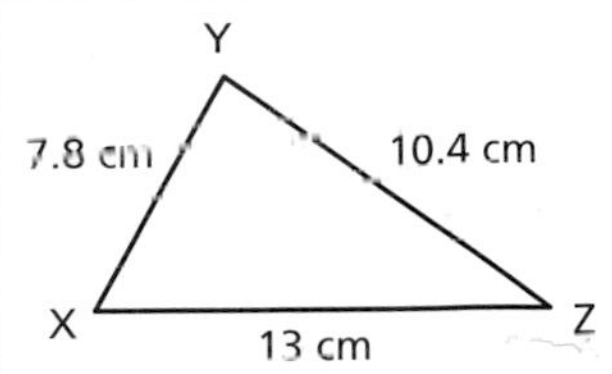

4

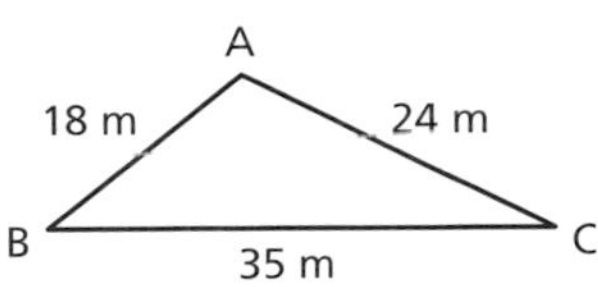

Hint

Use the Cosine Rule twice.

a Calculate the sizes of *all* the angles in triangle ABC.

b Copy and complete this table.

c Write down any observations you make about the relative sizes of the sides and angles.

Length of side	Size of opposite angle
$a = 35$ m	∠A
$b = 24$ m	∠B
$c = 18$ m	∠C

5 Calculate the size of the largest angle in triangle PQR.

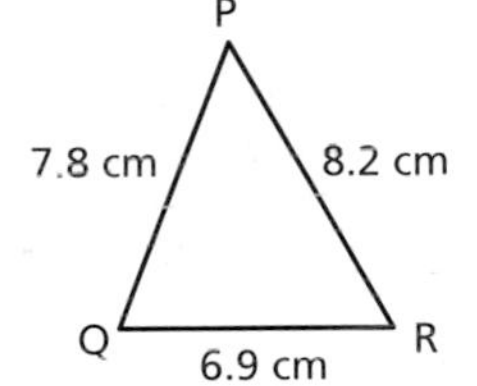

6

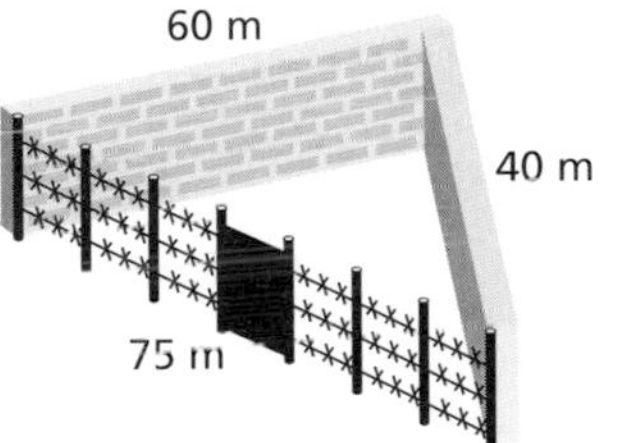

A field has walls on two sides and a fence on the other.
Calculate the angle between the walls.

7 Euan and Ralph are standing 24 m apart. A weather balloon is being tethered to the ground by two ropes. Euan's rope is 17 m long. Ralph's rope is 15 m long.
Calculate the angle of elevation of the balloon from:

a Euan ($e°$)

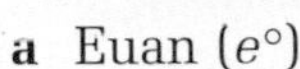

b Ralph ($r°$).

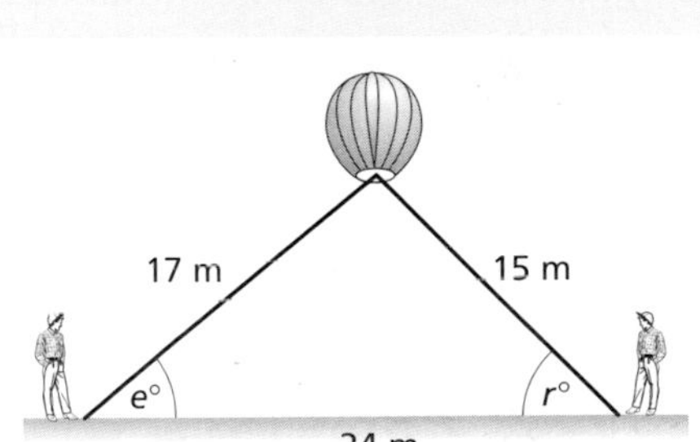

8

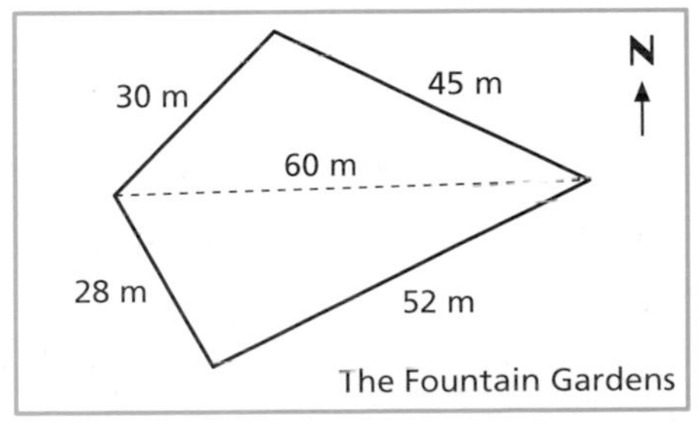

A surveyor takes measurements in a walled park and makes the sketch opposite.
Calculate the sizes of the four angles between the walls of the park.

9

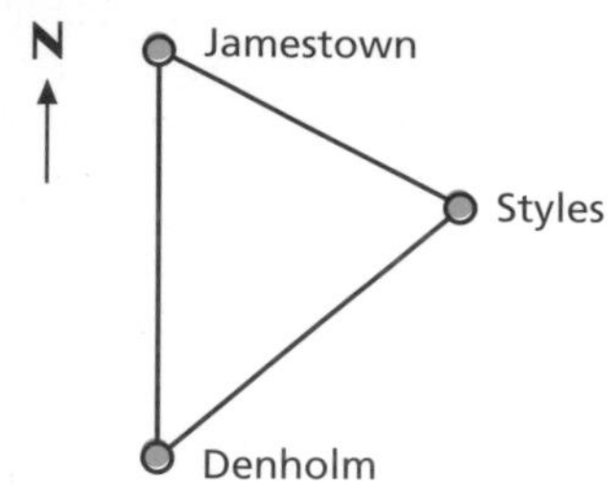

Three towns are positioned as in the diagram.
Jamestown is 36 km north of Denholm.
Styles is 23 km from Jamestown and 25 km from Denholm.
Calculate the bearing of Styles from Denholm.

10 A golfer is standing 17 m from a hole. She hits her ball and it travels 19 m. The ball is still 2.5 m from the hole.
By how many degrees was the ball off-line?

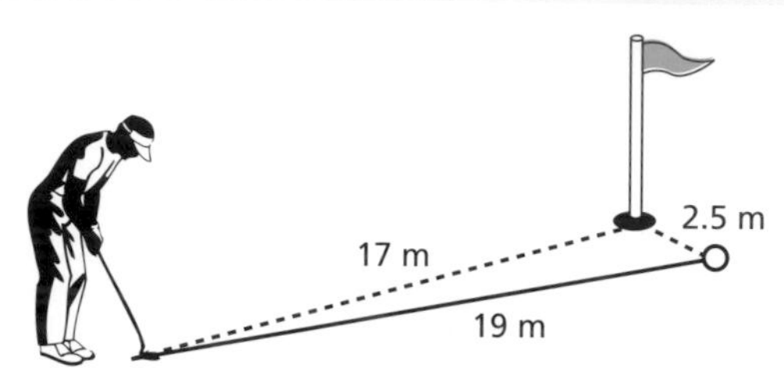

Challenge

Two cars leave an intersection at the same time.
Car A travels along one road at 70 km/h while car B travels along the other at 66 km/h. After half an hour the cars are 10 km apart.
Calculate the angle between the two roads.

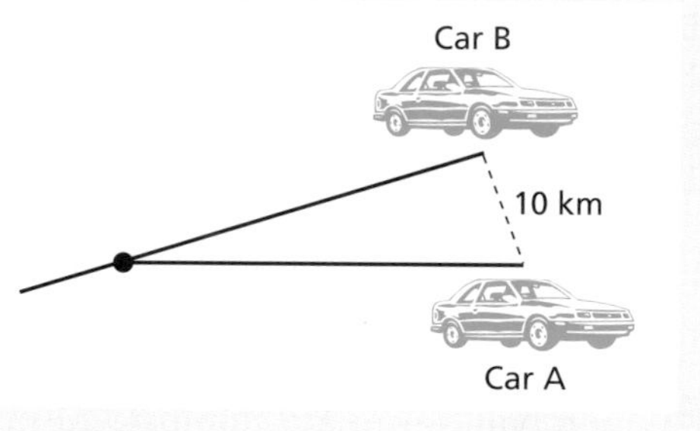

Solving triangles

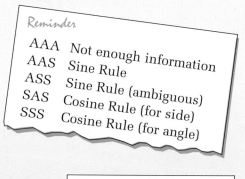

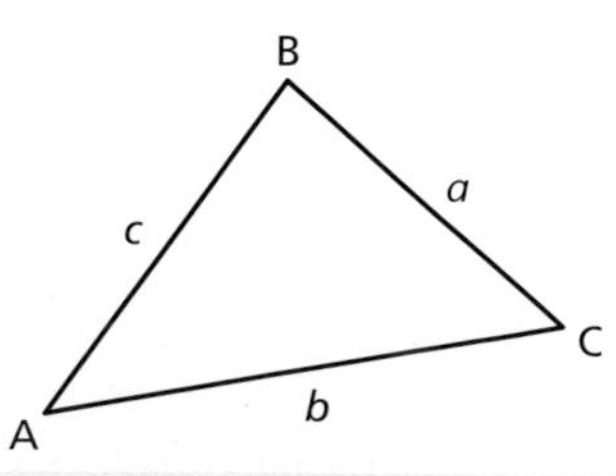

Reminder

AAA Not enough information
AAS Sine Rule
ASS Sine Rule (ambiguous)
SAS Cosine Rule (for side)
SSS Cosine Rule (for angle)

You know 3 angles (AAA) A, B and C … **Not enough information**

You know 1 side and 2 angles (AAS) A, a and C … **Use the Sine Rule**

It's a good policy to find the third angle.

You know 2 sides and an angle not included (ASS) A, b and a ...	Use the Sine Rule (ambiguous case)
You know 2 sides and the included angle (SAS) A, b and c ...	Use the Cosine Rule: $a^2 = b^2 + c^2 - 2bc \cos A$
You know 3 sides (SSS) a, b and c ...	Use the Cosine Rule: $\cos A = \dfrac{b^2 + c^2 - a^2}{2bc}$

EXERCISE 14

1 Calculate the value of x in each triangle.

a

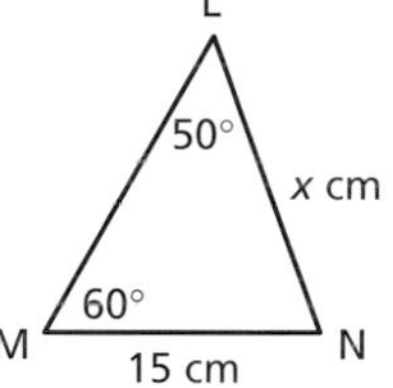

b

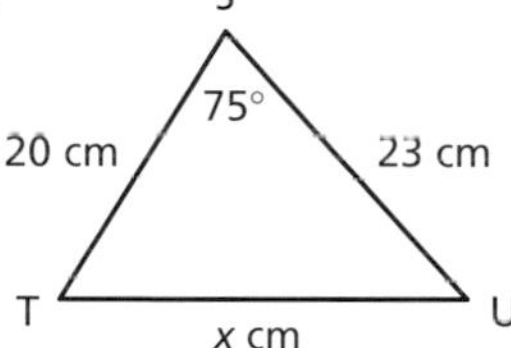

c

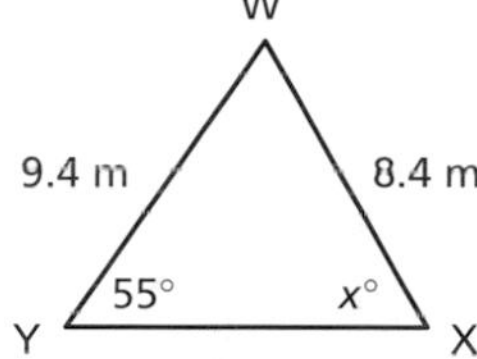

d

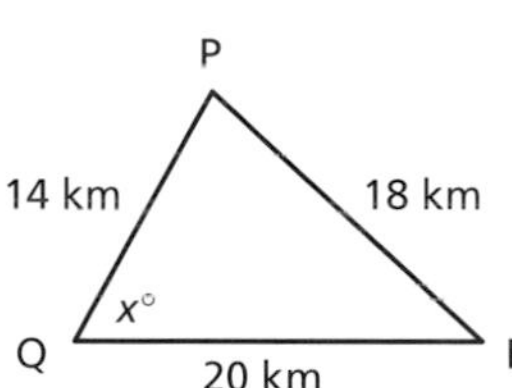

e

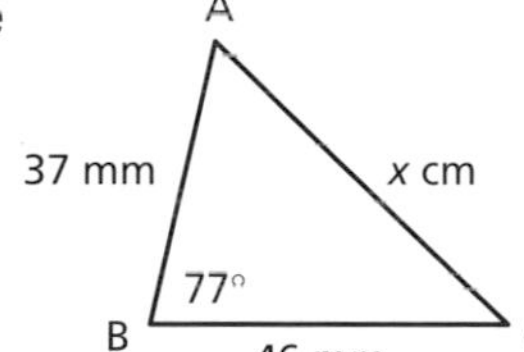

f

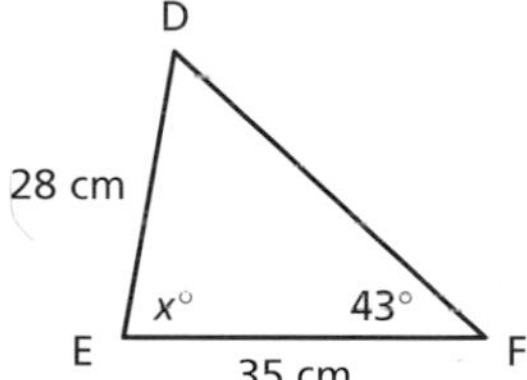

2 In these triangles calculate *all* the unknown angles and sides.

a

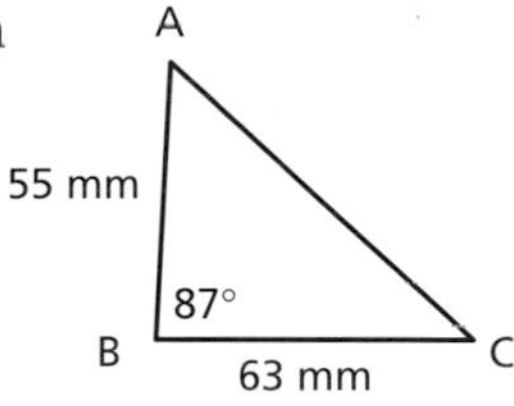

b

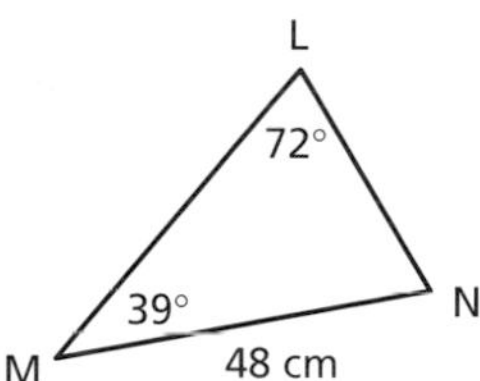

c

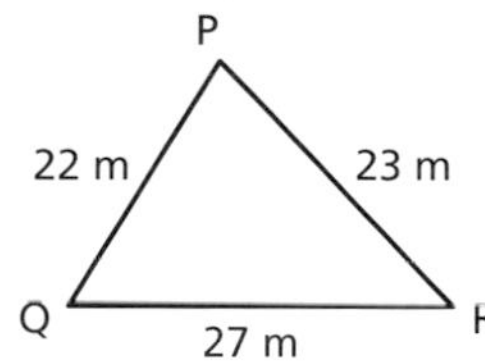

d

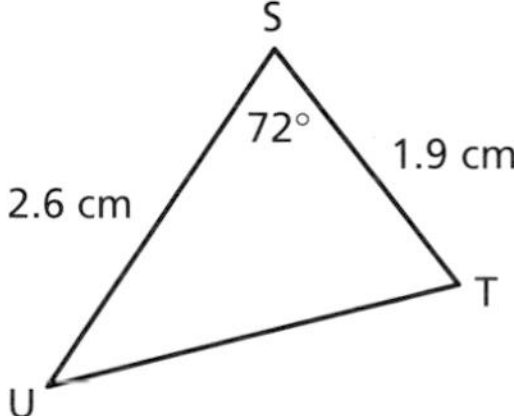

e

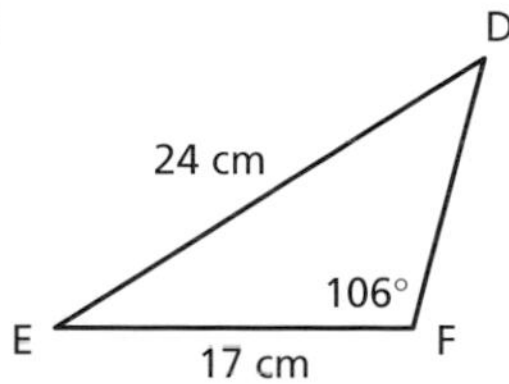

f

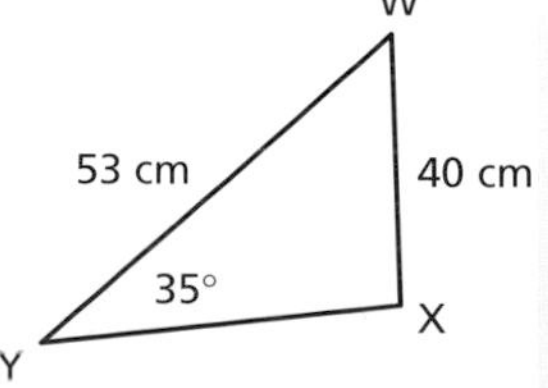

3 In a game of bowls the bowler is standing 24 m from the jack.
Her bowl travels 23 m in a straight line. It comes to rest 3.5 m from the jack.
By how many degrees was her bowl off-line?

4 A pastry cutter has edges measuring 16 cm. The angle between the straight edges is 75°.
Calculate the width of the cutter.

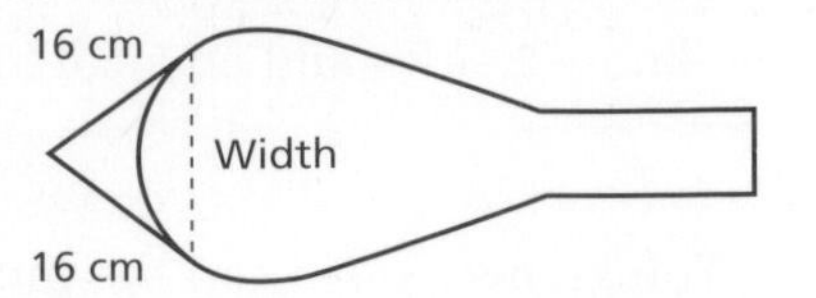

5

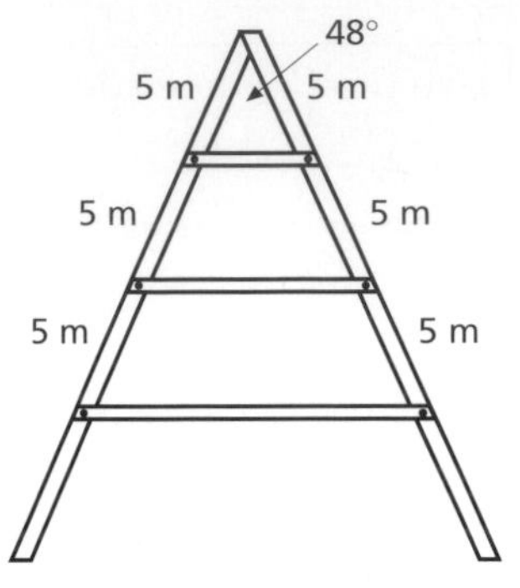

The design of an electricity pylon is shown in the diagram.
The cross-spars are bolted to the uprights every 5 m.
Calculate the length of each of the three cross-spars when the angle at the top of the pylon is 48°.

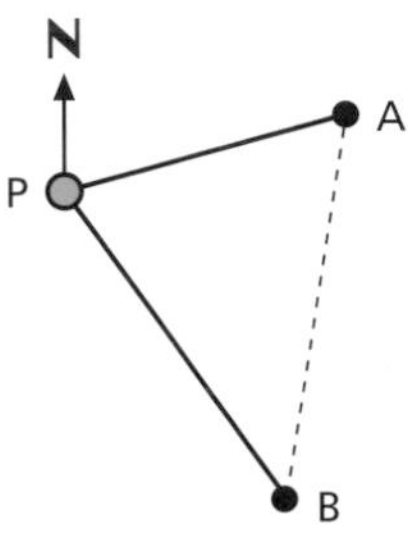

6 Ship A sails from port P on a bearing of 075° for 28 km.
Ship B sails from the port for 36 km on a bearing of 144°.

a Calculate the size of ∠APB.

b Calculate the distance between the two ships.

7

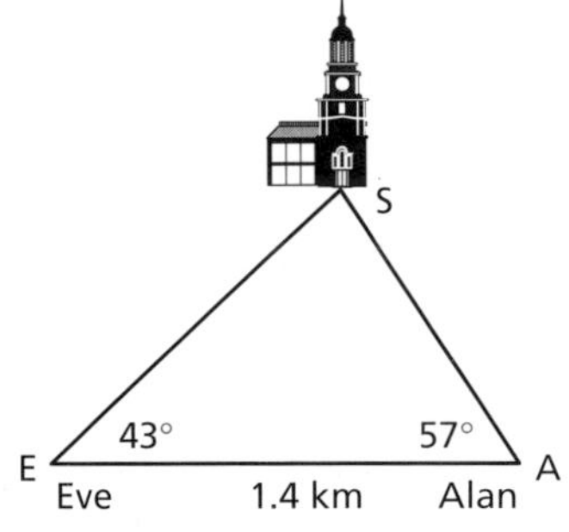

Eve and Alan are standing 1.4 km apart.
They both take a sighting on a steeple.
∠SEA is 43° and ∠SAE is 57°.

a Calculate ∠ESA.

b Calculate the distance from the steeple to:
(i) Eve **(ii)** Alan.

8 The wooden frame of a modern deckchair is shown.
Calculate the size of the four missing angles and the remaining side.

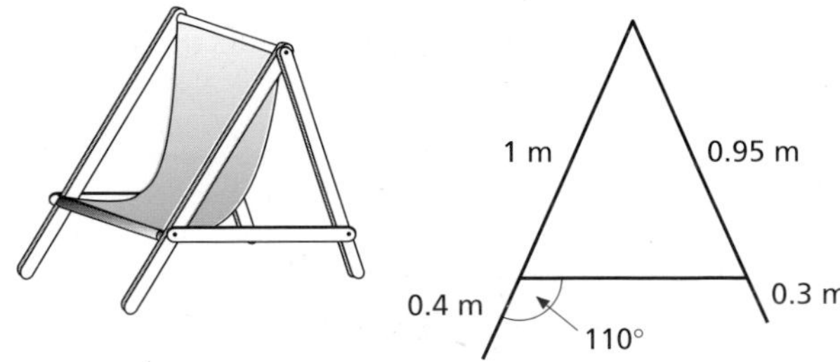

CHAPTER 8 REVIEW

1 Calculate the area of this triangle.

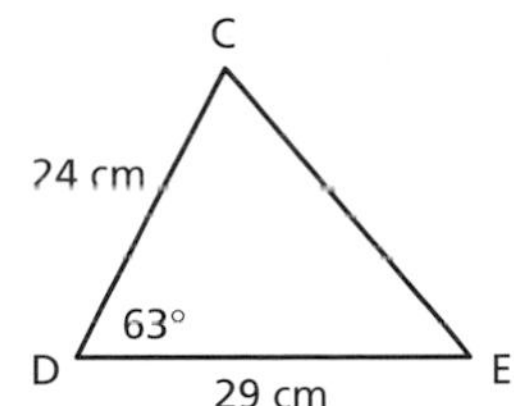

2 The manufacturer of stained glass windows uses two triangular pieces of glass.
   a Calculate the area of each piece of glass.
   b Which has the greater area, and by how much?

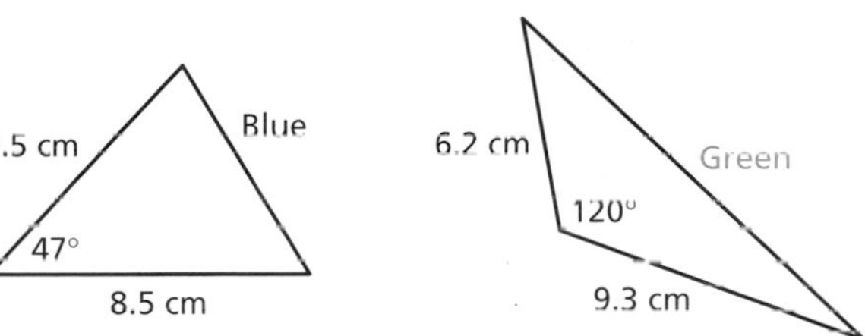

3 Calculate the length of KL.

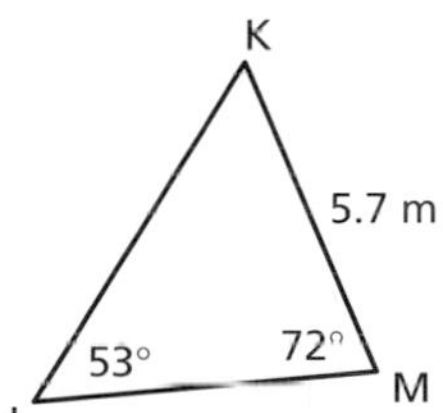

4 Calculate the size of angle FGH.

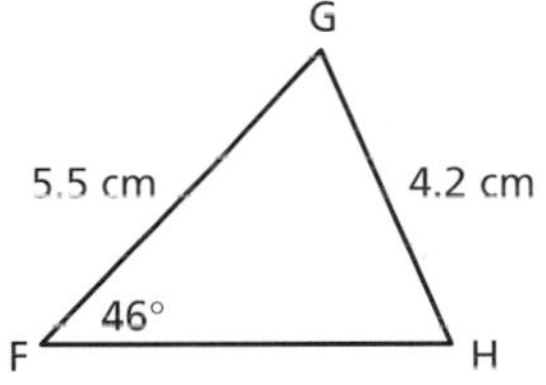

5 The frame for a chair for a lifeguard is triangular in shape.
One leg of the chair is 2.2 m long and makes an angle of 68° with the ground.
The other leg of the chair is 2.4 m long.
What angle does it make with the ground?

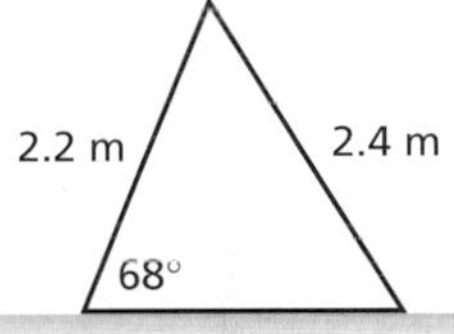

6 A tent pole is held in position by two guyropes.
One rope is 3.2 m long and makes an angle of 55° with the ground.
The other rope makes an angle of 62° with the ground.
How long is the second rope?

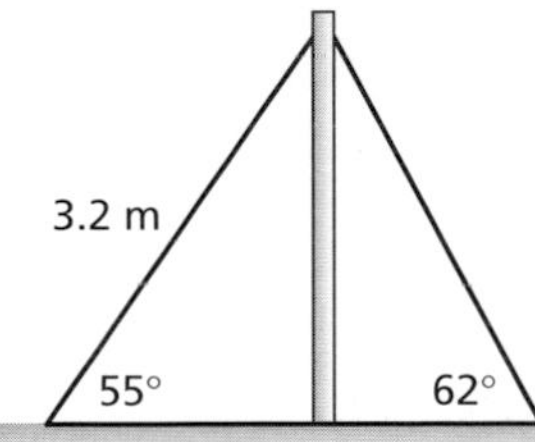

7 Calculate the length of DF.

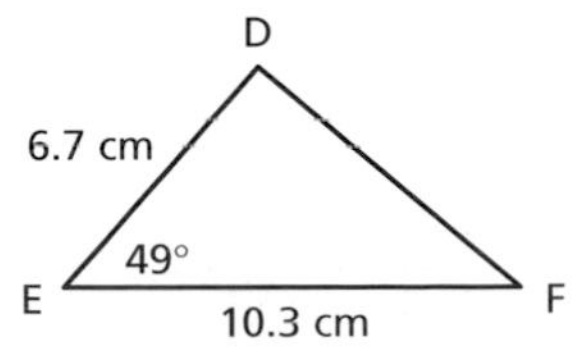

8 Calculate the size of angle PRQ.

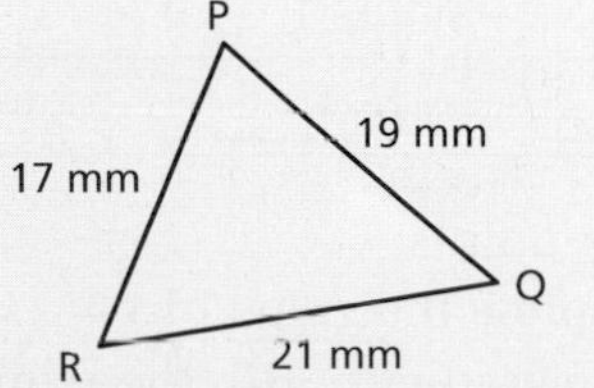

9 Simultaneous Linear Equations

Reminder

The equation $y = ax + b$ can be represented by a straight line which has a gradient of a and passes throught the point $(0, b)$.

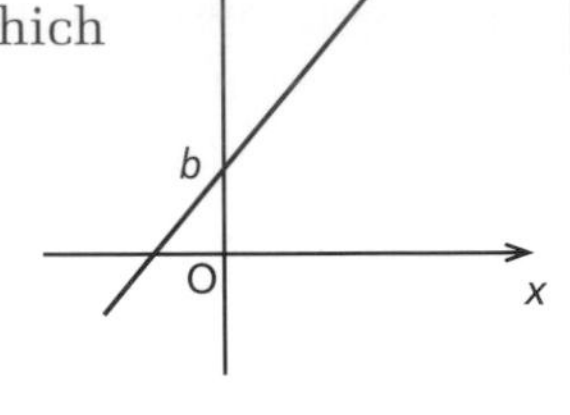

Example

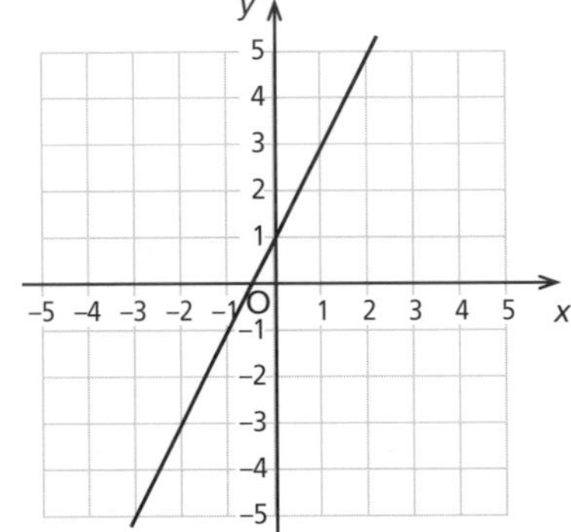

The line $y = 2x + 1$

STARTING POINTS

1 **a** Add the following pairs of terms.

(i) $3x$ and $2x$ **(ii)** $5x$ and $-5x$ **(iii)** $-y$ and $-2y$

(iv) $-m$ and $3m$ **(v)** k and $-5k$

b Subtract the second term from the first term.

(i) $8x$ and $2x$ **(ii)** $8x$ and $-2x$ **(iii)** $2y$ and $8y$

(iv) $-x$ and $-x$ **(v)** $-5y$ and $5y$

2 Calculate the value of:

a y where $y = 100 - 2x$ and $x = 15$

b Q where $Q = 1.6x + 2y$ and $x = 5$ and $y = 4.5$.

3 Solve:

a $2x + 5 = x + 8$ **b** $5x - 2 = 2x + 10$ **c** $7 - 4x = 2x + 19$

4 For $y = 2x + 3$:

a copy and complete the table

x	–3	–2	–1	0	1	2
y						

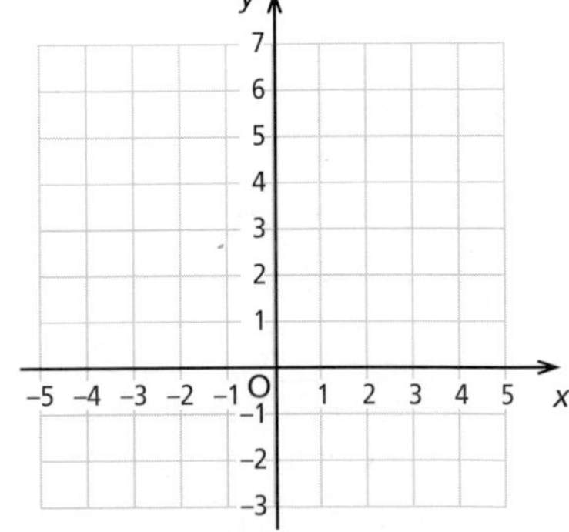

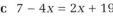

b plot the six points

c hence complete the graph of $y = 2x + 3$

d state **(i)** the gradient **(ii)** the y-intercept of the line.

5 Sketch the graph of:

a $y = x + 1$ **b** $y = 7 - x$ **c** $2x + y = 10$

6 Find formulae for:

a C, the cost in pounds of x CDs at £7 each

b N, the number of litres in a tank after t minutes when it is filling at the rate of 30 litres each minute.

c K, the cost in pounds of a party of a adults and c children going to the cinema when an adult ticket costs £3 and a child ticket costs £2.

Pairs of lines and intersections

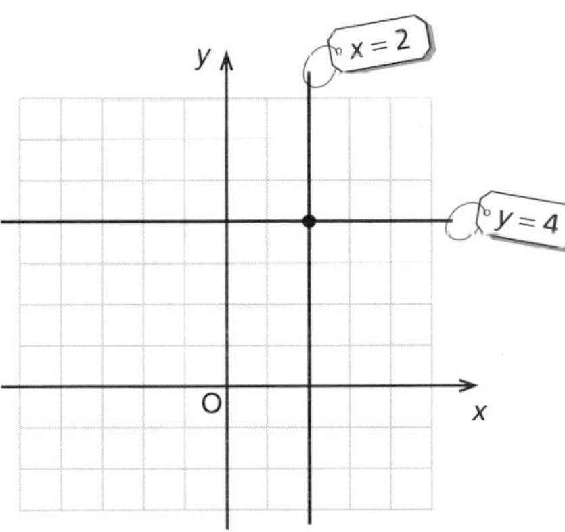

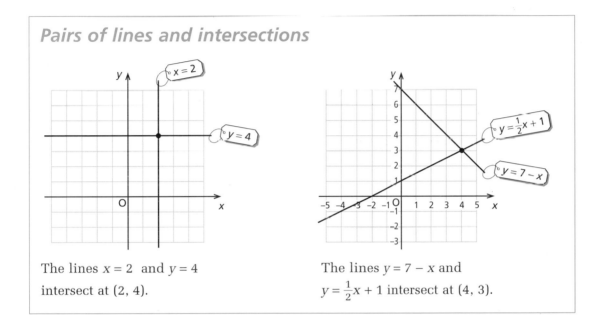

The lines $x = 2$ and $y = 4$ intersect at (2, 4).

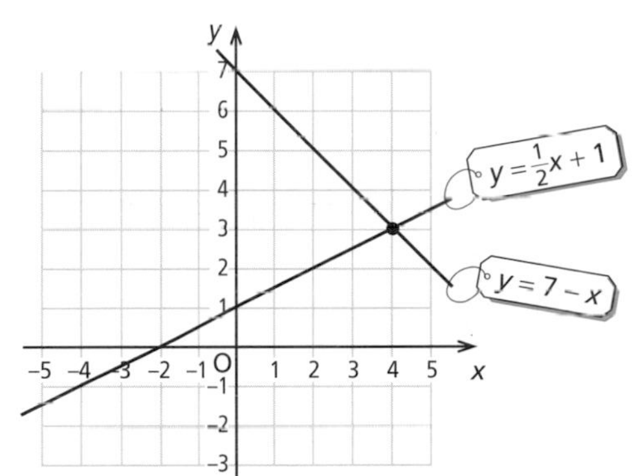

The lines $y = 7 - x$ and $y = \frac{1}{2}x + 1$ intersect at (4, 3).

EXERCISE 1

1 For each pair of equations: **(i)** draw the graphs **(ii)** state the point of intersection.

a $y = 2x + 1$, $y = x - 4$

b $y = 3x - 2$, $y = 6 - x$

c $y = x + 3$, $y = 2x - 1$

d $y = \frac{1}{2}x - 1$, $y = 5 - x$

2 For each equation:

(i) state the coordinates of three points which satisfy it

(ii) plot the points and draw the line.

a $x + y = 4$ **b** $2x + y = 6$ **c** $4x + 5y = 20$ **d** $x - y = 8$

3 For each pair of equations: **(i)** draw the graphs **(ii)** state the point of intersection.

a $x + y = 3$, $2x + y = 4$

b $x + 2y = 4$, $x - y = 1$

c $x + y = 5$, $3x + y = 9$

d $x - y = 8$, $3x + y = 0$

e $y + x = 4$, $y - x = 2$

f $2y - x = 3$, $2y + x = 5$

g $y + 2x = 2$, $2y - x = -6$

h $y - 2x = 1$, $y - x = 7$

i $3x + y - 3 = 0$, $x + 2y + 9 = 0$

j $2y - 3x - 8 = 0$, $2y + 5x + 8 = 0$

k $2y - 3x - 9 = 0$, $y - 3x = 0$

4 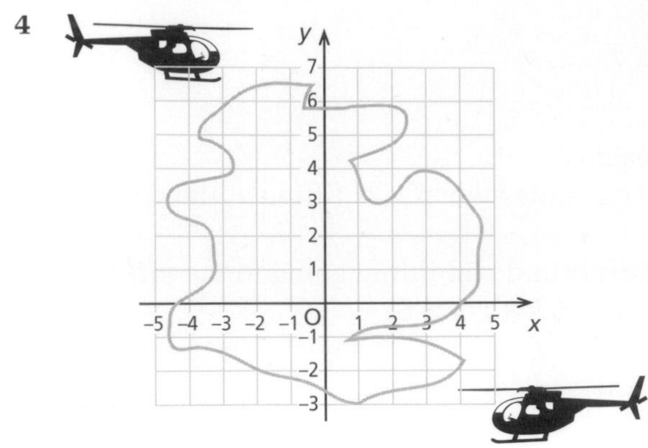

Three helicopters fly over an island. Their routes are straight lines which, with reference to a certain coordinate grid, have equations:

$y = x + 5$

$y = 0.4x + 2$

$y = -0.5x + 2.$

It is important to know where these routes cross.

On a grid like the one shown, draw each line and give the coordinates of the three points of intersection.

5 On a stylised map of the ski slopes, Run 1 is represented by the line $y = 3x - 2$, Run 2 by the line $y = 2 - x$ and Run 3 by $3y - x = 18$. Where do these runs cross?

The point of intersection

Example

Two tanks are being topped up.

Tank 1 has 10 litres of water in it and is being filled at the rate of 3 litres a minute.

Tank 2 has 15 litres to start and is being filled at a rate of 2 litres a minute.

10 litres

15 litres

Tank 1

Tank 2

The volume of water, V litres, after t minutes can be calculated using the formulae:

Tank 1 $V = 10 + 3t$

Tank 2 $V = 15 + 2t$

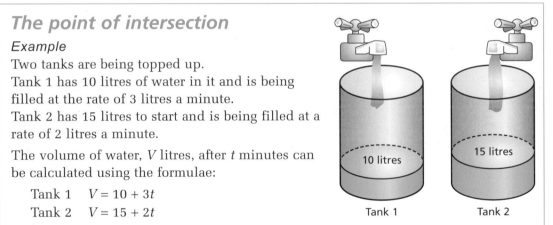

After how many minutes will the two tanks hold the same amount?

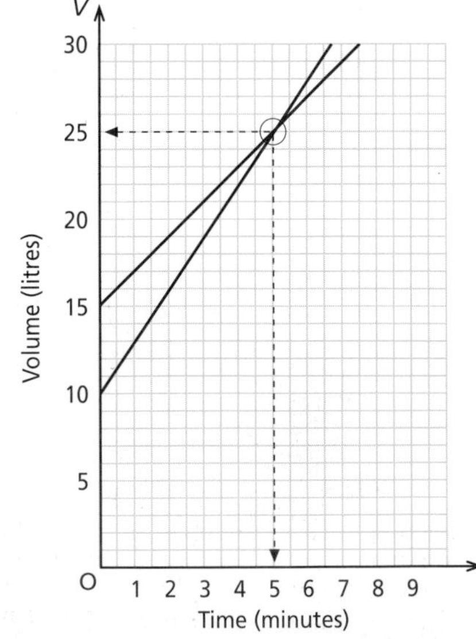

Drawing the lines lets you find the point of intersection, the point where the volumes are the same.

After 5 minutes both tanks contain 25 litres.

EXERCISE 2

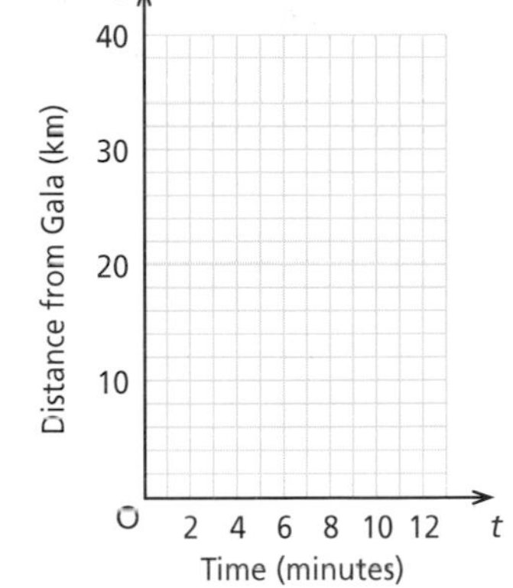

1 Two cars in a vintage car rally set off at noon.
One leaves Stow, a village 10 km from Gala, travelling at 2 km per minute. Its distance, d km, from Gala after t minutes can be calculated using the formula $d = 10 + 2t$.
The other car leaves Heriot, which is 20 km from Gala, travelling at a speed of 1 km per minute. Its distance, d km, from Gala after t minutes can be calculated using the formula $d = 20 + t$.

a Using a grid similar to that shown, draw graphs to represent the progress of both cars.

b By examining the point of intersection say **(i)** when and **(ii)** how far from Gala the cars are when one car overtakes the other.

2

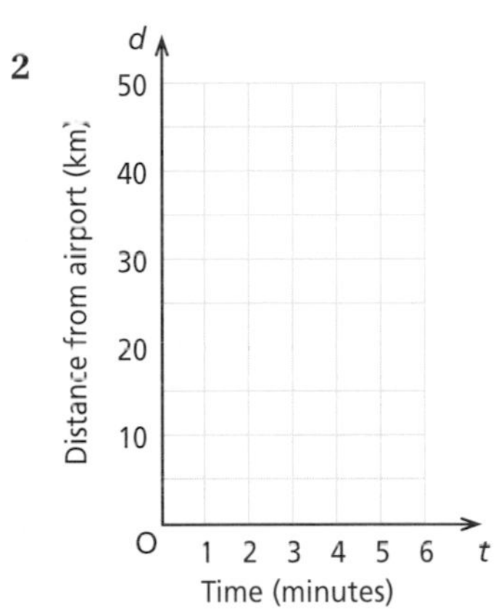

The movements of two aircraft near an airport can be modelled by the equations
$d = 40 - 3t$ (plane 1) and $d = 50 - 5t$ (plane 2)
where d km is the distance from the airport after t minutes of observation.

a Using a grid similar to that shown, draw graphs to represent the movements of the planes.

b **(i)** When are the two aircraft the same distance from the airport?
(ii) What is this distance?

3 The way two tanks are filled can be modelled by the equations:

Tank 1 $V = 5 + 4t$

Tank 2 $V = 15 + 2t$

where V litres is the volume in the tank after t minutes.

a Draw graphs to illustrate the tanks filling over a period of 6 minutes.

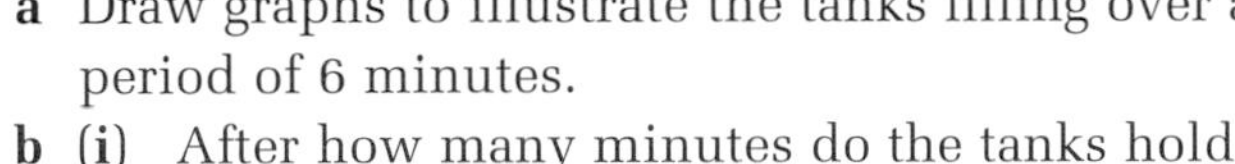

b **(i)** After how many minutes do the tanks hold the same volume?
(ii) What is this volume?

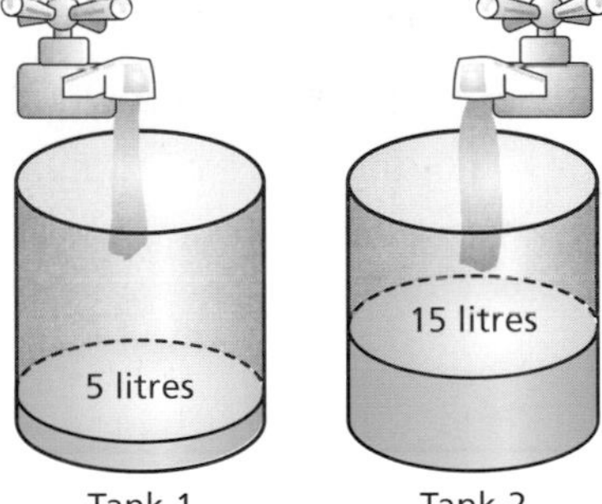

4 A botanist experiments with different plant nutrients. She models the growth of two different plants by the equations:

Plant 1 $L = 20 + 4t$

Plant 2 $L = 12 + 6t$

where L cm is the length of the plant after t days.

a Draw both lines on a suitable grid.

b **(i)** After how many days are the plants the same length?
(ii) What is this length?

5 A candlemaker experiments with different waxes.
A 10 cm candle made from wax type 1 burns according to the model $L = 10 - t$. A 15 cm candle made from wax type 2 burns according to the model $L = 15 - 3t$.
In both cases L cm is the length of the candle after t hours.

a Draw a graph to illustrate these models.
b What information can we get by examining the point of intersection of the two lines?

6

Two petrol tankers are being emptied.
ACCO unloads at the rate of 200 litres per minute.
TTT unloads at the rate of 150 litres per minute.

a ACCO starts with 1200 litres. Write down a formula for the volume, V litres, of petrol left in the tanker after t minutes.
b TTT starts with 900 litres. Write down a similar formula for the volume, V litres, of petrol left in the tanker after t minutes.
c Draw graphs of these volumes over the first 6 minutes.
d What information can we get by examining the point of intersection of the two lines?

7 When two balloonists are first observed, one is on the ground and the other is 14 m up. The one on the ground rises at a steady rate of 6 metres per minute. The other rises at a rate of 2 metres per minute.

a Write down a formula for the height, H m, of each balloon after t minutes.
b Draw graphs to illustrate these equations.
c Describe the moment when both balloons are at the same height.

8 Two planes are flying towards an airport. The table gives details of each flight from when observations began.

	Distance from airport	Speed
Plane 1	22 km	5 km/min
Plane 2	15 km	3 km/min

a Write down a formula for the distance, D km, of each aircraft from the airport after t minutes.
b With the aid of graphs, find when both planes are the same distance from the airport.

Problem solving with simultaneous equations

On a bus trip the Green family (2 adults and 3 children) paid a total of £12.
On the same trip the Whytes (1 adult and 1 child) paid £5.
What is the cost for **(i)** an adult **(ii)** a child?

Since we don't know these costs we let £x represent the cost of an adult and £y represent the cost of a child, giving us the two equations:

$$2x + 3y = 12$$
$$x + y = 5$$

Picking suitable points helps us draw the lines.

For $2x + 3y = 12$
when $x = 0$ then $y = 4$
when $y = 0$ then $x = 6$

For $x + y = 5$
when $x = 0$ then $y = 5$
when $y = 0$ then $x = 5$

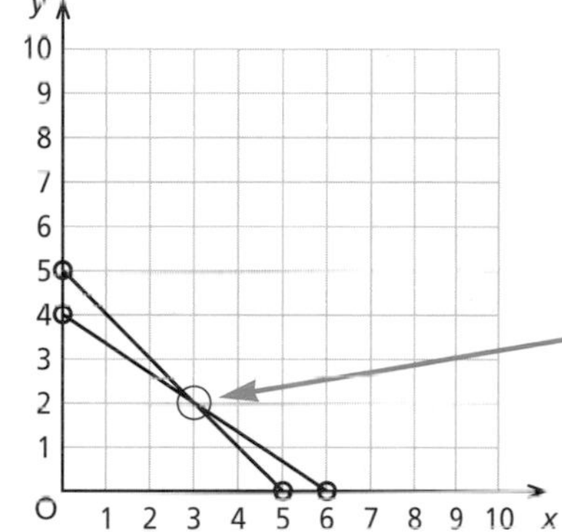

The one point which is on both lines gives us the set of values for x and y which fit both equations simultaneously.

$x = 3$ and $y = 2$

It costs £3 for an adult and £2 for a child.

EXERCISE 3

1 Pantomime tickets for 3 adults and 1 child cost £15.
Tickets for 1 adult and 2 children cost £10.

- **a** If an adult's ticket costs £x and a child's ticket costs £y, then the first statement leads to the equation $3x + y = 15$.
  Write down the equation to which the second statement leads.
- **b** Graph both equations and find the coordinates of the point of intersection.
- **c** State the cost of
  - **(i)** 1 adult
  - **(ii)** 1 child
  - **(iii)** 6 adults and 3 children.

2 Passengers travelling by public transport through a city take the bus and the Tube. Both modes of transport charge by the kilometre.

- **a** 4 km by Tube and 2 km by bus costs £7. This leads to the equation $4x + 2y = 7$.
  Explain carefully what x and y stand for.
- **b** 2 km by Tube and 6 km by bus costs £6. Write this as an equation in x and y.
- **c** By examining the intersection of two lines find the cost per kilometre of each mode of transport.
- **d** What is the cost of a 10 km journey, the first half of which is by Tube and the rest by bus?

3 A fertiliser is made by blending together two ingredients, Fastgrow and Greendip. Different blends produce different effects.
Blend A: 4 cups of Fastgrow and 3 cups of Greendip costs 20p.
Blend B: 2 cups of Fastgrow and 5 cups of Greendip costs 17p.

a If a cup of Fastgrow costs x pence and a cup of Greendip costs y pence, write down two different equations in x and y.

b By considering the intersection of two lines find the value of x and y.

c How much would a blend of 6 cups of Fastgrow with 1 cup of Greendip cost?

4

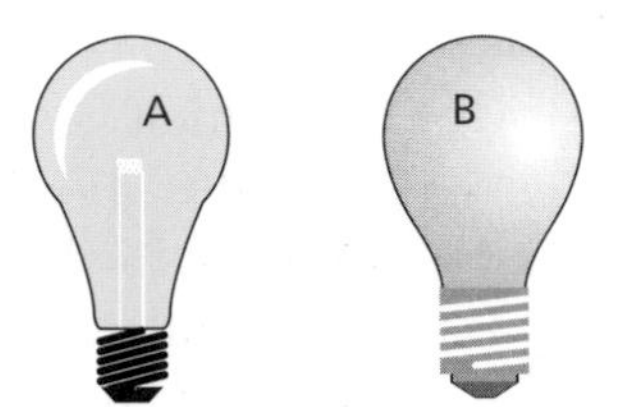

Two types of bulbs are set up on a test bench to see how efficient each is. The number of units each uses is measured.

On day 1, type A burns for 6 hours and type B for 5 hours.
The total number of units burned is 14.

On day 2, type A burns for 8 hours and type B for 3 hours.
The total number of units burned is 15.

Let type A burn x units per hour and type B burn y units per hour.

a Write down two equations in x and y.

b Make use of graphs to calculate the values of x and y.

c How many units are used if both bulbs burn for 24 hours?

5 Whole City Food Packers produce two nut mixes for their retail outlets.
Tropicana: 3 kg of pecan nuts and 4 kg of pistachios; total cost £25.
Crunch mix: 2 kg of pecan nuts and 5 kg of pistachios; total cost £26.
A third mix is suggested, Supernut: 5 kg of pecan nuts and 2 kg of pistachios.
How much will this new mix cost?

Solving simultaneous equations by substitution

It may not always be convenient to draw a graph.
Sometimes an algebraic method may be preferred.

Example

Solve the pair of equations $y = x + 1$ and $2y - 5x + 4 = 0$ simultaneously.

$y = x + 1$ .... ①

$2y - 5x + 4 = 0$ .... ②

Label them for easy reference.

Equation 1 tells us that y can be replaced by $x + 1$.
Do this in equation 2.

$2(x + 1) - 5x + 4 = 0$
$\Rightarrow 2x + 2 - 5x + 4 = 0$
$\Rightarrow 6 - 3x = 0$
$\Rightarrow 3x = 6$
$\Rightarrow x = 2$

This method is called **substitution**: y has been substituted by $x + 1$.

Equation 1 tells us that $y = x + 1$
$\Rightarrow y = 2 + 1$
$\Rightarrow y = 3$

Now check that this pair of values fit equation 2:

$2 \times 3 - 5 \times 2 + 4 = 0$ ✓

EXERCISE 4

1 Solve each pair of equations simultaneously. Use the method of substitution.

a $y = x - 1$ .... ①
$2y + x = 4$ .... ②

b $y = 2x$ .... ①
$3y - x = 15$....................... ②

c $x = y + 3$ .... ①
$3y - 2x = 1$ .... ②

d $y = 2x + 1$......................... ①
$y = x - 3$.......................... ②

e $y = 3x - 1$
$5x - y = 3$

f $y = 4x + 1$
$3y - 2x = 23$

g $x = 2y + 1$
$3y + 2x = 16$

h $y = 5 - 2x$
$2y - 3x = 17$

i $y = 2x - 3$
$4x - y = 15$

2 By first rearranging equation 1 into the form '$y = \ldots$' or '$x = \ldots$', solve the following simultaneous equations by substitution.

a $y - 2x = 3$
$3y - 2x = 17$

b $5y + x = 3$
$7y - x = 21$

c $8x - y = 3$
$2x - y = 3$

d $3x - y = 2$
$2x - y = - 1$

e $4x + y + 7 = 0$
$2y - 3x - 8 = 0$

f $y - 4x - 3 = 5$
$y + 7x - 30 = 0$

3 Part of Kiran's journey is by road and the rest is cross-country. Clue number 1: the distance by road is 3 km more than the cross-country distance. Clue number 2: the total distance to his destination is 13 km.

a Let x km be the distance by road and y km be the distance cross-country. Write down an equation in x and y which represents: **(i)** clue 1 **(ii)** clue 2.

b Solve the pair of equations simultaneously by substitution to help you describe the journey fully.

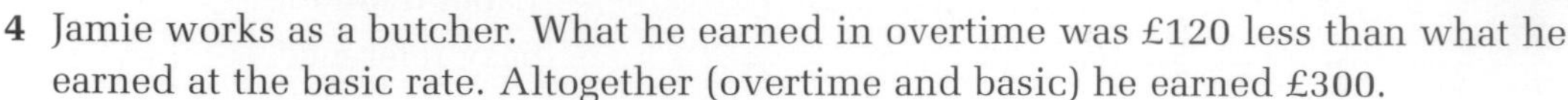

4 Jamie works as a butcher. What he earned in overtime was £120 less than what he earned at the basic rate. Altogether (overtime and basic) he earned £300.

a Let £x represent his overtime earnings. Let £y represent his basic earnings. Write down two equations in x and y.

b Solve these equations to find how much he earned:
(i) in overtime **(ii)** as a basic wage.

5 There are three times as many children as adults on a bus. An adult pays £3 and a child pays £2. The total fare collected is £54. Let x represent the number of adults on the bus. Let y represent the number of children.

a Write down two equations in x and y using the information given.

b Solve the equations simultaneously to find how many
(i) adults **(ii)** children are on the bus.

6 In one year Jenny's grandfather will be three times as old as she is just now. The difference between their ages is 41 years.

a Form a pair of simultaneous equations to model the situation.

b Solve the equations to find the age of each person.

7 In a snooker demonstration Jack Brown plays 12 games. He is a professional and is paid for each game he plays. He is paid £20 when he wins a game and £5 if he loses. Altogether he earns £180 for the 12 games.

a Letting x represent the number of games won and y the number lost, form a pair of simultaneous equations in x and y.

b Solve the equations simultaneously to to help you describe how Jack got on.

8 A hamburger stall sold coffee and hamburger rolls. If they had sold just 4 more coffees than they did then they would have sold twice as many coffees as rolls. Rolls cost £2 and coffees cost £1. They sold £100 worth of goods.
How many **a** coffees **b** rolls did they sell?

9 Sarah plans a 300 mile journey travelling on both a motorway and A roads. She estimates that at 70 mph on the motorway and 50 mph on the A roads it will take her a total of 5 hours.
Let x hours represent the time she expects to be on the motorway and y hours represent the time on the A roads.
Describe the planned journey giving **(i)** times **(ii)** distances.

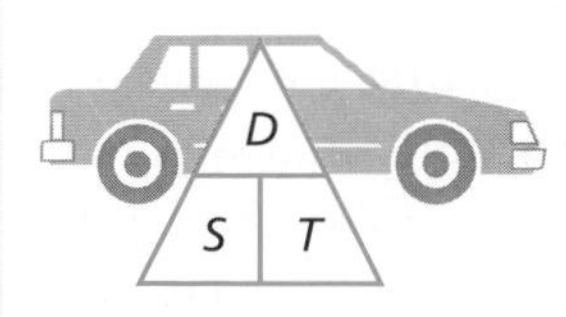

Solving simultaneous equations by elimination

Two types of cakes are shown: cream tops and toffee tops.
Can you use the clues to find the weight of each type?

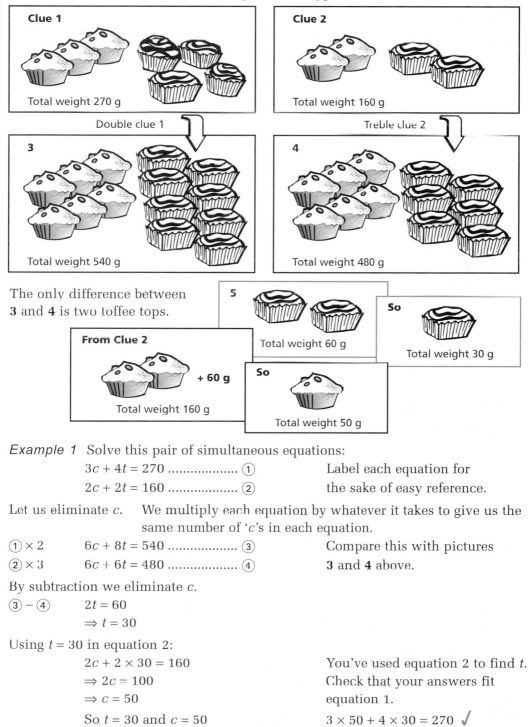

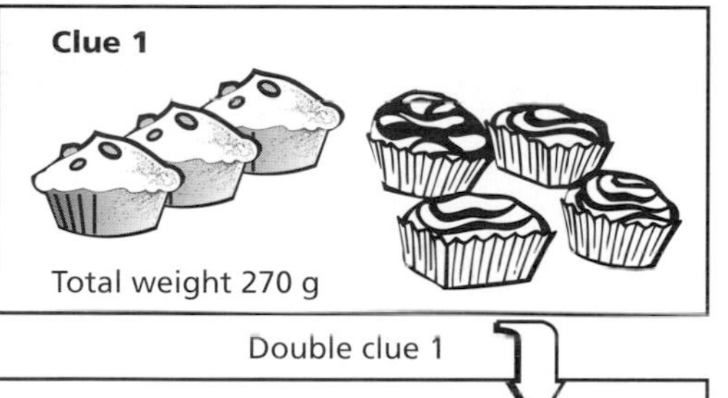

Double clue 1

Treble clue 2

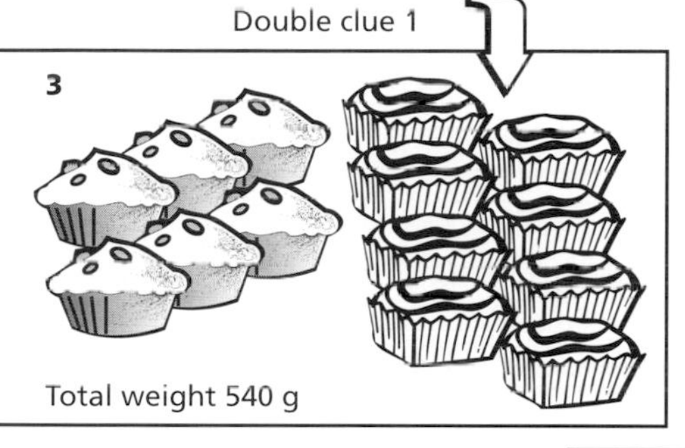

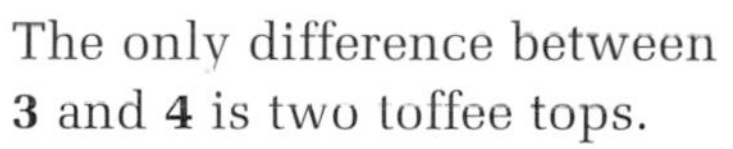

The only difference between **3** and **4** is two toffee tops.

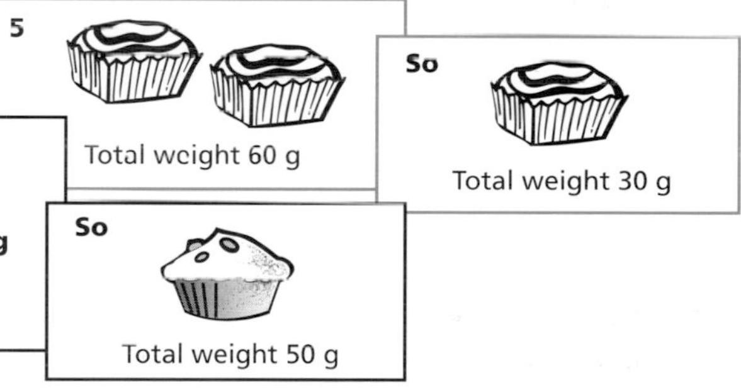

Example 1 Solve this pair of simultaneous equations:

$3c + 4t = 270$ .... ① Label each equation for

$2c + 2t = 160$ .... ② the sake of easy reference.

Let us eliminate c. We multiply each equation by whatever it takes to give us the same number of 'c's in each equation.

① × 2 $6c + 8t = 540$ .... ③ Compare this with pictures

② × 3 $6c + 6t = 480$ .... ④ **3** and **4** above.

By subtraction we eliminate c.

③ − ④ $2t = 60$

$\Rightarrow t = 30$

Using $t = 30$ in equation 2:

$2c + 2 \times 30 = 160$

$\Rightarrow 2c = 100$

$\Rightarrow c = 50$

So $t = 30$ and $c = 50$

You've used equation 2 to find t. Check that your answers fit equation 1.

$3 \times 50 + 4 \times 30 = 270$ ✓

Example 2 Solve this pair of equations simultaneously:

$2a - 3b = 1$ .... ①
$7a + b = 15$ .... ②

Label each equation for the sake of easy reference.

① × 1 $2a - 3b = 1$ .... ① ... leaving 1 untouched.

② × 3 $21a + 3b = 45$ .... ④

④ + ① $23a = 46$
$\Rightarrow a = 2$

Note that it is more convenient to add to eliminate b here.

Using $a = 2$ in equation 2: $7 \times 2 + b = 15$
$\Rightarrow b = 1$
So $a = 2$ and $b = 1$

EXERCISE 5

1 In the following pairs of simultaneous equations
(i) add or subtract to eliminate one variable
(ii) solve the equations.

a $2x + y = 5$, $x - y = 1$
b $4x + 2y = 14$, $2x - 2y = 4$
c $5x + 3y = 4$, $2x - 3y = 10$
d $-2x + 3y = 5$, $2x - y = 1$
e $3x + 2y = 8$, $x + 2y = 4$
f $5x + 3y = 20$, $3x + 3y = 6$
g $2x - 3y = 3$, $5x - 3y = 12$
h $4x + y = 14$, $4x + 3y = 26$
i $3x + 5y = 7$, $3x - 2y = 14$

Careful: $5y - (-2y) = 7y$

j $2x + y = 15$, $2x - 2y = 0$
k $7x - 2y = 3$, $7x + 5y = 17$
l $3x - y = 4$, $-5x - y = -4$
m $5x - 2y = 3$, $2x - 2y = 6$
n $a + b = 10$, $a - b = 4$
o $2m - n = 5$, $m - n = 2$
p $4x - 3y = 22$, $x - 3y = 1$
q $2p + 5q = 6$, $2p - 2q = -1$
r $3x - 4y = 1$, $-x + 4y = 13$

2 In the following pairs of simultaneous equations:
(i) multiply by whatever it takes to prepare one variable for elimination
(ii) add or subtract to eliminate one variable
(iii) solve the equations.

a $x + 4y = 9$, $2x - 2y = 3$
b $3a + 4b = 3$, $a - 8b = 1$
c $4x - 2y = 3$, $x + 4y = 3$
d $2m + 2n = 5$, $4m - n = 5$
e $d - 3e = -2$, $2d + e = 3$
f $5x - y = 1$, $x + 2y = -2$
g $6x + 2y = 1$, $2x + y = 0$
h $10x + y = -3$, $2x + 2y = 3$
i $3u - 8v = 11$, $u + 2v = -1$
j $3x + y = 12$, $10x - 3y = 40$
k $4a - 3b = 5$, $14a + 2b = 5$
l $4m - 6n = 7$, $5m - 8n = 8$

3 Solve the following pairs of simultaneous equations.

a $a = 2b + 1$ $a + b = 10$	**b** $3x + 2y = 8$ $x - y = 1$	**c** $5x - 6y = 12$ $2x - 6y = 3$
d $y = 4x - 1$ $2x - 3y = 23$	**e** $15d + 2e = 4$ $2d + e = 2$	**f** $3u + 2v = 2$ $2u + 3v = -2$
g $2x + y = 3$ $y = 5 - 4x$	**h** $a + 7b = 11$ $a - 3b = -4$	**i** $3w + 5y - 2 = 0$ $5w + 5y - 3 = 0$

4 An order of 3 hamburgers and 2 portions of chips came to £4.10.
A second order of 4 hamburgers and 3 portions of chips cost £5.70.
Let h pence represent the cost of 1 hamburger.
Let c pence represent the cost of a portion of chips.

a Write down two equations in h and c.

b Solve the equations simultaneously to find the cost of:
(i) a hamburger **(ii)** a portion of chips.

5 At a car factory a nose-to-tail queue of 4 model As and 6 model Bs is 34 m long.
A nose-to-tail queue of 5 model As and 2 model Bs is 26 m long.
Let a metres represent the length of a model A car.
Let b metres represent the length of a model B car.

a Write down two equations in a and b.

b Solve the equations simultaneously to find the length of:
(i) a model A **(ii)** a model B car.

6 The total cost of 5 second class and 7 first class stamps is 275 pence.
The total cost of 3 second class and 2 first class stamps is 110 pence.
By forming a suitable pair of simultaneous equations find the cost of:

a a first class stamp **b** a second class stamp.

7 With 4 Easytone cassettes and 3 Suresound cassettes we can record 540 minutes of music. With 2 of each type we can record 300 minutes.
How much can be recorded with 1 Easytone and 5 Suresound cassettes?

8 Three courses of brick make a wall 270 mm high. Four courses of brick make a wall 365 mm high.

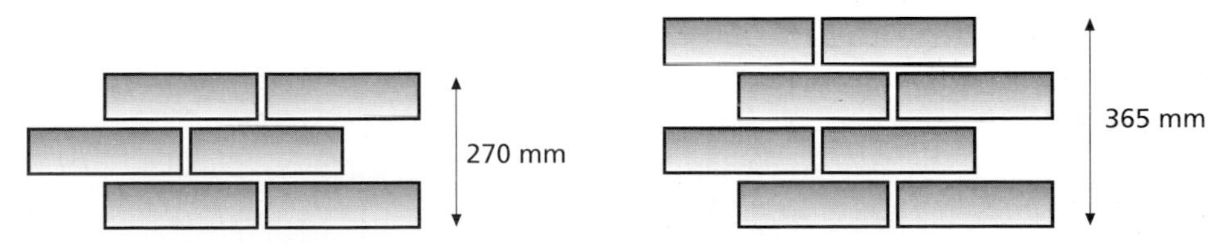

a If we assume that the bricklayer can keep the cement layers of equal thickness, calculate:
(i) the thickness of a brick and **(ii)** the thickness of a cement layer.

b How high will a ten course wall be?

CHAPTER 9 REVIEW

1 Two coaches are travelling to Aberdeen.
The first coach averages 80 km/h and starts 400 km from Aberdeen.
Its progress can be modelled by the equation $d = 400 - 80t$ where d km is the distance from Aberdeen after t hours.

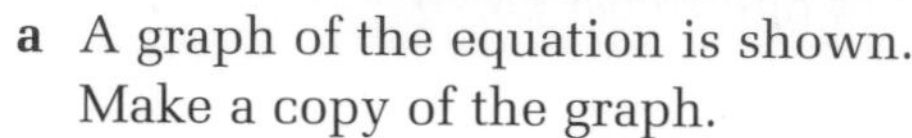

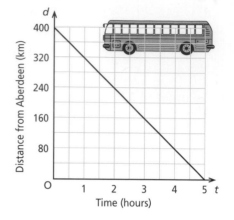

a A graph of the equation is shown. Make a copy of the graph.

b How far is coach 1 from Aberdeen an hour and a half into the journey?

c Coach 2 starts 240 km from Aberdeen and averages 40 km/h.

(i) Write down an equation to model its progress.

(ii) Draw its graph on your diagram.

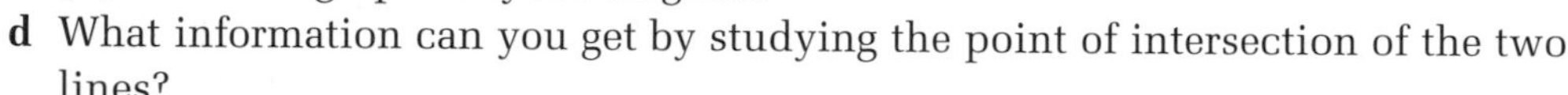

d What information can you get by studying the point of intersection of the two lines?

2 Solve each pair of simultaneous equations graphically.

a $y = 2x + 3$
$y = 12 - x$

b $2x + 5y = 20$
$2x - y = 8$

3 In the Bistro Bar, customers at one table ordered 3 glasses of wine and 2 coffees. Their bill came to £12.
At another table 4 glasses of wine and 4 coffees were ordered. This cost £18.

a What happened at the first table can be modelled by $3x + 2y = 12$. Explain what x and y stand for.

b Write down an equation to model what happened at table 2.

c Draw suitable graphs and write down the coordinates of the point of intersection.

d What is the cost of:

(i) a glass of wine

(ii) a cup of coffee

(iii) an order for 5 wines and 3 coffees?

4 Solve:

a by substitution $y = 5x - 2$
$3y - 2x = 33$

b by elimination $3x - 5y = 11$
$4x + 3y = 5$

c by the most suitable method

(i) $y = 3 - x$
$3x - 5y = 9$

(ii) $2x + 3y = 16$
$4x - 9y = 2$

(iii) $3a + 5b = -1$
$2a - 3b = 12$

10 Graphs, Charts and Tables

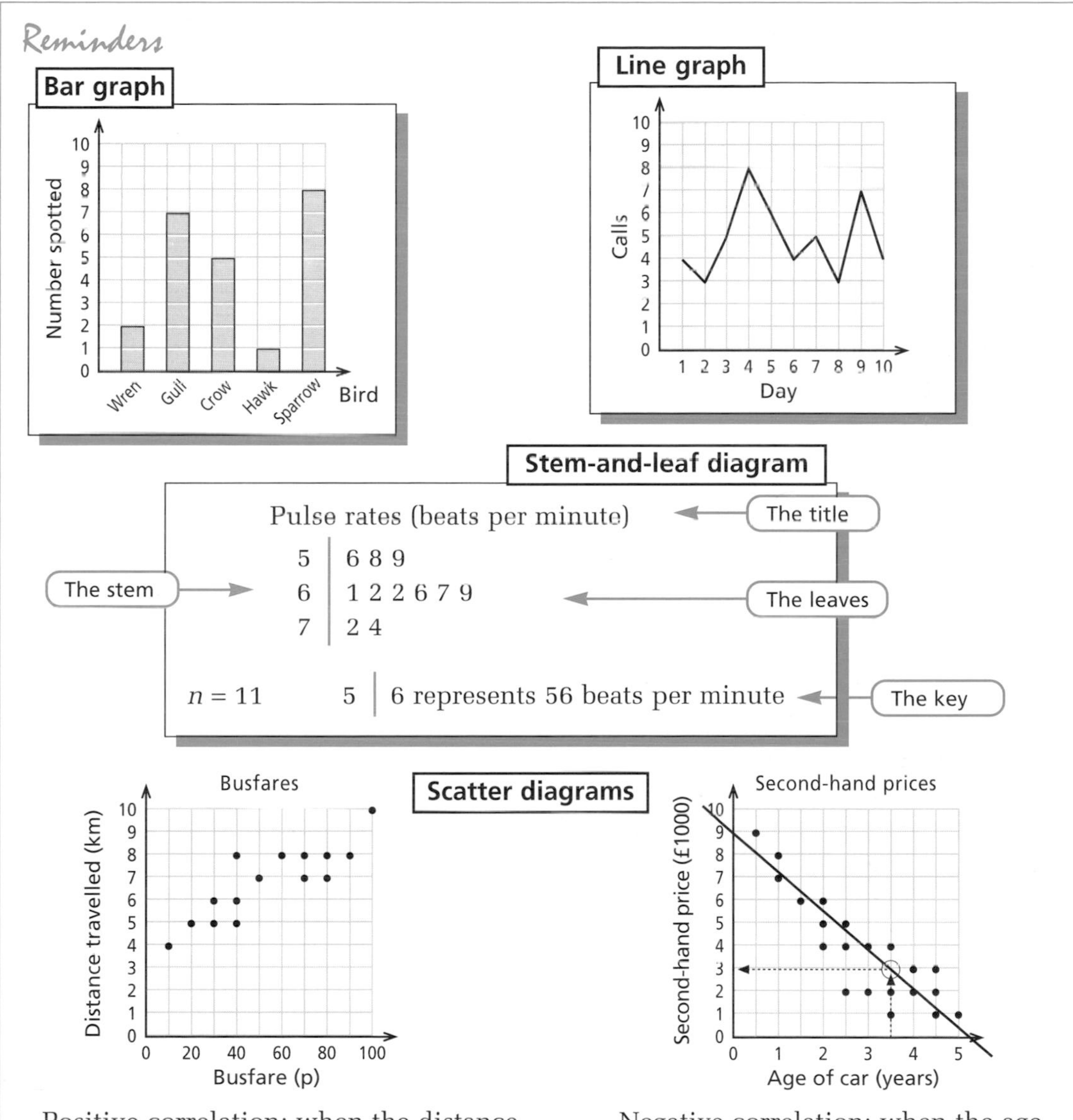

Positive correlation: when the distance increases, the fare increases.

Negative correlation: when the age increases, the price decreases.

Using our judgement we have drawn the best-fitting straight line on the second scatter diagram. We try to draw a line which:

a highlights the trend of the points

b has roughly the same number of points above as below it.

We can use the line to estimate the price of a car given its age.

STARTING POINTS

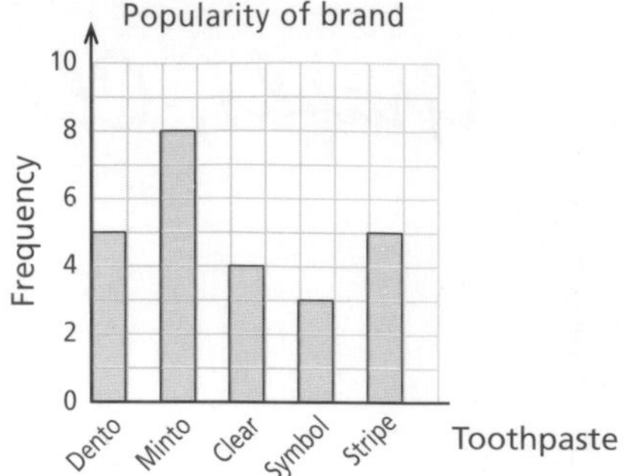

1 A quick survey in a supermarket on shoppers' preferred brand of toothpaste produced this bar chart.

a Which was the most popular brand?
b How many people preferred Symbol?
c How many people were questioned?
d What fraction preferred Stripe?

2 To administer the council tax, local authorities place homes into groups labelled A to H. Band A is the cheapest and band H is the dearest. An official lists the bands for homes in a particular area:

B C C A B B B C C D C D
C B B D D D E E D D D D
E F F D D C C C E E F F
B B B C C D D C C B A A
D D C C F F G G E E D D
H D F F B B C C C B B B

a Make a tally chart and find the total frequency for each band.
b Draw a bar chart to show this data.
c Which band is the mode?

3

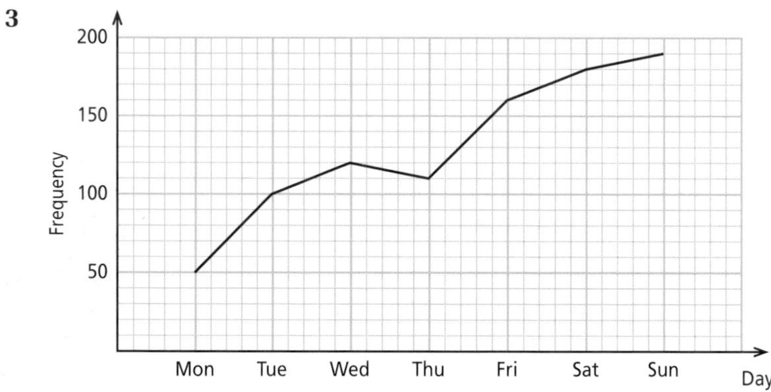

A mill has been turned into an industrial museum. The attendance figures for one week of the tourist season are illustrated in the line graph.

a How many attended on Wednesday?
b What is the mean attendance per day?
c Describe the trend.
d In one week out of season the attendance figures were as follows.

Mon	Tue	Wed	Thu	Fri	Sat	Sun
20	10	30	40	40	100	120

(i) Draw a line graph to illustrate these figures.
(ii) What features do the out-of-season and the in-season figures share?

4 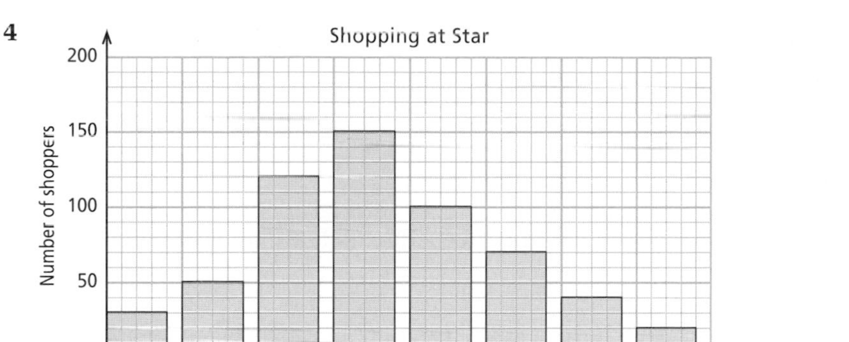

The bar graph gives the lengths of time customers say they take to do their shopping at Star supermarket.

a Which time is the mode?

b What is **(i)** the shortest **(ii)** the longest length of time on the graph?

c Use **b** to calculate the range of times spent shopping.

d How many customers say they spend over one hour in the supermarket?

5 The police set up a speed check in a 30 mph zone.
They noted the speeds correct to the nearest 10 miles per hour.

Speed (mph)	10	20	30	40	50
Number of cars	5	7	18	9	1

a Draw a line graph to illustrate the table.

b Which speed is the mode?

c How many motorists were recorded as doing 40 mph or more?

6 Market gardeners are testing a new variety of pea. The lengths of the pods are measured after picking.
The stem plot shows the results.

a What is **(i)** the longest
(ii) the shortest length?

b Which level has the most data?

c Which length occurred the most often?

d What is the length of the eighth longest pod?

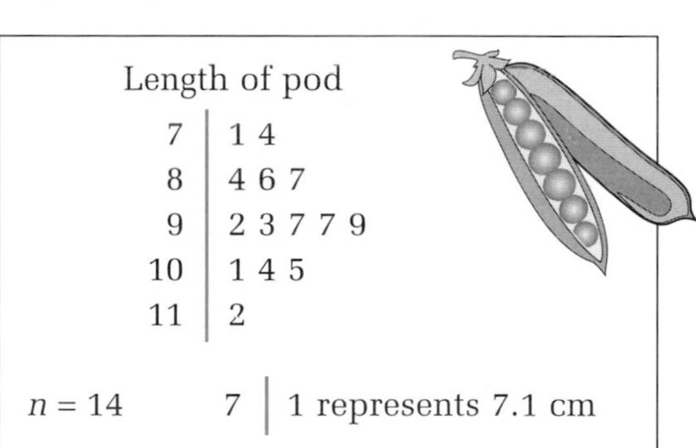

Length of pod

7	1 4
8	4 6 7
9	2 3 7 7 9
10	1 4 5
11	2

$n = 14$ 7 | 1 represents 7.1 cm

7 A check is made on the length of time spent on the phone in an office. Sixteen calls are monitored. The length of time of each is recorded to the nearest minute.

22 45 18 11 35 26 22 19
16 33 29 28 30 17 26 47

a Copy and complete this stem-and-leaf diagram.

b Calculate the range of these call lengths.

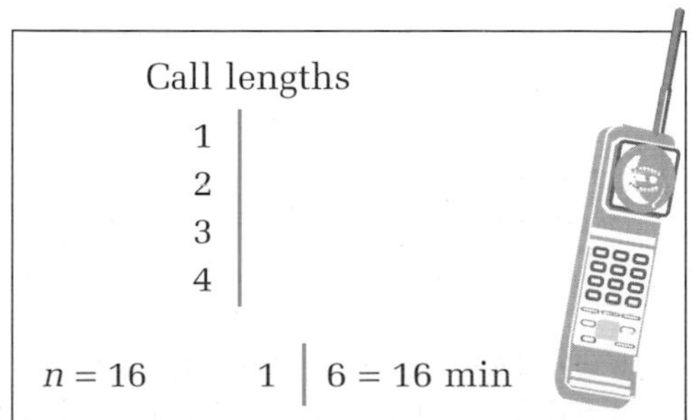

Call lengths

1	
2	
3	
4	

$n = 16$ 1 | 6 = 16 min

8 At the driving range a golfer records how many yards he can strike the ball.

108 115 132 121 141 122 138 127 165 142

118 127 149 120 139 136 131 141 111 129

137 110 101 103 118 122 154 146 131 126

Draw a stem-and-leaf diagram to illustrate the data.

9 The number of hours of TV watched, Monday to Friday, is tabulated along with the maths scores for ten students.

Candidate	A	B	C	D	E	F	G	H	I	J
Hours of TV	40	35	28	20	30	15	24	10	10	15
Maths mark	0	10	30	70	10	20	40	70	80	60

a On a suitable grid, make a scatter diagram from the data in the table.

b Is the correlation between score and hours of TV positive or negative?

10 A survey is done of wasps around a school. The number of wasps caught in collecting jars is noted. The date is recorded as a decimal, 7.5 being halfway through July.

The scatter diagram shows what is found.

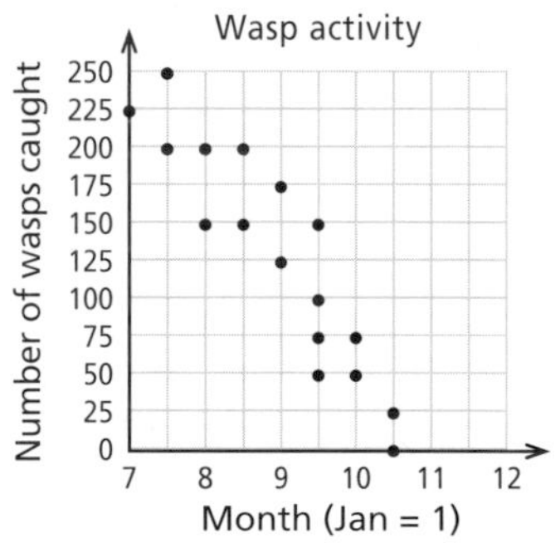

a Describe the correlation between the number of wasps and the date.

b Identify the best-fitting straight line. Use it to estimate how many wasps may be caught mid August.

c 115 wasps are collected one day. Which month was that most likely to be?

11 Ten students with part-time jobs are asked to say how many hours a week they work and how much they earn. The table shows their replies.

Student	A	B	C	D	E	F	G	H	I	J
Hours worked	5	8	8	10	9	6	5	8	6	11
Wage (£)	14	18	14	28	32	16	10	24	12	34

a On a grid like the one shown, draw a scatter diagram to illustrate the table.

b Draw the best-fitting straight line on your diagram.

c Use this line to estimate:

(i) the wage to expect for 7 hours of work

(ii) the hours you would need to work to earn £25.

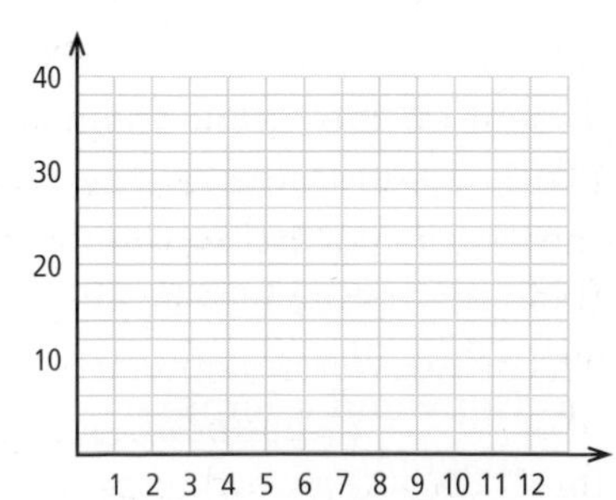

12

Record	1	2	3	4	5	6	7	8	9	10	11	12
Beaufort scale	1	4	6	2	5	7	3	8	4	9	10	11
Speed (mph)	3	19	30	10	26	38	15	50	17	55	63	70

Peter collects weather statistics. He records the wind speed at 12 different times. By listening to weather reports he is able to find out the strength of the wind as measured on the Beaufort Scale. The table shows his findings.

a With suitable axes draw a scatter diagram to illustrate the table.

b Draw the best-fitting straight line on your diagram.

c Use this line to estimate:

(i) the Beaufort number when the windspeed is 40 mph.

(ii) the windspeed when the Beauford number is given as 7.

Relative frequency

A supermarket keeps a record of wine sales, noting the country of origin of each bottle. The frequency table shows one day's sales.

Country	Frequency
France	120
Australia	30
Italy	27
Spain	24
Germany	18
Others	21
Total	240

120 of the bottles sold were French wines.

It may be of more interest that half of the sales were French.

120 ÷ 240 = 0.5

When we divide the frequency by the total frequency we get the *relative frequency.*

Country	Frequency	Relative frequency
France	120	0.5
Australia	30	0.125
Italy	27	0.1125
Spain	24	0.1
Germany	18	0.075
Others	21	0.0875
Total	240	1

Note the total of the relative frequencies is always 1.

The relative frequency is needed when you want to draw a pie chart.

If the supermarket wished to order 1000 bottles of wine they may start by assuming that the relative frequencies are fixed and order 500 French wines, 125 Australian wines, etc.

1000×0.5
1000×0.125

The relative frequency can be used as a measure of the likelihood of some event happening, e.g. when a customer comes in for wines half the time you would expect them to ask for French wine.

EXERCISE 1

1 The table gives a breakdown of the 5 hours of sport broadcast one Saturday on a particular channel. At the end of each minute the sport which was on was noted.

Sport	Frequency (min)	Relative frequency
Football	120	
Golf	60	
Swimming	45	
Athletics	30	
Equestrian	15	
Others	30	
Total		

a Copy and complete the table.
b Add the relative frequencies.
c Explain why your answer to **b** should be 1.
d On the Sunday the channel gives 1 hour to a summary of the Saturday sport. Assuming the same relative frequencies, how much time is given to swimming coverage?

2 The table shows the number of boys and girls born in a maternity unit out of 1000 births.

	Boys	Girls	Totals
Frequency	470	530	1000
Relative frequency			

a Calculate the relative frequency of **(i)** boys **(ii)** girls.
b Check that the total of the relative frequencies is 1.
c What would you normally expect the relative frequency of boys to be?

3 A shop sells three types of film: 12 exposure, 24 exposure and 36 exposure. The table shows the number sold one weekend.

Number of exposures	Frequency	Relative frequency
12	40	
24	160	
36	50	
Total		

a Copy the table and calculate the relative frequency for each type of film.
b Draw a pie chart of the film sales.
c The shop wishes to order 500 rolls of film. Using the relative frequencies as a guide, say how many of each type should be ordered.

4 A survey of the prices paid by students for their trainers produces this set of data:

Price (£)	Frequency	Relative frequency
10–19.99	92	
20–29.99	164	
30–39.99	78	
40–49.99	40	
50 or over	26	
Total		

a Copy the table and calculate the relative frequencies for each price group.
b What fraction of the students paid: (i) less than £20 (ii) less than £30?

5 The MacKenzies' quarterly phone bill lists different lengths and costs of telephone calls.

Type of call		Frequency	Relative frequency
Local	40p or less	108	
Local	more than 40p	126	
Regional and national	40p or less	24	
Regional and national	more than 40p	42	
	Total		

a Copy the table and calculate the relative frequency of each type of call.
b Draw a pie chart of the situation.
c The table below gives details of the next quarterly bill.

Type of call		Frequency	Relative frequency
Local	40p or less	84	
Local	more than 40p	98	
Regional and national	40p or less	18	
Regional and national	more than 40p	32	
	Total		

(i) Complete the relative frequency column, correct to 2 d.p.
(ii) Compare the phone use over the two quarters.

Reading pie charts

Newtown Wanderers have played 24 games.
The pie chart shows how they got on.

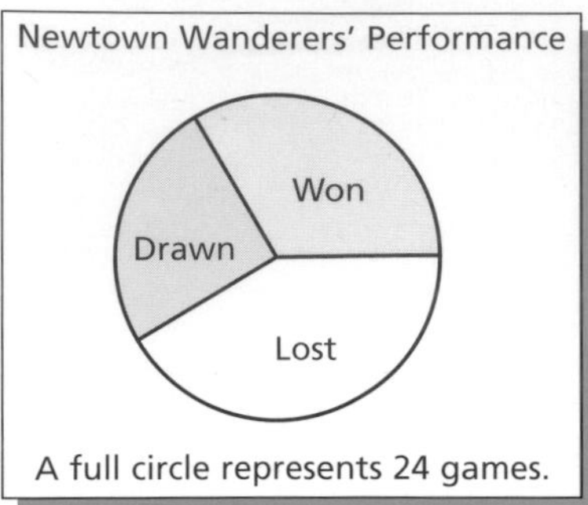

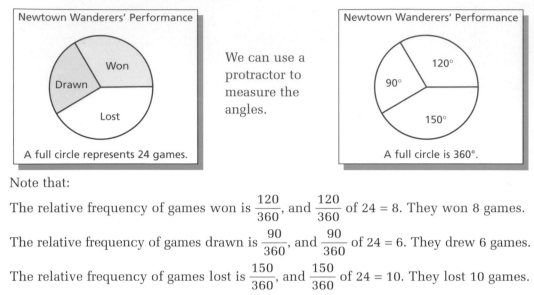

We can use a protractor to measure the angles.

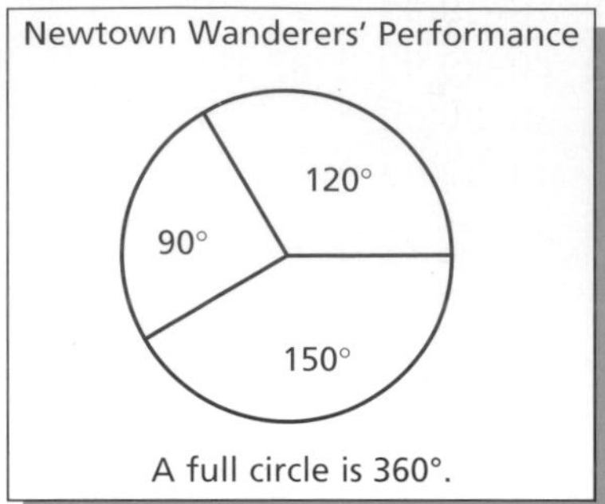

Note that:

The relative frequency of games won is $\frac{120}{360}$, and $\frac{120}{360}$ of 24 = 8. They won 8 games.

The relative frequency of games drawn is $\frac{90}{360}$, and $\frac{90}{360}$ of 24 = 6. They drew 6 games.

The relative frequency of games lost is $\frac{150}{360}$, and $\frac{150}{360}$ of 24 = 10. They lost 10 games.

Check that 8 + 6 + 10 = 24 games.

EXERCISE 2

1 500 people were asked how they made their way to the Continent.
The pie chart shows their replies.

- **a** Use a protractor to measure the angles at the centre of the circle.
- **b** Convert this information into relative frequencies.
- **c** How many used the car ferry?
- **d** How many more people used the hovercraft than the Chunnel?

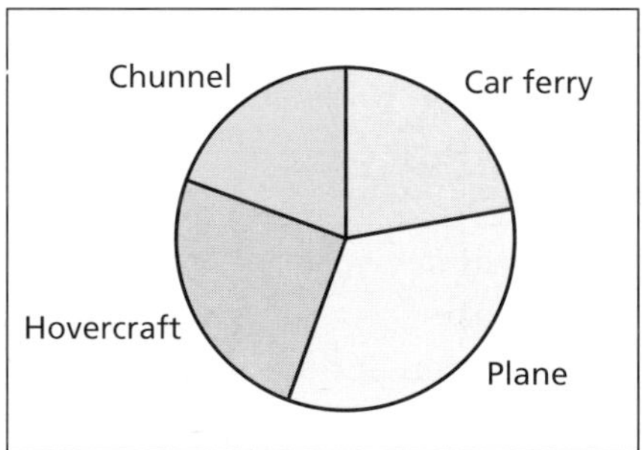

2 A timber merchant recorded which types of timber his last 1000 customers requested.
The pie chart illustrates the findings.

- **a** Use a protractor to measure the angles at the centre of the circle.
- **b** Convert this information into relative frequencies.
- **c** How many customers asked for
  (i) chipboard **(ii)** oak?
- **d** How many more people asked for teak than pine?

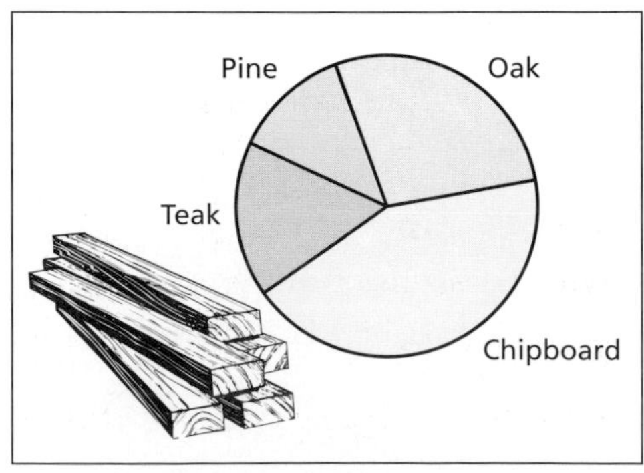

3 Over the Christmas holidays an art gallery had 5000 visitors. A survey classified them as youths, young adults, middle-aged and old-age pensioners. By studying the pie chart, find out how many visitors there were in each category.

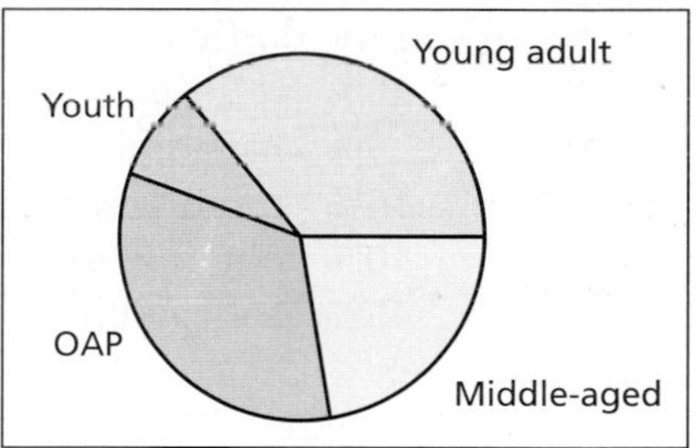

Constructing pie charts

A geologist examines pebbles on a beach to study drift.
She counts the types and makes a table of the information.

	Frequency	Relative frequency
Granite	43	$\frac{43}{150}$
Dolerite	52	$\frac{52}{150}$
Sandstone	31	$\frac{31}{150}$
Limestone	24	$\frac{24}{150}$
Total	150	

If 360° is to represent the whole sample of pebbles then (working to the nearest degree):

$\frac{43}{150}$ of 360° = 103° represents the granite pebbles

$\frac{52}{150}$ of 360° = 125° represents the dolerite pebbles

$\frac{31}{150}$ of 360° = 74° represents the sandstone pebbles

$\frac{24}{150}$ of 360° = 58° represents the limestone pebbles.

Hint
Working with common fractions avoids the dangers of rounding too early.

The pie chart looks like this:

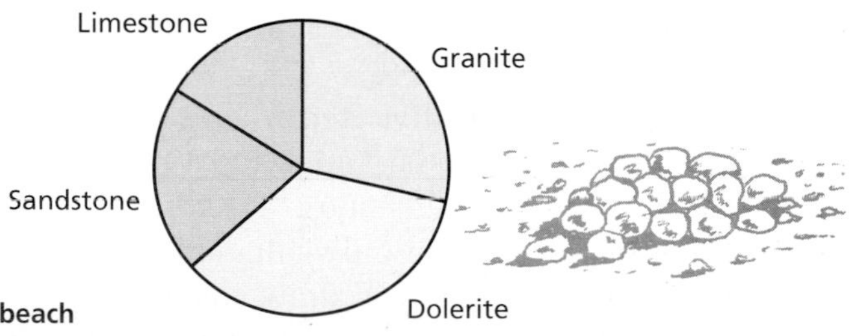

Pebbles on the beach

EXERCISE 3

1 When a raspberry crop is harvested it is found that:
$\frac{1}{20}$ are unripe; $\frac{1}{20}$ are over-ripe; $\frac{3}{20}$ are damaged by insects; $\frac{15}{20}$ are good.

a Calculate: **(i)** $\frac{1}{20}$ of 360° **(ii)** $\frac{3}{20}$ of 360° **(iii)** $\frac{15}{20}$ of 360°.

b Draw a pie chart to depict the raspberry crop.

2 A survey on the destinations of school leavers produces the following figures:

25% full-time job
5% part-time job
15% training scheme
10% out of work
45% college/university.

a Calculate:
(i) 25% of 360 (ii) 5% of 360 (iii) 15% of 360 (iv) 10% of 360.
b Construct a pie chart to show the destinations of school leavers.

3 There are 60 books on a shelf: 10 are reference books, 30 are fiction, 12 are poetry and 8 are biographies.
a Write down the relative frequency of each category of book.
b Draw a pie chart to depict the data.

4 A hundred motorists are asked about the fuel they use: 40 use 4-star petrol, 30 use unleaded, 10 use unleaded premium and 20 use diesel.
a Express each of these figures as a relative frequency.
b Draw a pie chart of the survey.

5 Two hundred people who suffer from allergies were asked about their allergy. The table summarises their replies.

Allergy	Stings	Nuts	Tomatoes	Others
Number of sufferers	60	80	20	40

a 30% of those asked were allergic to stings.
What percentage were allergic to: (i) nuts (ii) tomatoes (iii) others?
b Draw a pie chart to illustrate the figures.

6 An inspector studying train movements at a station puts the arrivals into four categories.
Early: 18 trains; on time: 59 trains; acceptably late: 12 trains; unacceptably late: 8 trains.
a Convert the data to relative frequencies.
b (i) Calculate the necessary angles to 1 decimal place.
(ii) Check that the total is 360°.
(iii) What happens if you only calculate the angles to the nearest degree?
(iv) How accurately can you draw angles?
c Keep the above in mind as you draw a pie chart to illustrate the data.

7 Divide the programmes from the TV page in a newspaper into different types: news and current affairs; soap operas; situation-comedy; films; documentaries or educational; others.
For each of the five terrestrial channels make a pie chart to show how they divide the time among the programme types.

Cumulative frequency

Fifty maths students are graded 1 to 10 where 10 is the best grade. The numbers achieving each grade are shown below.

Grade	Frequency	Cumulative frequency
1	0	0
2	2	2
3	4	6
4	10	16
5	11	27
6	10	37
7	6	43
8	4	47
9	2	49
10	1	50

A third column has been created which keeps a running total of the frequencies. These figures are called **cumulative frequencies**.

The cumulative frequency of grade 7 is 43.

This can be interpreted as '43 candidates are graded 7 or less'.

EXERCISE 4

1 At a bird sanctuary a warden records the arrival of a species of goose which spends the winter in Scotland.
In the frequency column the number of new arrivals, each day, is recorded. The cumulative frequency column gives the total number of geese that have arrived so far.

Day	Frequency (No. arriving each day)	Cumulative frequency (Total arrived so far)
1	2	2
2	8	10
3	15	25
4	24	49
5	20	69
6	16	85
7	5	90

a How many geese arrived on **(i)** day 1 **(ii)** day 4?
b How many, in total, had arrived by **(i)** day 4 **(ii)** day 7?

2 A medical officer records the number of new cases of flu reported each week in her area.
a Copy and complete the table.
b Which was the worst week?
c How many cases were reported altogether?
d By which week was the worst of the epidemic over?

Week	Frequency	Cumulative frequency
1	14	
2	38	
3	65	
4	26	
5	11	
6	2	

3 People were asked how long each week they spent watching TV soaps. The questionaire specified 0 hours, 1 hour, 2 hours, etc.

Time (t hours)	Frequency (%)	Cumulative frequency
0	10	
1	20	
2	25	
3	30	
4	10	
5	5	

a Copy and complete the table. **b** Which is the modal time?
c How many spend 3 hours or less watching soaps?

4 A traffic survey is conducted on a residential road one weekday morning. The line graph shows the number of vehicles passing the checkpoint each hour. The observer only records his count on the hour.

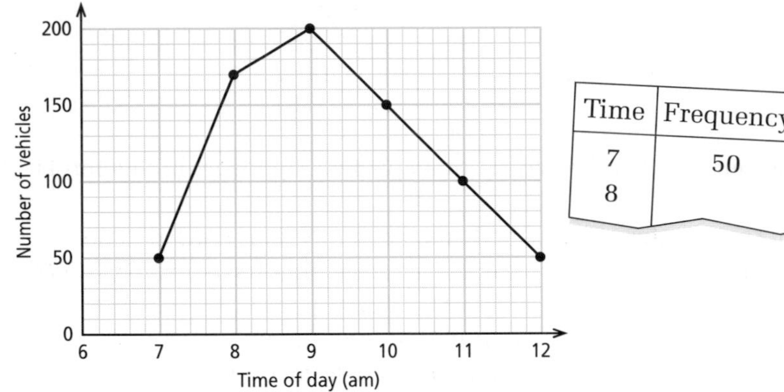

Time	Frequency	Cumulative frequency
7	50	50
8		

a Copy and complete the table. **b** How many vehicles were counted?
c By approximately what time had 500 vehicles been counted?

5 The graph shows the lengths of jumps a group of students managed to make from a standing start. Measurements were made to the nearest 10 cm.

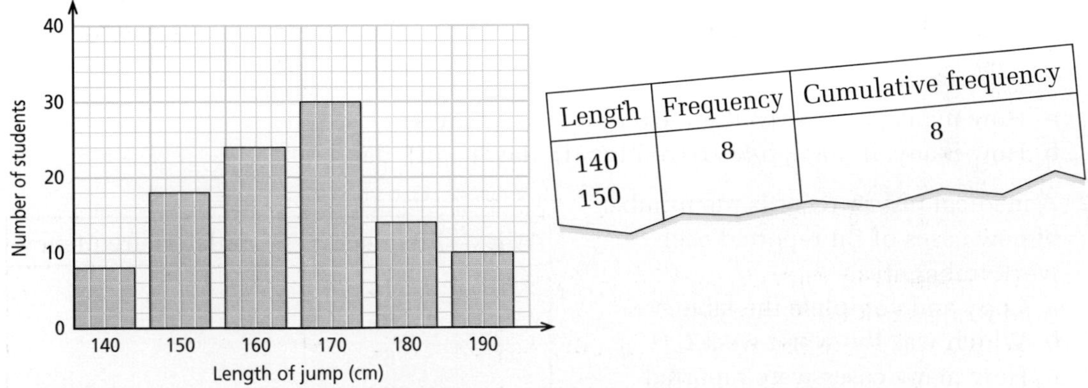

Length	Frequency	Cumulative frequency
140	8	8
150		

a Copy and complete the table.
b How many students jumped: **(i)** 180 cm or less **(ii)** less than 140 cm?
c How many students took part?

Cumulative frequency diagrams

The cumulative frequency table contains data from a survey on the petrol consumption of cars in a built-up area. Eighty cars were studied. The distance travelled on one gallon of fuel was estimated to the nearest 5 miles per gallon.

Miles travelled on 1 gallon (mpg)	Frequency	Cumulative frequency
20	3	3
25	8	11
30	19	30
35	23	53
40	16	69
45	7	76
50	4	80

Making a line graph of cumulative frequency against miles travelled on one gallon of petrol gives us a **cumulative frequency diagram**.

From this graph we can estimate information not found on the table. For example, around 40 vehicles have a petrol consumption of less than 32 miles per gallon.

Note we have plotted (15, 0) – no cars were studied with a petrol consumption of 15 mph.

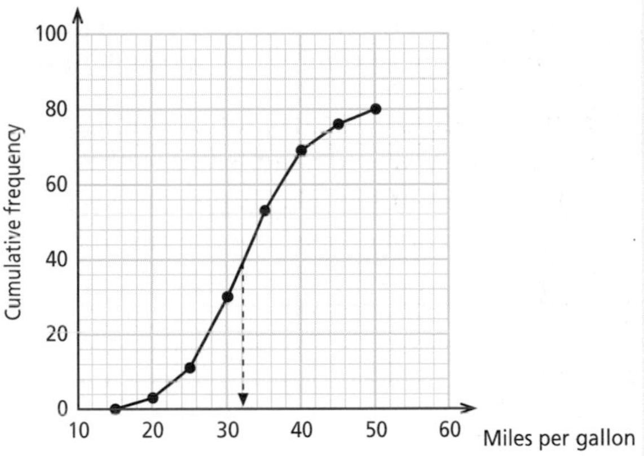

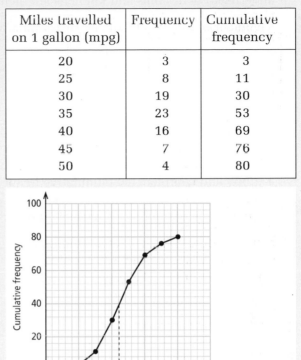

EXERCISE 5

1

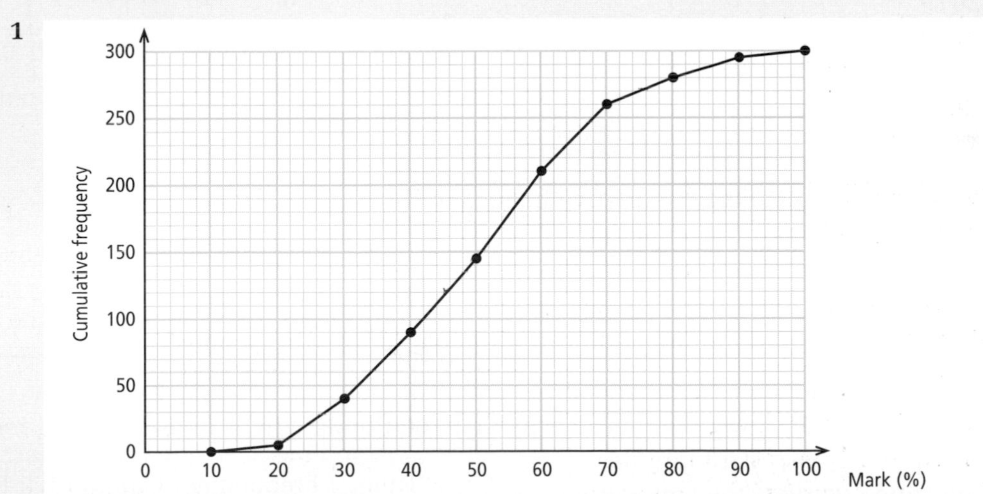

Three hundred students sit a Social Studies exam. The cumulative frequency diagram shows their marks.

a How many students scored **(i)** 50% or less **(ii)** more than 70%?

b The examiners decide that:

(i) to pass, a mark over 45% is required. How many students failed?

(ii) to achieve a grade A, over 75% is required. How many are awarded grade A?

2 An estate agent counts the number of rooms there are in each of 40 houses being advertised. Bathrooms and kitchens are included. The table shows the data.

Number of rooms	Frequency	Cumulative frequency
4	1	1
5	3	4
6	8	
7	12	
8	9	
9	5	
10	2	

a Copy and complete the cumulative frequency column.
b Draw a cumulative frequency diagram.
c How many of the houses have eight or more rooms?

3 A dental survey is carried out among two groups: 16-year-olds and 40-year-olds. The number of teeth each person has is recorded. The tables show the results.

16-year-olds		
Number of teeth	Frequency	Cumulative frequency
25	4	4
26	5	9
27	8	
28	15	
29	13	
30	5	

40-year-olds		
Number of teeth	Frequency	Cumulative frequency
24	4	4
25	7	11
26	8	19
27	8	
28	8	
29	6	
30	4	
31	3	
32	2	

a Copy and complete the cumulative frequency columns.
b On the same axes, draw cumulative frequency diagrams for both groups.
c Compare the number of teeth for the two groups.
Overall do the younger group have more teeth?
Why is the maximum number of teeth different for the two groups?

4 A new airline claims that its flights direct from Glasgow to Paris take 2 hours 45 minutes. The table shows the times for its first 100 flights. Flight times are recorded to the nearest 10 minutes.

a Copy and complete the cumulative frequency column.
b Draw a cumulative frequency diagram.
c Estimate the number of flights that take less than 2 h 45 min.
Is the airline's claim reasonable?

Time (t min)	Frequency	Cumulative frequency
160	9	
170	23	
180	32	
190	25	
200	11	

Dot plots

It is often useful to get a 'feel' for the location of a data set on the number line. A **dot plot** can be drawn for this purpose.

Example 1 A group of students measure their pulse rates when resting. The rates are 66, 69, 62, 58, 74, 56, 67, 72, 61, 62, 59.

Each piece of data becomes a data point sitting above the number line.

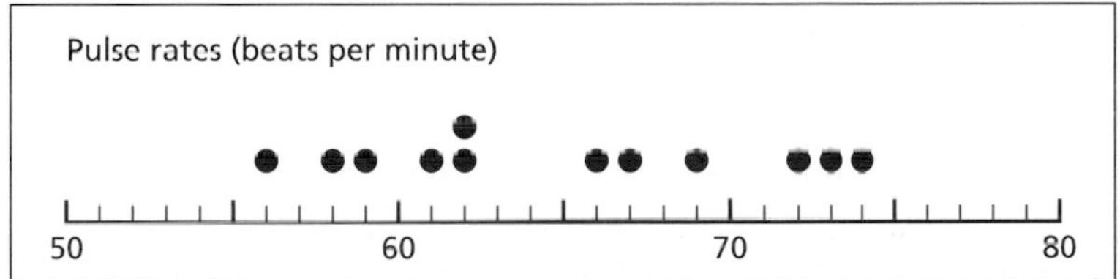

Some features of the distribution of figures become clearer:

- the lowest score is 56 beats per minute
- the highest score is 73 beats per minute
- the mode (most frequent score) is 62
- the median (middle score) is also 62
- the distribution is fairly flat.

Here are some common expressions relating to dot plots:

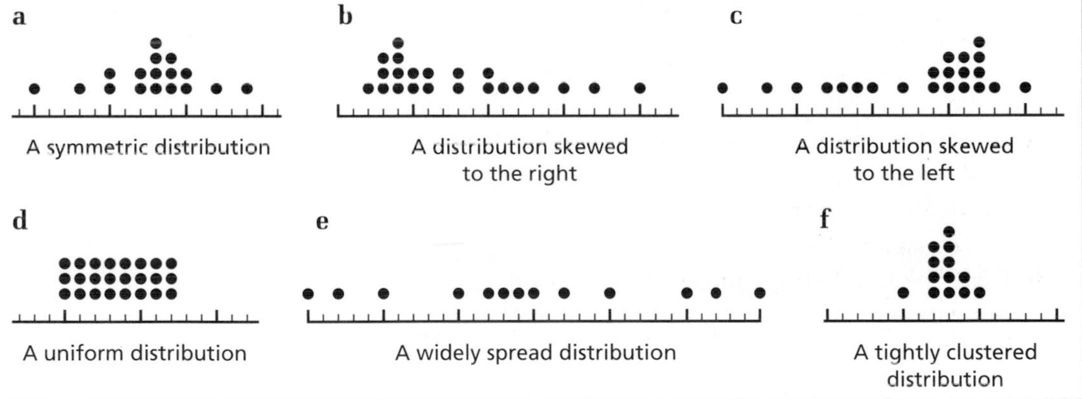

EXERCISE 6

1 A batch of watches is carefully checked to see how much time each watch gains over a given period. The dot plot shows the gains in seconds.

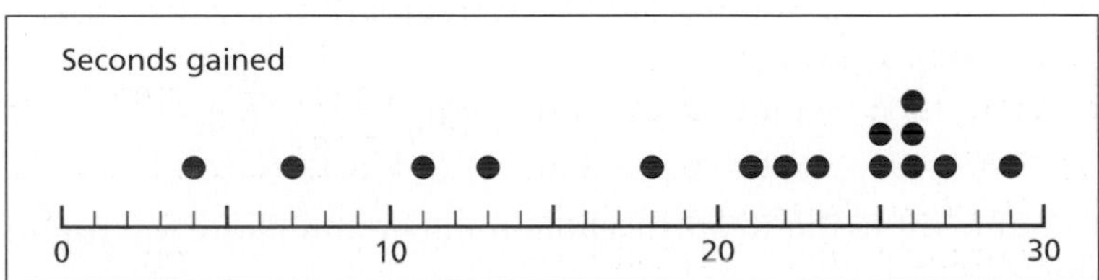

a List all the gains in order of size.

b Find **(i)** the biggest **(ii)** the smallest **(iii)** the median gain.

c Write a sentence describing the shape of the distribution.

2 A dice is thrown 30 times and the results recorded.

1	3	2	5	1	4
5	6	5	4	6	3
3	2	5	4	2	6
4	6	1	2	3	5
6	4	3	1	2	1

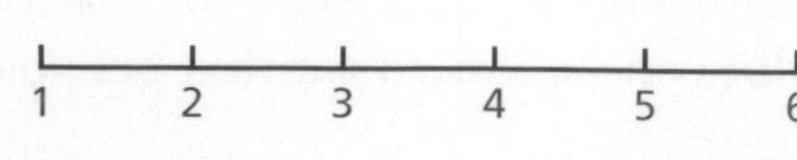

a Draw a dot plot on a suitable scale to illustrate the distribution of scores.
b State **(i)** the biggest **(ii)** the smallest **(iii)** the median score.
c Write a sentence describing the shape of the distribution.

3 A supermarket sells pre-packed mushrooms. A sample of 16 packets are inspected.
A count is made of the numbers of mushrooms in each packet. The dot plot shows the results.

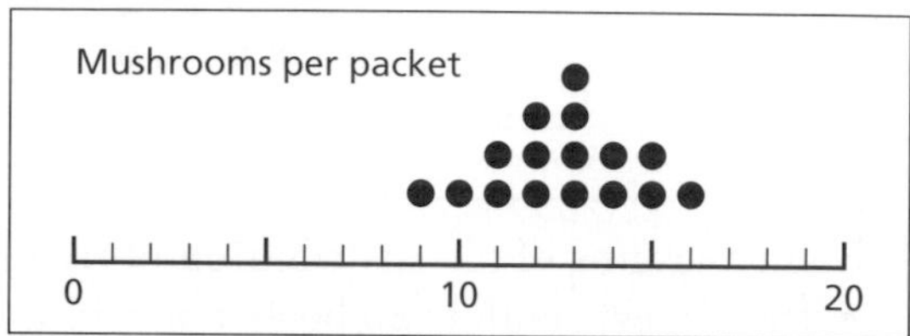

a What is **(i)** the greatest **(ii)** the least number of mushrooms per packet?
b Which amount occurred the most often?
c Describe the distribution.
d If the supermarket is going to print a description of the contents of a packet what might it say without being misleading?

4 A showroom has eleven cars priced as follows:
£10 400, £10 500, £10 500, £10 700, £11 200, £11 300,
£11 600, £12 300, £12 500, £13 400, £14 100.

a Use the figures to make a dot plot on a copy of: **(i)** scale 1
(ii) scale 2 (round the data to the nearest £1000).
b Describe the distribution as it appears on: **(i)** scale 1
(ii) scale 2.
c Which description gives a better idea of the pricing in the showroom?

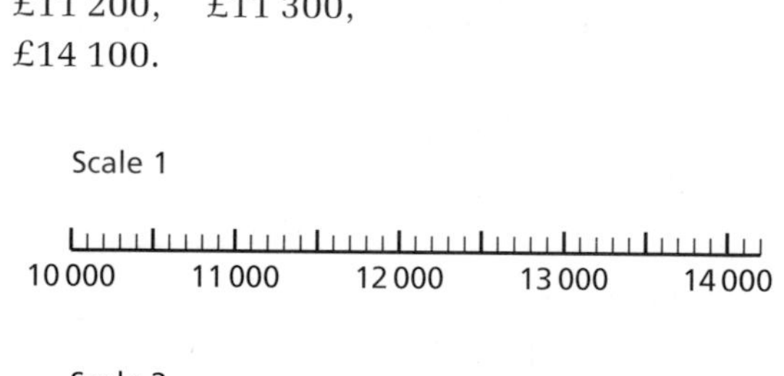

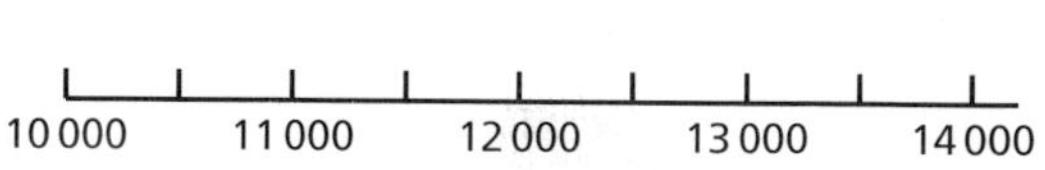

5 A health clinic gives people over 45 years old regular check-ups.
The cholesterol count is measured from blood samples.
One day, tests give these results:

4.3, 4.4, 4.6, 4.8, 4.8, 4.9, 5.0, 5.1, 5.3,
5.7, 5.8, 6.1, 6.2, 6.4, 6.6, 7.3, 8.1.

a Round the counts off to the nearest whole number and show the rounded figures on a dot plot.
b A count of 6 is considered reasonable. Higher than that is unhealthy.
How many people had a reading higher than that?
c Describe the distribution. Is the sample, on the whole, healthy?

6 A consumer advice bureau investigates the different interest rates on offer by banks and building societies in the High Street. This is a list of the percentage rates they find:

4.8, 6.2, 7.1, 5.6, 4.9,
5.2, 6.4, 7.5, 4.3, 5.4,
6.7, 7.6, 4.2, 5.5, 4.2,
4.5, 5.2, 6.0, 4.8, 5.0.

a Draw a dot plot of the rates:
(i) working to 1 decimal place **(ii)** working to the nearest whole number.
b Write a short sentence describing High Street interest rates.

Challenge

Carry out this investigation yourself. You will need squared paper.

Illustration 1

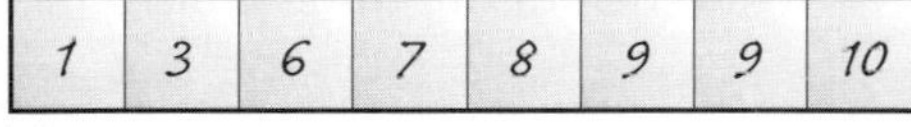

Illustration 2

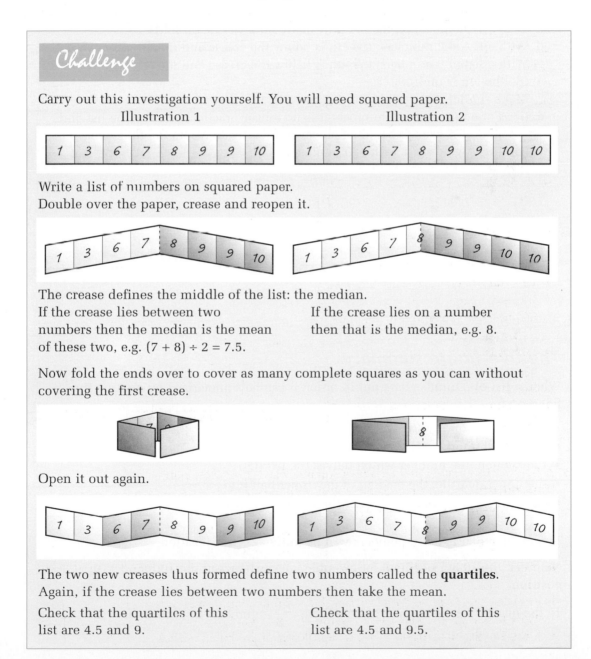

Write a list of numbers on squared paper.
Double over the paper, crease and reopen it.

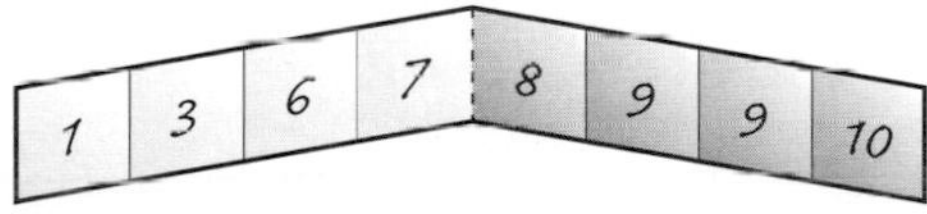

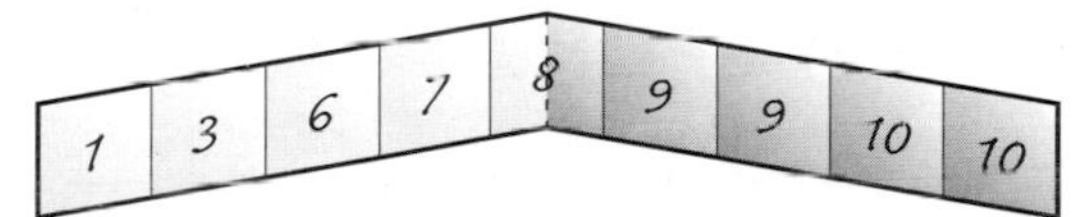

The crease defines the middle of the list: the median.

If the crease lies between two numbers then the median is the mean of these two, e.g. (7 + 8) ÷ 2 = 7.5.

If the crease lies on a number then that is the median, e.g. 8.

Now fold the ends over to cover as many complete squares as you can without covering the first crease.

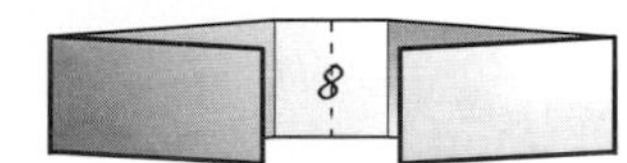

Open it out again.

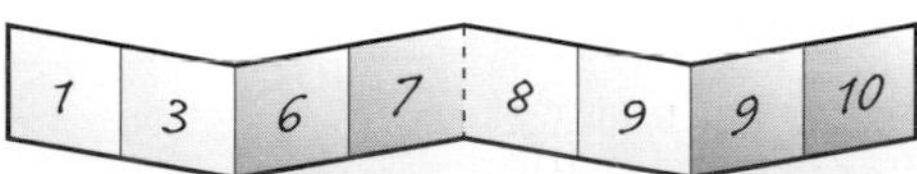

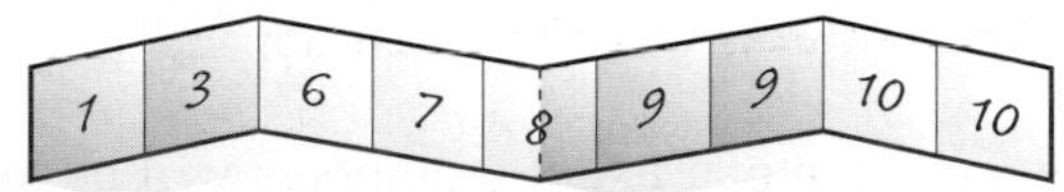

The two new creases thus formed define two numbers called the **quartiles**.
Again, if the crease lies between two numbers then take the mean.

Check that the quartiles of this list are 4.5 and 9.

Check that the quartiles of this list are 4.5 and 9.5.

a With 8 numbers on the list no number is creased.
With 9 numbers on the list one number is creased.
What will happen with a list of:
(i) 10 numbers
(ii) 11 numbers
(iii) 12 numbers?

b When 8 is divided by 4 the remainder is 0.
When 9 is divided by 4 the remainder is 1.
(i) List the remainder when dividing 10, 11 and 12 by 4.
(ii) How are the answers above related?

c With 121 numbers on the list how many numbers lie on folds?

d With a list of 8 numbers, the 4th is below the crease and the 5th is above it.
With a list of 9 numbers, the 4th is below the crease and the 6th is above it. (So the 5th is on it.)
Make similar discriptions for **(i)** 10 **(ii)** 11 **(iii)** 12 numbers.

e **(i)** For a list with 121 numbers it is no longer practical to write the list and fold. If it were to be done, however, investigate where the folds would be.
(ii) Investigate a list with 123 numbers.

The five-figure summary

When a list of n numbers are put in order, it can be summarised by quoting five figures:

- the highest number (H)
- the lowest number (L)
- the median, the number which halves the list (Q_2)
- the upper quartile, the median of the upper half (Q_3)
- the lower quartile, the median of the lower half (Q_1).

The median of a list of n numbers will be in the $\frac{n+1}{2}$th position.

Note that the 10.5th position, for example, means between the 10th and 11th position.

To the nearest whole number there will be $\frac{n-1}{2}$ numbers in each half.

Example 1 2 4 5 5 6 7 7 7 8 9 10

The highest number $H = 10$

The lowest number $L = 2$

There are 11 numbers so the median is in $(11 + 1) \div 2 = 6$th position … $Q_2 = 7$

$10 \div 2 = 5$. To the nearest whole number there are 5 numbers in each half.

$(5 + 1) \div 2 = 3$. Q_1 is in the 3rd position counting from L … $Q_1 = 5$

Q_3 is in the 3rd position counting from H … $Q_3 = 8$

If you imagine folding an evenly spaced list on a piece of paper, the quartiles lie on the folds.

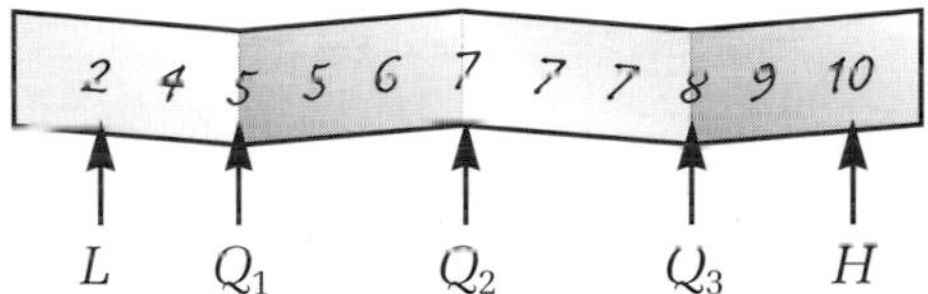

Example 2 2 4 5 5 6 7 7 8 9 10

There are 10 numbers in the list.

$(10 + 1) \div 2 = 5.5$. Q_2 lies between the 5th and 6th numbers …
$Q_2 = (6 + 7) \div 2 = 6.5$

$(10 - 1) \div 2 = 4.5$. To the nearest whole number there are 5 numbers in each half.

$(5 + 1) \div 2 = 3$. Q_1 lies in the 3rd position … $Q_1 = 5$
Q_3 lies in the 3rd position counting from H … $Q_3 = 8$

$L = 2$
$Q_1 = 5$
$Q_2 = 6.5$
$Q_3 = 8$
$H = 10$

Example 3 2 4 5 5 6 7 8 9 10

There are 9 numbers in the list.

$(9 + 1) \div 2 = 5$. Q_2 lies in the 5th position … $Q_2 = 6$

$(9 - 1) \div 2 = 4$. To the nearest whole number there are 4 numbers in each half.

$(4 + 1) \div 2 = 2.5$. Q_1 lies between the 2nd and 3rd numbers …
$Q_1 = (4 + 5) \div 2 = 4.5$
Q_3 lies between the 2nd and 3rd numbers counting from H … $Q_3 = 8.5$

$L = 2$
$Q_1 = 4.5$
$Q_2 = 6$
$Q_3 = 8.5$
$H = 10$

EXERCISE 7

1 Make a five-figure summary of each of the following distributions.

a 2 7 7 11 15 24 32 44 45 47 48
b 18 21 23 23 24 26 27 29 36 37
c 23 26 31 34 35 35 35 46 61
d 94 97 102 110 122 128 134 147

2 Put the following lists in numerical order and then make a five-figure summary.

a 17 23 4 21 18 17 25 8 11 16 10
b 56 43 23 17 29 23 18 30 27 31
c 88 75 83 72 73 89 80 84 84
d 12 8 7 19 23 25 20 14

Box plots

When we know the extremes, H and L, the median, Q_2, and the quartiles Q_1 and Q_3, we can illustrate the distribution effectively using a **box plot**.

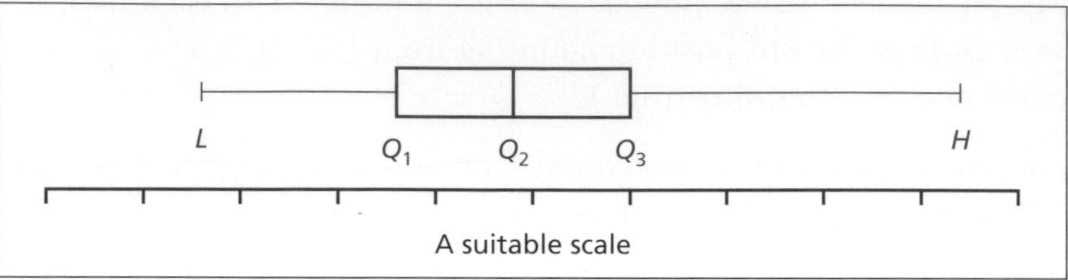

Example

Lowest score = 16; highest score = 94; $Q_1 = 36$; $Q_2 = 48$; $Q_3 = 60$

For an exam out of 100, the box plot would look like this:

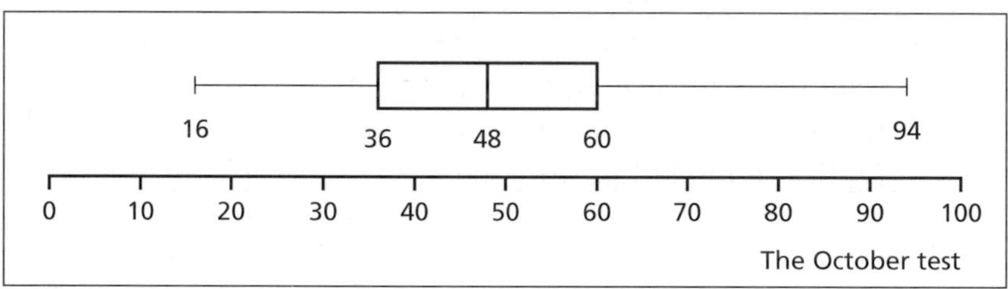

Note that: 25% of the candidates got between 16 and 36 (the lower whisker),
50% of the candidates got between 36 and 60 (in the box),
25% of the candidates got between 60 and 94 (the upper whisker).

EXERCISE 8

1 The points scored by ten rugby teams one weekend have been put in order.

3 5 8 14 21 22 26 34 50 50

a Make a five-figure summary.

b Copy and complete the box plot.

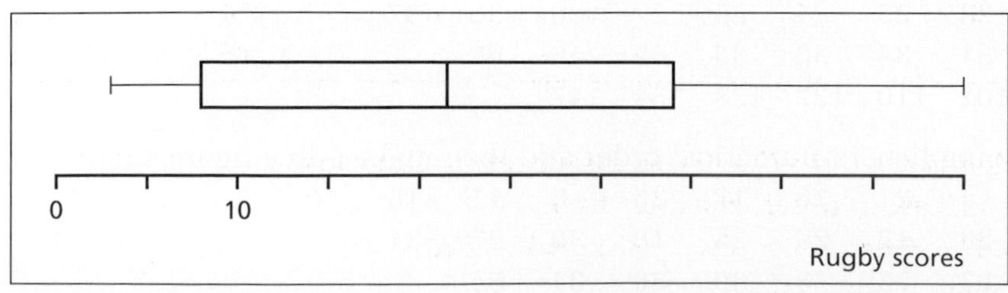

2 This box plot shows the number of shaves a group of men get out of a new brand of disposable razor.

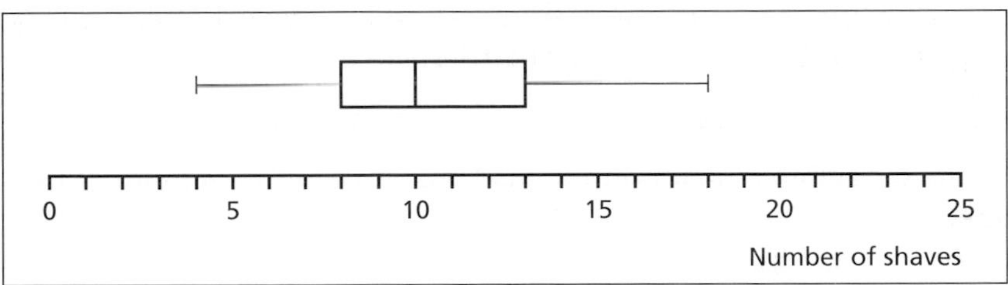

Write down: **a** **(i)** the least **(ii)** the greatest number of shaves

b the median

c **(i)** the lower **(ii)** the upper quartile values.

3 The Endurance Exhaust Company keeps a record of the number of car exhausts fitted each day. The box plot summarises the data.

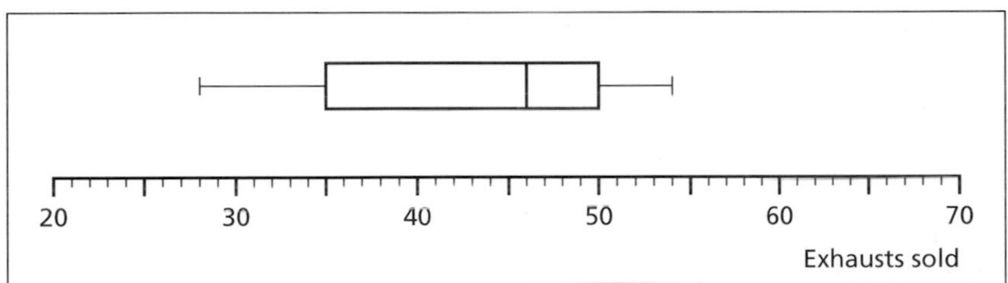

Write down: **a** **(i)** the lowest **(ii)** the greatest number fitted in a day.

b the median

c **(i)** the lower **(ii)** the upper quartile.

4 A cinema lists the lengths of its films, in minutes, for one month.
The times are given in order:

87 90 92 92 95 98 102 102 103 105 106 111 125 127 139

a Find the median time.

b Work out the lower quartile.

c Find the upper quartile value.

d Use this scale to draw a box plot.

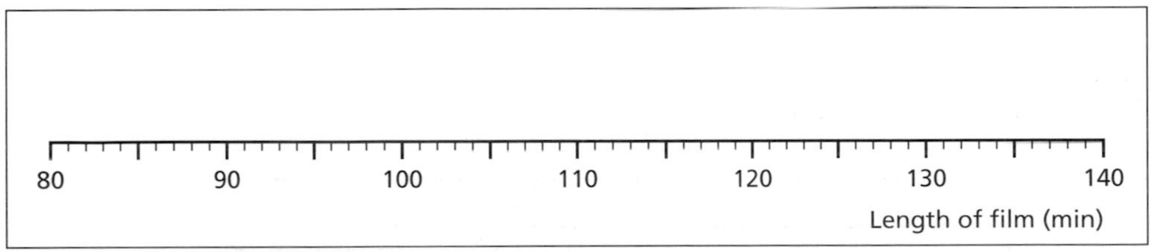

5 A group of friends compare the prices they paid for their jeans.
These are the prices, in order, cheapest first.

£18 £22 £27 £30 £32 £35 £39 £45 £50

a Make a five-figure summary.

b Draw a box plot.

6 The number of members attending a keep-fit class over 20 sessions is noted.

9 9 10 11 12 14 14 15 16 17

18 18 19 19 19 20 21 21 22 22

a Calculate the median and lower and upper quartiles.

b Draw a box plot.

7 A hairdresser records the number of appointments booked in for one month at the Cut and Curl Salon.

38 44 46 50 60 28 30 41 45 56

28 43 41 59 25 25 38 42 55 26

a Write the number of clients in order, least first.

b Make a five-figure summary.

c Draw a box plot.

Comparing distributions

When comparing distributions it is useful to consider two things:

a the central tendency (the mean, the mode or the median)

b how the marks spread out (the range can be used but more often the **interquartile range** or **semi-interquartile range** is used).

The interquartile range = $Q_3 - Q_1$ **The semi-interquartile range** = $\frac{Q_3 - Q_1}{2}$

Box plots can be used to help compare distributions.

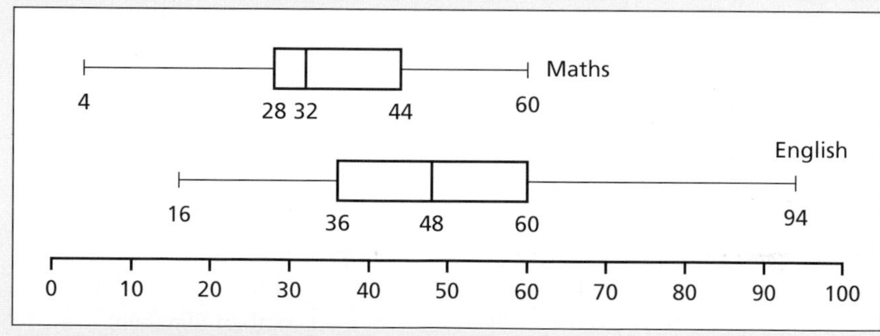

These box plots compare the results of two exams, one in maths and one in English. Note first that the maths results had a median of 32 and a semi-interquartile range of 8; the English results had a median of 48 and a semi-interquartile range of 12. On average English had better scores than maths (since the median is higher) but scores tended to be more variable (a bigger semi-interquartile range).

EXERCISE 9

1 A survey concerning gas consumption takes place in a small community. Twelve houses with loft insulation and twelve without insulation have their gas usage monitored for a month.
The meter measures cubic metres of gas.

With insulation	240	210	170	130	110	40	40	30	70	120	170	250
Without insulation	290	280	220	180	150	70	60	50	100	160	230	300

a Make a five-figure summary of the 'with insulation' data.
b Repeat for the 'without insulation' data.
c Draw box plots of each set of data on the same diagram.
d Compare the two plots.
(i) Does loft insulation tend to cut down gas consumption?
(ii) What other factors might play a relevant part in this survey?

2 Castle Estates build houses. At present they use two suppliers of roof tiles. They decide only to use one in future. They don't mind waiting for a reasonable length of time for deliveries. For planning purposes, however, deliveries must be consistent. They check the recent records for their two suppliers:

Reliable Roofs' last few orders took these number of days to arrive:
50, 30, 38, 49, 52, 21, 20, 36, 24, 47, 21.
Top Tiles' last few orders took these number of days:
48, 24, 43, 34, 37, 40, 35, 41, 37, 15, 30, 60, 39, 45, 36, 49.

a Draw a box plot for each company (on the same scale).
b Calculate the range for each.
c Calculate the semi-interquartile range for each.
d Explain what the statistics show. Which company would you recommend?

CHAPTER 10 REVIEW

1 Theatregoers were asked what kind of production they would like to see next. The pie chart illustrates their replies.

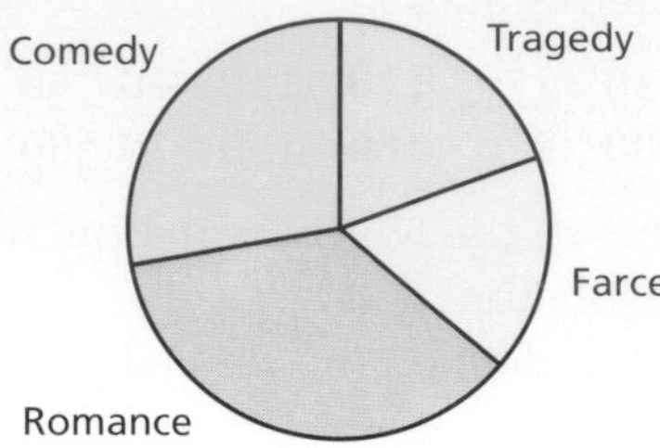

a Measure the size of the angles at the centre of the chart.

b 500 people were questioned.
Estimate the number of people who voted for each category.

2

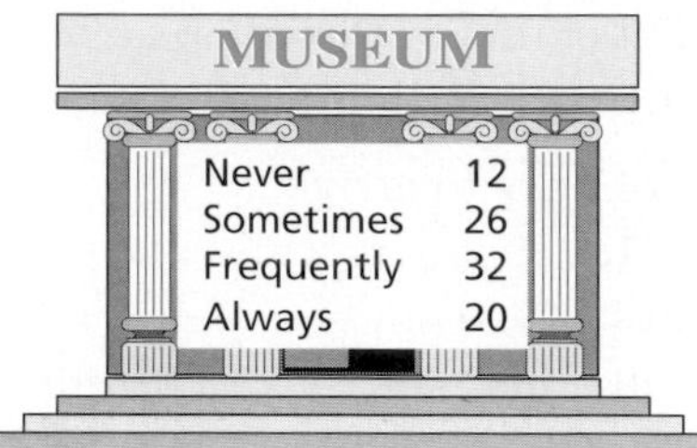

A museum carries out a survey to try to judge the usefulness of its coffee bar.
Visitors are asked 'When you visit the museum do you use the café
(i) never **(ii)** sometimes **(iii)** frequently **(iv)** always?'.
The responses are shown.
Make a pie chart to illustrate the results.

3 A travel agent asks clients to fill in a questionnaire about the total number of weeks they spend abroad in one year.

Number of weeks abroad	Frequency	Cumulative frequency
0	25	
1	70	
2	95	
3	65	
4	35	
5	10	

a Copy the table and complete the cumulative frequency column.

b How many people in the survey spend:

(i) 3 weeks or less abroad

(ii) 4 weeks or more abroad?

4 A consumer protection group carries out a survey into the bus fares of 20 journeys of similar distances. The dot plot illustrates their findings.

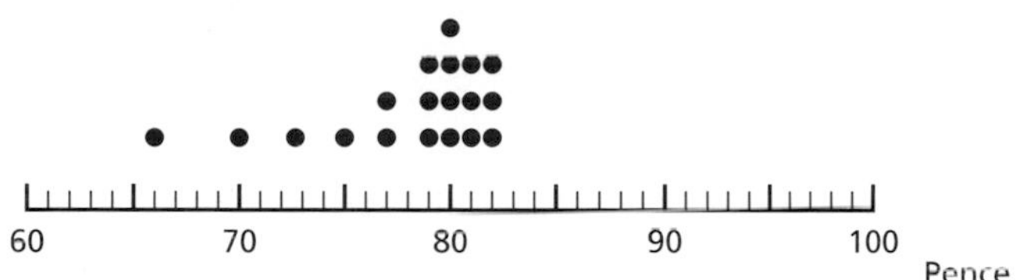

a What is the (i) highest (ii) lowest fare charged?
b What is the mode of the fares?
c Describe the distribution of the fares.

5 Staff at a garage check the number of kilometres that various types of car travel on one litre of petrol. These are the results:

12.3, 16.1, 12.9, 12, 11.5, 11.7, 12.2,
11.9, 13.3, 15.4, 12.4, 14.7, 14, 12.9, 15.7.

a Draw a dot plot of the data as given.
b Draw a dot plot rounding the data to the nearest whole number.
c What is the range of the data?
d Describe the shape of the distribution of the data.

6 Sarah rings round various catteries to see how many cats each can cater for. These are the replies:

18, 22, 26, 36, 40, 40, 37, 34, 30, 23, 16, 12, 10.

a List the numbers in order.
b Calculate the median and lower and upper quartiles.
c Draw a box plot to illustrate the figures.

7 The results of two exams are illustrated in the box plots.

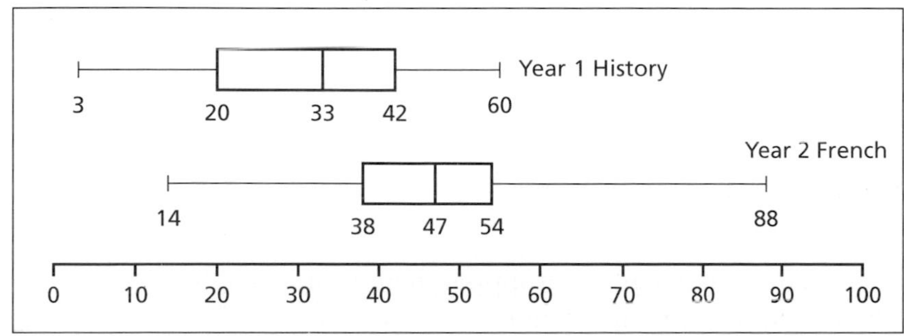

a For each boxplot find:
(i) the median (ii) the range (iii) the semi-interquartile range.
b Write a few sentences comparing the performances of the candidates sitting each exam.

11 Statistics

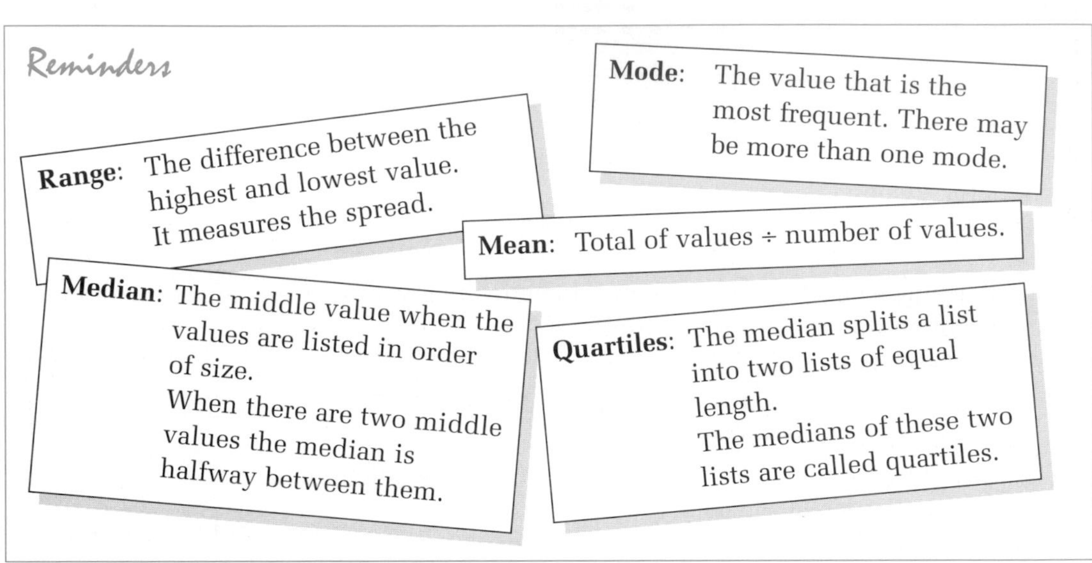

Reminders
Range: The difference between the highest and lowest value. It measures the spread.
Mode: The value that is the most frequent. There may be more than one mode.
Mean: Total of values ÷ number of values.
Median: The middle value when the values are listed in order of size.
When there are two middle values the median is halfway between them.
Quartiles: The median splits a list into two lists of equal length.
The medians of these two lists are called quartiles.

STARTING POINTS

1 Brass tacks come in boxes labelled 'Contents: 45 approx.'. The manufacturers don't check the whole output of boxes. They check a **sample** of boxes.
Here are the results from a sample of 16 boxes.

42	45	48	44
43	46	45	49
48	43	45	47
50	46	45	46

a What is **(i)** the highest count **(ii)** the lowest count **(iii)** the range?
b Calculate the mean number of tacks in the sample.
c Which count occurred most often (the **mode** or **modal** score)?
d Draw a bar chart to illustrate the data.
e Comment on the claim on the box.

2 Golf balls are tested for 'bounce' by dropping them from a height of 1 m and measuring the height of the rebound to the nearest 10 cm.

No balls only bounced to a height of 10 cm.

Rebound (cm)	10	20	30	40	50	60
Frequency	0	2	4	7	5	1

a How many rebounded **(i)** 30 cm **(ii)** less than 40 cm **(iii)** more than 40 cm?
b How many balls were tested (the **sample size**)?
c What was the most common interval of rebound (the **modal height**)?

3 The whole set of things under consideration in a situation is known as the **population**, whether it be everyone in a school or the whole output from the brass tacks factory or every ball in a golf shop.
When it is impractical to consider the whole population then a **sample** is examined.
Which of the following claims could be investigated by looking at the population rather than a sample?

a '48% of the students are girls.'
b 'The batteries we make last 100 hours.'
c '30% of people can't tell margarine from butter.'
d '24% of Jack's stamp collection are foreign.'
e '53% of the cars on the road are foreign.'

4 A sample of eggs is taken from one day's production and graded 1 to 7 according to size.

1	3	7	3	5
4	6	2	4	3
4	1	3	4	2
3	2	5	1	6
3	5	2	4	3

Weight (g)	Tally	Frequency
1		
2		
3		
4		

a Copy and complete the table to help organise the data.
b Illustrate the table by means of a bar graph.

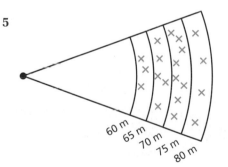

5

The diagram shows how far Tessa's practice javelin throws go.
She scores each throw according to the last marker that the javelin passes.

a Copy and complete the frequency table.
b How many throws did Tessa have?

Distance (m)	Frequency
60	3
65	
70	
75	

6 At the Phoenix Printing Company the weekly wages of the staff are £200, £100, £800, £160, £100, £380, £120 and £180.

a What is the mode? Why is this not typical?
b Calculate the mean. Is this typical of the wages? Explain.
c Calculate the median wage. Is this more representative?
d Calculate the range. Are the wages widely spread?

7 Max records his scores in a round of golf in a table like this:

Score	Frequency (holes)	Score × frequency
3	4	3 × 4
4	6	
5	7	
6	1	
Totals		

a Copy and complete the table.
b **(i)** What is his total score?
(ii) How many holes did he play?
(iii) Calculate the mean (total score ÷ total number of holes) correct to 1 d.p.
c What is the mode?
d His scores in order are 3, 3, 3, 3, 4, 4, 4, 4, 4, 4, 5, 5, 5, 5, 5, 5, 5, 6.
What is the median? Can you see how to find it from the table?
e Calculate the range of his scores.
f Is Max a good golfer?
g Which of the mode, median and mean is the most typical of his scores?

8 The Everbright Electricity Company carries out a survey of homes to find the number of light sockets in each.
Four different streets are visited with these results..

Hazel Road	8	9	12	13	13	14	14	15			
Ash Street	8	8	9	11	13	13	13	14	15		
Lime Grove	9	10	10	12	13	14	14	15	16	18	
Beech Lane	10	10	11	11	13	13	14	14	14	14	15

a Work out the median number of sockets for each street.
b Calculate the quartiles in the list for **(i)** Hazel Road **(ii)** Ash Street.
c **(i)** What is the upper quartile of the Lime Grove list?
(ii) What is the lower quartile of the Beech Lane list?

9 Consider what happens as a lorry gets older.
Copy these axes and plot points to show the type of correlation you would expect.
Describe the correlation.

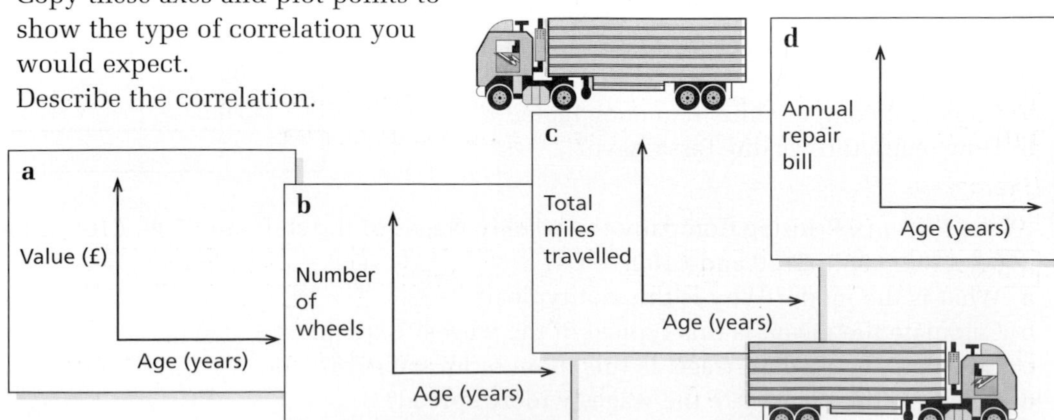

10 An estate agent lists the annual income of a few customers, together with the value of the house they buy.

Customer	A	B	C	D	E	F	G
Income (£1000)	35	50	15	12	18	24	28
House value (£1000)	68	100	32	22	35	46	56

a Plot a scatter graph.
b Describe the type of correlation.
c Draw the line of best fit.
d Estimate the value of a house bought by a customer with an income of £40 000.

Calculating the quartiles from a frequency table

To find the quartiles of an *ordered* list you consider its length.
You need to find three numbers which break the list into four smaller lists of equal length.

Example 1
For a list of 24 numbers, 24 ÷ 4 = 6 remainder 0:

[6 numbers] Q_1 [6 numbers] Q_2 [6 numbers] Q_3 [6 numbers]

The quartiles fall in the gaps between the 6th and 7th, the 12th and 13th, and the 18th and 19th numbers.

Example 2
For a list of 25 numbers, 25 ÷ 4 = 6 remainder 1:

[6 numbers] Q_1 [6 numbers] [1 no.] [6 numbers] Q_3 [6 numbers]

Q_2 (the 1 no.)

The lower quartile falls in the gap between the 6th and 7th numbers, the median falls on the 13th number and the upper quartile falls between the 19th and 20th numbers.

Example 3
For a list of 26 numbers, 26 ÷ 4 = 6 remainder 2:

[6 numbers] [1 no.] [6 numbers] Q_2 [6 numbers] [1 no.] [6 numbers]

Q_1 (the first 1 no.), Q_3 (the second 1 no.)

The lower quartile falls on the 7th number, the median falls between the 13th and 14th numbers and the upper quartile falls on the 20th number.

Example 4
For a list of 27 numbers, 27 ÷ 4 = 6 remainder 3:

[6 numbers] [1 no.] [6 numbers] [1 no.] [6 numbers] [1 no.] [6 numbers]

Q_1, Q_2, Q_3 (the three 1 no. boxes, in order)

The lower quartile falls on the 7th number, the median falls on the 14th number and the upper quartile falls on the 21st number.

EXERCISE 1

1 **a** Given a list of 34 numbers put in order, describe the position of:
(i) the lower quartile **(ii)** the median **(iii)** the upper quartile.
b Repeat part **a** for lists of length **(i)** 28 **(ii)** 33 **(iii)** 23.

2 **a** During a diving competition involving 30 contestants, the scores awarded by one judge were noted. They have been put in order.

1	1	1	2	2	2
2	3	3	3	3	3
4	4	4	4	5	5
5	5	6	6	6	6
6	7	7	7	8	8

a Describe the positions in the list of:
(i) the lower quartile **(ii)** the median **(iii)** the upper quartile.
b Work out the three numbers from the given list.

3 A stem-and-leaf diagram is a simple way of putting a big list in order. This particular list shows how candidates fared in their last maths assessment.
a How many numbers are in the list?
b Describe the positions of the median and quartiles.
c Work out the quartiles.

The maths scores

Stem	Leaf
0	0 1 7
1	2 3 5 6
2	2 2 4 4 5 5 6
3	3 3 3 6 7 7 7 8
4	5 6 6

$n = 25$ 4 | 5 represents a score of 45

4 Staff at a petrol station record the number of litres of petrol each customer buys one morning.
The figures are sorted in a stem-and-leaf diagram.
a Describe the position of the median and the two quartiles.
b Work out the values of the median and the quartiles.
c A useful measure of the spread of the 'scores' is called the **interquartile range**: IQR = $Q_3 - Q_1$. Work out the interquartile range in this case.

Petrol purchased (litres)

Stem	Leaf
1	8 8 9
2	5 6 6 7 8 8 8 9
3	1 1 2 2 3 5 5 5 5 6 6 7
4	0 0 1 1 1 2 2 3 3 4 4 4 4 5 5 6 6 7 7
5	0 1 1

$n = 45$ 1 | 8 represents 18 litres

5 Every 10 minutes the number of customers passing through the check-out in a supermarket is noted. The following is a copy of the record. It is not yet ordered.

12	23	30	24	41	31	44	13	48	17	50
21	23	26	43	49	37	35	20	44	50	27
13	15	19	26	26	35	46	28	20	27	44
27	35	30	35	47	48	50	33			

a Construct a stem-and-leaf diagram to order the data.
b Work out the values of the median and the quartiles.
c Work out the interquartile range.

Using a cumulative frequency column

Example The frequency table shows the length of phone calls (in minutes) made from an office in one day.
Calculate the median and quartiles of these times.

Time (min)	Frequency
1	2
2	3
3	5
4	8
5	4

A cumulative frequency column is added:

Cumulative frequency
2
5
10
18
22

There are 22 times

22 ÷ 4 = 5 remainder 2. The list is arranged:

[5 numbers] [1 no.] [5 numbers] [5 numbers] [1 no.] [5 numbers]

The lower quartile is the 6th number.
Note from the cumulative frequency column that when the list is put in order (i.e. 1 1 2 2 2 3 3 3 3 3 4 4 4 4 4 4 4 4 5 5 5 5), the 5th number is the last 2 minute call and the 10th number is the last 3 minute call.
So the 6th number is a 3 minute call. $Q_1 = 3$ minutes.

The median falls between the 11th and 12th numbers.
The cumulative frequency column tells us the 10th number is the last 3 minute call and the 18th number is the last 4 minute call.
So the 11th and 12th numbers are 4 minute calls. $Q_2 = 4$ minutes.

The upper quartile is the 17th number.
From the cumulative frequency column we can deduce that $Q_3 = 4$ minutes.

EXERCISE 2

1 A selection of schools were asked how many fifth year sections they had. The table summarises their replies.

No. of sections	No. of schools (frequency)	Cumulative frequency
4	3	
5	5	
6	8	
7	9	
8	8	

a Construct a cumulative frequency column.
b How many schools were considered?
c Work out the two quartiles and the median number of sections.

2 A survey on house size was conducted in the village of Newton. Residents were asked how many rooms their dwelling had. The results are shown in the table.

No. of rooms	No. of dwellings (frequency)	Cumulative frequency
5	6	
6	8	
7	10	
8	12	
9	6	

a Construct a cumulative frequency column.
b How many houses were examined?
c Work out the two quartiles and the median number of rooms.
d Work out the interquartile range.

3 In a survey on the overuse of the car in the urban environment, a study was made of the number of passengers in buses. Working to the nearest 10 passengers, a random sample of 70 buses produced the following table.

No. of passengers	No. of buses (frequency)	Cumulative frequency
0	2	
10	5	
20	13	
30	15	
40	19	
50	12	
60	4	

a Work out the two quartiles and the median number of passengers.
b Work out the interquartile range.
c Draw a box plot to illustrate the figures.

4 Malcolm works for a courier service. The number of deliveries he makes each day is logged.

No. of deliveries	No. of days (frequency)
0	1
5	18
10	28
15	26
20	37

a Calculate the median number of deliveries.
b Calculate **(i)** the quartiles
(ii) the interquartile range.

Cumulative frequency diagrams – estimating the quartiles

The number of light sockets were counted in each house in a village.
They were counted to the nearest 10 for simplicity.
A cumulative frequency column was created as shown and used to draw a cumulative frequency diagram.

Number of socket(s)	Cumulative frequency
10	2
20	9
30	24
40	34
50	39
60	40

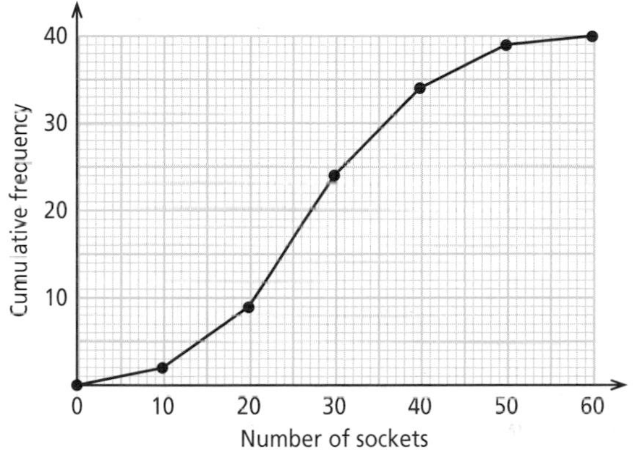

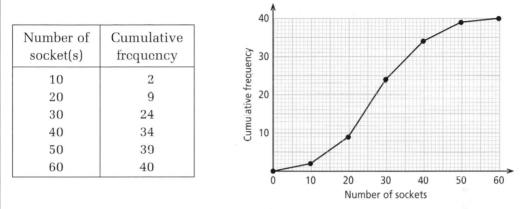

By splitting the cumulative frequency axis into four equal parts it is possible to estimate the quartiles and median from the graph.

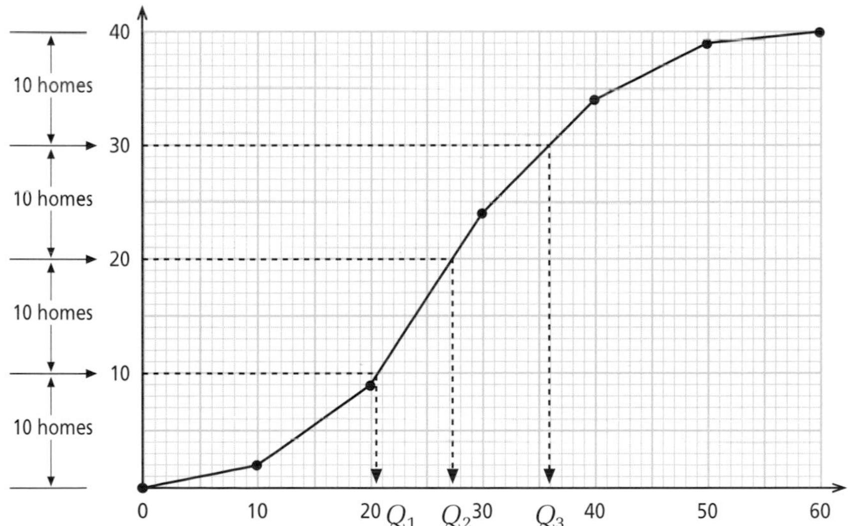

The lower quartile $Q_1 = 21$
The median $Q_2 = 27$
The upper quartile $Q_3 = 36$

We can now introduce another measure of spread known as the **semi-interquartile range**.

The interquartile range $Q_3 - Q_1 = 36 - 21 = 15$

The semi-interquartile range $= \dfrac{Q_3 - Q_1}{2} = 7.5$

EXERCISE 3

1 The heights of 100 male students were recorded.
A cumulative frequency diagram was constructed.

a Read the median value.
b Read the lower quartile (Q_1).
c Read the upper quartile (Q_3).
d Calculate the interquartile range ($Q_1 - Q_3$).
e Calculate the semi-interquartile range.
f Martin is 178 cm tall. Compare his height to the other students.

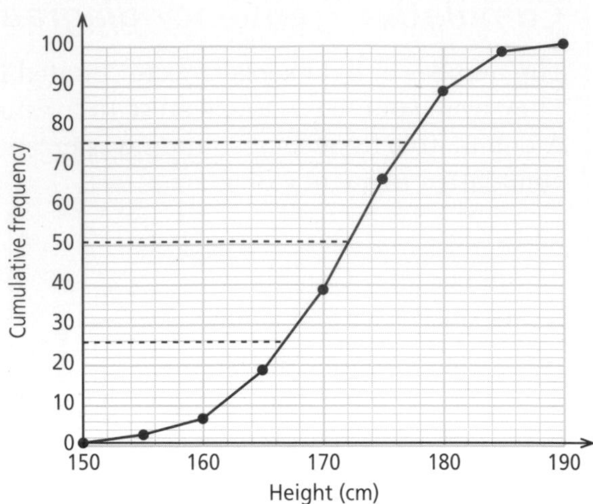

2

Cumulative frequency

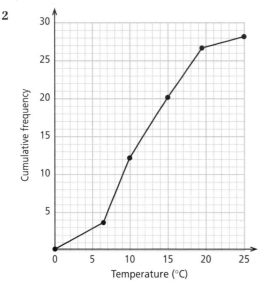

Temperature (°C)

A south coast seaside resort records the maximum temperature for each day in February. A cumulative frequency diagram is plotted.

a (i) What is a quarter of 28?
(ii) Read the median temperature.
b Read the lower and upper quartiles.
c Calculate the interquartile range.
d Calculate the semi-interquartile range.

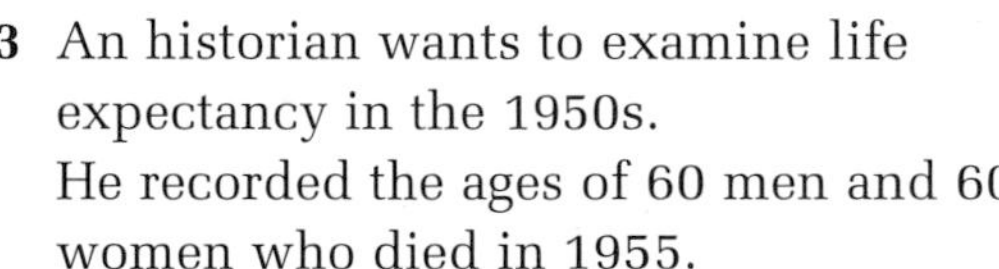

3 An historian wants to examine life expectancy in the 1950s.
He recorded the ages of 60 men and 60 women who died in 1955.

a Read the median life expectancy for men and women.
b Read the lower and upper quartiles and calculate the interquartile range and semi-interquartile range.
c Comment on the data.

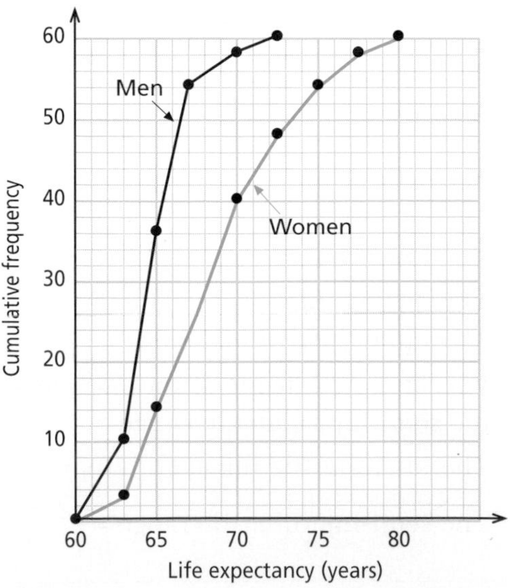

4 A store stocks two types of torch batteries, Everlast and PowerGlow. The frequency tables show how long, to the nearest hour, samples of 200 of each last.

Everlast

Hours of life	1	2	3	4	5	6	7	8	9	10
Frequency	0	10	10	10	20	30	40	30	30	20

PowerGlow

Hours of life	1	2	3	4	5	6	7	8	9	10
Frequency	5	15	25	30	30	20	10	5	20	40

a Construct cumulative frequency diagrams for both tables.
b Find the median life of each battery type.
c Calculate the interquartile range and the semi-interquartile range of each.
d Which battery would you recommend. Why?

Standard deviation

The **range** measures spread. Unfortunately any big change in either the largest or smallest score will mean a big change in the range, even though only one number may have changed.

The **semi-interquartile range** is less sensitive to a single number changing but again it is only really based on two of the scores.

A measure of spread which uses all the data is the **standard deviation**.

The **deviation** of a score is how much the score differs from the mean.

Example 1 Find the standard deviation of these five scores: 70, 72, 75, 78, 80.

Step 1
The mean is
375 ÷ 5 = 75

Step 2 Score − mean

Step 3

	Score	Deviation	$(\text{Deviation})^2$
	70	−5	25
	72	−3	9
	75	0	0
	78	3	9
	80	5	25
Totals	375	0	68

Step 4
The mean square deviation is
68 ÷ 5 = 13.6

The standard deviation is $\sqrt{13.6} = 3.7$ to 1 d.p.

Step 1 Calculate the mean.

Step 2 Write down the deviation of each score.
Note that a negative sign signifies that it is below the mean.
(If we tried to average these deviations we would end up with zero.)

Step 3 Square each deviation.
(This gets rid of the negative signs.)

Step 4 Add the squared deviations and divide by the number of scores.
(The mean square deviation.)

Step 5 Take the root of this value: $\sqrt{13.6} = 3.7$ (to 1 d.p.)
The standard deviation = 3.7.

Having squared and then taken the root, we know that the standard deviation is in the same units as the scores.

Example 2 Find the standard deviation of these six amounts of money:
£12, £18, £27, £36, £37, £50.

Mean score: 180 ÷ 6 = 30

Mean square deviation:
962 ÷ 6 = 160.33

Standard deviation:
$\sqrt{160.33} = 12.7$ (to 1 d.p.)

The mean is £30 and the standard deviation is £12.70.

	Score (£)	Deviation	$(\text{Deviation})^2$
	12	−18	324
	18	−12	144
	27	−3	9
	36	6	36
	37	7	49
	50	20	400
Totals	180		962

When the standard deviation is low it means the scores are close to the mean.

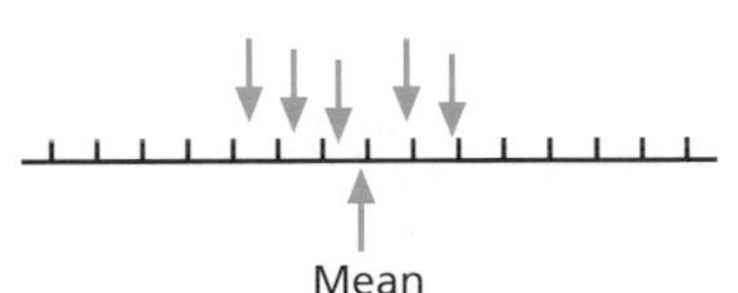

When the standard deviation is high it means the scores are spread out from the mean.

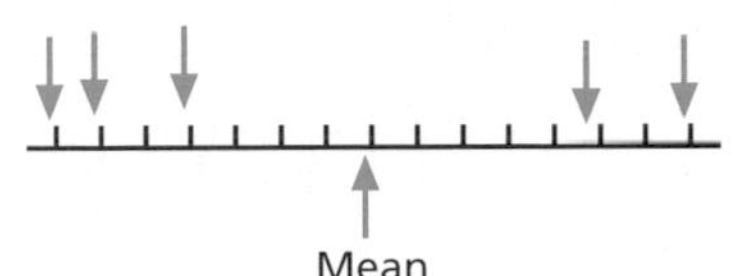

EXERCISE 4

1 Four friends compare the lengths of their Christmas holidays: Elaine 7 days, Frank 7 days, Gill 12 days and Harry 14 days.

a Check that the mean length of holiday is 10 days.

b Copy and complete the table.

c Find the mean square deviation (the mean of the last column).

d Find the standard deviation.

	Days	Deviation	(Deviation)^2
	7	−3	9
	7		
	12		
	14		
Totals			

2 a The shoe sizes of five girls are 3, 4, 4, 7 and 7.

(i) Calculate the mean shoe size.

	Size	Deviation	(Deviation)^2
	3		
	4		
	4		
	7		
	7		
Totals			

(ii) Copy and complete the table.

(iii) Calculate the standard deviation of the girls' shoe sizes.

	Size	Deviation	(Deviation)^2
	3		
	4		
	4		
	7		
	7		
Totals			

b The shoe sizes of five boys are 5, 7, 7, 7 and 9.

(i) Calculate the mean.

(ii) Calculate the standard deviation correct to 1 d.p.

(iii) Who has the larger feet, the girls or the boys?

(iv) Do the shoe sizes of the boys vary more than the girls?

Finding the standard deviation from a sample

The 300 employees of Statsys plc all live within a 25 km radius of the factory.
The table gives the actual distances to the nearest kilometre.
Notice that the standard deviation of the distribution is 7.09 km.

	1	2	3	4	5	6	7	8	9	10	11	12
1	25	12	21	15	5	2	7	10	5	20	24	17
2	24	14	4	6	18	20	21	24	25	15	15	22
3	15	8	9	11	13	2	17	17	16	18	15	1
4	15	6	22	16	24	4	17	20	19	16	4	4
5	25	12	20	22	7	8	16	13	17	20	18	19
6	5	22	19	10	14	6	8	21	5	21	7	7
7	22	15	7	10	9	15	19	2	4	20	11	1
8	22	10	12	19	7	22	10	5	14	2	6	2
9	8	1	14	25	13	25	5	8	13	13	19	10
10	18	2	15	24	9	2	11	12	20	14	22	24
11	19	6	23	18	25	6	10	16	23	15	2	11
12	5	7	13	17	18	8	1	5	19	11	18	21
13	10	25	25	18	9	8	4	5	19	15	11	6
14	23	13	23	21	10	14	7	8	15	12	11	24
15	23	8	7	3	15	6	6	21	3	12	8	20
16	4	17	23	11	20	22	20	8	9	11	5	2
17	2	14	19	19	13	1	25	3	5	3	5	10
18	10	17	14	22	22	13	9	25	20	17	7	8
19	4	4	19	11	25	14	10	5	12	3	4	9
20	4	22	11	10	4	20	22	15	1	14	5	10
21	6	4	18	17	3	20	8	4	19	10	22	22
22	2	11	22	2	13	13	16	23	25	8	10	6
23	21	16	12	12	24	23	4	14	25	1	1	7
24	4	1	8	19	15	17	19	16	3	6	19	13
25	12	7	3	10	12	11	1	15	10	24	15	24
								Standard deviation				7.09

It costs time and money to collect this complete set of data.
It would be cheaper to just take a sample.
How is the standard deviation of the sample connected to the standard deviation of the population?

Set your calculator to FIX mode with 0 decimal places.

Rand $\times$ 12 + 1 will generate a random number between 1 and 12.

Rand $\times$ 25 + 1 will generate a random number between 1 and 25.

Generate random number pairs which you can then use as coordinates to pick out a sample of six numbers from the table.

Calculate the standard deviation of the six numbers using the formula:
$\sqrt{((\text{sum of squared deviations})/n)}$
where n is the size of the sample.

Now use the formula:
$\sqrt{((\text{sum of squared deviations})/(n-1))}$

Try this several times. Average the results of your attempts.
Over many trials you should find that, on average, the second formula provides a better estimate for the standard deviation of the whole set of numbers than the first.

For the rest of the chapter we will assume we are always working with a sample and therefore will always work with the second formula.

$$\text{Mean} = \frac{\text{sum of scores}}{n}$$

$$\text{Standard deviation} = \sqrt{\left(\frac{\text{sum of squared deviations}}{n-1}\right)}$$

This formula is usually written as $s = \sqrt{\frac{\Sigma(x - \overline{x})^2}{n-1}}$ where $\overline{x}$ represents the sample mean and Σ stands for "the sum of".
When you calculate the mean and standard deviation of the sample in this manner, you are also finding an estimate for the mean and standard deviation of the underlying population.

EXERCISE 5

1 a The pulse rates of eight athletes are measured after completing strenuous exercise. The rates are 70, 72, 73, 74, 75, 76, 76 and 76 beats per minute.
Calculate the sample mean rate and the standard deviation (correct to 1 d.p.).

b Eight office staff take the same exercise as the athletes.
Their pulse rates are 80, 81, 83, 90, 94, 96, 96 and 100.

(i) Calculate the sample mean rate for the office staff.
(ii) Calculate the sample standard deviation correct to 1 d.p.
(iii) Who are fitter, the athletes or the office staff?
(iv) What do the standard deviations tell you?

2 At the start of a typing course a student recorded her mistakes per minute as follows:
0 1 2 2 3 5 7 8

a (i) Calculate the mean number of errors she made per minute.
(ii) Calculate the sample standard deviation.

b After several practice sessions she again recorded her mistakes per minute, with these results: 2 3 3 3 4 4 4 5

(i) Calculate her new mean and standard deviation.
(ii) Has her mean improved?
(iii) Has her consistency improved?

3 The number of frogs in various local ponds were counted for a wildlife survey.
The results were: 7 21 35 37 57 68 100

a Calculate:
(i) the range **(ii)** the semi-interquartile range
(iii) the sample standard deviation.

b A year later a second survey was done. The results this time were:
12 25 34 37 52 62 76. Calculate the new:
(i) range **(ii)** semi-interquartile range **(iii)** standard deviation.

c Which measure of spread was affected most by the small changes in the data?

Using the calculator

You need to be in STAT mode.   or  

It is good practice to clear all the memories. AC

Example You want to enter this list of numbers: 2, 3, 4, 5, 5, 6, 6, 7, 7.

2 M+ 3 M+ 4 M+ 5 M+ 5 M+ 6 M+ 6 M+ 7 M+ 7 M+

If you wish to know how many numbers have been entered, press

n In this example, the calculator will tell you 9.

If you wish to know the sum of the list, press

Σx In this case the answer is 45.

If you wish to know the mean of the list, press

$\bar{x}$ The answer here is 5.

If you wish to know the standard deviation of the list, assuming you are working with a sample, press

s_n The answer in this example is 1.73 (to 2 d.p.)

Note: When you are definitely dealing with a population then the standard deviation is calculated using σ_n

For the above example this will give you 1.63 (to 2 d.p.).
In this chapter we assume that all data are from samples.

Warning
Not all calculators behave in the same way. Check your manual. If in doubt, ask!

Warning
On some calculators you will need to press 

EXERCISE 6

1 Sure Start plc make car batteries. They set up an experiment which tests how long a batch will last. The results, to the nearest year, are:
4, 5, 3, 6, 1, 4, 3, 2, 4, 5, 6, 2, 2, 3, 1.
 a Calculate:
  (i) the mean
  (ii) the standard deviation correct to 1 d.p.
 b Their guarantee lasts for 3 years. Should they be pleased with this sample? Explain.
 c If the standard deviation is greater than 2 the manufacturing process has to be improved.
 What do the results of this sample suggest about the process?

2 A company is developing a central heating system controlled by a thermostat. The equipment is set to keep a room at 20 °C.

The actual temperatures recorded (in degrees Celsius) are:

21.5, 22.3, 19.4, 20.2, 18.8, 19.6, 21.1. 19.8, 18.5, 20.8.

a Calculate:

(i) the mean

(ii) the standard deviation correct to 1 d.p.

b To pass a quality control test the mean should be within 0.5 °C of the setting and the standard deviation should be less than 2 °C. What do the results show?

3 A company makes a machine that serves tennis balls for players to hit for practice. To test the machine it is set for 80 km/h and the actual speeds of the balls are recorded.

The speeds, in km/h, are:

82, 86, 75, 80, 79, 72, 75, 88, 86, 74,
84, 70, 80, 82, 73, 74, 86, 88, 84, 72.

a Calculate:

(i) the mean speed

(ii) the standard deviation correct to 1 d.p.

b If the mean speed is within 2 km/h of the setting and the standard deviation is less than 5 km/h the machine passes; if not, it needs adjusting. What action should be taken?

4 A consumer magazine is surveying vehicle breakdown and rescue companies. It produces a report on the times taken to reach broken down vehicles.

The times, in minutes, for samples of two companies are given.

Roadside Rescue: 30, 40, 28, 40, 25, 45, 30, 33, 45, 40, 41, 39.
Auto Assist: 38, 12, 18, 68, 11, 39, 77, 80, 13, 18, 14, 12.

a Calculate:

(i) the mean

(ii) the standard deviation for each company.

b Which of the two would you recommend? Give reasons.

5 A scientist compares the effect of two types of fertiliser on a cereal crop.

Fertiliser	A	B
Mean height	120 cm	80 cm
Standard deviation	15	40

Compare the two fertilisers to find which gives:

a the tallest growth

b the more consistent height.

Scatter graphs

Example In a science lesson Rachel records the length of a spring when extended by different weights.

Weight (W g)	100	400	800	500	650	250	700	600
Length of spring (L cm)	20	36	57	39	49	26	54	47

Follow these steps to try and find a connection between W and L.

Step 1 Draw a scatter graph.
It shows there is a strong positive relation between L and W.

It is often valuable to draw a line to represent this relation.

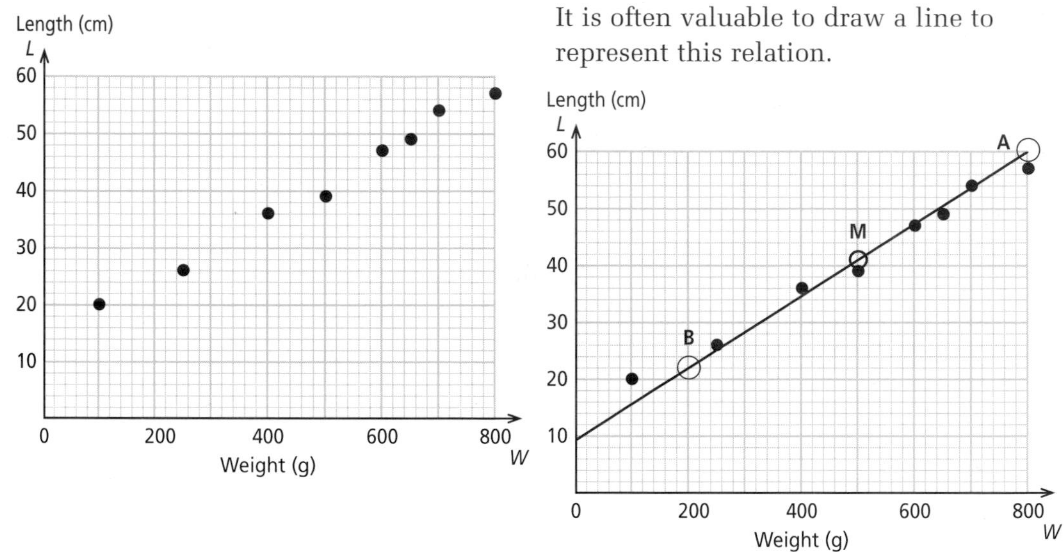

Step 2 Calculate the mean weight (500 g) and the mean length (41 cm).

Step 3 Plot the point M(500, 41).

Step 4 Draw the best-fitting straight line passing through M.

To find the equation of the line of best fit

A straight line equation has the form $y = mx + c$ or in this case $L = mW + c$ where m is the gradient and c is the intercept on the y axis.

Step 5 Find two suitable points on the line, e.g. A(800, 60) and B(200, 22).

Step 6 Calculate the gradient. $m = \frac{60 - 22}{800 - 200} = 0.063$

So $L = 0.063W + c$

Step 7 Find c by substituting one point into the equation:

$$22 = 0.063 \times 200 + c$$

$$c = 9.4$$

You can check this figure is reasonable using the graph.

Step 8 The equation of the line of best fit is $L = 0.063W + 9.4$.

EXERCISE 7

1 Kate investigated the link between shoe sizes (S) and lengths of hands (H cm) for a few friends.

Shoe sizes (S)	5	9	8	4	8	6	10	6
Hand lengths (H cm)	15	19	18	15	17	16	20	16

She plotted the points and drew the best-fitting straight line.

$H = mS + c$

a Check that the point given by the two means (M) is (7, 17).

b Check that the two points A (10, 20) and B (6, 16) lie on the line.

c Copy and complete to calculate the gradient m:

$$m = \frac{20 - 16}{10 - \ldots} = \ldots$$

d $H = mS + c$. Using A(10, 20) and your value for m, find c.

e Write down the equation of the line of best fit.

f Use your equation to estimate the length of someone's hand who has shoe size 11.

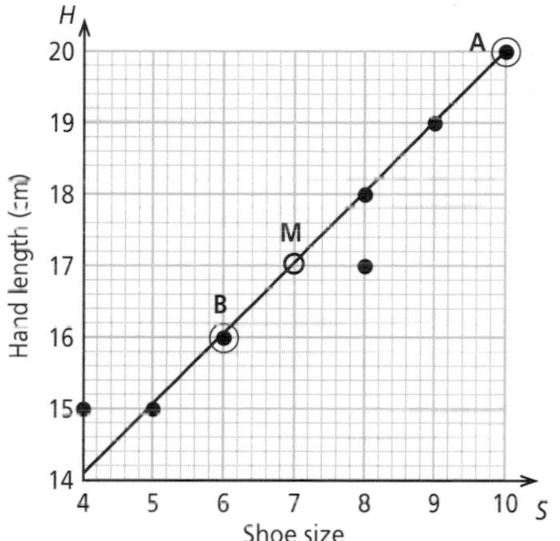

2

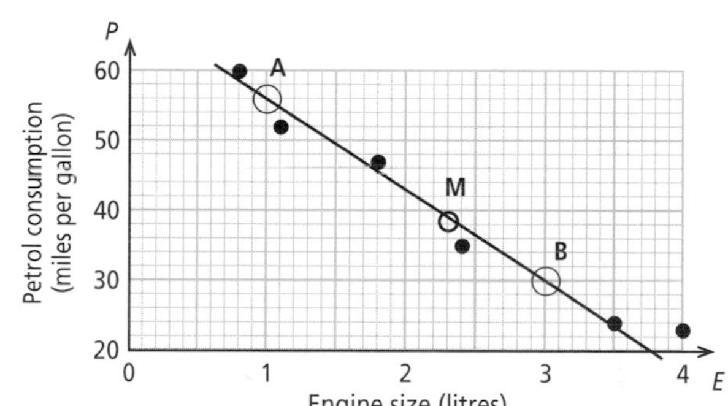

Mark thinks that there may be a link between the size of a car engine (E litres) and its petrol consumption (P miles per gallon).
He test drives a few cars and produces a scatter graph.
The points A(1, 56) and B(3, 30) lie on the best-fitting line.

a Use these points to calculate the gradient m. (Hint: it is negative.)

b The equation is $P = mE + c$. Calculate c.

c Write down the equation of the line of best fit.

d Estimate the consumption of a car with a 2 litre engine.

e Could you use this equation to find the size of engine needed to get 100 miles per gallon?

3 An estate agent lists the annual income of a few clients, together with the value of the house they buy.

Client	A	B	C	D	E	F	G
Income in £1000s (L)	35	50	15	12	18	24	28
House value in £1000s (V)	68	98	32	22	35	46	56

a Plot a scatter graph.
b Calculate **(i)** the mean income **(ii)** the mean house value.
c Draw the line of best fit.
d For the equation $V = mI + c$, find m and c.
Write down the equation of the line of best fit.
e A person has an income of £40 000. What price might they pay for a house?
f Could you use this equation to find out how much a person with an income of £6000 might pay for a house? Explain.

4 A certain weedkiller is applied to plants under laboratory conditions.
The increase in the length (x cm) of the plant before it died was charted against the number of days (y) it took to die.

Increase in the length (x)	1	2	3	3	4	5	5	6	6	7
Days to die (y)	5	6	6	7	7	7	8	8	9	10

a Plot a scatter graph.
b Draw the line of best fit.
c For the equation $y = mx + c$, find m and c.
Write down the equation of the line of best fit.
d A weed takes 3.5 days to die. Estimate its increase in length.
e Would it be sensible to use the line to estimate the increase in the length of a plant which took 20 days to die?

5 The owners of an orange grove are trying to grow bigger and bigger oranges, but they are worried that the bigger the orange the lower the sugar content.
Using a scale of 1 to 20 to measure sweetness and centimetres to measure radius, they produce the following data.

Sweetness	1	3	6	10	13	15	18	19
Radius (cm)	5.4	5	5	4.4	4.4	4	4	3.8

a Draw a line of best fit.
b Comment on the relationship between size and sweetness.
c Work out the equation of the line of best fit.

6 The rate of inflation is of concern to most politicians. It gives an idea of how fast prices are going up. The table gives the rate for various years since 1975.

Year	1975	1978	1981	1984	1987	1990	1993	1996	1999
Rate (%)	25	15	10	6	5	10	2	3	1

a Draw a scatter graph connecting year to rate of inflation.
b Draw the best-fitting straight line and find its equation.
c Comment on the usefulness of your line to estimate inflation in:
(i) 1960 **(ii)** 1994 **(iii)** 2001.

Probability

Throwing a dice randomly produces the numbers from 1 to 6.
By this we mean that each number is **equally likely** and that there is no way of predicting the outcome of a particular throw.

Simon predicts the outcomes of football results using a dice.
If he throws a 1, 2 or 3 he says the home team is going to win.
If he throws a 4 or 5 then the away team will win.
If he throws a 6 then it will be a draw.
What is the most likely outcome? How do we measure the likelihood of an event?

The most common way is to calculate the **probability** of the event.

This is calculated using the formula $\textbf{P(event)} = \dfrac{\textbf{number of favourable outcomes}}{\textbf{number of possible outcomes}}$

assuming each outcome is equally likely.

Example P(home win) $= \frac{3}{6} = 0.5$

P(away win) $= \frac{2}{6} = 0.33$ (to 2 d.p.)

P(draw) $= \frac{1}{6} = 0.17$ (to 2 d.p.)

You can see that by Simon's method a home win is the most likely result.

EXERCISE 8

1 A coin is tossed.
  a How many possible outcomes are there?
  b How many heads are there?
  c Calculate: **(i)** P(head) **(ii)** P(tail).

2 A card is chosen at random from a deck of 52 cards.
  a How many possible outcomes are there?
  b Calculate: **(i)** P(ace) **(ii)** P(heart) **(iii)** P(red) **(iv)** P(ace of hearts).

3 There are ten bays in a car park. The first car in the morning is equally likely to park in any one. What is: **a** P(park in bay 7) **b** P(park in bay 10)
  c P(park in a bay numbered less than 4)?

4 A normal dice is rolled.
  a Calculate: **(i)** P(4) **(ii)** P(even number).
  b Neil needs any number to win.
    (i) How many favourable outcomes are there?
    (ii) How many possible outcomes are there?
    (iii) Calculate P(Neil wins).
  c What is the probability of a certainty?
  d Sandra needs a 7 to finish.
    (i) How many favourable outcomes are there?
    (ii) How many possible outcomes are there?
    (iii) Calculate P(Sandra finishes).
  e What is the probability of an impossibility?

5 James sells 100 raffle tickets for charity.
Kalil buys 1 ticket. Sarah buys 10 tickets.
Calculate: **a** P(Kalil wins) **b** P(Sarah wins).

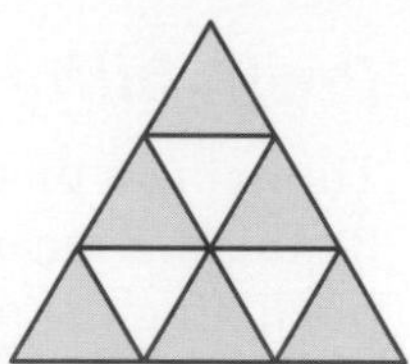

6 A pin is stuck, at random, into this network of congruent triangles.
Calculate: **a** P(white) **b** P(green).

7 In a card game, each letter of the alphabet is printed on its own card. A card is selected at random.
Calculate: **a** P(vowel) **b** P(consonant).

8 **a** In a row of houses, 25 have double-glazing and 15 have not.
If a double-glazing company sends advertising to a house chosen at random calculate:
(i) P(house double-glazed) **(ii)** P(house not double-glazed).

b The company decides only to send agents to a street if the probability of a house selected at random *not* having double-glazing is 0.4 or greater.
Which of the following streets will be targeted?
(i) Smith Street where 4 out of 9 don't have double-glazing.
(ii) Rose Street where 14 out of 30 don't have double-glazing.
(iii) Monarch Street where 12 out of 30 don't have double-glazing.

9 **a** A box of sweets contains 5 chocolates, 10 mints and 15 chews.
A sweet is selected at random.
Calculate: **(i)** P(chocolate) **(ii)** P(mint) **(iii)** P(chew).

b An Easter selection box contains 60 mixed sweets.
How many chocolates must there be if P(chocolate) = 0.4?

10 A coin and a dice are tossed at the same time.
a List all the possible outcomes.
b Calculate:
(i) P(H and 3)
(ii) P(H and even)
(iii) P(H and not a 6).

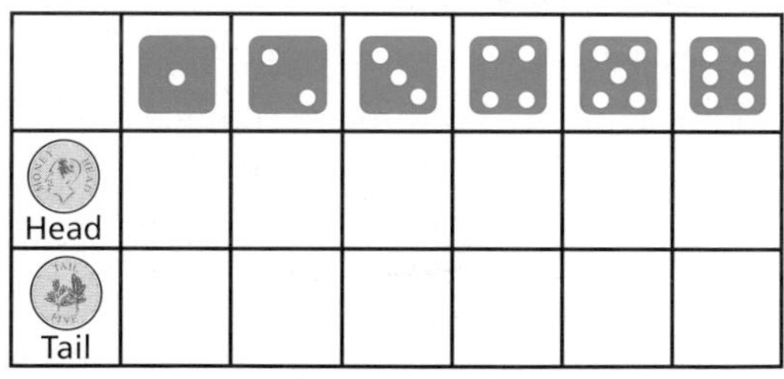

11 In a word game, a letter is chosen at random from each word:

a Calculate: **(i)** P(E) from PERCENTAGE **(ii)** P(A) from PARALLEL.
b Which is more likely:
(i) choosing an E from PERCENTAGE or **(ii)** choosing an A from PARALLEL?

Relative frequencies

A particular stretch of town road is thought to be overused. A survey of traffic produces these figures.

Vehicle	Frequency
Bike	5
Motorbike	8
Car	15
Van	7
Lorry	9
Bus	6
Total =	50

Sometimes it is more useful to know what fraction of the sample fall into a category rather than how many. At these times we calculate the relative frequencies.

Vehicle	Frequency	Relative frequency
Bike	5	$5 \div 50 = 0.1$
Motorbike	8	$8 \div 50 = 0.16$
Car	15	$15 \div 50 = 0.3$
Van	7	$7 \div 50 = 0.14$
Lorry	9	$9 \div 50 = 0.18$
Bus	6	$6 \div 50 = 0.12$
Total =	50	$50 \div 50 = 1$

$\frac{5}{50}$ or 0.1 of the traffic are bikes.

A good check: the relative frequencies add up to 1. Rounding errors may make a slight difference.

EXERCISE 9

1 A sports centre hall is used for a variety of activities. The table shows the number of sessions it is booked for each activity during one week.

Activity	Frequency
Badminton	6
5-a-side football	7
Aerobics	5
Dance	3
Basketball	4

a Add a relative frequency column.

b What is the relative frequency of:

(i) badminton

(ii) any game involving a ball?

c Draw a pie chart to illustrate the data.

2 An itemised phone bill allows you to see which service is most used.
The table shows the frequency of different types of calls on one phone bill.

Type of call	Frequency
Local	80
Long distance	20
Family and Friends	97
Business discount	64
Phonecard	39

a Add a relative frequency column (work to 2 d.p.).

b What is the relative frequency of these calls?

(i) phonecard

(ii) local

(iii) not local.

3 The table shows the sales recorded in a shoe shop one day.

a Add a relative frequency column (work to 2 d.p.).

b What is the relative frequency of:

(i) size 6 sales

(ii) sales of shoes bigger than size 8?

Shoe size	Frequency
6	8
7	3
8	5
9	9
10	12

The relative frequency of size 7 sales is 0.08, i.e. 0.08 of the sales were size 7.
If the shop orders more shoes they would be sensible to make 0.08 of them size 7.
If they ordered 200 more pairs of shoes, they should order 16 pairs of size 7 shoes (0.08 of 200 = 16).

c How many size 8 pairs should they order if they order 200 more pairs of shoes?

4 A book shop records this list of sales for one day.

a Add a relative frequency column (work to 2 d.p.).

b What is the relative frequency of:

(i) sales of romance novels

(ii) all sales except sci-fi?

c If another 500 books are to be ordered, how many of each category would be best?

Category	Frequency
Romance	20
Western	23
Sci-Fi	45
Historic	14
Detective	28

Probability from relative frequency

Three students carry out surveys to study left-handedness. Dennis asks 10 friends. Emma asks a class of 25 students. Felix surveys a whole year group (200 students).

	Number of LH students	Total asked
Dennis	2	10
Emma	3	25
Felix	20	200

Dennis finds 2 out of 10 are left-handed: the relative frequency is $\frac{2}{10} = 0.2$.

Emma finds 3 out of 25 are left-handed: the relative frequency is $\frac{3}{25} = 0.12$.

Felix finds 20 out of 200 are left-handed: the relative frequency is $\frac{20}{200} = 0.1$.

Because Felix asked a lot more people, his result is the most representative.
We can use Felix's data to estimate the probability of left-handedness.

$$\text{P(left-handed)} \approx 0.1$$

When the sum of the frequencies is large, the relative frequency of an outcome is a good estimate of the probability of the outcome.

EXERCISE 10

1 Jean, Ali and Claire each carry out a survey on house alarms. The table shows their results.

	Number of houses with alarms	Total in survey	Relative frequency
Jean	7	10	
Ali	12	20	
Claire	40	100	

a Calculate the relative frequency of house alarms for each person.
b Whose results would you use to estimate the probability of a house chosen at random having an alarm?
c Write down P(house has an alarm).

2 The soccer results one weekend are given in the table.
a Copy and complete the table.
b For a match chosen at random estimate:
(i) P(Home win) **(ii)** P(Draw) **(iii)** P(Away win).

Result	Frequency	Relative frequency
Home win	45	
Draw	20	
Away win	35	
Total		

3 A drawing-pin is dropped and the number of 'pin ups' recorded every 10 throws.

a Copy and complete the table.

'Pin up' frequency	5	11	12	14	18	20	22	24
Number of drops	10	20	30	40	50	60	70	80
Relative frequency of 'pin up'	0.5	0.55						

b What is the best estimate for the probability of 'pin up'?
c Try this experiment with a box of drawing-pins. Comment on the relative frequency of 'pin ups' as the number of pins used increases.

4 A bus driver on a regular route thinks that a particular set of traffic lights is nearly always against him. He records the number of times the lights are red every 20 trips.

Number of times on red	16	30	42	52	65
Number of trips	20	40	60	80	100
Relative frequency of red					

a Copy and complete the table.
b What is the best estimate for the probability of the lights being red?
c Was the bus driver correct? Comment.

Relative frequency is an estimate for probability. The bigger the sample, the better the estimate.

Random numbers

Dice, cards and balls are used to produce random numbers in a lottery.

RAND The calculator has a button which generates random numbers between 0 and 1 (usually to 3 d.p.). Check your calculator.

We can get the calculator to simulate (behave like) a dice.

Step 1 Put your calculator in FIX mode.

Step 2 Set the number of decimal places to zero.

Step 3 Set the constant facility to multiply by 5. (Note 5 and not 6.)

Step 4 Each time you press RAND = you will get one of 0, 1, 2, 3, 4, 5.

Treat the zero as the 6 and the calculator simulates a dice.

For a different range, change the constant in step 3.
For a coin make it 1.
For a lottery make it 48 (and ignore any duplicate numbers).

Simulation

Example

A garage is giving away medallions featuring the four top teams in a league. They are not all equally easy to collect.

P(Rovers) = 0.5 P(Stars) = 0.1
P(Wanderers) = 0.3 P(Saints) = 0.1

If you only get one medallion at each visit, how many visits is it likely to take to collect a full set?

Set the constant facility to 9. RAND =

Make up decision rules about what happens as each number comes up.

0, 1, 2, 3, 4 you get a Rovers' medallion.
5, 6, 7 you get a Wanderers' medallion.
8 you get a Stars' medallion.
9 you get a Saints' medallion.

Note how the rule matches the probabilities.

Set up a table

and start recording:

<table>
<tr><th>Rovers
0–4</th><th>Wanderers
5–7</th><th>Stars
8</th><th>Saints
9</th></tr>
<tr><td>卌 |||
8</td><td>|||
3</td><td>|
1</td><td>||
2</td></tr>
</table>

= 14 visits before collecting a full set.

Do the experiment several times and you should get a 'feel' for what is typical.

EXERCISE 11

1 A plant starts as a single shoot. It grows according to the following rules.

- Each branch grows 1 cm in a year.
- A branch can then do one of three things:

flower and die	P(flower) = 0.3
keep growing	P(keep growing) = 0.2
fork and grow	P(fork) = 0.5.

a Set up your calculator to randomly give 0–9.

b Simulate the growth of four different plants growing over three years.

2 At a supermarket there are three check-outs.
It is found that the probabilities of a customer going to a particular checkout are:

P(check-out A) = 0.6
P(check-out B) = 0.3
P(check-out C) = 0.1

a Set up your calculator to randomly give 0–9.

b **(i)** Make up a decision rule about what happens as each number comes up.
(ii) Use the rule to simulate the arrival of 12 customers at the check-out.

c After three numbers have been generated, allow one person to leave the queue of each check-out. (This customer has been served.)
Run the simulation again. Does a queue develop?

d An usher is employed to make sure that each check-out has an equal probability of being used. How does this affect the queueing?
(Hint: Set up your calculator to randomly give 0–2.)

3 Collect data at local traffic lights which will allow you to estimate:

a the probability of being stopped

b the mean number of cars coming per minute

c the phasing/timing of the lights.

Use your data to set up a simulation.

CHAPTER 11 REVIEW

1 Mrs Banks, Head of College, keeps a record of the absentee figures for one week. Note that 38 students were absent for only one day, 42 were absent for two days, etc.

Number of days absent	Frequency	Cumulative frequency
1	38	
2	42	
3	26	
4	14	
5	10	

a Copy and complete the table.
b How many students were absent in the week?
c Work out: **(i)** the median number of days absent
(ii) the quartiles.

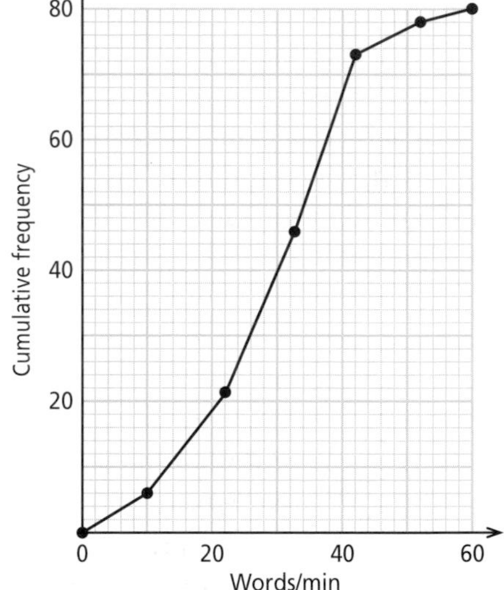

2 Mrs Wilson's word-processing evening class is making progress.
The cumulative frequency diagram shows how many words they can type per minute.
a From the graph find:
(i) the median number of words/minute
(ii) the lower quartile
(iii) the upper quartile.
b Calculate: **(i)** the interquartile range
(ii) the semi-interquartile range.

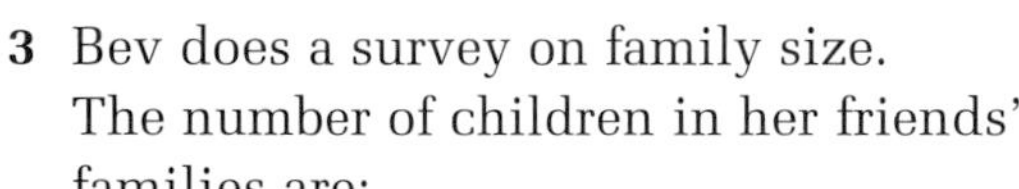

3 Bev does a survey on family size.
The number of children in her friends' families are:
1, 1, 2, 2, 2, 3, 4, 5.
a Without using the standard deviation key, work out the sample standard deviation of this list.
b Bev's family has four children.
How does this compare with the rest?

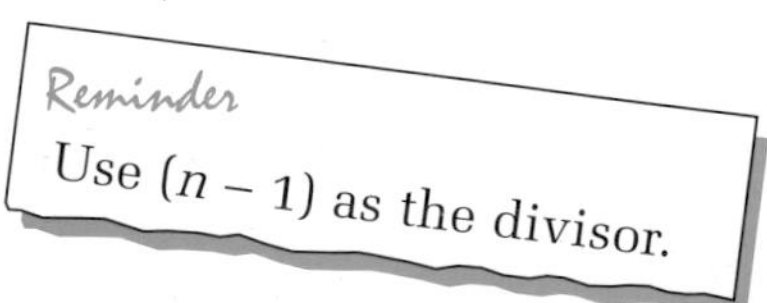

4 The Simpsons are wanting to buy a semi-detached house.
They list the prices of houses advertised in an estate agent's window:
£62 000, £80 000, £56 000, £50 000, £58 000, £65 000,
£74 000, £68 000, £62 000, £80 000, £73 000, £69 000.
Use a calculator to work out:
a the sample mean house price
b the standard deviation correct to the nearest £1000.

5 Natalie collects data for a scatter graph of the number of wins and the total points for teams in a soccer league.

Team	A	B	C	D	E	F	G	H
Wins W	5	2	8	7	4	3	10	9
Points P	18	6	28	26	15	9	35	31

a Plot a scatter graph using the horizontal axis for W.
b Calculate M and draw a line of best fit.
c For $P = mW + c$, find m and c.
d Write down the equation of the line of best fit.

6 The table shows the number of car drivers taking their test for the first time at the Oldtown Test Centre in one week.

Day	Mon	Tue	Wed	Thu	Fri	Sat	Total
Total	10	9	12	10	15	4	60
Relative Frequency							

a Calculate the relative frequency of the number taking the test each day.
This table shows the number who passed the test.

Day	Mon	Tue	Wed	Thu	Fri	Sat	Total
Passed	6	3	3	1	3	2	
Relative Frequency							

b How many passed during the week?
c Work out the relative frequency of passes each day.
d **(i)** How many sat the test during the week?
(ii) How many passed?
(iii) Estimate the probability of passing first time.

7 The Wheel of Fortune spins.
a Calculate:
(i) P(winning £100)
(ii) P(winning £10)
(iii) P(losing).
b Get your calculator to simulate 12 spins of the wheel at £10 a go.

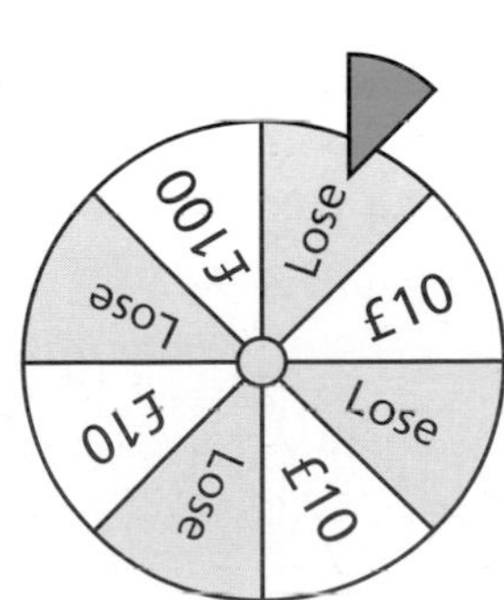

12 Revising Unit 2

Trigonometry

Reminders

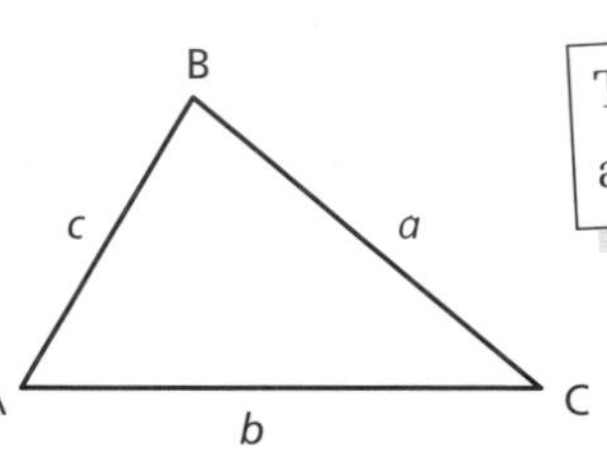

The Sine Rule: $\dfrac{a}{\sin A} = \dfrac{b}{\sin B} = \dfrac{c}{\sin C}$

The Cosine Rule for finding a side: $a^2 = b^2 + c^2 - 2bc \cos A$

The Cosine Rule for finding an angle: $\cos A = \dfrac{b^2 + c^2 - a^2}{2bc}$

A rule for finding the area of a triangle: Area $= \frac{1}{2}bc \sin A$

EXERCISE 1

1 Calculate the length a correct to 3 s.f.

a

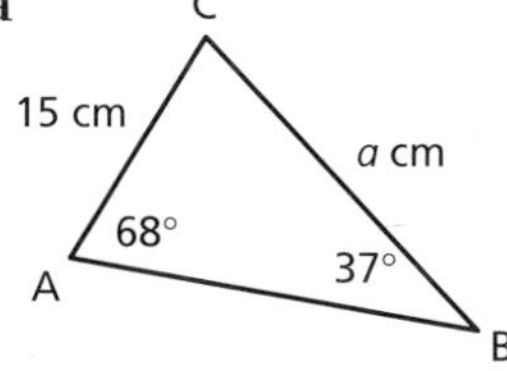

b

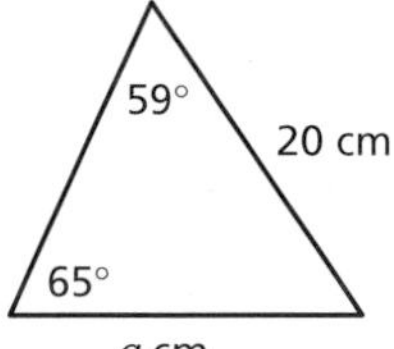

c

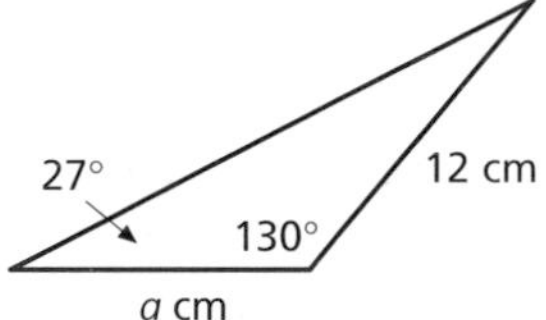

2 Calculate angle DFE correct to 1 d.p.

a

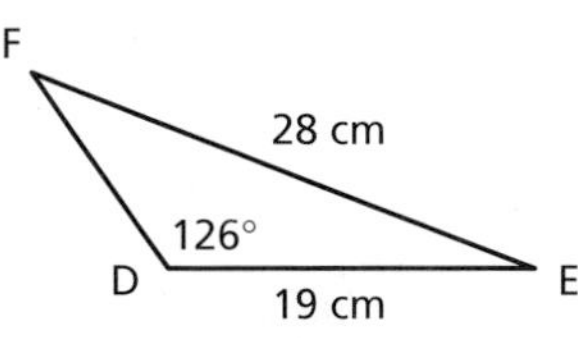

b

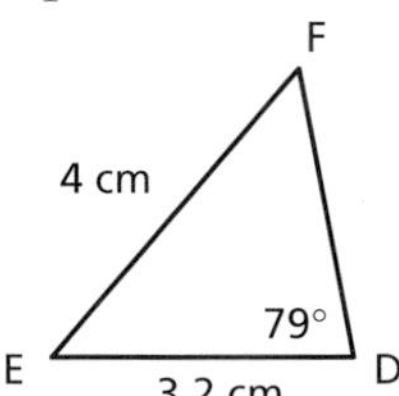

c

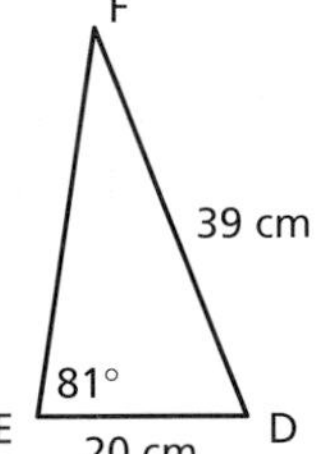

3 Calculate correct to 3 s.f.:

a the area of triangle JKL **b** the length JL.

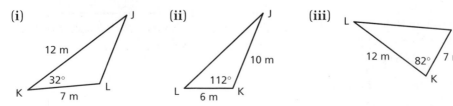

(i)

(ii)

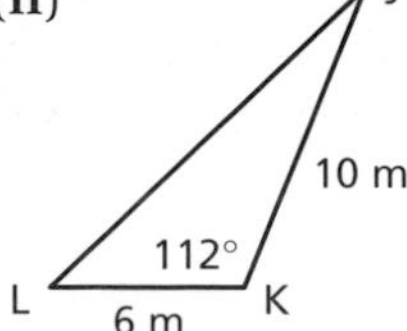

(iii)

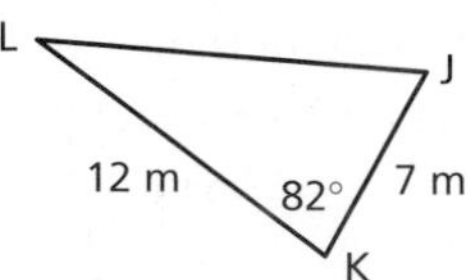

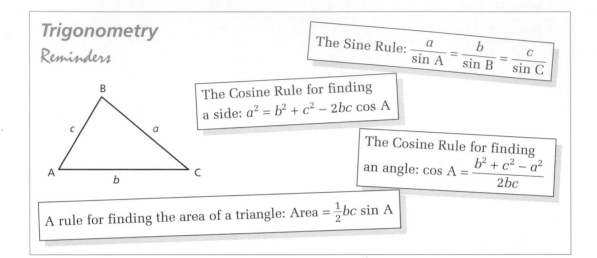

4 Calculate angle HGI correct to 1 d.p.

a

G 8.9 m I, 6.4 m, 7.2 m, H

b

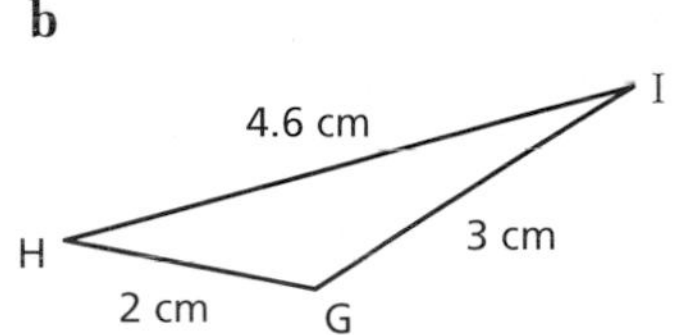

c

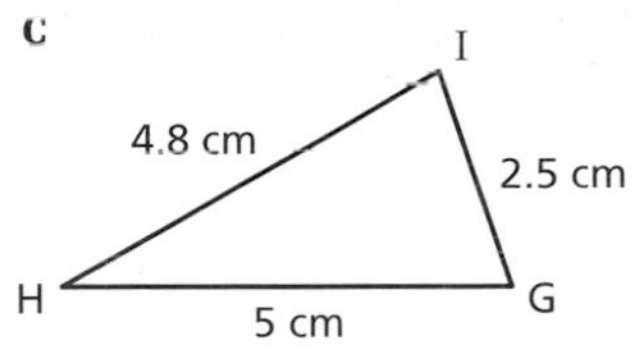

5 At a science-fiction convention two types of souvenir pennants are on sale. They are sold in tubes just long enough to contain them.

U, 30 cm, The Cassinni Division, 41°, V, 25 cm; X, 23 cm, TERRA FIRMA, 47°, Y, 28 cm

a **(i)** Which pennant has the greater area?

(ii) Calculate the difference between the areas.

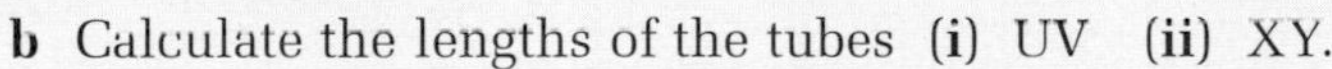

b Calculate the lengths of the tubes **(i)** UV **(ii)** XY.

c Which tube has the greater length? By how much?

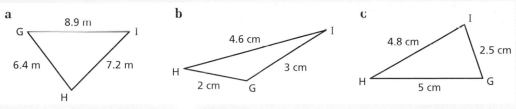

6 The supporting arm of a bracket is 2.2 m long. It can be locked in two positions, AB or AB′.

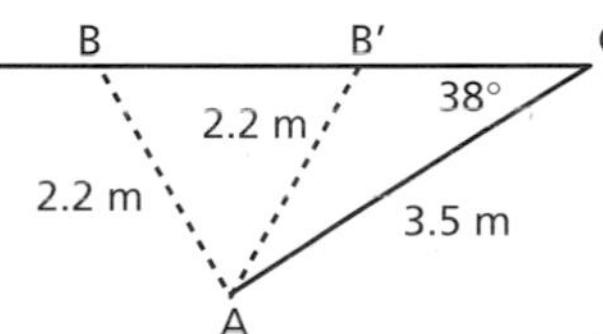

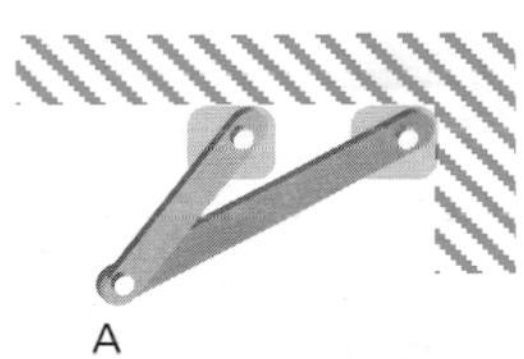

Calculate the two possible angles, ∠ABC and ∠AB′C, that the arm can make with the horizontal roof.

7 Two boats at M and N locate a wreck, P, on the sea bed.

a Calculate the angles at **(i)** M **(ii)** N **(iii)** P.

b Calculate the depth, d m, of the wreck below the surface.

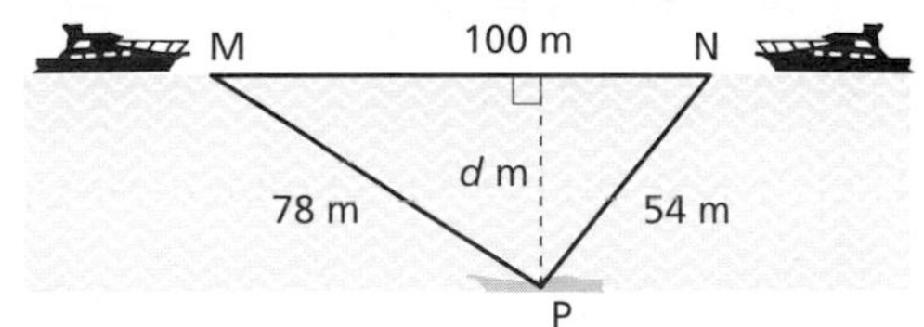

8

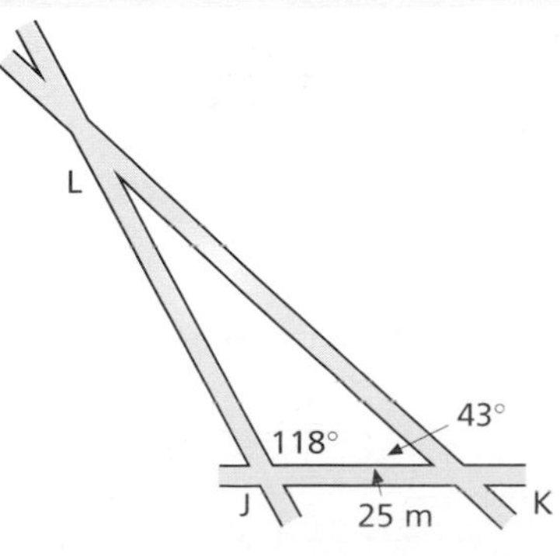

Three roads meet at a triangular junction. The island created in the centre has to be paved with a kerb fitted round it.

a Calculate the length: **(i)** LK **(ii)** LJ.

b What is the perimeter of the triangle JKL?

c Calculate the area of the island.

Simultaneous equations

Reminders

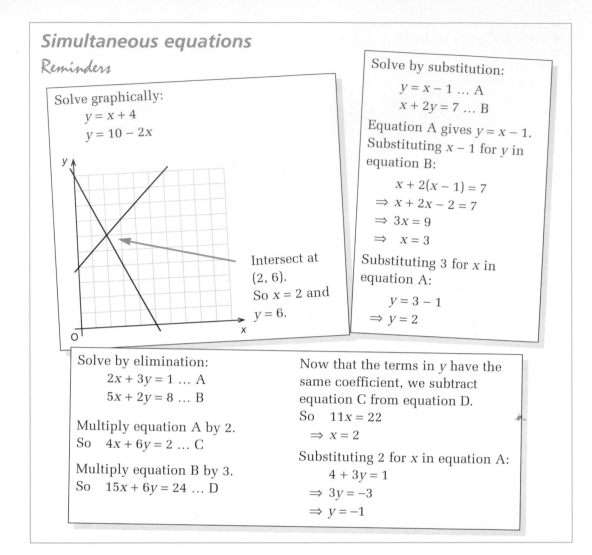

Solve graphically:

$y = x + 4$

$y = 10 - 2x$

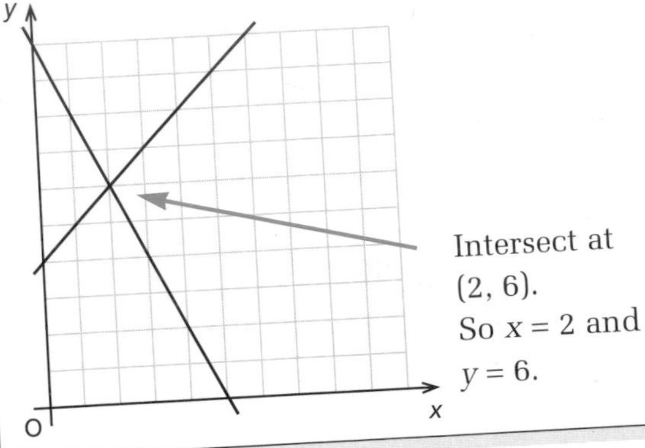

Intersect at (2, 6). So $x = 2$ and $y = 6$.

Solve by substitution:

$y = x - 1$ … A

$x + 2y = 7$ … B

Equation A gives $y = x - 1$. Substituting $x - 1$ for y in equation B:

$x + 2(x - 1) = 7$

$\Rightarrow x + 2x - 2 = 7$

$\Rightarrow 3x = 9$

$\Rightarrow x = 3$

Substituting 3 for x in equation A:

$y = 3 - 1$

$\Rightarrow y = 2$

Solve by elimination:

$2x + 3y = 1$ … A

$5x + 2y = 8$ … B

Multiply equation A by 2.
So $4x + 6y = 2$ … C

Multiply equation B by 3.
So $15x + 6y = 24$ … D

Now that the terms in y have the same coefficient, we subtract equation C from equation D.
So $11x = 22$

$\Rightarrow x = 2$

Substituting 2 for x in equation A:

$4 + 3y = 1$

$\Rightarrow 3y = -3$

$\Rightarrow y = -1$

EXERCISE 2

1 Copy and complete the graphs to solve each pair of simultaneous equations.

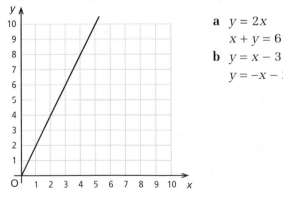

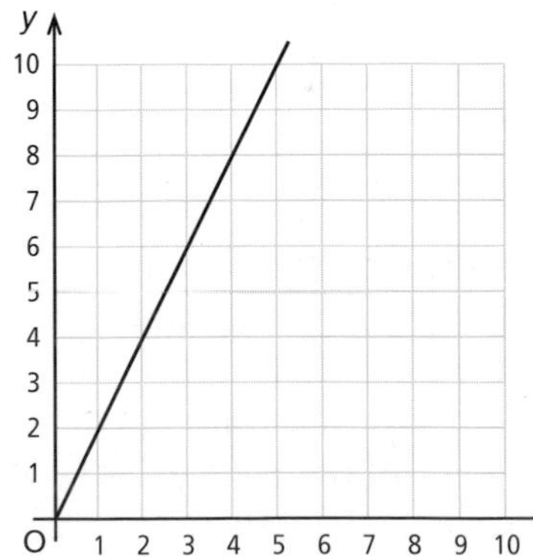

a $y = 2x$
$x + y = 6$

b $y = x - 3$
$y = -x - 2$

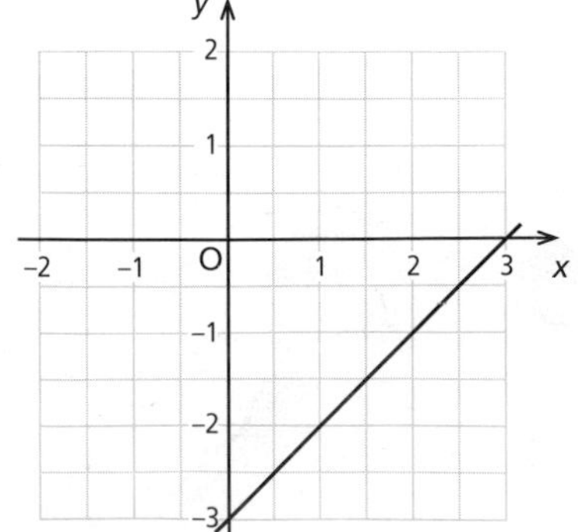

2 Solve this pair of equations using graphical methods.

$y = x + 2$

$y = 2x + 1$

3 Solve each pair of simultaneous equations by substitution.

a $y = 2x$
$y = x + 3$

b $y = 8 - x$
$y = 3x$

c $y = 4$
$y = x + 1$

d $y = 4x - 3$
$y = 2x + 1$

e $y = 3x$
$2x + y = 15$

f $y = 2x$
$5x - y = 3$

4 Solve each pair of simultaneous equations by elimination.

a $x + y = 10$
$x - y = 6$

b $3x + y = 17$
$x + y = 7$

c $2x + 3y = 3$
$x - y = -6$

d $3x - 2y = 16$
$2x - y = 11$

e $4x + 3y = 16$
$5x + 2y = 13$

f $2x - 3y = 7$
$3x + 4y = 2$

5 Two shops hire out mountain bikes. Their conditions of hire can be illustrated by this graph.

a What is the cost of hiring a bike from each company for:
(i) 3 days (ii) 6 days?

b (i) What is the number of days' hire when the cost is the same?
(ii) What is this cost?

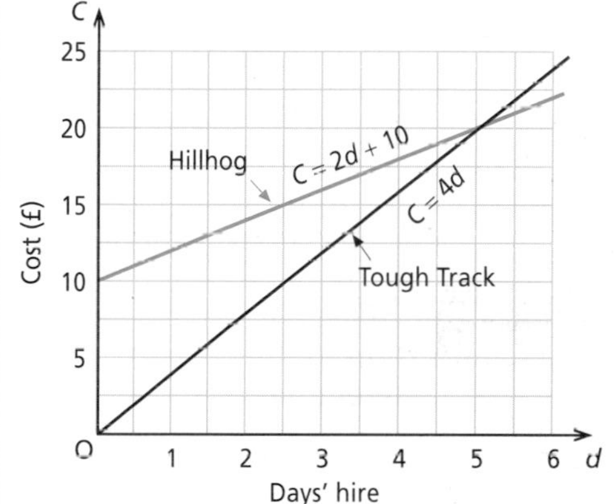

6 One water tank is being emptied while another is being filled.
The volume, V litres, of water in the tanks after m minutes can be calculated from the formulae $V = 90 - 6m$ and $V = 4m$.

a Which formula is for (i) the filling tank (ii) the emptying tank?

b On the same diagram draw graphs to show the volume of water in each tank for $t = 0$ to 15 minutes.

c (i) After how many minutes are the volumes equal?
(ii) What is the volume then?

7 Mike's father is three times as old as Mike. The difference in their ages is 22 years.

a Use x for Mike's age and y for his father's and form two equations.

b Solve them to find their ages.

8 Four bolts and three nuts together weigh 36 g. Two bolts and one nut weigh 16 g.

a Form two equations to show this information.

b Solve the equations to find the weight of (i) a bolt (ii) a nut.

9 On a holiday to Niagara Falls, the Morrisons exchanged £142 into 20 US dollars and 50 Canadian dollars. The following day they exchanged £108 into 40 US dollars and 20 Canadian dollars. The rate of exchange was the same on both days. Let x pounds per dollar be the US rate and y pounds per dollar be the Canadian rate.

a Form two equations in x and y.

b Solve these equations simultaneously to work out both exchange rates.

Graphs, charts and tables

Reminders

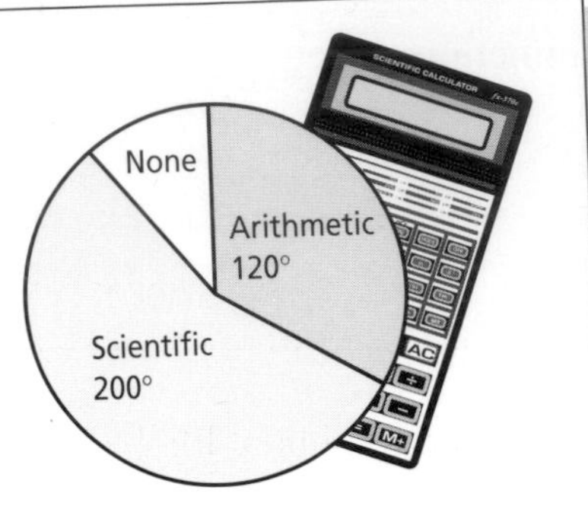

The chart shows calculator use among third year pupils.
There are 180 pupils in third year.

120° is a third of 360° so 60 pupils (a third of 180 pupils) use arithmetic calculators.

200° is five ninths of 360° so 100 pupils (five ninths of 180 pupils) use scientific calculators.

The rest, 20 pupils, use no calculator.

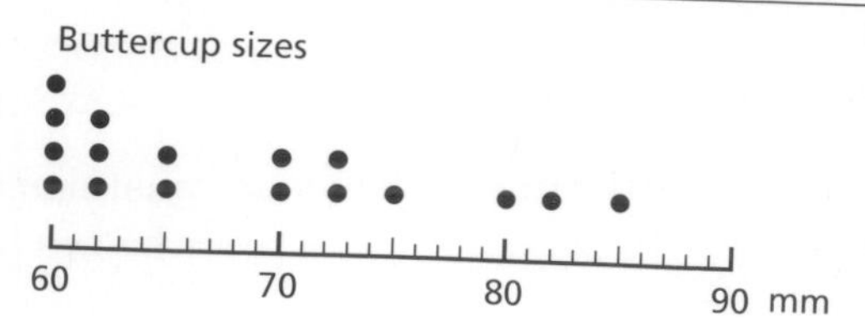

The length of the creeping buttercup is the subject of a survey. The dot plot illustrates the data collected.

Note that the distribution has a mode of 60 mm and is skewed to the right.

There are 17 numbers.
Q_1 lies between the 4th and 5th 61 mm
Q_2 is the 9th 65 mm
Q_3 lies between the 13th and 14th 74 mm
The highest piece of data is 85 mm.
The lowest piece of data is 60 mm.
The box plot illustrates the 5-figure summary.

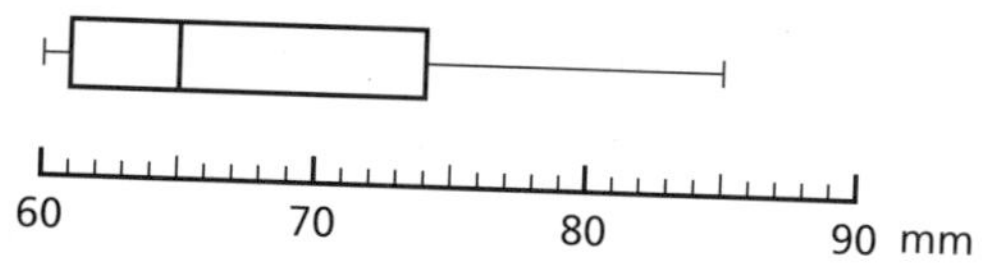

EXERCISE 3

1 A petrol station noted the types of fuel bought by different customers.

Fuel type	Frequency (no. of customers)
2-star	12
4-star	48
Unleaded	60
Derv. (diesel)	24

a Copy the table and add a relative frequency column. (Leave your answers as common fractions.)

b Hence or otherwise draw a pie chart to illustrate the data.

2 The length of time patients have to wait at a health centre is being studied. Patients are selected at random and their waiting time, in minutes, is recorded. The following represents one morning's data.

6 15 11 3 24 8 12 15
10 21 17 8 14 23 8 13

a Draw a dot plot to illustrate the data.
b Calculate the range of waiting times.
c Copy and complete this stem-and-leaf diagram.
d Use the diagram to help you work out:
(i) the median
(ii) the quartiles of the distribution.

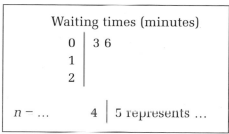

Waiting times (minutes)

	0	3 6
	1	
	2	
n = ...	4	5 represents ...

3 Asif checks the prices of second-hand items in the sales columns of his local newspaper. The prices, to the nearest £10, are:

40 70 60 40 40 50 60 70 50
60 50 50 30 80 70 50 30 20
90 20 80 90 40 60 20 80 40
90 50 60 80 30 30 40 80 80

a (i) Copy and complete this frequency table.
(ii) Complete the cumulative frequency column.
b How many items cost: (i) more than £70
(ii) £60 or less?
c Work out: (i) the median price
(ii) the lower quartile
(iii) the upper quartile of the distribution.
d Hence construct a box plot to illustrate the distribution of the prices.

Price (£)	Frequency	Cumulative frequency
20		
30		
40		
50		
60		
70		
80		
90		

4 Moira grows Bonsai trees. The table shows the heights, to the nearest centimetre, of some of her trees after a year.

a Copy and complete the table.
b Draw a cumulative frequency diagram.

Height (cm)	Frequency	Cumulative frequency
5	3	
6	5	
7	8	
8	12	
9	8	
10	4	

5 The box plot shows the number of letters in the surnames of a sample of students.

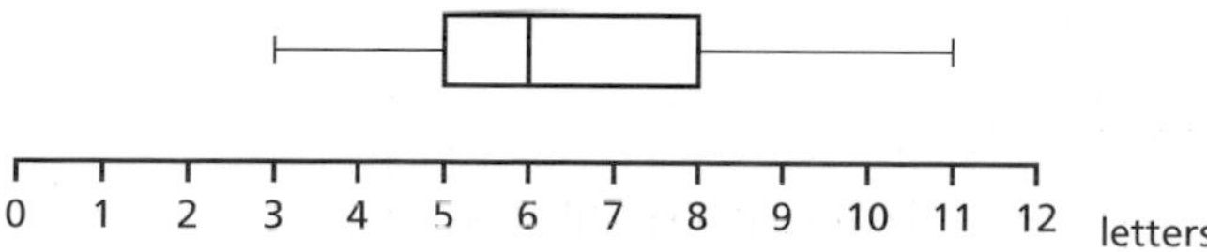

a How long is: (i) the shortest (ii) the longest surname?
b What is: (i) the lower quartile (ii) the upper quartile (iii) the median length?

6 Mr Watkins breeds tropical birds. The table shows the number of chicks raised in different nest boxes.

a Copy the table and complete the relative frequency column.

b Draw a pie chart to illustrate the data.

Number of chicks	Frequency	Relative frequency
1	3	
2	5	
3	8	
4	4	

7 These are the monthly salaries to the nearest £10 at the Force Ten double-glazing factory:

1340 1470 1680 1510 1600 1550
1750 1340 1820 1740 1450 1580
1310 1440 1670 1300 1770 1480
1670 1870 1340 1680 1790 1840
1430 1500 1380 1730 1800 1550.

a Copy and complete the stem-and-leaf diagram.

b Which level has the most entries?

c Work out **(i)** the median salary
(ii) the quartiles.

d Dennis earns £1450. How does his salary compare with the others?

Monthly salaries

13	
14	
15	
16	
17	
18	

$n = \ldots$ 13 | 4 represents …

8 Compare the growth rates of these two financial funds over a 15-year period.

Spread Investment:
6.9% 7.2% 7.0% 6.8% 7.2%
7.5% 7.7% 8.2% 7.3% 7.2%
8.1% 7.4% 7.2% 6.9% 7.1%

High Risk:
7.9% 8.2% 9.1% 8.3% 9.5%
9.6% 9.6% 8.2% 7.4% 6.2%
6.0% 5.8% 6.0% 5.8% 5.7%

a Construct separate dot plots for each year.

b Calculate: **(i)** the median **(ii)** the quartiles for each fund.

c Construct a box plot for each on the same diagram.

d What has happened to the two funds over the 15 years?

9 In the card game Bridge, players assess how good their hand is by counting the number of points:
ace = 4 points, king = 3 points, queen = 2 points, jack = 1 point.
(An average hand totals 10 points.)
Two players keep a record of the total number of points in their hands during an evening's play.

Marie: 9 12 6 10 13 8 4 11 7 9 8 13 11 8 6 9
Tony: 10 14 17 15 12 6 20 16 11 13 8 12 17 15 15

Note that Tony plays one hand less than Marie.

a Calculate the medians and quartiles for each player and make a 5-figure summary.

b Use the same scale to construct box plots for each player.

c Compare each player's luck that evening.
(The more points, the better the hand is likely to be.)

Statistics

Reminders

A sample of 18 people were asked in a trivia quiz how many of the 7 dwarves they could name. These are the results:

1 2 2 2 3 3 3 4 4 5 5 6 6 6 6 7 7 7

18 ÷ 4 = 4 remainder 2.

So the lists splits into four parts as follows:

4 numbers	1	4 numbers	4 numbers	1	4 numbers
	Q_1		Q_2	Q_3	

The lower quartile is the 5th number 3

The median falls between the 9th and 10th 4.5

The upper quartile is the 14th number 6

The semi-interquartile range $= (Q_3 - Q_1) \div 2 = 1.5$

Find the mean:

1 2 2 2 3 3
3 4 4 5 5 6
6 6 6 7 7 7

Check the mean = 4.4 to 1 d.p.

Work out how much each score deviates from the mean:

−3.4 −2.4 −2.4 −2.4 −1.4 −1.4 −1.4 −0.4 −0.4
0.6 0.6 1.6 1.6 1.6 1.6 2.6 2.6 2.6

Square each deviation:

11.56 5.76 5.76 5.76 1.96 1.96 1.96 0.16 0.16
0.36 0.36 2.56 2.56 2.56 2.56 6.76 6.76 6.76

Sum the squared deviations: 66.28

Divide the sum by $(n - 1)$ where n is the number of scores:

$66.28 \div (18 - 1) = 3.899$ to 3 d.p.

Standard deviation $= \sqrt{3.8999} = 2.0$ to 1 d.p.

The relative frequency of a score = frequency of the score ÷ total frequency

The relative frequency of a score can be used as an estimate of the probability of that score happening.

Probability of an event occuring:

$$\text{P(event)} = \frac{\text{no. of favourable outcomes}}{\text{total no. of outcomes}}$$

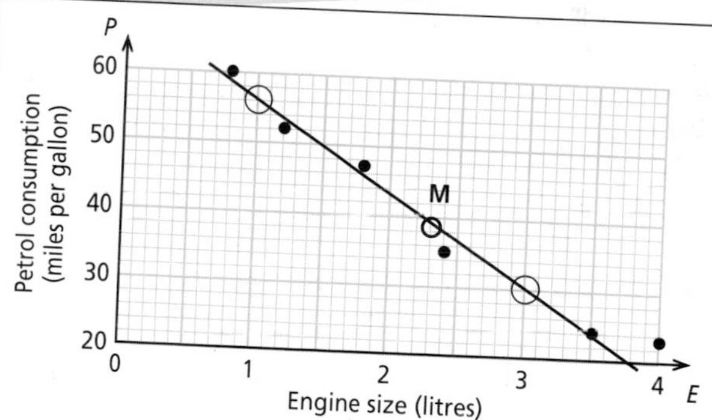

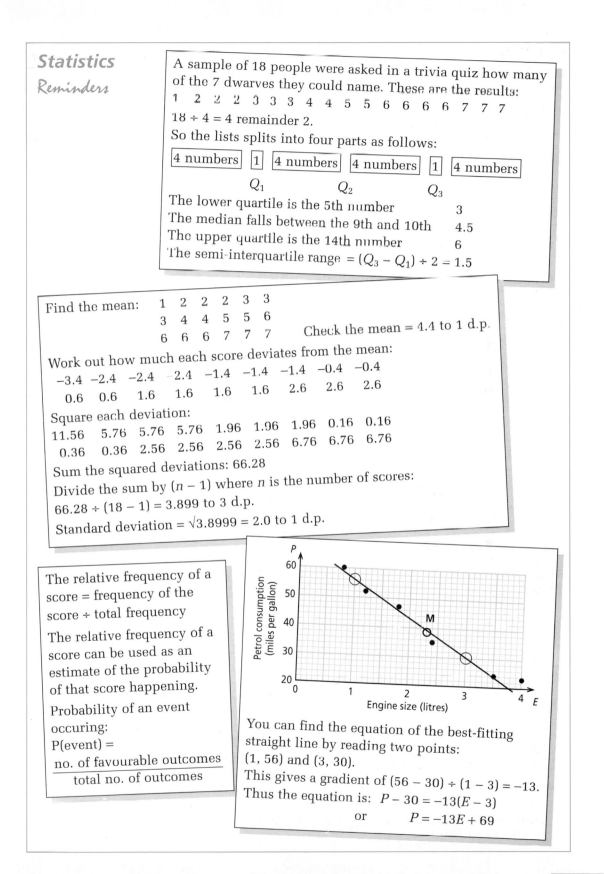

You can find the equation of the best-fitting straight line by reading two points: (1, 56) and (3, 30).

This gives a gradient of $(56 - 30) \div (1 - 3) = -13$.

Thus the equation is: $P - 30 = -13(E - 3)$

or $P = -13E + 69$

EXERCISE 4

1 The table shows the numbers of passengers who board the 77 bus at the start of its route. The counts were made to the nearest 5 passengers. Records have been kept for 50 journeys.

Passengers	Frequency	Cumulative frequency
5	7	
10	12	
15	15	
20	16	

a Copy and complete the table.
b What is the median number of passengers?
c Work out: **(i)** the quartiles **(ii)** the semi-interquartile range.

2 The times of entrants in a charity walk are recorded. This cumulative frequency diagram has been constructed from the data.

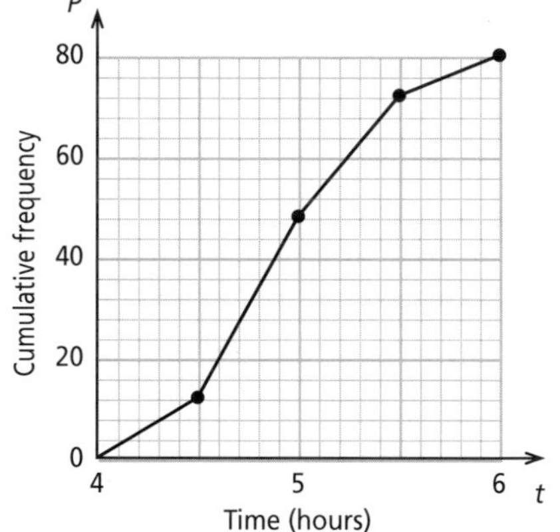

a From the diagram work out:
(i) the median
(ii) the lower quartile
(iii) the upper quartile.
b Calculate: **(i)** the interquartile range
(ii) the semi-interquartile range.

3 On a winter's day, the noon temperatures are recorded for various places.
Edinburgh 4 °C Belfast 6 °C Dublin 7 °C Cardiff 9 °C London 9 °C
a Calculate the mean temperature.

	Temperature (°C)	Deviation	(Deviation)^2
	4		
	6		
	7		
	9		
	9		
Totals			

b **(i)** Copy and complete the table.
(ii) Calculate the standard deviation.
(iii) Check your answer using the appropriate calculator button in STAT mode.

4 The scatter graph shows the charges a plumber makes for repair jobs which need different lengths of time. The points A and B lie on the line of best fit.

a Use these points to calculate the gradient m.

b The equation of the line is $C = mt + c$. Calculate c.

c Write down the equation of the line of best fit.

d What would you estimate a 3-hour job would cost?

e How long would you expect the plumber to have worked when the charge was £55?

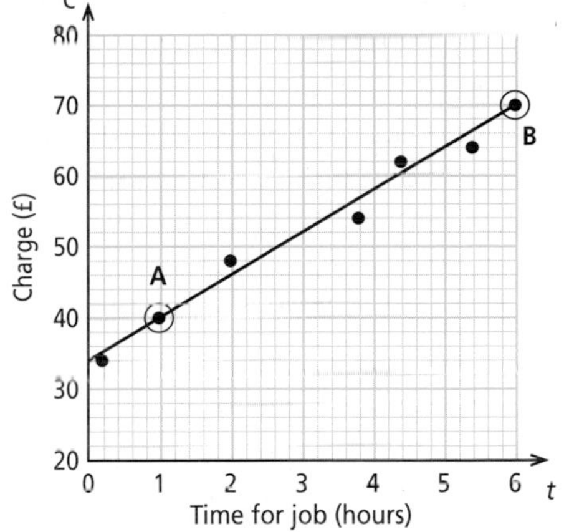

5

Front

☐	☐	☐	☐	☐
☐	☐	x	☐	☐
☐	☐	☐	☐	☐
☐	☐	☐	☐	☐

A room has four rows of five desks.
A person sits at a desk chosen at random.
Calculate each of the following probabilities:

a P(sits at desk x)

b P(sits in the front row)

c P(sits at a desk surrounded by other desks).

6 At an Indian restaurant one lunchtime, customers choose these curries from the business lunch menu:

a Add a relative frequency column.

b Estimate the probability that the next customer will select: **(i)** chicken **(ii)** vegetable.

Type	Frequency
Chicken	15
Lamb	8
Prawn	6
Beef	4
Vegetable	7

7 A group of graduates were asked about how much debt they had accumulated while at university. The table shows the results.

Debt	Frequency	Cumulative frequency
0	38	
1000	18	
2000	46	
4000	54	
6000	36	
8000	8	

a Copy and complete the table.

b Calculate the median debt.

c Work out: **(i)** the quartiles **(ii)** the semi-interquartile range.

d Martin has a debt of £3000. How does this compare with the median?

e How much does the median debt increase by if the 38 graduates with no debts are omitted?

8 A social club has two tickets for a pop concert to raffle.
One is raffled on Monday. Tim buys nine of the 200 tickets sold.
The other is raffled on Tuesday. Tania buys six of the 120 tickets sold.

a Calculate: **(i)** P(Tim wins a ticket) **(ii)** P(Tania wins a ticket).

b Who is more likely to win a ticket?

c How many more tickets would the person less likely to win have to buy to make these probabilities equal?

9 A study of 1000 male and 1000 female drivers over their driving life produced these statistics:

	Male	Female
Killed	3	1
Seriously injured	37	23
Slightly injured	132	117

a Make a new table showing the relative frequencies for:
(i) male drivers
(ii) female drivers.

b Estimate the probability that:
(i) a male will be killed
(ii) a female driver will be killed or seriously injured whilst driving.

c Compare the statistics for male and female drivers.

10 A fishing fleet keeps records of its catches. The weight, in tonnes, of fish caught recently are: 64, 42, 106, 35, 122, 53, 133 and 24.
Five years ago, for similar catches, the weights were:
160, 175, 132, 148, 156, 185, 153 and 182 tonnes.

a Calculate the mean and standard deviation for:
(i) the recent data
(ii) the 5-year-old data.

b Use your answer to help you describe what has happened over this period of time.

11 A golf club holds a competition.
These are the gross scores and handicaps of the players.

Player	A	B	C	D	E	F	G	H	I	J
Handicap (H)	8	20	2	11	16	4	18	7	13	24
Gross score (S)	83	95	75	85	88	76	92	80	86	97

a Plot a scatter graph and say whether the correlation is positive or negative.

b Draw the line of best fit.

c Find its equation in the form $S = mH + c$.

d Estimate the score for a player with a handicap of 9.

e A player scores 90. Estimate his handicap.

13 More Algebraic Operations

Reminders

Simplify $\frac{9}{6}$.

$$\frac{9}{6} = \frac{3 \times 3}{3 \times 2} = \frac{3}{3} \times \frac{3}{2} = 1 \times \frac{3}{2} = \frac{3}{2}$$

This is more usually written as:

$$\frac{9}{6} = \frac{\overset{1}{\cancel{3}} \times 3}{\underset{1}{\cancel{3}} \times 2} = \frac{3}{2}$$

Express $\frac{3}{4}$ as a number of eighths.

$4 \times 2 = 8$, so …

$$\frac{3}{4} = \frac{3 \times 2}{4 \times 2} = \frac{6}{8}$$

The multiples of 2 are 2, 4, 6, 8, 10, 12, 14, 16, 18, ...
The multiples of 3 are 3, 6, 9, 12, 15, 18, ...
Common to these lists are 6, 12 and 18.
The lowest of these is 6.
6 is called the **lowest common multiple** of 2 and 3.
We say the **lcm** of 2 and 3 is 6.

STARTING POINTS

1 Write each fraction in its simplest form.

a $\frac{8}{12}$ **b** $\frac{12}{16}$ **c** $\frac{10}{25}$ **d** $\frac{48}{32}$

2 Express:

a $\frac{1}{2}$ as a number of eighths **b** $\frac{2}{3}$ as a number of ninths

c $\frac{3}{4}$ as a number of twelfths **d** $\frac{2}{5}$ as a number of fifteenths

e $\frac{5}{7}$ as a number of fourteenths **f** $\frac{2}{9}$ as a number of twenty-sevenths

3 What is the lowest common multiple of each pair of numbers?

a 2, 5 **b** 2, 7 **c** 3, 4 **d** 6, 8 **e** 10, 12 **f** 20, 25

4 The lcm of 2 and 3 is 6. Copy and complete the following: $\frac{1}{2} + \frac{2}{3} = \frac{■}{6} + \frac{■}{6} = \frac{■ + ■}{6} = \frac{■}{6}$

5 Calculate, giving your answer in its simplest form:

a $\frac{1}{2} + \frac{1}{4}$ **b** $\frac{2}{3} - \frac{1}{2}$ **c** $\frac{3}{4} \times \frac{5}{6}$ **d** $\frac{2}{5} \div \frac{8}{15}$

6 Find the value of: **a** 2^3 **b** 3^4 **c** $\sqrt{100}$ **d** $\sqrt{64}$ **e** $\sqrt[3]{8}$

7 x^3 means $x \times x \times x$. Write down the meaning of: **a** y^4 **b** $\frac{1}{a^5}$

8 Multiply out: **a** $3(2x - 3y)$ **b** $x(x-1)$ **c** $(x+1)(x-1)$ **d** $x(2x - 3x^2)$

Simplest form

Example 1 $\frac{12}{15} = \frac{3 \times 4}{3 \times 5} = \frac{4}{5}$

Example 2 $\frac{y^2}{y} = \frac{y \times y}{y} = \frac{y}{1} = y$

Example 3 $\frac{2b}{6b^2} = \frac{2 \times b}{6 \times b \times b} = \frac{1}{3b}$

Example 4 $\frac{a^3}{a^2} = \frac{a \times a \times a}{a \times a} = \frac{a}{1} = a$

Example 5 $\frac{(y-1)^2}{(y-1)^3} = \frac{(y-1)(y-1)}{(y-1)(y-1)(y-1)} = \frac{1}{(y-1)}$

Each fraction has been reduced to its simplest form.

EXERCISE 1

Reduce each fraction to its simplest form.

1 **a** $\frac{9}{12}$ **b** $\frac{14}{20}$ **c** $\frac{15}{35}$ **d** $\frac{12}{18}$ **e** $\frac{40}{56}$

2 **a** $\frac{x^2}{x}$ **b** $\frac{x^3}{x^3}$ **c** $\frac{a}{a^2}$ **d** $\frac{m^3}{m^4}$ **e** $\frac{y^6}{y^3}$ **f** $\frac{b^4}{b^4}$ **g** $\frac{t}{t^4}$ **h** $\frac{d^2}{d^3}$

3 **a** $\frac{2m}{m}$ **b** $\frac{6y}{3y}$ **c** $\frac{8x}{4}$ **d** $\frac{9a}{9}$ **e** $\frac{4t}{6}$

4 **a** $\frac{3y^2}{y}$ **b** $\frac{x^2}{4x}$ **c** $\frac{8x}{6x^2}$ **d** $\frac{ab}{a}$ **e** $\frac{ab^2}{b}$

5 **a** $\frac{x^2y}{x}$ **b** $\frac{x^2y^3}{y^2}$ **c** $\frac{6xy}{3y}$ **d** $\frac{a^2b}{a^2b}$ **e** $\frac{x^2y^2}{xy}$

f $\frac{xy^2}{x^2y}$ **g** $\frac{2a^3}{a^2}$ **h** $\frac{9m^2}{6m^3}$ **i** $\frac{abc}{ac}$ **j** $\frac{def}{e}$

6 **a** $\frac{(x+1)^2}{(x+1)}$ **b** $\frac{(y-1)}{(y-1)^2}$ **c** $\frac{(y-1)^3}{(y-1)}$ **d** $\frac{(m-3)^2}{(m-3)^3}$ **e** $\frac{(a-2)^4}{(a-2)^3}$

f $\frac{(d-5)}{(d-5)^3}$ **g** $\frac{(2y+3)^2}{(2y+3)^3}$ **h** $\frac{(1+2x)^2}{(1+2x)^2}$ **i** $\frac{(2-x)^2}{(2-x)}$ **j** $\frac{(3a-2)^3}{(3a-2)}$

k $\frac{(6-2d)}{(6-2d)^3}$ **l** $\frac{(x^2-1)^3}{(x^2-1)^2}$ **m** $\frac{(8y+1)^2}{(1+8y)^4}$ **n** $\frac{(4-2y)^3}{(4-2y)^5}$ **o** $\frac{(1+2a+a^2)^3}{(1+2a+a^2)^2}$

7 **a** $\dfrac{(m-1)(m+1)}{(m+1)}$ **b** $\dfrac{(x-3)(x+3)}{(x-3)}$ **c** $\dfrac{(4y+5)}{(4y+10)(4y+5)}$

d $\dfrac{(2a+3)^2}{(2a-1)(2a+3)}$ **e** $\dfrac{(a+2)(a-2)}{(a-2)(a+2)}$ **f** $\dfrac{(5-y)^2(5+y)}{(5+y)^2(5-y)}$

g $\dfrac{(1-2x)^3(1+3x)^3}{(1-2x)(1+3x)^2}$ **h** $\dfrac{(4+2a)^2(4-2a)^3}{(5+2a)(4-2a)^2}$

Adding and subtracting fractions

Compare similarly numbered examples.

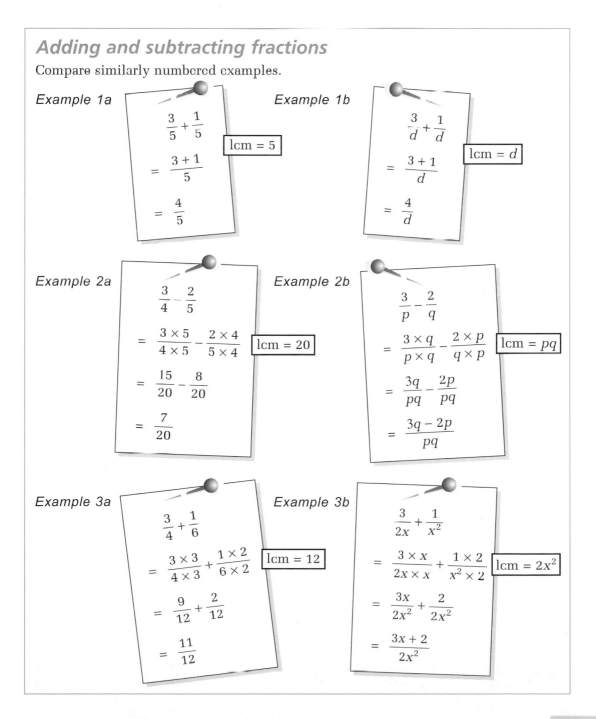

Example 1a

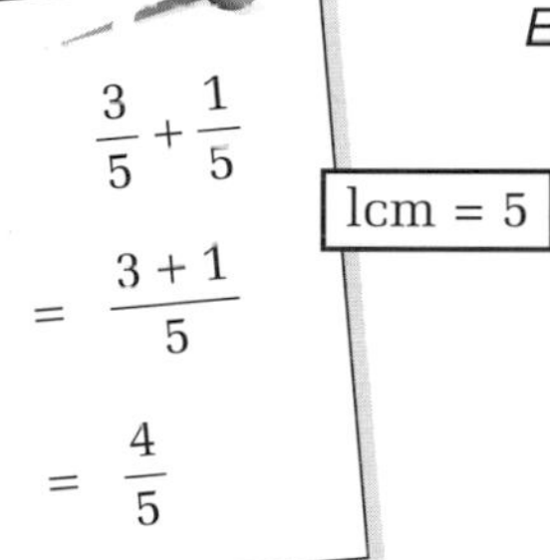

$$\frac{3}{5}+\frac{1}{5} = \frac{3+1}{5} = \frac{4}{5}$$

lcm = 5

Example 1b

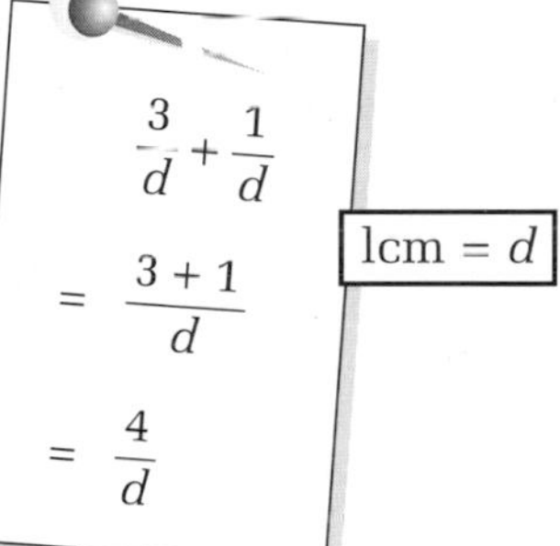

$$\frac{3}{d}+\frac{1}{d} = \frac{3+1}{d} = \frac{4}{d}$$

lcm = d

Example 2a

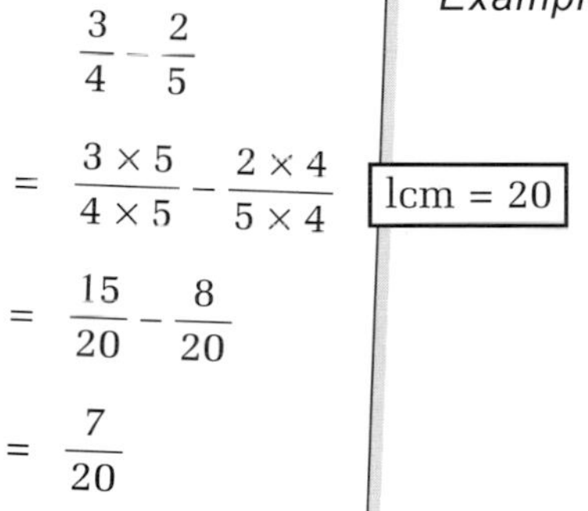

$$\frac{3}{4}-\frac{2}{5} = \frac{3\times 5}{4\times 5}-\frac{2\times 4}{5\times 4} = \frac{15}{20}-\frac{8}{20} = \frac{7}{20}$$

lcm = 20

Example 2b

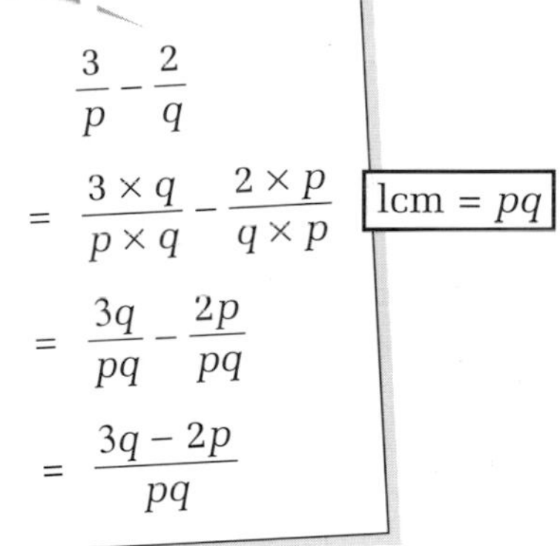

$$\frac{3}{p}-\frac{2}{q} = \frac{3\times q}{p\times q}-\frac{2\times p}{q\times p} = \frac{3q}{pq}-\frac{2p}{pq} = \frac{3q-2p}{pq}$$

lcm = pq

Example 3a

$$\frac{3}{4}+\frac{1}{6} = \frac{3\times 3}{4\times 3}+\frac{1\times 2}{6\times 2} = \frac{9}{12}+\frac{2}{12} = \frac{11}{12}$$

lcm = 12

Example 3b

$$\frac{3}{2x}+\frac{1}{x^2} = \frac{3\times x}{2x\times x}+\frac{1\times 2}{x^2\times 2} = \frac{3x}{2x^2}+\frac{2}{2x^2} = \frac{3x+2}{2x^2}$$

lcm = $2x^2$

EXERCISE 2

Perform these additions and subtractions.

1 a $\frac{1}{5}+\frac{2}{5}$ **b** $\frac{1}{3}+\frac{1}{4}$ **c** $\frac{2}{5}-\frac{1}{3}$ **d** $\frac{5}{6}-\frac{2}{3}$ **e** $\frac{3}{8}+\frac{5}{6}$

2 a $\frac{1}{a}+\frac{2}{a}$ **b** $\frac{2}{m}+\frac{3}{m}$ **c** $\frac{2}{a}-\frac{1}{b}$ **d** $\frac{5}{c}-\frac{2}{d}$ **e** $\frac{3}{e}+\frac{5}{f}$

3 a $\frac{4}{p}+\frac{1}{q}$ **b** $\frac{3}{p}+\frac{1}{k}$ **c** $\frac{3}{b}-\frac{7}{h}$ **d** $\frac{8}{m}-\frac{3}{n}$ **e** $\frac{1}{f}+\frac{3}{g}$

4 a $\frac{5}{y}-\frac{4}{y}$ **b** $\frac{2}{d^2}+\frac{3}{d^2}$ **c** $\frac{2}{3a}+\frac{1}{a}$ **d** $\frac{4}{a}-\frac{12}{a}$ **e** $\frac{1}{2c}+\frac{1}{3c}$

5 a $\frac{3}{2h}-\frac{2}{3h}$ **b** $\frac{3}{4m}+\frac{5}{6m}$ **c** $\frac{2}{3a}-\frac{1}{2b}$ **d** $\frac{3}{4c}+\frac{4}{3d}$ **e** $\frac{2}{5e}+\frac{7}{3f}$

6 a $\frac{3}{t^2}+\frac{1}{t}$ **b** $\frac{1}{m^2}-\frac{1}{m}$ **c** $\frac{2}{a}-\frac{3}{a^2}$ **d** $\frac{2}{x^2}-\frac{2}{x}$ **e** $\frac{3}{y^2}-\frac{3}{3y}$

Mutliplying and dividing fractions

Multiplication examples

$$\frac{3}{8}\times\frac{4}{5}=\frac{3\times\overset{1}{\cancel{4}}}{\underset{2}{\cancel{8}}\times 5}=\frac{3\times 1}{2\times 5}=\frac{3}{10}$$

$$\frac{5a}{6}\times\frac{3}{a^2}=\frac{5\overset{1}{\cancel{a}}\times\overset{1}{\cancel{3}}}{\underset{2}{\cancel{6}}\times\underset{a}{\cancel{a^2}}}=\frac{5\times 1}{2\times a}=\frac{5}{2a}$$

Division examples

$$\frac{4}{9}\div\frac{5}{6}=\frac{4}{9}\times\frac{6}{5}=\frac{4\times\overset{2}{\cancel{6}}}{\underset{3}{\cancel{9}}\times 5}=\frac{4\times 2}{3\times 5}=\frac{8}{15}$$

$$\frac{2xy}{3}\div\frac{5x}{y}=\frac{2xy}{3}\times\frac{y}{5x}=\frac{2\overset{1}{\cancel{x}}y\times y}{3\times 5\underset{1}{\cancel{x}}}=\frac{2y^2}{15}$$

EXERCISE 3

Perform these multiplications and divisions.

1 a $\frac{2}{3}\times\frac{3}{5}$ **b** $\frac{4}{5}\times\frac{3}{8}$ **c** $\frac{7}{12}\times\frac{8}{21}$ **d** $\frac{9}{32}\times\frac{8}{27}$ **e** $\frac{7}{45}\times\frac{5}{6}$

2 a $\frac{a}{4}\times\frac{a}{2}$ **b** $\frac{3}{y}\times\frac{5}{y}$ **c** $\frac{a}{4}\times\frac{2}{a}$ **d** $\frac{2m}{3}\times\frac{5}{3m}$ **e** $\frac{3a}{4b}\times\frac{14}{6a}$

3 a $\frac{1}{3}\div\frac{2}{3}$ **b** $\frac{5}{6}\div\frac{4}{9}$ **c** $\frac{3}{5}\div\frac{6}{25}$ **d** $\frac{18}{35}\div\frac{6}{25}$ **e** $\frac{32}{49}\div\frac{4}{7}$

4 a $\frac{t}{3}\div\frac{t}{6}$ **b** $\frac{1}{a}\div\frac{5}{a}$ **c** $\frac{y}{3}\div\frac{2}{y}$ **d** $\frac{4n}{3}\div\frac{6n}{5}$ **e** $\frac{4a}{6}\div\frac{6}{5a}$

5 a $\frac{m^2}{2}\times\frac{1}{m}$ **b** $\frac{c}{3}\times\frac{3}{c^2}$ **c** $\frac{4t^2}{3}\times\frac{9}{2t}$ **d** $\frac{cd}{2}\times\frac{c}{d}$ **e** $\frac{6a}{b}\times\frac{ab}{3}$

6 **a** $\dfrac{5y}{4} \div \dfrac{9y^2}{8}$ **b** $\dfrac{3}{xy} \div \dfrac{9}{4y}$ **c** $\dfrac{2ab}{3} \div \dfrac{5a}{b}$ **d** $\dfrac{8u^2v^2}{3} \div \dfrac{4u}{v}$

e $\dfrac{4m^2n}{3} \div \dfrac{m}{6n}$

7 **a** $\dfrac{7v}{12u^2} \times \dfrac{3uv}{21}$ **b** $\dfrac{2a^2}{5} \times \dfrac{10}{a^3}$ **c** $\dfrac{5ab^2}{2} \times \dfrac{4}{ab}$ **d** $\dfrac{(1+x)^2}{(1+y)} \times \dfrac{(1+y)^2}{(1+x)}$

e $\dfrac{(a-2)}{(a+2)^2} \div \dfrac{(a-2)^2}{(a+2)^3}$

8 You cannot divide by zero. In each of the following fractions give one value that x cannot take.

a $\dfrac{1}{(1-x)}$ **b** $\dfrac{1}{(2+x)}$ **c** $\dfrac{1}{(3+2x)}$

If you need to divide by, say, $(1 - x)$ then you should add $x \neq 1$.

Changing the subject of simple formulae

The formula to work out the cost of an order for calculators is

$C = nu$

where C is the cost in £,

n is the number of calculators ordered and

u is the cost in £ of one calculator.

Since the formula works out C, then C is known as the subject of the formula.

In some cases you might know how much you have to spend (C) and need to work out how many calculators you can buy. You would then like n to be the subject.

Here are two ways of making n the subject.

Method 1

Step 1

Imagine the formula as a number machine which inputs n:

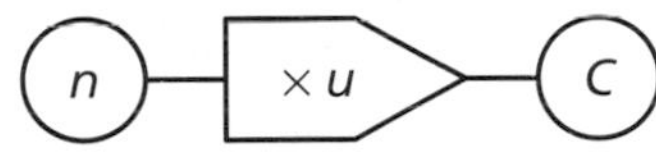

Step 2 Reverse the machine:

(i) reverse the order **(ii)** reverse each process.

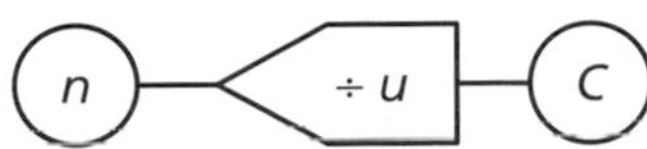

Step 3 Express the machine as a formula: $n = \dfrac{C}{u}$

Method 2

$$C = nu$$

$$\Rightarrow \quad \frac{C}{u} = \frac{nu}{u}$$

$$\Rightarrow \quad \frac{C}{u} = n$$

$$\Rightarrow \quad n = \frac{C}{u}$$

Here is another example.
The perimeter, P, of a rectangular plot of land is computed using the formula $P = 2(l + b)$ where l is the length and b is the breadth of the rectangle.
Make b the subject of the formula.

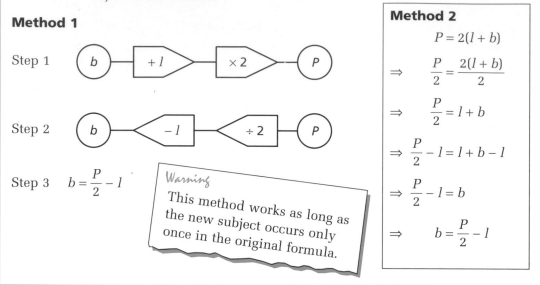

Method 1

Step 1

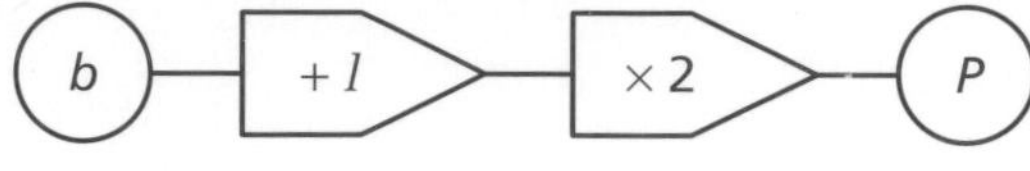

Step 2 — b ← $-\,l$ ← $\div\,2$ ← P

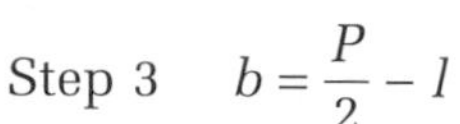
Step 3 $b = \frac{P}{2} - l$

Warning
This method works as long as the new subject occurs only once in the original formula.

Method 2

$$P = 2(l + b)$$

$$\Rightarrow \quad \frac{P}{2} = \frac{2(l + b)}{2}$$

$$\Rightarrow \quad \frac{P}{2} = l + b$$

$$\Rightarrow \quad \frac{P}{2} - l = l + b - l$$

$$\Rightarrow \quad \frac{P}{2} - l = b$$

$$\Rightarrow \quad b = \frac{P}{2} - l$$

EXERCISE 4

1 Change the subject of each formula to the letter indicated in square brackets.

a (i) $x = y + 3$ [y] **(ii)** $p = q - 7$ [q] **(iii)** $a = b + c$ [b] **(iv)** $d = e - f$ [e]

b (i) $a = \frac{b}{4}$ [b] **(ii)** $c = \frac{8}{d}$ [d] **(iii)** $S = \frac{D}{T}$ [D] **(iv)** $S = \frac{D}{T}$ [T]

c (i) $a = 3x + 2$ [x] **(ii)** $g = 4h - 9$ [h] **(iii)** $y = 4s - t$ [s] **(iv)** $y = mx + c$ [x]

d (i) $p = 3(q + 2)$ [q] **(ii)** $m = n(q + 6)$ [q] **(iii)** $v = u(x + y)$ [x] **(iv)** $a = b(c - d)$ [b]

2 The total cost of hiring a digger, £D, is worked out using the formula $D = d + m$ where £d is the cost of the driver and £m is the cost of the machine.
Make m the subject of the formula.

3

A stamp designer works out the total length of perforation, P mm, using the formula $P = 2(a + b)$ where a mm is the length and b mm is the breadth of the stamp.
Make a the subject of the formula.

4 The formula for the cost of hiring a car is $T = f + 6k$ where £T is the total cost, £f is the fixed charge and k is the number of kilometres travelled.
Change the subject of the formula to: **a** f **b** k.

5 The formula for the capacity of a container truck, V cubic metres, is $V = lbh$ where l, b and h are the length, breadth and height respectively.
Change the subject to: **a** l **b** b **c** h.

6 The circumference of the wheel can be worked out using $C = 2\pi r$.
Make r the subject of the formula.

7 The size of the frog population, P, in a pool next year can be estimated from the formula $P = (1 + r)F$ where r is the growth factor and F is the size of the population this year.
Change the subject to:
a F **b** r.

8 The total cost, £T, of a party of people going to the theatre is $T = 12A + 7C$ where A and C stand for the number of adults and children respectively.
Change the subject to:
a A **b** C.

Squares and square roots

If $a^2 = 25$ then $a = \pm\sqrt{25} = \pm 5$
In some cases either 5 or −5 will be inappropriate.

Example 1
The force, F newtons, of the air against a train can be calculated from the formula $F = ks^2$ where s is the speed of the train in km/h and k is a constant.

To make s the subject: $s^2 = \frac{F}{k}$

So $s = \sqrt{\frac{F}{k}}$ (Negative speed is not considered.)

Example 2
The thickness, t cm, of hawser required to lift a weight of T tonnes can be worked out using the formula $t = \frac{4\sqrt{T}}{9}$.

To make T the subject: $t = \frac{4\sqrt{T}}{9}$

$$\Rightarrow \frac{9t}{4} = \sqrt{T}$$

$$\Rightarrow T = \left(\frac{9t}{4}\right)^2$$

$$\Rightarrow T = \frac{81t^2}{16}$$

EXERCISE 5

1 The cover of a floppy disk is square. The length of its side can be calculated using $L = \sqrt{A}$ where A is its area. Make A the subject of the formula.

2 The cost, £C, of getting an enclosed space to a temperature, T °C, is governed by the formula $C = kT^2$ where k is a constant. Make T the subject of the formula. (Note: temperatures can be negative. Look for two answers.)

3 The volume, V ml, of a fridge can be worked out using $V = hw^2$ where h cm is the height and w cm is the width of the fridge.
Make w the subject of the formula. (Can you have negative widths?)

4 A pendulum swings according to the law $T^2 = kL$ where T seconds is the time taken for one swing and L cm is the length of the pendulum.
a Make T the subject of the formula.
b Make L the subject.

5 The following formulae are used in the physics of free-falling objects.

$v = u + at$

a Change the subject of this formula to: **(i)** u **(ii)** t.

$s = ut + 0.5at^2$

b Change the subject of this formula to: **(i)** u **(ii)** a.

$v^2 = u^2 + 2as$

c Change the subject of this formula to: **(i)** a **(ii)** u.

6 The area of a drum skin can be calculated using $A = \pi r^2$.
Change the subject to r.

7 The volume of a tin of paint can be calculated from $V = \pi r^2 h$.
Change the subject to: **a** h **b** r.

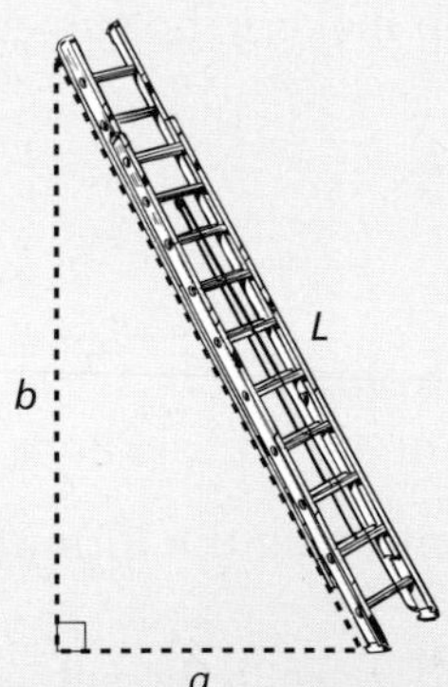

8 Using the Theorem of Pythagoras, $L^2 = a^2 + b^2$.
L^2 is the subject of the formula.
a Make a^2 the subject.
b If we make L the subject, then $L = \sqrt{(a^2 + b^2)}$.
Make **(i)** a **(ii)** b the subject.

9 The cost of a computer can be worked out from the formula $C = P\left(1 + \frac{r}{100}\right)$ where r is the rate of VAT and P is the price before tax.
Change the subject to: **a** P **b** r.

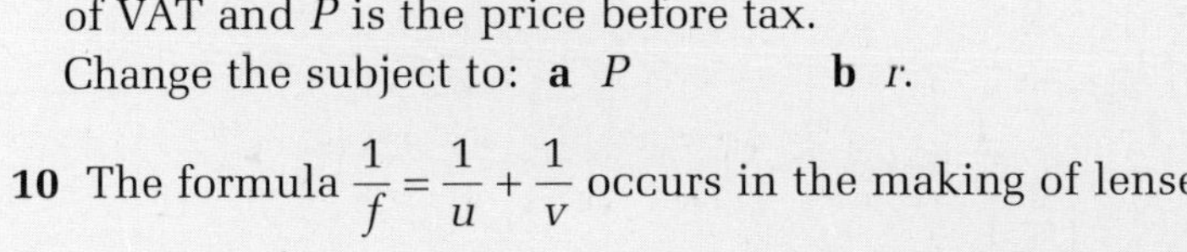

10 The formula $\frac{1}{f} = \frac{1}{u} + \frac{1}{v}$ occurs in the making of lenses.

a Make $\frac{1}{u}$ the subject.
b By adding fractions and inverting, make f the subject.
c Make u the subject.

Surds

When a number can be expressed as the result of a division of two integers we call it **rational**.

Examples 4, 0.5, 0.333 333 3... are all rational.

$4 = 4 \div 1$

$0.5 = 1 \div 2$

$0.333\,333\,3... = 1 \div 3$

You may think that all numbers are rational, but there are certain numbers which it can be proved are not. These we call **irrational** numbers.

$\sqrt{1}$, $\sqrt{4}$, $\sqrt{9}$, $\sqrt{0.25}$, $\sqrt[3]{8}$, $\sqrt[4]{81}$ and many other roots of numbers have rational values.

Many other roots, however, have irrational values, e.g. $\sqrt{2}$, $\sqrt{3}$, $\sqrt{5}$, $\sqrt{6}$, $\sqrt[3]{4}$, $\sqrt[4]{100}$ ...
These numbers are called **surds.**

We usually leave such numbers in surd form rather than provide a decimal approximation.
If asked to provide an *exact* value then we must leave such numbers in surd form.

EXERCISE 6

1 **(i)** Which of these numbers are surds?
(ii) Write down the value of each number which is not a surd.

a $\sqrt{16}$ **b** $\sqrt{20}$ **c** $\sqrt{25}$ **d** $\sqrt{30}$ **e** $\sqrt{50}$ **f** $\sqrt{81}$

g $\sqrt[3]{27}$ **h** $\sqrt[3]{64}$ **i** $\sqrt[3]{30}$ **j** $\sqrt[3]{216}$ **k** $\sqrt[4]{256}$ **l** $\sqrt[4]{10\,000}$

2 Evaluate:

a **(i)** $\sqrt{(9 \times 64)}$ **(ii)** $\sqrt{9} \times \sqrt{64}$ **(iii)** $\sqrt{(16 \times 25)}$ **(iv)** $\sqrt{16} \times \sqrt{25}$
(v) $\sqrt{(81 \times 100)}$ **(vi)** $\sqrt{81} \times \sqrt{100}$

b **(i)** $\sqrt{(16 + 9)}$ **(ii)** $\sqrt{16} + \sqrt{9}$ **(iii)** $\sqrt{(25 + 144)}$ **(iv)** $\sqrt{25} + \sqrt{144}$
(v) $\sqrt{(36 + 64)}$ **(vi)** $\sqrt{36} + \sqrt{64}$

c **(i)** $\dfrac{\sqrt{81}}{\sqrt{9}}$ **(ii)** $\sqrt{\dfrac{81}{9}}$ **(iii)** $\dfrac{\sqrt{100}}{\sqrt{25}}$ **(iv)** $\sqrt{\dfrac{100}{25}}$
(v) $\dfrac{\sqrt{18}}{\sqrt{8}}$ **(vi)** $\sqrt{\dfrac{18}{8}}$

d **(i)** $\sqrt{(225 - 144)}$ **(ii)** $\sqrt{225} - \sqrt{144}$ **(iii)** $\sqrt{(169 - 25)}$ **(iv)** $\sqrt{169} - \sqrt{25}$
(v) $\sqrt{(841 - 400)}$ **(vi)** $\sqrt{841} - \sqrt{400}$

Parts **a** and **c** show us $\sqrt{(ab)} = \sqrt{a} \times \sqrt{b}$ and $\sqrt{\dfrac{a}{b}} = \dfrac{\sqrt{a}}{\sqrt{b}}$

Parts **b** and **d** show us $\sqrt{(a + b)} \neq \sqrt{a} + \sqrt{b}$
$\sqrt{(a - b)} \neq \sqrt{a} - \sqrt{b}$

These results can be used to simplify surds.

Example 1 Simplify $\sqrt{32}$.

$\sqrt{32} = \sqrt{(16 \times 2)}$
$= \sqrt{16} \times \sqrt{2}$
$= 4\sqrt{2}$

Hint
Look for factors which are perfect squares.

Example 2 Simplify $\sqrt{\frac{8}{50}}$.

$\sqrt{\frac{8}{50}} = \sqrt{\frac{(4 \times 2)}{(25 \times 2)}}$
$= \frac{\sqrt{4} \times \sqrt{2}}{\sqrt{25} \times \sqrt{2}}$
$= \frac{2}{5}$

Example 3 Simplify $\sqrt{0.09}$.

$\sqrt{0.09} = \sqrt{\frac{9}{100}}$
$= \frac{\sqrt{9}}{\sqrt{100}}$
$= \frac{3}{10} = 0.3$

EXERCISE 7

Simplify the following without the aid of a calculator.
Leave your answer in surd form where appropriate.

1 **a** $\sqrt{8}$ **b** $\sqrt{12}$ **c** $\sqrt{20}$ **d** $\sqrt{81}$ **e** $\sqrt{50}$
f $\sqrt{27}$ **g** $\sqrt{48}$ **h** $\sqrt{72}$ **i** $\sqrt{32}$ **j** $\sqrt{75}$

2 **a** $\sqrt{108}$ **b** $\sqrt{288}$ **c** $\sqrt{150}$ **d** $\sqrt{90}$ **e** $\sqrt{900}$
f $\sqrt{490}$ **g** $\sqrt{4900}$ **h** $\sqrt{160}$ **i** $\sqrt{1600}$ **j** $\sqrt{2500}$

3 **a** $\sqrt{\frac{12}{27}}$ **b** $\sqrt{\frac{12}{75}}$ **c** $\sqrt{\frac{18}{32}}$ **d** $\sqrt{\frac{27}{75}}$ **e** $\sqrt{\frac{24}{16}}$
f $\sqrt{\frac{12}{49}}$ **g** $\sqrt{\frac{25}{18}}$ **h** $\sqrt{\frac{64}{100}}$ **i** $\sqrt{\frac{20}{45}}$ **j** $\sqrt{\frac{54}{72}}$

4 **a** $\sqrt{0.01}$ **b** $\sqrt{0.36}$ **c** $\sqrt{0.004}$ **d** $\sqrt{0.25}$ **e** $\sqrt{0.0016}$
f $\sqrt{0.49}$ **g** $\sqrt{0.0064}$ **h** $\sqrt{0.000\,009}$ **i** $\sqrt{0.0025}$ **j** $\sqrt{0.81}$

5

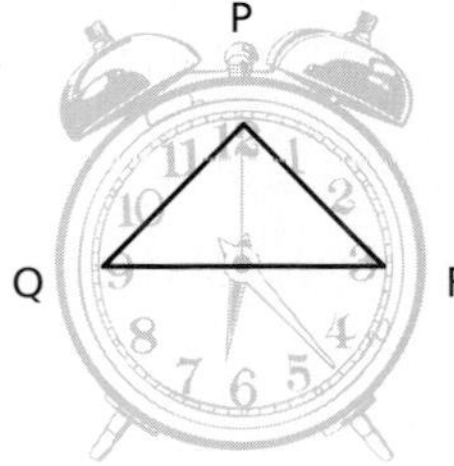

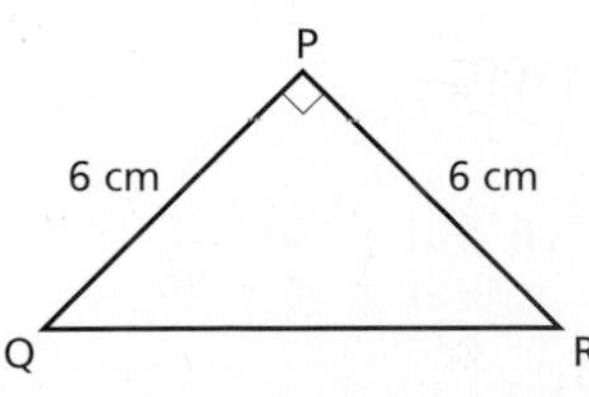

Triangle PQR is right-angled. PQ = PR = 6 cm.
Calculate the diameter of the clock face, leaving your answer as a simplified surd.

6 Each box has a square base.
The length of the base, b cm, can be worked out using the formula $b = \sqrt{\dfrac{V}{h}}$ where V cm^3 is the volume and h cm is the height.

Calculate the length of the base, leaving your answer in surd form:

a $V = 50,\ h = 9$
b $V = 48,\ h = 25$
c $V = 80,\ h = 81$

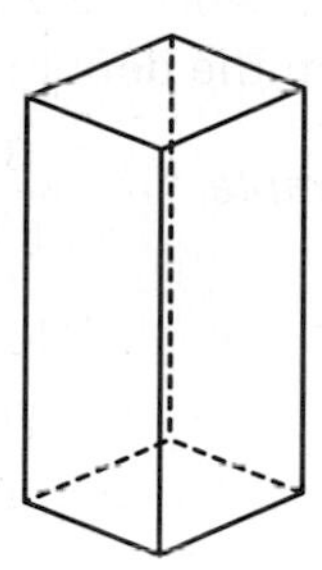

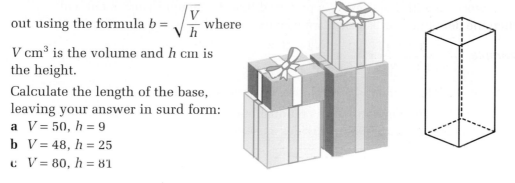

Further simplification

$$\sqrt{a} \times \sqrt{b} = \sqrt{(ab)}$$

$$\frac{\sqrt{a}}{\sqrt{b}} = \sqrt{\frac{a}{b}}$$

Example 1

Simplify $\sqrt{3} \times \sqrt{12}$.

$\sqrt{3} \times \sqrt{12} = \sqrt{(3 \times 12)}$
$= \sqrt{36}$
$= 6$

Example 2

Simplify $\dfrac{\sqrt{12}}{\sqrt{3}}$.

$\dfrac{\sqrt{12}}{\sqrt{3}} = \sqrt{\dfrac{12}{3}}$
$= \sqrt{4}$
$= 2$

Example 3

Simplify $\sqrt{6} \times \sqrt{8}$.

$\sqrt{6} \times \sqrt{8} = \sqrt{(6 \times 8)} = \sqrt{48}$
$= \sqrt{(16 \times 3)}$
$= \sqrt{16} \times \sqrt{3}$
$= 4\sqrt{3}$

EXERCISE 8

Simplify each of the following, leaving your answer in surd form where appropriate.

1 **a** $\sqrt{5} \times \sqrt{20}$ **b** $\sqrt{3} \times \sqrt{27}$ **c** $\sqrt{8} \times \sqrt{2}$ **d** $\sqrt{2} \times \sqrt{98}$ **e** $\sqrt{2} \times \sqrt{18}$

2 **a** $\dfrac{\sqrt{8}}{\sqrt{2}}$ **b** $\dfrac{\sqrt{27}}{\sqrt{3}}$ **c** $\dfrac{\sqrt{5}}{\sqrt{20}}$ **d** $\dfrac{\sqrt{2}}{\sqrt{72}}$ **e** $\dfrac{\sqrt{112}}{\sqrt{7}}$

3 **a** $\sqrt{3} \times \sqrt{8}$ **b** $\sqrt{8} \times \sqrt{5}$ **c** $\sqrt{10} \times \sqrt{2}$ **d** $\sqrt{6} \times \sqrt{12}$ **e** $\sqrt{5} \times \sqrt{15}$

4 **a** $\dfrac{\sqrt{18}}{\sqrt{6}}$ **b** $\dfrac{\sqrt{12}}{\sqrt{2}}$ **c** $\dfrac{\sqrt{24}}{\sqrt{3}}$ **d** $\dfrac{\sqrt{60}}{\sqrt{5}}$ **e** $\dfrac{\sqrt{3}}{\sqrt{60}}$

5 **a** $\sqrt{3} \times \sqrt{33}$ **b** $\sqrt{48} \times \sqrt{6}$ **c** $\sqrt{56} \times \sqrt{2}$ **d** $\dfrac{\sqrt{5}}{\sqrt{250}}$ **e** $\dfrac{\sqrt{5}}{\sqrt{90}}$

Rationalising the denominator

When working with fractions it is preferred that the denominator is rational. When the denominator is a surd we usually proceed as follows.

Example 1 $\frac{3}{\sqrt{2}} = \frac{3}{\sqrt{2}} \times \frac{\sqrt{2}}{\sqrt{2}} = \frac{3\sqrt{2}}{\sqrt{4}} = \frac{3\sqrt{2}}{2}$

Remember $\frac{\sqrt{2}}{\sqrt{2}} = 1$ so we have just multiplied by 1.
The denominator is rational but the fraction still has the same value.
(The calculator provides a useful check.)

In general: $\frac{a}{\sqrt{b}} = \frac{a}{\sqrt{b}} \times \frac{\sqrt{b}}{\sqrt{b}} = \frac{a\sqrt{b}}{\sqrt{b^2}} = \frac{a\sqrt{b}}{b}$

Example 2 $\frac{2}{3\sqrt{5}} = \frac{2}{3\sqrt{5}} \times \frac{\sqrt{5}}{\sqrt{5}} = \frac{2\sqrt{5}}{3\sqrt{25}} = \frac{2\sqrt{5}}{15}$

Example 3 $\frac{6 - \sqrt{3}}{\sqrt{3}} = \frac{6 - \sqrt{3}}{\sqrt{3}} \times \frac{\sqrt{3}}{\sqrt{3}} = \frac{(6 - \sqrt{3})\sqrt{3}}{\sqrt{9}} = \frac{6\sqrt{3} - 3}{3} = \frac{3(2\sqrt{3} - 1)}{3} = 2\sqrt{3} - 1$

EXERCISE 9

Rationalise the denominators of these fractions.

1 a $\frac{1}{\sqrt{2}}$ **b** $\frac{2}{\sqrt{2}}$ **c** $\frac{3}{\sqrt{2}}$ **d** $\frac{2}{\sqrt{3}}$ **e** $\frac{3}{\sqrt{3}}$ **f** $\frac{9}{\sqrt{3}}$

g $\frac{10}{\sqrt{3}}$ **h** $\frac{1}{\sqrt{5}}$ **i** $\frac{3}{\sqrt{5}}$ **j** $\frac{10}{\sqrt{5}}$ **k** $\frac{7}{\sqrt{7}}$ **l** $\frac{10}{\sqrt{7}}$

2 a $\frac{5}{\sqrt{10}}$ **b** $\frac{9}{\sqrt{6}}$ **c** $\frac{6}{\sqrt{15}}$ **d** $\frac{1}{2\sqrt{2}}$ **e** $\frac{1}{4\sqrt{3}}$ **f** $\frac{1}{5\sqrt{5}}$

3 a $\frac{1 + \sqrt{2}}{\sqrt{2}}$ **b** $\frac{1 - \sqrt{5}}{\sqrt{5}}$ **c** $\frac{3 + \sqrt{6}}{\sqrt{6}}$ **d** $\frac{9 + 3\sqrt{3}}{\sqrt{3}}$ **e** $\frac{6 - 2\sqrt{10}}{\sqrt{10}}$

Rationalising denominators of the form $a \pm \sqrt{b}$

Remember the difference of two squares: $(x + y)(x - y) = x^2 - y^2$

Example 1 $(4 + \sqrt{3})(4 - \sqrt{3}) = 4^2 - (\sqrt{3})^2 = 16 - 3 = 13$

Note: $(a + \sqrt{b})(a - \sqrt{b}) = a^2 - (\sqrt{b})^2 = a^2 - b$
$(a + \sqrt{b})$ and $(a - \sqrt{b})$ are called **conjugate** surds.
When multiplied together they produce a **rational** answer.
This can be used to help rationalise the denominator in many cases.

Example 2 $\frac{6}{2 + \sqrt{3}} = \frac{6}{2 + \sqrt{3}} \times \frac{2 - \sqrt{3}}{2 - \sqrt{3}} = \frac{6(2 - \sqrt{3})}{(2 + \sqrt{3})(2 - \sqrt{3})} = \frac{6(2 - \sqrt{3})}{4 - 3} = 6(2 - \sqrt{3})$

Example 3 $\frac{5}{\sqrt{5} - 4} = \frac{5}{\sqrt{5} - 4} \times \frac{\sqrt{5} + 4}{\sqrt{5} + 4} = \frac{5(\sqrt{5} + 4)}{(\sqrt{5} - 4)(\sqrt{5} + 4)} = \frac{5(\sqrt{5} + 4)}{5 - 16} = \frac{5(\sqrt{5} + 4)}{-11}$

EXERCISE 10

1 Simplify:

a $(2 + \sqrt{5})(2 - \sqrt{5})$ b $(3 - \sqrt{2})(3 + \sqrt{2})$ c $(\sqrt{2} + 1)(\sqrt{2} - 1)$ d $(\sqrt{5} - 3)(\sqrt{5} + 3)$

2 Rationalise the denominators of these fractions.

a $\dfrac{1}{2 + \sqrt{3}}$ b $\dfrac{1}{\sqrt{2} + 1}$ c $\dfrac{1}{4 - \sqrt{2}}$ d $\dfrac{1}{\sqrt{5} - 1}$ e $\dfrac{1}{5 + \sqrt{3}}$

f $\dfrac{3}{2 - \sqrt{2}}$ g $\dfrac{7}{4 + \sqrt{3}}$ h $\dfrac{1}{\sqrt{3} - 2}$ i $\dfrac{3}{1 - \sqrt{2}}$ j $\dfrac{14}{1 + \sqrt{8}}$

Indices

A definition: a^n is shorthand for $a \times a \times a \times \dots \times a$ (n factors).
a is called the **base** and n is called the **index**.
(The plural of index is indices.)

Some rules: 1 What is $a^3 \times a^5$? $\underline{a \times a \times a} \times \underline{a \times a \times a \times a \times a} = a^8$

To multiply numbers with the same base, add the indices.

2 What is $\dfrac{a^6}{a^2}$?

$$\frac{a^6}{a^2} = \frac{a \times a \times a \times a \times a \times a}{a \times a} = a \times a \times a \times a = a^4$$

To divide numbers with the same base, subtract the indices.

In general: $\boldsymbol{a^m \times a^n = a^{m+n}}$

$\boldsymbol{a^m \div a^n = a^{m-n},\ a \neq 0}$

EXERCISE 11

Simplify the following, leaving all answers in index form.

1 a $a^2 \times a^3$ b $a^3 \times a^6$ c $a^1 \times a^3$ d $m^5 \times m^5$ e $t^2 \times t$

2 a $y^2 \times y^4$ b $(0.1)^2 \times (0.1)^3$ c $p^4 \times p$ d $\left(\frac{1}{8}\right)^3 \times \left(\frac{1}{8}\right)^5$ e $h^{10} \times h^{10}$

3 a $\dfrac{2^4}{2^3}$ b $\dfrac{3^6}{3^2}$ c $\dfrac{2^{10}}{2^5}$ d $\dfrac{5^5}{5^2}$ e $\dfrac{10^3}{10^3}$

4 a $a^6 \div a^5$ b $a^8 \div a^4$ c $t^4 \div t$ d $m^8 \div m^2$ e $y^{12} \div y^3$

5 a $2y^2 \times 4y^3$ b $a^3 \times 5a^3$ c $3t^4 \times 4t^3$ d $8m^4 \times m^2$ e $12y^5 \times y$

6 a $\dfrac{8c^8}{4c}$ b $\dfrac{12t^6}{9t^3}$ c $\dfrac{25a^4}{5a}$ d $\dfrac{4m^4}{3m^3}$ e $\dfrac{6c^5}{2c^2}$

7 a $a^2 \times a^3 \times a^4$ b $2y^2 \times 3y \times 4y^2$ c $\dfrac{t^8}{t^2 \times t^4}$ d $\dfrac{a^2 \times a^3}{a^4}$

Negative indices

1

$$\left.\begin{array}{l}\dfrac{a^2}{a^5} = \dfrac{a \times a}{a \times a \times a \times a \times a} = \dfrac{1}{a^3} \\ \text{but by the division rule: } \dfrac{a^2}{a^5} = a^{2-5} = a^{-3}\end{array}\right\} \text{so } \frac{1}{a^3} = a^{-3}$$

2

$$\left.\begin{array}{l}\dfrac{a^5}{a^5} = \dfrac{a \times a \times a \times a \times a}{a \times a \times a \times a \times a} = 1 \\ \text{but by the division rule: } \dfrac{a^5}{a^5} = a^{5-5} = a^0\end{array}\right\} \text{so } a^0 = 1$$

3 Using the multiplication rule:

$$\left.\begin{array}{r}(a^5)^3 = a^5 \times a^5 \times a^5 = a^{15} \\ (a^3)^5 = a^3 \times a^3 \times a^3 \times a^3 \times a^3 = a^{15}\end{array}\right\} \text{so } (a^5)^3 = (a^3)^5 = a^{5 \times 3}$$

In general: $\mathbf{\dfrac{1}{a^n} = a^{-n}}$

$\mathbf{a^0 = 1}$

$\mathbf{(a^m)^n = a^{mn}}$

Examples Write each of these using negative indices.

a $\dfrac{1}{x^4} = x^{-4}$ **b** $\dfrac{2}{3a^5} = \dfrac{2a^{-5}}{3}$ **c** $\dfrac{1}{y^{-3} \times y^5} = \dfrac{1}{y^2} = y^{-2}$

EXERCISE 12

1 Rewrite each expression using negative indices.

a $\dfrac{1}{y^2}$ **b** $\dfrac{1}{a^3}$ **c** $\dfrac{1}{x^5}$ **d** $\dfrac{3}{y^4}$ **e** $\dfrac{10}{x^3}$

f $\dfrac{2}{a^5}$ **g** $\dfrac{1}{6y^4}$ **h** $\dfrac{1}{2m^6}$ **i** $\dfrac{3}{7x^2}$ **j** $\dfrac{6}{5y^3}$

2 Rewrite each expression using positive indices.

a a^{-4} **b** b^{-2} **c** y^{-6} **d** $2m^{-4}$ **e** $7t^{-3}$

f $\dfrac{y^{-4}}{5}$ **g** $\dfrac{x^{-4}}{4}$ **h** $\dfrac{3c^{-4}}{2}$ **i** $\dfrac{4a^{-4}}{3}$ **j** $\dfrac{2x^{-4}}{7}$

3 Simplify each expression.

a $(x^2)^3$ **b** $(y^4)^2$ **c** $(t^3)^4$ **d** $(g^2)^7$ **e** $(h^2)^{-3}$

f $(a^{-5})^3$ **g** $(p^{-3})^3$ **h** $(q^5)^{-4}$ **i** $(k^{-3})^{-2}$ **j** $(a^{-4})^{-5}$

4 Simplify each expression using positive indices.

a $a^2 \times a^{-3}$ **b** $y^3 \times y^{-5}$ **c** $a^{-6} \times a^3$ **d** $d^{-4} \times d^3$

e $3t^{-2} \times 2$ **f** $2h^2 \times 4h^{-3}$ **g** $6m^{-2} \times 3m^{-3}$ **h** $2a^{-6} \times 3a^{-1}$

i $a^2 \div a^6$ **j** $y^3 \div y^4$ **k** $2a^4 \div 4a^5$ **l** $9c \div 6c^4$

m $t^{-2} \times t^2$ **n** $h^5 \times h^{-5}$ **o** $3m^4 \times 2m^{-4}$ **p** $5a^{-6} \times 3a^6$

5 Simplify each expression so that the variable only appears on the numerator.

a $\frac{a^2a^3}{a^7}$ **b** $\frac{y^{-1}y}{y^7}$ **c** $\frac{x^{-2}x^{-3}}{x^{-4}}$ **d** $\frac{m^5m^{-6}}{m^{-1}}$

e $\frac{1}{t^2t^3}$ **f** $\frac{1}{y^2y^5}$ **g** $\frac{3}{m^4m^{-1}}$ **h** $\frac{2}{x^{-2}x^{-6}}$

i $\frac{a^2}{a^3}$ **j** $\frac{c^5}{c^8}$ **k** $\frac{t^{-3}}{5t^2}$ **l** $\frac{3y^{-1}}{4y^2}$

6 Multiply out, leaving any negative indices in the answer.

Example $x^3(x^{-2} + x^{-5}) = x^3x^{-2} + x^3x^{-5} = x^{3+(-2)} + x^{3+(-5)} = x + x^{-2}$

a $y^2(y^{-3} + 2y^{-4})$ **b** $m^{-1}(m^{-1} - 5m^{-5})$ **c** $t^{-5}(3t^3 + 7t)$ **d** $2a^{-4}(4a^{-3} - 5a^3)$

Fractions as indices

What meaning can we give fractional indices?

$a^{\frac{1}{2}} \times a^{\frac{1}{2}} = a^{\frac{1}{2}+\frac{1}{2}} = a^1 = a$, Now $\sqrt{a} \times \sqrt{a} = a$, so $a^{\frac{1}{2}} = \sqrt{a}$

$a^{\frac{1}{3}} \times a^{\frac{1}{3}} \times a^{\frac{1}{3}} = a^{\frac{1}{3}+\frac{1}{3}+\frac{1}{3}} = a^1 = a$, $\sqrt[3]{a} \times \sqrt[3]{a} \times \sqrt[3]{a} = a$, so $a^{\frac{1}{3}} = \sqrt[3]{a}$

In general: $\boldsymbol{a^{\frac{1}{n}} = \sqrt[n]{a}}$

Also: $\left(a^{\frac{1}{3}}\right)^2 = a^{\frac{1}{3}} \times a^{\frac{1}{3}} = a^{\frac{1}{3}+\frac{1}{3}} = a^{\frac{2}{3}}$

Example 1

Find the value of $8^{\frac{2}{3}}$.

$$8^{\frac{2}{3}} = \left(\sqrt[3]{8}\right)^2 = (2)^2 = 4$$

Example 2

Simplify $\frac{a}{\sqrt[3]{a}}$.

$$\frac{a}{\sqrt[3]{a}} = a^1 \div a^{\frac{1}{3}} = a^{1-\frac{1}{3}} = a^{\frac{2}{3}}$$

Example 3

Simplify $\frac{a^{\frac{3}{4}}}{2a^{\frac{1}{4}}}$.

$$\frac{a^{\frac{3}{4}}}{2a^{\frac{1}{4}}} = \frac{a^{\frac{3}{4}-\frac{1}{4}}}{2} = \frac{a^{\frac{1}{2}}}{2}$$

EXERCISE 13

1 Evaluate:

a $16^{\frac{1}{2}}$ **b** $27^{\frac{1}{3}}$ **c** $81^{\frac{1}{4}}$ **d** $125^{\frac{1}{3}}$ **e** $1000^{\frac{1}{3}}$

f $81^{\frac{3}{4}}$ **g** $125^{\frac{2}{3}}$ **h** $16^{\frac{3}{4}}$ **i** $64^{\frac{2}{3}}$ **j** $1000^{\frac{2}{3}}$

2 Simplify, writing your answers with positive indices.

a $a^{\frac{1}{5}} \times a^{\frac{1}{5}}$ **b** $3y \times y^{\frac{1}{2}}$ **c** $2m^{\frac{1}{3}} \times 3m^{\frac{2}{3}}$ **d** $4a^2 \times 2a^{\frac{1}{3}}$

3 Simplify, writing your answers with positive indices.

a $\dfrac{a^{\frac{1}{2}}}{a^{\frac{1}{4}}}$ **b** $\dfrac{2x^{\frac{5}{3}}}{3x^{\frac{2}{3}}}$ **c** $\dfrac{3b^{\frac{1}{2}} \times b^{\frac{1}{2}}}{b^{\frac{1}{3}}}$ **d** $\dfrac{c}{c^{\frac{1}{5}}}$ **e** $k^{\frac{1}{3}} \times k^{-\frac{1}{3}}$

f $m^{\frac{2}{3}} \times m^{-\frac{5}{3}}$ **g** $y^{-\frac{3}{4}} \times y^{-\frac{3}{4}}$ **h** $2u^{-\frac{5}{3}} \times 3u^{\frac{1}{3}}$ **i** $10k^{\frac{4}{5}} \times 5k^{-2}$

4 Simplify, using positive indices.

a $\dfrac{3a^{\frac{1}{4}}}{4a^{\frac{3}{4}}}$ **b** $\dfrac{b^{\frac{2}{3}} \times b^{\frac{4}{3}}}{b^{\frac{8}{3}}}$ **c** $\dfrac{5c^{-2}}{c^{-\frac{1}{5}} \times c^{-\frac{3}{5}}}$ **d** $\dfrac{3d^{\frac{1}{3}} \times 6d^{\frac{1}{3}}}{2d^{\frac{5}{6}}}$

5 Simplify, using negative indices.

a $a^{-\frac{1}{5}} \times a^{-\frac{3}{5}}$ **b** $c \times c^{-\frac{8}{3}}$ **c** $\dfrac{h^{-\frac{2}{5}}}{h^{\frac{4}{5}}}$ **d** $\dfrac{3k^{\frac{1}{3}}}{4k^{\frac{7}{3}}}$ **e** $\dfrac{m^{\frac{1}{4}}}{m^{\frac{3}{4}}}$ **f** $\dfrac{4p^{-\frac{1}{5}}}{p^{\frac{1}{5}}}$

g $\dfrac{t^{\frac{2}{3}}}{2t^{3}}$ **h** $\dfrac{n^{-\frac{2}{3}}}{3n^{-\frac{1}{3}}}$

And finally ...

Example 1 $\left(a^{\frac{1}{3}}\right)^4 = a^{\frac{1}{3}} \times a^{\frac{1}{3}} \times a^{\frac{1}{3}} \times a^{\frac{1}{3}} = a^{\frac{4}{3}}$

In general: $\left(\boldsymbol{a}^{\frac{1}{m}}\right)^{\boldsymbol{n}} = \boldsymbol{a}^{\frac{n}{m}} = \left(\boldsymbol{a}^{\boldsymbol{n}}\right)^{\frac{1}{m}}$

Since $a^{\frac{1}{m}} = \sqrt[m]{a}$ we get $\left(\sqrt[m]{\boldsymbol{a}}\right)^{\boldsymbol{n}} = \boldsymbol{a}^{\frac{n}{m}} = \sqrt[m]{\boldsymbol{a}^{\boldsymbol{n}}}$

Example 2 $\left(y^{\frac{3}{4}}\right)^8 = y^{\frac{24}{4}} = y^6$

Example 3 $16^{\frac{3}{4}} = \left(\sqrt[4]{16}\right)^3 = \left(2\right)^3 = 8$

Example 4 $27^{-\frac{5}{3}} = \dfrac{1}{27^{\frac{5}{3}}} = \dfrac{1}{(\sqrt[3]{27})^5} = \dfrac{1}{3^5} = \dfrac{1}{243}$

Example 5 $(2a^2b^3)^4 = 2^4a^8b^{12} = 16a^8b^{12}$

Example 6 Changing to index form: $\dfrac{2}{\sqrt{5a^{-3}}} = \dfrac{2}{(5a^{-3})^{\frac{1}{2}}} = \dfrac{2}{5^{\frac{1}{2}}a^{\frac{-3}{2}}} = \dfrac{2a^{\frac{3}{2}}}{5^{\frac{1}{2}}}$

Example 7 Changing to surd form: $\left(3m^{-4}\right)^{\frac{1}{3}} = 3^{\frac{1}{3}}m^{-\frac{4}{3}} = \dfrac{3^{\frac{1}{3}}}{m^{\frac{4}{3}}} = \dfrac{\sqrt[3]{3}}{\sqrt[3]{m^4}} = \sqrt[3]{\dfrac{3}{m^4}}$

EXERCISE 14

1 Simplify:

a $\left(a^{3}\right)^{2}$ **b** $\left(x^{2}\right)^{3}$ **c** $\left(y^{4}\right)^{0}$ **d** $\left(c^{0}\right)^{4}$ **e** $\left(h^{\frac{1}{4}}\right)^{3}$

f $\left(k^{\frac{2}{3}}\right)^{-1}$ **g** $\left(m^{-\frac{1}{2}}\right)^{2}$ **h** $\left(n^{-2}\right)^{-3}$ **i** $\left(t^{-\frac{1}{3}}\right)^{-3}$ **j** $\left(u^{\frac{3}{4}}\right)^{-\frac{1}{2}}$

k $\left(3b^{2}\right)^{2}$ **l** $\left(2a^{4}\right)^{3}$ **m** $\left(9c^{4}\right)^{\frac{1}{2}}$ **n** $\left(8h^{6}\right)^{\frac{1}{3}}$ **o** $\left(2u^{-\frac{1}{3}}\right)^{-2}$

p $\left(xy^{2}\right)^{3}$ **q** $\left(2a^{2}b^{3}\right)^{2}$ **r** $\left(3p^{3}q^{4}\right)^{-3}$ **s** $\left(5u^{-\frac{1}{3}}v^{-\frac{3}{4}}\right)^{-2}$ **t** $\left(4a^{2}b^{\frac{1}{3}}\right)^{\frac{1}{2}}$

u $\left(3xy^{2}\right)^{2}$ **v** $\left(a^{-1}b^{3}\right)^{2}$ **w** $\left(3m^{\frac{1}{3}}n^{\frac{1}{2}}\right)^{-3}$

2 Find the value of:

a $8^{\frac{1}{3}}$ **b** $16^{\frac{1}{4}}$ **c** $8^{\frac{2}{3}}$ **d** $16^{\frac{3}{4}}$ **e** $125^{\frac{2}{3}}$

f $25^{-\frac{1}{2}}$ **g** $8^{-\frac{1}{3}}$ **h** $81^{-\frac{1}{4}}$ **i** $4^{\frac{3}{2}}$ **j** $4^{-\frac{3}{2}}$

k $\left(\frac{1}{9}\right)^{\frac{3}{2}}$ **l** $1^{-\frac{5}{2}}$

3 Write these numbers in index form.

a $\sqrt{a}$ **b** $\sqrt[3]{c}$ **c** $\left(\sqrt{y}\right)^{3}$ **d** $\sqrt[3]{m^{2}}$ **e** $\sqrt{a^{-1}}$

f $\sqrt{h^{-3}}$ **g** $\left(\sqrt[4]{t}\right)^{5}$ **h** $\sqrt{9x^{4}}$ **i** $\sqrt{4y^{6}}$ **j** $\sqrt{9a^{-3}}$

k $\sqrt{25c^{-2}}$ **l** $\frac{1}{\sqrt{16a^{8}}}$ **m** $\frac{1}{\sqrt{5t^{4}}}$ **n** $\frac{6}{\sqrt[3]{8y^{6}}}$ **o** $\frac{2}{\sqrt{8x^{5}}}$

4 Write these numbers in surd form.

a $a^{\frac{1}{3}}$ **b** $w^{\frac{1}{4}}$ **c** $c^{-\frac{1}{2}}$ **d** $h^{-\frac{1}{3}}$ **e** $y^{-\frac{1}{5}}$

f $2x^{\frac{1}{2}}$ **g** $5y^{\frac{1}{3}}$ **h** $9a^{-\frac{1}{2}}$ **i** $8c^{-\frac{1}{3}}$ **j** $\left(3a\right)^{-\frac{1}{2}}$

CHAPTER 13 REVIEW

1 Simplify these fractions:

a $\frac{3ab}{12abc}$ **b** $\frac{5y^4}{y^3}$ **c** $\frac{u^3v^2w}{uv^2w^3}$ **d** $\frac{(3-4a)^3}{(3-4a)}$

2 Calculate:

a $\frac{2}{x}+\frac{3}{x}$ **b** $\frac{3}{a}+\frac{4}{b}$ **c** $\frac{m}{2}+\frac{3}{m}$ **d** $\frac{4}{5u}+\frac{2}{uv}$

e $\frac{3}{4}-\frac{2}{x}$ **f** $\frac{2}{a}-\frac{3}{b}$ **g** $\frac{1}{2k}-\frac{3}{k}$ **h** $\frac{k}{5}-\frac{1}{k}$

i $\frac{3}{4}\times\frac{2}{9}$ **j** $\frac{2x}{y}\times\frac{3}{x}$ **k** $\frac{4d}{9p}\times\frac{3p}{16d}$ **l** $\frac{3y^2}{25}\times\frac{15q}{2y}$

m $\frac{12}{35}\div\frac{6}{7}$ **n** $\frac{2x}{9y}\div\frac{3x}{4x}$ **o** $\frac{xk}{2y}\div\frac{2xy}{4k}$ **p** $\frac{y^2}{2z^3}\div\frac{5y^3}{8z^2}$

3 a A telephone company calculates the bill, £B, using the formula $B = f + 2u$ where f is a fixed charge and u is the number of units used.
Change the subject to u.

b Every day Mike takes £m to work and spends £n at the canteen.
In a week he saves £K where $K = 5(m - n)$.
Make **(i)** m **(ii)** n the subject of the formula.

4 Simplify, leaving your answer in surd form:

a $\sqrt{2}\times\sqrt{6}$ **b** $\frac{\sqrt{96}}{\sqrt{3}}$ **c** $\sqrt{24}$ **d** $\frac{1}{\sqrt{50}}$ **e** $\sqrt{\frac{27}{8}}$

5 Express each of these with rational denominators:

a $\frac{5}{\sqrt{5}}$ **b** $\frac{2}{3\sqrt{3}}$

6 Simplify:

a $y^2\times y^4$ **b** $\frac{a^6}{a^3}$ **c** $\frac{y^{12}}{y^3\times y^4}$ **d** $\frac{2m^3\times m^{-3}}{m^2}$ **e** $3t^{-\frac{2}{3}}\times 2t$

7 Simplify, leaving your answer with negative indices:

a $4a^{\frac{3}{4}}\times 2a^{-2}$ **b** $\frac{8y}{y^{-\frac{1}{2}}\times 4y^3}$

8 Rationalise the denominator: **a** $\frac{22}{4-\sqrt{5}}$ **b** $\frac{18}{\sqrt{7}+1}$

9 Simplify: **a** $\left(x^{-3}\right)^2$ **b** $\left(x^{\frac{1}{3}}\right)^3$

14 Quadratic Functions

Reminders

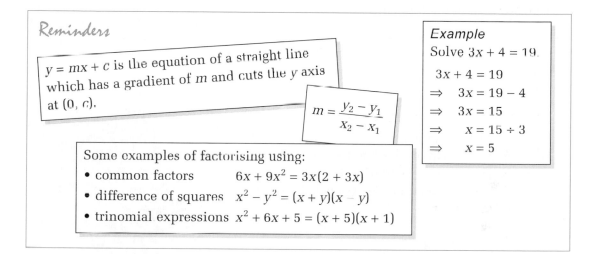

$y = mx + c$ is the equation of a straight line which has a gradient of m and cuts the y axis at $(0, c)$.

$$m = \frac{y_2 - y_1}{x_2 - x_1}$$

Some examples of factorising using:

- common factors $6x + 9x^2 = 3x(2 + 3x)$
- difference of squares $x^2 - y^2 = (x + y)(x - y)$
- trinomial expressions $x^2 + 6x + 5 = (x + 5)(x + 1)$

Example

Solve $3x + 4 = 19$.

$3x + 4 = 19$

$\Rightarrow \quad 3x = 19 - 4$

$\Rightarrow \quad 3x = 15$

$\Rightarrow \quad x = 15 \div 3$

$\Rightarrow \quad x = 5$

STARTING POINTS

1 Which of the given equations matches the line of best fit in this scatter graph?

(i) $y = 3x$

(ii) $y = 2x + 3$

(iii) $y = 3x - 2$

(iv) $y = 2x - 3$

(v) $y = 3x + 2$

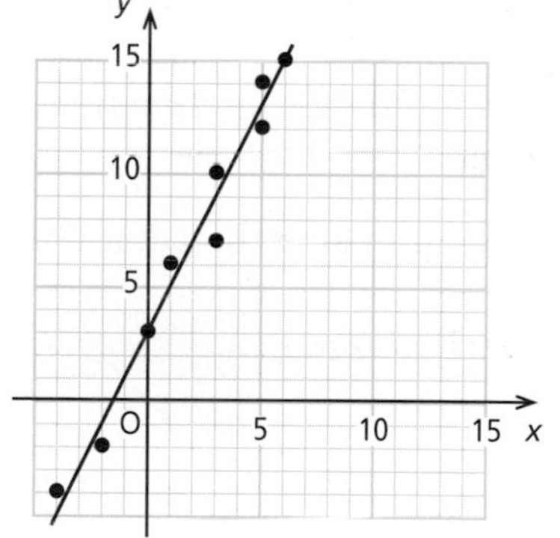

2 Write down **(i)** the gradient **(ii)** the point where the line cuts the y axis for the following lines: **a** $y = 4x + 2$ **b** $y = -2x + 7$ **c** $y = 0.5x - 4$.

3

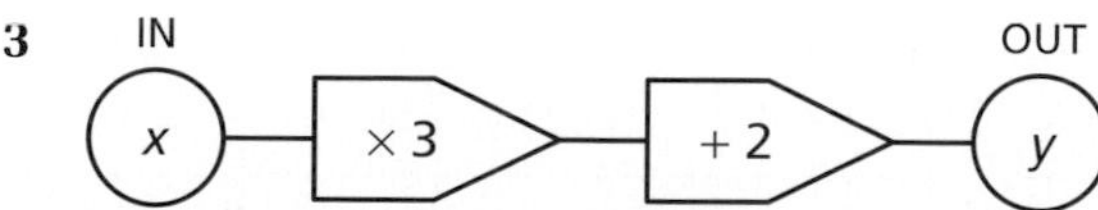

a Use the function machine to find the value of y when $x =$ **(i)** 0 **(ii)** 1 **(iii)** 2 **(iv)** 3 **(v)** 4 **(vi)** 5.

b Use your results to help you complete the table.

x	0	1	2	3	4	5	6
y	2	5					

c Plot all the points (x, y) and join them to make the line $y = 3x + 2$.

4 Evaluate each of the formulae using the given data:

a $A = lb$ when $l = 4$ and $b = 3.5$

b $C = 2\pi r$ when $r = 6$

c $T = u^2 + 3$ when $u = 2$.

5 Solve each of the following equations:

a $3x + 1 = 19$ **b** $4x + 5 = 29 - 2x$ **c** $x^2 = 4$ (two answers)

6 Factorise each of the following:

a **(i)** $3x + 12x^2$ **(ii)** $8y - 12xy$

b **(i)** $a^2 - b^2$ **(ii)** $4a^2 - 9b^2$

c **(i)** $x^2 + 5x + 6$ **(ii)** $x^2 - 4x - 12$

Functions

A roll of carpet is 5 m wide. It is sold in strips by the area. If the length of a strip is x m then the area, A square metres, is given by $A = 5x$. The value of A depends on the value of x. We say A is a **function** of x. We usually write:

$$A(x) = 5x$$

$A(1)$ is the value of A when $x = 1$ $5 \times 1 = 5$

$A(2)$ is the value of A when $x = 2$ $5 \times 2 = 10$

$A(7)$ is the value of A when $x = 7$ $5 \times 7 = 35$

$A(t)$ is the value of A when $x = t$ $5 \times t = 5t$

Using the formula for the function, we can make a table:

x	0	1	2	3	4	5	6
A	0	5	10	15	20	25	30

or draw a graph using the values of A as the y-coordinates: $y = A(x)$

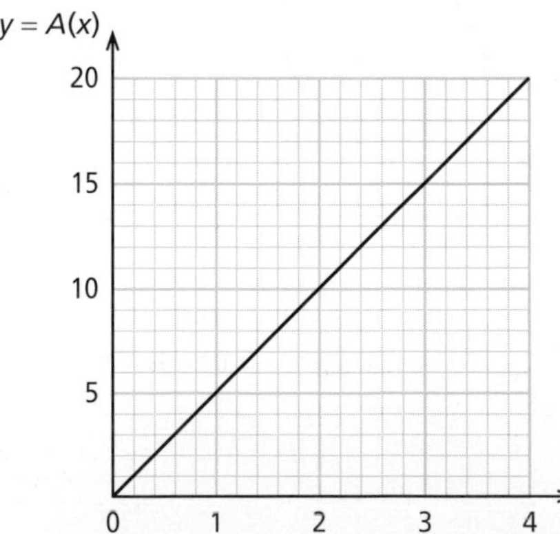

In this case the graph is a straight line. $A(x) = 5x$ is called a **linear function**.

EXERCISE 1

1 **a** $P(x) = 3x$. Work out the value of: **(i)** $P(1)$ **(ii)** $P(2)$ **(iii)** $P(5)$.

b $Q(x) = 7x$. Work out the value of: **(i)** $Q(0)$ **(ii)** $Q(4)$ **(iii)** $Q(6)$.

c $R(x) = x$. Work out the value of: **(i)** $R(4)$ **(ii)** $R(8)$ **(iii)** $R(10)$.

d $S(x) = 1.5x$. Work out the value of: **(i)** $S(2)$ **(ii)** $S(6)$ **(iii)** $S(8)$.

e $T(x) = \frac{1}{2}x$. Work out the value of: **(i)** $T(0)$ **(ii)** $T(2)$ **(iii)** $T(1.2)$.

2 Tickets for a swimming gala cost £2.50 each. The cost of a party of people is a function of the number in the party. $C(x) = 2.5x$ where £C is the cost and x is the number of people.

a Calculate: **(i)** $C(0)$ **(ii)** $C(5)$.

b Copy and complete the table.

x	0	1	2	3	4	5	6
$C(x)$							

c Draw a graph of the function.

3 For each of the following functions, without drawing the graph, state:
(i) where the line cuts the y axis **(ii)** the gradient of the line.

a $f(x) = 5x + 8$ **b** $f(x) = 7x + 4$ **c** $f(x) = 2x - 3$ **d** $f(x) = x - 2$
e $f(x) = -2x + 3$ **f** $f(x) = -3x - 1$ **g** $f(x) = -x - 5$ **h** $f(x) = -x$

4

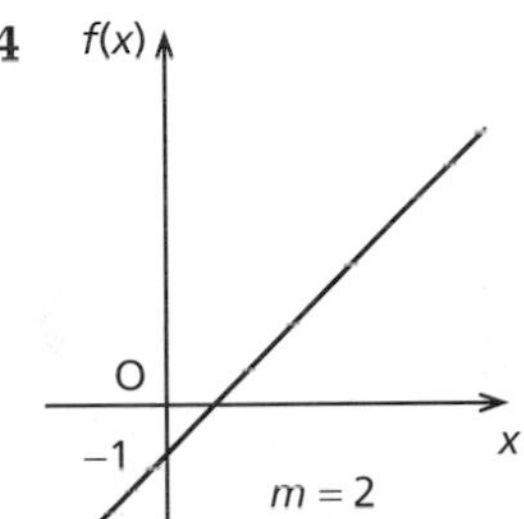

This is a sketch of the graph of $f(x) = 2x - 1$. Note the y-intercept and the gradient are marked.

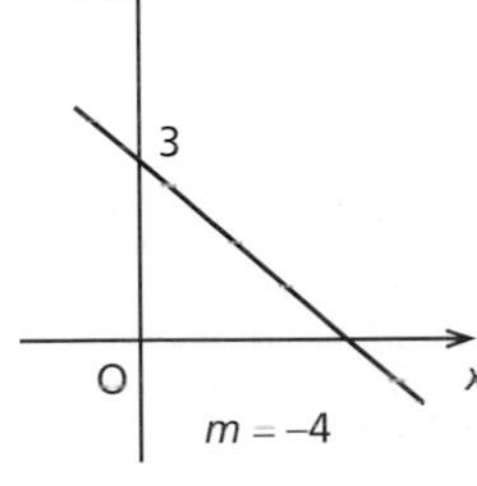

This is a sketch of the graph of $f(x) = -4x + 3$. Note the y-intercept and the negative gradient are marked.

Make sketches of the graphs of the following functions:

a $f(x) = 2x + 3$ **b** $f(x) = x + 1$ **c** $f(x) = 3x - 2$ **d** $f(x) = -x + 2$
e $f(x) = -3x$ **f** $f(x) = -2x - 1$ **g** $f(x) = x - 2$ **h** $f(x) = -2x - 4$

5 A fencer charges a basic rate of £20 plus £2 for every metre of fence he builds. Let C = total cost in £ and x = the number of metres of fence he uses. Then $C(x) = 2x + 20$.

a Using axes as shown, draw a graph of the function $y = C(x)$.

b Calculate the value of: **(i)** $C(5)$ **(ii)** $C(8)$.

c What is the cost of: **(i)** a 6 m fence (what is $C(6)$?) **(ii)** a 10 m fence?

d A fence costs £100 to build. How long is it? (For what value of x is $C(x) = 100$? Hint: Solve $2x + 20 = 100$.)

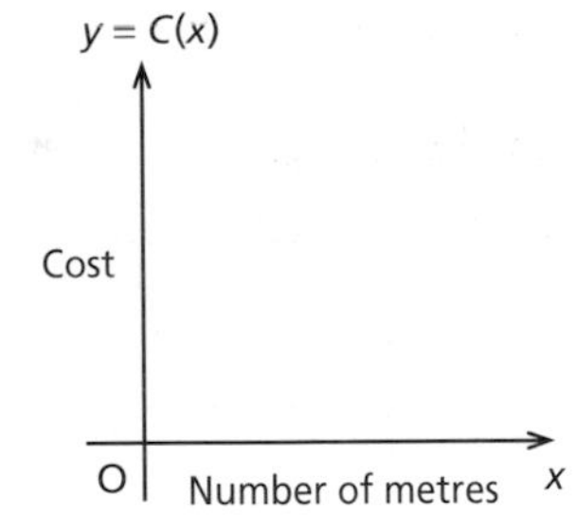

6 The gardeners at a park do a survey on a certain type of tree. They record:

- x, the number of years since the tree was planted
- H, the height of the tree.

The head gardener believes $H(x) = x + 2$.
The assistant gardener says $H(x) = 0.5x + 2$.

a Transfer the scatter diagram onto graph paper.

b Draw the graphs of: **(i)** $y = x + 2$ **(ii)** $y = 0.5x + 2$.

c Who do you think is correct?

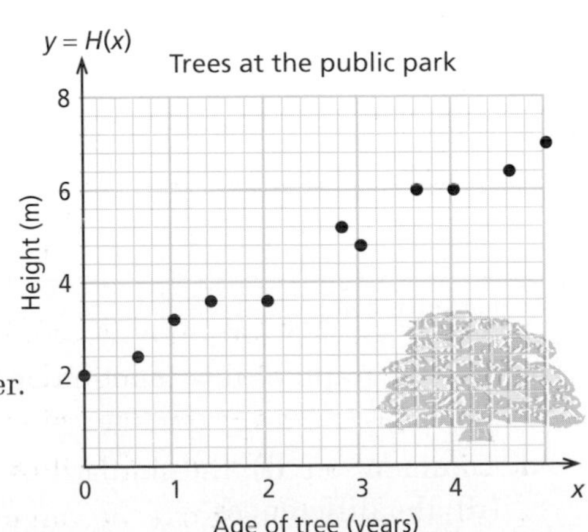

7 The cost in pounds of taking a vehicle on the ferry, $V(x)$, is a function of the number of people, x, in the vehicle. Four people in a minibus are charged £92. Seven people in a similar minibus are charged £152.

  a Assuming the function is linear, find a formula for the function.

  b What will ten people in a minibus be charged?

  c What is the charge for an empty minibus?

Quadratic functions

A function of the form $f(x) = ax^2 + bx + c$ is called a **quadratic function**.
a, b and c are constants and $a \neq 0$.

The simplest quadratic function is $f(x) = x^2$.
We can sketch the graph of $y = f(x)$ by first making a table of values.

x	−3	−2	−1	0	1	2	3
$f(x)$	9	4	1	0	1	4	9

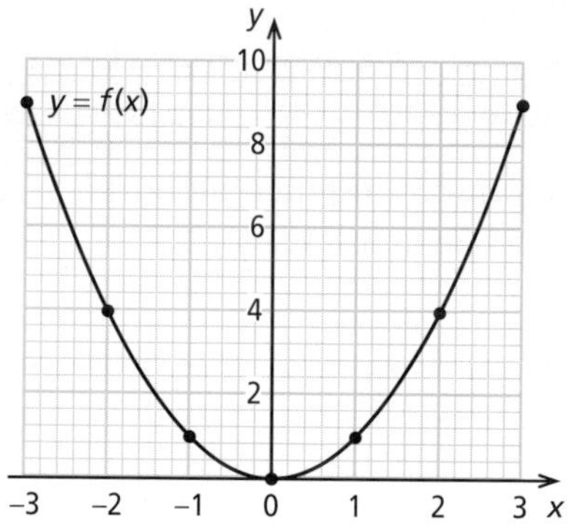

The curve is called a parabola.
It has an axis of symmetry, $x = 0$.
It has a **vertex** at (0, 0).
It cuts the x axis when $f(x) = 0$.

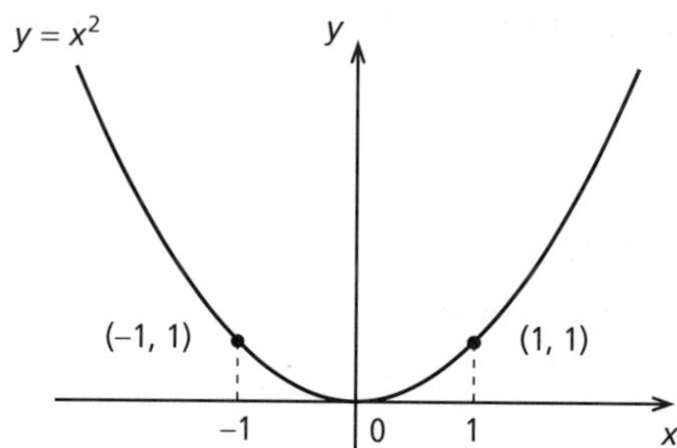

EXERCISE 2

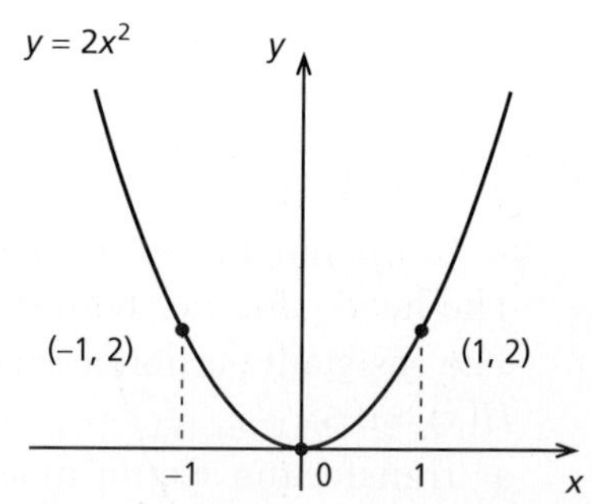

1 a Make your own copy of the graph $y = x^2$.

  b Copy and complete the table of values for the function $f(x) = 2x^2$.

x	−3	−2	−1	0	1	2	3
$f(x)$	18						

  c Make a graph of this function on the same diagram as $y = x^2$.

  d Comment on **(i)** the similarities
  (ii) the differences.

2 Each of the following functions is of the form $f(x) = ax^2$.
Using the same diagram for each:
(i) complete the table
(ii) draw a graph of $y = f(x)$
(iii) comment on the width of the curve where $y = a$.

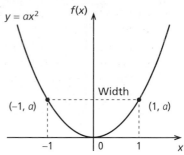

a $f(x) = 3x^2$

x	−3	−2	−1	0	1	2	3
$f(x)$	27	12	3				

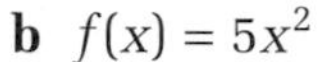

b $f(x) = 5x^2$

x	−3	−2	−1	0	1	2	3
$f(x)$	45	20	5				

c $f(x) = -x^2$

x	−3	−2	−1	0	1	2	3
$f(x)$	−9	−4					

d $f(x) = -2x^2$

x	−3	−2	−1	0	1	2	3
$f(x)$	−18	−8					

Check for each of the examples explored that the graph of $f(x) = ax^2$:
(i) is a parabola
(ii) has an axis of symmetry, the y axis.
(iii) has a vertex at (0, 0).

Example

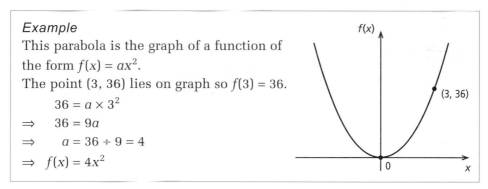

This parabola is the graph of a function of the form $f(x) = ax^2$.
The point (3, 36) lies on graph so $f(3) = 36$.

$$36 = a \times 3^2$$
$$\Rightarrow \quad 36 = 9a$$
$$\Rightarrow \quad a = 36 \div 9 = 4$$
$$\Rightarrow \quad f(x) = 4x^2$$

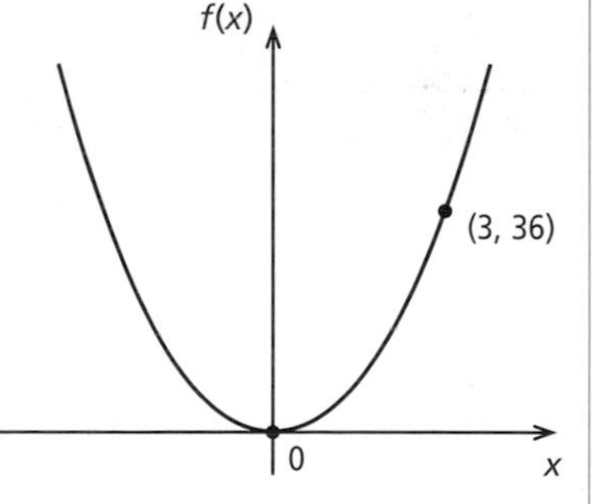

3 Find the formulae of the quadratic functions illustrated here.

a

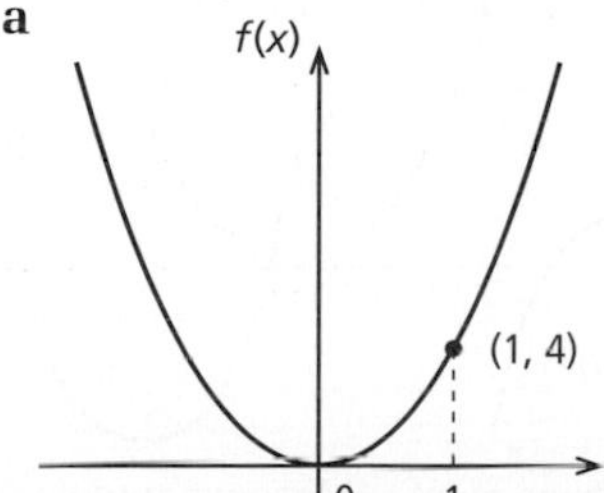

b

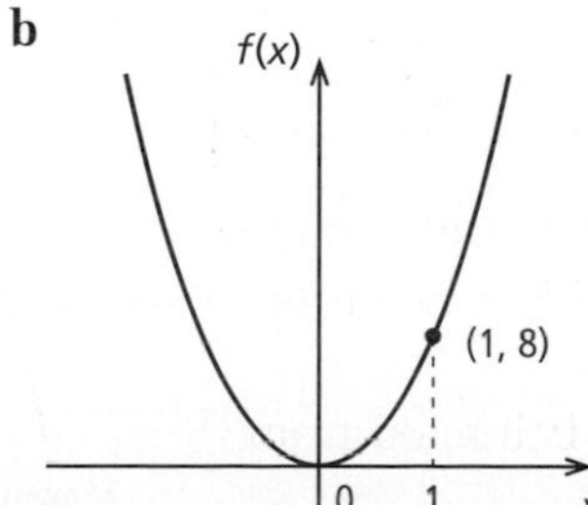

c

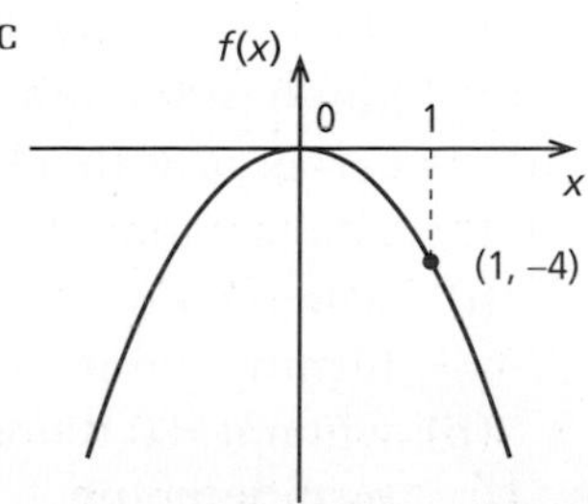

d

f(x); (2, 20); 0; x

e

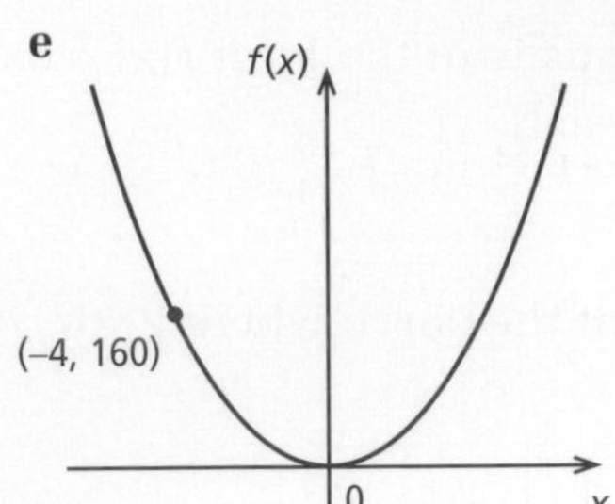

f

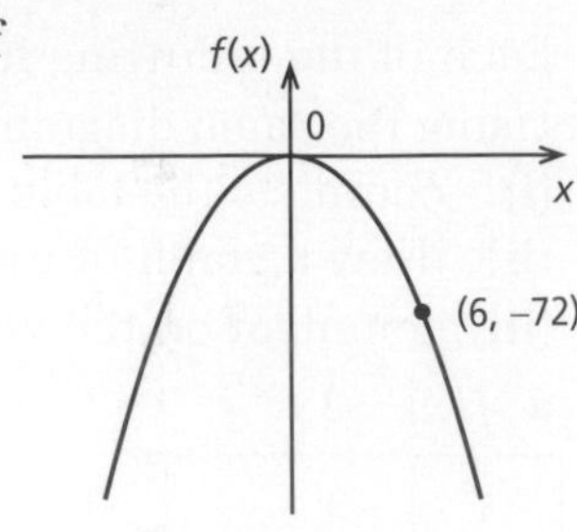

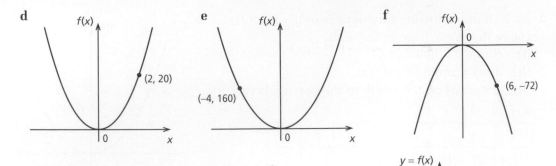

4 Look at the function with equation $y = x^2 + 2$.
First make a table ...

x	–3	–2	–1	0	1	2	3
$f(x)$	11	6	3	2	3	6	11

... and then draw a graph.

a Give the coordinates of the curve's vertex.

b What is the axis of symmetry?

y = f(x); 12; 10; 8; 6; 4; 2; –3; –2; –1; 0; 1; 2; 3; x

5 For each of the following functions:

(i) draw a graph

(ii) state the coordinates of its vertex

(iii) give its axis of symmetry.

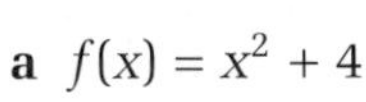

a $f(x) = x^2 + 4$

x	–3	–2	–1	0	1	2	3
$f(x)$	13	8	5				

b $f(x) = x^2 - 1$

x	–3	–2	–1	0	1	2	3
$f(x)$	8	3					

c $f(x) = 3x^2 - 1$

x	–3	–2	–1	0	1	2	3
$f(x)$	26	11					

d $f(x) = -x^2 + 3$

x	–3	–2	–1	0	1	2	3
$f(x)$	–6	–1					

e $f(x) = -2x^2 - 2$

x	–3	–2	–1	0	1	2	3
$f(x)$	–20						

6 Check the following details using the graphs you have drawn in question **5**.
In the graph of the function $f(x) = ax^2 + c$:

a the vertex is at $(0, c)$

b the axis of symmetry is $x = 0$, the y axis

c **(i)** when $a > 0$ the vertex is a minimum turning point

(ii) when $a < 0$ the vertex is a maximum turning point.

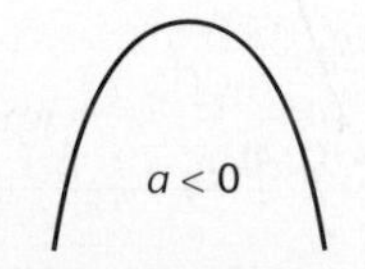

Maximum turning point

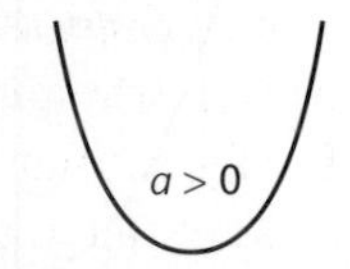

Minimum turning point

Example

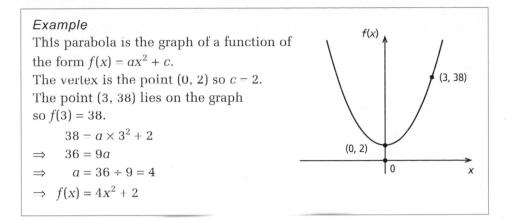

This parabola is the graph of a function of the form $f(x) = ax^2 + c$.
The vertex is the point (0, 2) so $c = 2$.
The point (3, 38) lies on the graph so $f(3) = 38$.

$$38 = a \times 3^2 + 2$$
$$\Rightarrow \quad 36 = 9a$$
$$\Rightarrow \quad a = 36 \div 9 = 4$$
$$\Rightarrow \quad f(x) = 4x^2 + 2$$

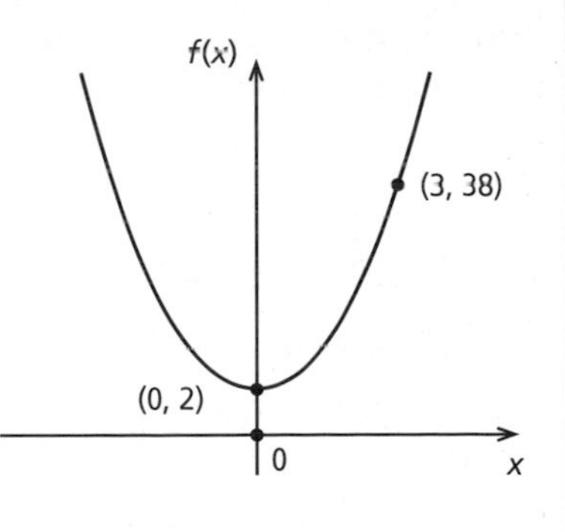

7 Find the equation of each of these functions. (The sketches are not drawn to scale.)

a

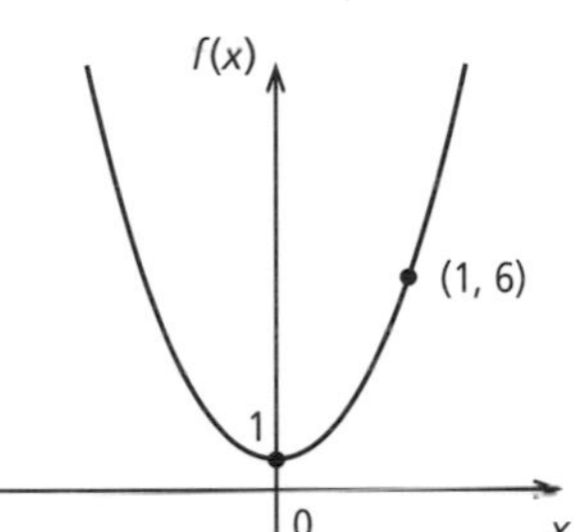

b

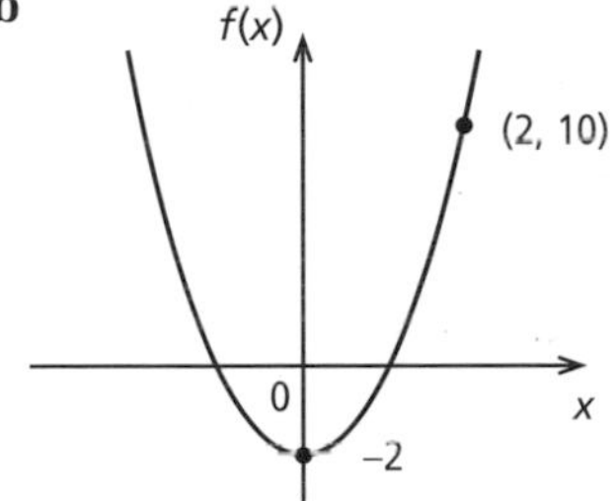

c

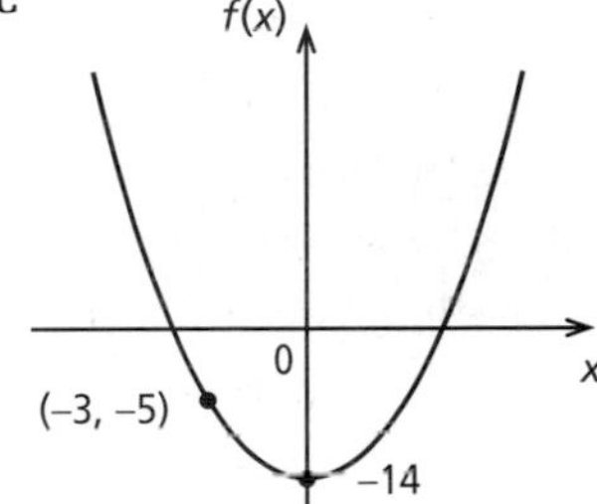

d

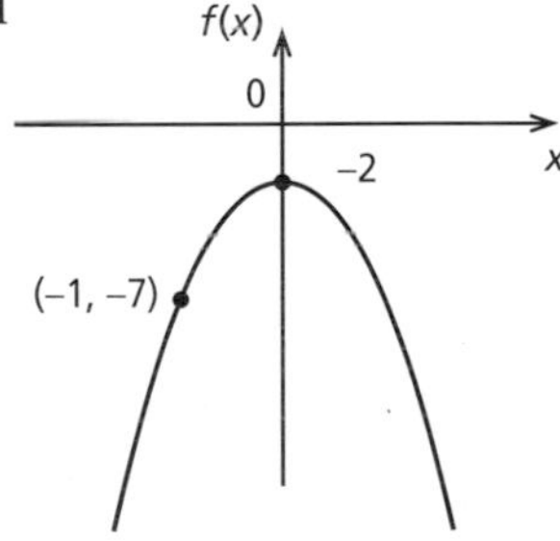

e

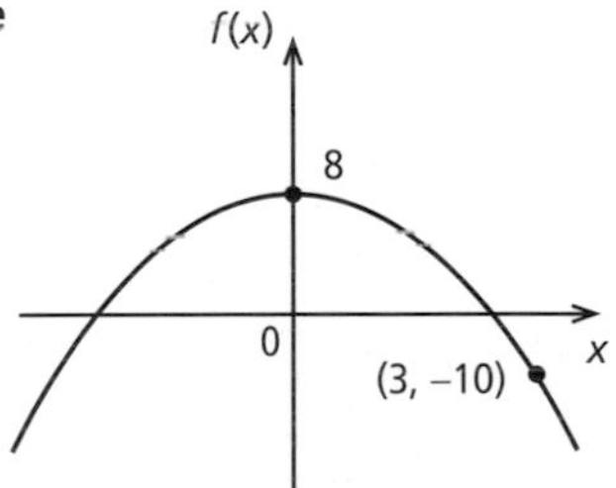

f

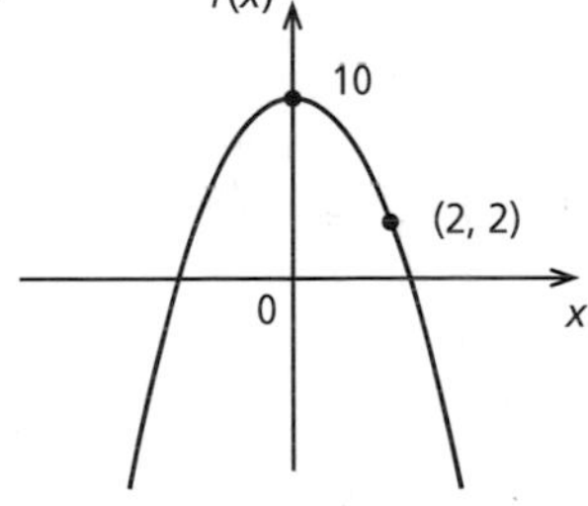

EXERCISE 3

1 Look at the function with equation $f(x) = (x - 1)^2$.
First make a table ...

x	–3	–2	–1	0	1	2	3	4
$f(x)$	16	9	4	1	0	1	4	9

... and then draw a graph.

a Give the coordinates of the curve's vertex.
b Check that the equation of the axis of symmetry is $x = 1$.

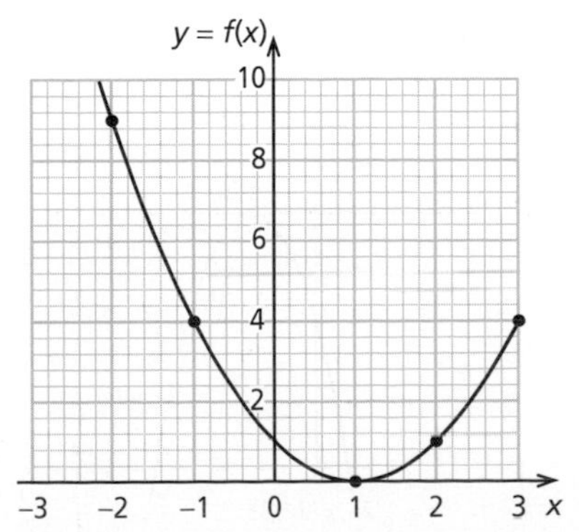

2 For the following functions, using the x values suggested:
(i) draw a graph **(ii)** state the coordinates of the vertex
(iii) give the equation of the axis of symmetry.

a $f(x) = (x - 3)^2;\ 0 \le x \le 6$
b $f(x) = (x + 4)^2;\ -7 \le x \le -1$
c $f(x) = (x + 1)^2;\ -4 \le x \le 2$
d $f(x) = 2(x - 3)^2;\ 0 \le x \le 6$
e $f(x) = -(x + 1)^2;\ -4 \le x \le 2$

3 Check the following details using the graphs you drew in question **2**.
In the graph of the function $f(x) = a(x - b)^2$:
a the vertex is at $(b, 0)$
b the axis of symmetry is $x = b$
c **(i)** when $a > 0$ the vertex is a minimum turning point
(ii) when $a < 0$ the vertex is a maximum turning point.

Example

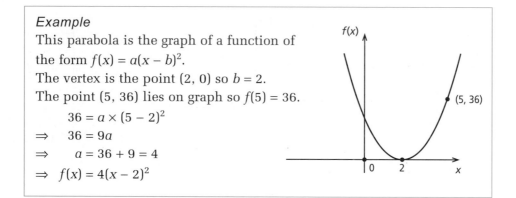

This parabola is the graph of a function of the form $f(x) = a(x - b)^2$.
The vertex is the point (2, 0) so $b = 2$.
The point (5, 36) lies on graph so $f(5) = 36$.

$$36 = a \times (5 - 2)^2$$
$$\Rightarrow \quad 36 = 9a$$
$$\Rightarrow \quad a = 36 + 9 = 4$$
$$\Rightarrow \quad f(x) = 4(x - 2)^2$$

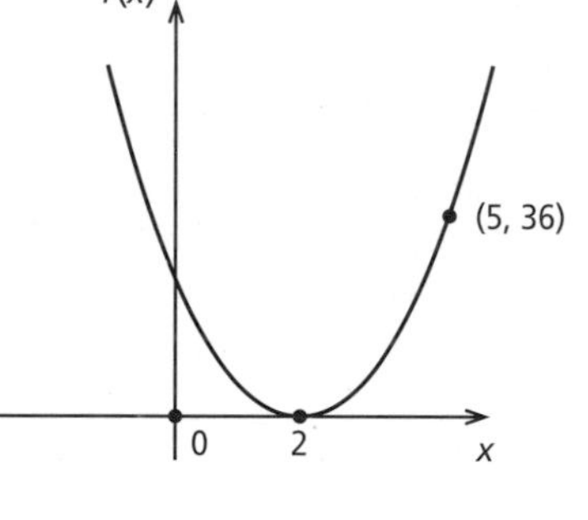

4 Find the equation of each of these functions.

a

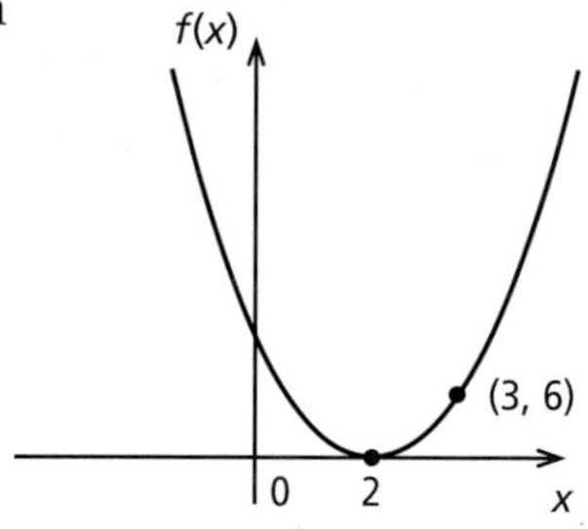

b

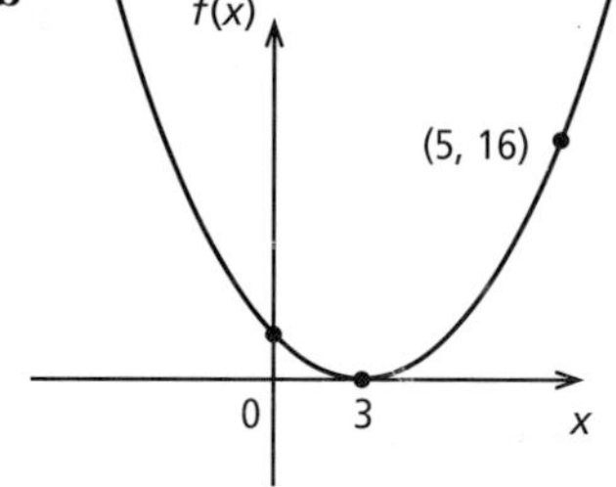

c

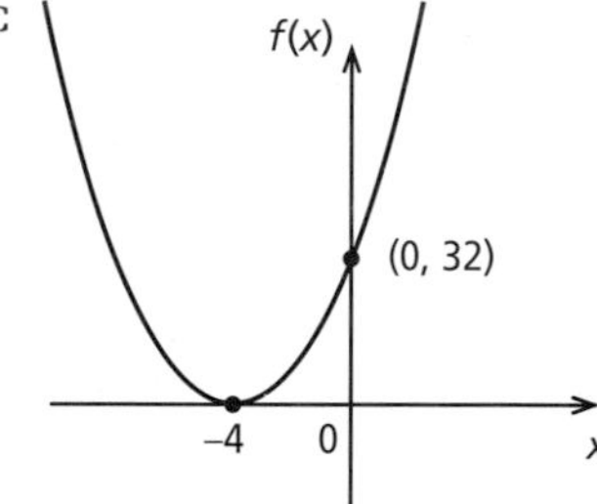

d

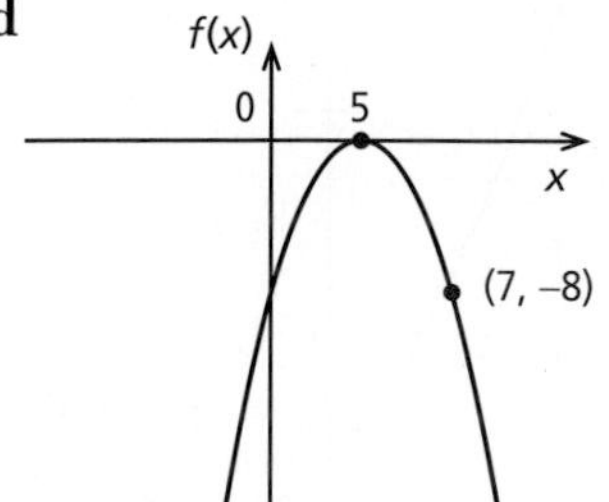

e

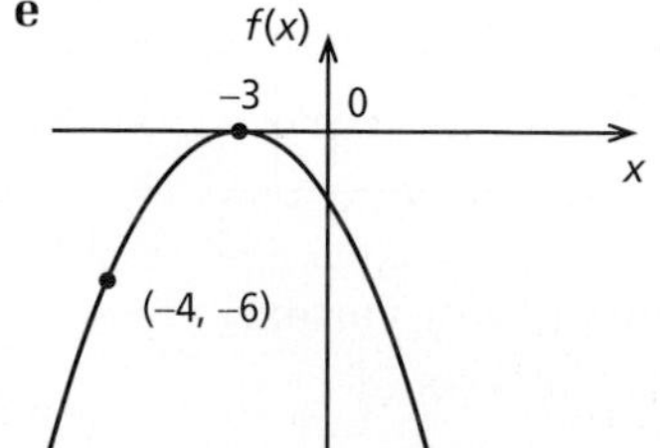

f

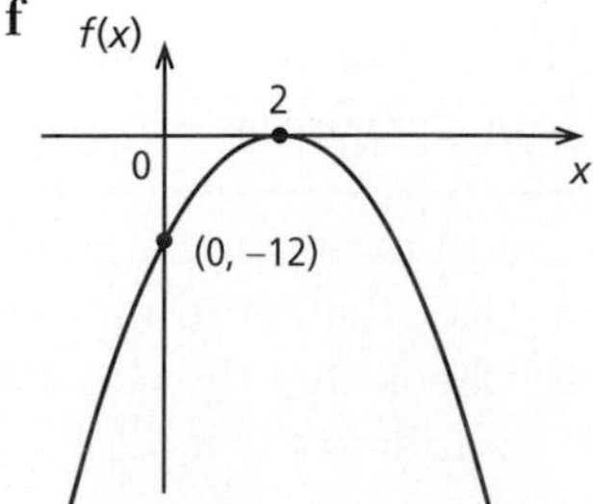

5 Match the following graphs with the equations.

a

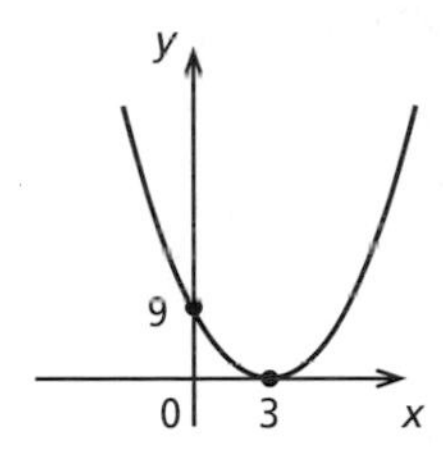

b

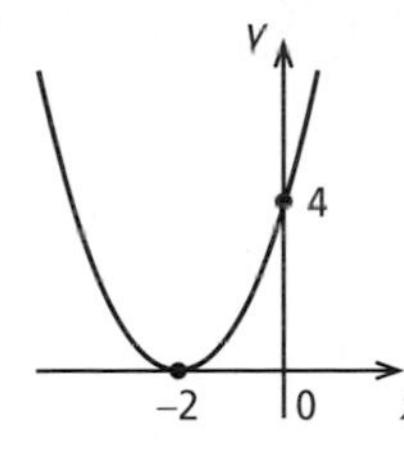

c

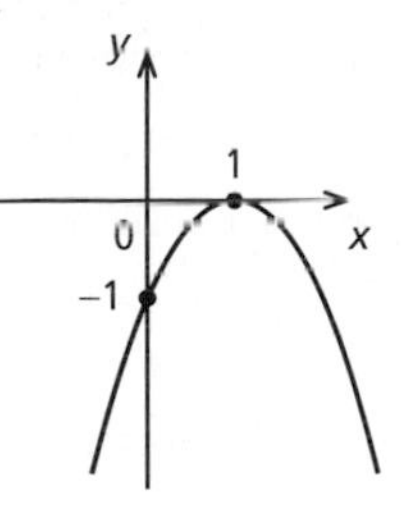

d

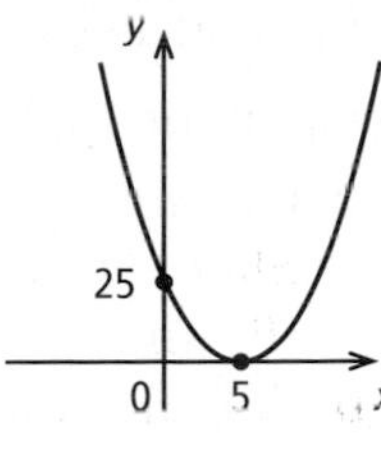

(i) $y = (x - 5)^2$ **(ii)** $y = (x + 2)^2$ **(iii)** $y = -(x - 1)^2$ **(iv)** $y = (x - 3)^2$

EXERCISE 4

1 A satellite TV dish is a parabola in cross-section. With axes as shown its equation is $y = \frac{1}{50}x^2$. The dish is 2 m wide.

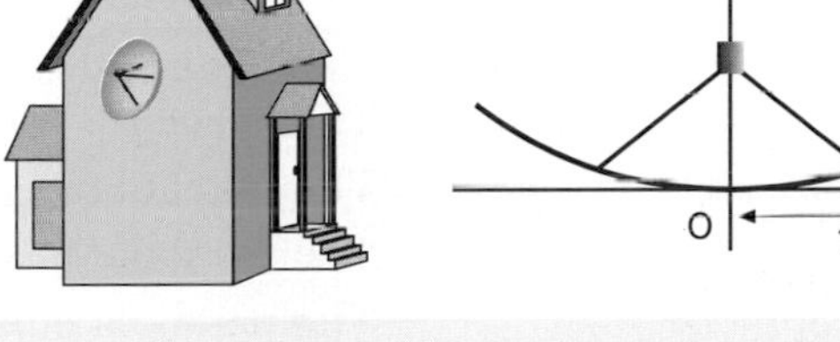

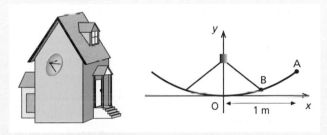

a What are the coordinates of the point A?

b The rod is connected at the point B whose x coordinate is 0.25. How high above the x axis is it?

2

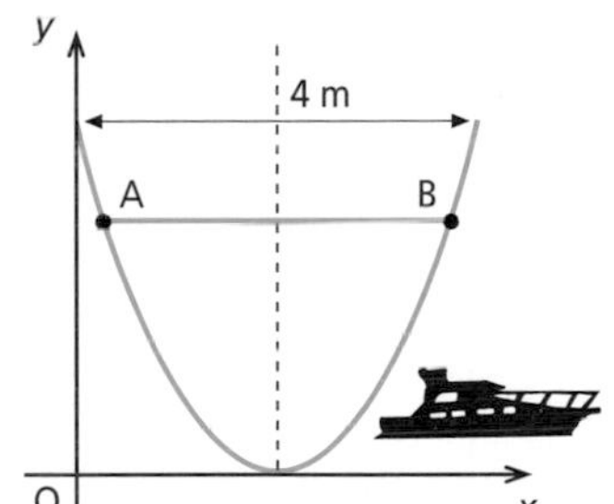

The cross-section of a boat in dry dock is a parabola with equation $y = (x - 2)^2$.

a Write down:

(i) the coordinates of the vertex

(ii) the equation of the axis of symmetry.

b The x coordinate of the point A is 0.2. Calculate its y coordinate.

c Use symmetry to find the coordinates of B.

d AB is the deck of the boat. How wide is it?

3

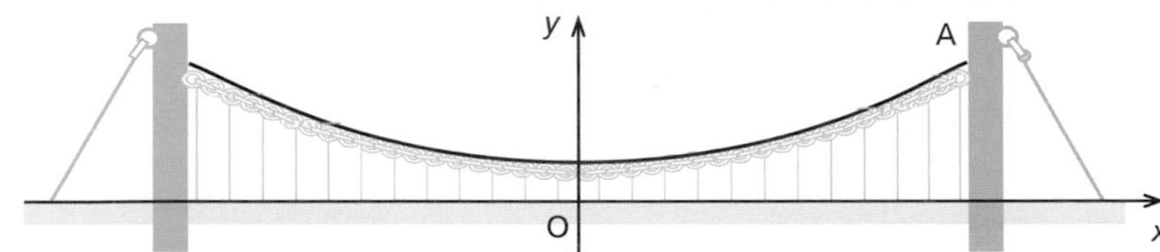

The supporting chains of a bridge form a parabola.

Its equation is $y = \frac{1}{600}x^2 + 50$ where x and y are measured in metres.

a Write down: **(i)** the coordinates of the vertex

(ii) the equation of the axis of symmetry.

b The chain meets a supporting pier at A. The x coordinate of A is 300. How high is the point A from the road (the x axis)?

c How far apart are the piers?

4 A helicopter is directly above a boat. Viewed from the helicopter, a distress flare from the boat has a parabolic flight path with equation $y = -\frac{1}{4}(x - 14)^2$ where x and y are measured in metres.

a State: **(i)** the coordinates of the vertex
(ii) the axis of symmetry of the flight of the flare.

b Calculate how far the boat, B, is below the helicopter.

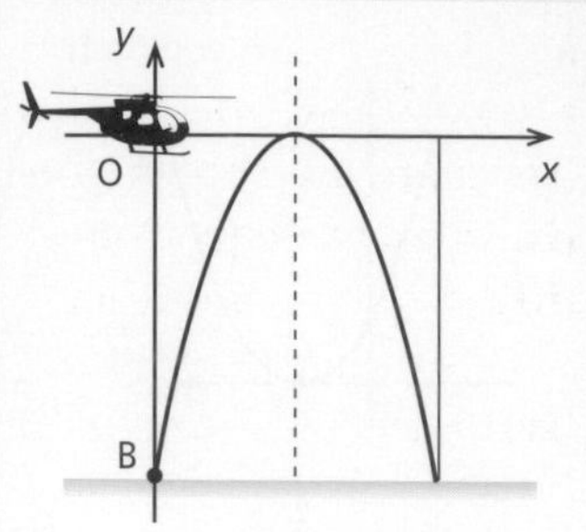

The general quadratic function

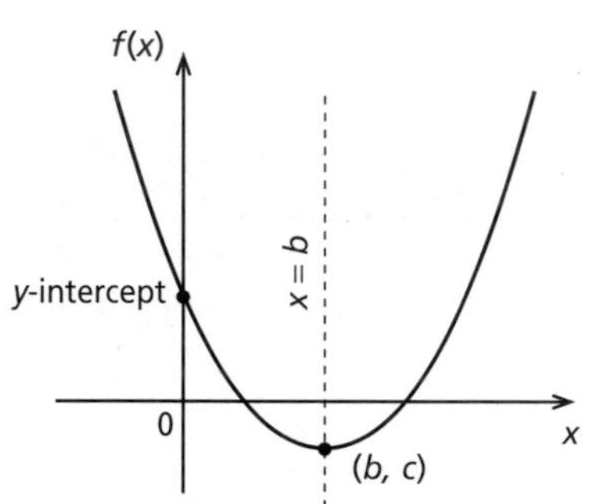

Every quadratic function can be written in the form

$$f(x) = a(x - b)^2 + c.$$

The curve $y = f(x)$ is a parabola.
The parabola has an axis of symmetry, $x = b$.
The parabola has a vertex or turning point (b, c).
The parabola cuts the y axis when $x = 0$, $y = ab^2 + c$.
When $a > 0$ the vertex is a minimum turning point.
When $a < 0$ the vertex is a maximum turning point.

Example 1

Sketch the graph of $f(x) = 2(x - 3)^2 + 1$.

$a = 2$, $b = 3$, $c = 1$

The graph cuts the y axis at $2 \times 3^2 + 1 = 19$.
The axis of symmetry is $x = 3$.
The vertex is $(3, 1)$.
Since $a > 0$ the vertex is a minimum turning point.
These points help you sketch the curve.

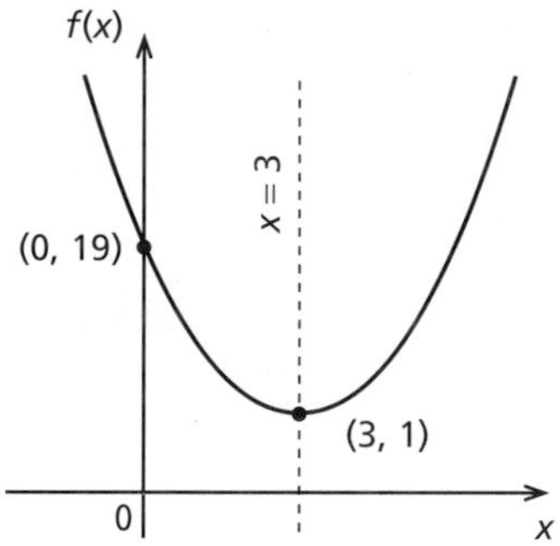

Example 2 Write down the equation of this curve in the form $y = a(x - b)^2 + c$, given that $a = 1$ or $a = -1$.

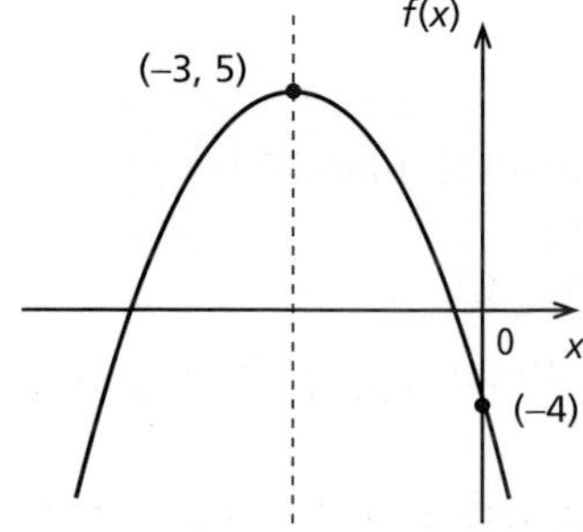

By inspection the vertex is $(-3, 5)$ so $b = -3$ and $c = 5$.
The vertex is a maximum turning point so $a = -1$.
The equation is $y = -(x + 3)^2 + 5$.

EXERCISE 5

1 For each equation of the form $a(x - b)^2 + c$:

(i) state the values of a, b and c

(ii) give the equation of the axis of symmetry

(iii) give the coordinates of the vertex and say whether it is a maximum or minimum turning point

(iv) calculate the y-intercept

(v) sketch the graph of the function.

a $y = (x - 3)^2 + 2$ **b** $y = (x - 7)^2 + 5$ **c** $y = (x + 4)^2 + 2$

d $y = (x + 6)^2 + 3$ **e** $y = (x - 1)^2 + 9$ **f** $y = (x + 2)^2 + 1$

g $y = -(x - 1)^2 - 4$ **h** $y = -(x - 2)^2 - 7$ **i** $y = -(x + 2)^2 - 3$

j $y = -(x + 5)^2 - 2$ **k** $y = -(x + 1)^2 - 8$ **l** $y = -(x - 4)^2 - 10$

2 In the following graphs, $a = 1$ or $a = -1$. In each case:

(i) state the value of a, b and c

(ii) give the equation of the curve

(iii) work out the coordinates of the point where the curve cuts the y axis.

a

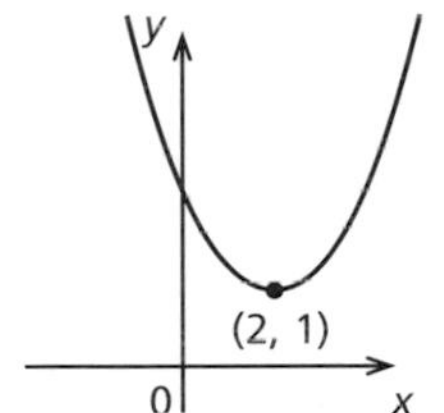

b

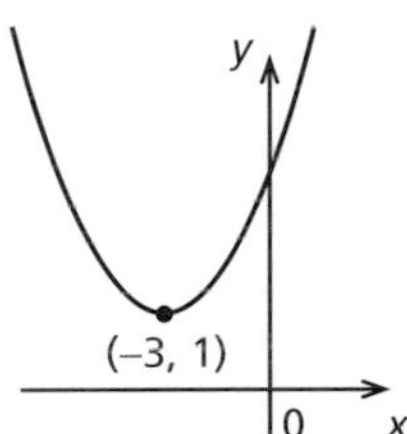

c

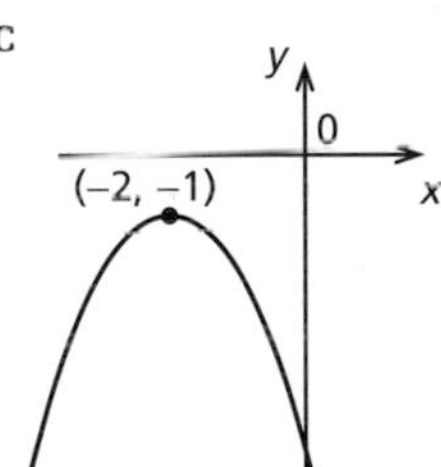

d

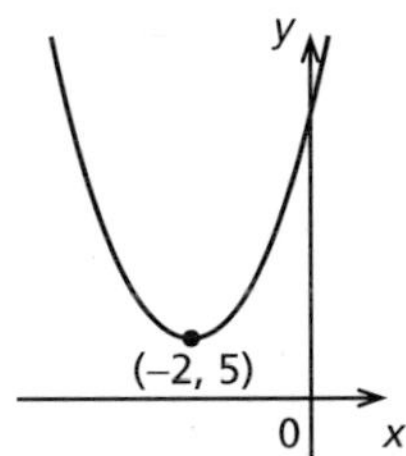

e

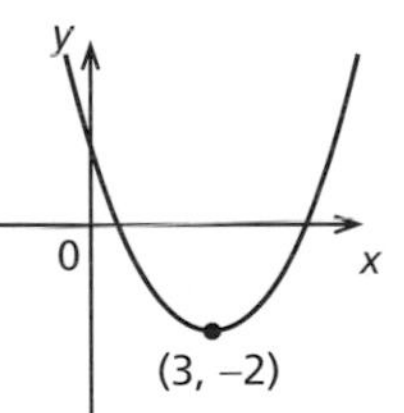

f

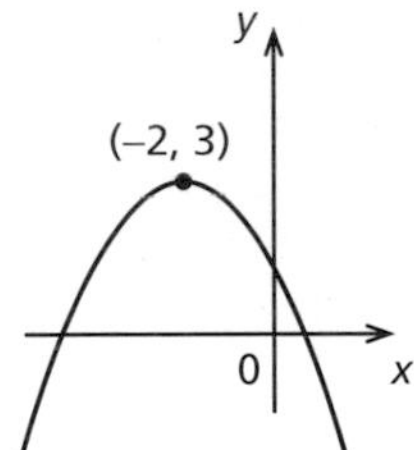

g

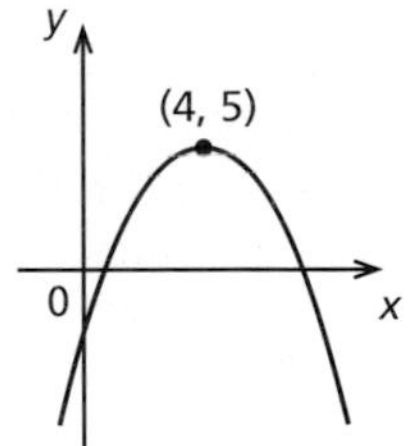

h

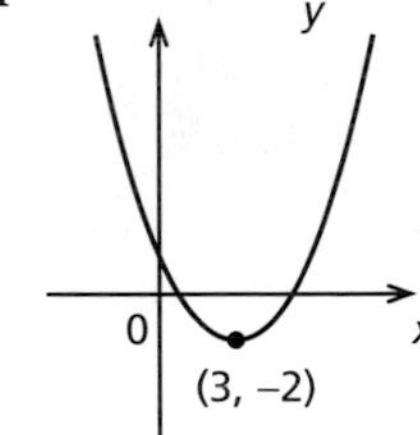

Minima and maxima

Example

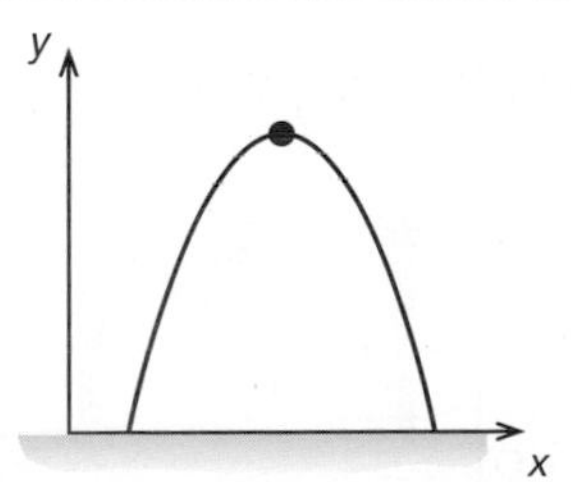

The height of a golf ball, $f(x)$, is a function of the horizontal distance of the ball, x, from the origin.

$$f(x) = -0.01(x - 60)^2 + 16$$

What is the maximum height reached?

By inspection, the vertex is a maximum turning point at (60, 16).

So the maximum height reached is 16 m when $x = 60$.

EXERCISE 6

1 This rectangle is x cm wide and $(6 - x)$ cm long. Its area is $x(6 - x)$ cm^2. We can write it like this: $A = x(6 - x)$.

x cm

(6 – x) cm

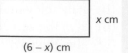

a Copy and complete the table.

x	0	1	2	3	4	5	6
A	0	5					

b Draw the graph of $A = x(6 - x)$.
c Where does the graph cut the x axis?
d What is the maximum area of the rectangle? (Hint: highest reading on the y axis.)
e For what value of x does the maximum area occur?
f Write out the equation of the curve in the form $y = a(x - b)^2 + c$.

2 A fencing contractor has 20 m of fencing. He wishes to fence off a rectangular plot of land backing onto a hedge. The area of the plot is given by $A = x(20 - 2x)$.

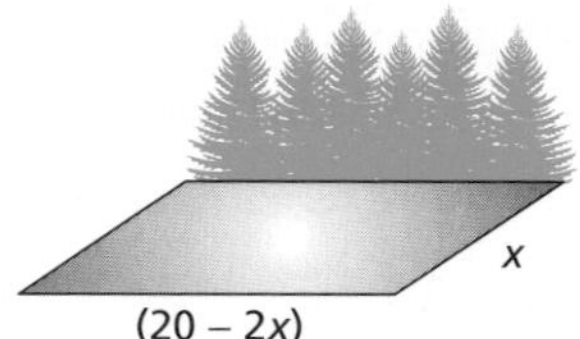

a Copy and complete this table.

x	0	2	4	5	6	8	10
A	0	32	48				

b Draw the graph of the function.
c Where does the graph cut the x axis?
d What is the equation of the axis of symmetry?
e What is the maximum area of the rectangle?
f Write out the equation of the function in the form $y = a(x - b)^2 + c$.

3 A distress flare is fired skyward from the deck of a yacht, such that $D = 8t - t^2$ where D is the height and t is the time, both measured in suitable units.

a Copy and complete this table.

t	0	1	2	4	6	8
D	0	7	12			

b Draw a graph of the equation.
c How long does it take the flare to land in the sea?
d After how many units of time is it highest from the sea?
e What is its maximum height?

4 Sitting in a test frame, the reflector for a car headlamp has a parabolic cross-section. Its equation is $y = \frac{1}{16}\left(x - 16\right)^2 + 7$ where x and y are measured in centimetres.

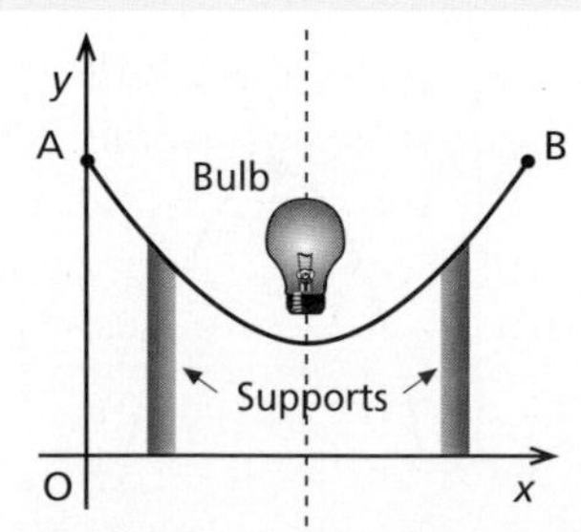

a State:
(i) the minimum turning point of the parabola
(ii) the equation of its axis of symmetry.
b Calculate the y coordinate of the point A.
c Use symmetry to calculate the coordinates of B.

5 The roof of an aerodrome hangar is parabolic. Its equation is

$y = -\frac{3}{125}\left(x - 25\right)^2 + 25$ where x and y are measured in metres.

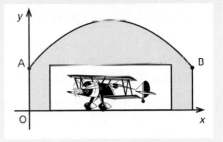

a State:

  (i) the maximum turning point of the parabola

  (ii) the equation of its axis of symmetry.

b Calculate the y coordinate of the point A.

c Use symmetry to calculate the coordinates of B.

d **(i)** How wide is the hangar? **(ii)** How high does the hangar reach?

Other forms of the quadratic function

Example $y = (x - 2)(x - 4)$

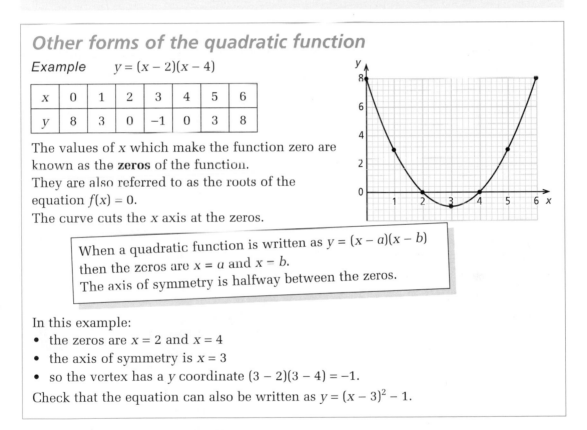

x	0	1	2	3	4	5	6
y	8	3	0	−1	0	3	8

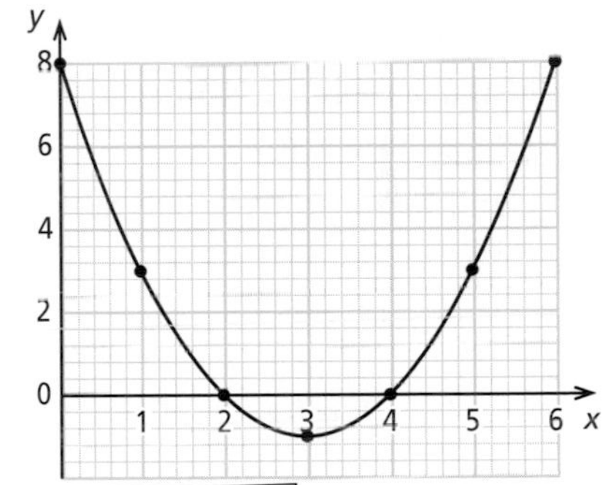

The values of x which make the function zero are known as the **zeros** of the function.
They are also referred to as the roots of the equation $f(x) = 0$.
The curve cuts the x axis at the zeros.

> When a quadratic function is written as $y = (x - a)(x - b)$ then the zeros are $x = a$ and $x = b$.
> The axis of symmetry is halfway between the zeros.

In this example:

- the zeros are $x = 2$ and $x = 4$
- the axis of symmetry is $x = 3$
- so the vertex has a y coordinate $(3 - 2)(3 - 4) = -1$.

Check that the equation can also be written as $y = (x - 3)^2 - 1$.

EXERCISE 7

1 For each of the following quadratic functions:

  (i) state the zeros of the function

  (ii) write down the axis of symmetry of its graph

  (iii) work out the coordinates of the vertex

  (iv) work out where the curve cuts the y axis.

a $y = (x - 1)(x - 5)$ **b** $y = (x - 6)(x - 2)$ **c** $y = (x - 3)(x - 5)$

d $y = (x - 3)(x + 1)$ **e** $y = (x - 2)(x + 4)$ **f** $y = (x + 3)(x + 1)$

Careful!

2 a Check that the table has been worked out correctly for the given function.
$y = -(x - 2)(x - 4)$

x	0	1	2	3	4	5	6
y	−8	−3	0	1	0	−3	−8

b Sketch the graph of the function using the table.
c Check that $y = (2 - x)(x - 4)$ gives the same table.

3 Match each of the graphs with an equation.

a
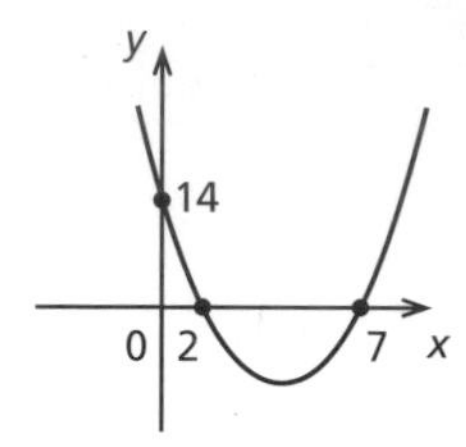

b
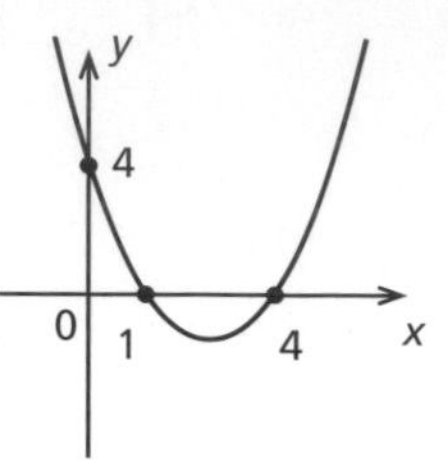

c
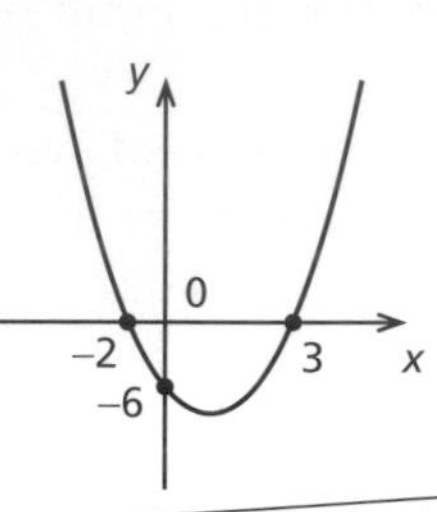

d
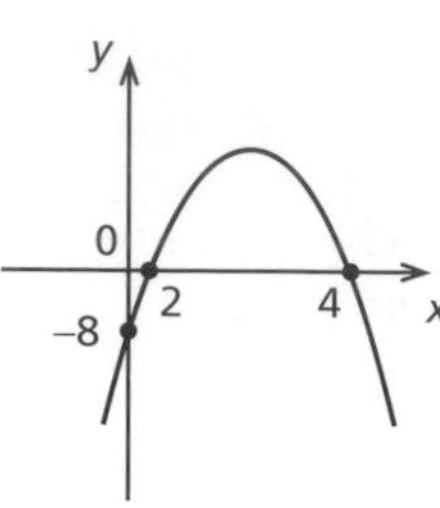

$y = (x - 1)(x - 4)$

$y = -(x - 2)(x - 4)$

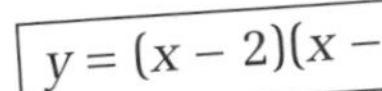

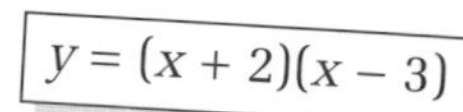

4 a Make a table of values of the function $y = x^2 - 6x + 8$.
b Compare this with the table for $y = (x - 2)(x - 4)$. Comment.

x	0	1	2	3	4	5	6
y							

Solving quadratic equations 1: a graphical approach

Using a graphics calculator, or forming a graph by using a table of values, we find the graph of the function $y = x^2 - x - 2$ looks like this:

Note that the curve cuts the x axis at $x = -1$ and $x = 2$.
That is when $y = 0$ then $x = -1$ or $x = 2$.

By drawing the graph of $y = x^2 - x - 2$ we can solve the equation $x^2 - x - 2 = 0$.

The **roots** or **solutions** of the quadratic equation $x^2 - x - 2 = 0$ are $x = -1$ and $x = 2$.

We can check our reading of the graph by substitution.

$x = -1$: $(-1)^2 - (-1) - 2 = 1 + 1 - 2 = 0$; -1 satisfies the equation.

$x = 2$: $(2)^2 - (2) - 2 = 4 - 2 - 2 = 0$; 2 satisfies the equation.

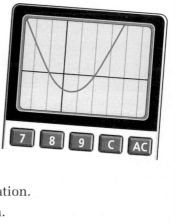

EXERCISE 8

1 By drawing a suitable graph, find the roots of these quadratic functions. Check each root by substitution.

a $x^2 - x = 0$ **b** $x^2 + 2x - 3 = 0$ **c** $3x - x^2 = 0$

d $x^2 - x - 2 = 0$ **e** $x^2 + x - 6 = 0$ **f** $2 - x - x^2 = 0$

g $x^2 - 4x + 3 = 0$ **h** $x^2 + 3x + 2 = 0$ **i** $x^2 - 5x + 6 = 0$

2 The height, h metres, of a rocket after t seconds is given by $h = 24t - 4t^2$.

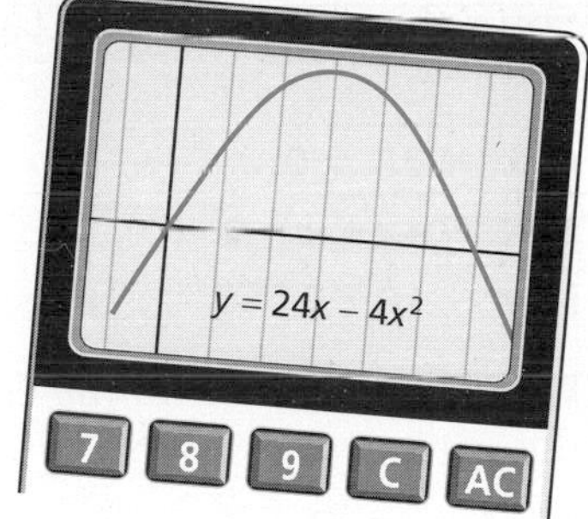

a Use the graph display to find the roots of $24t - 4t^2 = 0$. (Check by substitution.)
b For how long was the rocket in the air?
c When was the rocket at its highest? (Find the value of t halfway between the two roots.)
d Calculate its greatest height.

3 The temperature, T °C, of a chemical mixture t seconds after being mixed is given by $T = t^2 - 6t + 5$.
a At the start ($t = 0$) what was the temperature of the mixture?
b Use the display to find the roots of $t^2 - 6t + 5 = 0$. (Check by substitution.)
c Find the lowest temperature of the mixture.

4 a Draw the graph of $y = 4x^2 - 16x + 15$.
b Notice it cuts the x axis between $x = 1$ and $x = 2$. So one root of the equation $4x^2 - 16x + 15 = 0$ lies between 1 and 2. Where is the other root?

5 By drawing a suitable graph, estimate where the roots of each of the following equations are to be found.
a $x^2 - x - 5 = 0$ b $x^2 - 4x + 1 = 0$ c $x^2 + 4x - 6 = 0$
If you are using a graphics calculator then zoom in to refine the estimates.

Solving quadratic equations 2: using factors

When a number is multiplied by zero the result is zero.
If $7b = 0$ then $b = 0$.
If $ab = 0$ then either $a = 0$ or $b = 0$.
If $(x - 2)(x + 4) = 0$ then either $(x - 2) = 0$ or $(x + 4) = 0$.

Example 1 $2x^2 - x - 1 = 0$
Factorising:
$(2x + 1)(x - 1) = 0$
$\Rightarrow$ either $2x + 1 = 0$ or $x - 1 = 0$
$\Rightarrow$ either $x = -0.5$ or $x = 1$
Check by substitution.

Example 2 $y^2 + 3y = 0$
Factorising:
$y(y + 3) = 0$
$\Rightarrow$ either $y = 0$ or $y + 3 = 0$
$\Rightarrow$ either $y = 0$ or $y = -3$
Check by substitution.

EXERCISE 9

1 Solve:
a $(y - 1)(y + 2) = 0$ b $3x(x + 1) = 0$ c $(x + 1)(x + 2) = 0$
d $(m - 3)(m + 4) = 0$ e $2x(x - 5) = 0$ f $(2x - 1)(x + 3) = 0$
g $(a + 2)(a + 2) = 0$ h $(3x - 1)(2x + 1) = 0$ i $(c - 5)(2c - 3) = 0$

2 Solve these equations by factorising first:

a $x^2 + 2x + 1 = 0$ b $y^2 - y - 2 = 0$ c $x^2 - 4 = 0$

d $k^2 + 2k = 0$ e $n^2 + n - 6 = 0$ f $x^2 + 5x + 4 = 0$

g $x^2 - 4x + 4 = 0$ h $e^2 + 2e - 3 = 0$ i $x^2 - 5x + 6 = 0$

j $x^2 - 16 = 0$ k $x^2 - 3x = 0$ l $p^2 - p = 0$

3 For each display find the coordinates of the points of intersection of the graph with the x axis.

a $y = x^2 - 3x + 2$

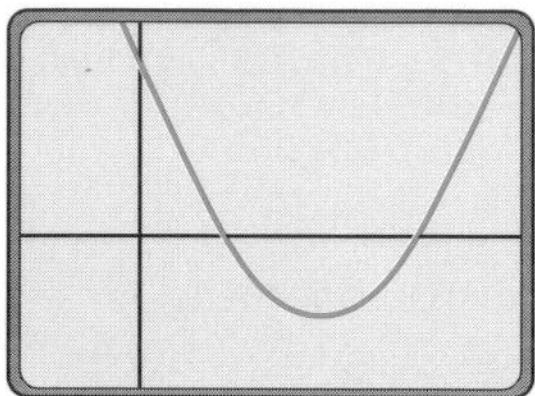

b $y = x^2 - x - 6$

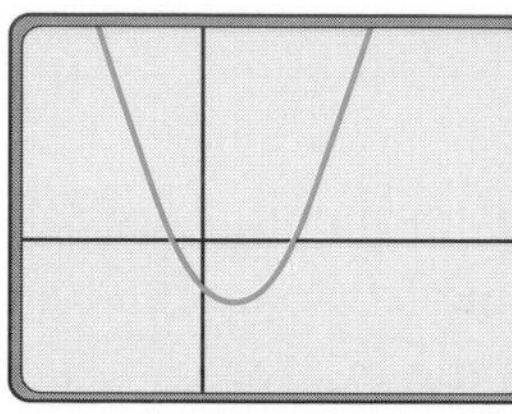

c $y = x^2 + 4x - 5$

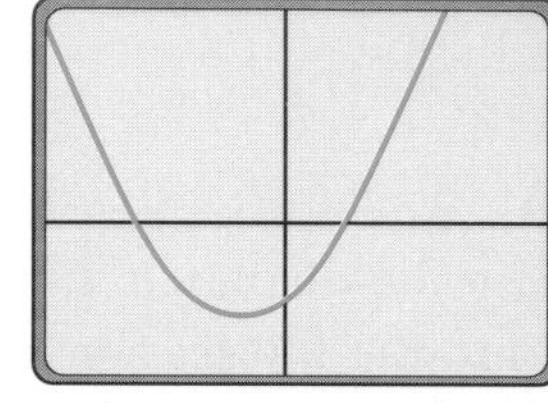

d $y = 4x - x^2$

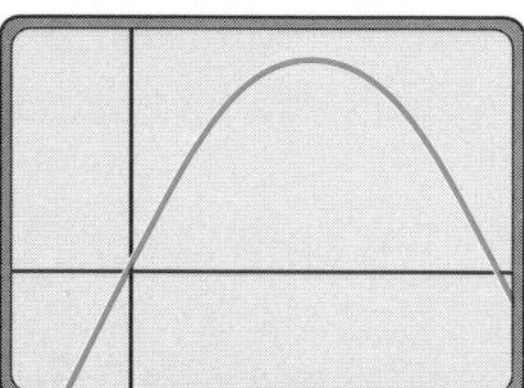

e $y = x^2 - 6x + 9$

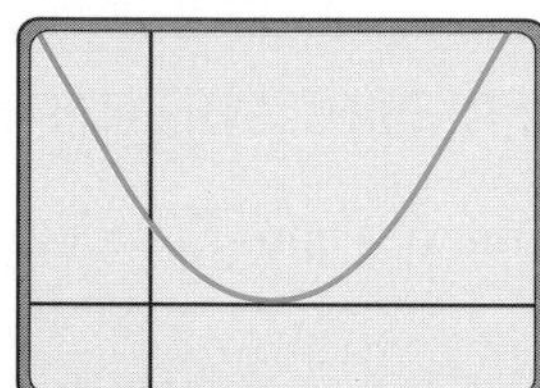

f $y = 2x^2 + x$

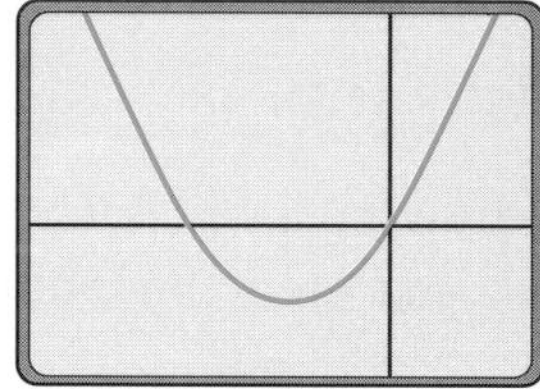

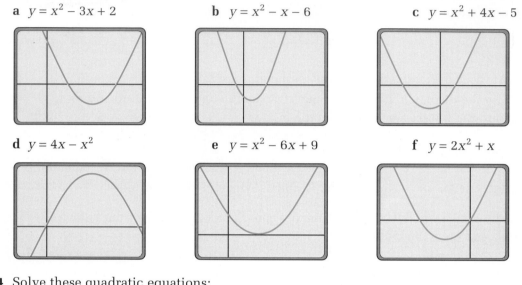

4 Solve these quadratic equations:

a $y^2 - 9 = 0$ b $y^2 + 3y - 10 = 0$ c $x^2 + x - 12 = 0$

d $m^2 - m - 12 = 0$ e $n^2 + 4n - 12 = 0$ f $y^2 + 9y + 20 = 0$

g $x^2 + 2x - 8 = 0$ h $y^2 - y - 12 = 0$ i $k^2 - 2k - 15 = 0$

j $a^2 - 4a - 12 = 0$ k $x^2 - 4x = 0$ l $m^2 - m - 30 = 0$

5 Find the roots of these quadratic equations:

a $2y^2 + 3y + 1 = 0$ b $3y^2 + 5y - 2 = 0$ c $2x^2 + x - 6 = 0$

d $4m^2 - 15m + 9 = 0$ e $3n^2 + n - 4 = 0$ f $4y^2 - 8y + 3 = 0$

g $9x^2 - 4 = 0$ h $6y^2 - 7y - 3 = 0$ i $9k^2 - 6k - 8 = 0$

6 The shape of a lens is modelled by the curve with equation $y = x^2 - 8x - 20$.

a Find the coordinates of A and B, the ends of the lens.

b x is measured in centimetres. Find the width of the lens, AB.

c y is measured in millimetres. If the lens is perfectly symmetrical then find its greatest thickness.

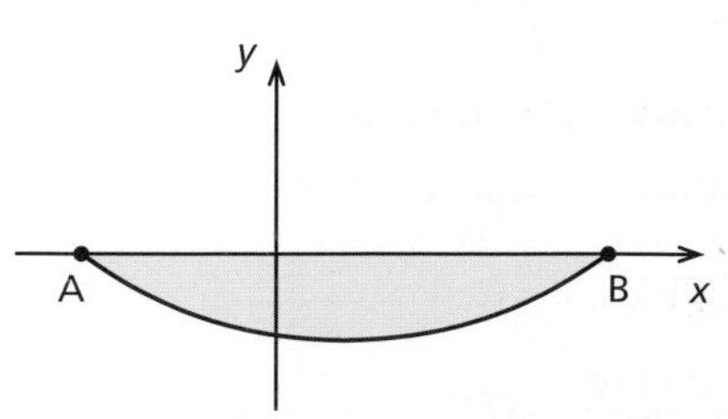

Solving quadratic equations 3: using a formula

Trying to solve the equation $x^2 + 6x - 5 = 0$ we quickly see that it cannot be factorised. Drawing a graph we can see there is a root between 0 and 1 and another between -6 and -7. But how do we find these roots?

Around the end of the first millennium this method was used.

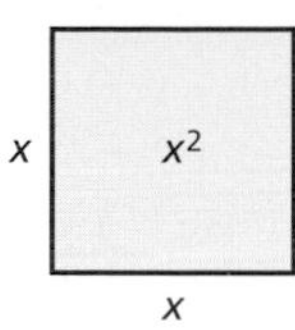

Take a square of side x. The area of this shape is x^2.

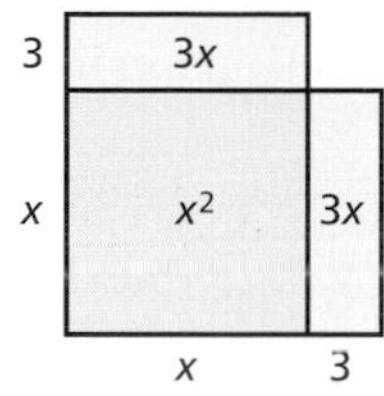

Note that $3x$ is half of $6x$.

Add two rectangles as shown. The area of this shape is $x^2 + 6x$.

3 | 3x | 9
x | x^2 | 3x
x | 3

The area of the shape can also be written as $(x + 3)^2 - 9$.

$$x^2 + 6x = (x + 3)^2 - 9.$$

So our equation $x^2 + 6x - 5 = 0$ can be written as $(x + 3)^2 - 9 - 5 = 0$.

$$(x + 3)^2 - 9 - 5 = 0$$
$$\Rightarrow (x + 3)^2 = 14$$
$$\Rightarrow (x + 3) = \pm\sqrt{14}$$
$$\Rightarrow x = -3 + \sqrt{14} \text{ or } -3 - \sqrt{14}$$
$$\Rightarrow x = 0.742 \text{ or } -6.742 \text{ (to 3 d.p.)}$$

Based on this ancient method a formula was devised which, under certain circumstances, can be used to solve quadratic equations:

> If $ax^2 + bx + c = 0$
>
> then $x = \dfrac{-b \pm \sqrt{(b^2 - 4ac)}}{2a}$

The circumstances are:

- we want to divide by a so $a \neq 0$
- we wish $\sqrt{(b^2 - 4ac)}$ so $(b^2 - 4ac) \geq 0$.

Example 1

Solve $x^2 + 6x - 5 = 0$.

We see that $a = 1$, $b = 6$, $c = -5$.

$$\text{So } x = \frac{-6 \pm \sqrt{(6^2 - 4 \times 1 \times (-5))}}{2 \times 1}$$

$$x = \frac{-6 + \sqrt{56}}{2} \text{ or } x = \frac{-6 - \sqrt{56}}{2}$$

$x = 0.742$ or $x = -6.742$ (to 3 d.p.)

Example 2

Solve $2x^2 + 3x - 1 = 0$.

We see that $a = 2$, $b = 3$, $c = -1$.

$$\text{So } x = \frac{-3 \pm \sqrt{(3^2 - 4 \times 2 \times (-1))}}{2 \times 2}$$

$$x = \frac{-3 + \sqrt{17}}{4} \text{ or } x = \frac{-3 - \sqrt{17}}{4}$$

$x = 0.281$ or $x = -1.781$ (to 3 d.p.)

EXERCISE 10

Give answers correct to 2 decimal places where appropriate.

1 Solve each of the following quadratic equations:
(i) by factorisation **(ii)** using the formula.

a $x^2 + 3x + 2 = 0$ **b** $x^2 + x - 2 = 0$ **c** $x^2 - 4x + 3 = 0$ **d** $x^2 - 2x + 1 = 0$
e $x^2 - 2x - 3 = 0$ **f** $x^2 - 2x - 8 = 0$ **g** $x^2 + 4x - 5 = 0$ **h** $x^2 + 5x + 6 = 0$

2 Solve each of the following quadratic equations using the formula.
Give answers correct to 1 d.p.

a $2x^2 + 4x + 1 = 0$ **b** $x^2 + 3x - 3 = 0$ **c** $2x^2 - 7x + 4 = 0$ **d** $x^2 - 8x - 1 = 0$
e $x^2 + 3x - 2 = 0$ **f** $3x^2 + 5x - 7 = 0$ **g** $x^2 - 2x - 2 = 0$ **h** $4x^2 - 5x - 3 = 0$
i $5x^2 - 9x + 3 = 0$ **j** $3x^2 - 3x - 5 = 0$ **k** $x^2 - 12x + 5 = 0$ **l** $-x^2 - 6x + 1 = 0$

3 Work out where each of the following curves cut the x axis.

a $y = x^2 + 5x - 1$ **b** $y = 2x^2 - 3x - 2$ **c** $y = 1 + 4x - 2x^2$ **d** $y = 3 + 4x - x^2$

4

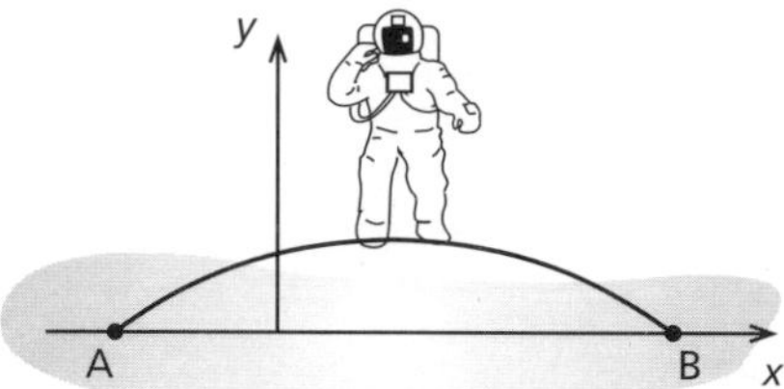

Giant steps. A lunar leap made by an astronaut has the equation $y = 5 + 0.5x - 0.1x^2$, relative to a certain set of axes.
y represents the height and x the distance from the origin, both measured in metres. Calculate the coordinates of the points A and B, the points where his height is zero.

5

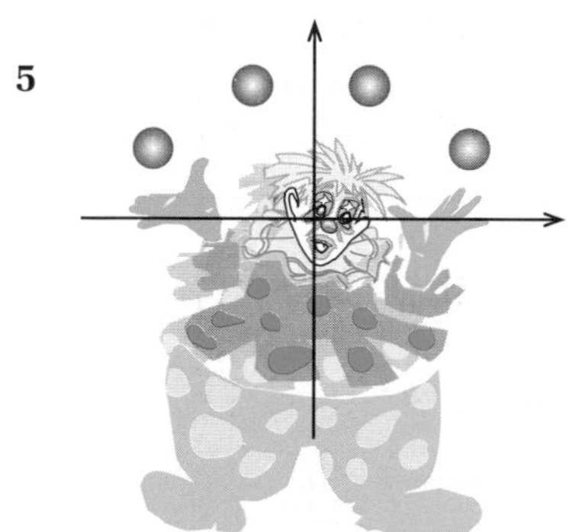

Modelling the motion of the juggling balls produces the equation $y = 3.5 - 1.5x - 2x^2$ where x and y are measured in convenient units and where the x axis is the juggler's eye level.
Solve the equation $3.5 - 1.5x - 2x^2 = 0$ to find the points where the balls are at eye level.

6 Express each of these quadratic equations in the form $ax^2 + bx + c = 0$ and then solve for x.

a $x^2 = 11(x + 1) + 1$ **b** $4x^2 = 3x + 2$ **c** $x^2 - 5 = 12x$
d $3x(x - 1) = 5$ **e** $5x - 1 = x^2$

CHAPTER 14 REVIEW

1 Find the value of $f(3)$ when $f(x) = 2x + 5$.

2 A plumber charges £20 for a call-out. He also charges £10 per hour. His total charge is $C(x)$ pounds for x hours of work.

a Write down a formula for $C(x)$.

b Sketch a graph of the function.

3 **a** Draw the graph of $y = (x - 2)^2$.

b **(i)** Give the equation of its axis of symmetry.

(ii) State the coordinates of its vertex.

c Is the vertex a maximum or minimum turning point?

4 For the graph of each of the following functions:

(i) state the coordinates of its vertex **(ii)** give the equation of the axis of symmetry **(iii)** work out where it cuts the y axis **(iv)** sketch the graph.

a $y = (x - 4)^2 + 2$ **b** $y = (x - 6)^2 + 1$ **c** $y = -(x - 5)^2 - 3$ **d** $y = 3(x - 2)^2 + 1$

5 Work out the equation of each of the graphs in the form $y = a(x - b)^2 + c$.

a

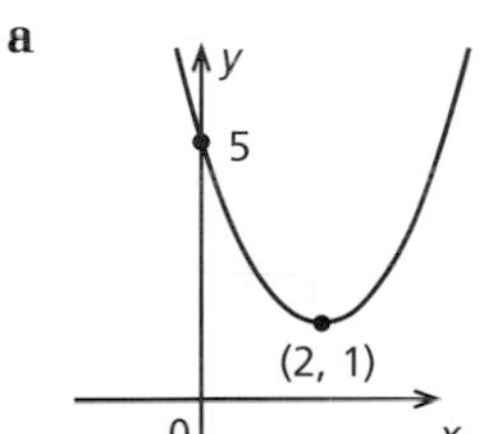

b

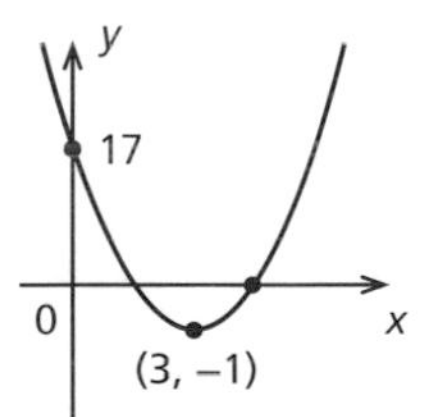

c

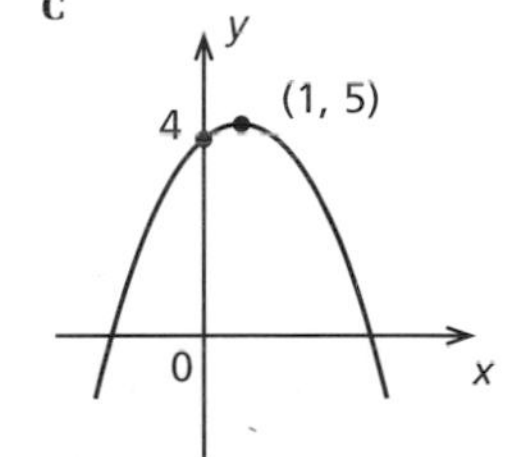

d

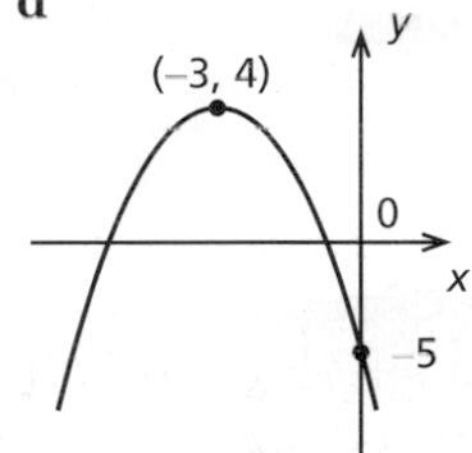

6 The area of a rectangular piece of land can be worked out from the equation $A(x) = 40x - 2x^2$.

a By drawing a table and graph, work out the maximum area the rectangle can be.

b Rewrite the formula in the form $A(x) = a(x - b)^2 + c$.

7 Use the display to solve $4 + 3x - x^2 = 0$.
Check each root by substitution.

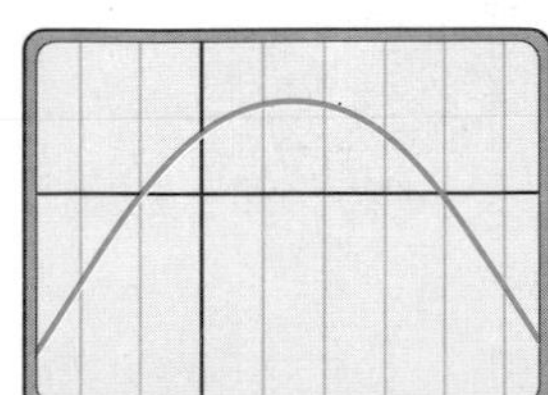

Graph of $y = 4 + 3x - x^2$

8 Solve each equation by first factorising:

a $x^2 - 2x - 8 = 0$ **b** $3x^2 + x - 2 = 0$

9 Find the roots of each equation correct to 1 d.p.

a $2x^2 - x - 7 = 0$ **b** $2x + 4 = 8 - x^2$

15 Further Trigonometry

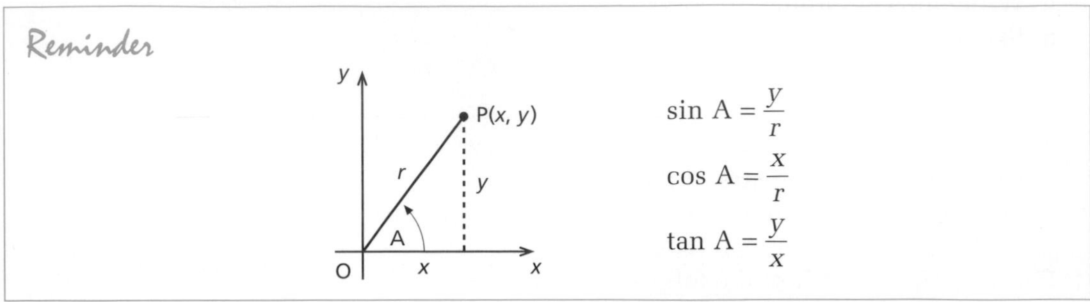

$$\sin A = \frac{y}{r}$$

$$\cos A = \frac{x}{r}$$

$$\tan A = \frac{y}{x}$$

In this chapter, unless otherwise stated, answers which are inexact should be rounded to 1 d.p. for angles and to 3 s.f. for all others.

STARTING POINTS

1 Use your calculator to find:

a sin 30° **b** cos 45° **c** tan 45° **d** cos 90° **e** sin 0°
f tan 70° **g** cos 190° **h** sin 200° **i** tan 320°

2 Report what happens when you ask your calculator for: **a** tan 90° **b** tan 270°.

3 Use your calculator to find the acute angle in each case.

a $\sin x° = 0.596$ **b** $\cos y° = 0.218$ **c** $\tan a° = 4.45$
d $\cos x° = 1$ **e** $\sin b° = 0.778$ **f** $\tan y° = 2.36$

4 Calculate the size of the angle marked $x°$ in each triangle.

a

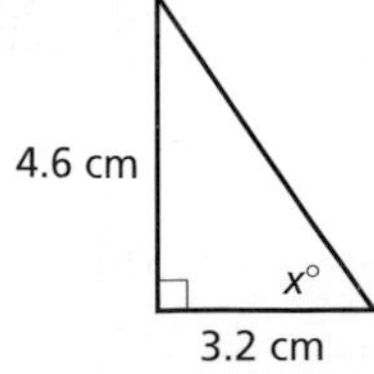

b

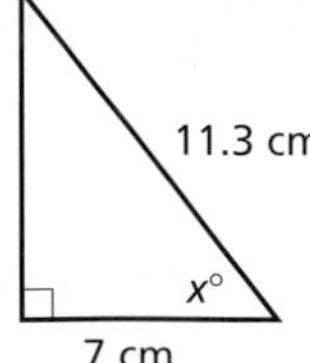

c

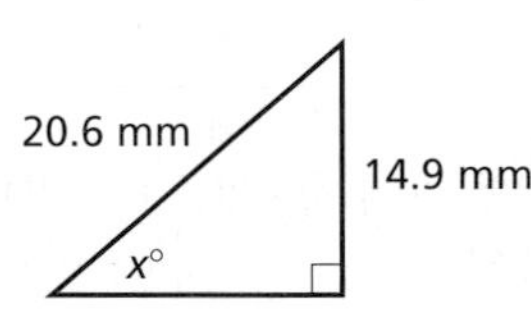

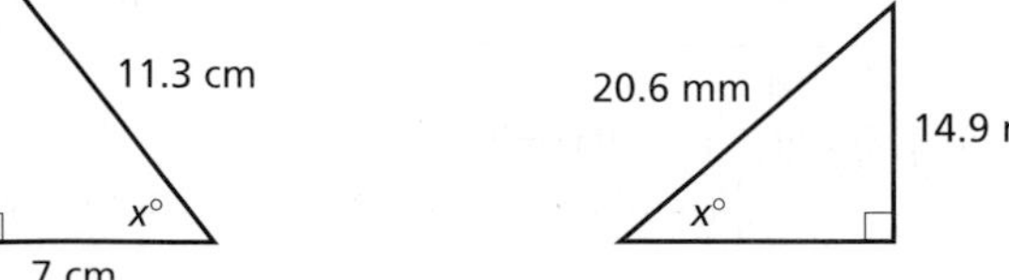

5 $f(x) = x^2 - 4x$

a Calculate the value of: **(i)** $f(3)$ **(ii)** $f(-3)$ **(iii)** $f(1)$ **(iv)** $f(0)$.

b Copy and complete the table.

x	−3	−2	−1	0	1	2	3
$f(x)$							

c Make a graph of $f(x)$.

d State the zeros of the function.

e **(i)** State the coordinates of the turning point.

(ii) Is it a maximum or minimum turning point?

The sine function

This graph of $y = \sin x°$ has been drawn for $0° \le x \le 90°$ with the aid of a calculator.

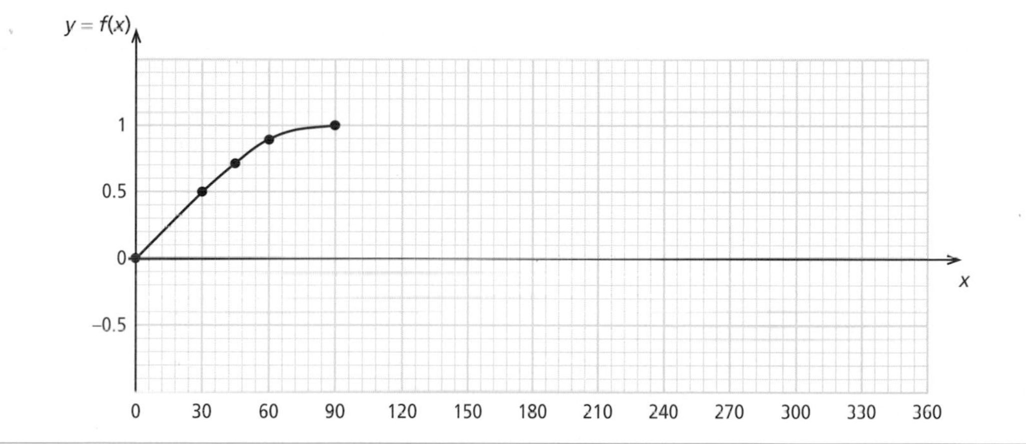

EXERCISE 1

1 **a** Copy the above graph on suitable graph paper.

b Copy and complete the table (work to 2 d.p. where necessary).

x	0	30	45	60	90	120	135	150	180	210	225	240	270	300	315	330	360
sin x	0	0.5	0.71	0.87	1												

c Use the table to draw the graph of $y = \sin x°$ for $0 \le x \le 360$.

d Answer the following, using $0 \le x \le 360$.

(i) What is the maximum value of the function?

(ii) What is the minimum value?

(iii) Give the coordinates of the turning points.

(iv) State the zeros of the function.

e Between what values is: **(i)** $\sin x°$ positive **(ii)** $\sin x°$ negative?

f Explain why the calculator gives an error report when we ask it to work out the angle whose sine is 2.

The graph you have drawn is known as the **sine wave**.
If you were to draw the graph beyond the domain $0 \le x \le 360$ then you would find that the wave repeats every 360°.

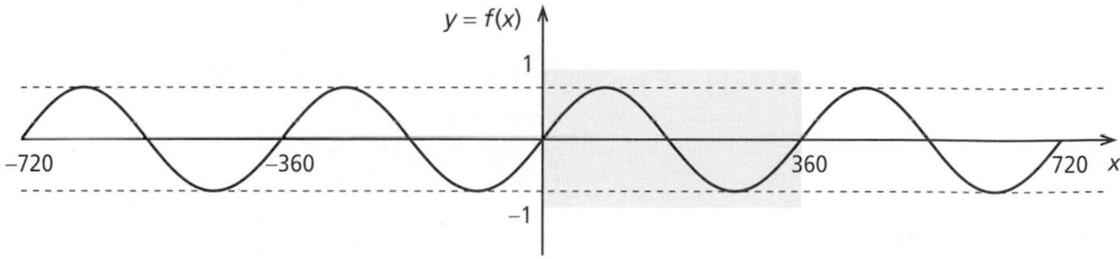

We say the function is **periodic** and that it has a period of 360°.

2 For $360° \leq x \leq 720°$:

a give the coordinates of the turning points

b state the zeros of the function.

3 a Copy and complete the table.

x	0	30	45	60	90	120	135	150	180	210	225	240	270	300	315	330	360
$\sin x°$	0	0.5	0.71	0.87	1												
$2 \sin x°$	0	1	1.42	1.73	2												
$3 \sin x°$	0	1.5	2.12	2.60	3												
$\frac{1}{2} \sin x°$	0	0.25	0.35	0.43	$\frac{1}{2}$												

b Comment on the zeros of each function.

c Comment on the period of each function.

d What is the maximum value of:

(i) $\sin x°$ **(ii)** $2 \sin x°$ **(iii)** $3 \sin x°$ **(iv)** $a \sin x°$?

4 We can make a sketch of a sine wave by showing the maximum and minimum turning points and the zeros.
Make similar sketches of:

a $y = 2 \sin x°$

b $y = 3 \sin x°$

c $y = \frac{1}{2} \sin x°$

d $y = 5 \sin x°$

e $y = 0.6 \sin x°$

f $y = 2.5 \sin x°$

g $y = a \sin x°$ where $a > 0$.

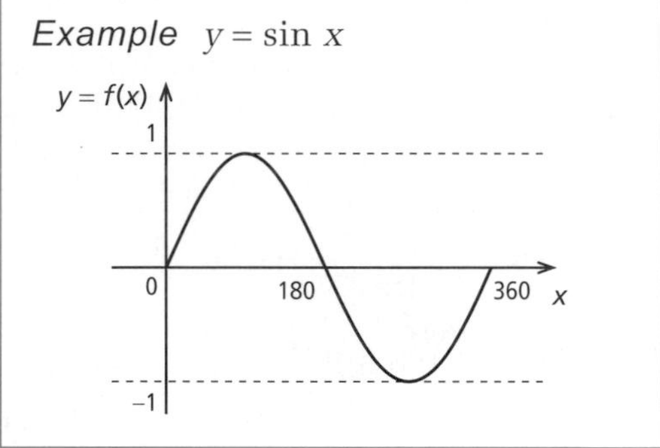

5 a Copy and complete the table.

x	0	30	45	60	90	120	135	150	180	210	225	240	270	300	315	330	360
$\sin x$	0	–0.5			–1												
$-2 \sin x$	0	–1			–2												

b Use this information to sketch: **(i)** $y = -\sin x°$ **(ii)** $y = -2 \sin x°$.

c Make similar sketches of:

(i) $y = -3 \sin x°$

(ii) $y = -4 \sin x°$

(iii) $y = -0.5 \sin x°$

(iv) $y = -a \sin x°$ where $a > 0$.

6 Suggest what the equation of this curve might be.

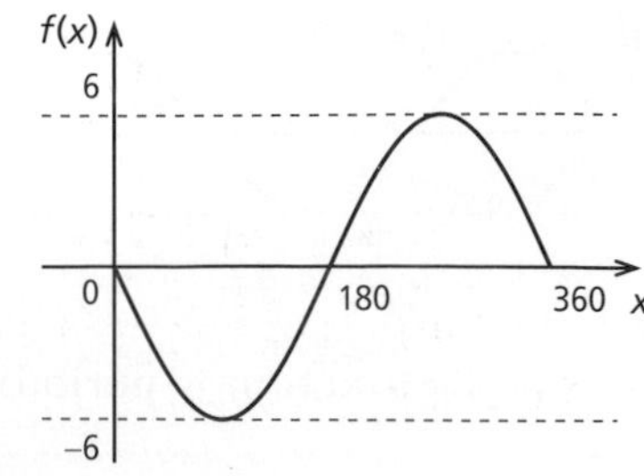

7 The minute hand on a clock is 6.5 cm long. The tip of the hand is y cm vertically above the centre. The hand makes an angle of $x°$ with the horizontal.
From the triangle you see $y = 6.5 \sin x°$.
Here is a graph of the height, y cm, against the angle, $x°$.

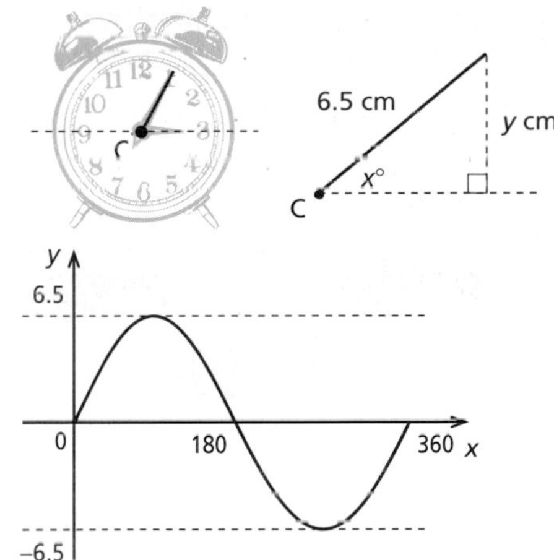

a What is the maximum height of the tip?
b What is the minimum height?
c State at what angles the height is zero.
d The hour hand is 5 cm long. The vertical height above the centre of its tip is given by $y = 5 \sin x°$. Make a sketch of the y against x in this case.

8

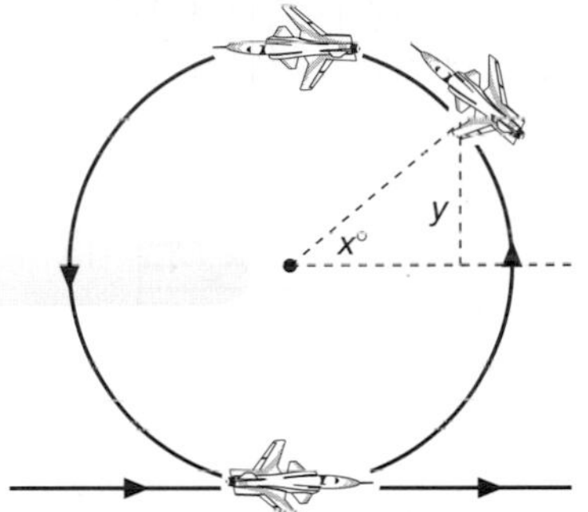

A stunt plane loops-the-loop at an air display. The vertical height, y m, of the plane above the centre of the loop is given by $y = 55 \sin x°$ where $x°$ is the angle that the radius of the circle to the plane makes with the horizontal.
a Make a sketch of y against x.
b What is the maximum height of the plane above the centre of the loop?
c What is the radius of the loop?

9 Viewed from above, the tip of the rotor blade of a helicopter is y m forward of the line AB when the blade makes an angle of $x°$ with it.
This is the graph of y against x.
a What is the maximum value of y?
b For what values of x is y zero?
c What is the radius of the circle?
d State the relation between y and x in the form $y = \ldots$

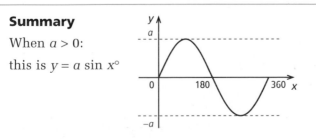

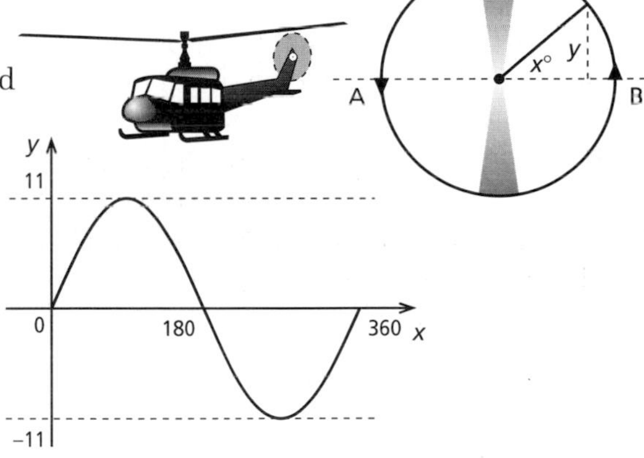

Summary

When $a > 0$:

this is $y = a \sin x°$

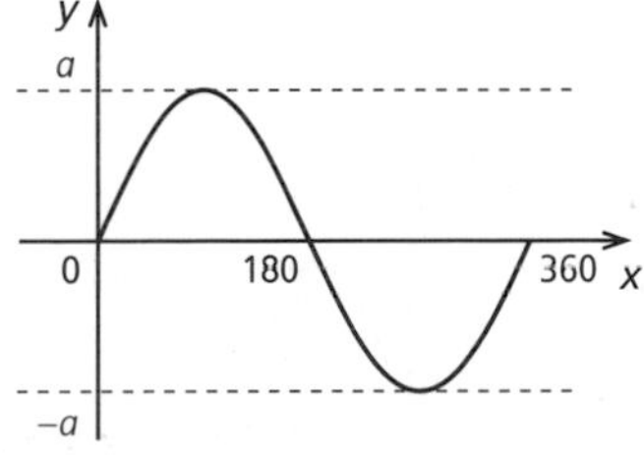

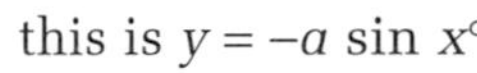
this is $y = -a \sin x°$

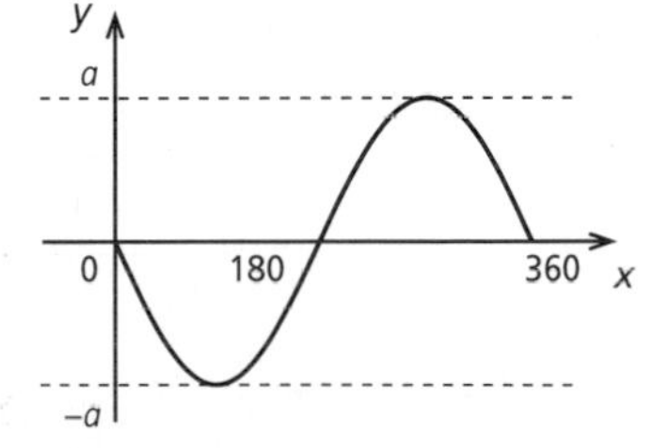

Note that the graph of $y = -f(x)$ is the reflection of $y = f(x)$ in the x axis.

Periodicity

When a pattern repeats itself over and over, it is said to be **periodic**. The period is the length of one complete part of the pattern. This can be measured between any part and its next occurrence.

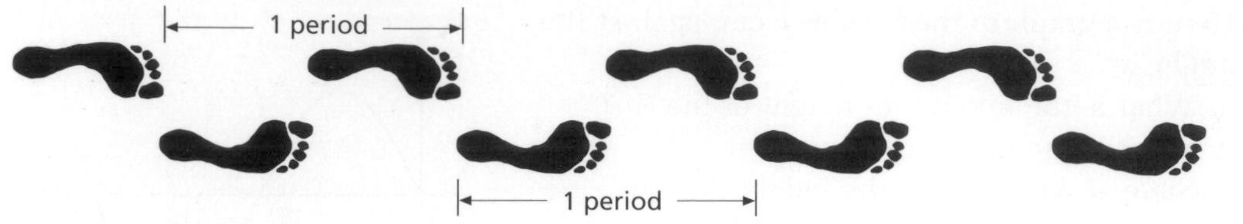

EXERCISE 2

1 Use a ruler to help you describe the period of each pattern.

a

b

c

2 This recurring decimal has a period of 3 digits: 0.425 425 425 425 425 425.

a Divide each of the following by 99 and comment on the period of each decimal.
(i) 23 (ii) 54 (iii) 1 (iv) 98

b Divide each of the following by 999 and comment on the period of each decimal.
(i) 23 (ii) 543 (iii) 21 (iv) 6

c Investigate other recurring decimals in like manner.

d Suggest a division which will lead to the recurring decimal
0.012 340 123 401 234 012 ...

3 Describe the period of the sine function using degrees as the unit of measurement.

a $y = \sin x°$

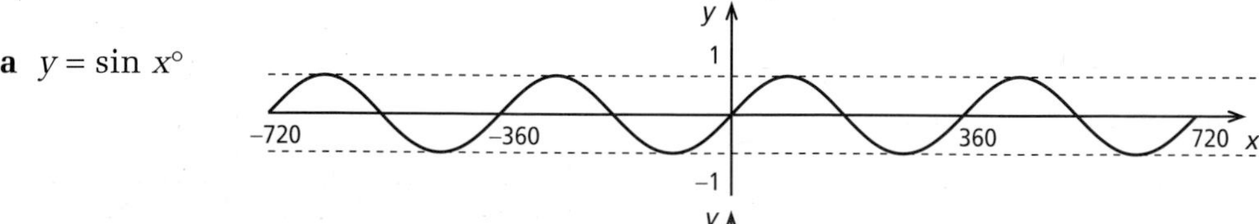

b $y = 3 \sin x°$

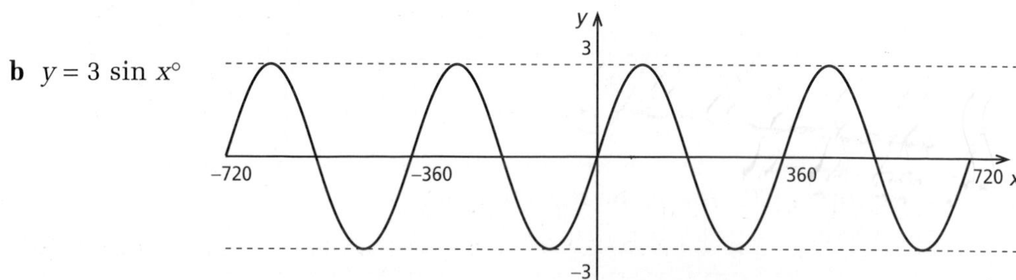

4 a Copy and complete this table, to 2 d.p. where necessary.

x	0	30	45	60	90	120	135	150	180	210	225	240	270	300	315	330	360
$\sin x^\circ$	0	0.5	0.71	0.87	1												
$\sin 2x^\circ$	0	0.87	1	0.87	0												
$\sin 3x^\circ$	0	1	0.71	0	−1												
$\sin \frac{1}{2}x^\circ$	0	0.26	0.38	0.5	0.71												

b For $y = \sin 2x^\circ$ give:
(i) the maximum value of y **(ii)** the minimum value of y **(iii)** the period.

c Repeat this for: **(i)** $y = \sin 3x^\circ$ **(ii)** $y = \sin \frac{1}{2}x^\circ$.

d By possibly considering more examples, suggest the period of:
(i) $y = \sin 4x^\circ$ **(ii)** $y = \sin 6x^\circ$.

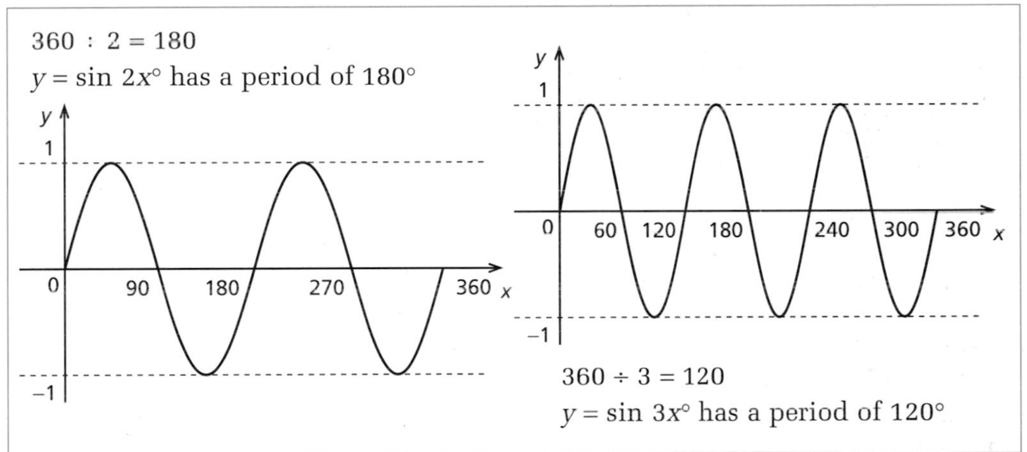

5 In a similar fashion draw sketches of:
a $y = \sin 4x^\circ$ **b** $y = \sin 6x^\circ$ **c** $y = \sin 5x^\circ$ **d** $y = \sin \frac{1}{2}x^\circ$
marking in where the curve cuts the x axis.

Note that in the function
$y = a \sin bx^\circ$,
a gives the maxima and minima,
$360^\circ \div b$ gives the period.

$360 \div 3 = 120$
$y = 2 \sin 3x^\circ$ has a period of 120°,
a maximum value of 2 and
a minimum of –2.

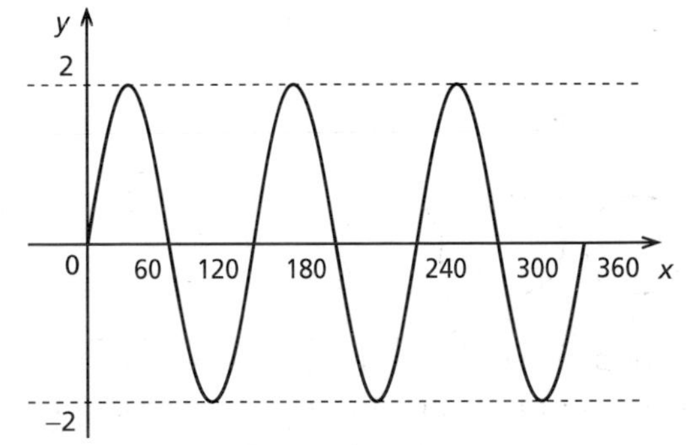

6 Use this information to help you draw sketches of:
a $y = 3 \sin 2x^\circ$ **b** $y = 3 \sin 4x^\circ$ **c** $y = 4 \sin 3x^\circ$ **d** $y = 2 \sin \frac{1}{2}x^\circ$

7 Each of the following are sketches of functions of the form $y = a \sin bx°$. For each:

(i) state the maximum value of the function and hence the value of a

(ii) find the length of one wave, w, and hence the value of b $(360 \div w)$

(iii) state the equation of the function.

a

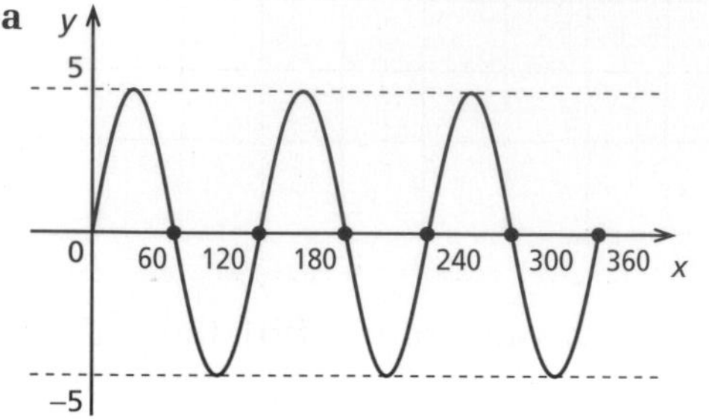

b

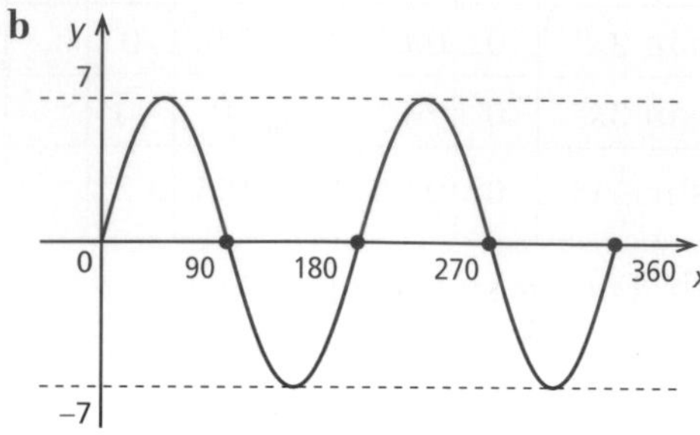

c

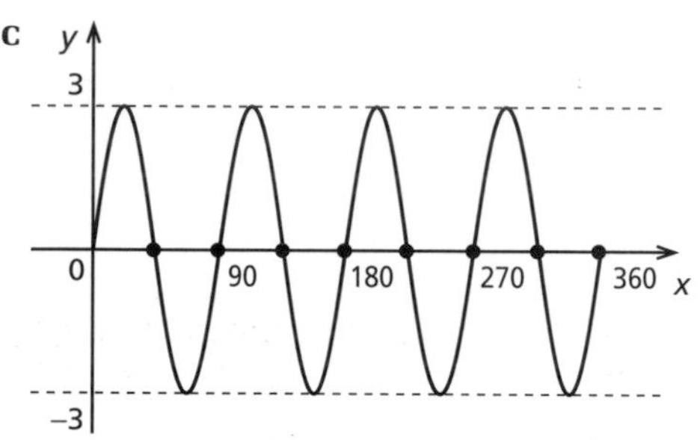

d

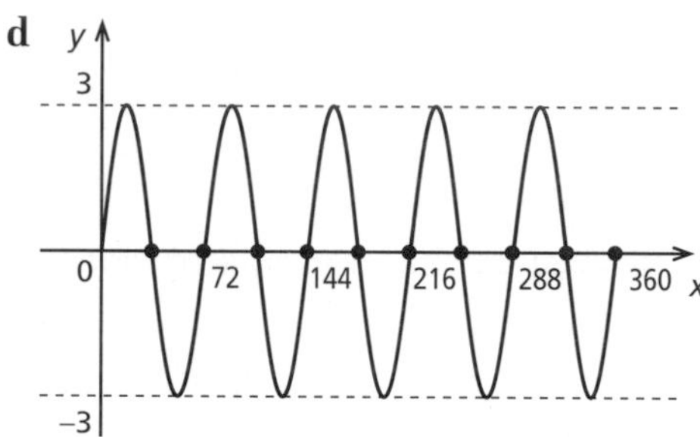

8 In each of these examples $y = a \sin bx°$, and a is negative.

a What feature of the graph indicates that a is negative?

b Write down the equation of each wave.

(i)

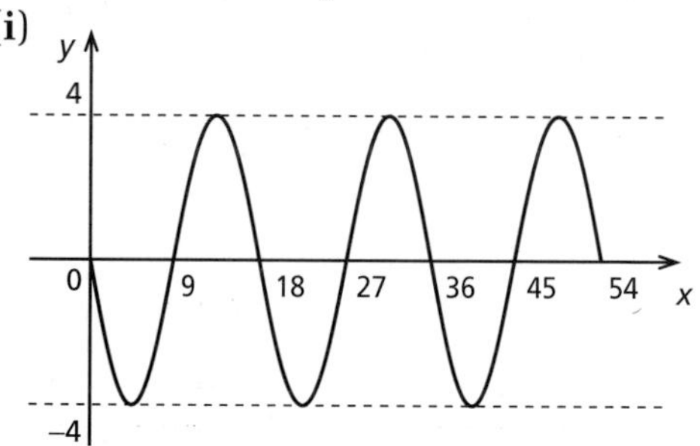

(ii)

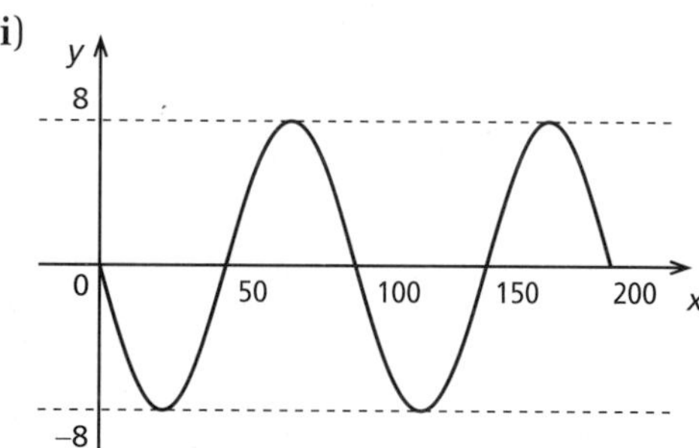

9 Sketch the following curves over two wave lengths.
Label where the curve cuts the x axis.

a $y = 3 \sin 10x°$ **b** $y = 2 \sin 5x°$ **c** $y = -3 \sin 2x°$ **d** $y = -4 \sin 6x°$

10

–4 –3 –2 –1 0 1 2 3 4

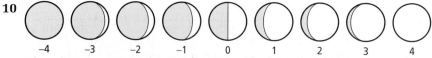

The phases of the moon can be numbered as shown.
Over a month the phase can be modelled by $y = 4 \sin 13x°$ where x is the number of days since the beginning of the month.

a Make a sketch of the function.

b Show on your sketch where the full moon is.

c Give, to 1 d.p., the length of 1 lunar cycle (1 wave length).

The cosine function

This is the graph of $y = \cos x°$ for $0° \leq x \leq 90°$.

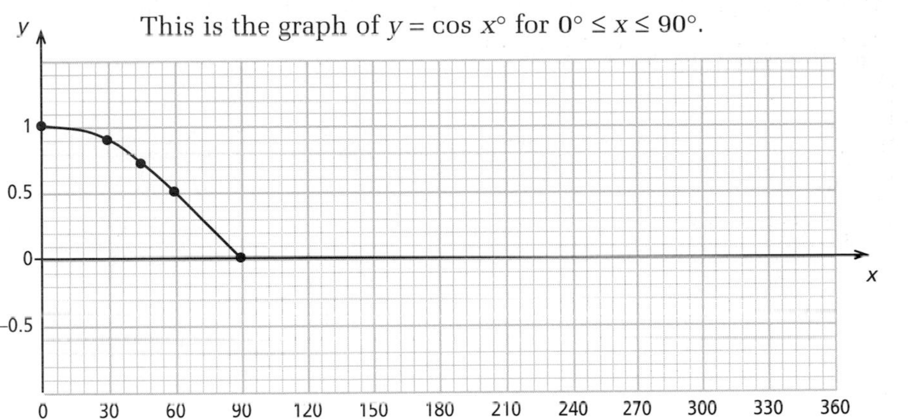

EXERCISE 3

1 **a** Copy and complete the table.

x	0	30	45	60	90	120	135	150	180	210	225	240	270	300	315	330	360
$\cos x$	1	0.87	0.71	0.5	0												

b Use the data to help you draw a cosine curve for $0 \leq x \leq 360$.

Like the sine wave, the graph of the cosine function is also a wave.
If the equation of the function is $y = a \cos bx°$ then a lets you work out the maxima and minima and b lets you work out the period.

Example 1 $y = 3 \cos 2x°$

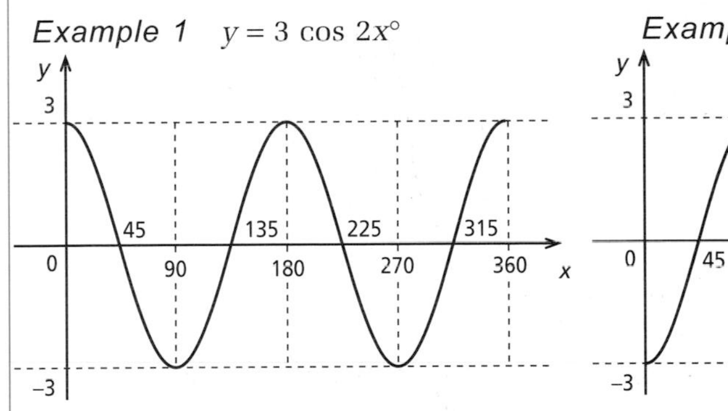

Example 2 $y = -3 \cos 2x°$

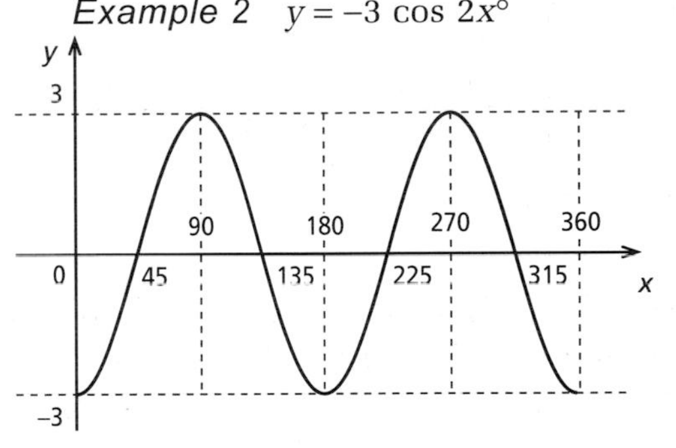

2 For each of the examples identify:

a the value of **(i)** the maxima **(ii)** the minima

b the values of x which make the function zero for $0 \leq x \leq 360$

c the period of the function.

3 Draw sketches of the following, marking the maxima, minima and zeros.
You need only draw one complete wave.

a $y = 7 \cos x°$ **b** $y = \cos 3x°$ **c** $y = 4 \cos 2x°$

d $y = -2 \cos x°$ **e** $y = -3 \cos 2x°$

4 These are both graphs of functions of the form $y = a \cos bx°$.

(i) Identify the maximum value of the function.

(ii) Identify the period and hence the value of b ($360 \div \text{period} = b$).

(iii) State the equation of the curve.

a

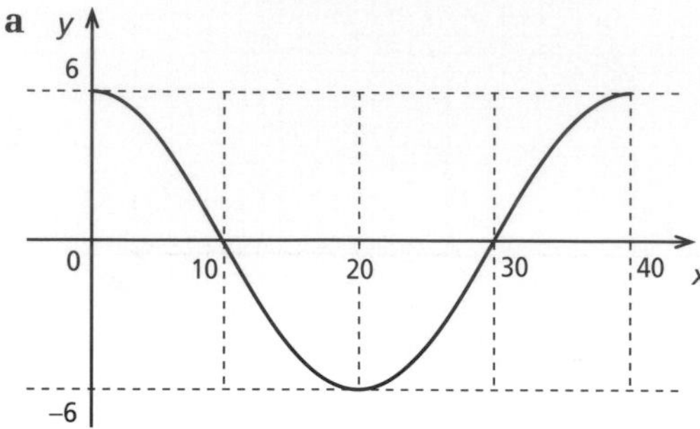

b

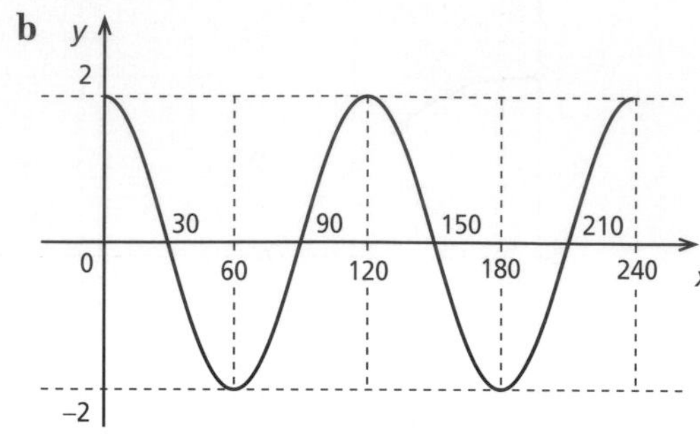

5

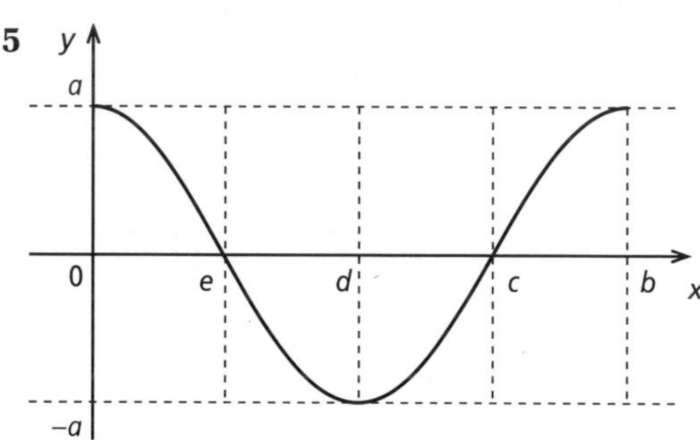

On a rough day-to-day basis, the depth of water in a harbour can be modelled by the formula $y = 4 \cos 30x$ where y is measured in metres from the mean sea-level (e.g. –2 is 2 m below mean sea-level) and x is the number of hours since high tide.

a State the value of:

(i) a **(ii)** b **(iii)** c **(iv)** d.

b High tide occurred at 3 pm one day. When is the first low tide after this?

6 The equation of each of the following curves is either of the form $y = a \sin x°$ or $y = a \cos x°$. Write down this equation in each case.

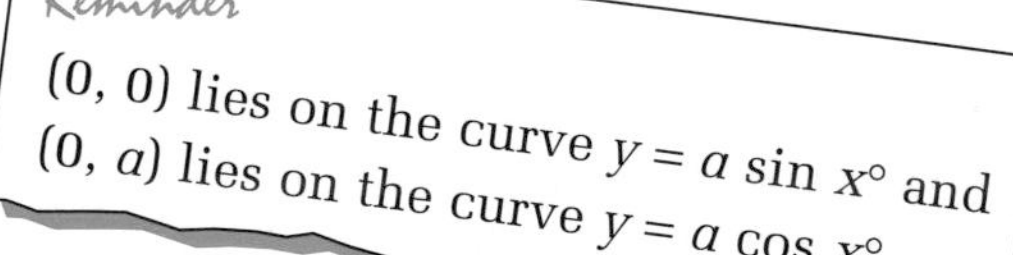

a

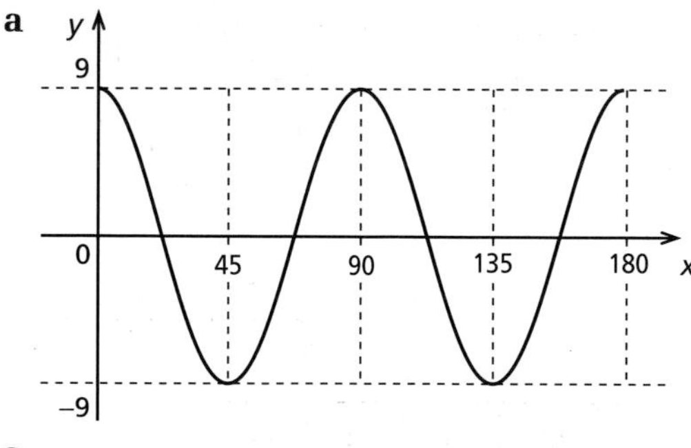

b

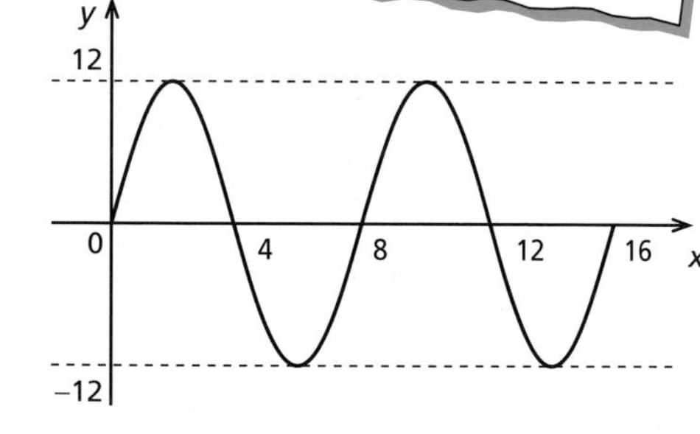

c

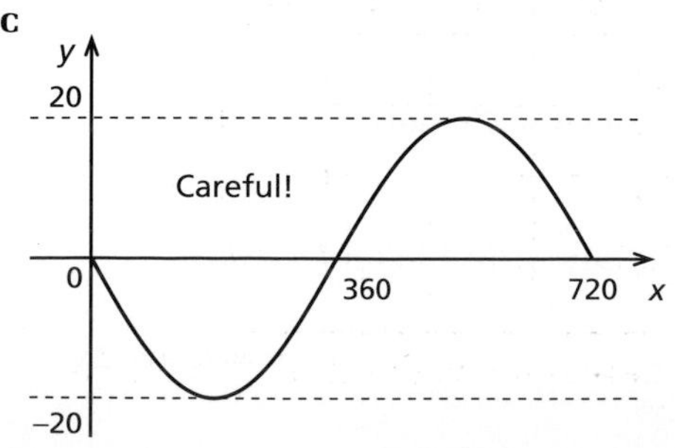

d

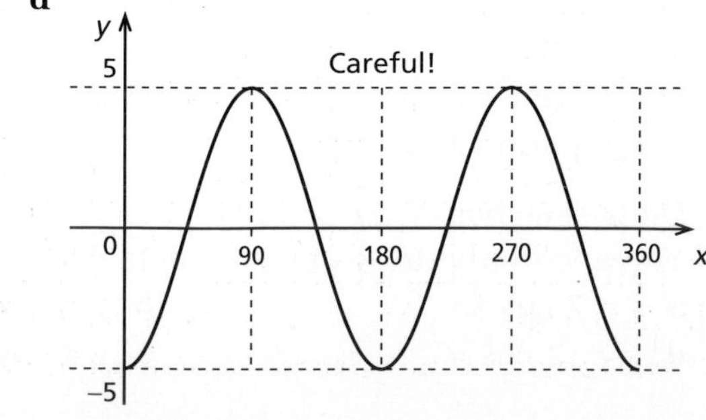

The tangent curve

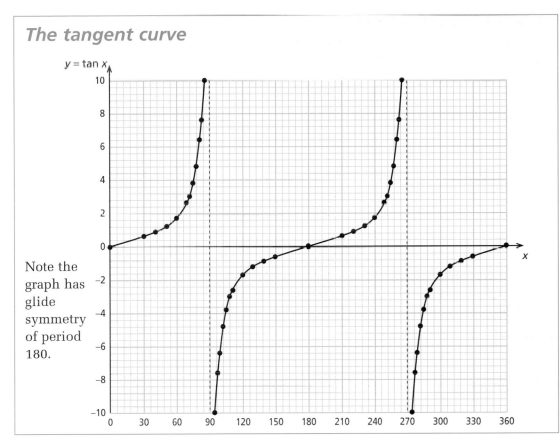

Note the graph has glide symmetry of period 180.

EXERCISE 4

1 **a** Use your calculator to check the plotted points in the graph above for $0 \le x < 90$.

b **(i)** What happens to the value of tan $x°$ as x approaches 90°? (Try 85°, 89°, 89.5°, 89.6°.)

(ii) What does the calculator do when you request tan 90° or tan 270°?

(iii) Using the definition that $\tan A = \frac{y}{x}$ can you explain the error message? (Think what happens to the length x as A approaches 90°.)

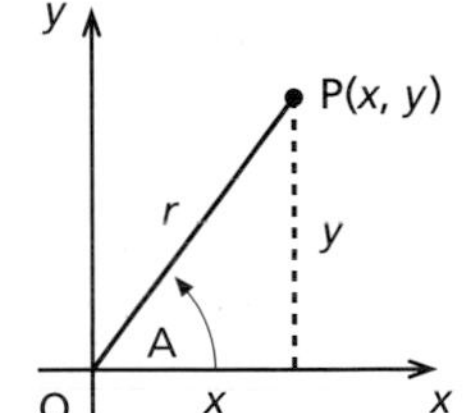

c What is the period of the tangent function?

2 **a** Copy and complete the table.

x	0	10	20	30	40	50	60	70	80	90
tan $x°$	0	0.18	0.36	0.58	0.84					
2 tan $x°$	0	0.35	0.73	1.15	1.68					
3 tan $x°$	0	0.53	1.09	1.73	2.52					
$\frac{1}{2}$ tan $x°$	0	0.09	0.18	0.29	0.42					

b In the graph of $y = a \tan x°$ what effect does altering the value of a have on the steepness of the curve? Graphs might help.

3 a Copy and complete the table.

x	0°	10°	20°	30°	40°	50°	60°	70°	80°	90°
tan $x°$	0	0.18	0.36	0.58	0.84					
tan $2x°$	0	0.36	0.84	1.73	5.67					
tan $3x°$	0	0.58	1.73	E	−1.73					
tan $4x°$	0	0.84	5.67	−1.73	−0.36					

b In the graph of $y = \tan bx°$ what effect does the value of b have?

4

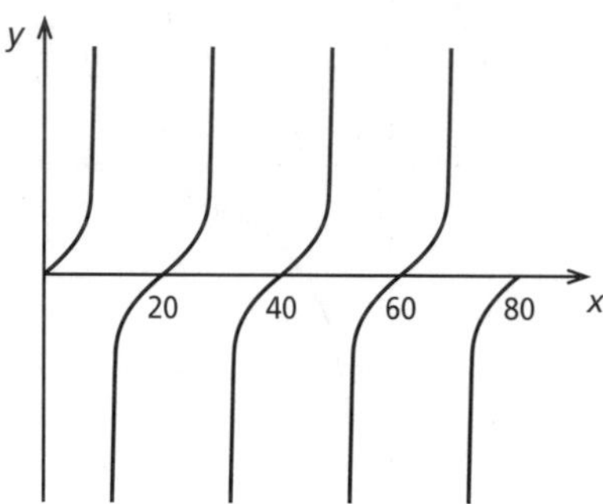

a What is the period of this function?

b The curve has an equation of the form $y = a \tan bx°$.
What is the value of b? (180 ÷ 20)

c The point (5, 2) lies on the curve.
Calculate the value of a.
(Hint: $2 = a \tan (5 \times b)$)

5 Find the equation of each of these curves. They are both of the form $y = a \tan bx°$.

a

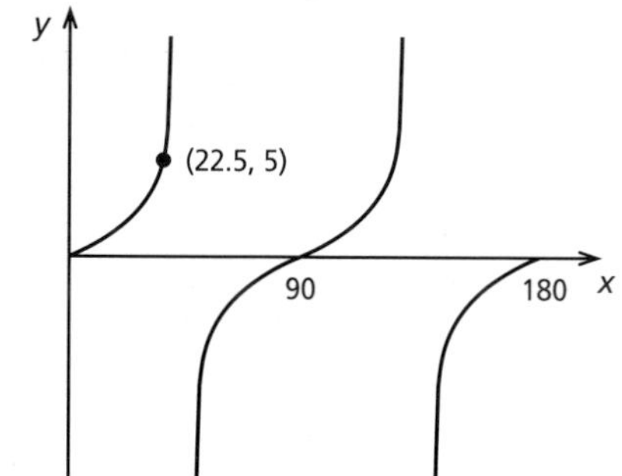

b

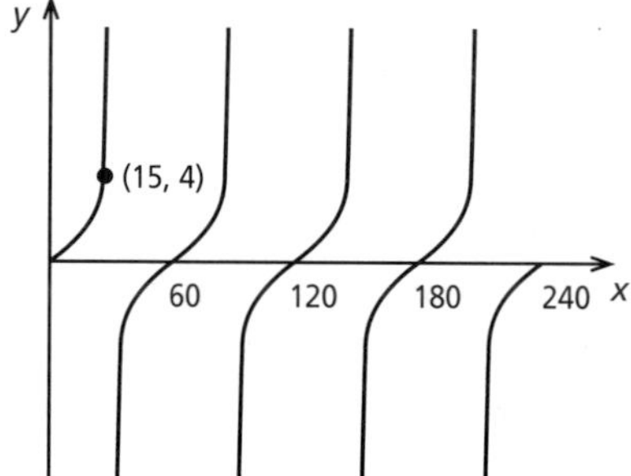

6 a As a balloon rises it is observed from a station at A. Its height is a function of the angle of elevation, $x°$.

$$y = a \tan x°$$

What is the value of a?

b Make a sketch of the function.

c As the balloon rises, what happens to the size of:
(i) AB **(ii)** BC **(iii)** tan $x°$?

C
$y°$
$x°$
A 100 m B

7 Make a sketch of $y = -\tan x°$.

How does a graphics calculator cope with the fact that tan 90° is not defined, when drawing the graph of $y = \tan x°$?

Phase angle

In a function such as $y = \sin (x - a)^\circ$ or $y = \cos (x - a)^\circ$, a is called the **phase angle**. Its effect on the graph of the function can be easily seen by constructing a table.

x	0°	10°	20°	30°	40°	50°	60°	70°	80°	90°
$\sin (x)^\circ$	0	0.18	0.36	0.58	0.84	0.77	0.87	0.94	0.98	1
$\sin (x - 10)^\circ$	−0.17	0	0.18	0.36	0.58	0.84	0.77	0.87	0.94	0.98
$\sin (x - 20)^\circ$	−0.34	−0.17	0	0.18	0.36	0.58	0.84	0.77	0.87	0.94
$\sin (x - 30)^\circ$	−0.5	−0.34	−0.17	0	0.18	0.36	0.58	0.84	0.77	0.87

Notice how the values seem to be displaced 10° to the right when the phase angle is 10°, and 20° to the right when the phase angle is 20°, and so on.

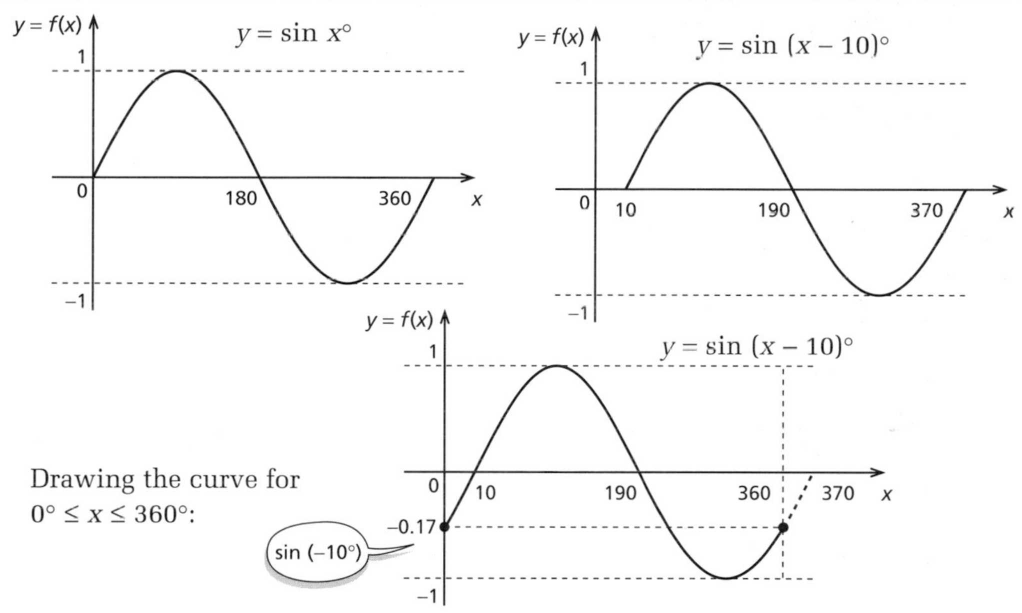

The same thing happens with the cosine and tangent curves.

EXERCISE 5

1 Each curve is of the form $y = a \sin (x - b)^\circ$. Read off the values of a and b.

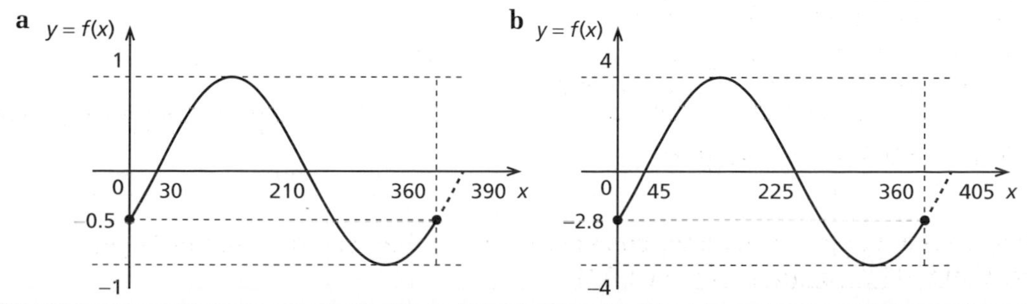

2 Each curve is of the form $y = a\cos(x - b)°$.

a Read off the values of a and b.

(i)

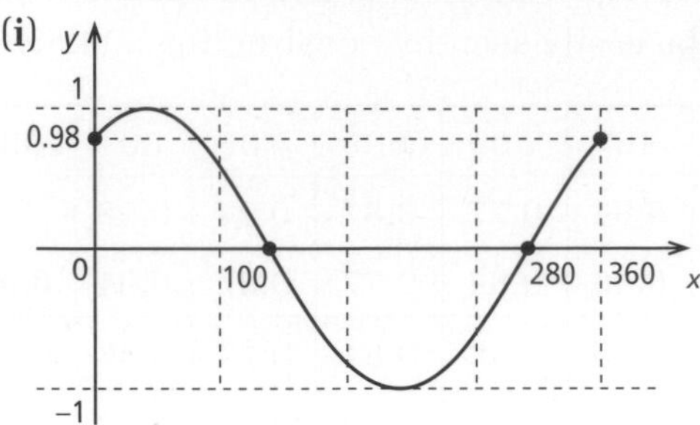

(ii)

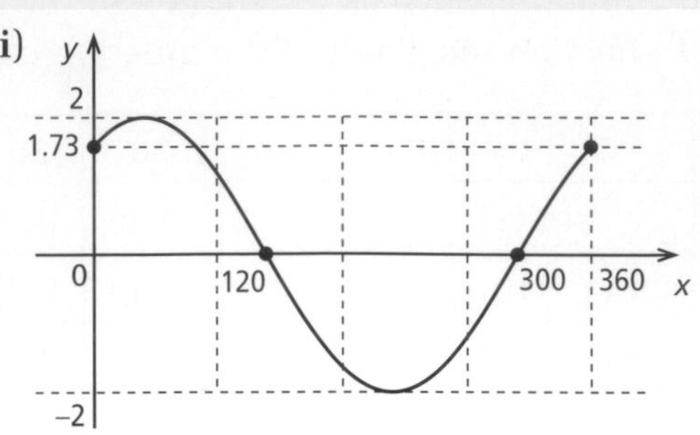

b Write down the maximum and minimum turning points in each case for $0° \le x \le 360°$.

3 Each curve is of the form $y = \tan(x - b)°$. Read off the value b.

a

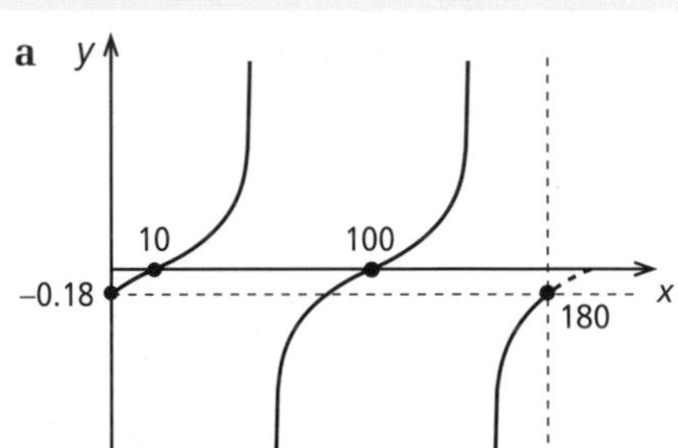

b

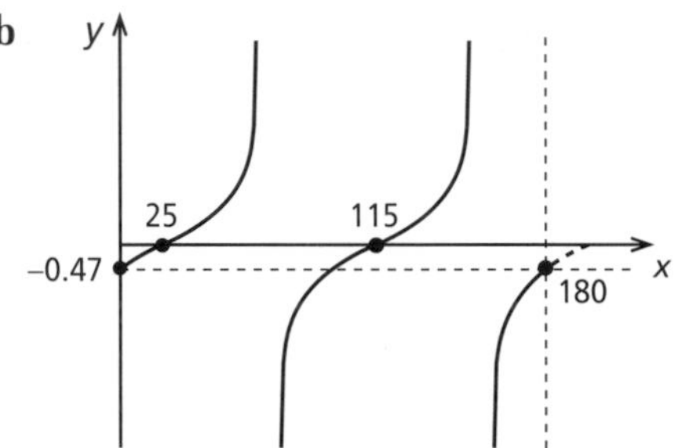

4 a Complete the table of values for **(i)** $y = \cos(x - 90)°$ **(ii)** $y = \sin x°$ and comment.

x	0°	10°	20°	30°	40°	50°	60°	70°	80°	90°
$\sin(x)°$	0									
$\cos(x - 90)°$	0									

b If $\sin(x - b)° = \cos x°$ what is the smallest b could be?

c What simpler function does $y = \sin(x - 360)°$ equal?

Hint
How far would you need to shift a sine wave to the right before it fits exactly onto the cosine wave?

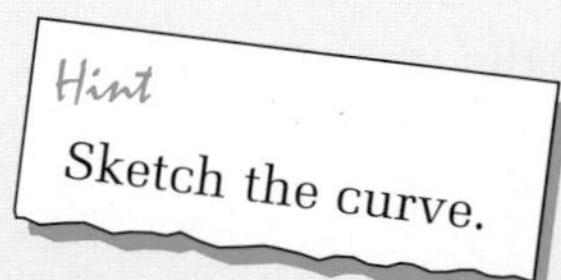

5 a Copy and complete the table.

b Comment on the results.

x	0°	10°	20°	30°	40°	50°	60°	70°	80°	90°
$\sin(x - 20)°$										
$\sin(x + 340)°$										

Moving the sine wave a° to the right has the same effect as moving it $(360 - a)$° to the left.

6 This curve can be looked at as:

(i) a cosine wave moved 20° to the right; $y = \cos(x - 20)°$

(ii) a cosine wave moved 340° to the left; $y = \cos(x + 340)°$

(iii) a sine wave moved 290° to the right; $y = \sin(x - 290)°$

(iv) a sine wave moved 70° to the left; $y = \sin(x + 70)°$.

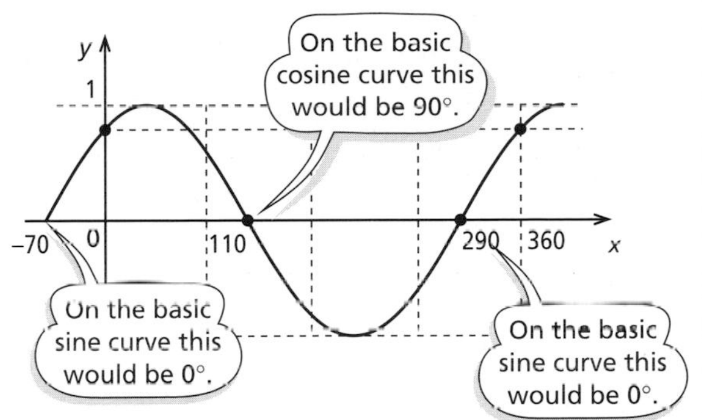

a Use your calculator to check that these forms all produce the same results.

b Similarly, write the equations of the following curves in four ways.

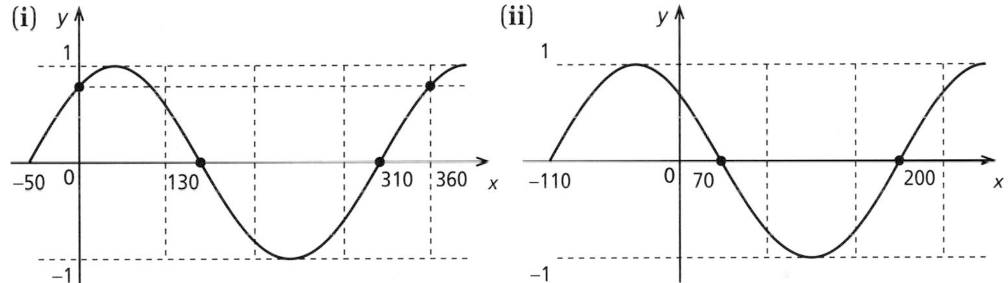

7

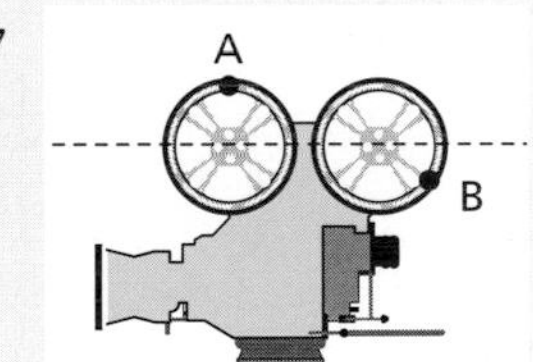

A film projector has two reels. The height, y units, of the point A on one reel is given by $y = \sin(x - 20)°$ where $x°$ is the angle through which the wheel has turned.

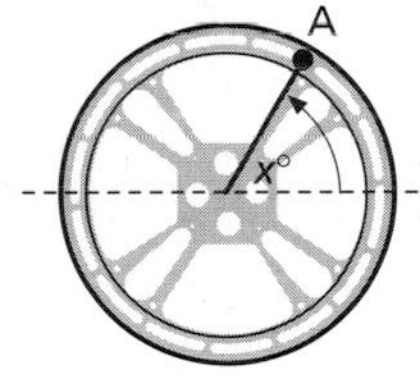

a Make a sketch of y against x for $0 \le x \le 360$.

On the other reel the height of B is given by $y = \sin(x + 120)°$.

b Sketch this curve on the same diagram.

c Estimate for what values of x the height of A and B is the same.

Challenge

You have examined the curve $y = a \sin bx°$ and $y = \sin(x - c)°$.

a Write a report on the effect each of a, b and c has on the curve.

b Consider how the curve $y = d + \sin(x - c)°$ differs from $y = \sin x$.
How does d affect the curve?

Solving equations

(i) Sines

Example 1 Solve $\sin x° = 0.561$.
(By this we mean 'find the angles which make this statement true'.)

Solution 1 The calculator gives:  SIN 0.561 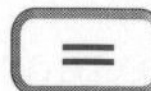 34.1° (to 3 s.f.)

Solution 2

The symmetry of the graph shows us that $180° - 34.1° = 145.9°$ is also a solution.

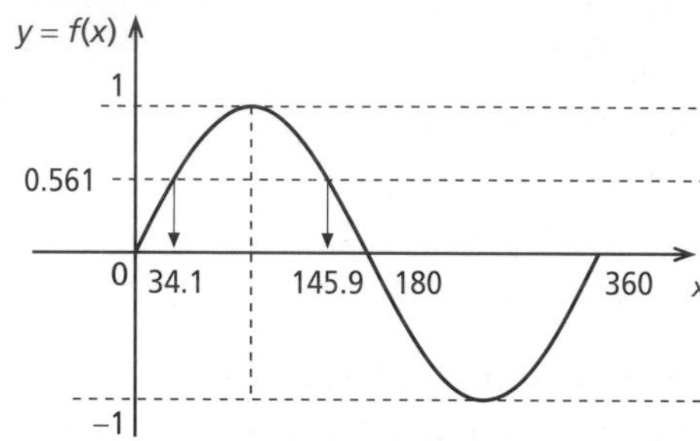

More solutions

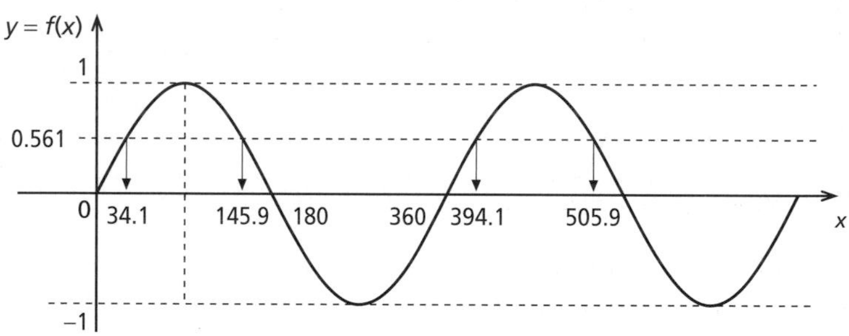

The periodicity of the sine wave produces an infinite list of solutions:

$34.1 + 360 = 394.1°$
$145.9 + 360 = 505.9°$
$394.1 + 360 = 754.1°$
$505.9 + 360 = 865.9°$
$754.1 + 360 = \ldots$

So if $\sin x° = 0.561$ then $x° = 34.1°, 145.9°, 394.1°, 505.9°, 754.1°, 865.9°, \ldots$
We are often told to limit ourselves to the solutions $0 \le x \le 360$.

Example 2 Solve $3 \sin x° + 1 = 0$, $0 \le x \le 360$.

$3 \sin x° = -1$
$\Rightarrow \sin x° = -0.333$ (to 3 s.f.)

$\Rightarrow x = -19.5$ (calculator)
or $x = 180 - (-19.5) = 199.5$ (symmetry of sine curve)
or $x = -19.5 + 360 = 340.5$ (periodicity of sine wave)
or $x = 199.5 + 360 = 559.5$ (periodicity of sine wave)

Since $0 \le x \le 360$ then $x° = 199.5°$ or $340.5°$.

EXERCISE 6

1 Solve the following, listing:
  (i) the calculator answer
  (ii) the answer provided by the symmetry
  (iii) two answers provided by the periodicity.

  a $\sin x° = 0.8$ b $\sin x° = 0.236$ c $\sin x° = 0.910$
  d $\sin x° = 0.179$ e $\sin x° = 0.227$ f $\sin x° = 0.73$

2 Solve the following where $0 \le x \le 360$:

  a $\sin x° = -0.7$ b $\sin x° = -0.512$ c $\sin x° = -0.781$
  d $\sin x° = -0.699$ e $\sin x° = -0.358$

3 Solve the following equations for $0 \le x \le 360$:

  a $2 \sin x° - 1 = 0$ b $5 \sin x° = 4$ c $7 \sin x° - 2 = 1$ d $4 \sin x° + 3 = 0$
  e $6 \sin x° + 1 = 0$ f $4 + 2 \sin x° = 3$ g $2 - 5 \sin x° = 3$ h $3 \sin x° + 5 = 6$
  i $8 \sin x° + 5 = 0$ j $7 + 9 \sin x° = 0$

4 In a harbour a computer measures the depth of water every few minutes. This depth, y m, is given by $y = 6 \sin x° + 8$ where x is the reading number.
  a How deep is the water at reading 50?
  b For which readings does the depth of water in the harbour equal 13.2 m?

(ii) Cosines

Example Solve $\cos x° = 0.625$.

$x = 51.3°$ (calculator)
or $x = 360 - 51.3 = 308.7°$ (symmetry)
or $x = 360 + 51.3 = 411.3°$ (periodicity)
or $x = 360 + 308.7 = 668.7°$ (periodicity)

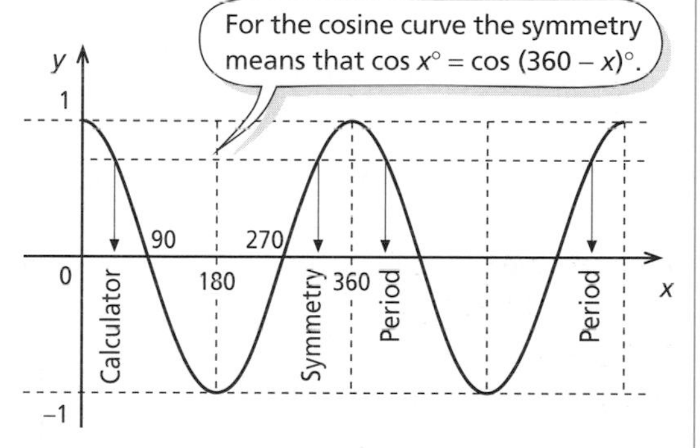

5 Solve the following, listing:
  (i) the calculator answer
  (ii) the answer provided by the symmetry
  (iii) two answers provided by the periodicity.

  a $\cos x° = 0.7$ b $\cos x° = 0.45$ c $\cos x° = 0.718$
  d $\cos x° = 0.811$ e $\cos x° = 0.697$

6 Solve the following where $0 \le x \le 360$:

  a $\cos x° = -0.8$ b $\cos x° = -0.591$ c $\cos x° = -0.184$
  d $\cos x° = -0.601$ e $\cos x° = -0.1$

7 Solve the following equations for $0 \le x \le 360$:

  a $3 \cos x° - 1 = 0$ b $6 \cos x° = 3$ c $9 \cos x° - 4 = 2$ d $5 \cos x° + 2 = 0$
  e $7 \cos x° + 3 = 0$ f $7 + 9 \cos x° = 2$ g $1 - 8 \cos x° = 4$ h $6 \cos x° + 2 = 3$

8

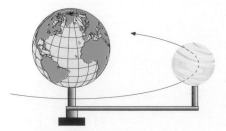

A clockwork model of the Earth and Moon is as shown. The distance of the Moon from its starting position can be calculated using $y = 5 \cos x° + 5$ where y is the distance in centimetres and x is the number of seconds since the model was activated.

a Calculate the value of y when x is **(i)** 20 **(ii)** 80.
b In the first 360 seconds, for what values of x is the distance 6 cm?

(iii) Tangents

Example Solve $\tan x° = 2$.

$x = 63.4$ (calculator)
or $x = 180 + 63.4 = 243.4$ (symmetry – glide)
or $x = 63.4 + 360 = 423.4$ (periodicity)
or $x = 243.4 + 360 = 603.4$ (periodicity)
or $x = \ldots$

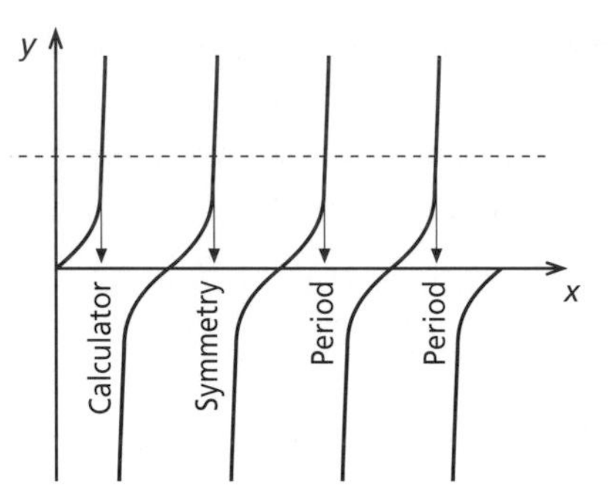

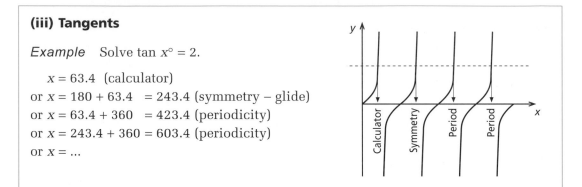

9 Solve the following, listing:
(i) the calculator answer
(ii) the answer provided by the glide symmetry
(iii) two answers provided by the periodicity.

a $\tan x° = 3$ **b** $\tan x° = 0.77$ **c** $\tan x° = 5$
d $\tan x° = 0.912$ **e** $\tan x° = 12$

10 Solve the following where $0 \le x \le 360$:

a $\tan x° = -2$ **b** $\tan x° = -0.561$ **c** $\tan x° = -5.912$
d $\tan x° = -3.34$ **e** $\tan x° = -0.599$

11 Solve the following equations for $0 \le x \le 360$:

a $2 \tan x° - 5 = 0$ **b** $8 \tan x° = 2$ **c** $3 \tan x° - 6 = 17$ **d** $4 \tan x° + 3 = 12$
e $2 \tan x° + 7 = 0$ **f** $5 + 2 \tan x° = 8$ **g** $4 - 5 \tan x° = 6$ **h** $7 \tan x° + 4 = 1$

12

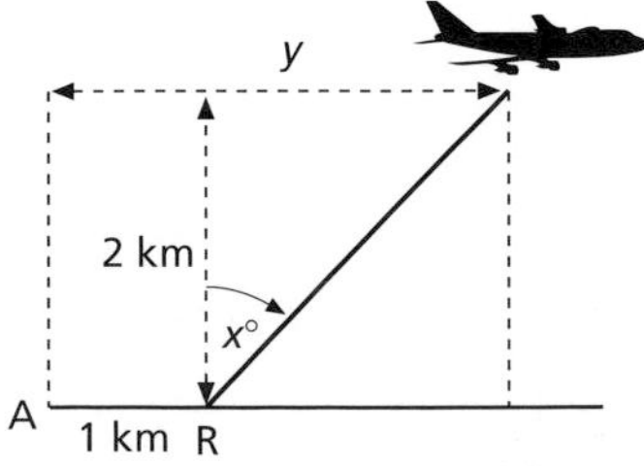

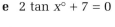

Radar at R is tracking an aircraft. The angle through which it moves is x °. The distance from the airport, y km, is calculated using the formula $y = 2 \tan x° + 1$.

a How far from the airport is the craft when x is **(i)** 30° **(ii)** 43°?
b **(i)** For $0 \le x \le 360$ find the values of x when $y = 12$.
(ii) Which answer is possible in the story?

(iv) Mixed examples

First answer:	calculator
Second answer:	symmetry
Third answer:	Periodicity
Fourth answer:	Periodicity
and so on…	

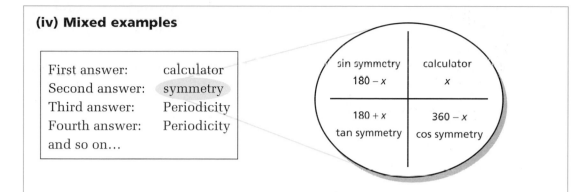

sin symmetry $180 - x$	calculator x
$180 + x$ tan symmetry	$360 - x$ cos symmetry

13 Solve the following, listing:

(i) the calculator answer

(ii) the answer provided by the symmetry

(iii) two answers provided by the periodicity.

a $\sin x° = 0.45$ **b** $\tan x° = 7.12$ **c** $\cos x° = 0.521$ **d** $\tan x° = 1.20$

e $\sin x° = 0.93$ **f** $\cos x° = -0.7$ **g** $\sin x° = -0.506$ **h** $\tan x° = -4.9$

i $\sin x° = -0.309$ **j** $\cos x° = -0.399$

14 Solve the following equations for $0 \leq x \leq 360$:

a $3 \tan x° - 7 = 0$ **b** $8 \sin x° + 5 = 1$ **c** $3 \cos x° + 5 = 7$ **d** $2 \tan x° + 7 = 11$

e $7 \cos x° + 1 = 0$ **f** $5 + 9 \sin x° = 3$ **g** $3 - 5 \cos x° = 5$ **h** $8 \tan x° + 3 = 9$

Sin, cos and tan connections

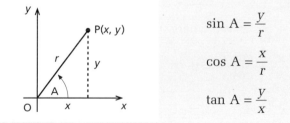

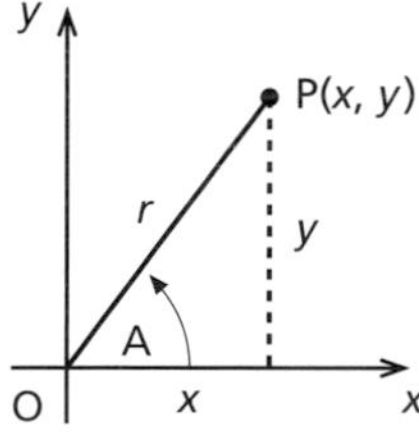

$$\sin A = \frac{y}{r}$$

$$\cos A = \frac{x}{r}$$

$$\tan A = \frac{y}{x}$$

A The Theorem of Pythagoras tells us that: $x^2 + y^2 = r^2$

Dividing by r^2 gives: $\frac{x^2}{r^2} + \frac{y^2}{r^2} = \frac{r^2}{r^2}$

Using the definitions: $\mathbf{\sin^2 A + \cos^2 A = 1}$

B By definition: $\tan A = \frac{y}{x}$

Divide numerator and denominator by r: $\tan A = \frac{y/r}{x/r}$

Using the definitions: $\mathbf{\tan A = \frac{\sin A}{\cos A}}$

EXERCISE 7

$\sin^2 A + \cos^2 A = 1$

1 Check that the relation $\sin^2 A + \cos^2 A = 1$ works when x equals:

a 30° **b** 90° **c** −130° **d** 320° **e** 507°.

2 Use the relation $\sin^2 A + \cos^2 A = 1$ to:

a express $\sin^2 A$ in terms of $\cos^2 A$

b express $\cos^2 A$ in terms of $\sin^2 A$

c prove $\sin A = \sqrt{(1 - \cos^2 A)}$ where A is acute

d express $\cos A$ in terms of $\sin A$ where A is acute.

3 **a** Given that $\sin^2 A = 0.2$, state the value of $\cos^2 A$.

b Given that $\cos^2 A = 0.31$, state the value of $\sin^2 A$.

c Given that $\cos A = 0.5$, state the value of $\sin^2 A$.

d Given that $\cos A = 0.6$ and A is acute, state the value of $\sin A$.

e Given that $\cos A = 0.6$ and A is reflex, state the value of $\sin A$.

4 Simplify the following:

a $\sqrt{(1 - \sin^2 x°)}$; $0 \le x \le 90$ **b** $\dfrac{1 - \sin^2 x°}{\cos^2 x°}$ **c** $\dfrac{1 - \cos^2 x°}{\sin x°}$

d $(\cos x° + \sin x°)(\cos x° - \sin x°)$ **e** $(\cos x° + \sin x°)^2 - 2 \cos x° \sin x°$

5 Simplify:

$\tan A = \dfrac{\sin A}{\cos A}$

a $\dfrac{(1 - \cos^2 x°)}{\sin x°}$ **b** $\dfrac{(1 - \cos^2 x°)}{\cos^2 x°}$ **c** $\dfrac{2 \sin^2 x°}{(1 - \sin^2 x°)}$

Example

Solve the equation $\sin x° + \cos x° = 0$ where $0 \le x \le 360$.

Dividing by $\cos x°$: $\dfrac{\sin x°}{\cos x°} + \dfrac{\cos x°}{\cos x°} = 0$

So $\tan x° + 1 = 0$

$\tan x° = -1$

$x = -45$ (calculator)

or $x = 180 + (-45) = 135$ (symmetry)

or $x = 360 + (-45) = 315$ (periodicity)

or $x = 360 + (135) = 495$ (periodicity)

so $x° = 135°$ or $315°$

6 Solve the following equations in a similar manner.

a $\sin x° = \cos x°$ **b** $2 \sin x° - \cos x° = 0$

c $5 \sin x° - 2 \cos x° = 0$ **d** $4 \sin x° + 3 \cos x° = 0$

e $5 \sin x° = 3 \cos x°$ **f** $4 \sin x° + \cos x° = 0$

g $7 \sin x° + 3 \cos x° = 0$ **h** $5 \sin x° - \cos x° = 0$

CHAPTER 15 REVIEW

1 Make a sketch of:
(i) the sine function $y = \sin x°$, $0 \le x \le 360$
(ii) the cosine function $y = \cos x°$, $0 \le x \le 360$.
Label the turning points and the zeros.

2 Draw graphs of each of the following functions:
a $y = 2 \sin x°$ **b** $y = 3 \cos 2x°$ **c** $y = 2 \sin 5x°$ **d** $y = -4 \sin x°$.
For each graph write down:
(i) the periodicity (ii) maximum and minimum turning points
(iii) zeros of the function.

3 Identify the equations of the following functions from the graphs.

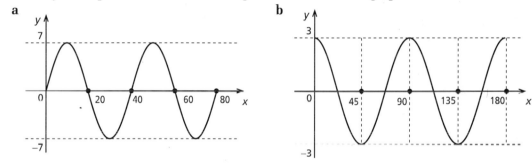

a

b

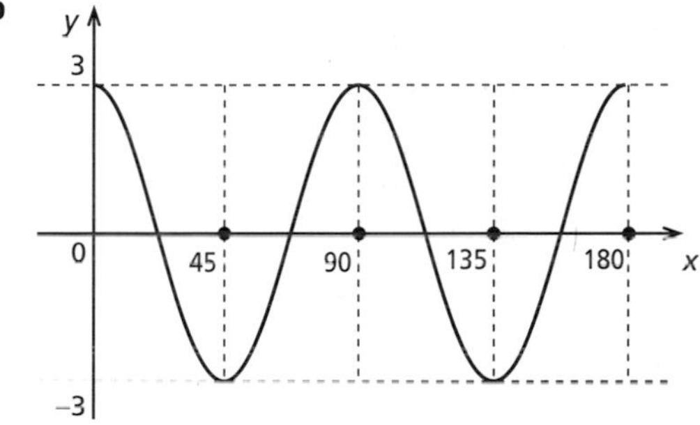

4 Draw a sketch of the function $y = \tan x°$.

5 Solve the following equations for $0° \le x \le 360°$:
a $2 \sin x° - 1 = 0$ **b** $4 \cos x° + 2 = 0$ **c** $6 \sin x° + 2 = 0$
d $3 \cos x° - 2 = 0$ **e** $2 \tan x° - 1 = 0$ **f** $2 \sin x° + 3 = 7$

6 Draw a sketch of the function $y = \cos (x - 30)°$.

7 This curve has an equation of the form $y = a \sin(x - b)°$
Work out the value of a and b.

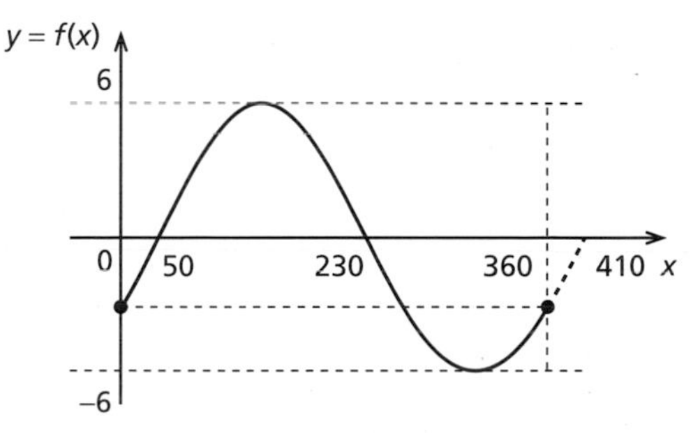

8 Simplify: **a** $\sin^2 x° + \cos^2 x°$ **b** $\dfrac{\sin x°}{\cos x°}$ **c** $\dfrac{2\sqrt{(1 - \cos^2 x°)}}{\sin x°}$; $0 \le x \le 90$.

9 Solve for $0 \le x \le 360$:
a $5 \sin x° - 2 \cos x° = 0$ **b** $3 \sin x° + \cos x° = 0$.

16 Revising Unit 3

Algebraic operations

Reminders

Make denominators the same when adding and subtracting:

$$\frac{3}{4a} + \frac{1}{a^2}$$
$$= \frac{3a}{4a^2} + \frac{4}{4a^2}$$
$$= \frac{3a + 4}{4a^2}$$

Multiplying:

$$\frac{3}{a} \times \frac{a^2}{12}$$
$$= \frac{3a^2}{12a}$$
$$= \frac{a}{4}$$

Dividing:

$$\frac{3}{a} \div \frac{a^2}{12}$$
$$= \frac{3}{a} \times \frac{12}{a^2}$$
$$= \frac{36}{a^3}$$

Surds:

a $\sqrt{3} \times \sqrt{5} = \sqrt{3 \times 5} = \sqrt{15}$

b $\frac{\sqrt{21}}{\sqrt{3}} = \sqrt{\frac{21}{3}} = \sqrt{7}$

c $\sqrt{8} = \sqrt{(4 \times 2)} = \sqrt{4} \times \sqrt{2} = 2 \times \sqrt{2} = 2\sqrt{2}$

d $\sqrt{8} + \sqrt{18} = 2\sqrt{2} + 3\sqrt{2} = 5\sqrt{2}$

Indices:

a $a^n = a \times a \times \ldots \times a$ (n factors)

b $a^m \times a^n = a^{m+n}$

c $a^m \div a^n = a^{m-n}$

d $(a^m)^n = a^{mn}$

e $1 = a^0$

f $\frac{1}{a^m} = a^{-m}$

g $a^{\frac{1}{2}} = \sqrt{a}$

h $a^{\frac{1}{n}} = \sqrt[n]{a}$

i $(a^m)^{\frac{1}{n}} = a^{\frac{m}{n}} = \sqrt[n]{a^m}$

EXERCISE 1

1 Calculate:

a $\frac{1}{a} + \frac{2}{a}$ **b** $\frac{3}{y^2} - \frac{1}{y^2}$ **c** $\frac{1}{x} + \frac{1}{2x}$ **d** $\frac{1}{m} - \frac{1}{3m}$

e $\frac{1}{2m} + \frac{1}{3m}$ **f** $\frac{1}{3t} - \frac{1}{4t}$ **g** $\frac{2}{3y} + \frac{5}{2y}$ **h** $\frac{2}{c^2} + \frac{3}{c}$

i $\frac{2}{a} + \frac{a}{4}$ **j** $\frac{1}{3c} - \frac{2c}{5}$ **k** $\frac{1}{x^2} + \frac{1}{2x}$ **l** $\frac{3}{2y} + \frac{4}{5y^2}$

2 Simplify:

a $c^2 \times c^3$ **b** $y^3 \times y^4$ **c** $m^6 \div m^2$ **d** $\frac{a^9}{a^3}$ **e** $\frac{m^2}{m^3}$

f $\frac{(k+3)^9}{(k+3)^3}$ **g** $\frac{(a-3)^3}{(a-3)}$ **h** $\frac{(2t-1)^3}{(2t-1)^4}$ **i** $\frac{(x-1)^{10}}{(x-1)^9}$ **j** $(n-5)^2 \times (n-5)^3$

3 Change the subject of each of these formulae to that indicated in the brackets.

a $P = 4L$; $[L]$ **b** $x = y + 4$; $[y]$ **c** $B = \frac{1}{3}C$; $[C]$

d $m = 6n + p$; $[n]$ **e** $8T = 2u + v$; $[u]$ **f** $A = 3(B + C)$; $[B]$

4 Simplify:

a $\frac{6}{a} \times \frac{a}{2}$ **b** $\frac{4}{c} \times \frac{3}{c}$ **c** $\frac{3y}{5} \times \frac{10}{9y}$ **d** $\frac{2}{m} \div \frac{5}{m}$

e $\frac{6t}{5} \times \frac{20}{3t^2}$ **f** $\frac{2w^2}{3} \div \frac{8w}{9}$ **g** $\frac{3n}{4m} \times \frac{m^2n}{6}$ **h** $\frac{4uv}{3} \times \frac{v^2}{9u}$

5 Simplify:

a $\sqrt{3} \times \sqrt{2}$ **b** $\sqrt{32} \times \sqrt{2}$ **c** $\sqrt{2} \times \sqrt{5} \times \sqrt{10}$

d $\frac{\sqrt{75}}{\sqrt{3}}$ **e** $\frac{\sqrt{500}}{\sqrt{5}}$ **f** $\frac{\sqrt{6} \times \sqrt{8}}{\sqrt{3}}$

6 Follow the example to help you rationalise the denominator in each fraction.

Example $\frac{3}{\sqrt{5}} = \frac{3 \times \sqrt{5}}{\sqrt{5} \times \sqrt{5}} = \frac{3\sqrt{5}}{5}$

a $\frac{1}{\sqrt{5}}$ **b** $\frac{1}{\sqrt{7}}$ **c** $\frac{2}{\sqrt{6}}$ **d** $\frac{10}{\sqrt{10}}$ **e** $\frac{4}{3\sqrt{8}}$

7 Simplify:

a $a^3 \times a^{-2}$ **b** $y^{-4} \times y^2$ **c** $m^{-1} \times m^{-2}$ **d** $n^3 \times n^{-3}$

e $t^{-4} \times t^{-3}$ **f** $u^{-\frac{1}{2}} \times u^{-\frac{1}{2}}$ **g** $w^{-\frac{3}{2}} \times w^{\frac{1}{2}}$ **h** $y^{-\frac{5}{2}} \times y^{-\frac{7}{2}}$

i $a^{-3} \div a^2$ **j** $c^{-1} \div c^3$ **k** $h^{-4} \div h^{-1}$ **l** $k^{\frac{2}{3}} \div k^{-\frac{2}{3}}$

8 Express each in its simplest surd form:

a $\sqrt{20}$ **b** $\sqrt{27}$ **c** $\sqrt{32}$ **d** $\sqrt{45}$ **e** $\sqrt{2} \times \sqrt{6}$

f $\sqrt{80}$ **g** $\sqrt{98}$ **h** $\sqrt{108}$ **i** $\sqrt{112}$ **j** $\frac{\sqrt{24}}{\sqrt{3}}$

9 Simplify:

a $\frac{3m^2}{2} \times \frac{4}{m}$ **b** $\frac{6}{t} - \frac{3}{2t}$ **c** $\frac{10}{y} \div \frac{4}{y^2}$ **d** $\frac{10}{y} + \frac{4}{y^2}$

10 Express in the form ax^n:

a $\frac{1}{x^2}$ **b** $\frac{2}{x^2}$ **c** $\frac{1}{2x^2}$ **d** $\frac{3}{4x^5}$ **e** $\frac{1}{x^{\frac{2}{3}}}$ **f** $\frac{2}{x^{-\frac{1}{4}}}$

g $\frac{3}{4x^{\frac{1}{2}}}$ **h** $\frac{1}{\sqrt{x}}$ **i** $\frac{3}{\sqrt{x}}$ **j** $\frac{1}{5\sqrt{x}}$ **k** $\frac{7}{3\sqrt{x}}$ **l** $\frac{4}{5\sqrt[3]{x}}$

11 Simplify:

a $a^{\frac{1}{4}} \times a^{\frac{3}{4}}$ b $c^{\frac{2}{3}} \times c^{\frac{2}{3}}$ c $m \times m^{\frac{1}{2}}$ d $h^{\frac{4}{5}} \div h^{\frac{1}{5}}$

e $k^2 \times k^{\frac{1}{2}}$ f $t^{\frac{1}{2}} \times t^{\frac{1}{2}}$ g $y^{\frac{2}{3}} \times y^{\frac{4}{3}}$ h $x^{\frac{5}{4}} \div x^{\frac{1}{4}}$

12 Change the subject:

a $A = \frac{1}{3}B - C$ to (i) C (ii) B

b $P = \frac{T+R}{V}$ to (i) V (ii) T

c $2A = BC - D$ to (i) D (ii) C

d $p = 3(q + 2r)$ to (i) q (ii) r

e $M = \frac{1}{4}(N - P)$ to (i) N (ii) P

f $T = \frac{5(u+v)}{W}$ to (i) W (ii) u.

13 For each rectangle, find an expression for
(i) its area
(ii) its perimeter.

a 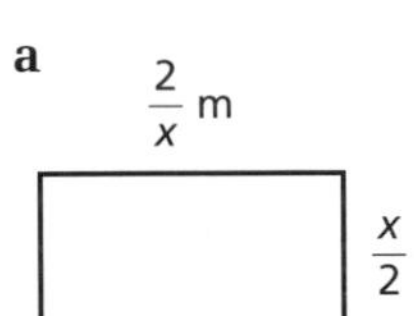

b 

14 Find an expression for:
a the total length of the two sections of rod
b the difference in their lengths.

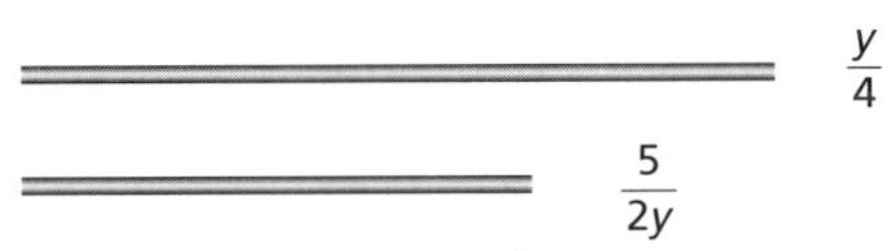

15 Express each of these as three separate terms with fractional indices:

a $\frac{5x^2 + 3x - 2}{\sqrt{x}}$ b $\frac{4x^2 - x + 5}{\sqrt[3]{x}}$

16 $y = x^{\frac{3}{2}}\left(4x^{-\frac{1}{2}} - x^{-\frac{3}{2}}\right)$

a Remove the brackets.
b Hence or otherwise make x the subject of the formula.

17 Express each fraction with a rational denominator:

a $\frac{1}{1 + \sqrt{2}}$ b $\frac{1}{3 - \sqrt{5}}$ c $\frac{2}{\sqrt{10} - 3}$ d $\frac{9}{5 + \sqrt{7}}$

18 Simplify:

a $\left(x^2\right)^3$ b $\left(x^3\right)^2$ c $\left(y^4\right)^3$ d $\left(a^{\frac{1}{2}}\right)^3$ e $\left(a^3\right)^{\frac{1}{2}}$ f $\left(m^{\frac{1}{3}}\right)^{\frac{1}{2}}$

g $\left(2c\right)^3$ h $\left(3h\right)^{-2}$ i $\left(4k\right)^{-1}$ j $\left(4m\right)^{-\frac{1}{2}}$ k $\left(8t^2\right)^{\frac{1}{3}}$ l $\left(16t^{-\frac{2}{3}}\right)^{\frac{3}{2}}$

19 Express in the form ax^n:

a $\frac{1}{\sqrt[3]{x^2}}$ b $\frac{1}{\sqrt[3]{8x^3}}$ c $\frac{1}{\sqrt{5x^4}}$ d $\frac{2}{3\sqrt{6x}}$ e $\frac{x}{4\sqrt{x^5}}$ f $\frac{2x}{3\sqrt{x^3}}$

Quadratic functions

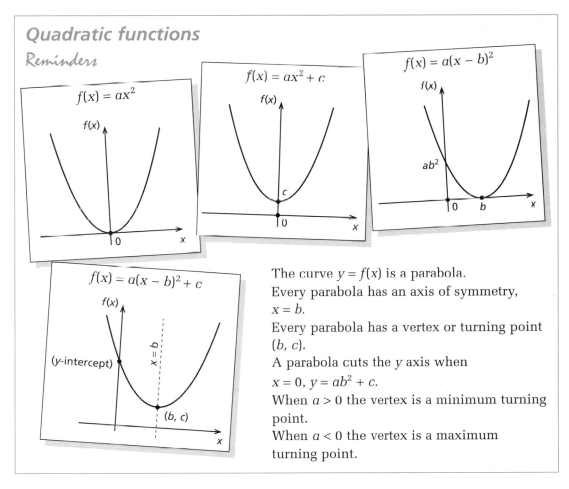

Reminders

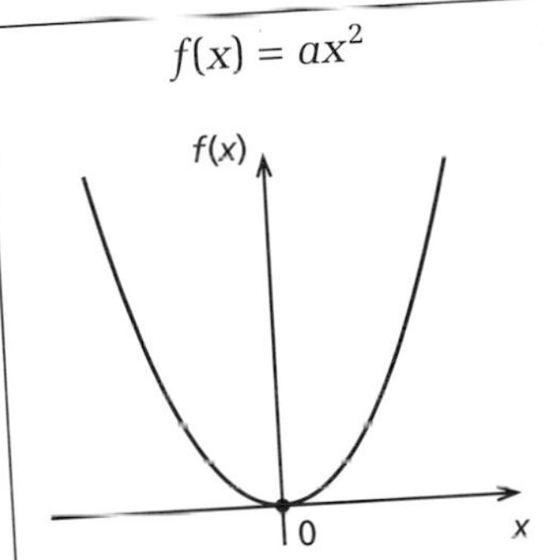

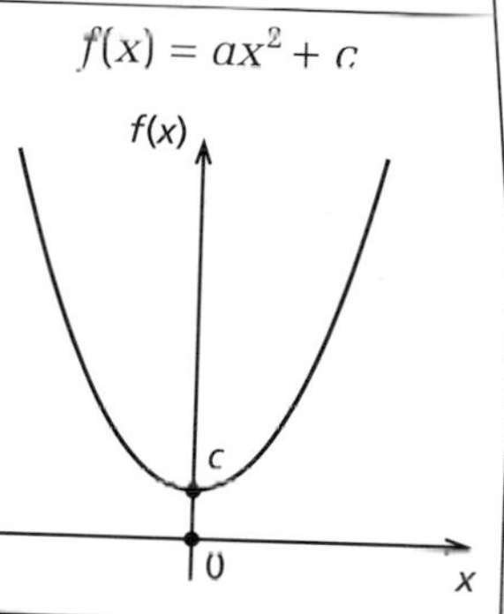

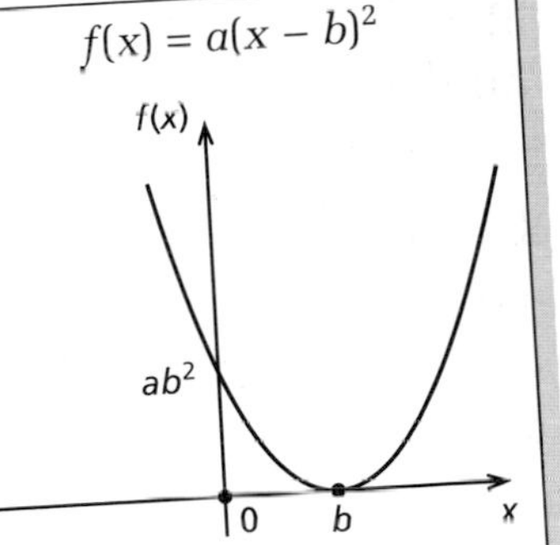

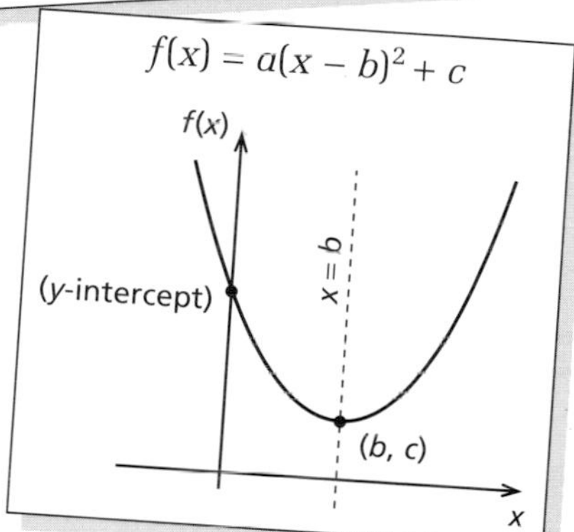

The curve $y = f(x)$ is a parabola.
Every parabola has an axis of symmetry, $x = b$.
Every parabola has a vertex or turning point (b, c).
A parabola cuts the y axis when $x = 0$, $y = ab^2 + c$.
When $a > 0$ the vertex is a minimum turning point.
When $a < 0$ the vertex is a maximum turning point.

EXERCISE 2

1 Each graph shows a parabola whose vertex is at the origin.
Write down the equation of each graph in the form $y = kx^2$.

a

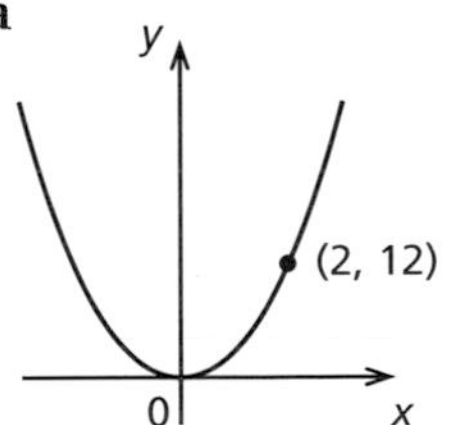

b

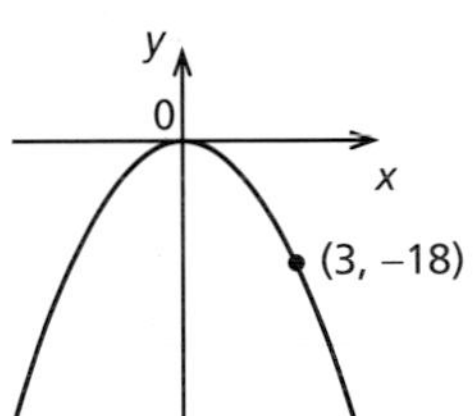

c

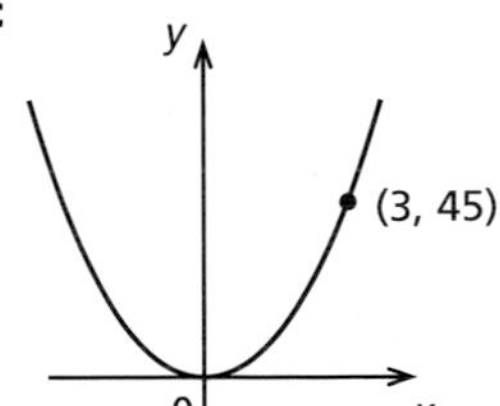

2 Write down the equation of each parabola in the form $y = k(x - a)^2 + b$ where $k = \pm 1$.

a

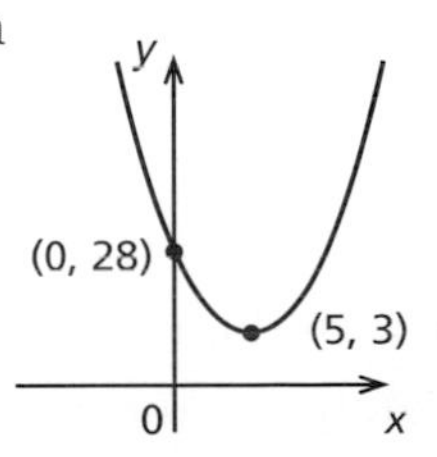

b

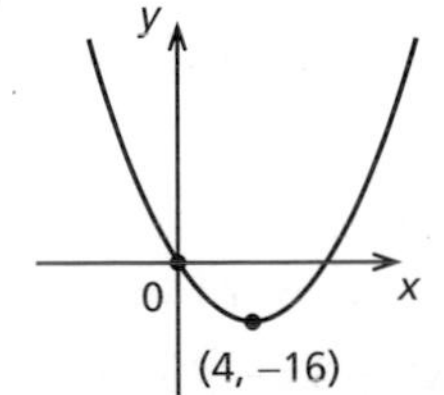

c

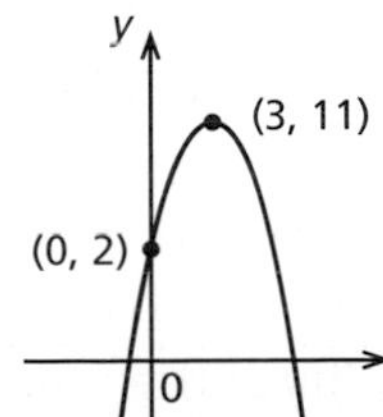

d

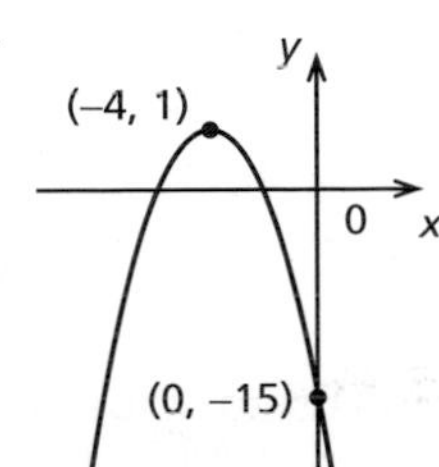

3 For each of the quadratics write down:

(i) the coordinates of its vertex

(ii) the nature of the turning point

(iii) the equation of the axis of symmetry.

a $y = (x - 1)^2 - 5$ b $y = 4 - (x - 3)^2$

4 Sketch the graph of the quadratic given by:

a $y = x^2 - 3$ b $y = (x + 1)^2 - 6$ c $y = -3 - (x - 7)^2$

5 Write down the roots of these quadratics:

a $(x + 1)(x - 3) = 0$ b $(x + 6)(x + 2) = 0$ c $x(x + 5) = 0$

6 a Copy and complete the table for the quadratic $y = x^2 + 2x - 3$.

x	-6	-4	-2	0	2	4	6
y							

b Draw the graph of $y = x^2 + 2x - 3$ on 2 mm graph paper.

c Use your graph to help you solve $x^2 + 2x - 3 = 0$.

d What is the axis of symmetry of the curve?

7 a Copy and complete the table for the quadratic function $y = 14 + 5x - x^2$.

x	1	2	3	4	5	6	7	8
y								

b Plot the points in the table on a coordinate diagram.

c Write down:

(i) the equation of the axis of symmetry of the quadratic function

(ii) the roots of $14 + 5x - x^2 = 0$.

d Find the coordinates of the vertex.

e Draw the graph of $y = 14 + 5x - x^2$.

8 Solve these equations by first factorising the quadratic expression.

a $x^2 + 6x + 9 = 0$ b $x^2 + 5x + 6 = 0$ c $x^2 + 5x + 4 = 0$ d $x^2 + 2x - 3 = 0$

e $x^2 - x - 6 = 0$ f $x^2 - 5x - 14 = 0$ g $x^2 + x - 20 = 0$ h $x^2 + 5x - 14 = 0$

i $x^2 - 5x + 6 = 0$ j $x^2 - 7x + 6 = 0$ k $x^2 + x - 12 = 0$ l $x^2 - 4x - 12 = 0$

9 If $ax^2 + bx + c = 0$ then $x = \dfrac{-b \pm \sqrt{(b^2 - 4ac)}}{2a}$

Use this formula to solve these quadratic equations correct to 3 s.f.

a $x^2 + 2x - 5 = 0$ b $x^2 - x - 3 = 0$ c $x^2 - 4x + 2 = 0$ d $x^2 + 5x + 3 = 0$

10 a Copy and complete the table of values for the quadratic function $y = x^2 - 3x - 7$.

x	-3	-2	-1	0	1	2	3	4	5	6
y										

b On 2 mm graph paper draw the graph of $y = x^2 - 3x - 7$.

c Write down: (i) the coordinates of the vertex

(ii) the equation of the axis of symmetry

(iii) the coordinates of the point of intersection with the y axis.

d From your graph estimate the roots of $x^2 - 3x - 7 = 0$ as accurately as you can.

11 Factorise the quadratic expressions and hence solve the equations.

a $3 - 2x - x^2 = 0$ **b** $12 + x - x^2 = 0$ **c** $6 + 5x - x^2 = 0$ **d** $-12 + 7x - x^2 = 0$

12 Try to solve $x^2 + 2x + 5 = 0$ using the quadratic formula. What do you notice?

13 The difference between two whole numbers is 7.
When the numbers are multiplied together the answer is 198.
Let the numbers be n and $n - 7$.

a Show that $n^2 - 7n - 198 = 0$.

b Solve the quadratic equation.

c Hence or otherwise find the two numbers.

14 The sum of two whole numbers is 37. When they are multiplied together the answer is 312. Let the numbers be n and $37 - n$.

a Form a quadratic equation in n.

b Solve the equation to help you find the two numbers.

15 The floor area of a rectangular games hall is $432\ \text{m}^2$.
Its length is x m and its breadth is $(x - 6)$ m.

a Show that $x^2 - 6x - 432 = 0$.

b Solve the quadratic equation and hence find the dimensions of the games hall.

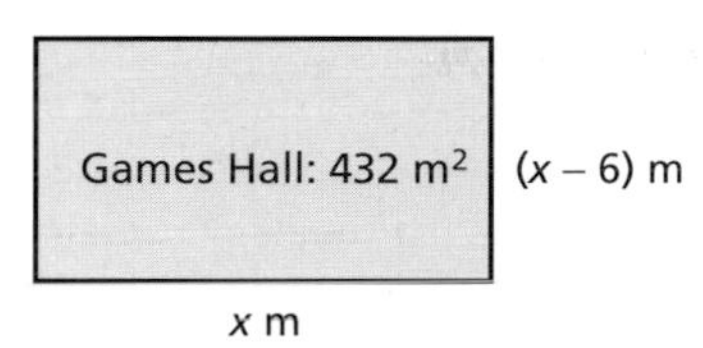

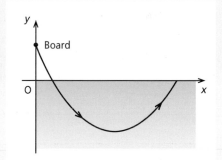

16 Another rectangular games hall has a floor area of $560\ \text{m}^2$.
Its breadth is 8 m less than its length.
Form a quadratic equation and solve it to find the dimensions of the games hall.

17 The diagram shows the path of a diver from the moment she leaves the diving board until she re-surfaces. Her path is modelled by the quadratic $y = x^2 - 9x + 8$, with x measured in metres.

a How far from the water's edge (point O) is the diver as she:

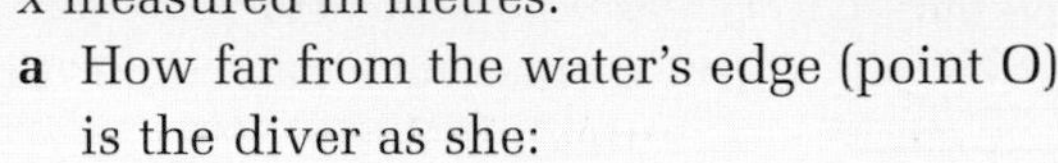

(i) enters the water (ii) re-surfaces?

b How high is the diving board?

c How deep is the dive?

18 First factorise the quadratic expression and then solve the equation.

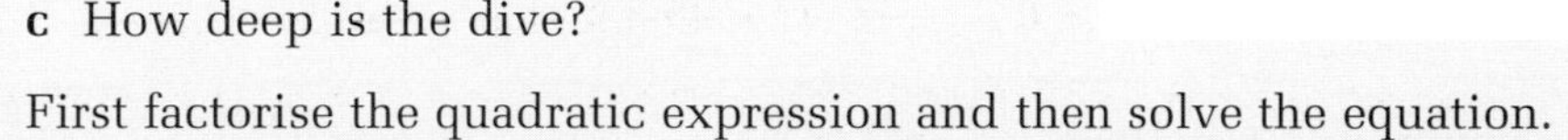

a $2x^2 + 7x + 3 = 0$ **b** $2x^2 + 7x + 6 = 0$ **c** $2x^2 - 9x - 5 = 0$

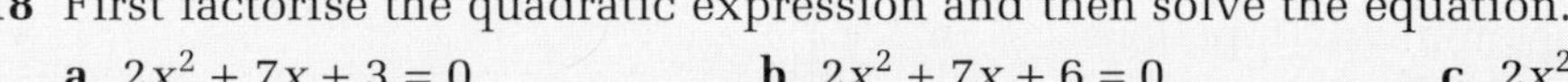

d $2x^2 - 9x + 10 = 0$ **e** $3x^2 + 10x + 3 = 0$ **f** $3x^2 - 8x + 4 = 0$

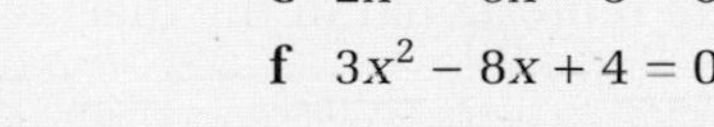

g $3x^2 - 11x + 6 = 0$ **h** $5x^2 - 8x - 4 = 0$

19 Use the quadratic formula to solve these equations correct to 3 s.f.

a $2x^2 + 5x + 1 = 0$ **b** $2x^2 - 6x + 3 = 0$ **c** $3x^2 + 2x - 2 = 0$

d $3x^2 + 7x - 1 = 0$

Further trigonometry

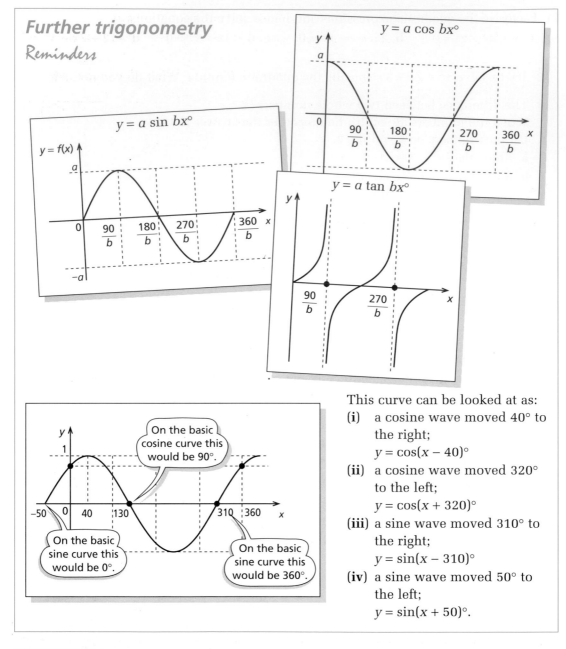

Reminders

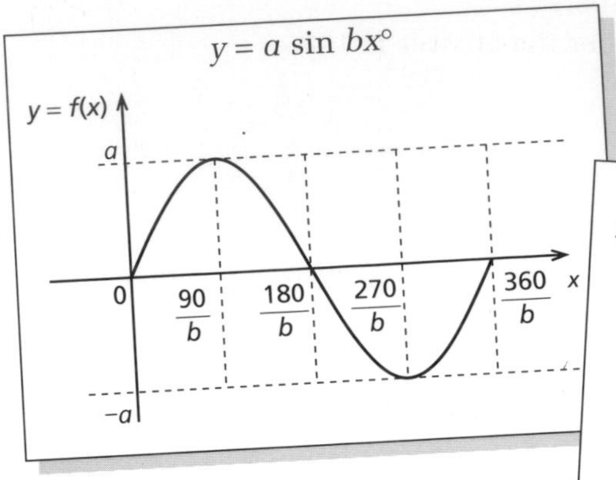

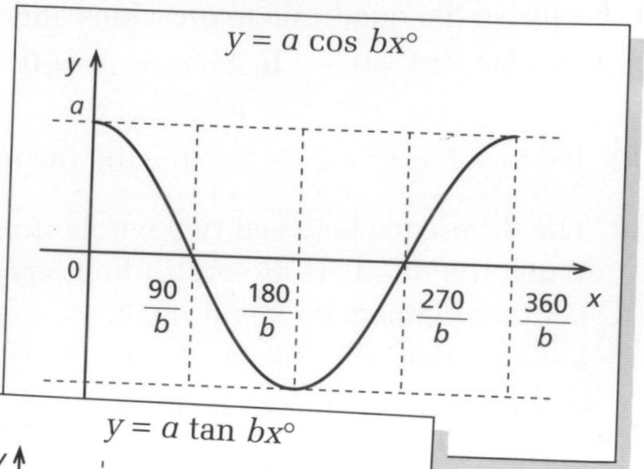

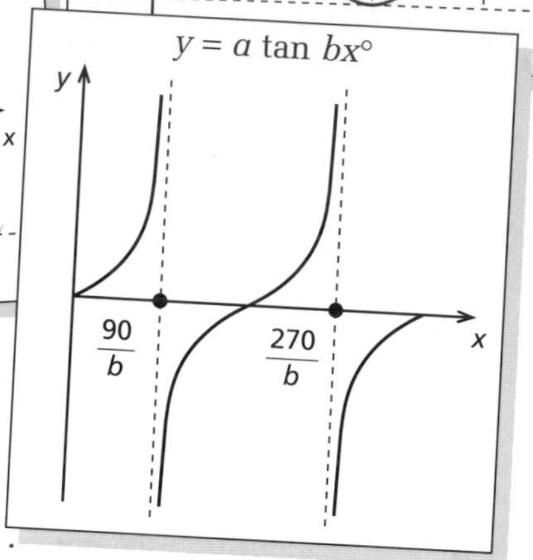

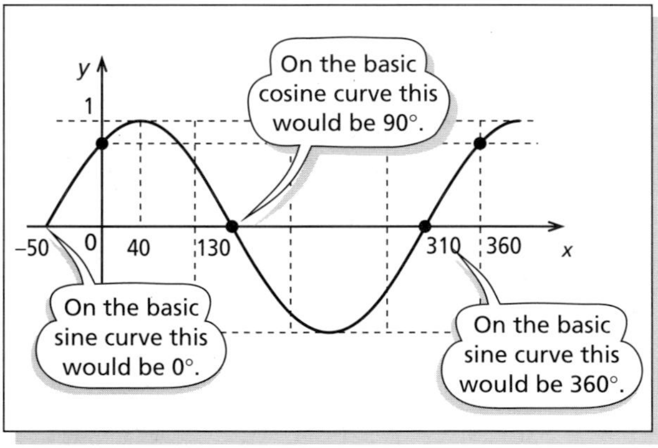

$y = a \sin bx°$

$y = a \cos bx°$

$y = a \tan bx°$

On the basic cosine curve this would be 90°.

On the basic sine curve this would be 0°.

On the basic sine curve this would be 360°.

This curve can be looked at as:

(i) a cosine wave moved 40° to the right;
$y = \cos(x - 40)°$

(ii) a cosine wave moved 320° to the left;
$y = \cos(x + 320)°$

(iii) a sine wave moved 310° to the right;
$y = \sin(x - 310)°$

(iv) a sine wave moved 50° to the left;
$y = \sin(x + 50)°$.

EXERCISE 3

1 What three trigonometric functions are represented in the diagrams?

a

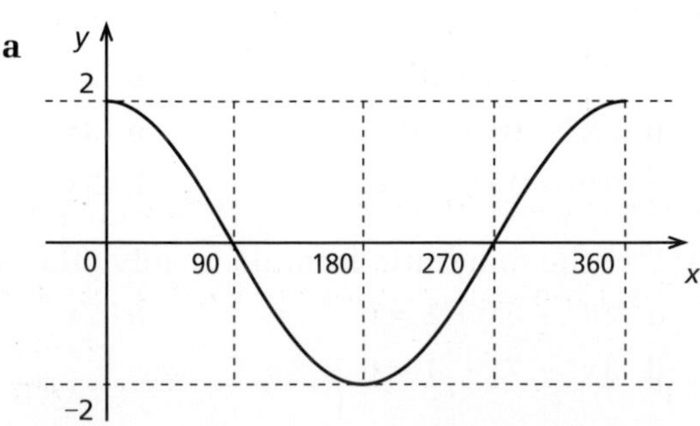

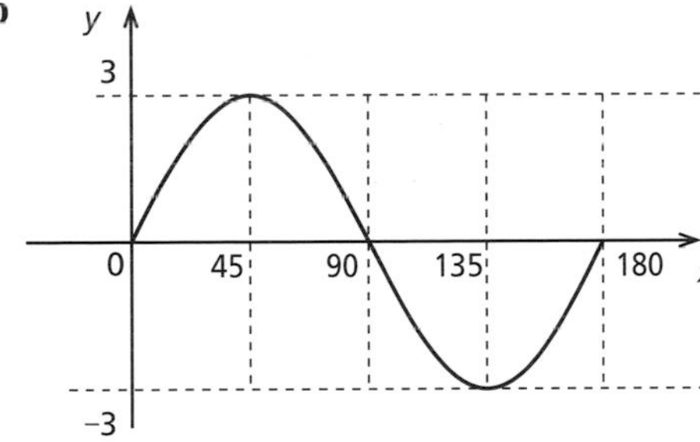

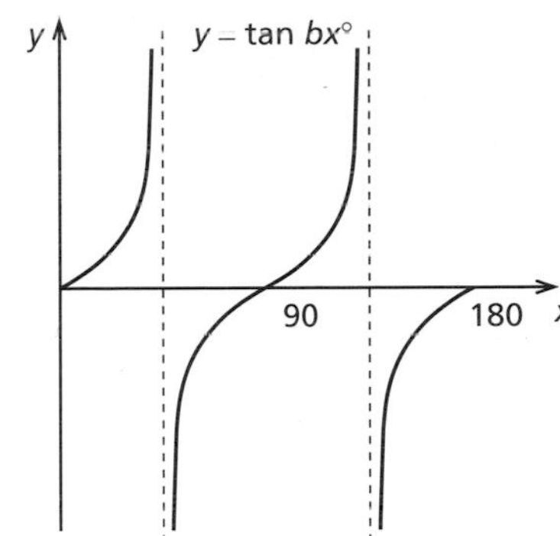

2 **a** On 2 mm graph paper draw the graph of $y = 3 \sin x°$ for $0 \le x \le 360$.

b What is the period of $y = 3 \sin x°$?

c From the graph solve $3 \sin x° = 0$ for $0 \le x \le 360$.

3 **a** Make a sketch of the graph of $y = \cos 2x°$ for $0 \le x \le 360$.

b What is its period?

c From the sketch, write down the values of x for which:

(i) $\cos 2x° = 0$ for $0 \le x \le 360$

(ii) $\cos 2x° = -1$ for $0 \le x \le 360$.

4 Determine the equations of these trigonometric functions from their sketches.

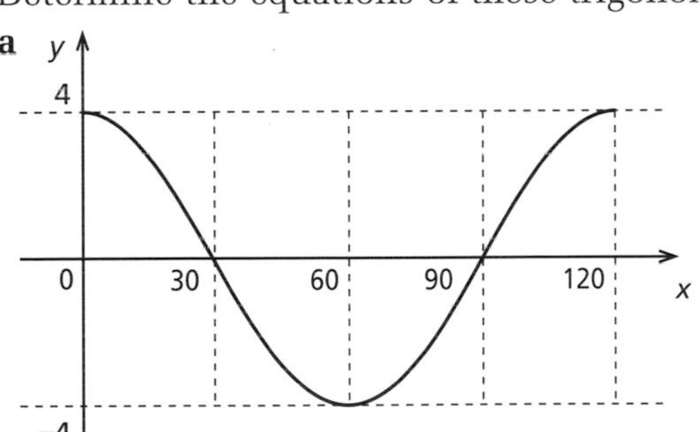

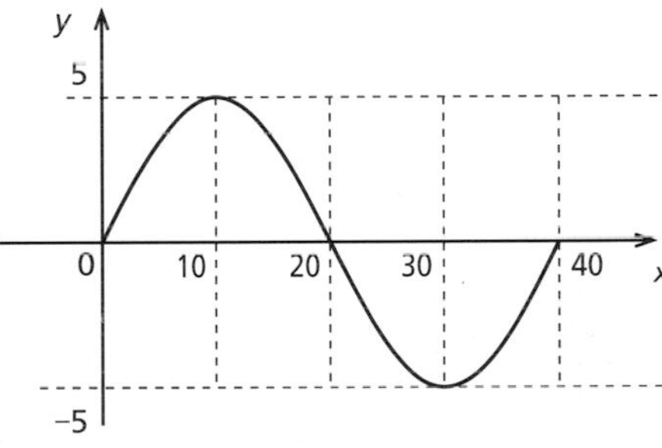

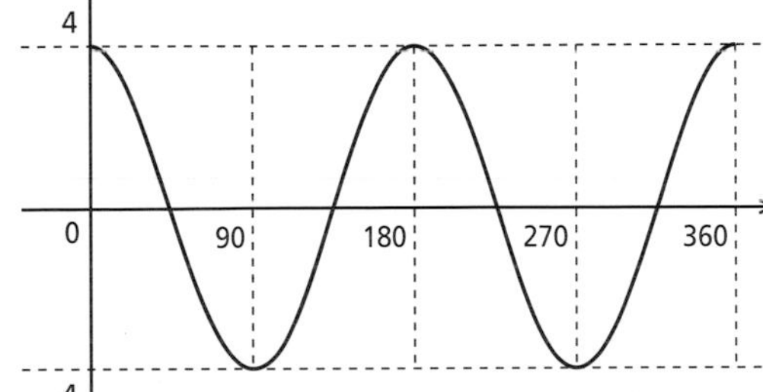

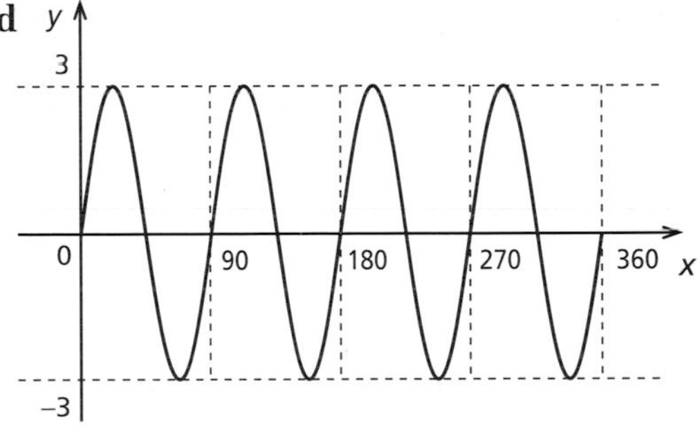

5 Write down the period of each trigonometric function in question **4**.

6 Find the two solutions of each of these equations for $0 \le x \le 360$:

a $\sin x° = 0.6$ **b** $\cos x° = 0.2$ **c** $\tan x° = 1.5$

d $\cos x° = -0.8$ **e** $\sin x° = -0.25$ **f** $\tan x° = -2.4$

7 Solve these equations for $0 \le x \le 360$:

a $\cos x° - 1 = 0$ **b** $\sin x° + 1 = 0$ **c** $2 \cos x° + 1 = 0$ **d** $\tan x° - 3 = 2$

e $3 \sin x° - 1 = 0$ **f** $4 \cos x° - 3 = 0$ **g** $5 \cos x° + 3 = 0$ **h** $3 \sin x° + 2 = 0$

8 **a** Sketch the graph of $y = 2 \cos \frac{1}{2}x°$ for $0 \le x \le 720$.

b From the graph solve:

(i) $2 \cos \frac{1}{2}x° = 0$ for $0 \le x \le 360$ **(ii)** $2 \cos \frac{1}{2}x° = 2$ for $0 \le x \le 720$.

c What is the period of $y = 2 \cos \frac{1}{2}x°$?

9 Sketch the graph of each trigonometric function for $0 \le x \le 360$:

a $f(x) = \cos(x + 90)°$ **b** $g(x) = \sin(x + 30)°$

c $h(x) = \sin(x - 30)°$ **d** $k(x) = \cos(x - 30)°$

10 Use the graphs in question **9** to help you solve these equations for $0 \le x \le 360$:

a $\cos(x + 90)° = 0$ **b** $\cos(x + 90)° = -1$ **c** $\sin(x + 30)° = 1$

d $\sin(x - 30)° = -1$ **e** $\cos(x - 30)° = -1$ **f** $\cos(x - 30)° = 1$

11 Simplify these trigonometric expressions:

a $\dfrac{1 - \cos^2 x°}{1 - \sin^2 x°}$ **b** $\dfrac{\sin^3 x° + \sin x° \cos^2 x°}{\cos x°}$

c $\dfrac{\tan x° \cos x°}{\sin x°}$ **d** $\dfrac{\sin A - \sin^3 A}{\cos^3 A}$

12 The wave motion of water in an experimental tank can be modelled by $y = 3 \sin 4x°$, where x m is the horizontal distance travelled from the edge of the tank and y m is the height of the wave.

a How high is the crest of a wave?

b What is the period of the wave?

c How high is the wave when it has travelled:

(i) 30 m **(ii)** 50 m from the edge of the tank?

13 A player's golf shot is modelled by $h = 10 \sin \frac{3}{4}x°$, where h m is the height of the ball and x m is the horizontal distance travelled by the ball. The model is only good for a certain range of values of x.

a What was the greatest height reached by the ball?

b What horizontal distance had it travelled at that point?

c How far from the golfer did the ball land?

d Where does the model break down?

14 A ball is hit with a tennis racquet. Its path is modelled by the equation $h = 12 \sin(x + 10)°$ for $0 \le x \le 170$.

h is the height of the ball in metres.

a How high did the ball go?

b What horizontal distance had it covered when it was at its greatest height?

c What was the total horizontal distance travelled by the ball before it landed?

d How far from the ground was the ball when it was hit by the racquet?

17 Calculations in a Social Context

Earning
Saving
National Insurance
Gross
Borrowing
Bonus
Tax
Spending
Credit
Commission
Net

STARTING POINTS

1 Match each term with the sentence which describes it.

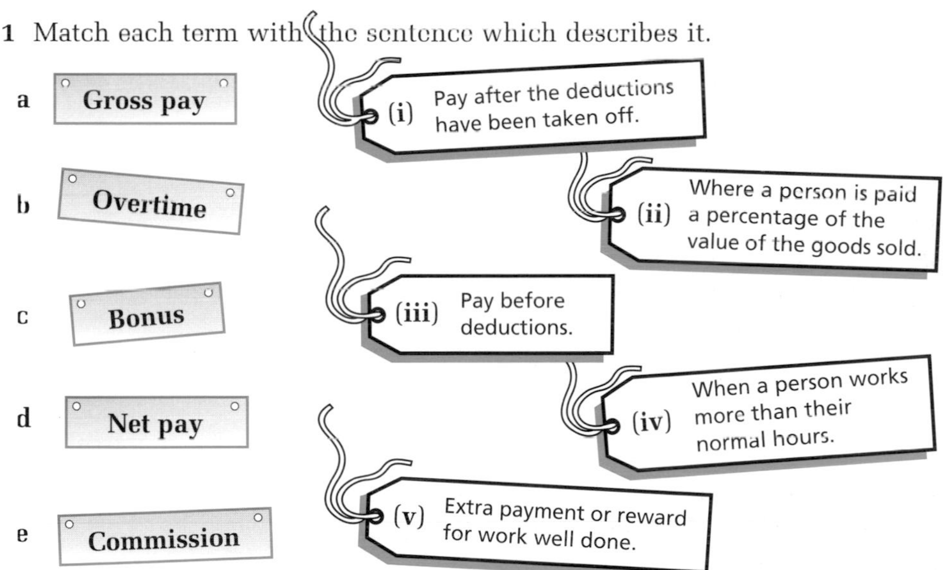
a Gross pay
b Overtime
c Bonus
d Net pay
e Commission
(i) Pay after the deductions have been taken off.
(ii) Where a person is paid a percentage of the value of the goods sold.
(iii) Pay before deductions.
(iv) When a person works more than their normal hours.
(v) Extra payment or reward for work well done.

2 Calculate: **(a)** 6% of £1020 **(b)** 2.5% of £19 740.

3 Kerry works 32 hours for £5 per hour and does 2 hours of overtime at double time. How much is her gross pay?

4 Express in minutes: **(a)** 0.5 hour **(b)** 0.25 hour **(c)** 0.75 hour.

5 Jamila's gross annual salary is £15 852. How much is her gross monthly salary?

6 Calum has a net annual pay of £12 292.80. What is his net weekly wage?

7 How many years are in **(a)** 36 months **(b)** 60 months?

8 Steve takes out a personal loan. The terms are £186 per month for 3 years. How much will Steve pay in total for the loan?

9 Chaz has a Europa Express credit card. The interest rate on purchases is 1.2% per month. One month his purchases totalled £1268.40. How much was he charged for interest?

Overtime

One way of earning more than a basic wage is to work overtime.
Not all jobs offer the opportunity of working overtime.
It is more common in jobs paid at an hourly rate rather than a fixed annual salary.

People can be paid overtime when they work at unsociable times such as at nights, weekends or holidays, or when they work more than their normal working day.

The most common rates are time and a half and double time but there are others.

F is the overtime factor.

Double time	$\times 2$
Time and a half	$\times 1.5$
Time and a quarter	$\times 1.25$

Basic pay is worked out by multiplying the basic rate by the number of hours worked at the basic rate. **Basic** $= B \times H$

Overtime can be worked out by multiplying the basic rate by the number of hours worked at overtime, then multiplying by the overtime factor. **Overtime** $= B \times H \times F$

Example Calculate 4 hours of overtime at time and a half if the basic rate of pay is £6 per hour.

$$6 \times 4 \times 1.5 = 36$$

Overtime pay = £36

EXERCISE 1

1 Calculate each of the following overtime payments.

	Basic hourly rate	Hours of overtime	Overtime factor	Overtime pay (£)
a	£5.00	3	Double time	
b	£4.00	5	Time and a half	
c	£7.00	3	Time and a half	
d	£6.00	4.5	Time and a quarter	
e	£3.40	4	Double time	
f	£4.80	6	Time and a half	
g	£10.00	4	Time and a half	
h	£5.40	8	Time and a quarter	
i	£4.50	2.25	Double time	
j	£4.95	3.75	Time and a third	

2 Katie is given a choice of overtime. She has been offered $2\frac{1}{2}$ hours work on Friday night at time and a third or 2 hours on Saturday morning at time and a half. Her basic rate of pay is £6.00 an hour. Which overtime offer would give her more money?

3 Here are some weekly wageslips. Find the total amount paid in each.

a

PAYMENTS			
DESCRIPTION	HOURS	RATE	AMOUNT
Basic	40	6.25	
Overtime	4	Double time	
Total			

b

PAYMENTS			
DESCRIPTION	HOURS	RATE	AMOUNT
Basic	38.75	6.80	
Overtime	3.5	Time and a half	
Total			

c

PAYMENTS			
DESCRIPTION	HOURS	RATE	AMOUNT
Basic	37	4.00	
Overtime	3.5	6.00	
Total			

d

PAYMENTS			
DESCRIPTION	HOURS	RATE	AMOUNT
Basic	39	5.50	
Overtime	3	8.25	
Total			

4 Andrew has a summer job in an electronics factory. He works a basic week of 35 hours at £4.50 per hour. One week he is asked to work on a Saturday morning from 7 to 11 o'clock at time and a third. How much is Andrew's gross pay this week?

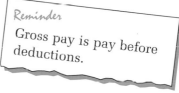

Reminder
Gross pay is pay before deductions.

5 Here are timesheets for three workers in a factory. They work a basic 7-hour day, Monday to Friday.

Overtime rates are:

Monday to Friday	time and a third
Saturday	time and a half
Sunday	double time

a

Name: **Jim Bond**	
	Hours
Mon	7 h
Tue	7 h
Wed	9 h
Thu	7 h
Fri	7 h
Sat	4 h
Sun	2 h

Jim's basic pay is £4.50 per hour.

b

Name: **Kerry Tate**	
	Hours
Mon	7 h
Tue	8 h
Wed	7 h
Thu	10 h
Fri	7 h
Sat	3 h
Sun	

Kerry's basic pay is £5.70 per hour.

c

Name: **Matt Wallace**	
	Hours
Mon	7 h
Tue	7 h
Wed	9 h
Thu	7 h
Fri	7 h
Sat	4 h
Sun	2 h

Matt's basic pay is £4.80 per hour.

Calculate each person's gross weekly wage.

Commission

Commission is a form of payment, usually a fixed percentage of the amount of goods sold.
It is an incentive scheme which encourages the sales staff to sell.

Example A salesperson is paid a basic pay of £600 per month plus 3% commission on all her sales. Her sales for one month amounted to £12 000. Calculate her gross pay for the month.

3% of 12 000 = 360
360 + 600 = 960

The salesperson earns £960 in the month.

EXERCISE 2

1 Ricky Gaunt is a car salesman. He earns £735 per month. One month he sells £19 600 worth of cars. He earns 2.5% commission.
Calculate: **a** his commission **b** his gross pay that month.

2 Ya Wing is a department manager. His basic monthly pay is £843. His rate of commission is 2.75%. His sales one month are £28 400.
Calculate his gross pay for the month.

3 The notes show how two sales executives did one month.

a Calculate the gross pay for each executive.
b Which executive earned more for their sales?
c Who earned the bigger gross pay?

4 Network selling is another way to earn commission from sales. It is usual to invite people to have parties in their homes where goods are displayed and sold. The network seller is paid commission on sales made.
Marjorie is a network seller of jewellery. For each party her commission is as follows.
If the sales are £500 or less she gets 25% commission.
If the sales are over £500 she gets 33% commission.
She keeps a record of her parties.

Date	Name/address	Total sales	Commission
23/07	Thom/Springbank	£460.20	
24/07	Hanna/Abbotseat	£348.70	
29/07	Gollan/Bramdean	£611.90	
02/08	Gaddis/Grovehouse	£704.50	

Calculate her commission for each party.

5 Helen Johnston makes a living by selling make-up. She invites people to have parties in their homes. She is paid the following per party.

Commission	Sales
20%	The first £300
25%	The next £200
35%	The rest

Example: £220 will attract 20% commission

Example: £400 will attract 20% of £300 plus 25% of £100

How much does Helen earn from a party if she sells:

a £100 **b** £450 **c** £610 worth of make-up?

Payslips

Wages and salaries are usually paid into a bank account of your choice. So that you may check your pay you are normally given a payslip or pay advice. This is a record of your earnings and deductions.

Gross pay – Deductions = Net pay

The main deductions are itemised below.

If your annual salary is above a set amount you *must* pay:

- **income tax** (a percentage of your salary). The percentage rate of tax and the amount you can earn before tax is set annually in the budget.
- **National Insurance** (a percentage of your salary, usually between 2% and 10%). This money goes towards the National Health Service and pensions.

You may choose to pay:

- **superannuation** (an extra pension scheme)
- **AVCs** (additional voluntary contributions towards a pension)
- **a union fee** (money you pay to be a member of a trades union)
- **a charity donation** (you may wish to pay towards a specific charity)
- **a social fund contribution** (some employees save each week towards social activities).

You may have to pay:

- **other deductions** (depending on circumstances).

Example Graham Payton has a holiday job in a supermarket. Here is one of his weekly payslips.

Pay Advice

Date	Tax code	Employee name
10/07/98	404L	**Payton, Graham**

Payments				Deductions	
Description	Hours	Rate	Amount	Description	Amount
Basic	34.75	4.00	139.00	Tax	12.20
				National Insurance	9.02
		Gross	139.00	Total deductions	21.22
				Net pay:	117.78

EXERCISE 3

1 Examine Graham's payslip carefully and answer the following questions.
  a What is his basic rate of pay?
  b Check that his hourly rate times his hours gives the amount earned.
  c Did he do any overtime?
  d How much income tax did he pay?
  e Check his total deductions are correct.
  f How is his net pay calculated? Check it is correct.

2 Here are the payslips for two other temporary workers at the supermarket. For each employee work out the values of A, B, C, D and E.

a

Date	Tax code	Employee name	
10/07/98	404L	**McMillan, Mark**	Pay Advice

Payments				Deductions	
Description	Hours	Rate	Amount	Description	Amount
Basic	28.5	4.00	**A**	Tax	14.30
Overtime	4	6.00	**B**	National Insurance	8.03
		Gross	**C**	Total deductions	**D**
				Net pay:	**E**

b

Date	Tax code	Employee name	
10/07/98	404L	**Sylvester, Kerry**	Pay Advice

Payments				Deductions	
Description	Hours	Rate	Amount	Description	Amount
Basic	35.00	4.50	**A**	Tax	18.40
Overtime	2.5	7.00	**B**	National Insurance	10.17
		Gross	**C**	Total deductions	**D**
				Net pay:	**E**

3 These wageslips give details of people's weekly wages and deductions. Calculate: **(i)** the gross wage **(ii)** the total deductions and **(iii)** the net wage for each.

a

Employee No. 00784		Month 04		
Basic Wage	Overtime	Bonus	Expenses	Gross Wage
£410.30	£54.60	£0.00	£0.00	
Income Tax	Nat. Ins.	Superannuation	Other	Total Deductions
£67.35	£17.48	£0.00	£1.20	
Name:	**Simon Potter**		Net Wage:	

b

Employee No. 00784		Month 04		
Basic Wage	Overtime	Bonus	Expenses	Gross Wage
£380.96	£0.00	£33.74	£43.84	
Income Tax	Nat. Ins.	Superannuation	Other	Total Deductions
£50.06	£15.44	£22.80	£0.00	
Name:	**Sheila Stencil**		Net Wage:	

4 Ned Findly is paid monthly. Here is his pay advice.

a Calculate: **(i)** his total deductions and **(ii)** his net pay.

Pay and Allowances	Amount (£)	Deductions	Amount (£)
SALARY	1776.25	TAX N.I. SUPERANN	272.65 131.88 106.58
TOTAL PAYMENTS		TOTAL DEDUCTIONS	
CUMULATIVE TOTALS	Taxable Gross 6747.99 Tax Deducted 1106.23 N.I. Contribution 533.58 Superannuation 426.31		NET PAYABLE on 28/11/97 by BACS

b The cumulative totals give a running total of how much he has earned and paid out since the start of the financial year. Calculate the total deductions so far.

5 This timesheet and payslip is for a factory worker who is on **flexitime**. (He can clock in and out when he wants, within limits.)

	In	Out	In	Out	No. of hours
Mon	8 am	12 noon	1 pm	5 pm	8
Tue	8.30 am	12 noon	1 pm	5 pm	7.5
Wed	8.30 am	12 noon	1 pm	5 pm	7.5
Thu	8 am	12 noon	1 pm	4 pm	7
Fri	7 am	12 noon	1 pm	2 pm	6
Sat	8 am	11.30 am			3.5
Sun	10 am	12 noon			2

Basic Pay: 35 hours at £6.90 = ...

Overtime:

(Mon to Sat) ... hours at time and a third = ...

(Sunday) ... hours at double time = ...

Gross Pay =

Deductions:

Income Tax = £53.91

National Insurance = £17.44

Union Dues = £6.00

Total Deductions =

Net Pay =

a Check that the number of hours entered are correct.

b How many hours did he work in total, Monday to Saturday?

c After working 35 hours Monday to Saturday the rest is overtime. How much Monday to Saturday overtime has he done?

d All work on a Sunday is overtime.
Calculate: **(i)** the worker's gross pay **(ii)** his total deductions **(iii)** his net pay.

Tax

We are allowed to earn some money free of tax. This amount is called our **allowance**. Whatever we earn more than our allowance is taxable.

Taxable income = Income – Allowances

There are many kinds of allowances but the main one is called **personal allowance**.

Example

Vincent Hanna earned £19 676 in the year 1997–98.
His allowances totalled £5272.
His taxable income = 19 676 − 5272 = 14 404.
He paid tax on £14 404 of his income.

14 404 − 4100 = 10 304 (less than 22 000)
20% of 4100 = 820
23% of 10 304 = 2369.92
total = 3189.92

He paid £3189.92 in tax that year.

Rates of tax (1997–98)
Taxable income is taxed at the following rates:
lower rate 20% on the first £4100
basic rate 23% on the next £22 000
higher rate 40% on the income over £26 100.

EXERCISE 4

1 Using the rates of tax shown above, calculate:
(i) the taxable income **(ii)** the tax due for each of the following people.

		Annual gross income (£)	Allowances (£)	Taxable income (£)	Tax due (£)
a	Ed McLean	15 234	4045		
b	Meg Bateman	18 720	3120		
c	Fadi Roy	35 421	5875		

2 Look at Vincent Hanna's salary and tax again.
We can divide the figures by **12** or **52** to show that:
(i) his monthly pay is £1639.67 and his monthly tax is £265.83
(ii) his weekly pay is £378.38 and his weekly tax is £61.34.

a For Ed McLean, calculate his gross weekly pay and weekly tax.
b For Meg Bateman, calculate her gross weekly pay and weekly tax.
c For Fadi Roy, calculate his gross monthly pay and his monthly tax.

3 Andy has a job as a hairdresser in a city salon. In a year he earns a basic wage of £12 619.80. He also earns £2000 in tips. He has a personal allowance of £4045.
Calculate:
a his gross annual income (pay plus tips)
b his taxable income
c his weekly gross wage
d his weekly tax.

4 Phil is a car salesman. Last year he had a basic gross of £21 985. He made £20 000 in sales and he was paid 2.2% commission on these sales. He is a married man and gets the higher personal allowance of £4045. Other allowances include union payments of £500, personal expenses of £320 and travelling expenses related to his job of £700.
a Calculate:
(i) his gross annual income **(ii)** his total allowances **(iii)** his taxable income.
b Phil pays tax at the rates given above.
Calculate: **(i)** the tax payable for the year **(ii)** his monthly tax.

Tax codes

If you work and pay tax you will have a tax code. A tax code is made up of numbers and a letter. It appears on notices from the Inland Revenue and on a P60 form from your employers. The *letter* in the code denotes whether you get the higher (H) or lower (L) personal allowance. The *number* is your total allowance divided by 10, ignoring any remainder.

Example 1

Peter Samuels is married and so gets the higher personal allowance.
This year his total allowances come to £6345. His tax code is therefore 634H.

Example 2

Tina Bryars is single and gets the lower personal allowance.
This year her total allowances come to £3129. Her tax code is therefore 312L.

EXERCISE 5

1 Work out the tax code for each person.

a Ed McLean (single), total allowances £4059
b Meg Bateman (single), total allowances £3998
c Peter Rally (married), total allowances £5612
d Meg Taylor (higher), total allowances £7112

2 Say what the following tax codes tell you about each person.

a 452H **b** 239L **c** 418H **d** 421L

3 Frank Maithers has a total income of £25 342 this year. His tax code is 564H.

a Estimate **(i)** his allowances **(ii)** his taxable income.
b If he is taxed at 24% for all of his taxable income, estimate his tax bill.

4 Repeat question **3** for these people.

a Geraldine Smith: income £12 782; tax code 342L; rate of tax 25%
b Usman Aslam: income £22 124; tax code 672H; rate of tax 30%
c Heather Jones: income £35 000; tax code 829L; rate of tax 24%

Borrowing and saving

Reminder

When working out interest on your calculator over several periods, errors due to rounding can build up. This can be avoided by making your calculator work to 2 decimal places.

Check your calculator manual on how to do this.
It may be FIX and TAB 2 or MODE 72.

The calculator displays 2 decimal places at each step but retains in its memory 8 to 10 decimal places and uses them in the next steps.

In the following sections it is assumed your calculator is set up in this way.

Example

Work out the interest on a loan of £500 over 12 months at a rate of 2.5% per month.
Note: at the end of a month you have 100% + 2.5% = 102.5% of the amount you had at the start of the month. (100 + 2.5) ÷ 100 = 1.025

Method 1

Set up your calculator constant facility to multiply by 1.025 (102.5%).
Type 500 (the initial amount).
Press '=' 12 times. Each time you press it the amount at the end of each month is displayed.
The final amount is £672.44.

Method 2

Enter $500 \times (1.025)^{12} =$
Check that this also gives £672.44.

Since you started with £500, the interest is £672.44 – £500 = £172.44.

EXERCISE 6

1 When the interest rate is 2.5% then the multiplier is (100 + 2.5) ÷ 100 = 1.025.
State the multiplier for the following rates:
a 10% **b** 5% **c** 3.5% **d** 1% **e** 0.5%.

2 Use method 1 to **(i)** calculate the interest for 12 months
(ii) record the amount after 6 months on the following:
a £600 at 3% per month **b** £1000 at 2.6% per month
c £100 at 1.8% per month.

3 Use method 2 to calculate the interest for 12 months on the following:
a £400 at 2.6% per month **b** £850 at 3.1% per month
c £670 at 1.1% per month.

4 Calculate 12 months' interest on £100 at the following rates:
a 3% per month **b** 1.5% per month
c 3.8% per month **d** 1.53% per month
e 0.8% per month **f** 2.21% per month

The rate of interest per month can be quite misleading. In all advertisements loan companies and banks must quote the **annual percentage rate (APR)**.

Example

If the monthly rate of interest is 1.53%, what is the annual percentage rate?
Consider £1 being borrowed for 1 year at 1.53% per month.

The amount due at the end of the year = $£1 \times (1.0153)^{12}$ = £1.20 to 2 d.p.
The interest is 20 pence. The APR is 20%.

5 Use the same method to work out the APR when the monthly rate of interest is:
a 0.8% **b** 2.21% **c** 1.17% **d** 1.39%.

Repayments

When a loan is made, regular and equal repayments are usually agreed. The size of these repayments depends on:

(i) how much is borrowed
(ii) the annual percentage rate (APR)
(iii) the time over which the loan is made.

The calculations involved are too complex for the average person and so tables are usually set up. This table shows the monthly repayments required for 12, 24, 36 or 48 months. The APR is given in the left-hand column.

APR on £1000	12 months	24 months	36 months	48 months
10	£87.72	£45.95	£32.07	£25.16
12	£88.56	£46.79	£32.92	£26.03
14	£89.40	£47.62	£33.78	£26.91
16	£90.23	£48.46	£34.63	£27.80
18	£91.05	£49.28	£35.49	£28.68
20	£91.86	£50.10	£36.34	£29.57
22	£92.66	£50.92	£37.19	£30.46
24	£93.45	£51.73	£38.04	£31.35
26	£94.24	£52.54	£38.88	£32.24
28	£95.02	£53.34	£39.73	£33.12
30	£95.79	£54.14	£40.57	£34.01

Example 1 £1000 is borrowed for 36 months at an APR of 26%.

The table shows us that £38.88 is paid each month.

Example 2 £3000 is borrowed for 24 months at an APR of 28%.

The table shows us that each £1000 costs £53.34.
So for £3000 we pay $3 \times 53.34 =$ £160.02 a month.

You will also be given the option of taking out a **loan protection policy** along with your loan. Paying a little extra each month can give you some security and peace of mind. In the event of illness, accident or redundancy your monthly repayments will be taken care of for a certain period of time. In the event of your death the loan will be fully repaid.

Monthly payments including loan protection.

APR on £1000	12 months	24 months	36 months	48 months
10	£93.86	£50.54	£36.23	£28.93
12	£94.76	£51.47	£37.20	£29.94
14	£95.66	£52.39	£38.17	£30.95
16	£96.54	£53.30	£39.14	£31.97
18	£97.42	£54.21	£40.10	£32.98
20	£98.29	£55.11	£41.06	£34.00
22	£99.14	£56.01	£42.02	£35.03
24	£99.99	£56.91	£42.98	£36.05
26	£100.83	£57.79	£43.94	£37.07
28	£101.67	£58.68	£44.89	£38.09
30	£102.49	£59.55	£45.85	£39.12

Example £2500 is borrowed. It is paid back over 24 months at an APR of 22%.
Loan protection is taken out.
Calculate: **a** the monthly repayments
b the total repayment
c the cost of the loan.

a From the table, £1000 costs £56.01 per month.
$2.5 \times 56.01 = 140.03$
So for £2500 we pay £140.03 per month.

b $140.03 \times 24 = 3360.72$
The total repayment over the term of the loan is £3360.72.

c $3360.72 - 2500 = 860.72$
The cost of the loan is £860.72.
Compare this with the cost if no protection is taken out.

EXERCISE 7

Use the above table and the one on page 273 in questions **1** to **6**.

1 Kenneth takes out a loan of £3500 payable over 12 months, without loan protection. The APR is 20%.
 a How much is the monthly repayment?
 b How much more is the same loan with loan protection?

2 Hari borrows £4000 over 36 months with loan protection. The APR is 24%.
 a How much is the monthly repayment?
 b What is the total amount repaid?
 c What is the cost of this loan?

3 Helen wants to borrow £3000 over 24 months when the APR is 18%.
 a What will it cost her a month without loan protection?
 b How much *more* will it cost her a month if she wants loan protection?

4 Compare the costs with and without loan protection for a loan of £4000 over 36 months at 26% APR.

5 Steven wants to take out a loan for a new kitchen. He wants a loan over 36 months with loan protection. He is offered terms at 24% APR. He wonders whether to borrow £3000 or £3500.
   a How much is his monthly repayment on (i) £3500 (ii) £3000?
   b How much more would he pay, in total, for the larger loan?
   c He decides on a loan of £3000. He has to pay an administrative fee of 1% of the loan. How much is the administrative fee?

6 Ruth needs a loan. She works out that the most she can afford to pay is £170 per month. She wants the biggest loan she can get over 2 years and doesn't want to take out protection.
   a How much can she borrow at 18% APR?
   b How much is the monthly premium?
   c She has to pay an administrative fee of 1% of the loan. How much is this fee?

7 Josie wants a conservatory added to her home. The architect says it will cost her £10 000. These are the two loan offers she looks at.

REGAL BANK Personal Loans

60 months 13.9% APR on Loans of £10 000

Loan amount (£)	Monthly repayment	Total to repay
10 000	268.77	

LOANSAFE Personal Loans

60 months	Amount of loan	Total paid	Monthly payment
APR 12.9%	£10 000		£263.88

   a How long is each loan for?
   b Work out the total repayment on each loan.
   c (i) Which monthly payment is cheaper?
      (ii) By how much?
   d If all else is equal, which loan should Josie take?

8 Study this loan table carefully and then answer the questions.

Loan amount	£2500 at 17.9% APR		£5000 at 14.9% APR		£8000 at 14.9% APR	
Repayment Term	Monthly Repayment	Total Repayment	Monthly Repayment	Total Repayment	Monthly Repayment	Total Repayment
12 months	244.55		482.03	5784.36	771.25	9255.00
36 months	101.52	3654.72	194.82		311.71	11 221.56
60 months		4287.60	137.49	8249.40	219.99	

   a How many years are in 60 months?
   b How much is the APR on a loan of £8000?
   c How much is the monthly repayment on a loan of £2500 over 36 months?
   d How much is the monthly repayment on a loan of £8000 over 12 months?
   e Calculate the total repayment on a loan of £5000 payable over 36 months.
   f What is the total repayment on a loan of £2500 payable over a year?
   g How much is the loan if the monthly repayment is £194.82 taken over 36 months?
   h How much more is the APR on a loan of £2500 than on a loan of £8000?
   i How much more is the monthly repayment on a loan of £5000 if it is repaid over 36 months rather than over 60 months?
   j How much would you be borrowing if the total repayment is £11 221.56?

Credit cards

Convenient

Cash in hand

Worldwide spending power

Credit cards can be used to pay for goods and services up to an agreed credit limit which depends on how much you earn and your circumstances. You can use your card to obtain cash advances from banks and cash dispensers at home and abroad. Account fees and interest charges vary from card to card.
Here are some examples.

	Europa Bank	Northern Gold	A1	Vantage
Annual fee	£10	No fee	£15	£10
Monthly rate of interest	2.2%	1.5%	1.67%	1.3%
Annual percentage rate (APR)	29.8%	19.5%	21.9%	16.7%
Minimum monthly repayment	£5 or 3%	£5 or 5%	£5 or 3%	£5 or 5%

Minimum monthly repayment: the percentage shown (of amount owing) or £5, whichever is the greater.
If you settle your account in full within 25 days of the statement date, you can obtain interest-free credit on purchases and balance transfers.

EXERCISE 8

1 a How much is the monthly rate of interest on an A1 card?

b You spend £500 one month using an A1 card. You do not settle the account in full.
What monthly rate of interest is charged?

c How much is the APR on a Europa Bank card?

d How much more is the APR on a Northern Gold card than on a Vantage card?

e Which is greater and by how much, £5 or 3% of £157?

f Which of the above cards gives the most favourable rate of monthly interest?

g Madge spends £135 on her Northern Gold card one month.

(i) What is her minimum repayment?

(ii) She is charged one month's interest on the rest. How much interest is this?

2 Here is a credit card comparison guide.

		Purchases		Cash advances	
Credit card	Annual fee	APR	Monthly interest rate	APR	Monthly interest rate
ABC Fortune	Nil	21.9%	1.66%	23.8%	1.8%
Gold Wise	£10	21.5%	1.63%	23.3%	1.76%
World Express	£20	20.9%	1.6%	22.8%	1.72%
Capitol Bank	£12	20.6%	1.57%	22.5%	1.7%

This table lists only some of the features of the cards named.
The way in which interest is calculated varies from card to card.

a How much more is the APR for cash advances than for purchases with a Capitol Bank card?

b How much is the APR for cash advances with a Gold Wise card?

c How much interest would you be charged one month if you have £1500 owing for cash advances on a Gold Wise card?

3 Mary uses her World Express card for some purchases. She buys a new duvet and curtains for her bedroom The bill comes to £215. She pays with her card.
How much is she charged for interest that month on this money?

4 Harry Peterson used his ABC Fortune card to buy material worth £244.67.

a Calculate the interest due at the end of the month.

b What does he owe, in total, at the end of the month?

c He is asked to make a minimum payment of 5% of this bill. How much is this?

5 Here is part of Melissa's monthly account from Gold Wise. Calculate the missing amounts.

Purchases	£		
Frazers	167.50	Monthly interest at 1.63%	= b
Gulp	39.60	Total amount due	= c
Saxony	89.99	Minimum monthly repayment	= 3% of total amount due
Scot Travel	54.80		
Total	a		= £ d

Payment is due by 21 09 99.
Payment can be sent direct or through a bank account.

6 Phil has used his World Express Card. Here is his monthly statement. Calculate the missing amounts.

Cash advances	£		
01 09 99	50	Monthly interest at b %	= c
10 09 99	30	Total amount due	= d
14 09 99	60	Minimum monthly repayment	= 3% of total amount due
18 09 99	25		
Total	a		= £ e

Payment is due by 21 09 99.
Payment can be sent direct or through a bank account.

7 Mohini is going to New York on holiday. She pays for her flight with her ABC Fortune card. It costs £540.99. This is the only item on her monthly bill. She pays the total amount due after 30 days.
Including one month's interest, how much does she pay?

CHAPTER 17 REVIEW

1 Dave is saving for his holidays. He works 2 hours of overtime on Friday night at time and a third, and 3 and a half hours on Saturday morning at time and a half. If his basic rate of pay is £5.70 per hour, how much is he paid for his overtime?

2 Calculate the total gross amount paid on this weekly payslip.

PAYMENTS			
DESCRIPTION	HOURS	RATE	AMOUNT
Basic	39	7.00	
Overtime	3.5	Time and a half	
Total			

3 Tessa Hendry is the manager of the children's clothes department in a large department store. She is paid commission on all her sales. Here is part of her salary slip for one month.

Pay			Amount (£)
Salary			905
Commission	Percentage rate 2.2%	Sales (£) 20 400	a
Total 31/08/97	Hendry, Tessa		b

Calculate: **a** her commission for that month **b** her total monthly gross pay.

4 Bruce is an apprentice joiner. Here is his payslip for one week.
Calculate the missing entries.

Payments				Deductions	
Description	Hours	Rate	Amount	Description	Amount
Basic	37	4.50	a	Tax	20.40
Overtime	2.5	6.75	b	National Insurance	13.17
	Total		c	Total	d
Date	Tax code	Employee name		Net pay:	e
10/07/98	305L	Sylvester, Bruce			

5 Stan Brown is a garage mechanic. He is single and has an annual gross income of £16 785. His allowances for the year are £4045. He pays tax at the following rates: 20% on the first £4000, 25% on the rest.
Calculate:

a his taxable income
b the amount of tax he pays in a year
c his net annual pay
d his net weekly pay
e his tax code.

6 **a** Sue Halley gets the higher personal allowance.
Her total allowances come to £6193.
What is her tax code?

b Ben Carrington's tax code is 712L. Describe, as best you can, his allowances.

7 Here is a loan table.

Loan amount	£2000 at 16.7% APR		£5000 at 15.9% APR		£8000 at 14.8% APR	
Repayment Term	Monthly Repayment	Total Repayment	Monthly Repayment	Total Repayment	Monthly Repayment	Total Repayment
12 months	181.08	(i)	451.01	5412.12	718.00	(iii)
36 months	69.92	2517.12	173.03	(ii)	(iv)	9831.96

a Study it carefully and calculate the missing amounts.
b On a loan of £8000 how much is the APR?
c How much more is the monthly repayment on a loan of £5000 if it is repaid over 12 months rather than 36 months?
d You take out a loan. The total repayment is £6229.08.
(i) How much are you borrowing?
(ii) Over what period of time is the loan taken?

8 Here are some details of Liz Harper's credit card.
Here is a copy of her monthly account from Trust Card.
Calculate the missing amounts.

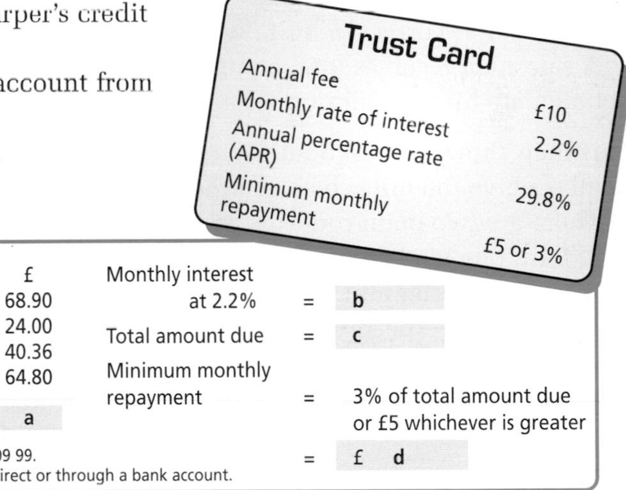

Purchases	£			
D & E	68.90	Monthly interest at 2.2%	=	b
Grape	24.00	Total amount due	=	c
A.B. Smith	40.36	Minimum monthly repayment	=	3% of total amount due or £5 whichever is greater
Scot Travel	64.80			
Total	a		=	£ d

Payment is due by 21 09 99.
Payment can be sent direct or through a bank account.

18 Logic Diagrams

STARTING POINTS

1 Here is an uncompleted bill for some art materials.

	A	B	C	D	E	F
1	Item	Price (£)	Number	Cost (£)	VAT at 17.5% (£)	Cost inc VAT (£)
2	A4 paper	2.53	3	7.59	1.33	8.92
3	Finetip pen	1.49	10			
4	Sable brush	2.07	5			

a The word 'Item' is in box A1.
When completed, what is in box: **(i)** A3 **(ii)** D3 **(iii)** E3 **(iv)** F3?

b Complete row 4 of the table.

c Find the total cost of the bill (including VAT).

2 **a** Calculate the 'average' (mean) of 26.7, 83.4, 21.5, 26.4, 32.7 and 55.9.

b Two paintings have dimensions 1.3 m × 0.9 m and 1.5 m × 0.8 m.
Which has the greater area and by how much?

c $V = \pi r^2 h$ gives the volume, V cm^3, of a cylinder where r cm is the radius of the base and h cm is the height.
Calculate V, correct to 3 s.f., when $r = 2.6$ cm and $h = 10.2$ cm.

d A salesman receives 8% commission on all sales over £10 000 each month.
Calculate his commission for a month when his sales were £23 000.

3 This map shows part of South Ayrshire. The numbers give the miles between the places.

a There are two main routes from Ballantrae to Barr, one via Penkill and one via Colmonell. Which is shorter and by how much?

b At an average speed of 36 mph how long would it take to travel from Girvan to Barrhill?

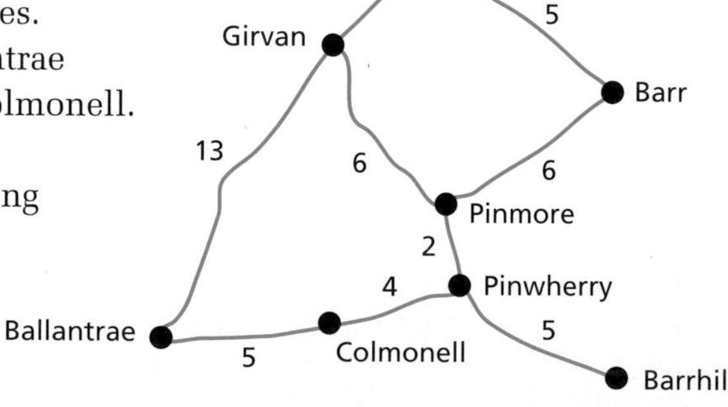

4

	Fife Ness	Peterhead	Fraserburgh	Banff	Buckie
Peterhead	78				
Fraserburgh	94	16			
Banff	111	33	18		
Buckie	124	46	31	15	
Lossiemouth	134	56	41	25	11

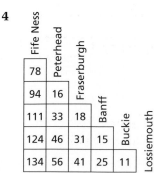

Look at this distance table for sea routes (distances are in nautical miles).
The distance from Peterhead to Banff is 33 miles.

a Give the distance from Fife Ness to Buckie.

b A boat travels from Lossiemouth stopping at Banff and Peterhead on its way to Fife Ness. How far did it travel?

Spreadsheets

A spreadsheet is open on a computer. The display shows a grid. Each box in the grid is called a **cell**.

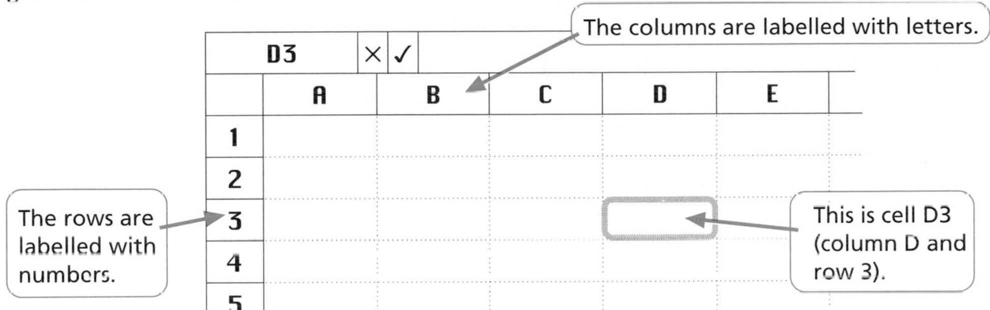

The columns are labelled with letters.
D3
A
B
C
D
E
1
2
3
4
5
The rows are labelled with numbers.
This is cell D3 (column D and row 3).

When the pointer (usually shaped ✥ in a spreadsheet) is over cell B2 and clicked,

B2	× ✓		
	A	B	C
1			
2			

the cell B2 is selected.

Any typing done will appear in the Edit bar at the top of the spreadsheet.

B2	× ✓ any typing		
	A	B	C
1			
2			

B3	× ✓		
	A	B	C
1			
2		any typing	
3			

Pressing the 'Return' key makes the typing appear in cell B2. The highlighted cell moves down to B3.

Pressing the 'Tab' key instead makes the highlighted cell move to the right to C2.

C2	× ✓		
	A	B	C
1			
2		any typing	

B2	× ✓		
	A	B	C
1			
2		any typing	

Clicking the tick in the Edit bar keeps the highlighting at B2.

EXERCISE 1

B3	× ✓	51.26		
	A	**B**	**C**	**D**
1	Year	Wage	Hours	Price index
2	0	£40.19	46	100
3	1	£51.26	46	115
4	2	£62.80	45	127
5	3	£75.12	44	133
6	4	£79.33	44	165

1 a Name the cell containing:
(i) 'Year'
(ii) 45
(iii) 'Hours'.

b Which cell is selected?

c 'Return' is pressed.
(i) Which cell is selected?
(ii) What will appear in the Edit bar?

d If cell C5 is selected and 'Tab' is pressed, what will appear in the Edit bar?

2 Which cell is selected after:
(i) 'Return'
(ii) 'Tab' is pressed for these spreadsheets?

a (cell A2 selected)

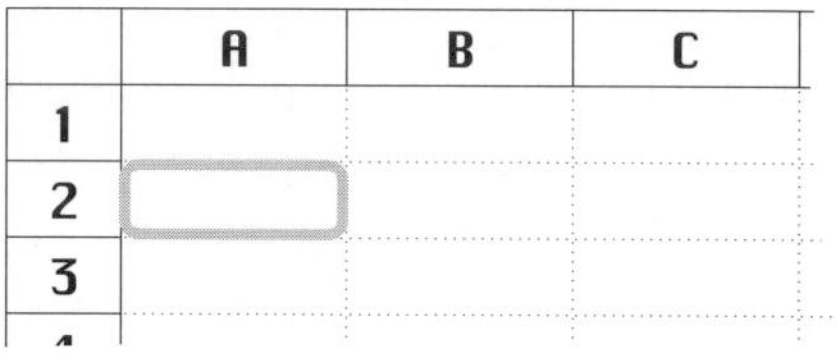

	A	B	C
1			
2	▭		
3			

b (cell C1 selected)

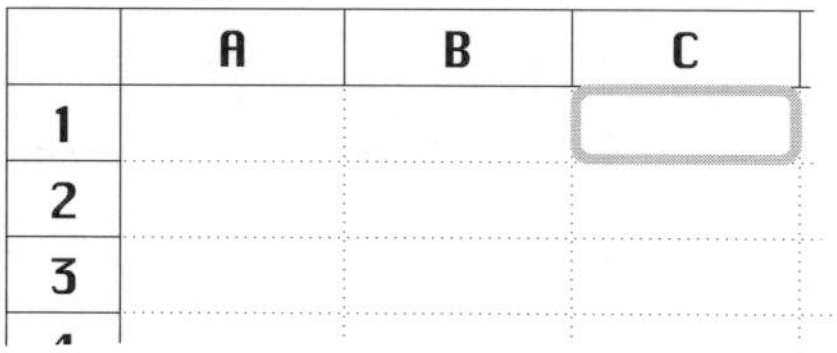

	A	B	C
1			▭
2			
3			

c (cell C3 selected)

	A	B	C
1			
2			
3			▭

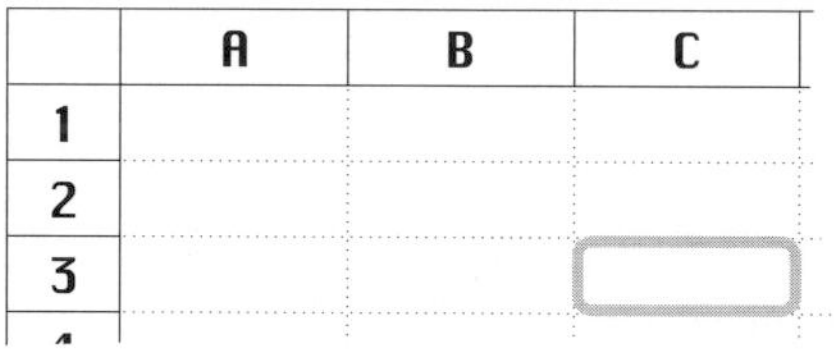

3 Look at these Edit bars.

a	D5	× ✓	135
b	B3	× ✓	Peter
c	D7	× ✓	= D8 + C4
d	A3	× ✓	A15

For each say:
(i) which cell is selected at the moment
(ii) which cell will be selected if 'Return' is pressed
(iii) which cell will be selected if 'Tab' is pressed.

4 If you are working at the computer then open a new spreadsheet page.

a These Edit bars tell you which cells to select and what to type.
After each one press 'Return' or 'Tab' to enter the typing into the cell.

(i)	A1	× ✓	Round	(ii)	A2	× ✓	Score
(iii)	B1	× ✓	1	(iv)	B2	× ✓	76
(v)	C1	× ✓	2	(vi)	C2	× ✓	85
(vii)	D1	× ✓	3	(viii)	D2	× ✓	72
(ix)	E1	× ✓	4	(x)	E2	× ✓	73

b You should have a spreadsheet like this:

	A	B	C	D	E
1	Round	1	2	3	4
2	Score	76	85	72	73

It gives golf scores over 4 rounds.
(i) Which round is the best? **(ii)** Which is the worst?
(iii) What is the average score over the 4 rounds?

Challenge

You can select a cell, then go to Format menu and choose Alignment with option Centre. This alters the way the typing is displayed in the cell. There are other options in the Format menu. Alter the format of cells in your spreadsheet to improve the presentation of the information.

	A	B
1	Ian	Aligned
2	135	right
3	135	left
4	135	centre

5 Each arrow key [↓] [→] [←] [↑] moves the highlighted cell in the direction of the arrow. Name the next selected cell when:

a C2 is highlighted and [↑] is pressed **b** B2 is highlighted and [→] is pressed

c A2 is highlighted and [↓] is pressed **d** E5 is highlighted and [←] is pressed.

6 This spreadsheet gives the monthly sales, in thousands of litres, of petrol sold at a petrol station.

	A	B	C	D	E
1		Jan	Feb	Mar	Apr
2	1997	12.2	13.6	15.2	14.9
3	1998	13.6	14.2	15.6	15.2
4	Increase	1.4			

It has been set up to examine how sales have increased from 1997 to 1998. The entry in cell B4 is 1.4. The January increase is 1400 litres.

a What number should appear in cell
(i) C4
(ii) D4
(iii) E4?

b The data in cell B3 is wrong. It should read 14.6. To overwrite the 13.6 entry:
- select B3
- type 14.6
- press 'Tab'.

The entry in B4 will now be wrong. What should it be?

c If you are at the computer:
(i) make up the spreadsheet
(ii) make the corrections
(iii) experiment with the Format menu to make your spreadsheet look like this:

F5 × ✓

	A	B	C	D	E
1		Jan	Feb	Mar	Apr
2	*1997*	12.2	13.6	15.2	14.9
3	*1998*	14.6	14.2	15.6	15.2
4	*Increase*	2.4			

7 This spreadsheet shows the profit or loss that will be made at a disco for various numbers of tickets sold.

	A	B	C	D	E
1	Tickets sold	Income (£)	Expenses (£)	Profit (£)	Result
2	0	0	80	-80	Loss
3	10	50	100	-50	Loss
4	20	100	120	-20	Loss
5	30	150	140	10	Profit
6	40		160		

Examine the spreadsheet.

a What is the income from one ticket?

b What entry should be made in cell **(i)** B6 **(ii)** D6 **(iii)** E6?

c The entry in cell C6 is incorrect. It should be 180.
Describe the steps you have to take to correct it.

d If you are at the computer:
(i) make the spreadsheet
(ii) make the corrections.

e Experiment with the Format menu, especially the 'number' option (fixed precision 2) to make your spreadsheet look like this:

	A	B	C	D	E
1	Tickets sold	Income (£)	Expenses (£)	Profit (£)	Result
2	0	0.00	80.00	-80	Loss
3	10	50.00	100.00	-50	Loss
4	20	100.00	120.00	-20	Loss
5	30	150.00	140.00	10.00	Profit
6	40		180.00		

Formatting cells

The number 12.345 has been entered in each cell in the A column.
The Format menu allows you to pick how the number should be displayed.
If you choose 'fixed' then you should also choose 'precision', the number of decimal places you want fixed.
If you choose 'currency' then a £ sign appears (*do not type it in*) and the precision is fixed at 2 automatically.
To format a cell or block of cells you must first select them by dragging.
Try to format the cells to make your spreadsheets look professional.

A1	×✓	Useful formats	
	A	B	C
1		Format	Precision
2	12.345	general	
3	12	fixed	0
4	12.3	fixed	1
5	12.35	fixed	2
6	12.345	fixed	3
7	£12.35	currency	2 forced
8	1235%	per cent	0 forced

Entering formulae

This spreadsheet calculates the perimeter of different-sized rectangles.
Cell C2 is selected. It contains a formula which you can see in the Edit bar.

C2	×✓	= 2*(A2 + B2)	
	A	B	C
1	Length	Breadth	Perimeter
2	5	6	22
3	7.2	3	20.4
4	4	2.7	13.4
5	1	0.5	3

This may be entered by following these steps.

- Select cell C2
- Type = 2*(— Pressing '=' tells the computer you are entering a formula.
- Click on A2 — A2 becomes a variable in the formula.
- Type + — + (add); – (subtract); * (multiply); / (divide).
- Click on B2 — B2 becomes a variable in the formula.
- Type)
- Press 'Return' or click the tick in the Edit bar.

Cell C2 contains the formula = 2*(A2 + B2)
but what shows is '22', the value of the formula when A2 holds 5 and B2 holds 6.

Note: In cell C3 the formula becomes = 2*(A3 + B3) (what shows is 20.4)
In cell C4 the formula becomes = 2*(A4 + B4) (what shows is 13.4)
In cell C5 the formula becomes = 2*(A5 + B5) (what shows is 3).

EXERCISE 2

1 a In the above spreadsheet A1 contains a label, A2 contains data and C2 contains a formula. Describe the contents of: **(i)** B1 **(ii)** C3 **(iii)** A4.

b If this spreadsheet were to be continued for two more rows, what formula would be in cell: **(i)** C6 **(ii)** C7?

2 Look again at the last spreadsheet on the previous page.

a If the data in A2 were altered to read 10, the entry in C2 would change. To what?

b The spreadsheet is altered to display the perimeter of rectangles with the following dimensions: 2.5 cm × 12 cm; 3.5 cm × 10 cm; 8.4 cm × 0.9 cm; 26.2 cm × 31.3 cm. Write down the corresponding entries in column C.

3 Often we need the sum of a collection of cells.
Here are the absentee figures over one week for first, second and third year classes.

G2	× ✓	= B2 + C2 + D2 + E2 + F2				
	A	B	C	D	E	F	G
1	Year	Monday	Tuesday	Wednesday	Thursday	Friday	Weekly total
2	*1st*	25	12	8	7	15	
3	*2nd*	12	11	11	10	16	
4	*3rd*	14	15	20	23	39	
5	*Total*	51	38	39	40	70	

a Cell G2 contains the formula = B2 + C2 + D2 + E2 + F2, the weekly total of first year absences. What value will appear in cell G2?

b What formula will be in: **(i)** G3 **(ii)** G4?

c What formula could be in cell G5?

4 We can make use of the = SUM( ) formula, as shown in these examples.

Example 1 To find the first year weekly total:

G2	× ✓	= SUM(B2..F2					
	A	B	C	D	E	F	G
1	Year	Monday	Tuesday	Wednesday	Thursday	Friday	Weekly total
2	*1st*	25	12	8	7	15	

- select G2
- type = SUM(
- hold down the button on the mouse and drag the pointer from B2 to F2
- type)
- press 'Return'.

Check the formula reads = SUM(B2..F2).

Example 2 To find the Monday total:

G2	× ✓	= SUM(B2..B4	
	A	B	C
1	Year	Monday	Tuesday
2	*1st*	25	12
3	*2nd*	12	11
4	*3rd*	14	15
5	*Total*		38

- select B5
- type = SUM(
- hold down the button on the mouse and drag the pointer from B2 to B4
- type)
- press 'Return'.

Check the formula reads = SUM(B2..B4).

Example 3 To put the grand total for the week in cell G5:

G5	× ✓	= SUM(B2..F4					
	A	B	C	D	E	F	G
1	Year	Monday	Tuesday	Wednesday	Thursday	Friday	Weekly total
2	*1st*	25	12	8	7	15	67
3	*2nd*	12	11	11	10	16	60
4	*3rd*	14	15	20	23	39	111
5	*Total*	51	38	39	40	70	238

- select G5
- type = SUM(
- drag the pointer from B2 to F4
- type)
- press 'Return'.

Check the formula reads = SUM(B2..F4).

a By this method B5 contains the formula = SUM(B2..B4).
What formula is in: **(i)** C5 **(ii)** E5?

b G2 contains the formula = SUM(B2..F2).
What formula is in: **(i)** G3 **(ii)** G4?

5 This spreadsheet calculates the circumference and area of circles with different radii. **PI( )** is used for π.

B2	× ✓	= 2*PI()*A2	
	A	B	C
1	Radius	Circumference	Area
2	1.2	7.54	4.52
3	1.3	8.17	5.31
4	1.4	8.80	6.16
5	1.5	9.42	7.07

Cells B2 to C5 are formatted for 'fixed precision 2'.
(B2 to C5 means the block of cells defined by B2 as the top left-hand cell and C5 the bottom right-hand cell.)

a Write down the formula in: **(i)** B3 **(ii)** B4 **(iii)** C2 **(iv)** C3.

b If you are at the computer, construct the above spreadsheet.
Use your spreadsheet to help you search for the radius (to 3 s.f.) of a circle with area 10 cm^2.

Reminder
If you are at a computer you should construct each spreadsheet.

6 This spreadsheet calculates the discount and sale price of items of furniture. Cells B2 to D4 have been formatted for currency.

C2	× ✓	= B2/3		
	A	B	C	D
1	Item	*Original price*	*Discount*	*Sale price*
2	Drawers	£234.00	£78.00	£156.00
3	Table	£312.00		
4	Chair	£79.00		

a Column C calculates the discount. C2 contains = B2/3
What formula is entered in: **(i)** C3 **(ii)** C4?

b The sale price is the original price less the discount.
What formula is entered in: **(i)** D2 **(ii)** D3 **(iii)** D4?

7 This spreadsheet to calculate the electricity bill contains only three pieces of data: the two meter readings and the price per unit, 15.47 pence.

	A	B	C	D
1		Electricity Bill		
2	*Meter Readings*			
3	Previous	Present	Units used	Price per unit
4	12729	12995	266	15.47
5			Sub total	£41.15
6			VAT at 8%	£3.29
7			Total bill	£44.44

Work out the four formulae used.

Copying and pasting formulae

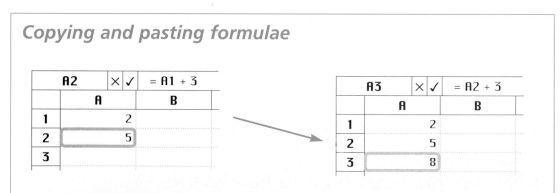

A2	× ✓	= A1 + 3
	A	B
1	2	
2	5	
3		

A3	× ✓	= A2 + 3
	A	B
1	2	
2	5	
3	8	

The piece of data '2' has been entered in A1.
The formula = A1 + 3 has been entered in A2.

- With A2 selected, chose 'copy' from the Edit menu.
- Select A3 and choose 'paste' from the Edit menu.

A copy of the formula is copied from cell A2 to A3.
Note, however, that it has altered from = A1 + 3 to = A2 + 3.

Here is a quick way to paste a formula into a block of cells.

A3	× ✓	= A2 + 3
	A	B
1	2	
2	5	
3	8	
4		
5		
6		
7		
8		
9		
10		

- Select the block, having the cell with the desired formula as the top cell.
- Select 'fill down' from the Calculate menu.
- 'Fill right' can be used in a similar manner.

A3	× ✓	= A2 + 3
	A	B
1	2	
2	5	
3	8	
4	11	
5	14	
6	17	
7	20	
8	23	
9	26	
10	29	

EXERCISE 3

1 This spreadsheet calculates the volume of cylinders using the formula $V = \pi r^2 h$.
A2 and B2 contain the numbers 1 and 5 respectively.
A3 contains the formula = A2 + 0.1.

A3	× ✓	= A2 + 0.1	
	A	B	C
1	Radius	Height	Volume
2	1	5	15.71
3	1.1		
4			

a Cells A3 to A10 are selected and 'fill down' is chosen.
   (i) What formula is contained in A10?
   (ii) What number is displayed in A10?
b B2 to B10 are selected and 'fill down' is chosen. What is the result?
c Write down the formula used in cell C2.
d Describe the formatting used for cell C2.
e Construct the spreadsheet to calculate the volumes of cylinders of height 5 cm with radius from 1 cm to 1.8 cm in steps of 0.1 cm.

2 This spreadsheet contains a different number pattern in each column.

E11				
	A	B	C	D
1	3	30	256	1
2	6	28	128	3
3	12	26	64	7
4	24	24	32	15
5	48	22	16	31
6	96	20	8	63
7	192	18	4	127
8	384	16	2	255
9	768	14	1	511
10	1536	12	0.5	1023

a What formula has been put into A2 and 'filled down' to create pattern A?

b Answer this question for: **(i)** B2 **(ii)** C2 **(iii)** D2.

3 Here are some useful functions:

SQRT(A2) … the square root of A2

A2^3 … A2 raised to the power 3.

Row 2 in this spreadsheet contains numbers. All other cells in subsequent rows contain formulae.

Write down the formula in cell:

a A6 **b** B4

c C5 **d** D3.

E10				
	A	B	C	D
1	Number	Square	Square Root	Cube
2	1	1	1	1
3	2	4	1.41	8
4	3	9	1.73	27
5	4	16	2.00	64
6	5	25	2.24	125
7	6	36	2.45	216
8	7	49	2.65	343
9	8	64	2.83	512
10	9	81	3.00	729

4

	A	B	C
1	x	x^2 - 4x	3x^2 - 2x + 1
2	-4	32	57
3	-3	21	34
4	-2	12	17
5	-1	5	6
6	0	0	1
7	1	-3	2
8	2	-4	9
9	3	-3	22
10	4	0	41

In this spreadsheet a couple of quadratic functions have been tabulated.

a What formulae have been entered in:
(i) B2 **(ii)** C2?
The headings in B1 and C1 should help.

b By looking at the spreadsheet, solve the equation $x^2 - 4x = 0$.

5 A manufacturer makes juice cartons. Each carton has a square base. The volume of a carton is the area of the base times the height. The makers want the carton to have a height of 7 cm and a volume of 1000 cm^3.
This spreadsheet is set up to work out the volume for different bases.

	A	B	C	D
1	Width	Area of base	Height	Volume
2	1	1	7	7

a A2 contains 1.
A3 contains = A2 + 1.
A3 is copied down to row 10.
What happens in column A?

b B2 contains = A2*A2.
B2 is copied down to row 10.
(i) What formula is in B7?
(ii) What value appears in B5?

c C2 contains 7.
C2 is copied down to row 10.
Comment on what happens.

d D2 contains = B2*C2.
D2 is copied to row 10.
(i) What is the formula in D6?
(ii) What is the value in D10?

e Check that row 10 works out as shown.

8	7	49	7	343
9	8	64	7	448
10	9	81	7	567

We have found a carton with a volume of 567 cm^3.
We want 1000 cm^3. We must go further.

f Copy row 10 by dragging.
Paste it into rows 11 to 14 by dragging.

11	10	100	7	700
12	11	121	7	847
13	12	144	7	1008
14	13	169	7	1183

(i) What is the first row with a volume greater than 1000 cm^3?
(ii) What width of base must the manufacturer use?

6

	A	B
1	$C = n^2 - 24n + 152$	
2	Workers (n)	Cost (C) £1000s
3	1	129
4	2	108
5	3	89
6	4	72
7	5	57
8	6	44
9	7	33

The cost C, measured in thousand pounds, of building a house depends on n, the number of workers employed, and is given by $C = n^2 - 24n + 152$.

a Create a spreadsheet that calculates this cost.

b Use your spreadsheet to determine the ideal number of workers to employ to keep the costs to a minimum.

Finding the mean on a spreadsheet

A spreadsheet uses the term AVERAGE for the mean.
= AVERAGE(D2..D6) is a formula for the mean of the numbers from D2 to D6.

EXERCISE 4

If you are at a computer you should construct each spreadsheet.

1 This spreadsheet gives the marks of five students over two tests.

B7 ✕ ✓ = AVERAGE(B2..B6)

	A	B	C	D
1		Test 1	Test 2	Total
2	Yasmin	23	47	70
3	Siobhan	43	49	92
4	Michael	37	38	75
5	Peter	31	36	67
6	John	15	12	27
7	Mean	29.8	36.4	66.2

a What formula goes into cell D2 to work out Yasmin's total?

b The formula is copied into cells D3 to D6. What formula is in cell D6?

c Cell B7 holds the formula for calculating the mean mark of test 1, namely = AVERAGE(B2..B6).

(i) What formula goes into C7 to do a similar job for test 2?

(ii) What formula goes into D7 to calculate the mean of column D?

2 This spreadsheet shows the amount due on a £100 loan with interest accumulating at 2% per month.

C15 ✕ ✓ = AVERAGE(C3..C14)

	A	B	C
1	Month	Amount owed	Interest in month
2	Jan	£100.00	
3	Feb	£102.00	£2.00
4	Mar	£104.04	£2.04
5	Apr	£106.12	£2.08
6	May	£108.24	£2.12
7	Jun	£110.41	£2.16
8	Jul	£112.62	£2.21
9	Aug	£114.87	£2.25
10	Sep	£117.17	£2.30
11	Oct	£119.51	£2.34
12	Nov	£121.90	£2.39
13	Dec	£124.34	£2.44
14	Jan	£126.82	£2.49
15	APR	26.82	£2.24

a Write down the formula that is entered in cell B3 and 'filled down' column B. The cells in column B are formatted for currency.

b The yearly rate, or APR, is therefore 26.82%. What formula goes into B15 to calculate this rate?

c A third column is added to calculate the extra interest due each month. What formula is entered in C3 and 'filled down' the column?

d In cell C15 the AVERAGE formula is used to calculate the mean interest per month. Find this value.

3 Using a spreadsheet similar to the one in question **2** above, find
(i) the APR **(ii)** the mean interest per month for a loan of:

a £500 at 1.6% per month for a year **b** £1500 at 1.4% per month for a year

c £12 000 at 0.9% per month for a year.

Graphs in spreadsheets

All spreadsheet packages can display data graphically.

Example

This spreadsheet shows the numbers of different coloured pencils in stock in a shop.

Highlight cells A1 to B5, then select the Chart menu.

You will usually have a wide choice of possible charts:

	A	B
1	Colour	Amount
2	Red	260
3	Green	150
4	Blue	312
5	Black	560

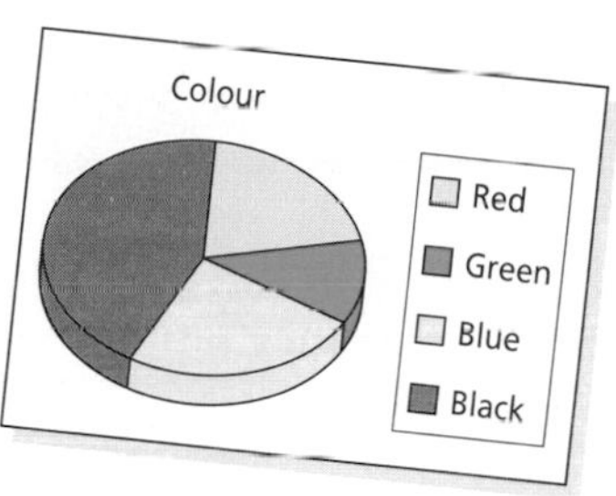

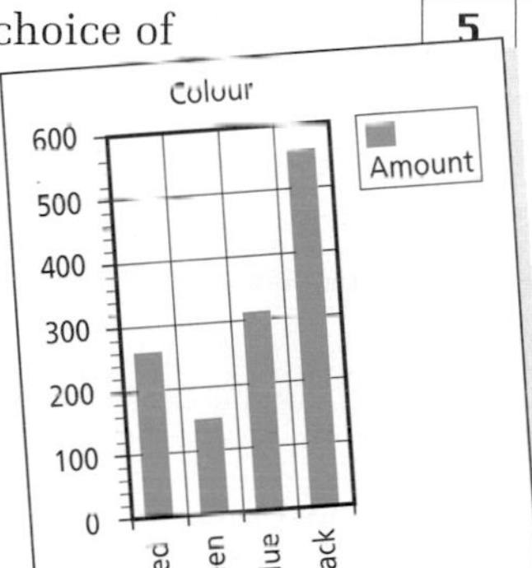

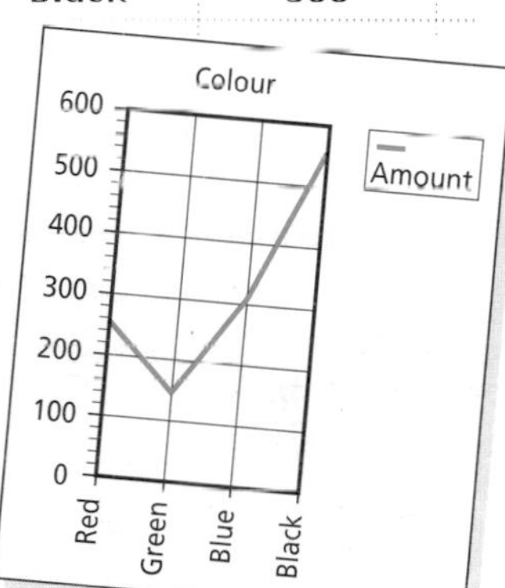

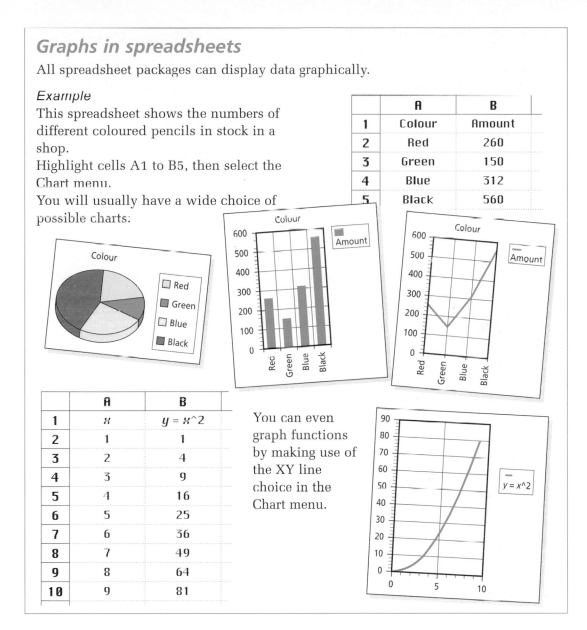

	A	B
1	x	$y = x$^2
2	1	1
3	2	4
4	3	9
5	4	16
6	5	25
7	6	36
8	7	49
9	8	64
10	9	81

You can even graph functions by making use of the XY line choice in the Chart menu.

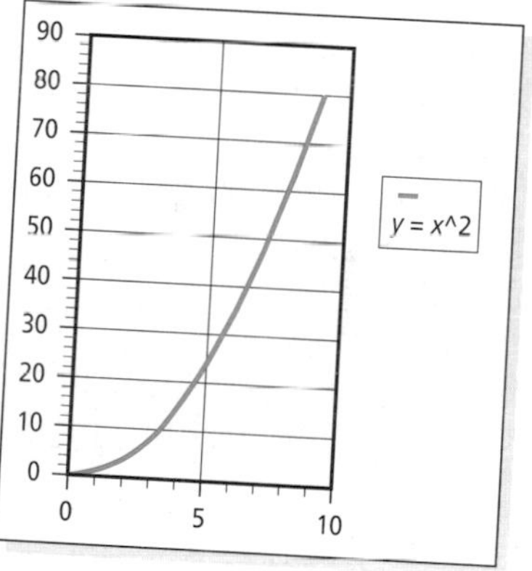

EXERCISE 5

1 This spreadsheet gives data about the number of lunches ordered by students in different years attending a college for one week in March.

	A	B	C	D	E
1		1st year	2nd year	3rd year	4th year
2	Mon	34	27	30	18
3	Tue	32	28	19	12
4	Wed	36	28	12	10
5	Thu	34	31	13	10
6	Fri	36	18	18	8

a Construct this spreadsheet, adding daily totals in column F and totals for the different years in row 7. Add a grand total in cell F7.

b Use the Graph options to present this information in a variety of useful ways.

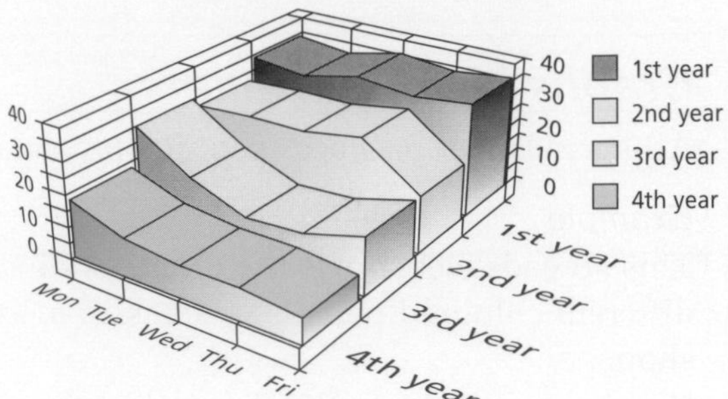

2 It was discovered that crop yield Y, in kg/m^2, was related to the amount of fertiliser x units/m^2, by the formula $Y = 14.4 + 6x - 0.6x^2$.

a Construct a spreadsheet to calculate the yields for $x = 0$ to $x = 12$.

b Present the data in a useful graphical form.

c Use the results you obtained to give practical advice to a farmer on the best use of this fertiliser.

3 Construct a spreadsheet to calculate the results of investing £1000 in the following four investment schemes.

	1st year	2nd year	3rd year	
Scheme 1	10%	9%	8%	Rate decreases 1% each year.
Scheme 2	1%	2%	3%	Rate increases by 1% each year.
Scheme 3	1%	1.5%	2.25%	Rate multiplied by 1.5 each year.
Scheme 4	0.1%	0.2%	0.4%	Rate doubled each year.

For each scheme, entry is by fixed term with a maximum term of 12 years. Give a potential investor advice in an easy to understand graphical format.

4 The simultaneous equations $y = 0.5x - 1$ and $y = 2x - 7$ can be solved using a spreadsheet. When cells A1 to D7 are selected and the 'Make chart' option 'x-y-line' is chosen, the resulting graph indicates a solution $x = 4$, $y = 1$. This can be checked by substitution in the equations.

A1 × ✓ x

	A	B	C	D
1	x	0.5x - 1	x	2x - 7
2	1	-0.5	1	-5
3	2	0	2	-3
4	3	0.5	3	-1
5	4	1	4	1
6	5	1.5	5	3
7	6	2	6	5

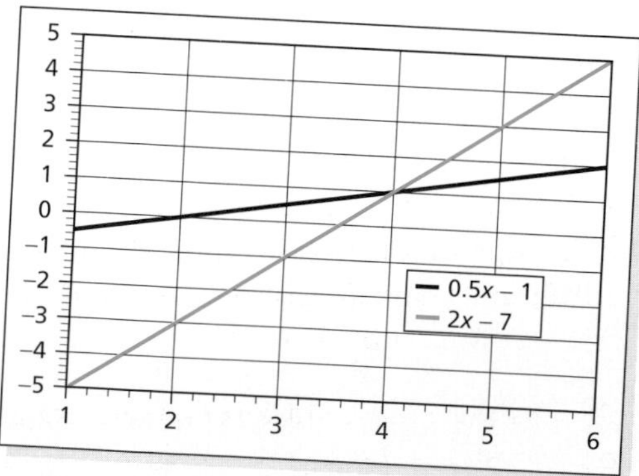

In a similar way, solve these simultaneous equations using a spreadsheet and showing the solutions graphically. (Check the solutions by substitution.)

a $y = 2x + 1$
$y = -1.5x + 8$

b $y = -2x + 5$
$y = 1.5x - 2$

c $y = -1.5x + 3$
$y = 0.5x - 5$

d $y = 0.4x - 2$
$y = x + 1$

Challenge

Where does the line $y = 0.5x + 3$ meet the parabola $y = x^2 - 2x - 3$?
Use a spreadsheet to find the answer as accurately as you can.

Tree diagrams

A vending machine offers tea or coffee; with or without sugar; and with or without milk. What is the variety of drinks on offer?

Examine the diagram below.

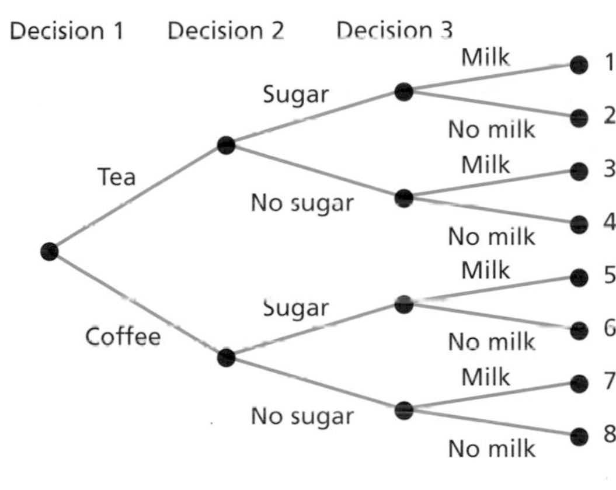

We see that, at each decision, the diagram branches. Mainly for that reason, it is referred to as a **tree diagram**.

We see that there are eight endings. So there must be eight varieties of drink.

We can list each variety by following each branch to its tip, recording the decisions as we go.

For example: ending 6 represents coffee, with sugar, without milk.

EXERCISE 6

1 Describe the variety of drink represented by:

a ending 3 **b** ending 4 **c** ending 5 **d** ending 8.

2 An automatic washing machine offers a hot or cold wash, the option to include a rinse and the option to include a spin-drying cycle.

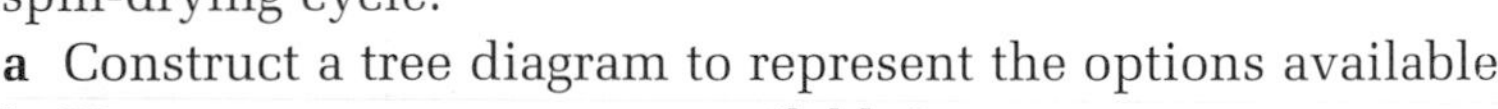

a Construct a tree diagram to represent the options available.

b How many programs are available?

c If a fourth option, to include a tumble dry, were possible, how many programs would then be available?

3 Alan, Betty and Cara form the social committee of an office. One has to be chairperson, one the secretary and one the treasurer.
Copy and complete the tree diagram to find all possible ways that the committee can be structured.

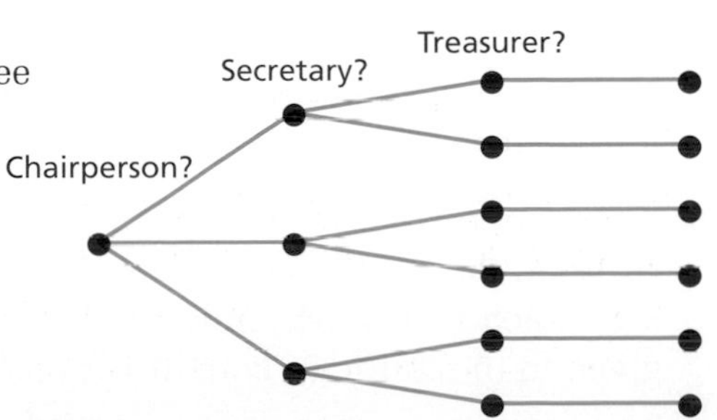

4 Mark has a password to get onto the computer network. For the sake of security he changes it often. He always uses a four-letter rearrangement of his name.

a Construct a tree diagram to show all possible rearrangements of the name 'MARK'.

b Assuming he never actually uses his name, how many passwords are available to Mark?

5 A tree diagram can be used to 'untangle' route systems. The map shows five villages in the country. The local doctor wants the quickest route between places. A tourist wants to see as much as possible without revisiting the same village twice.

Here is a tree diagram exploring the routes from A to D.

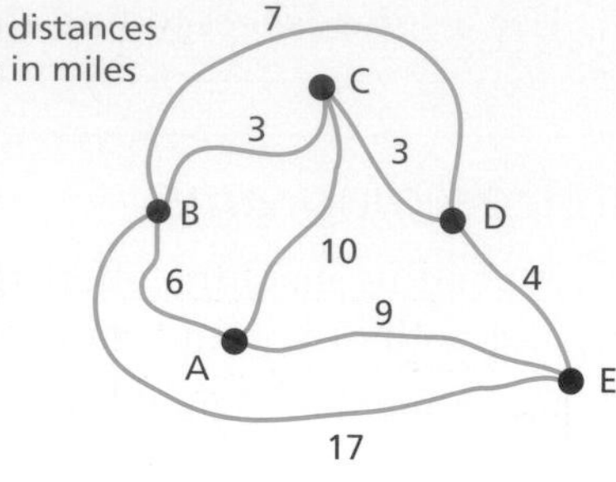

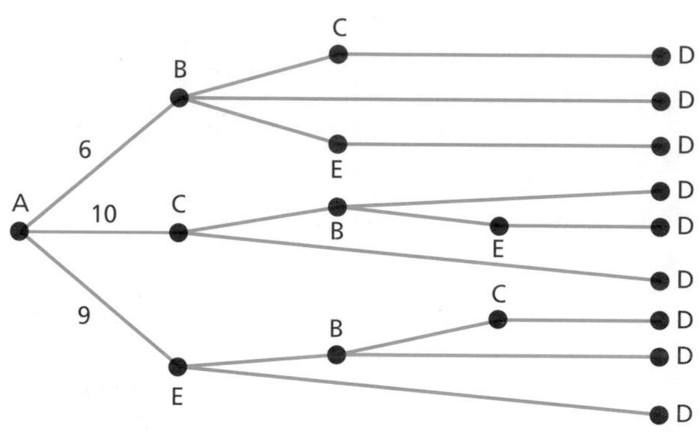

a Complete the tree, adding the mileage between villages.

b At the end of each branch put the total mileage travelled along that branch.

c Which route would be chosen by: **(i)** the doctor **(ii)** the tourist?

d Draw a diagram to help you explore the routes between B and E.

6 Try and devise a tree diagram to explore the routes between places in your school. You may have to consider one-way systems.

7 Since tree diagrams are useful in listing possibilities they are often employed in probability problems. This tree diagram helps you list the possible outcomes, when a dice and a coin are cast at the same time. (Note: it is easier to consider the event with the bigger number of outcomes first.)

a How many possible outcomes are there?

c What is the probability of:

(i) a head and an even number

(ii) a tail and a number bigger than 4

(iii) a 4 with a tail?

Dice
1 2 3 4 5 6
H (1, H) T (1, T)
H (2, H) T (2, T)
H (3, H) T (3, T)
H (4, H) T (4, T)
H (5, H) T (5, T)
H (6, H) T (6, T)

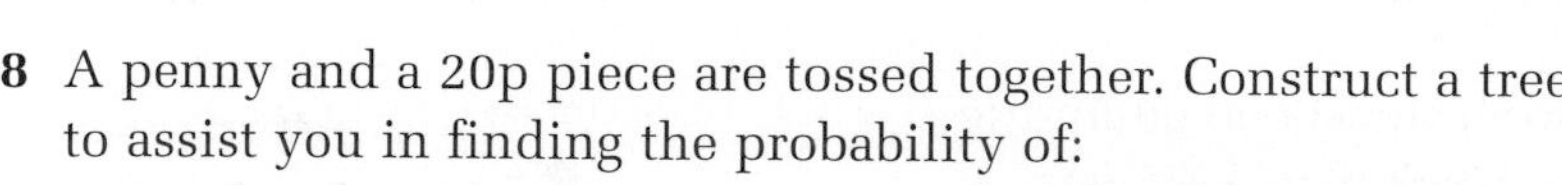

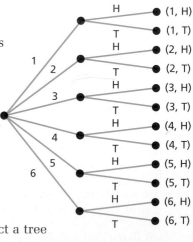

8 A penny and a 20p piece are tossed together. Construct a tree to assist you in finding the probability of:

a two heads **b** a head and a tail.

9 There are three sets of roadworks on John's route to work. At each, the traffic is controlled by a man turning a 'Go/Stop' sign. Each man works independently, making sure that the time given to the traffic in both directions is shared equally.

a Construct a tree diagram to show all possible outcomes as John makes his way to work past these three men.

b What is the probability of:

(**i**) being stopped

(**ii**) being stopped exactly twice

(**iii**) not being stopped?

Network diagrams

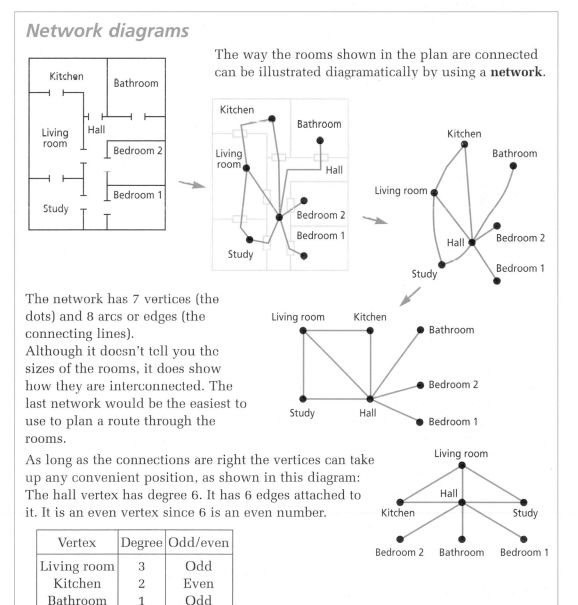

The way the rooms shown in the plan are connected can be illustrated diagramatically by using a **network**.

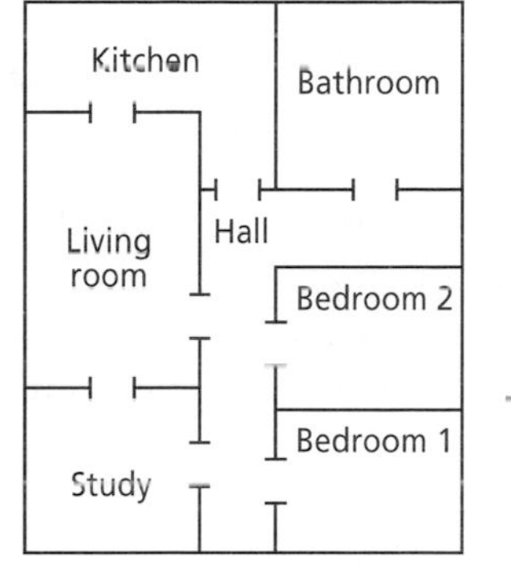

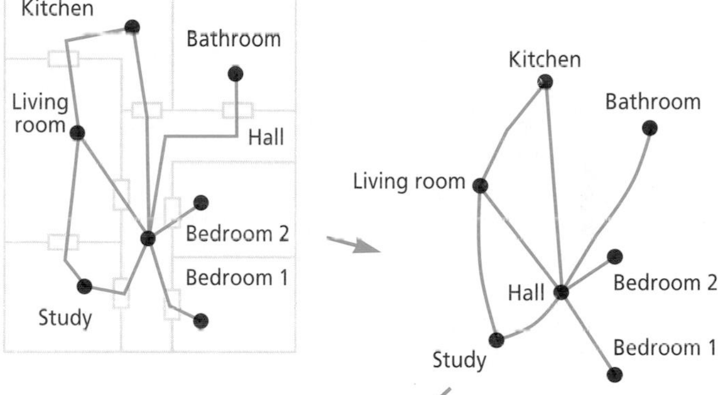

The network has 7 vertices (the dots) and 8 arcs or edges (the connecting lines).
Although it doesn't tell you the sizes of the rooms, it does show how they are interconnected. The last network would be the easiest to use to plan a route through the rooms.

As long as the connections are right the vertices can take up any convenient position, as shown in this diagram:
The hall vertex has degree 6. It has 6 edges attached to it. It is an even vertex since 6 is an even number.

Vertex	Degree	Odd/even
Living room	3	Odd
Kitchen	2	Even
Bathroom	1	Odd
Bedroom 1	1	Odd
Bedroom 2	1	Odd
Hall	6	Even
Study	2	Even

Here is a degree table for this particular network diagram.

EXERCISE 7

1 Draw a network diagram for each house plan.

(i) State the total number of vertices and arcs for each diagram.

(ii) Construct a degree table for the diagram.

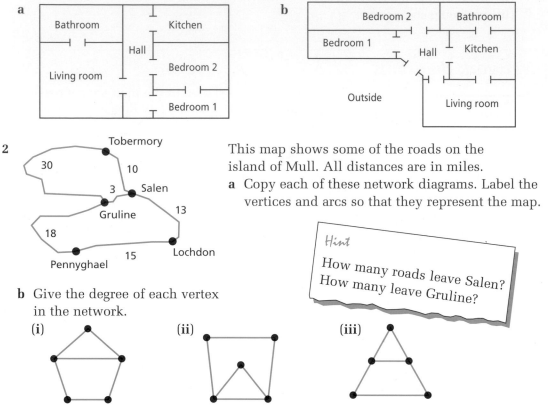

a

Bathroom
Kitchen
Hall
Bedroom 2
Living room
Bedroom 1

b

Bedroom 2
Bathroom
Bedroom 1
Hall
Kitchen
Outside
Living room

2

Tobermory
30
10
3
Salen
Gruline
13
18
Pennyghael
15
Lochdon

This map shows some of the roads on the island of Mull. All distances are in miles.

a Copy each of these network diagrams. Label the vertices and arcs so that they represent the map.

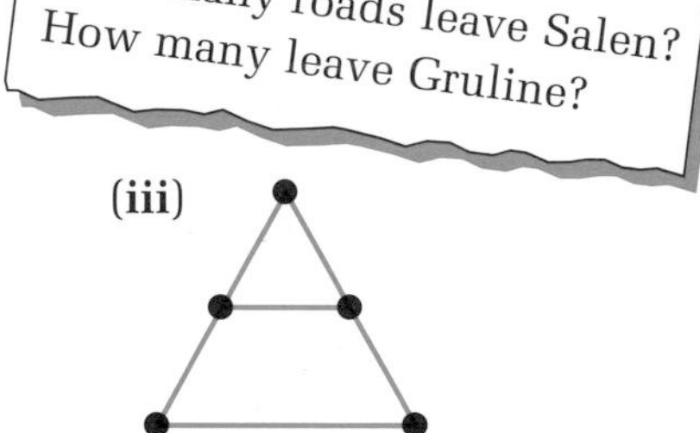

Hint
How many roads leave Salen?
How many leave Gruline?

b Give the degree of each vertex in the network.

(i)

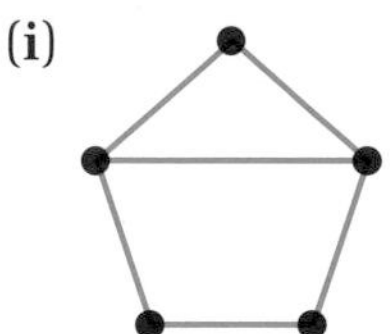

(ii)

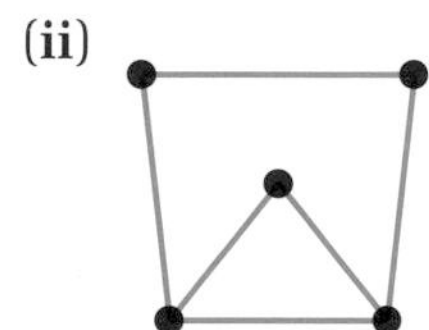

(iii)

c Find the shortest route from Tobermory to Pennyghael. How long is it?

3 A road repair team wants to check the whole network of roads shown here. (All distances are in miles.) They wish to start at Lower Largo and finish at Anstruther. They don't mind passing through a town twice but they do mind travelling the same stretch of road.

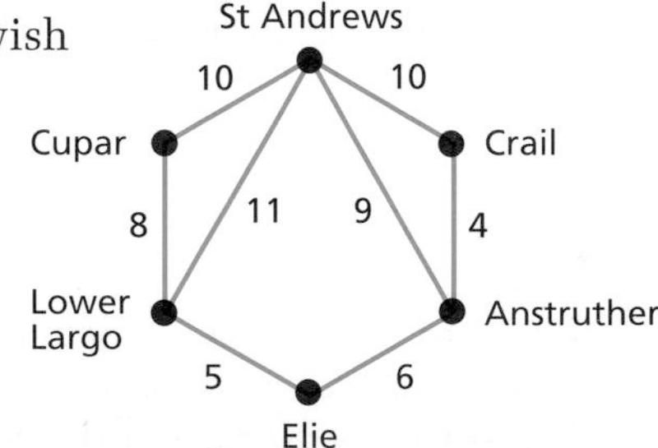

a **(i)** Describe a route that would suit them.

(ii) How long is the route?

b Copy and complete this table.

Vertex	Degree	Even/odd
St Andrews	4	Even
Cupar	2	Even
Lower Largo	3	Odd
Elie		
Anstruther		
Crail		

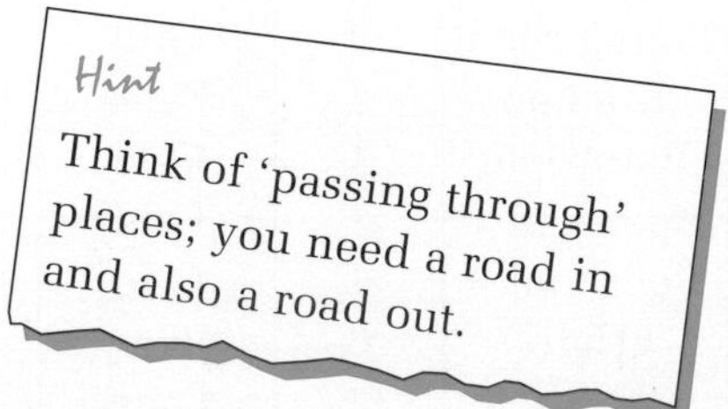

11
9

6

Hint
Think of 'passing through' places; you need a road in and also a road out.

c Try to explain why your route had to start at an odd vertex and end at an odd vertex.

4 a Draw a network to represent each of these maps. Label the vertices to show the places. Label the arcs to show the distances. (Distances are in miles.)

(i)

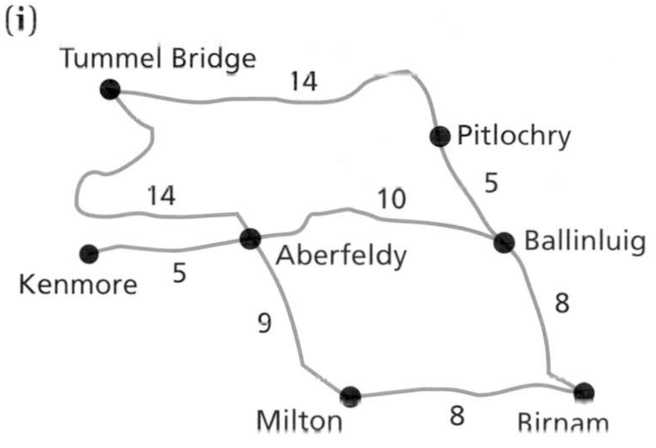

(ii)

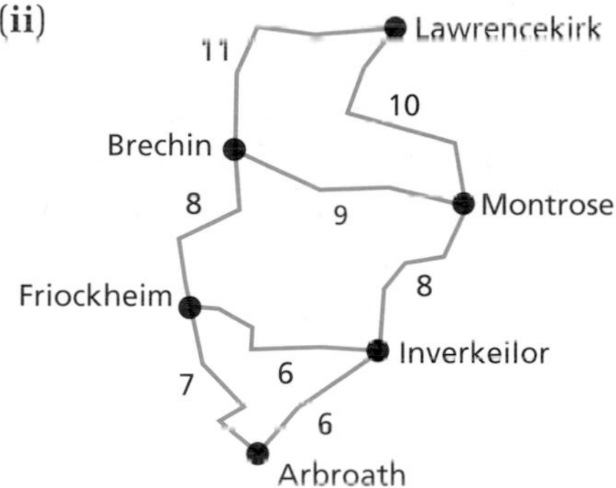

b Find a route covering all 73 miles of map (**i**).

c Is it possible to find such a route for map (**ii**)? Give a reason for your answer. When such a route is possible in a network, we say the network is **traversable**.

Hint

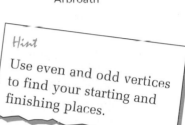

Use even and odd vertices to find your starting and finishing places.

Reminder

If there are more than two odd vertices then the network can't be covered without going over at least one arc twice.

- If you are just passing through a vertex you create a road in and a road out (even).
- If you start at a vertex you create a single path out (odd).
- If you finish at a vertex you create a single path in (odd).

5 All of these networks are traversable. Copy each network diagram by starting at one vertex and finishing at another vertex, without lifting your pencil. You are not allowed to retrace any of the arcs.

a

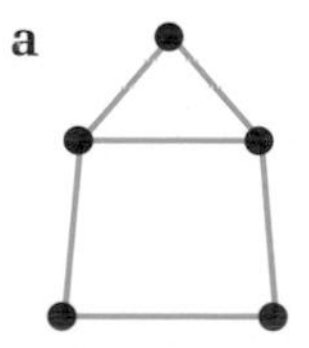

b

c

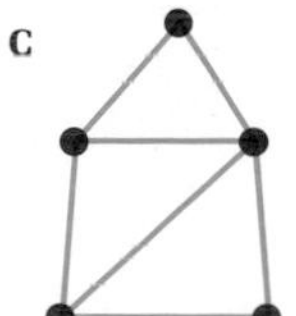

d

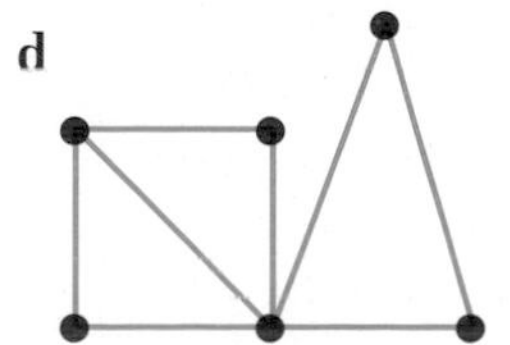

6 These network diagrams show the tunnels in a mine. Air is pumped into the mine at one of the labelled vertices, travels through all the tunnels once and is extracted at another.

a

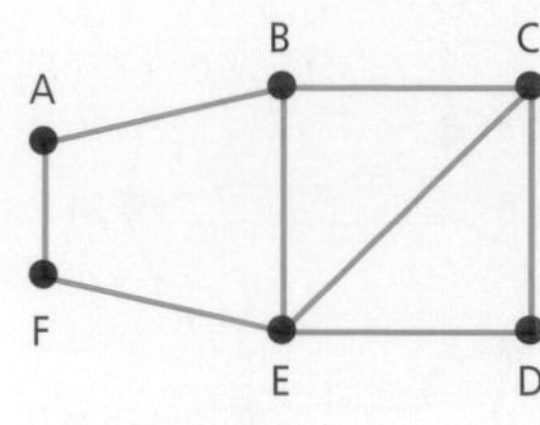

b

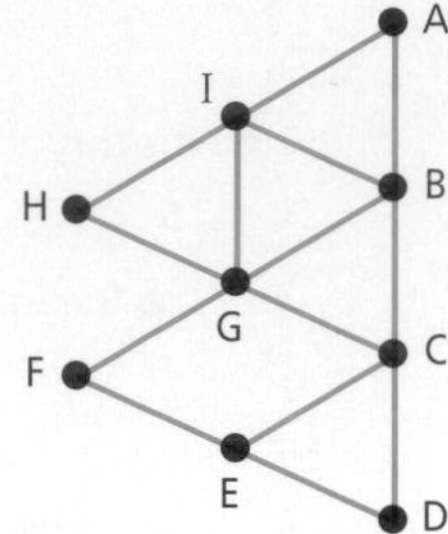

By using degree tables identify possible entry and exit vertices for the air. Show a suitable route for the air in each case.

7 Can these rooms be connected by a single unbroken wire that runs through each doorway only once?

a Make a network for each of these plans.

b Use the network to help you find a wiring route. (One of the problems is impossible.)

(i)

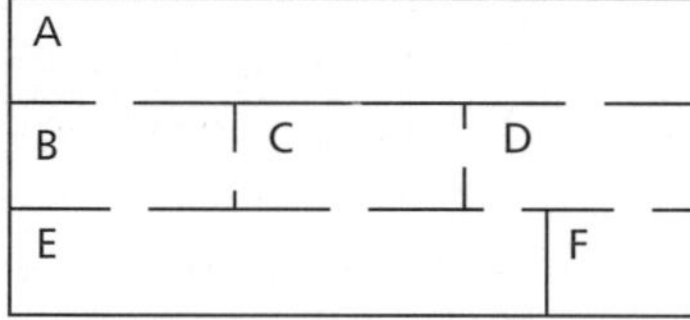

(ii)

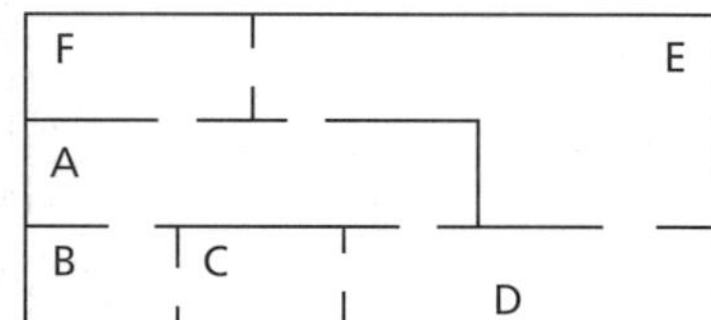

(iii)

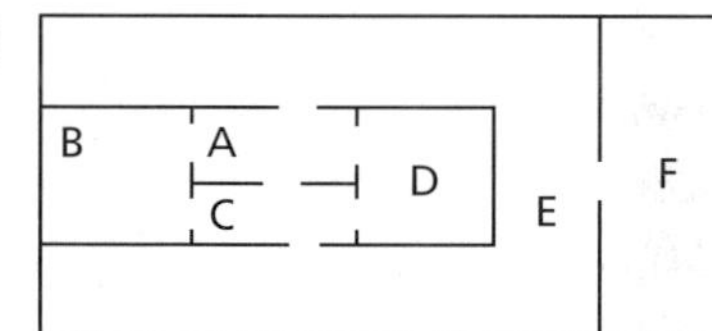

Activity networks

In this kind of network the vertices represent the start and finish of a step in a job. The arc represents the step.
Each arc is labelled with the step description and the time it takes to do the step.

Example 1

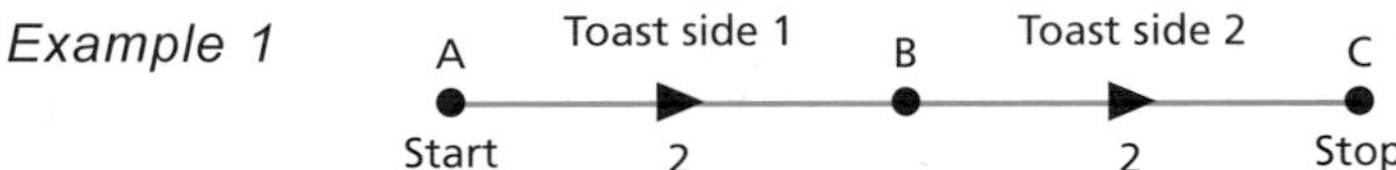

This simple network describes how to make a piece of toast under the grill. The times are in minutes. Note that it takes 2 + 2 = 4 minutes to make the toast.

Example 2

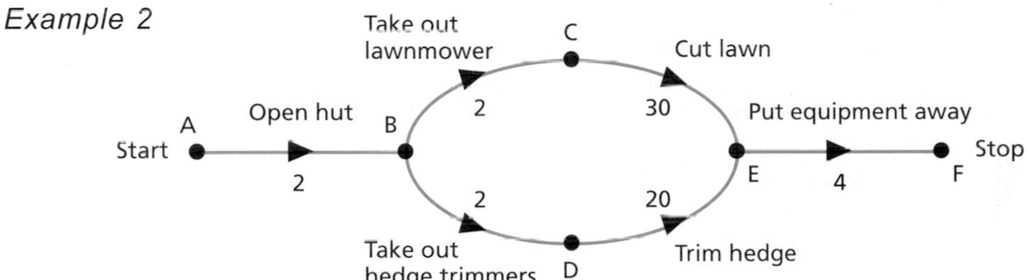

If there is more than one person doing the job it is possible for two steps to happen at the same time. This network shows two people doing the garden. Times are in minutes.
Note that the longest path is ABCEF, a total of 2 + 2 + 30 + 4 = 38 minutes. So, from start to finish, doing the garden will take 38 minutes. This longest path is often called the **critical path**.

EXERCISE 8

1 This network describes cooking a meal of meat and two vegetables. All times are in minutes. There are three rings on the cooker. This lets all the pieces cook at the same time if you wish.

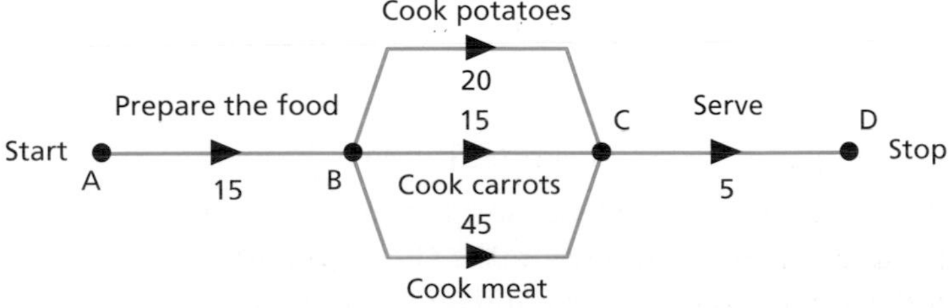

a How many **(i)** vertices **(ii)** arcs does the network have?
b How long does it take to **(i)** prepare the food **(ii)** serve the food?
c **(i)** What is the length of the longest path?
(ii) How long then does it take to do the job?

2 A man hires a cement mixer to make himself a concrete path.
The network describes the job of making the path. All times are in hours.

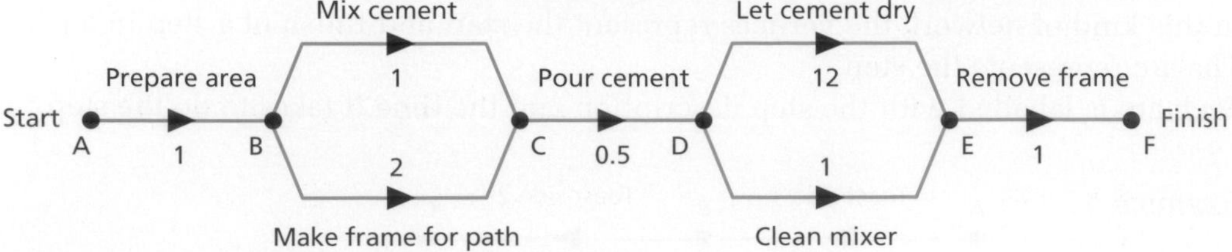

a What is **(i)** the longest **(ii)** the shortest part of the job?
b What is the quickest time in which the whole job can be done?

3 In this activity network, each vertex indicates the start of a step.
The arc leaving a vertex is labelled with the time required to complete the step.
Times are in hours. (Note that it takes 0 hours to start.)

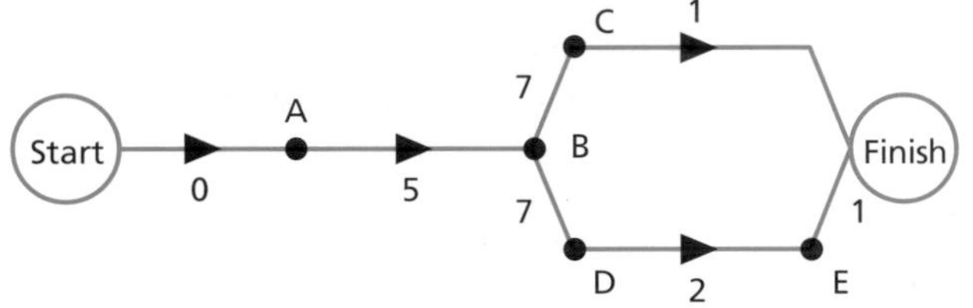

Decorating
A: Paint woodwork
B: Hang wallpaper
C: Put up curtains
D: Lay carpet
E: Set up furniture

a How long does it take to lay the carpet?
b What is done after the carpet is laid?
c Which three tasks have to wait until after the wallpaper has been hung?
d What is the shortest possible time to complete the whole task?

4

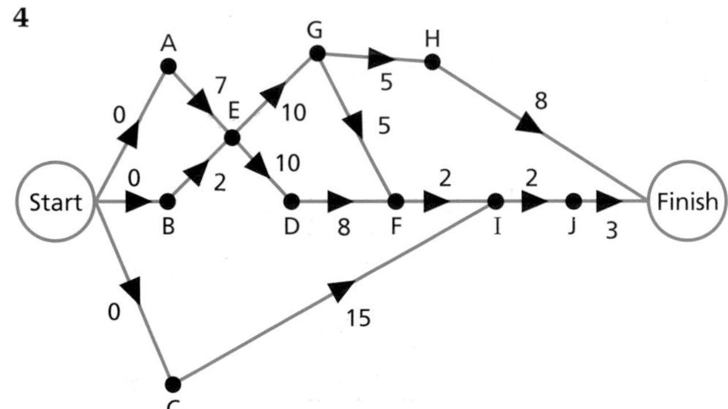

Building a garage
A: Lay foundations
B: Make doors and window frames
C: Lay drains
D: Electrical and plumbing tasks
E: Walls
F: Ceiling
G: Roof
H: Install doors and windows
I: Gutters
J: Paint

> *Example* How long after task E is started can task F begin?
> E takes 10 days, at which point tasks G and D can both begin.
> However, before task F can begin, both tasks G and D have to be completed.
> This requires 8 days, not 5 days. So the longer path of 18 days must be chosen.

The longest path, from start to finish, is called the critical path.
It will give the minimum time needed to complete the garage.
Find the critical path for the whole job and state the minimum time required.

5 a Construct an activity network for the following 'Making breakfast' tasks. All times are in minutes.

A: Grind coffee beans 1
B: Slice bread 2
C: Heat pan 3
D: Set table 5
E: Make toast 3
F: Make coffee 2
G: Cook bacon 5
H: Cook tomato 2
I: Cook eggs 3

Note you will have to complete:
A before F
B and C before E
C before G
E, F and I before H
B, C, E and G before I.

b Find the critical path through the network and calculate the minimum time needed to prepare breakfast.

Flowcharts

This is an example of a flowchart. This one helps you to calculate the interest when a certain amount is invested for a year.

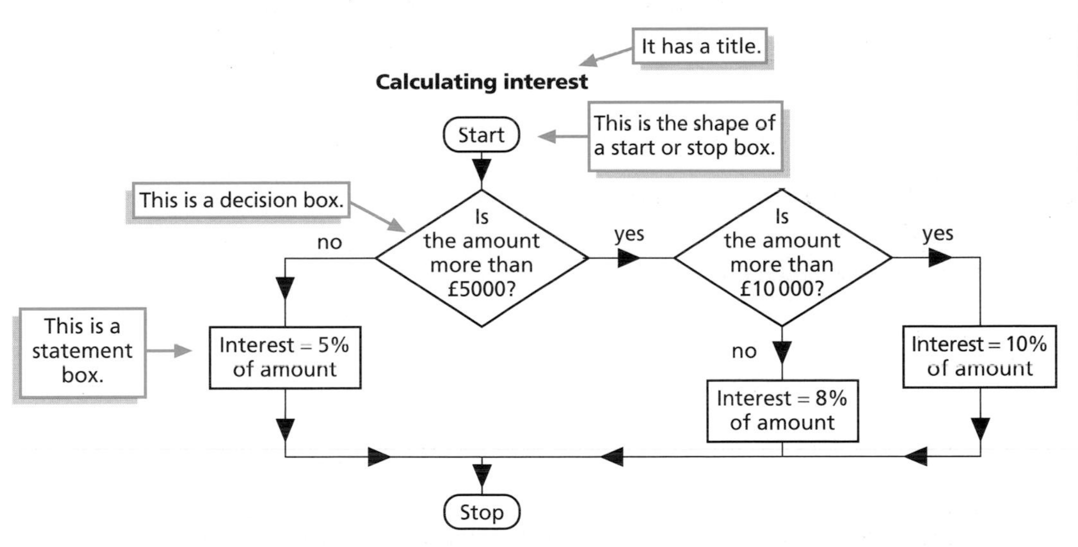

Follow the arrows, read the questions and act on the statements.

EXERCISE 9

1 Use the flowchart above to calculate the interest earned if the amount is:

a £12 000 b £2000 c £10 000 d £5000.

2 This flowchart helps you work out a salesperson's wage based on commission.

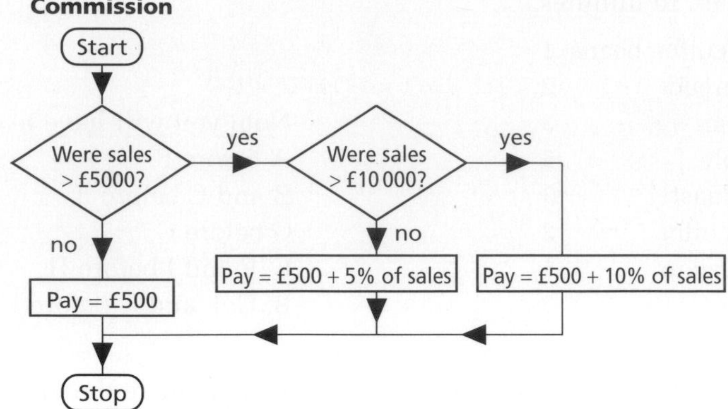

Calculate the wages for salespeople with sales of:

a £8000 **b** £250 **c** £12 000 **d** £10 000.

3 The charge for yachting lessons depends on various things, as shown in the flowchart.
What is the charge for:

a 1 trial lesson
b 8 lessons
c 14 lessons?

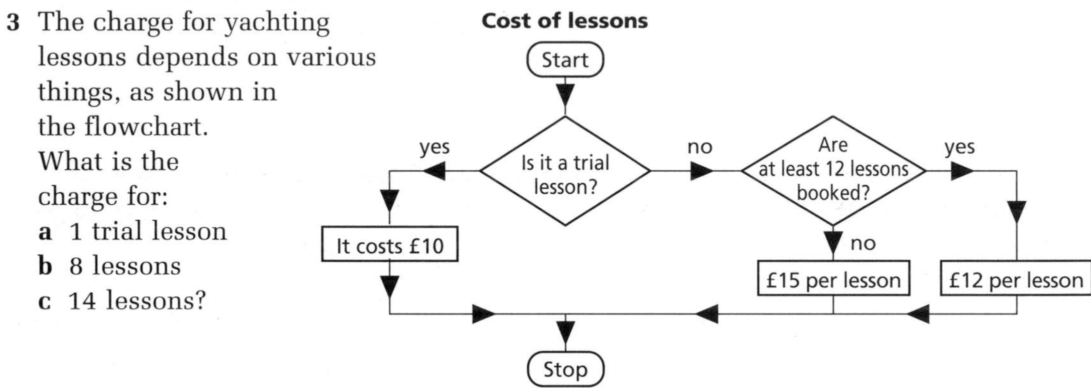

4 The playground area, A m^2, required at a secondary school depends on the number of students, N, at the school.

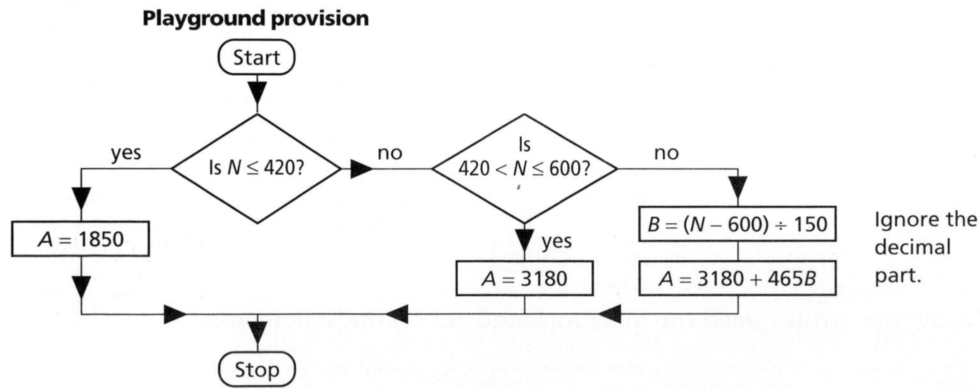

a Calculate the size of playground, in m^2, required for a school with:
(**i**) 300 (**ii**) 600 (**iii**) 1000 (**iv**) 1500 students.

b By trial and improvement (or otherwise) find the size of school that would require a playground of 1 hectare (1 hectare = 10 000 m^2).

Challenge

Find out if the playground at your school, or one near you, is of adequate size.

5 The maximum flow, P people per minute, in corridors or stairs of width W cm, is given by this flowchart.

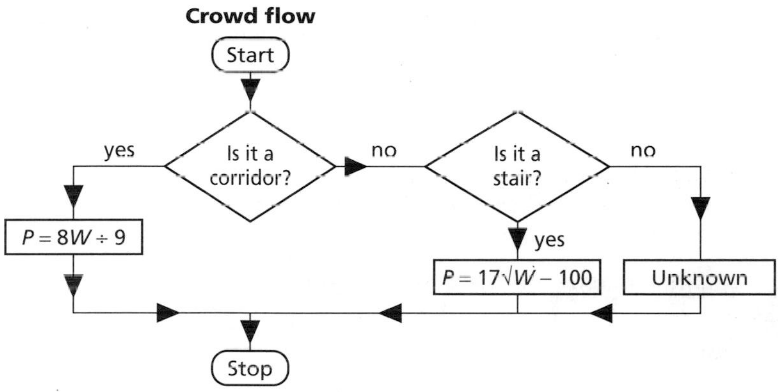

The entrance corridor to a cinema is 2.3 m wide and the stairs are 2.9 m wide.
If there are 250 people in the cinema, what is the shortest time they will take to go:

a down the stairs **b** out the corridor entrance?

Decision tree diagrams

These diagrams are related to flowcharts and can be used to sort items into categories. Each question asked will double the number of categories.

Example

A number between 1 and 4 is to be chosen. Two questions are needed to guarantee that the number can be found.

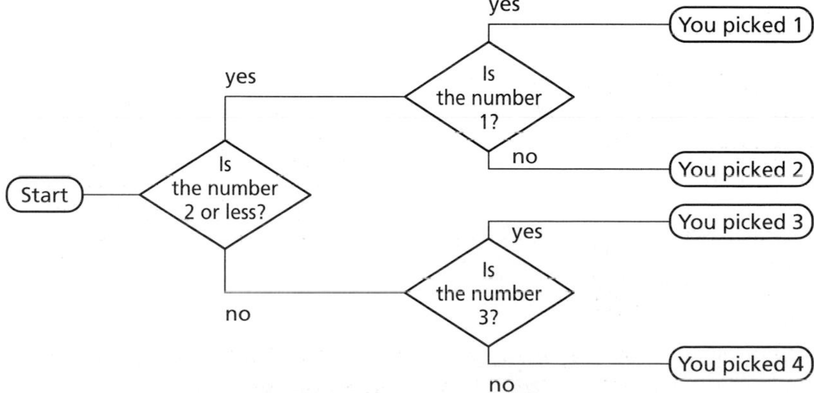

At a more complicated level this can be used to program computers to be **expert systems** and diagnose disease, etc.

EXERCISE 10

1 This decision tree is to sort out triangles into three types:
 (i) equilateral
 (ii) isosceles
 (iii) scalene.

Start
Does triangle have turn symmetry?
yes → It is …
no → Does triangle have line symmetry?
yes →
no →

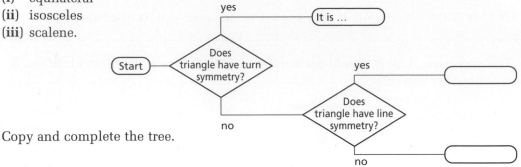

Copy and complete the tree.

2 One person is chosen from these eight people. Devise a decision tree which will guarantee you can identify the chosen person after three questions.

3 Devise a decision tree diagram which will help you categorise the quadrilaterals according to their symmetries.

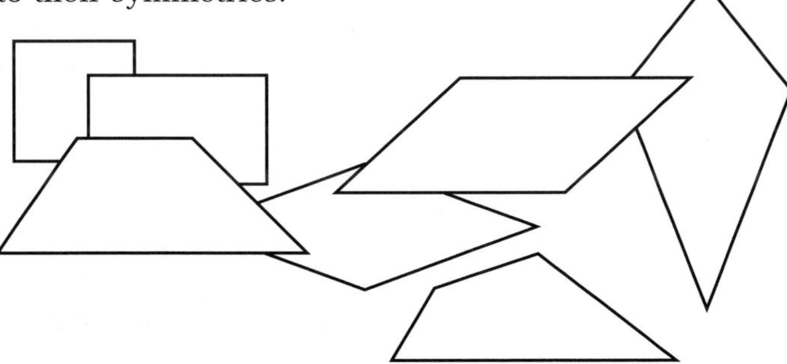

4 Aziz and Majid are playing a guessing game. One makes up a number between 1 and 1000. The other must guess it in the minimum of tries.
 a What is the minimum number of guesses needed?
 b Investigate the minimum number of guesses needed for guessing a number between 1 and 1 000 000.

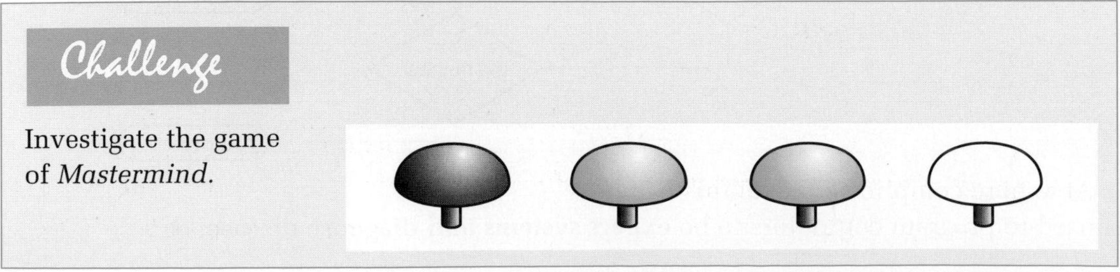

Challenge

Investigate the game of *Mastermind*.

CHAPTER 18 REVIEW

1 This spreadsheet calculates the areas of circles with different radii.

a Formulae are entered in cells A3 and B2 and then 'filled down' the columns.
What formula is in: **(i)** A3 **(ii)** B2 **(iii)** A5 **(iv)** B6?

b If B7 is selected what formula will appear in the Edit bar?

c Describe the formatting options used for cells B2 to B9.

d Describe the effect of changing A2 to 4 instead of 5.

	A	B
1	Radius	Area
2	5	78.54
3	5.1	81.71
4	5.2	84.95
5	5.3	88.25
6	5.4	91.61
7	5.5	95.03
8	5.6	98.52
9	5.7	102.07

2 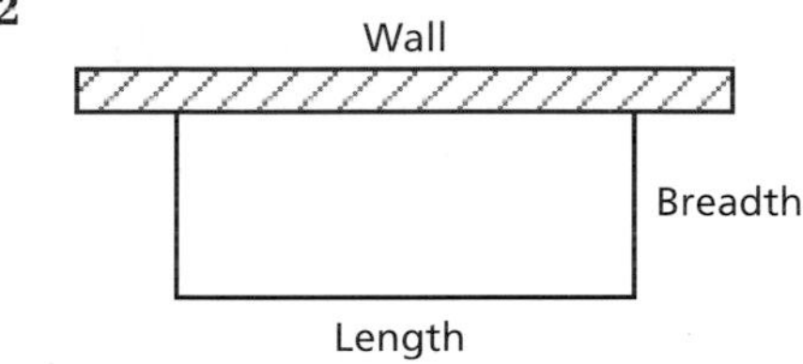

You have 50 m of fencing to make an enclosure against a wall, as shown in the diagram.

a Construct a spreadsheet that will calculate:
(i) the breadth for a given length
(ii) the area of the enclosure for that length and breadth.

b Graph the data for the area to find the dimensions that give the maximum area.

3 Here is an activity network. Find the critical path and give the minimum time for completion of the whole task.
Times are given in days.

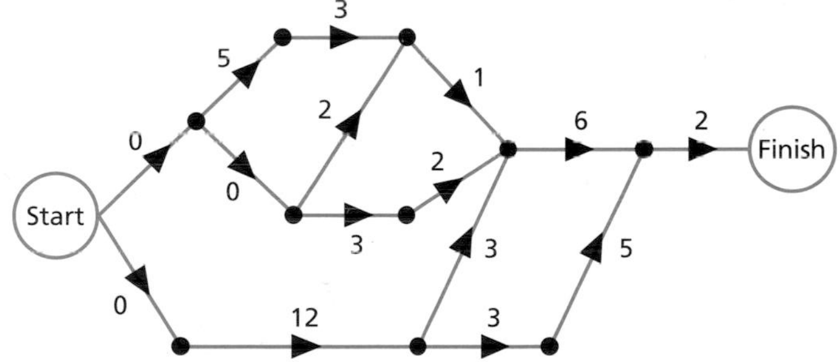

4 The temperature, T °C, of a chemical reaction depends on the quantity, Q mg, of a substance X. The flowchart shows you how to calculate T when Q is known.

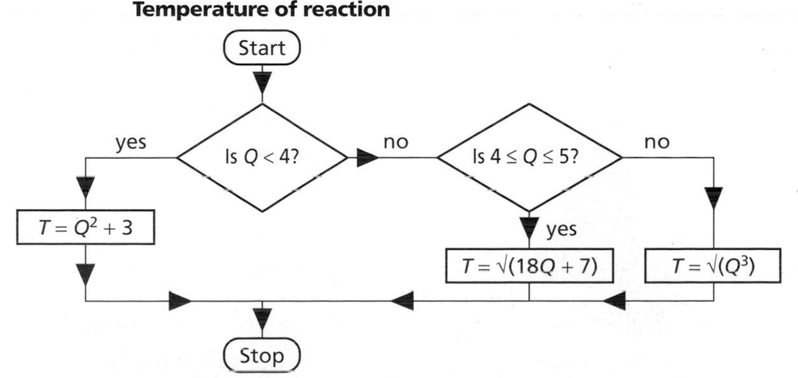

Calculate the temperature of reactions involving:

a 2.3 mg
b 4 mg
c 6.8 mg
d 5 mg of substance X.

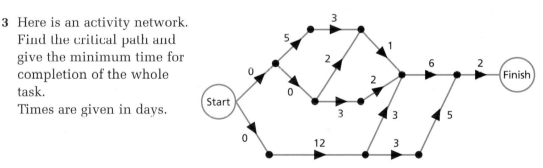

19 Formulae

Reminder

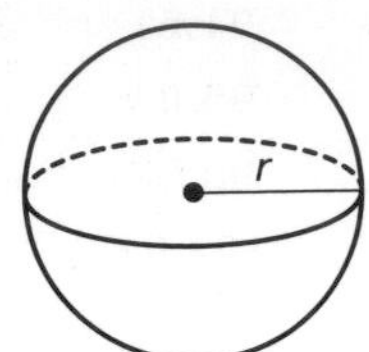

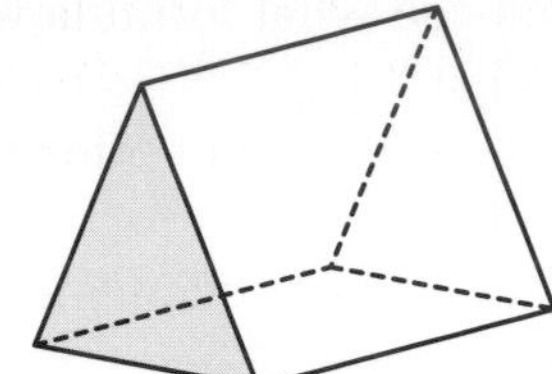

$V = \frac{4}{3}\pi r^3$ $V = \frac{1}{3}\pi^2 h$ Volume = area of end (A) times length (l).

STARTING POINTS

1 If $a = 6$ and $b = 2$ find:

a $a + b$ **b** $a - b$ **c** $2(a + b)$ **d** $a^2 + b$ **e** $\frac{a}{b}$

2 The equation of a straight line is $y = 2x - 3$.
Find the values of y to complete the table.

x	−3	−2	−1	0	1	2	3
y	−9						

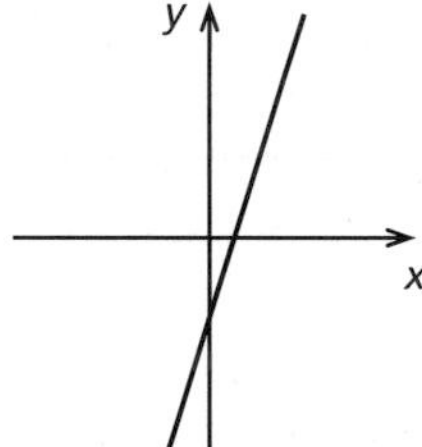

3 Calculate the circumference of the following circles using the formula given.

$C = 2\pi r$

C is the circumference
r is the radius

a

6 cm

b

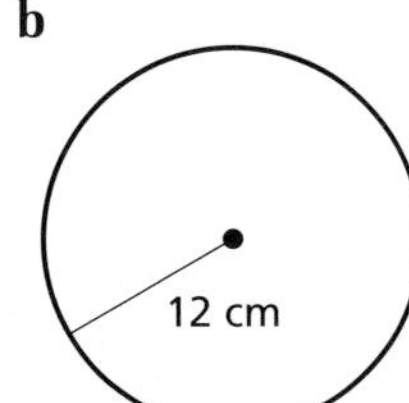

4 Calculate the volume of each solid.

a

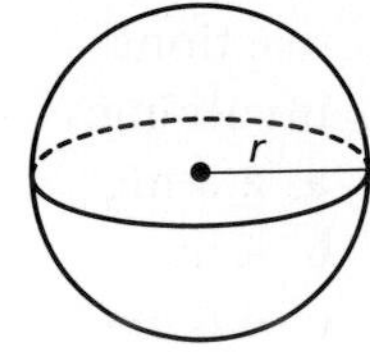

Radius = 10 cm

b

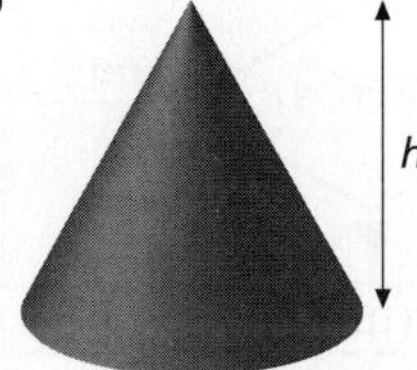

Radius = 6 cm
Height = 4 cm

c

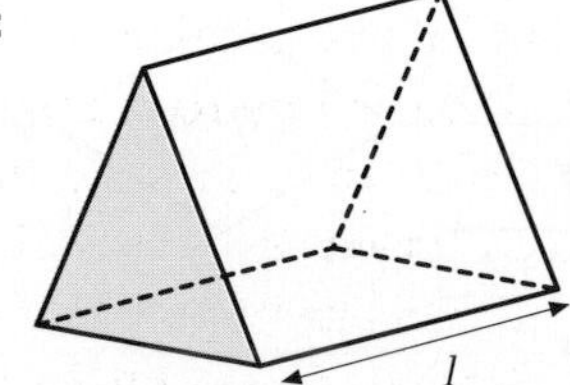

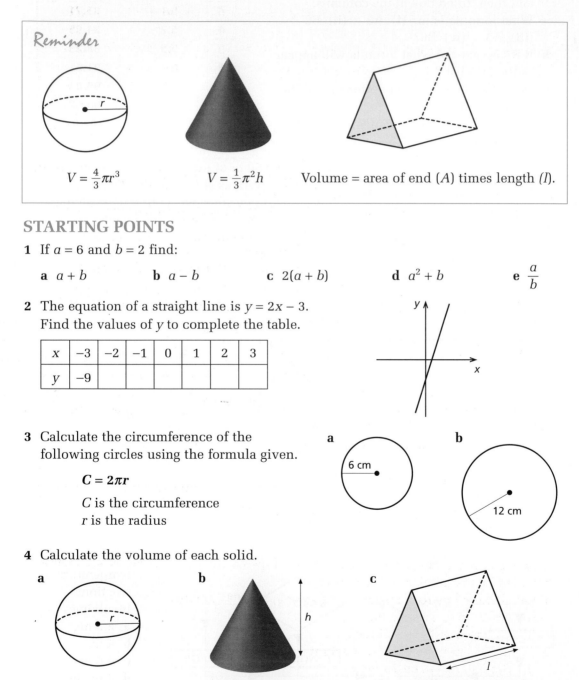

Area of end = 4 cm²
Length = 6 cm

Using formulae expressed as words

Often a formula will be given as a sentence rather than a set of symbols in an equation.

Example

The average speed of a journey is the total distance travelled divided by the total time taken.

Calculate the average speed when a journey of 72 miles takes one and a half hours.

$72 \div 1.5 = 48$ The average speed is 48 miles per hour.

EXERCISE 1

1 Use the formula above to calculate the average speed for the following journeys.

a Total distance travelled is 25 km; total time taken is half an hour.

b Total distance travelled is 500 km; total time taken is two and a quarter hours.

2

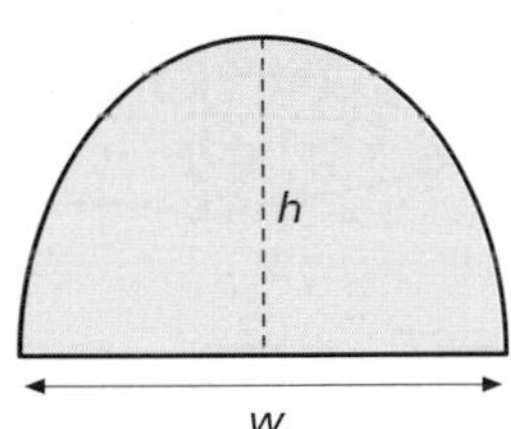

a The area of the front of an aircraft hangar of the type shown is two thirds the height times the width.

Calculate the area of a hangar with the following dimensions:

(i) height 10 m, width 20 m

(ii) height 15 m, width 23 m

(iii) height 18 m, width 35 m.

b The volume of the hangar is the area of the opening times the length of the hangar.

What is the volume of a hangar with dimensions:

(i) height 8 m, width 9 m, length 15 m

(ii) height 18 m, width 25 m, length 28 m

(iii) height 21 m, width 16 m, length 22 m?

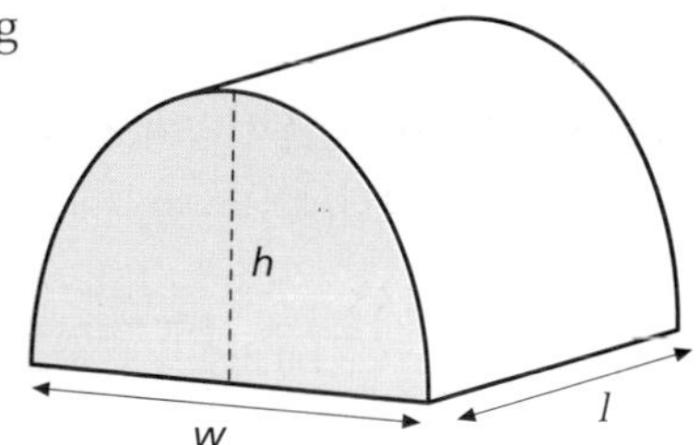

3 A car's petrol consumption can be calculated by dividing the number of kilometres travelled by the number of litres used.

a Calculate the petrol consumption for each of the following:

(i) 18 km on 2 litres of fuel

(ii) 25 km on 2.3 litres of fuel.

b In tests two cars performed as follows:

(i) Simba 179 km on 25 litres

(ii) Cougar 85 km on 12 litres.

Which car had the better petrol consumption?

4 We still measure speed in miles per hour. On the Continent they use kilometres per hour. At sea we measure a boat's speed in knots.
We can change:

- miles per hour to knots by multiplying by 0.869
- knots to kilometres per hour by multiplying by 1.852
- kilometres per hour to miles per hour by multiplying by 0.621.

a How many knots are equal to:
(i) 30 mph **(ii)** 45 mph **(iii)** 1.15 mph? (Give your answers to 2 d.p.)

b How many kilometres per hour are equal to:
(i) 10 knots **(ii)** 6 knots **(iii)** 1 knot? (Give your answers to 2 d.p.)

c How many miles per hour are equal to:
(i) 50 km/h **(ii)** 32 km/h **(iii)** 22 km/h? (Give your answers to 2 d.p.)

d Giving each answer to 1 d.p., convert:
(i) 1 mph into knots
(ii) your answer to **(i)** into km/h
(iii) your answer to **(ii)** into mph.

e Comment on your answers to **d**.

5 a The average depth of a swimming pool like the one shown is half the sum of the depth at the shallow end and the depth at the deep end. What is the average depth for the following?

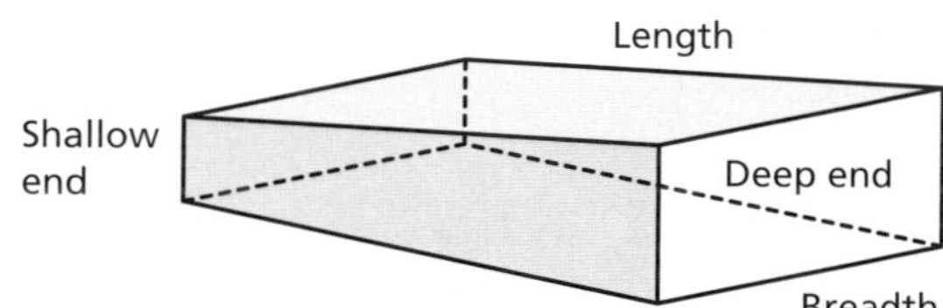

(i) shallow end = 1 m; deep end = 3 m
(ii) shallow end = 1.2 m; deep end = 1.8 m

b The volume of the pool is the average depth times the length times the breadth. Calculate the volume of the following pools.
(i) average depth = 3 m; length = 20 m; breadth = 12 m
(ii) average depth = 2 m; length = 25 m; breadth = 18 m

c Calculate the volume of this pool.

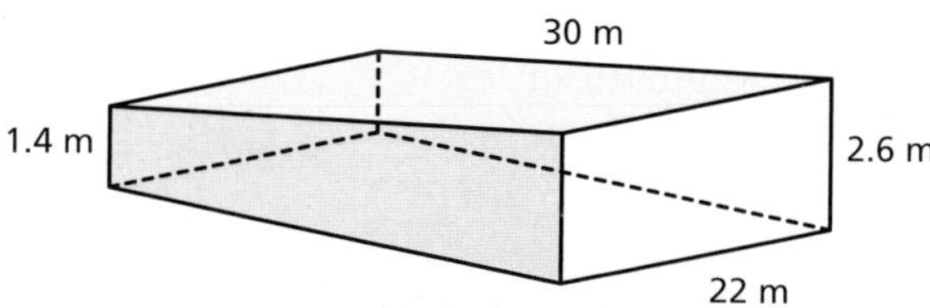

6 You can convert a temperature in degrees Celsius into degrees Fahrenheit by multiplying the Celsius temperature by 9, then dividing by 5 and finally adding on 32.

a Convert the following into Fahrenheit temperatures: **(i)** 25 °C **(ii)** 100 °C.

b Jamie is an trainee heat engineer. As a quick rule he just doubles the Celsius temperature and adds 30. Use Jamie's rule to convert the following:
(i) 5 °C **(ii)** 10 °C **(iii)** 20 °C.

c Compare Jamie's answers to the accurate answers and comment on his quick rule.

7 We can use this formula to change from a foreign currency to pounds sterling:

amount in pounds = amount in foreign currency ÷ exchange rate

Use the exchange rate table to find the equivalent sums in pounds sterling.

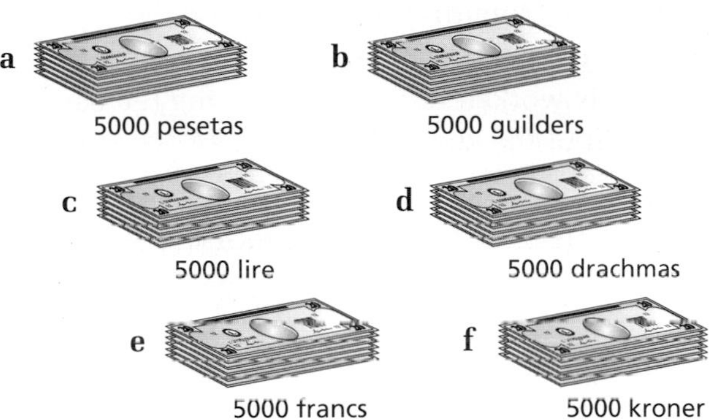

Today's tourist rates	
Country	Exchange rate for £
Denmark	11.05 kroner
France	9.75 francs
Greece	456 drachmas
Holland	3.24 guilders
Italy	2825 lire
Spain	243 pesetas

8 The height of a prism can be found by dividing the volume by the area of the base.

$$\text{Height} = \frac{\text{Volume}}{\text{Area of base}}$$

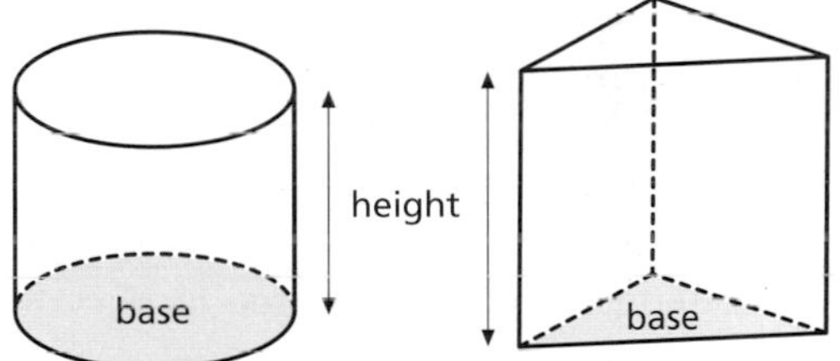

A drinks manufacturer wants a carton to hold 500 cubic centimetres of juice. He considers various prisms. Calculate the height of each.

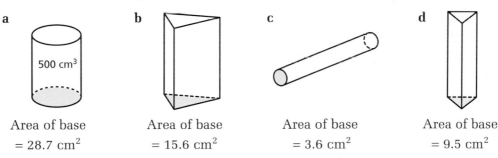

a

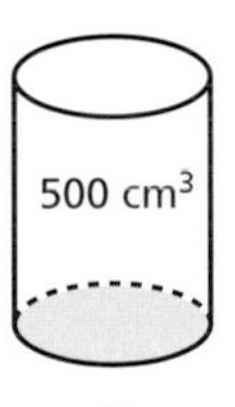

Area of base = 28.7 cm²

b

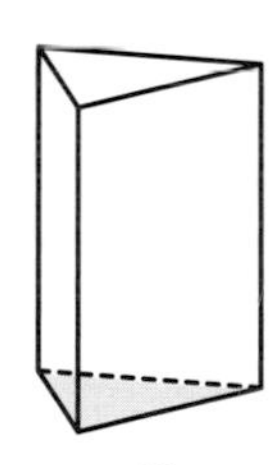

Area of base = 15.6 cm²

c

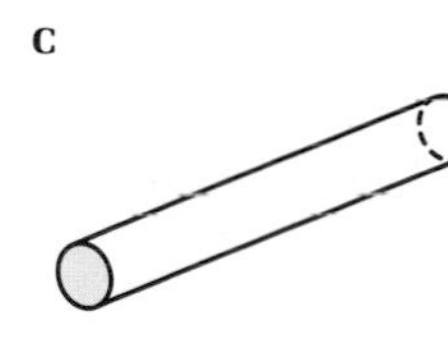

Area of base = 3.6 cm²

d

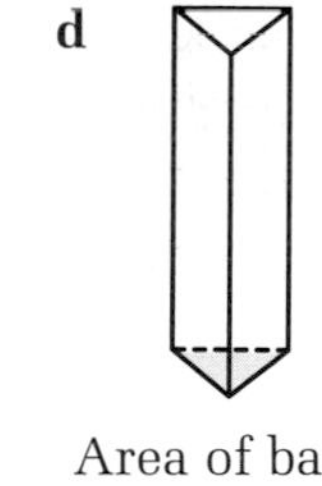

Area of base = 9.5 cm²

9 A sales representative always drives more than 1000 miles a month. She claims monthly travel expenses using the following formula:

28p per mile for the first 1000 miles
plus 19p per mile for travel over 1000 miles.

Use the formula to calculate her expenses for the months shown.

a January 1894 miles
b February 2256 miles
c March 3763 miles

10 The cost of electricity before VAT can be worked out by multiplying the number of units used by the cost per unit and adding on the standing charge.

a Calculate the cost of electricity in the following circumstances:

(i) 1200 units used at 13.7 pence per unit; standing charge = £18.24

(ii) 972 units used at 18.4 pence per unit; standing charge = £25

(iii) 2034 units used at 24 pence per unit; standing charge = £45.23.

b The final bill, after 8% VAT is added, is worked out by multiplying the basic bill by 1.08. Calculate the final bill on each of the above.

11 The power needed to run an electric circuit can be worked out by squaring the current and multiplying by the resistance. (Power is measured in watts when the current is measured in amps and the resistance is measured in ohms.) How much power is needed:

a to run a fire when the current is 10 amps and the resistance is 10 ohms

b to light a bulb when the current is 2 amps and the resistance is 15 ohms

c to run an appliance when the current is 5 amps and the resistance is 120 ohms?

Formulae expressed as symbols

The power needed to run an electric circuit can be worked out by squaring the current and multiplying by the resistance. This is quite cumbersome and can be shortened as long as we agree on the shorter form:

Power = square of current × resistance

or even better $P = I^2R$

where P is the power measured in watts, I is the current measured in amps and R is the resistance measured in ohms.

Example Calculate the power used when a current of 5 amps is passed through a resistance of 20 ohms.

$P = I^2R$

$\Rightarrow P = 5 \times 5 \times 20 = 500$

$\Rightarrow$ Power is 500 watts.

EXERCISE 2

1 How much a spring stretches, L mm, depends on two things:

G, a number which is different for every material,

W, the load in grams on the spring.

The formula is $L = GW$.

Calculate:

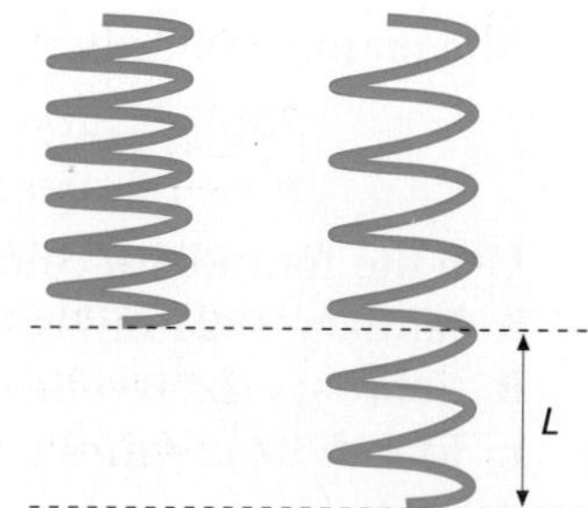

a L when (i) $G = 3$ and $W = 12$ (ii) $G = 13$ and $W = 23$

b G when (i) $L = 25$ and $W = 5$ (ii) $L = 10$ and $W = 2$

c W when (i) $L = 60$ and $G = 3$ (ii) $L = 5$ and $G = 2$.

2 A magnet exerts a force F newtons at a distance of d cm.
The force and the distance are connected by the formula $F = 3 \div d^2$.
a Calculate the force when the distance is: **(i)** 3 cm **(ii)** 5 cm **(iii)** 10 cm.
b What happens as the distance increases?

3 An ecologist studying small populations of a certain type of bat says that the population follows the formula

$$\frac{P = L(100 - L)}{100}$$

where P is the population next year and L is the population this year.

Calculate next year's population for a colony of size:
a 20 **b** 30 **c** 40 **d** 50.

4 The focal length of a lens, f mm, can be calculated if you know the distance to the object being magnified, u mm, and the distance to the image, v mm.

$$f = \frac{u \times v}{u + v}$$

Work out f when: **a** $u = 6$ mm and $v = 12$ mm
b $u = 14$ mm and $v = 182$ mm **c** $u = 18$ mm and $v = 63$ mm.

5 There is no fixed size for a brick.
The only restriction is that the brick's dimensions must obey the formula $L = 2W + T$ where L is the length, W is the width and T is the thickness of the space between bricks, all measured in centimetres.

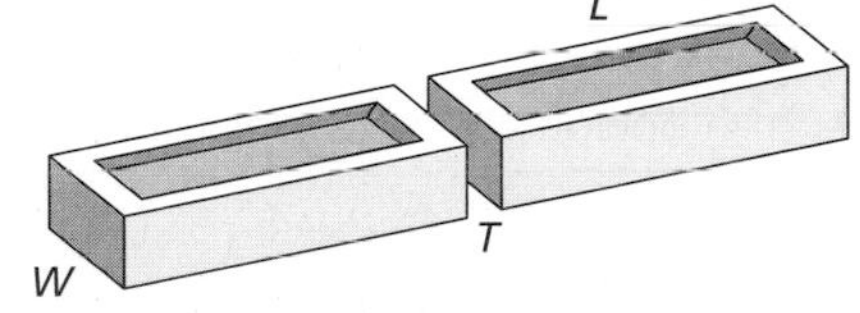

a Calculate L when: **(i)** $W = 3$ cm and $T = 1$ cm **(ii)** $W = 4$ cm and $T = 0.8$ cm.
b Work out T when: **(i)** $L = 11$ cm and $W = 5$ cm **(ii)** $L = 12$ cm and $W = 3.5$ cm.
c Calculate W when: **(i)** $L = 15$ cm and $T = 1$ cm **(ii)** $L = 12$ cm and $T = 0.8$ cm.

6 We tend to think of distances in metres but car speeds in miles per hour.
When braking we have to consider two things:
T metres, the thinking distance
(the distance travelled before we start to apply the brakes)
B metres, the braking distance
(the distance travelled by the car once the brakes have been applied).
These formulae can help us calculate these distances:

$\boxed{T = 0.3V}$ and $\boxed{B = 0.015V^2}$ where V is the car's speed in miles per hour.

Use the formulae to calculate:
a the thinking distance at **(i)** 30 mph **(ii)** 45 mph **(iii)** 70 mph
b the braking distance at **(i)** 20 mph **(ii)** 60 mph **(iii)** 70 mph
c the overall stopping distance at **(i)** 25 mph **(ii)** 70 mph.

7 Caterers who organise banquets reckon on 70 cm of space per person at the table.
In a dining room with identical circular tables the formula for seating is

$$P = \frac{N\pi r}{35}$$

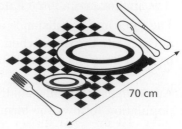

where P is the number of people who can be seated, N is the number of tables and r is the radius of a table.

a How many people can be seated at a banquet where there are 14 tables of radius 1.5 m?

b **(i)** What is the circumference of one table?
(ii) Where does the 35 come from in the formula?

8 The area of the washer can be calculated from the formula

$$A = \pi(R^2 - r^2)$$

where A is the shaded area, R is the radius of the outside of the washer and r is the radius of the hole.
Calculate the area of a washer when:

a $R = 10$ cm and $r = 4$ cm
b $R = 8$ mm and $r = 6$ mm
c $R = 25$ mm and $r = 4$ mm.

9 In electronics, resistors can either be connected

like this: 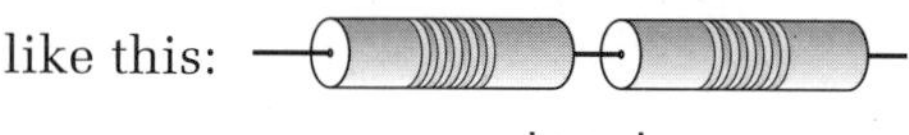

in series

or like this: 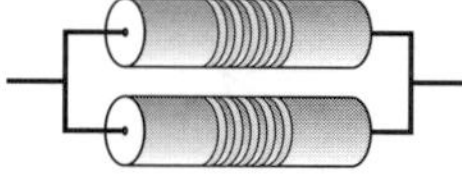

in parallel

The overall resistance, R ohms, can be worked out using these formulae.

For series: $R = r_1 + r_2$ For parallel: $R = \frac{r_1 \times r_2}{r_1 + r_2}$

where r_1 and r_2 are the resistances of the two resistors.

a Calculate the overall resistance for a pair of resistors set up in series when:
(i) $r_1 = 12$ and $r_2 = 14$ **(ii)** $r_1 = 6.1$ and $r_2 = 3.4$ **(iii)** $r_1 = 0.9$ and $r_2 = 8.4$.

b Calculate the overall resistance for a pair of resistors set up in parallel when:
(i) $r_1 = 12$ and $r_2 = 24$ **(ii)** $r_1 = 14$ and $r_2 = 35$ **(iii)** $r_1 = 21$ and $r_2 = 28$.

10 The speed at which a motorcyclist starts to slip on a corner is worked out using the formula $V = K\sqrt{r}$ where V is the speed in metres per second, r is the radius of the bend in metres and K is a measure of how good the surface is.

a Calculate the slipping speed when:
(i) $K = 2$ and $r = 49$ m **(ii)** $K = 2$ and $r = 81$ m.
Comment on the effect the radius of the bend has on the slipping speed.

b Calculate the slipping speed when:
(i) $K = 1$ and $r = 36$ m **(ii)** $K = 0.5$ and $r = 36$ m.

c A motorcyclist is arriving at a bend quite fast. Is he hoping for:
(i) a large or small value for K **(ii)** a large or small value for r?

11 The pendulum in a clock swings according to the law

$$T = 2\pi\sqrt{\left(\frac{L}{10}\right)}$$

where T is the time in seconds of one swing and L is the length of the pendulum.

a Calculate the time it takes to complete one swing when the length of the pendulum is:

(i) 16 cm **(ii)** 25 cm **(iii)** 81 cm.

b A swing takes 0.5 second. You want it to slow down.
Do you make the pendulum longer or shorter?

12 The capacity of a fire hydrant can be worked out using the formula

$$V = \frac{1}{3}\pi r^2 h$$

a Calculate the capacity of a hydrant which has a radius of 10 cm and a height of 25 cm.

b Fire safety officers recommend a hydrant containing 4 litres for a certain hall.
Is a hydrant of radius 12 cm and height 26 cm good enough?

13

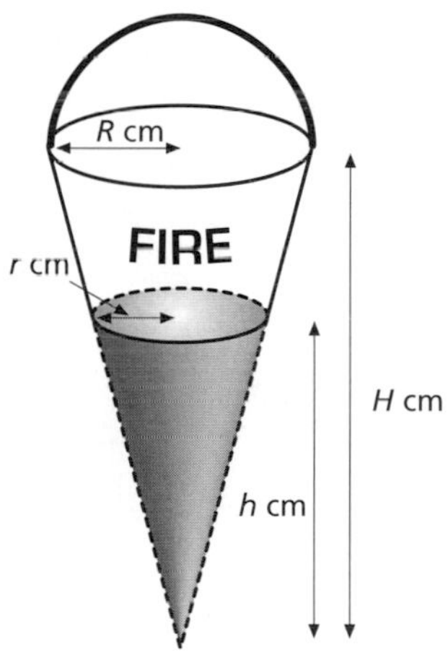

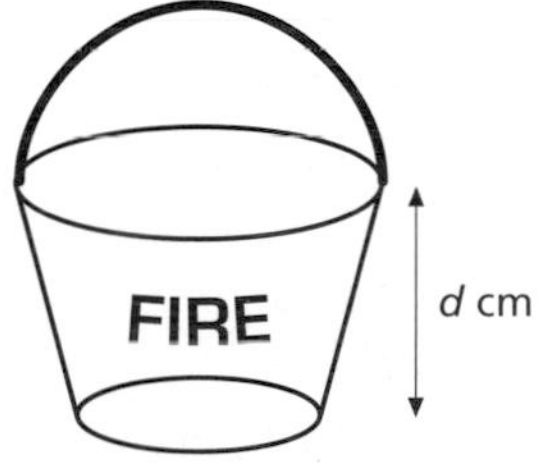

A fire bucket is made from a truncated cone, a cone with its vertex cut off.
Its volume can be found by subtracting the volumes of two cones:

$$V = \frac{1}{3}\pi R^2 H - \frac{1}{3}\pi r^2 h$$

where the symbols represent the measurements in the diagram.

a Calculate correct to 1 d.p. the volume of the bucket when:

(i) $R = 30$ cm; $r = 25$ cm; $H = 72$ cm; $h = 60$ cm

(ii) $R = 27$ cm; $r = 21$ cm; $H = 81$ cm; $h = 63$ cm.

b If you were given a bucket you would find it very difficult to measure H and h.
You could, however, measure d cm which is the depth of the bucket.
Note that $d = H - h$.
In terms of R, r and d, the volume can be shown to be $V = \frac{1}{3}\pi d(R^2 + Rr + r^2)$.
Check that the formula works for the data in part **a**.

Surface areas

We can refer to the surface area as S units^2.

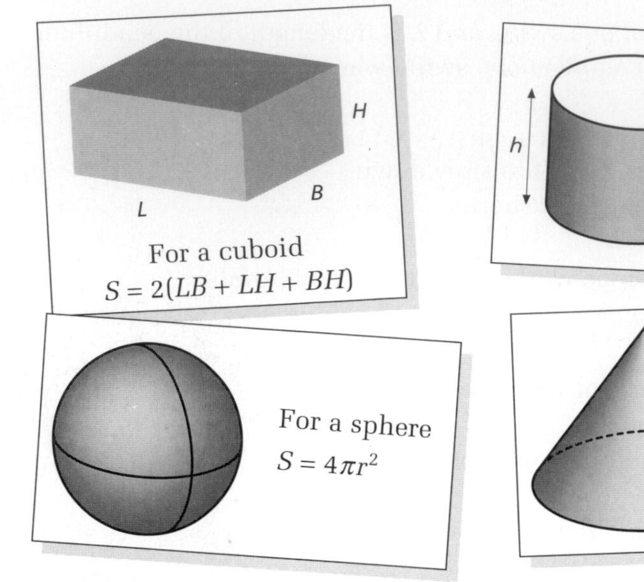

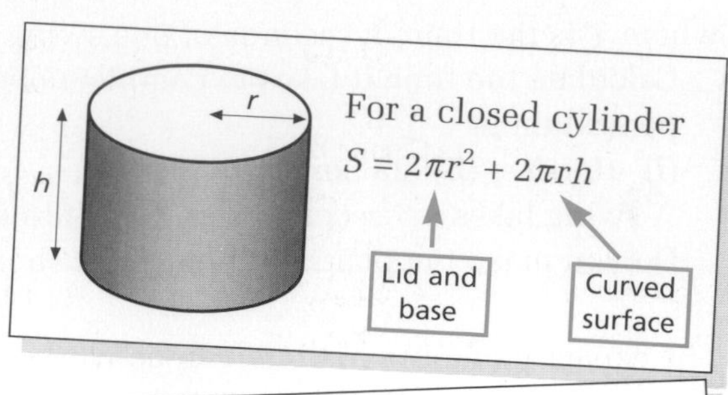

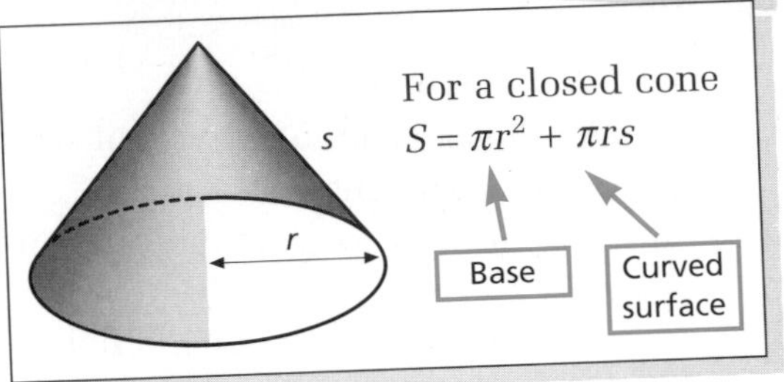

EXERCISE 3

1 Calculate the surface area of each solid.

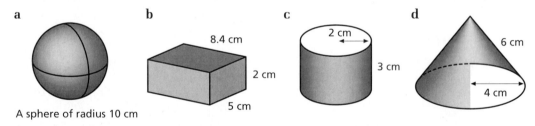

a A sphere of radius 10 cm

b 8.4 cm, 2 cm, 5 cm

c 2 cm, 3 cm

d 6 cm, 4 cm

2

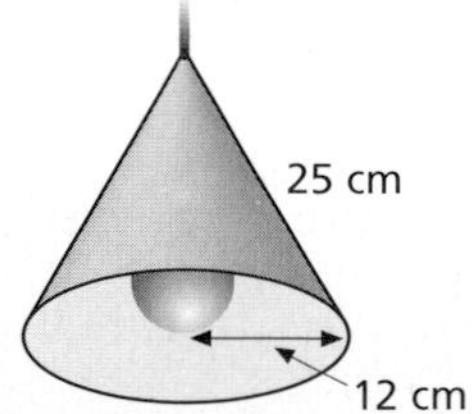

This lampshade is a cone without a base.

a Write down a formula for the area of its curved surface.

b Calculate the curved surface area.

3 The plastic piping shown is a cylinder with neither lid nor base.

a Write down a formula for its surface area.

b Calculate its surface area.

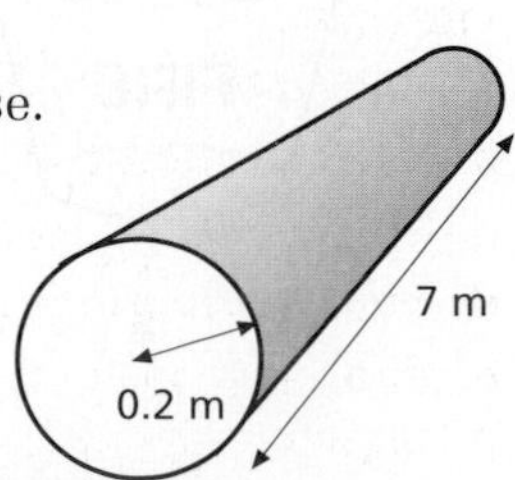

4 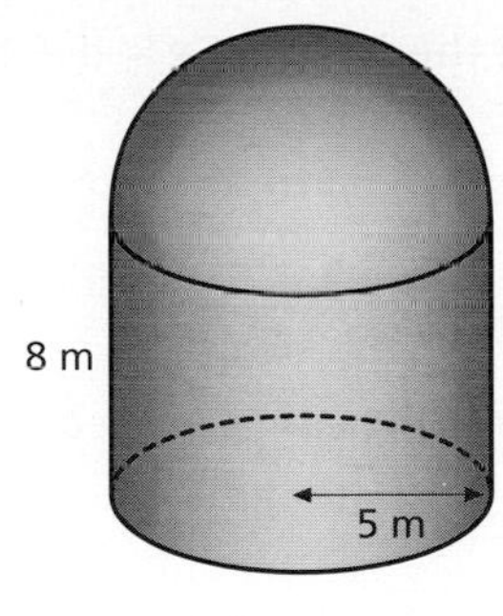

A silo made of metal is in the shape of a hemisphere on top of a cylinder.
The whole thing is to be painted.
Calculate:

a the area of the hemisphere

b the area of the curved surface of the cylinder

c the area to be painted.

5 A medicine capsule is made of a cylinder with two hemisperical ends. It has a total length of 10 mm.
The cylinder has a length of 5 mm.

a Calculate the radius of the hemispheres and cylinder.

b Calculate the surface area of the capsule.

c Find a formula for the surface area of a capsule where the total length is D mm and the cylinder length is C mm.

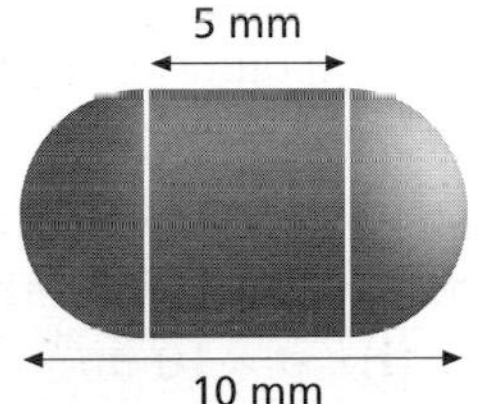

Finding the value of a variable which is not the subject

Example

In the formula $v = lbh + k$, v is called the subject of the formula.
What is the value of b given that $v = 1000$, $l = 4$, $h = 25$ and $k = 500$?

Method 1

Substitute: $v = lbh + k$

$\Rightarrow 1000 = 4 \times b \times 25 + 500$

$\Rightarrow 1000 = 100 \times b + 500$

Solve for b: $500 = 100b$

$\Rightarrow b = 500 \div 100$

$\Rightarrow b = 5$

Method 2

Change the subject: $v = lbh + k$

$\Rightarrow v - k = lbh$

$\Rightarrow b = \dfrac{v - k}{lh}$

Substitute: $b = \dfrac{1000 - 500}{4 \times 25}$

$\Rightarrow b = \dfrac{500}{100}$

$\Rightarrow b = 5$

EXERCISE 4

1 In each of the following, substitute then solve an equation to find the required variable.

a Find a when $c = b - a$; $c = 4$ and $b = 12$.

b Find a when $b = 3a$; $b = 7.2$.

c Find b when $c = 2ab$; $c = 54$ and $a = 9$.

d Find c when $b = 2(c - a)$; $b = 16$ and $a = 4$.

e Find k when $m = 3k - 2g$; $m = 7$ and $g = 1$.

f Find t when $w = 3tg - 2t$; $w = 32$ and $g = 2$.

2 When a body falls, its velocity at time t can be found using the formula $v = u + 10t$ where u m/s is the initial velocity.

a Calculate v when $u = 5$ m/s and $t = 12$ seconds.

b Substitute then solve an equation to calculate:

(i) u when $v = 64$ and $t = 4$ (ii) t when $v = 60$ and $u = 20$.

3 The perimeter of a rectangle, P cm, can be found using the formula $P = 2(l + b)$ where l is the length and b is the breadth of the rectangle.

a Calculate P when $l = 2$ cm and $b = 5$ cm.

b Substitute then solve an equation to calculate:

(i) l when $P = 92$ and $b = 5$ (ii) b when $P = 12$ and $l = 3.8$.

4 The distance, s m, travelled by a body falling can be calculated from the formula $s = ut + 5t^2$ where u is the starting velocity and t the time in seconds since observations began.

a Calculate the value of s when:

(i) $u = 10$ m/s and $t = 4$ seconds

(ii) $u = 5$ m/s and $t = 6$ seconds.

b Substitute then solve an equation to help you find:

(i) u when $S = 28$ m and $t = 1$ second

(ii) u when $s = 99$ m and $t = 3$ seconds

(iii) t when $S = 0$ m and $u = 5$ m/s.

5 A metal rod expands when it is heated up. Its new length, L cm, is given by $L = l(1 + kt)$ where l is the original length, t °C is the rise in temperature and k is a number which depends on the type of metal.

Calculate the value of:

a L when $l = 12$, $k = 0.002$ and $t = 40$

b l when $L = 22$, $k = 0.001$ and $t = 20$

c t when $L = 50$, $k = 0.003$ and $l = 15$

d k when $L = 40$, $t = 20$ and $l = 39$.

6 The power of a car engine used to be measured in horsepower.

It could be calculated from the formula $p = \dfrac{nd^2}{1613}$

where n is the number of cylinders and d mm is the diameter of a cylinder.

a Calculate p when $n = 4$ and $d = 80$.

b Calculate d when $n = 6$ and $p = 10$.

c Calculate n when $d = 78$ and $p = 15$.

(Remember this should be a whole number.)

7 In a Christmas shop window display, a bouncing Santa goes up and down.

Its height, h cm, can be calculated using the formula $h = 25 \sin (x + 90)$.

a Calculate h when $x =$ (i) 30 (ii) 55.

b Calculate x when $h =$ (i) 0.6 (ii) 0.8 (iii) –0.3.

CHAPTER 19 REVIEW

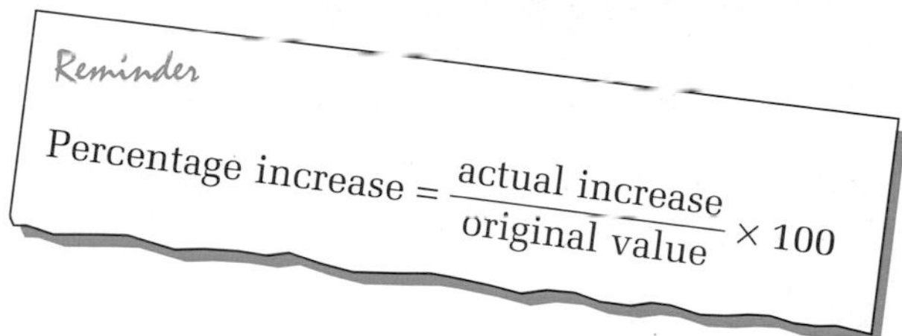

Reminder
Percentage increase = $\frac{\text{actual increase}}{\text{original value}} \times 100$

1 **a** A metal bar is heated. It expands from 560 mm to 568 mm.
Calculate the percentage increase in its length.

b The estimated cost of a building is £2 500 000.
By completion the cost had risen to £2 950 000.
Calculate the percentage rise in cost.

2 When a room is built like a cuboid, the total surface area of its walls is worked out by multiplying the perimeter of the room by its height.
Calculate the surface area of the walls of a room with:

a perimeter 30 m, height 3 m

b perimeter 25 m, height 2.5 m.

3 The surface area, A cm^2, of a ball can be calculated using the formula
$A = \frac{C^2}{\pi}$ where C is the circumference of the ball.

a Calculate the surface area of a ball with circumference: **(i)** 30 cm **(ii)** 2.5 cm.

b The earth has a circumference of 40 000 km. Calculate its surface area.

4 A famous scientist, Johannes Kepler, discovered that for every body in the solar system $T = \sqrt{(R^3)}$ where T is the time it takes in years for the body to go round the Sun and R is the distance from the Sun in astronomical units.

a The Earth is 1 astronomical unit from the Sun.
How long does it take the Earth to go round the Sun?

b Calculate the time it takes for each of the following planets:

(i) Jupiter, 5.2 astronomical units from the Sun

(ii) Mars, 1.52 astronomical units from the Sun.

5 The length, L m, of the chain in a suspension bridge can be worked out using $L = \frac{3S^2 + 8D^2}{6S}$ where
S is the span and D is the drop.

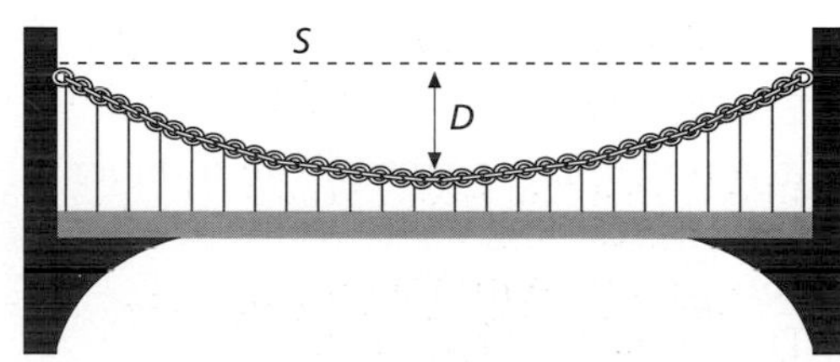

a Calculate L when $S = 100$ and $D = 20$.

b Find, by substituting and solving an equation, the value of D when $L = 500$ and $S = 300$.

20 Statistical Assignment

STARTING POINTS

1 For the sake of record-keeping, candidates in an exam were graded 1 to 5 according to performance. The bar chart illustrates the results.

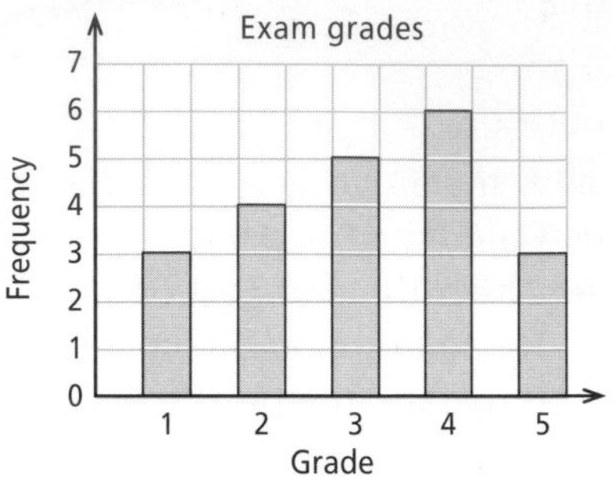

a How many achieved a grade 2?

b What is the modal grade?

c How many candidates were there?

d The table shows the same data.

Grade	1	2	3	4	5
Frequency	3	4	5	6	3

Use the table to find the mean grade.

2 Deluxe Taxi Hire uses a series of standard charges rather than mileage. The table shows the number of each type of charge the firm had over an evening.

Charge (£)	Frequency	Cumulative frequency
1	8	
2	12	
3	45	
4	21	
5	12	
6	2	

a Copy and complete the table.

b Draw a cumulative frequency diagram.

c Use the diagram to help you estimate:

(i) the median charge

(ii) the quartiles.

d Calculate the semi-interquartile range.

You will encounter different kinds of data when carrying out surveys. Sometimes the data can be counted; sometimes it is measured.

Example 1

If you wanted to survey the number of bees entering a particular area, you would count them.
The number of bees is an example of **discrete** data.

Example 2

If you wanted to examine the heights of cars, you would measure their heights.
The height of a car is an example of **continuous** data.

When there are a lot of data or when the set of data is well spread out, we often group the data for compactness and easier handling.

Number of bees	Frequency
0–4	3
5–9	5
10–14	7
15–19	1

0–4 means 0, 1, 2, 3 or 4 bees.
0 and 4 are the class limits and are both included in the group.
The table tells us that on three occasions either 0, 1, 2, 3 or 4 bees were counted in the area.

This would generally be illustrated by a bar graph where the scale on the x axis shows discrete groups.

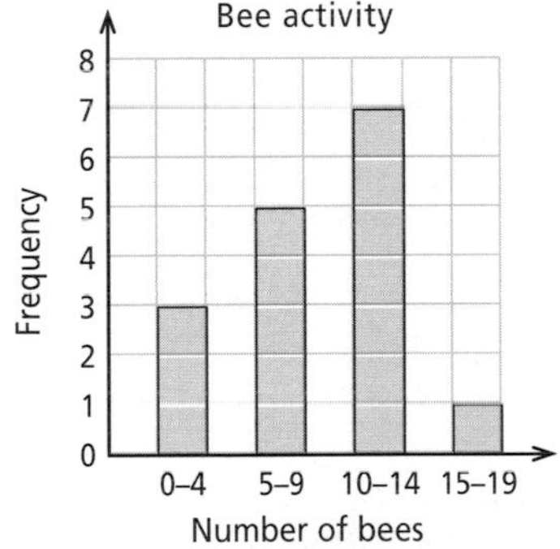

Note that the modal class is 10–14.

Height of car (cm)	Frequency
$130 \le L < 140$	2
$140 \le L < 150$	3
$150 \le L < 160$	7
$160 \le L < 170$	5

$130 \le L < 140$ refers to all the possible lengths, L cm, between 130 cm and 140 cm and has:

- a class width of $140 - 130 = 10$ cm
- a lower limit of 130 cm which is in the interval
- an upper limit of 140 cm which is not in the interval
- a mid-point of 135 cm.

This would generally be illustrated by a histogram, where the scale on the x axis is continuous.

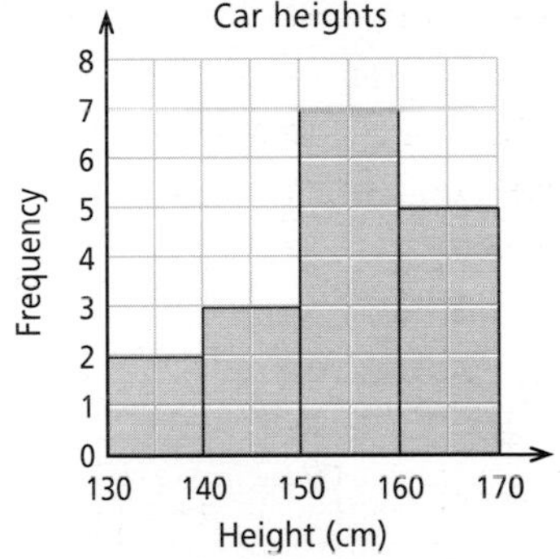

Note that the modal class is $150 \le L < 160$.

The mode itself can be estimated using the histogram.

- Identify the modal class limits, 150 and 160.
- Mark two points at 150:
  - (i) top of previous interval
  - (ii) top of modal interval.
- Mark two points at 160:
  - (i) top of modal interval
  - (ii) top of next interval.
- Join them in a cross as shown.
- Read the value on the x axis which corresponds to the intersection.
  In this case it is 157. The mode is 157 cm.

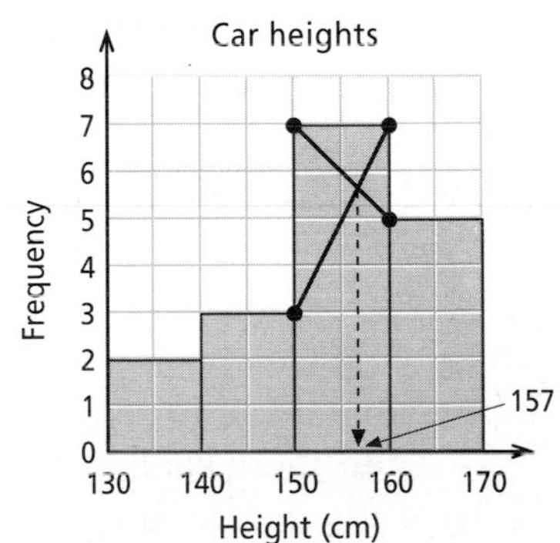

This technique can be used with discrete data if it is treated as continuous and a histogram is drawn.

EXERCISE 1

1 The table shows the time, in minutes, of the first goals scored in soccer league matches one weekend.

a Illustrate the data in a histogram.

b What is the modal class?

c Estimate the value of the mode.

Time (t min)	Frequency
$0 \le t < 10$	4
$10 \le t < 20$	9
$20 \le t < 30$	6
$30 \le t < 40$	5
$40 \le t < 50$	4
$50 \le t < 60$	4
$60 \le t < 70$	2
$70 \le t < 80$	3
$80 \le t < 90$	3

2 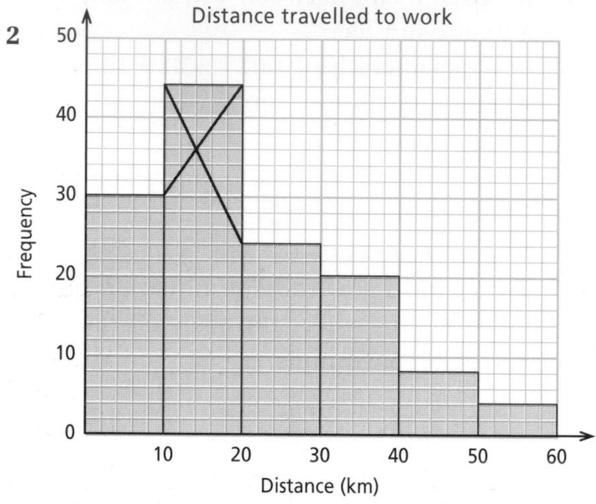

A survey of city workers is carried out to discover the distance each employee travels to work. The histogram shows the results.

a What is the modal class?

b Estimate the mode to the nearest kilometre.

c How many people took part in the survey?

3 This histogram shows the cost of quarterly telephone bills in a sample of homes.

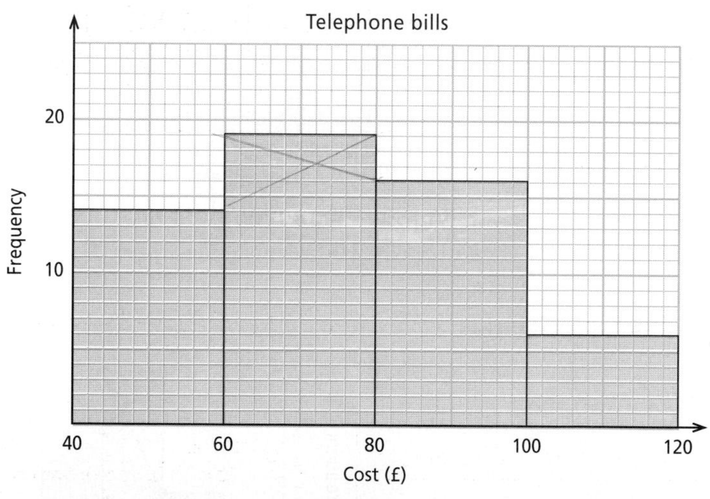

a What is the modal class?

b Estimate the mode to the nearest pound.

c How many homes were in the survey?

4 The Bonne Cuisine restaurant opened last year. The frequency table shows the number of customers who have eaten there each evening.

a Treat the data as if it were continuous and draw a histogram.

b What is the modal class number of customers each evening?

c Make a construction to estimate the mode.

Number of customers	Frequency
21–30	20
31–40	36
41–50	54
51–60	26

5 Fergus, a forestry worker, measures the heights of a sample of 100 trees in a conifer plantation. The frequency table gives the heights of the trees in metres.

a Draw a histogram of the heights of the trees.

b What is the modal class height?

c Make a construction to estimate the mode, correct to 1 d.p.

Height (h metres)	Frequency
$6 \le h < 7$	9
$7 \le h < 8$	18
$8 \le h < 9$	29
$9 \le h < 10$	26
$10 \le h < 11$	18

Estimating the mean

When data have been grouped the mean can be estimated by using the mid-values to represent the intervals.

Example

The table records the weights of 29 boys.
A third column of mid-values has been added, then a fourth column showing mid-values times frequency.
The frequency column is totalled to give the number of recordings (Σf).

Weight (kg)	f frequency	x mid-value	fx
$35 \le W < 45$	1	40	40
$45 \le W < 55$	5	50	250
$55 \le W < 65$	8	60	480
$65 \le W < 75$	12	70	840
$75 \le W < 85$	3	80	240
Totals	$\Sigma f = 29$		$\Sigma fx = 1850$

(Σ is the Greek letter *sigma*. Σf is short for 'the sum of the column headed f'.)
The last column is totalled to give an estimate of the total of all the weights (Σfx).

$$\text{mean} = \frac{\Sigma fx}{\Sigma f}$$

$$= 1850 \div 29 = 63.8 \text{ to 1 d.p.}$$

EXERCISE 2

1 A company keeps a record of the lengths of its employees' phone calls one week.

a Copy and complete the table.

Time (t minutes)	Mid-value	Frequency	Mid-value × frequency
$0 \le t < 2$	1	48	48
$2 \le t < 4$	3	69	207
$4 \le t < 6$		40	
$6 \le t < 8$		31	
$8 \le t < 10$		12	
	Total		

Note:
48 calls lasted between 0 and 2 minutes;
we assume they all lasted 1 minute.
So 48 calls at 1 minute gives 48 minutes.

This is the number of calls.

This is the total time of all the calls.

b Copy and complete the calculation to find the mean.
Mean length = total time ÷ number of calls
= ... ÷ ...
= ... minutes.

2 These are the marks of 80 students in a maths test.

Mark	Mid-value	Frequency	Mid-value × frequency
1–10	5.5	4	$5.5 \times 4 = 22$
11–20	15.5	16	$15.5 \times 16 =$
21–30		28	
31–40		20	
41–50		12	
Total		80	S

a Copy and complete the table.
b Calculate the mean: total of marks (S) ÷ 80.
c Alison scored 32. How does her mark compare with the others?

3 A survey is carried out to see how long people at the swimming baths spend in the water during the Early Bird session.

Time (min)	Mid-value	Frequency	Mid-value × frequency
$35 \leq t < 40$	37.5	8	$37.5 \times 8 =$
$40 \leq t < 45$	42.5	30	
$45 \leq t < 50$		34	
$50 \leq t < 55$		20	
$55 \leq t < 60$		8	
Total			S

a Copy and complete the table.
b Calculate the mean.
c Alan spends 45 minutes in the water. In which group is his time recorded?
d Flora swims for 55 minutes. How does her time compare with the others?

4 A ten-pin bowling club records the scores of its members in one competition.

Score(s)	Mid-value	Frequency	Mid-value × frequency
$80 \leq s < 100$		7	
$100 \leq s < 120$		15	
$120 \leq s < 140$		19	
$140 \leq s < 160$		11	
Total			

a Copy and complete the table.
b How many members are there?
c Calculate the mean.
d Alexa scored 127. Is she above or below the mean?

The median and quartiles

When working with grouped data we can estimate the value of the median and the quartiles by first drawing a suitable cumulative frequency diagram.

Example Look at this summary of test results.
Note that ten students scored between 30 and 40.

Class interval	Frequency	Cumulative frequency
$0 \le x < 10$	0	0
$10 \le x < 20$	2	2
$20 \le x < 30$	4	6
$30 \le x < 40$	10	16
$40 \le x < 50$	11	27
$50 \le x < 60$	10	37
$60 \le x < 70$	6	43
$70 \le x < 80$	4	47
$80 \le x < 90$	2	49
$90 \le x < 100$	1	50

- The cumulative frequency is plotted against the *upper* class limit. The points are then joined by straight line segments. (Note: When the points are joined by a smooth curve, the curve is often referred to as an **ogive**.)
- The vertical axis, up to the top cumulative frequency, is divided into 4 equal lengths by 3 boundaries ($50 \div 4 = 12.5$). The boundaries are: 12.5, 25, 37.5.
- The scores corresponding to the boundaries are the estimates required.

  $Q_1 = 39$ (lower quartile)
  $Q_2 = 48$ (median)
  $Q_3 = 60$ (upper quartile).

The semi-interquartile range $= \dfrac{60 - 39}{2} = 10.5$

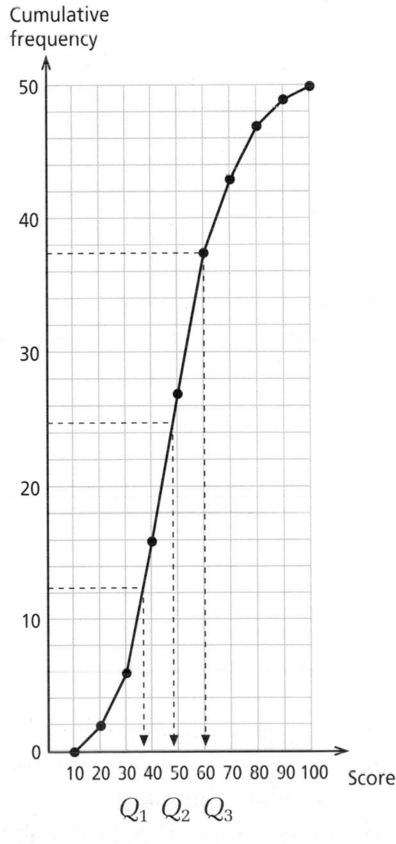

EXERCISE 3

1 The police set up a speed check in a 30 mph zone.

Speed (mph)	$0 \le S < 10$	$10 \le S < 20$	$20 \le S < 30$	$30 \le S < 40$	$40 \le S < 50$
Number of cars	5	7	18	9	1

a Draw a cumulative frequency diagram.
b Estimate the value of:
(i) the lower quartile (ii) the median (iii) the upper quartile.
c Calculate the semi-interquartile range.

2 An environmental organisation involved in water conservation collects data about the length of time people spend showering in the morning. These are the times, to the nearest 10 seconds, given by the sample:

210, 190, 150, 200, 230, 300, 190, 180, 210, 180, 260, 160, 170, 230, 150,
320, 280, 310, 190, 250, 270, 220, 330, 280, 200, 320, 240, 300, 290, 180
330, 240, 200, 340, 330, 180, 270, 240, 300, 320, 270, 280, 260, 170, 240
310, 280, 220, 290, 300, 340, 290, 180, 240, 310, 280, 190, 320, 280, 250.

a Make a frequency table with class intervals:
$150 \le t < 180$, $180 \le t < 210$, $210 \le t < 240$, etc.
b Add a cumulative frequency column.
c Draw a cumulative frequency diagram.
d Estimate the value of: (i) the lower quartile (ii) the median (iii) the upper quartile.
e Calculate the semi-interquartile range.

3 A travel agent asks clients to fill in a questionnaire about the total number of days they spend abroad in one year.
a Copy the table and complete the cumulative frequency column.
b Draw a cumulative frequency graph.
c How many people, in the survey, spend:
(i) ten days or less abroad
(ii) two weeks or more abroad?
d Estimate the values of:
(i) the median (ii) the quartiles
e Calculate the semi-interquartile range.

Number of days abroad	Frequency	Cumulative frequency
0–5	25	
6–10	70	
11–15	95	
16–20	65	
21–25	35	
26–30	10	

4

Length of loan (days)	Frequency	Cumulative frequency
0–5	4	
6–10	11	
11–15	28	
16–20	47	
21–25	36	
26–30	19	
31–35	5	

A library keeps a record of how long books are out on loan.
The table shows one morning's returns.
a Copy the table and complete the cumulative frequency column.
b Draw the cumulative frequency graph.
c Estimate the semi-interquartile range.

Your statistical assignment

Your statistical assignment is intended to give you a chance to show the statistics you have learned on your course.

It should include:

a collecting data (describe its source)
b analysis of the data and comments on findings, or analysis and comparison of two data sets
c using grouped data
d using the estimated mean, median and/or mode and quartiles
e a short report with a sensible conclusion.

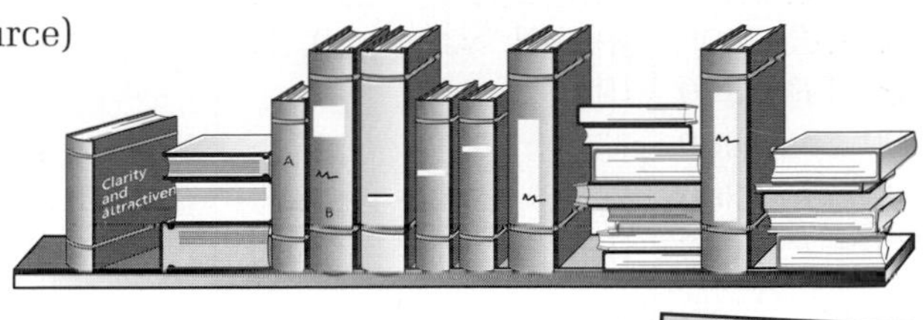

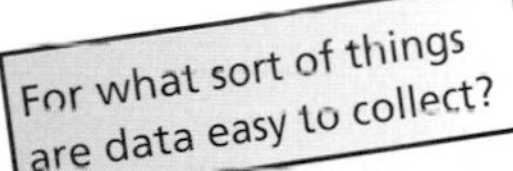

Sources:
Newspapers
Ceefax
Internet
Other people
Experiments

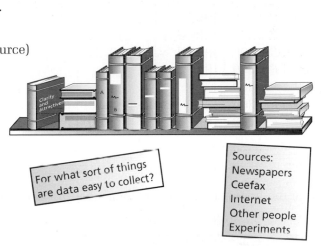

An example of a statistical assignment

Topic: *The Price of Mountain Bikes*

Task: I am going to collect information on the price of mountain bikes. I will compare the prices of new and second-hand bikes. I will collect my data from shops and advertisements in newspapers.

Data collected (in £):

Forty new bikes:
200, 180, 220, 410, 295, 400, 225, 368,
190, 260, 700, 250, 795, 790, 172, 350,
199, 250, 349, 620, 530, 270, 359, 320,
670, 279, 320, 180, 745, 325, 350, 220,
369, 475, 199, 259, 339, 799, 415, 239.

Sixty second-hand:
55, 70, 80, 85, 150, 225, 90, 400, 200, 165,
130, 60, 100, 95, 60, 85, 75, 45, 275, 130,
130, 85, 70, 90, 200, 95, 60, 80, 85, 100,
65, 50, 150, 60, 69, 85, 90, 190, 140, 145,
55, 100, 430, 200, 185, 445, 350, 400, 300, 325,
85, 400, 280, 140, 100, 95, 70, 99, 50, 150.

Data organised, displayed and analysed

New bikes

Price (£P)	Tally	Frequency
$100 \le P < 200$	卌 |	6
$200 \le P < 300$	卌 卌 ||	12
$300 \le P < 400$	卌 卌	10
$400 \le P < 500$	||||	4
$500 \le P < 600$	|	1
$600 \le P < 700$	||	2
$700 \le P < 800$	卌	5
Total		40

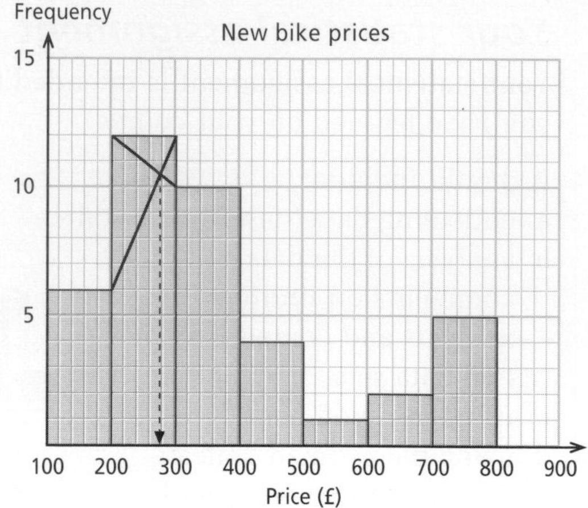

Modal class is $200 \le P < 300$ (£200–£300)

From the histogram I estimate the modal price for a new bike is £275.

Second-hand bikes

Price (£P)	Tally	Frequency
$0 \le P < 50$	|	1
$50 \le P < 100$	卌 卌 卌 卌 卌 ||||	29
$100 \le P < 150$	卌 卌	10
$150 \le P < 200$	卌 |	6
$200 \le P < 250$	||||	4
$250 \le P < 300$	||	2
$300 \le P < 350$	||	2
$350 \le P < 400$	|	1
$400 \le P < 450$	卌	5
Total		60

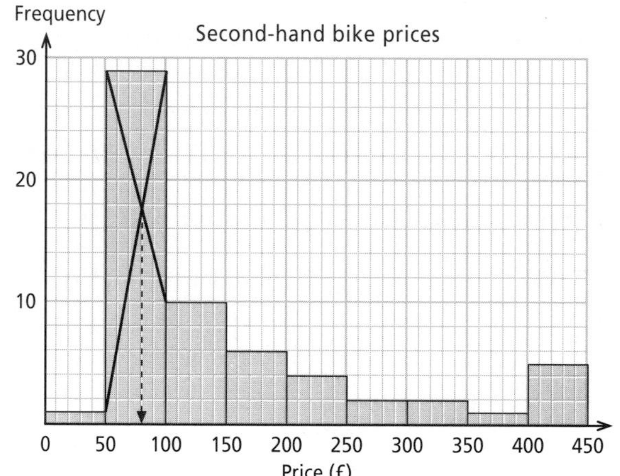

Modal class is $50 \le P < 100$ (£50–£100)

From the histogram I estimate the modal price for a second-hand bike is £80.

The mean

New bikes

Price (£P)	Mid-value	Frequency	Mid-value × frequency
$100 \le P < 200$	150	6	900
$200 \le P < 300$	250	12	3000
$300 \le P < 400$	350	10	3500
$400 \le P < 500$	450	4	1800
$500 \le P < 600$	550	1	550
$600 \le P < 700$	650	2	1300
$700 \le P < 800$	750	5	3750
	Totals	40	14 800

$14\,800 \div 40 = 370$

Mean price of a new bike = £370

Second-hand bikes

Price (£P)	Mid value	Frequency	Mid-value × frequency
$0 \le P < 50$	25	1	25
$50 \le P < 100$	75	29	2175
$100 \le P < 150$	125	10	1250
$150 \le P < 200$	175	6	1050
$200 \le P < 250$	225	4	900
$250 \le P < 300$	275	2	550
$300 \le P < 350$	325	2	650
$350 \le P < 400$	375	1	375
$400 \le P < 450$	425	5	2125
	Totals	60	9100

$9100 \div 60 = 152$

Mean price of a second-hand bike = £152

Median and quartiles

New bikes

Price (£P)	Frequency	Cumulative frequency
$100 \le P < 200$	6	6
$200 \le P < 300$	12	18
$300 \le P < 400$	10	28
$400 \le P < 500$	4	32
$500 \le P < 600$	1	33
$600 \le P < 700$	2	35
$700 \le P < 800$	5	40
Totals		

Second-hand bikes

Price (£P)	Frequency	Cumulative frequency
$0 \le P < 50$	1	1
$50 \le P < 100$	29	30
$100 \le P < 150$	10	40
$150 \le P < 200$	6	46
$200 \le P < 250$	4	50
$250 \le P < 300$	2	52
$300 \le P < 350$	2	54
$350 \le P < 400$	1	55
$400 \le P < 450$	5	60
Totals	60	

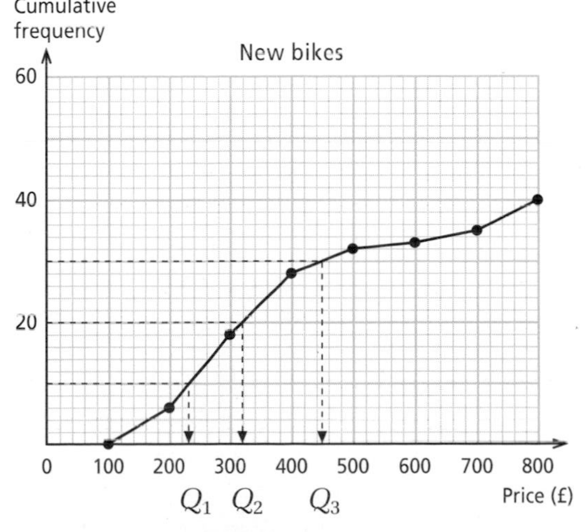

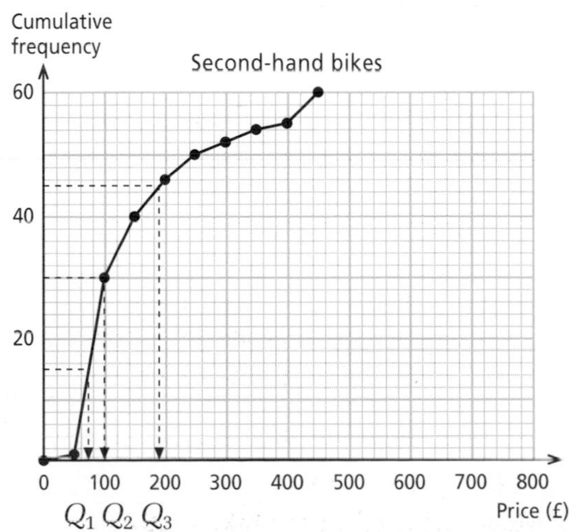

Median = £320
Lower quartile Q_1 = £240
Upper quartile Q_3 = £460
Interquartile range = £460 – £240
= £220
Semi-interquartile range = £220 ÷ 2
= £110

Median = £100
Lower quartile Q_1 = £75
Upper quartile Q_3 = £190
Interquartile range = £190 – £75
= £115
Semi-interquartile range = £115 ÷ 2
= £57.5

Data summary		
	New bike	Second-hand bike
Modal class	£200–£300	£50–£100
Mode	£275	£80
Mean	£370	£152
Median	£320	£100
SIQR	£110	£57.50

Conclusion

- The mode of a second-hand bike (£80) is much less than the mode of a new one (£275). I thought that it might be about half the price but it is less than a third.
- The mean prices for both new and second-hand bikes are quite a lot higher than the mode. This is because a few special bikes are very expensive and just one or two high prices can push the mean up a lot.
- The median prices are a bit higher than the mode. The median prices give a good idea of how much a typical bike might cost. There are a lot of second-hand bikes in the £50–£100 price class and so if I wanted to buy one in this class I ought to have quite a few to choose from.
- There are not many new bikes for less than £200 and it is unlikely that I could buy a second-hand one for less than £50.
- The interquartile ranges (the middle 50%) for both new (£220) and second-hand (£140) show a wide spread. As the range of prices of new bikes is likely to be much higher than that of second-hand ones it is not surprising that the interquartile range for second-hand ones is much less than that for new ones.

CHAPTER 20 REVIEW

1 Eggs are graded into sizes by weight. The table gives the sizes.

Size	Weight (g)	Frequency
7	$40 \le W < 45$	
6	$45 \le W < 50$	
5	$50 \le W < 55$	
4	$55 \le W < 60$	
3	$60 \le W < 65$	
2	$65 \le W < 70$	
1	$70 \le W < 75$	
	Total	

These are the weights, in grams, of the eggs collected one day at Chirpy Chick Farm:

52, 63, 47, 66, 51, 49, 61, 67, 48, 57,
63, 68, 44, 66, 54, 56, 71, 58, 63, 65,
61, 54, 58, 49, 44, 68, 69, 53, 70, 65,
69, 70, 46, 57, 62, 67, 45, 58, 62, 69,
68, 58, 52, 67, 62, 58, 48, 62, 74, 66.

a Copy and complete the table.
b How many eggs were collected?
c Which is the modal size?
d Draw a histogram of the data, plotting weight against frequency.
e Estimate the modal weight.

2 A collection of magazines was surveyed to see how many pages were devoted to advertisements. The following cumulative frequency diagram was produced from the data.

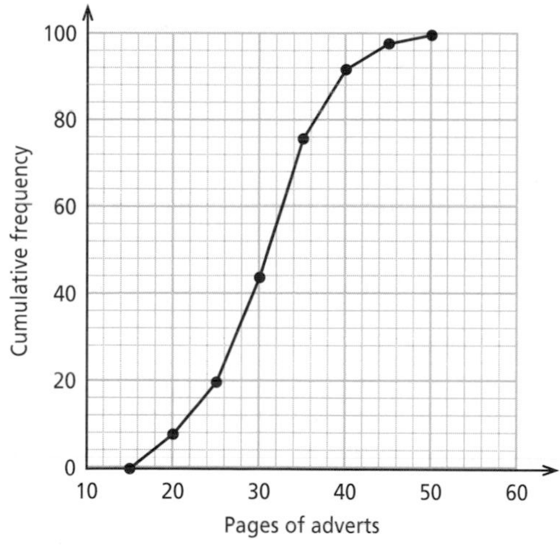

Pages	Frequency
11–15	0
16–20	8
21–25	12
26–30	24
31–35	32
36–40	16
41–45	7
46–50	1

a How many magazines were in the survey?
b How many magazines had:
(i) less than 30 pages of adverts **(ii)** more than 40 pages?
c Estimate:
(i) the median number of pages **(ii)** the quartiles
(iii) the semi-interquartile range.
d By making use of mid-values, calculate an estimate for the mean number of pages.

21 Revising Unit 4

Calculations in a social context: earnings

Reminders

A simple wageslip:

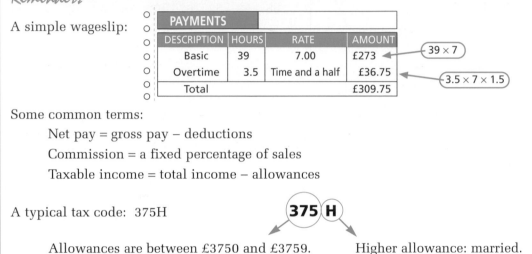

PAYMENTS			
DESCRIPTION	HOURS	RATE	AMOUNT
Basic	39	7.00	£273
Overtime	3.5	Time and a half	£36.75
Total			£309.75

39×7

$3.5 \times 7 \times 1.5$

Some common terms:

Net pay = gross pay − deductions

Commission = a fixed percentage of sales

Taxable income = total income − allowances

A typical tax code: 375H

375 H

Allowances are between £3750 and £3759. Higher allowance: married.

EXERCISE 1

1 Simon works at a textile mill.
He does 3 hours of overtime on Friday night at time and a half, and 4 and a half hours on Saturday morning at double time.
If his basic rate of pay is £6.00 per hour, how much is he paid for his overtime?

2 Calculate the total gross amount on this weekly payslip.

PAYMENTS			
DESCRIPTION	HOURS	RATE	AMOUNT
Basic	35	6.50	
Overtime	8.5	Time and a half	
Total			

3 Helen McCann is a salesperson in a major department store.
She is paid 3% commission on all her sales.
One month she made £15 000 worth of sales.
Her basic monthly salary is £1100.

a Calculate: **(i)** her commission for that month **(ii)** her total monthly gross pay.

b That month she paid £294 in tax and £93 in National Insurance payments.
A payment of £7 was also deducted for union subscriptions.
Calculate: **(i)** the total deductions **(ii)** Helen's net salary.

4 Tessa Dayton is an apprentice plumber. Here is her payslip for one week. Calculate the missing entries.

Payments				Deductions	
Description	Hours	Rate	Amount	Description	Amount
Basic	35	4.40	a	Tax	39.29
Overtime	8	6.60	b	National Insurance	12.41
	Total		c	Total	d

Date	Tax code	Employee name	Net pay:	e
10/07/98	345L	Tessa Dayton		

5 a Mr Pascal gets the higher personal allowance. His total allowances come to £7159. What is his tax code?

b Marjory Lemington has 647L for a tax code. Describe, as best you can, her allowances.

6 Peter Marshal is a technical assistant. He is married and has an annual gross income of £26 792. His allowances for the year are £5614. He pays tax on his taxable income at the following rates: 20% on the first £4000 and 25% on the rest. Calculate:

a his taxable income

b the amount of tax he pays in a year

c his net annual pay

d his net weekly pay

e his tax code.

7 Martha Cummings, a building surveyor, is paid £22 450 a year. Last year she received a summer holiday bonus of £155, a Christmas bonus of £500 and an expenses payment of £1000.

a Calculate her total income for the year.

b Her total annual allowances come to £5196. Calculate her taxable income.

c Tax is levied at a rate of 24%. Calculate:
(i) the tax Martha pays (ii) her annual income after tax.

8 As a photographer for a newspaper Malik is paid an annual salary of £35 000.
He is also given holiday bonuses which are worth £1200 to him.
When his photographs are sold to other papers he is paid 8% commission on the sale.
This particular year he is to receive commission on £12 000 worth of sales.

a Calculate his total income this year.

b His tax allowances come to £3100. Calculate his taxable income.

c Tax is levied at the following rates: 18% of the first £4000, 25% of the next £20 000, 30% of the rest.
Calculate: (i) the total tax due (ii) Malik's net annual salary.

Calculations in a social context: borrowing

Without protection				
APR on £1000	12 months	24 months	36 months	4 mo
18	£91.05	£49.28	£35.49	£2
19	£91.45	£49.69	£35.91	£2
20	£91.86	£50.10	£36.34	£2
21	£92.26	£50.51	£36.76	£2
22	£92.66	£50.92	£37.19	£
23	£93.06	£51.33	£37.61	£
24	£93.45	£51.73	£38.04	£
25	£94.85	£52.14	£38.46	£
26	£94.24	£52.54	£38.88	£
27	£94.63	£52.94	£39.31	£
28	£95.02	£53.34	£39.73	£

With protection				
APR on £1000	12 months	24 months	36 months	48 months
18	£97.42	£54.21	£40.10	£32.98
19	£97.85	£54.66	£40.58	£33.49
20	£98.29	£55.11	£41.06	£34.00
21	£98.72	£55.56	£41.54	£34.52
22	£99.14	£56.01	£42.02	£35.03
23	£99.57	£56.46	£42.50	£35.54
24	£99.99	£56.91	£42.98	£36.05
25	£100.42	£57.35	£43.46	£36.56
26	£100.83	£57.79	£43.94	£37.07
27	£101.25	£58.24	£44.42	£37.58
28	£101.67	£58.68	£44.89	£38.09

Example £3500 is borrowed and repaid over 24 months at an APR of 23%. Loan protection is not wanted. Calculate: **a** the monthly repayments **b** the total amount paid **c** the cost of the loan.

a From the first table the repayment per £1000 is £51.33.
So $3.5 \times 51.33 = 179.66$
The monthly repayments are £179.66.

b $24 \times 179.66 = 4311.84$
The total amount paid is £4311.84.

c $4311.84 - 3500 = 811.84$
The cost of the loan is £811.84.

EXERCISE 2

1 This table converts monthly interest rates to the equivalent APR.
It also gives the size of the repayments for each £1000 borrowed over 12 months.

What the monthly rate means when you repay in equal amounts over one year.		
Monthly rate (%)	APR	12 payments of
1.0	12.68	£88.85
1.1	14.03	£89.41
1.2	15.39	£89.98
1.3	16.77	£90.54
1.4	18.16	£91.11
1.5	19.56	£91.68
1.6	20.98	£92.25
1.7	22.42	£92.83
1.8	23.87	£93.40
1.9	25.34	£93.98
2.0	26.82	£94.56
2.1	28.32	£95.14

a State the APR which is equivalent to the following monthly rates:
(i) 1.3% (ii) 1.8% (iii) 2.0%.

b 18% APR is equivalent to a monthly rate of between 1.3% and 1.4%.
Make similar statements about the following:
(i) 16% APR (ii) 20% APR (iii) 25% APR.

c State the monthly repayments when £1000 is borrowed over a year at a monthly rate of:
(i) 1.1% (ii) 1.5% (iii) 2.1%.

d Calculate the monthly repayments when:
(i) £3000 is borrowed for a year at 1.6% per month
(ii) £5500 is borrowed for a year at 1.3% per month
(iii) £60 000 is borrowed for a year at 2% per month.

e £2000 is borrowed over 12 months. Calculate the total amount repaid if the interest rate is:
(i) 1.3% per month (ii) 1.4% per month.

f Give a guide as to how much it will cost to borrow £2000 over 12 months at an APR of 18%. Use your answers to part **e** to help you.

g Give a guide as to how much it will cost to borrow £4000 over 12 months at an APR of 19%.

In questions **2** to **5** refer to the tables above the start of this exercise.

2 Florence McLean took out a £2000 loan to pay for a skiing holiday. She paid it back in 12 equal instalments at an APR of 19%. She did not take out loan protection.
a What is her monthly repayment?
b What is the total repayment?
c What is the cost of the loan?

3 Transco Unlimited want to renovate their fleet of trucks. They take out a loan of £100 000. The APR is 22%. The loan is taken out over 3 years. They don't want loan protection.
a Calculate:
(i) the monthly repayments (ii) the total repayment (iii) the cost of the loan.
b If they are told that loan protection is part of the conditions of the loan, what then is the total cost of the loan?

4 Mr and Mrs Jacobson want to borrow £5000 to buy some furniture.
They feel £250 a month is as much as they can cope with as a monthly repayment.
The APR is 23%. They are not sure whether to take out loan protection.
a Work out their repayments over: (i) 24 months (ii) 36 months.
b Which of these plans is affordable?
c Calculate the total cost of the affordable plan.

5 Margaret Millar takes out a loan of £12 000 over 2 years, without protection, to buy a 4×4 truck.
a At an APR of 23% what is: (i) the monthly repayment (ii) the total repayment?
b Before she can take out the loan the interest rate rises to 24% APR.
How much more will the truck cost her, assuming she is still willing to take out the loan over 2 years?

6 Here are some details of Jack Brown's credit card.

Gold Card	
Annual fee	£10
Monthly rate of interest	2.2%
Annual percentage rate (APR)	29.8%
Minimum monthly repayment	£5 or 3%

Here is a copy of his monthly account from Gold Card. Calculate the missing amounts.

Purchases	£	Monthly interest at 2.2%	=	b
Tailor	217.90			
Thomson & Son	45.76	Total amount due	=	c
F. Brown	97.99			
Transcard	13.45	Minimum monthly repayment	=	3% of total amount due or £5 whichever is greater
Total	a			
Payment is due by 21 11 99. Payment can be sent direct or through a bank account.			=	£ d

Spreadsheets

Reminder

B2	✕ ✓ = A2*4
	A	**B**

	A	B
1	Number	4 times table
2	1	4
3	2	8
4	3	12
5	4	16
6	5	20
7	6	24
8	7	28
9	8	32
10	9	36
11	10	40
12		

Cell B2 is selected.
Its contents show up in the Edit bar: = A2 *4

A1 contains a label: Number
A2 contains a number: 1
A3 contains a formula: = A2 + 1
B2 contains a formula: = A2*4

Both columns are 'filled down' to row 11 with equivalent formulae so that, for example:
A11 contains the formula = A10 + 1
B11 contains the formula = A11*4

Cells A12 and B12 are empty.

The purpose of the spreadsheet is to show the 4 times table.

EXERCISE 3

1 Many rectangles have an area of 12 cm^2. What is the length and breadth of the rectangle with an area of 12 cm^2 which has the smallest perimeter? This spreadsheet resulted from an attempt to tackle this problem. All cells have been formatted for fixed precision 2. Row 1 contains labels. Only cell A2 contains a number. The rest contain formulae.

	A	B	C	D
1	Length	Breadth	Area	Perimeter
2	1.00	12.00	12.00	26.00
3	2.00	6.00	12.00	16.00
4	3.00	4.00	12.00	14.00
5	4.00	3.00	12.00	14.00
6	5.00	2.40	12.00	14.80
7	6.00	2.00	12.00	16.00
8	7.00	1.71	12.00	17.43
9	8.00	1.50	12.00	19.00
10	9.00	1.33	12.00	20.67
11	10.00	1.20	12.00	22.40
12	11.00	1.09	12.00	24.18
13	12.00	1.00	12.00	26.00

a What formula is in cell: **(i)** A3 **(ii)** A4 **(iii)** A5?

b We need A2 times B2 to make 12. What formula goes into cell: **(i)** B2 **(ii)** B3 **(iii)** B4?

c Column C is used to check and reinforce the idea that the area is indeed always 12. What formula goes into: **(i)** C2 **(ii)** C3 **(iii)** C4?

d What formula goes into cell: **(i)** D2 **(ii)** D3 **(iii)** D4?

e Examine column D and state between which two rectangles the one with the smallest perimeter is to be found.

f The spreadsheet is adjusted as shown to refine the search.

	A	B	C	D
1	Length	Breadth	Area	Perimeter
2	3.00	4.00	12.00	14.00
3	3.10	3.87	12.00	13.94
4	3.20	3.75	12.00	13.90
5	3.30	3.64	12.00	13.87
6	3.40	3.53	12.00	13.86
7	3.50	3.43	12.00	13.86
8	3.60	3.33	12.00	13.87
9	3.70	3.24	12.00	13.89
10	3.80	3.16	12.00	13.92
11	3.90	3.08	12.00	13.95

(i) What change has been made to the number in A2?

(ii) A formula has been put in A3 and 'filled down'. What is this formula?

(iii) Examine column D and describe the two rectangles between which the one with the smallest perimeter is to be found.

g (i) Another set of adjustments is made as shown. Describe the adjustment to cell A2, column A, column D.
(ii) Why was the adjustment to column D needed?
(iii) The rectangle required seems to be a square of side 3.46 or 3.47. What is special about the number?

	A	B	C	D
1	Length	Breadth	Area	Perimeter
2	3.40	3.53	12.00	13.859
3	3.41	3.52	12.00	13.858
4	3.42	3.51	12.00	13.858
5	3.43	3.50	12.00	13.857
6	3.44	3.49	12.00	13.857
7	3.45	3.48	12.00	13.857
8	3.46	3.47	12.00	13.856
9	3.47	3.46	12.00	13.856
10	3.48	3.45	12.00	13.857
11	3.49	3.44	12.00	13.857
12	3.50	3.43	12.00	13.857
13	3.51	3.42	12.00	13.858

2 This spreadsheet calculates the wages of employees in a small firm.

F6 ×✓

	A	B	C	D	E	F
1	Employee	Basic rate	Hours	Pay	Hours (time & half)	Overtime pay
2	Dan Kenneth	£6.25	35	£218.75	6	£56.25
3	Harry McLean	£5.80	37	£214.60	12	£104.40
4	Tom McCann	£4.90	48	£235.20	0	£0.00

a Column D works out the basic wage. What formula is in cell D2?
b Column F works out the overtime pay. What formula goes in cell F2?
c Column G is to be created to work out the total wage of each employee. What formula goes in cell G2?
d Write down a formula for cell G5 which will give the total wage bill for the firm.

3 Experiments are carried out to see if dice are fair. Each dice is thrown ten times and the results averaged.

B2 ×✓ = 5*RAND() + 1

	A	B	C	D	E	F	G	H	I	J	K	L
1	Dice											Average
2	1	1	1	1	3	5	3	5	3	4	2	2.92
3	2	5	2	4	3	1	3	4	6	4	6	3.80
4	3	6	2	3	3	5	6	5	4	3	1	3.74
5	4	6	6	4	3	4	6	5	2	1	6	4.29
6	5	3	6	1	2	2	5	3	4	1	5	3.28
7	6	5	2	3	4	3	3	4	4	4	3	3.55
8	7	1	4	5	3	2	2	2	4	1	2	2.75
9												3.48

a What average do you expect from a fair dice?
(What is the average of 1, 2, 3, 4, 5 and 6?)

b The spreadsheet has had the data for 7 dice entered.

(i) L2 holds the formula for calculating the average of the throws in B2 to K2. How would this appear in the Edit bar?

(ii) What formula is held in L6?

c L9 holds the formula for the average for all the throws.
Write down two different formulae which would do the job.

d As you can see in the Edit bar we didn't have dice to throw.
We got the spreadsheet to simulate dice.
First we format the required cells to fixed precision 0.
Then the formula = 5 *RAND() + 1 does the trick.
(It has been entered in cells B2 to K8.)
Altering the 5 alters the range of numbers you get.
Enter one less than you want.
Design a spreadsheet which will provide you with six numbers for the lottery.

4

	A	B	C	D
1	x	$2x + 1$	x	$5 - 3x$
2	-5	-9	-5	20
3	-4	-7	-4	17
4	-3	-5	-3	14
5	-2	-3	-2	11
6	-1	-1	-1	8
7	0	1	0	5
8	1	3	1	2
9	2	5	2	-1
10	3	7	3	-4
11	4	9	4	-7
12	5	11	5	-10
13	6	13	6	-13
14	7	15	7	-16

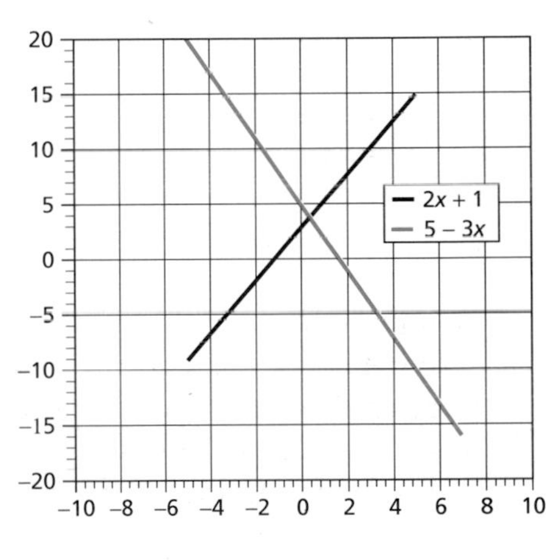

This spreadsheet has been constructed to help solve the pair of simultaneous equations $y = 2x + 1$ and $y = 5 - 3x$.

a A2 contains the number –5. The rest of the row contains formulae. Describe these formulae.

b The chart on the right has been made by the spreadsheet. What solutions does it suggest?

c Construct the spreadsheet and refine it to obtain more accurate solutions.

Network diagrams

Reminder

A network

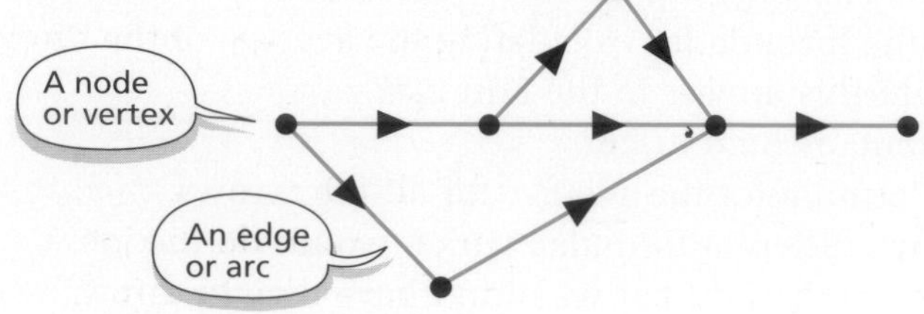

A school extension can be described diagramatically by a network as shown. Arrows can be added to indicate any one-way system.

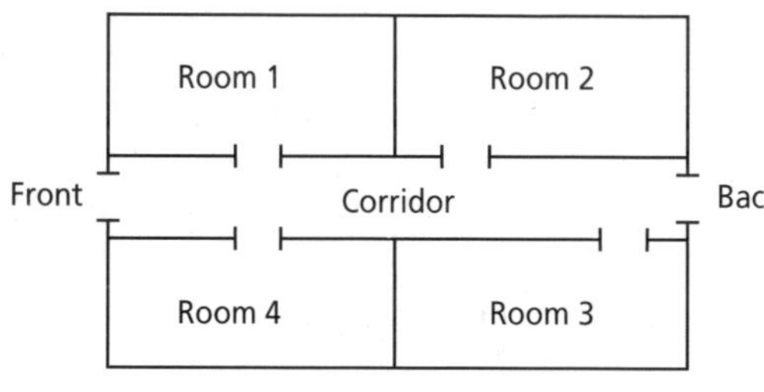

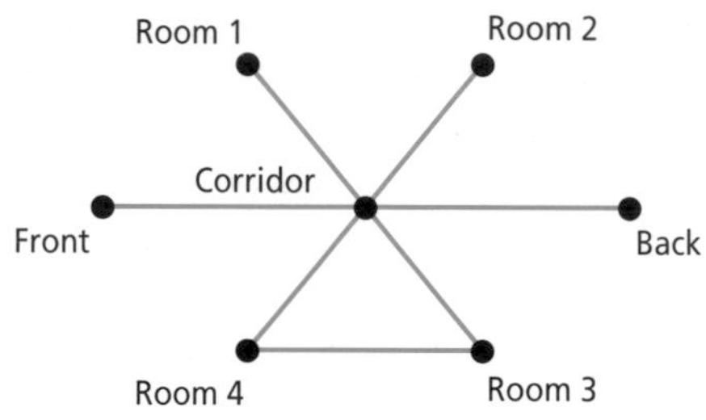

EXERCISE 4

1 Draw networks to represent the following room systems.

a

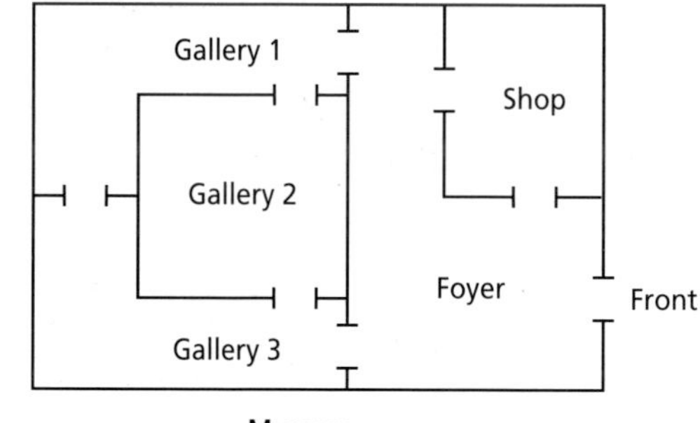

b

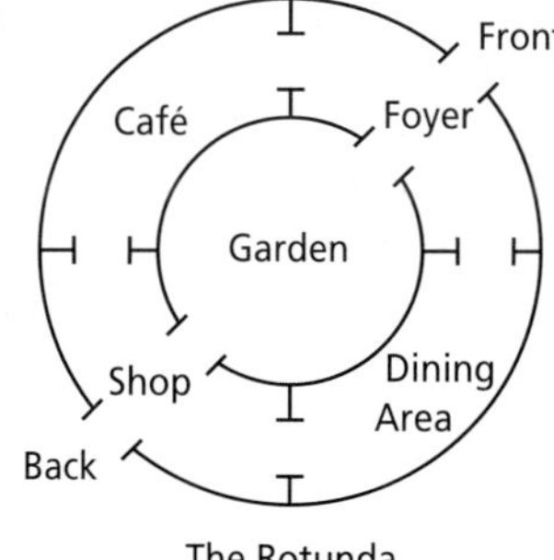

2 This is a plan of the ground floor of an art gallery which is housing a special exhibition.

a Draw a network to represent the layout.

b Find an efficient route through the network, visiting every arc once only. (Note: two arcs will join Galleries 1 and 2; one vertex is enough to represent outside.)

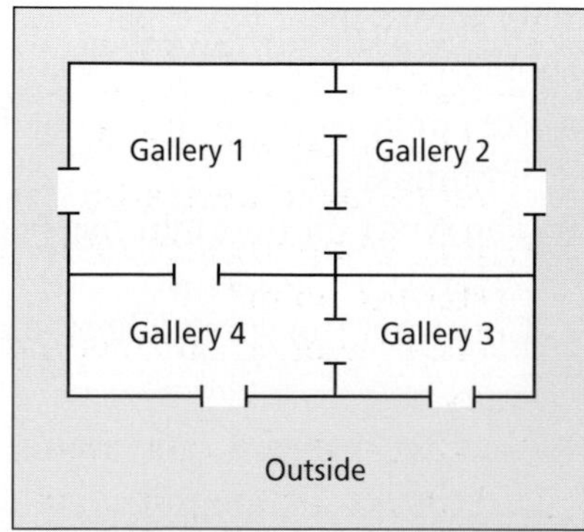

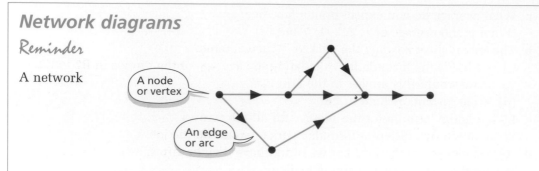

3

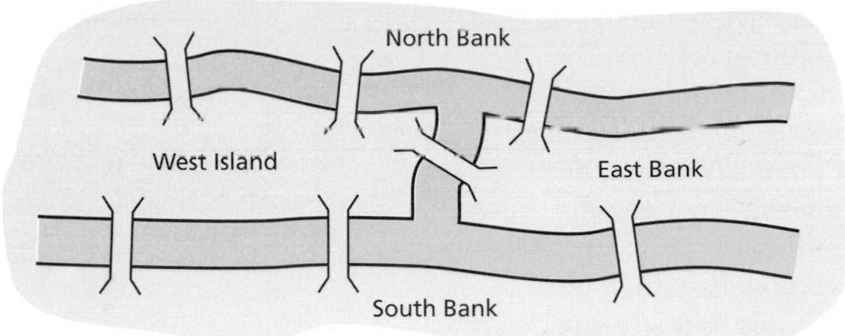

The diagram shows the Konigsberg bridges.
An island sits at a fork in a river. The three banks and the island were connected by seven bridges. On Sundays, people would go for a walk and try to cross each bridge only once before returning to their starting point.

a Make a network to represent the situation. Let a bit of land be represented by a vertex and a bridge by an arc.

b How many odd nodes are there in the network. Is it possible to do the described walk?

c Suggest minimal alterations which would make the walk possible.

4

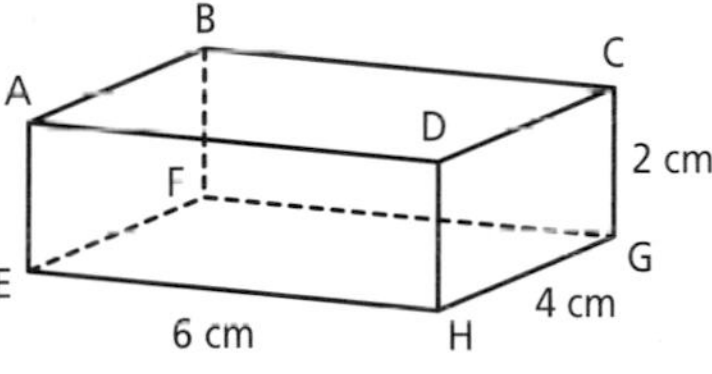

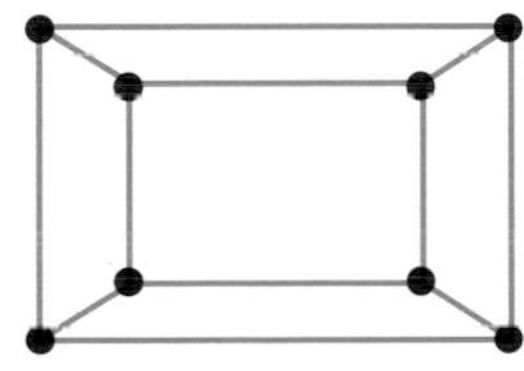

The cuboid ABCDEFGH can be represented by a network of the form shown.

a **(i)** Label each vertex. **(ii)** Mark the length of each edge.

b A spider walks along the edges, visiting each vertex once and only once.
Find: **(i)** any route which does this
(ii) the shortest such route
(iii) the longest such route.

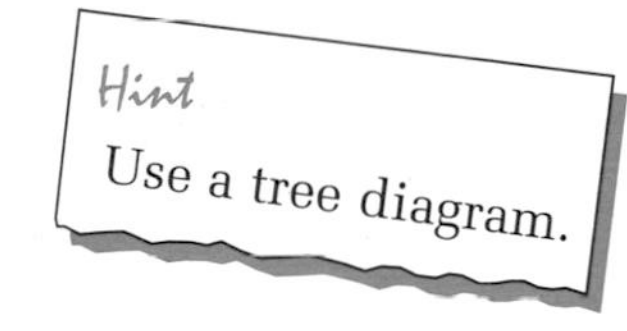

5 The map forms a network of roads and towns.

a A bread delivery man has to visit each town to supply the shops. What is the shortest route through the network:
(i) if he is not worried about returning to his starting point
(ii) if it is important to return to his starting point?

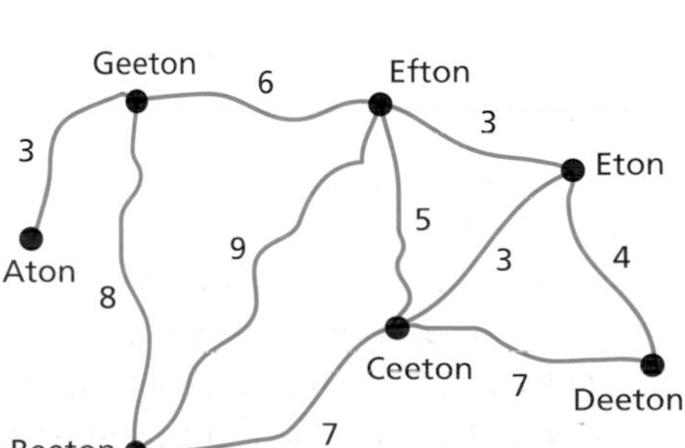

b This is a region of outstanding scenic beauty.
(i) What is the shortest route which takes in every road?
(ii) What is the longest route which doesn't go along the same road twice?

6 Michaela delivers papers. The network shows the possible routes between the supply shop and her home. The numbers on the arcs represent potential customers. She wants to find a route between the shop and her home which doesn't run along the same street (arc) twice, although she is happy to pass the same corner (vertex) more than once. She also wants to supply as many customers as possible. Suggest a suitable route.

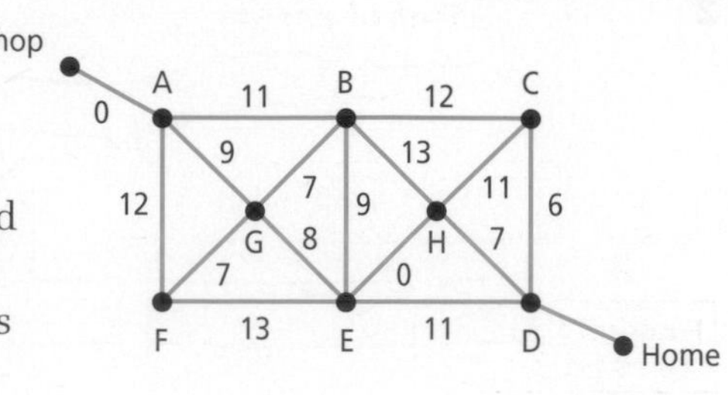

7 The network gives a logical breakdown of the steps in resurfacing a road. Each vertex represents the completion of a task. Each arc represents the task being done. The associated number is the time taken to do the task in hours.

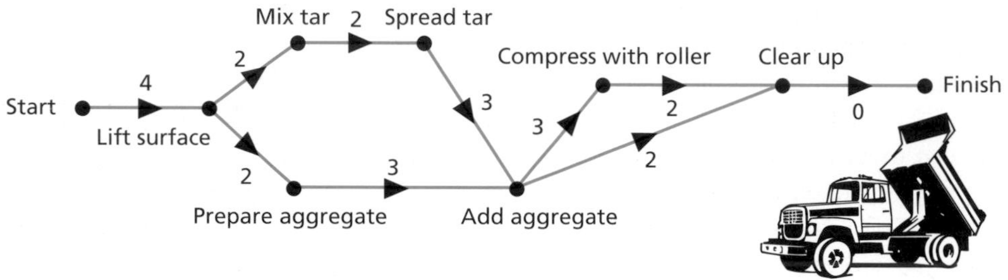

Find the longest route through the network and hence the quickest the job can be done.

Flowcharts

Reminder

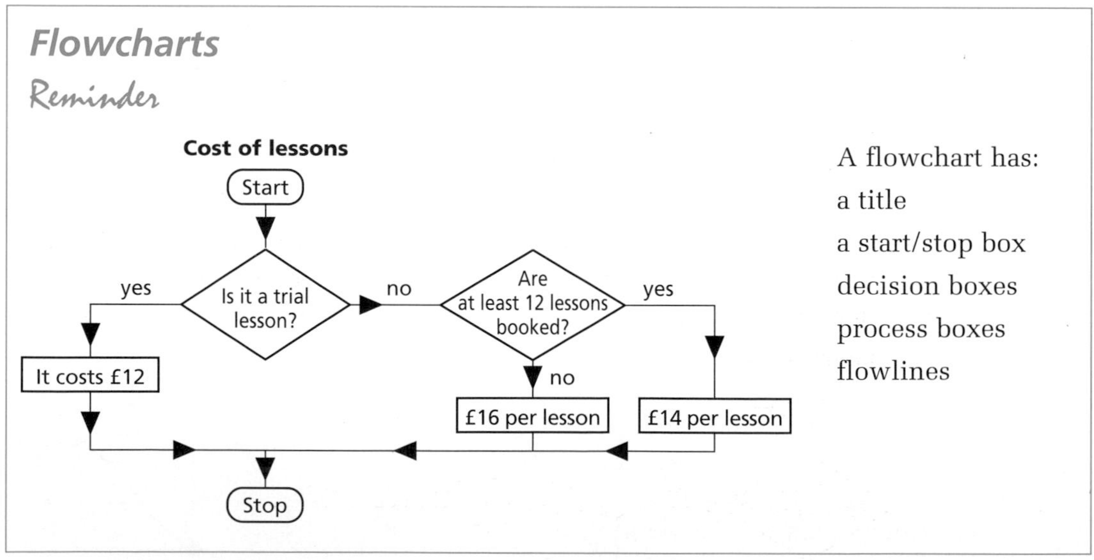

A flowchart has:
a title
a start/stop box
decision boxes
process boxes
flowlines

EXERCISE 5

1 Use the above flowchart to help you calculate the charge for:

a 1 trial lesson

b 8 lessons

c 14 lessons.

2

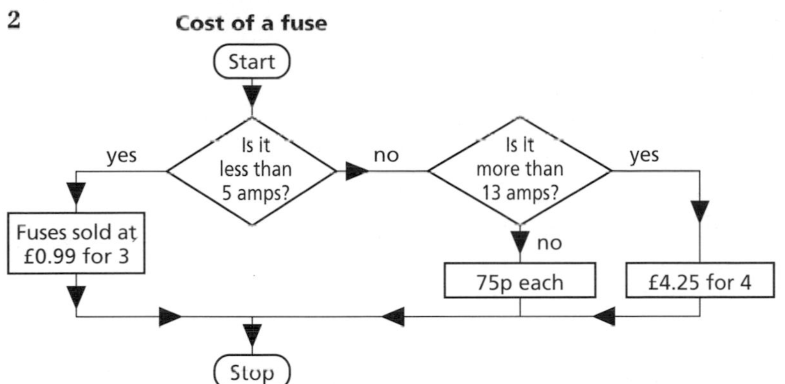

The cost of a fuse depends on its rating.
What is the cost of:

a a 13 amp fuse
b six 3 amp fuses
c twelve 15 amp fuses?

3 Margaret Weir works for £6.80 per hour. She can earn overtime.
If she meets her targets she is paid a bonus.

a What does she earn when she works for 34 hours but isn't paid the bonus?
b Calculate her earnings when she works for 50 hours and gets the bonus.
c How much is the bonus?

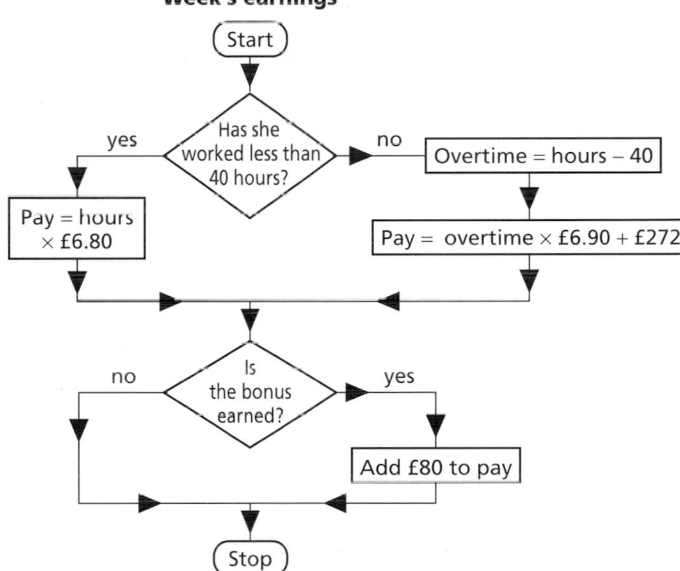

4 Maureen is a saleswoman. She doesn't start to get commission on sales until they are over £6000. If the sales go over £12 000 she is paid a special bonus commission.
Calculate her salary when her sales were: **a** £8000 **b** £18 000 **c** £5000.

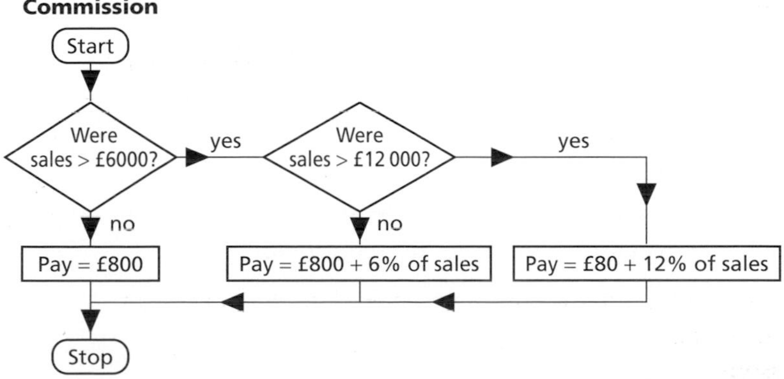

Can you work out why this process box reads as it does? Pay – £80 + 12% of sales

5

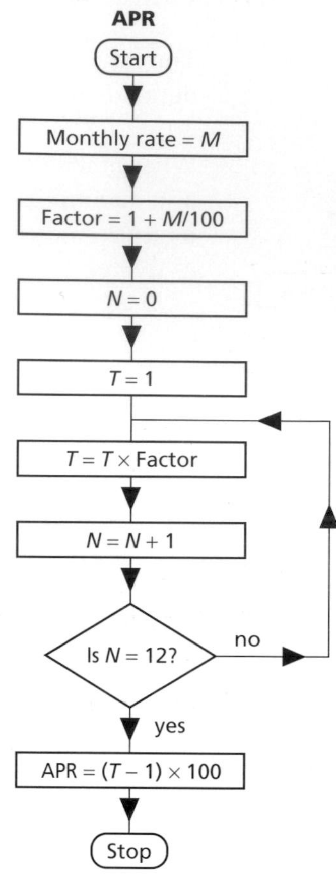

This flowchart helps you calculate the APR when the monthly rate, $M\%$, of interest is known.

a The boxes which read $N = 0$ and $N = N + 1$ form what is known as a **count**. What is it counting up to?

b With the aid of a calculator, fixed to 2 d.p., calculate the APR when $M =$ **(i)** 1 **(ii)** 3 **(iii)** 5.

c With the aid of the button y^x calculate (factor)^{12} to check your answers.

6 **a** Construct a flowchart to calculate a person's wage when the hours are known.
- The person's basic rate is £6 per hour.
- Any time over 35 hours is paid at double time.

b Test your flowchart using: **(i)** 30 hours **(ii)** 40 hours.

7 Construct a flowchart to calculate a man's wage when the hours and his age are known.
- If he is under 25 years his basic rate is £5 per hour.
- If he is 25 years or over then his basic wage is £6.50 per hour.
- Any time over 35 hours is paid at time and a half.

8 If you use a Scotia Bank credit card the charge at the end of the month is 4% of the amount due.
If you use Barland Credit the rate is 5% of the amount due.
However, if the amount due in either bank is less than £100, then there is no charge.
Construct a flowchart to illustrate these options.

Formulae

Reminder

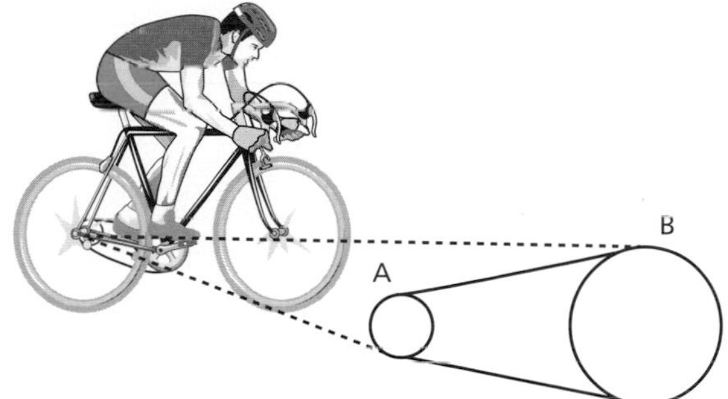

In a bicycle, cogwheel B turns and the chain makes cogwheel A turn.

Formula expressed in words

The speed of A (in revolutions per minute)

$= \frac{\text{the diameter of B} \times \text{the speed of B}}{\text{the diameter of A}}$

Formula expressed in symbols

$$S_A = \frac{D_B \times S_B}{D_A}$$

where D_A cm is the diameter of A
D_B cm is the diameter of B
S_A rpm is the speed of A
S_B rpm is the speed of B.

If the diameter of A = 6 cm, the diameter of B = 12 cm and the speed of B = 150 rpm, then the speed of A = (12 × 150) ÷ 6 = 300 rpm.

EXERCISE 6

1 Use the above formula to help you calculate the speed of A when:

a the diameter of A = 8 cm, the diameter of B = 12 cm and the speed of B = 200 rpm.

b D_A = 9 cm, D_B = 21 cm and S_B = 250 rpm.

2 The perimeter of a square is 4 times the square root of its area. Find the perimeter of a square whose area is:

a 16 cm^2 **b** 196 cm^2 **c** 10 000 m^2.

3 A wall is built on a hill. Its top, however, remains horizontal. Its ends remain vertical. When the wall is being repointed, the builder estimates the cost by first calculating the area. Area of wall = average of the two ends multiplied by its length. Calculate the area of each wall.

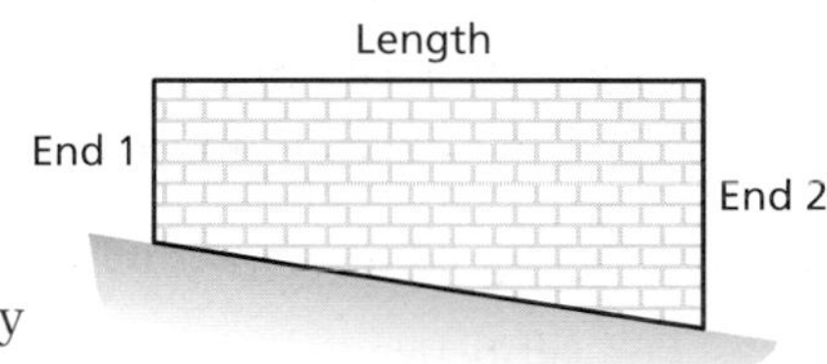

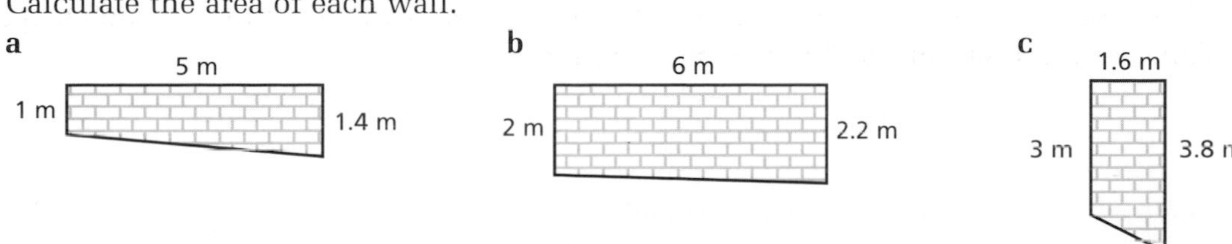

4 Galileo discovered that the time it takes for a pendulum to swing depends on its length. The length, L cm, of a pendulum can be worked out when you know the time, T seconds, of the swing you desire.

$$L = \frac{8T^2}{\pi^2}$$

How long is a pendulum whose swing lasts for:

a 3 seconds **b** 2.4 seconds? (Answer to 2 d.p.)

5 When something travels in a straight line with constant acceleration, the acceleration, a cm per second per second, after t seconds can be calculated using the formula

$$a = \frac{V - U}{t}$$

where V cm per second is the final velocity and U cm per second is the initial velocity. Calculate a when:

a $V = 5$, $U = 1$ and $t = 2$ **b** $V = 22$, $U = 8$ and $t = 5$ **c** $V = 8.9$, $U = 1.4$ and $t = 3.2$.

6 A plastics firm makes pipes.

The volume, V cm^3, of plastic needed to make a pipe of length L m, internal radius r m and external radius R m, can be worked out using the formula

$$V = \pi L(R - r)(R + r).$$

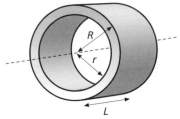

a What volume of plastic is needed to make a pipe:

(i) of length 10 m, internal radius 1 m, external radius 1.3 m

(ii) of length 5.5 m, internal radius 1.2 m, external radius 1.4 m?

b Calculate V when (i) $L = 6$, $R = 2.5$, $r = 1.9$

(ii) $L = 2.3$, $R = 2.4$, $r = 1.8$

7 A road barrier, 10 m long, can be raised or lowered, as shown.

A weight, W kg, is d cm from the pivot. This is balanced by a counterweight c kg.

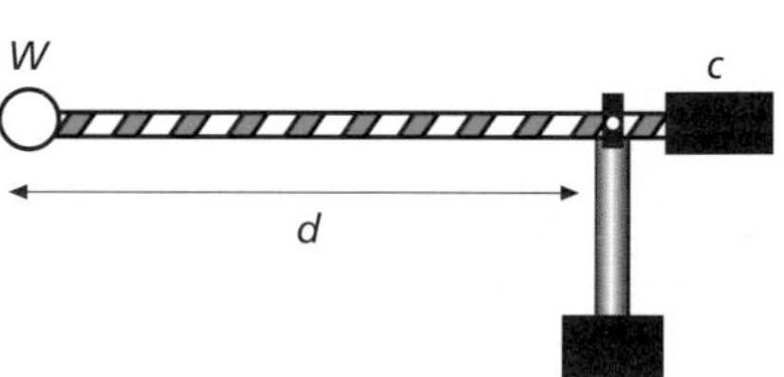

These are related by the formula $d = \frac{1000c}{W + c}$

a Calculate d when: (i) $W = 10$ and $c = 50$

(ii) $W = 5$ and $c = 80$.

b Calculate W when $d = 800$ and $c = 100$.

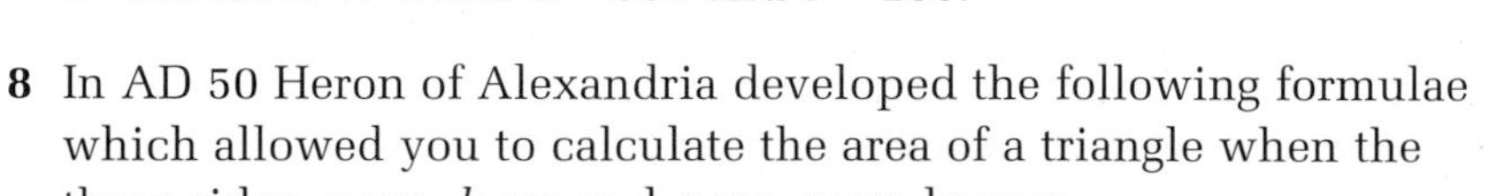

8 In AD 50 Heron of Alexandria developed the following formulae which allowed you to calculate the area of a triangle when the three sides, a cm, b cm and c cm, were known.

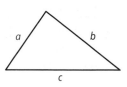

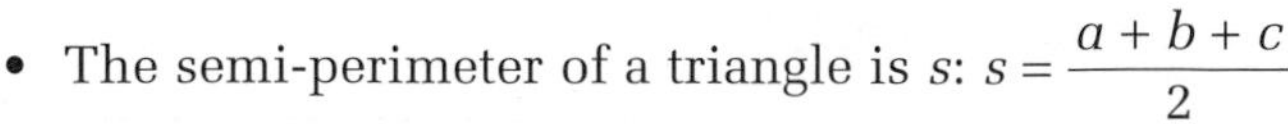

- The semi-perimeter of a triangle is s: $s = \frac{a + b + c}{2}$

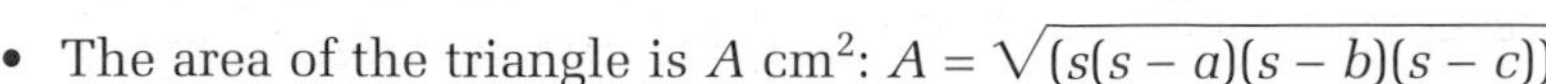

- The area of the triangle is A cm^2: $A = \sqrt{(s(s - a)(s - b)(s - c))}$

a Calculate the semi-perimeter of a triangle whose sides are:

(i) 3 cm, 4 cm and 5 cm long

(ii) 4 cm, 6 cm and 8 cm long

(iii) 2.9 cm, 5.7 cm and 6.1 cm long.

b Now calculate the area of each triangle.

Mode, median and mean

Reminder

In an office health check, 30 men had their weights recorded. The table shows the results.

Mode

Weight (kg)	Frequency
$50 \le w < 55$	1
$55 \le w < 60$	3
$60 \le w < 65$	6
$65 \le w < 70$	9
$70 \le w < 75$	8
$75 \le w < 80$	2
$80 \le w < 85$	1

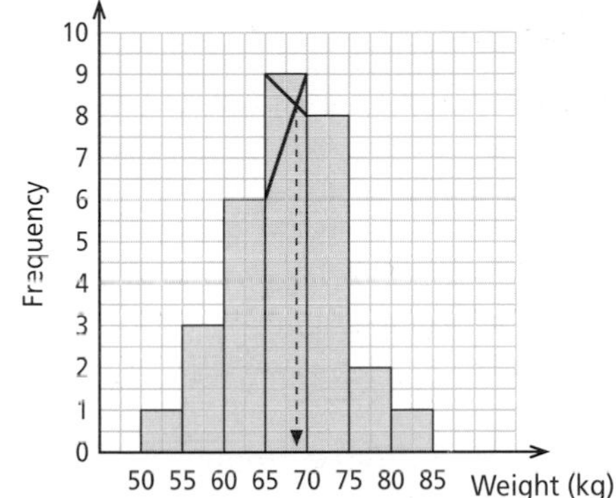

A histogram of the grouped data suggests a mode of approximately 68 kg.

Median

Plotting cumulative frequency against the upper class limit gives us estimates for:
the lower quartile, $Q_1 = 63$
the median, $Q_2 = 68$
the upper quartile, $Q_3 = 72$.

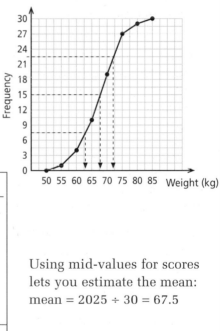

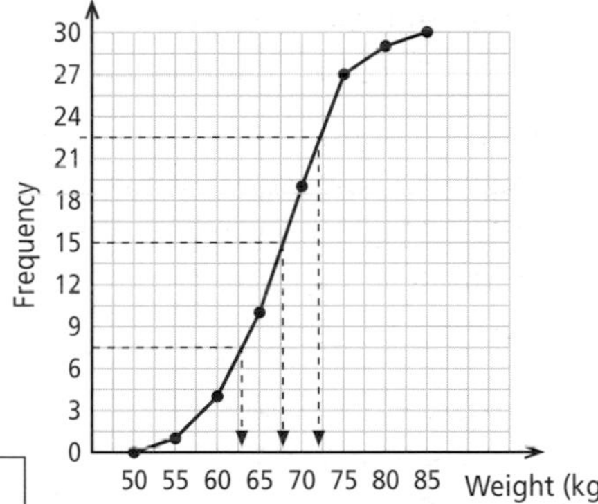

Mean

Weight (kg)	Frequency	Mid-value	fx
$50 \le w < 55$	1	52.5	52.5
$55 \le w < 60$	3	57.5	172.5
$60 \le w < 65$	6	62.5	375.0
$65 \le w < 70$	9	67.5	607.5
$70 \le w < 75$	8	72.5	580.0
$75 \le w < 80$	2	77.5	155.0
$80 \le w < 85$	1	82.5	82.5
Totals	30		2025

Using mid-values for scores lets you estimate the mean:
mean $= 2025 \div 30 = 67.5$

EXERCISE 7

1 A toy manufacturer tests the batteries for toys by running a sample of them to exhaustion.

a What is the modal class interval?

b Draw a histogram to illustrate the figures.

c Estimate the mode.

Life time (L hours)	Frequency
$5 \le L < 6$	3
$6 \le L < 7$	5
$7 \le L < 8$	9
$8 \le L < 9$	6
$9 \le L < 10$	2

2 A machine is meant to fill tins with 1000 ml of paint. A batch of tins is checked.

Volume (V ml)	Frequency
$970 \le V < 980$	1
$980 \le V < 990$	4
$990 \le V < 1000$	7
$1000 \le V < 1010$	10
$1010 \le V < 1020$	8
$1020 \le V < 1030$	7

a Draw a histogram of the figures.
b Estimate the modal volume.
c Do you think the machine is doing its job properly?

3 An electrical company manufactures resistors. In order to check that they are up to specification the resistance of a sample is measured.

a Make a cumulative frequency diagram.
b Use your diagram to estimate the value of:
  (i) the median resistance
  (ii) the quartiles of the distribution
  (iii) the semi-interquartile range.

Resistance (Ω ohms)	Frequency
$94 \le \Omega < 96$	1
$96 \le \Omega < 98$	2
$98 \le \Omega < 100$	9
$100 \le \Omega < 102$	12
$102 \le \Omega < 104$	11
$104 \le \Omega < 106$	8

4 Sticky tape is sold in rolls which are advertised as holding 100 m of tape. The table shows the data found when this claim was examined.

Length (L m)	Frequency
$98.5 \le L < 99.0$	3
$99.0 \le L < 99.5$	4
$99.5 \le L < 100.0$	7
$100.0 \le L < 100.5$	8
$100.5 \le L < 101.0$	12
$101.0 \le L < 101.5$	13

a Construct a cumulative frequency diagram.
b Estimate the value of:
  (i) the median length
  (ii) the quartiles of the distribution
  (iii) the semi-interquartile range.
c Comment on the advertised claim.

5 Police do a speed check on a sample of vehicles on a certain stretch of road.

Speed (S km/h)	Frequency
$20 \le S < 30$	3
$30 \le S < 40$	5
$40 \le S < 50$	12
$50 \le S < 60$	24
$60 \le S < 70$	13
$70 \le S < 80$	9

a How many vehicles did they check?
b Copy the table and add a mid-value column.
c Calculate, to 1 d.p., an estimate for the mean of the sample.

6 The table shows the results of a survey on the heights of young children.

Height (h cm)	Frequency
$60 \le h < 62$	6
$62 \le h < 64$	7
$64 \le h < 66$	18
$66 \le h < 68$	13
$68 \le h < 70$	11
$70 \le h < 72$	10

a Calculate, to 1 d.p., an estimate for the mean of the sample.

A second group of children is also surveyed, as shown in this table.

Height (h cm)	Frequency
$60 \le h < 62$	1
$62 \le h < 64$	2
$64 \le h < 66$	9
$66 \le h < 68$	15
$68 \le h < 70$	22
$70 \le h < 72$	13

b Calculate the mean of this group and compare both groups.

7 A new fertiliser is being tried out. Young plants in one bed are regularly given the fertiliser while others in another bed are given none. The heights of both sets of plants are recorded.

Without fertiliser

Height (p cm)	Frequency
$8.0 \le p < 8.1$	6
$8.1 \le p < 8.2$	9
$8.2 \le p < 8.3$	12
$8.3 \le p < 8.4$	11
$8.4 \le p < 8.5$	10
$8.5 \le p < 8.6$	9

With fertiliser

Height (p cm)	Frequency
$8.0 \le p < 8.1$	4
$8.1 \le p < 8.2$	5
$8.2 \le p < 8.3$	9
$8.3 \le p < 8.4$	14
$8.4 \le p < 8.5$	18
$8.5 \le p < 8.6$	15

a Find the mean of both groups.
b Estimate the median and quartiles of both groups.
c Take 8.0 and 8.6 to be the lowest and highest measurements and summarise each table by means of box plots.
d Compare the two groups of plants.

▪A▪N▪S▪W▪E▪R▪S▪

UNIT 1

1 Significant Figures

Page 1 Starting Points

1 **a** 3.44 **b** 0.47 **c** 81.26 **d** 79.05 **e** 0.02 **f** 0.01
2 **a** 7.2 **b** 4.1 **c** 2.1 **d** 0.6 **e** 8.9 **f** 0.5
3 **a** £2083.33 **b** £480.77
4 **a** 12.77 km per litre **b** 0.08 litre per km
5 **a** 3.41×10^2 **b** 7.814×10^3 **c** 9.3127×10^4 **d** 2.71×10^{-2} **e** 5×10^{-4}
6 **a** 3940 **b** 810 000 **c** 60 **d** 0.110 **e** 0.006 69
7 **a** 1.86×10^8 miles **b** 5.84×10^8 miles

Page 3 Exercise 1

1 **a** 2 **b** 3 **c** 3 **d** 2 **e** 2 **f** 4 **g** 1 **h** 4 **i** 4 **j** 1
2 **a** 3 **b** 1 **c** 2 **d** 4 **e** 5 **f** 3
3 **a, d** and **f** Further information needed **b** 5 **c** 5 **e** 4 **g** 3 **h** 3
4 **a** 3 **b** 3 **c** 4 **d** 4 **e** 3 **f** 5 **g** 6 **h** 4 **i** 3 **j** 2 **k** 1 **l** 2 **m** 4 **n** 3 **o** 1 **p** 3 **q** 2 **r** 2 **s** 2 **t** 1
5 **a** **(i)** 49 000 **(ii)** 49 500
b **(i)** 51 000 **(ii)** 50 800
c **(i)** 3500 **(ii)** 3460
d **(i)** 250 000 **(ii)** 246 000
e **(i)** 7000 **(ii)** 7010
f **(i)** 78 **(ii)** 77.8
g **(i)** 370 **(ii)** 365
h **(i)** 1.8 **(ii)** 1.79
i **(i)** 810 **(ii)** 809
j **(i)** 20 **(ii)** 20.1
6 **a** 20 **b** 6 **c** 0.0004 **d** 0.9 **e** 10 **f** 40 **g** 0.7 **h** 0.03
7 **a** 1.89 **b** 2.26 **c** 3.17 **d** 2.67 **e** 25.1 **f** 37.7 **g** 20.4 **h** 28.3
8 **a** £8750 **b** £6820 **c** £15 200 **d** £28 000
9 **a** **(i)** 13.0 cm **(ii)** 176 cm **(iii)** 785 mm
b **(i)** 13.0 cm **(ii)** 177 cm **(iii)** 785 mm
c To 3 s.f. 177 cm is more accurate than 176 cm as π is a more accurate measurement than 3.14.
10 **a** 69 cm^3 **b** 86 cm^3 **c** 63 cm^3

Page 5 Exercise 2

1 **a** 5.0×10^2 **b** 3.7×10^3 **c** 4.0×10^3 **d** 8.0×10^2 **e** 4.1×10^{-1} **f** 4.7×10^{-3}
2 **a** 6210 **b** 83.6 **c** 3.14 **d** 0.09 **e** 0.0081 **f** 599
3 **a** **(i)** £256.20 **(ii)** £375 **(iii)** £103.77
b **(i)** 230 000 km^2 **(ii)** 588 000 km^2 **(iii)** 2 180 000 km^2
c **(i)** 118 **(ii)** 139 **(iii)** 164
d **(i)** 104 000 hours **(ii)** 10 600 days
4 **a** **(i)** £348 **(ii)** £38.20 **(iii)** £64.40
b **(i)** £348.08 **(ii)** £38.15 **(iii)** £64.40
c Decimal places, to give the answer to the nearest penny

Page 6 Review

1 **a** 2 **b** 1 **c** 4 **d** 1 **e** 2
2 **a** 350 **b** 2.4 **c** 0.14 **d** 0.010
3 **a** £70.50 **b** £1050
4 **a** 4.5×10^8 km **b** 1.4×10^9 km

2 Calculations Involving Percentages

Page 7 Starting Points

1 **a** £12.50 **b** £30 **c** £2.12
2 £12.60
3 21 out of 25 is 4% better
4 **a** £36.75 **b** £34 **c** £25.80 **d** £11.98
5 **a** 55% **b** **(i)** 10p **(ii)** 14%
6 **a** £2975 **b** £378 **c** £5100

Page 8 Exercise 1

1 **a** £70 **b** £84 **c** £45.50 **d** £193.20
2 **a** £5950 **b** £4165 **c** £10 115 **d** £19 635
3 **a** **(i)** £22.50 **(ii)** £23
b **(i)** £76.50 **(ii)** £78.20
c **(i)** £157.50 **(ii)** £161
d **(i)** £324 **(ii)** £331.20
4 **a** **(i)** £237.25 **(ii)** £629 **(iii)** £7.84 **(iv)** £25.83
b £9.98, £173.38, £120.42, £765

5 a £154, £704 b £282.75, £1732.75
c £12.50, £512.50 d £350, £3150

Page 9 Exercise 2

1 a £20.50 b £61.20 c £235.12
d £105.06 e £157.62 f £187.29
g £334.27 h £113.25 i £21.55
j £419.96 k £1081.46 l £301.66
2 d
3 a £311.65
b Simple interest would be £288, £23.65 less
4 £13.17
5 a £5241.92 b £10 241.92
6 £18.25, £229.21, £436.13, £484.88, £604.01, £1329.95
7 £28 100 360
8 £5097.06

Page 10 Challenge

£500 000

Page 11 Exercise 3

1 a 1.03 b 1.07 c 1.1 d 1.12
e 1.08 f 1.25 g 1.125
2 a (i) £1687.30 (ii) £187.30
b (i) £2084.28 (ii) £334.28
3 a £1243.72 b £2400.67 c £5022.47
4 a £113.02 b £424.58 c £19 876.95
5 a £8000 at 6% b £1373.23
6 £252 763 923

Page 12 Exercise 4

1 £13 680 2 £2139
3 £1147.50 4 £3643.20
5 £37 679.14 6 13.3%
7 34.0% 8 21%
9 £859.78 10 £45 639
11 a (i) £18 200 (ii) £16 562 (iii) £15 071
b After 8 years
12 a (i) £2460 (ii) £1356
b After 10 years
13 a (i) £25 750 (ii) £27 318
b After 7 years
14 a (i) £660 (ii) £966
b After 6 years

Page 14 Exercise 5

1 a 2.16% b 2.12 %
2 30 000%
3 a £29 988 b £29 988
4 £1532
5 £1.45
6 £14 000
7 a (i) £108 000 (ii) £136 000 (iii) £147 000
b (i) £92 000 (ii) £71 600 (iii) £65 900
c (i) £200 000 (ii) £207 600 (iii) £212 900
d (i) £5300 (ii) 2.55% to 3 s.f.

Page 15 Exercise 6

1 a £21.20 b £3300 c £1224
2 a £42 400 b £44 732 c £46 969
d £50 726
3 a £330 b £346.50 c £367.57
d £373.08
4 7.27%; it is higher than the 1989 rate of inflation.
5 a (i) £1296 (ii) £1387 (iii) £1525
b (i) £1365 (ii) £1420 (iii) £1519
c 1991
6 a (i) £1 (ii) £1.08 (iii) £1.11
b 1994
7 £215.64
8 a (i) £103.50 (ii) £107.64 (iii) £113.02
b (i) £101.50 (ii) £103.53 (iii) £106.64
9 By 1994 Helen's wage is £17 821, Tommy's is £17 760, but Tommy has had more money to spend in 1992 and 1993.
10 No. It means prices are rising by a smaller amount.

Page 17 Exercise 7

1 £150
2 £12
3 £18 000, £22 000, £25 900
4 £73.86
5 £169 811
6 a £1200 b £1500

Page 18 Review

1 a £120 b £30
2 a £283.72 b £2083.73
3 £2266.56
4 28.1%
5 68.9%
6 a £130 b £1572
7 £22 816
8 a No. 20% increase is twice the inflation rate in 1990
b (i) £4.20 (ii) £4.46

3 Volume of Solids

Page 19 Starting Points

1 a 64 cm^2 b 1.08 m^2 c 154 mm^2
d 10.85 cm^2 e 3848 mm^2 f 227 cm^2
2 a cube b cone c sphere
d cuboid e square pyramid
3 a 125 cm^3 b 800 cm^3
4 a 17.5 b 0.085 c 97 500
5 a 4.9 b 77.92 c 53.29
d 551.368
6 a 39.48 b 181.5

Page 20 Exercise 1

1 a 905 cm^3 b 51 000 mm^3 c 11.5 m^3
d 3050 cm^3 e 28 300 mm^3

2 a 24 400 mm^3 b 14.1 m^3

3 905 cm^3, 5580 cm^3, 14 100 cm^3

4 a 268 mm^3 b 26 800mm^3

5 a 2250 cm^3 b 0.113 cm^3 c 19 900

6 1909

7 230 000 cm^3

8 452 cm^3

9 718 cm^3, 2090 cm^3, 4600 cm^3

Page 22 Exercise 2

1 a 288 cm^3 b 4.71 m^3 c 3540 mm^3

2 a 29.3 cm^3 b 2120 cm^3 c 945 cm^3

3 132 cm^3

4 70.7 cm^3

5 47.1 cm^3

6 a 115 cm^3 b 885 cm^3

7 b

Page 24 Exercise 3

1 a sphere
b cuboid (rectangular prism)
c triangular prism
d cone
e hexagonal prism
f cube (square prism)
g cylinder (circular prism)
h pentagonal prism
i irregular prism
j square-based pyramid

2 a f
b b, it could be a cuboid with a square base

Page 25 Exercise 4

1 a 180 cm^3 b 10 724 mm^3
c 353.6 cm^3 d 2.16 m^3

2 a 1008 cm^3 b 151.68 cm^3
c 499.8 cm^3 d 12 912 mm^3
e 3.817 m^3

3 1104 cm^3

4 a 1.5 m^2 b 2.25 m^3

5 a 50.3 cm^2 b 9054 cm^3

6 288 cm^3

7 a 37.5 m^2 b 375 m^3

8 203.4 cm^3

9 5.64 m^3

10 0.4 cm

11 a 1130 cm^3 b 41 800 mm^3 c 15 200 cm^3

12 a 263 cm^3, 464 cm^3, 867 cm^3
b 3 or 4 servings

13 a 10 000 cm b 7854 cm^3 c 55 000 cm^3

14 a 240 m^2 b 8640 m^3

15 a 64 cm^2 b 960 cm^3 c 18 528 g

16 4.47 m^3

Page 28 Exercise 5

1 a 2.4 m^3 b 191 cm^3 c 140 cm^3
d 151 cm^3 e 3.96 m^3

2 3.6 m^3

3 19.8 m^3

4 a 2.5 m b 91.6 m^3

5 a (i) 6 mm (ii) 3 mm
b 4 mm
c (i) 113 mm^3 (ii) 113 mm^3 (iii) 226 mm^3

6 a 8 cm b 2145 cm^3 c 4825 cm^3
d 6970 cm^3

7 a 3 cm b 101 cm^3

8 a 67 021 cm^3 b 130 900 cm^3 c 63 880 cm^3

9 a 2827 cm^2 b 1963 cm^2 c 864 cm^2
d 864 000 cm^3

10 a 8.18 m^3 b 14.14 m^3 c 5.96 m^3

11 5.81 cm^3

12 7750 cm^3

Page 31 Review

1 a 77.0 cm^3 b 202 cm^3 c 624 cm^3

2 a 107 cm^3 b 776 cm^3 c 1984 mm^3
d 15 700 cm^3

3 241 000 cm^3

4 38.8 cm^3

5 94.2 cm^3

4 Linear Relationships

Page 32 Starting Points

1 A(5, 4), B(−6, 2), C(−3, −4), D(2, −3), E(0, −6), F(3, 0), G(−4, 7)

2

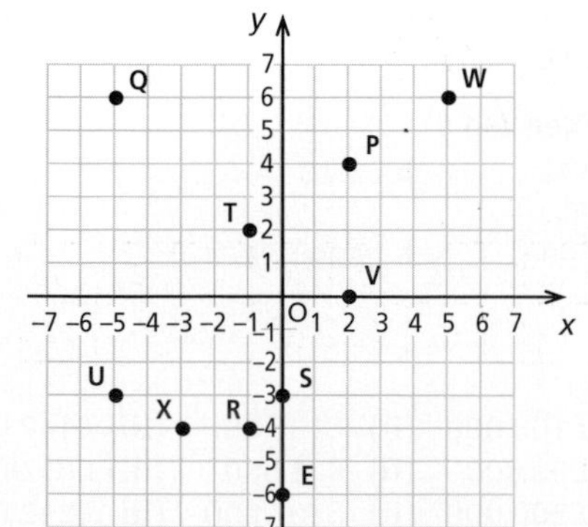

3 a (iii) $x = 1$ **(iv)** $x = -3$ **(v)** $y = 2$
(vi) $y = -3$

b $x = 1$, $y = -3$

c (4, 2)

d (1, −6)

4 a

x	0	1	2	3	4	5	6
y	0	6	12	18	24	30	36

b y is a cost

c Whole number of tickets

d

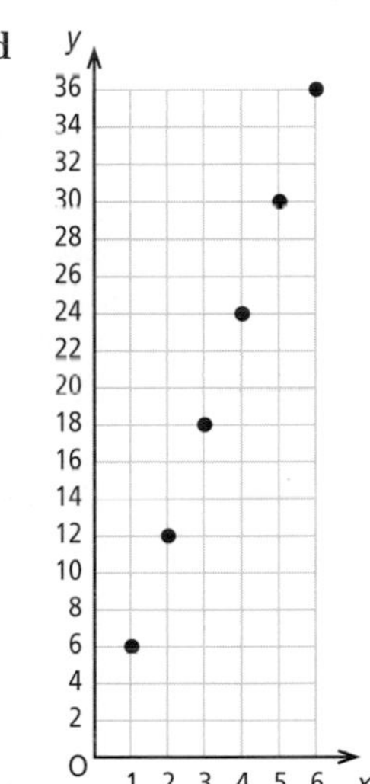

e Only whole tickets are sold

5 a

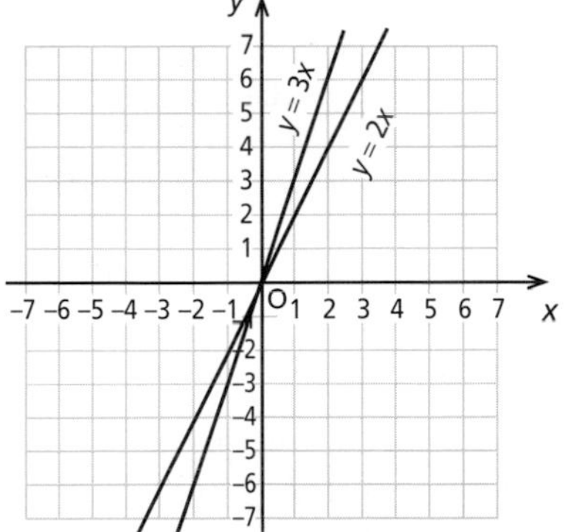

b $y = 3x$

6 a

x	−3	−2	−1	0	1	2	3
y	−2	0	2	4	6	8	10

b

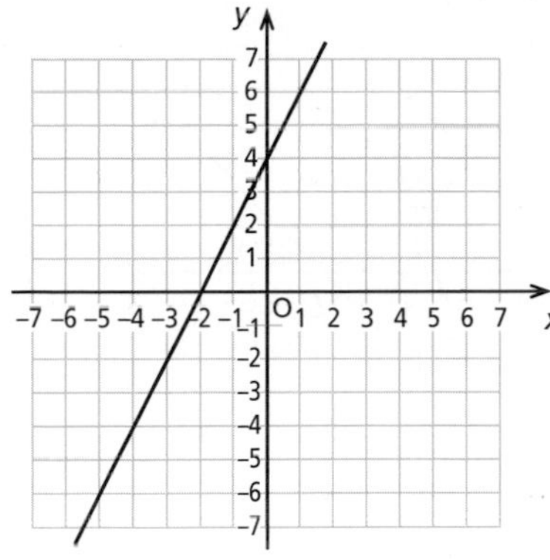

c Below

Page 33 Exercise 1

1 a

x	0	1	2
y	−1	0	1

b

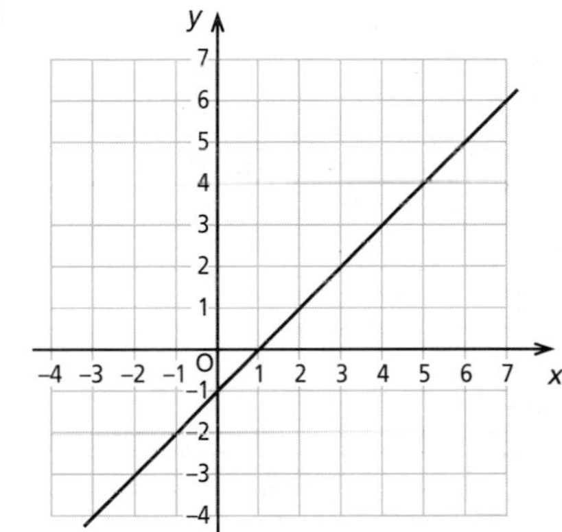

2 a

x	0	1	2
y	0	−1	−2

b

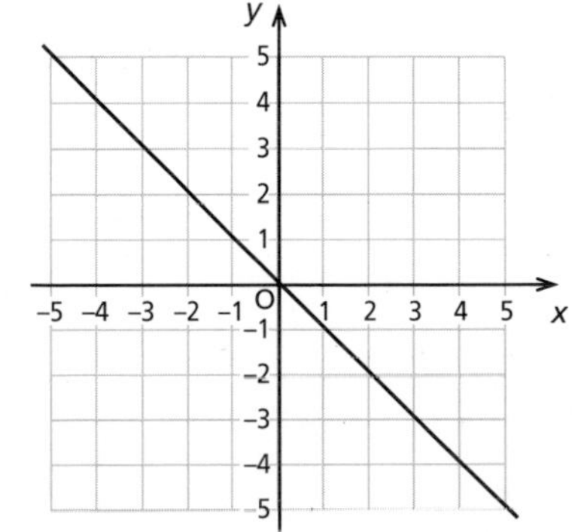

3

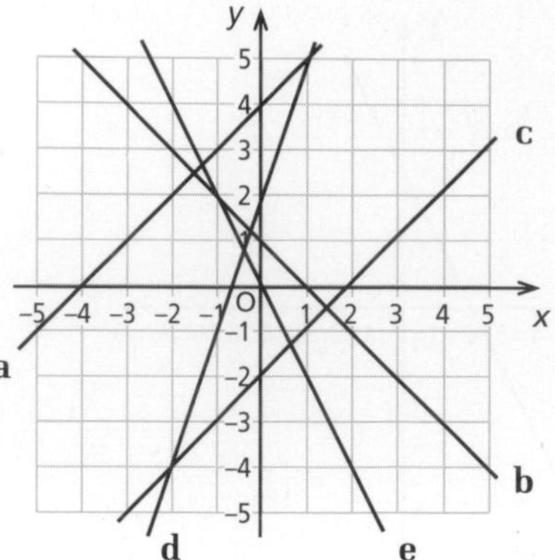

4 a

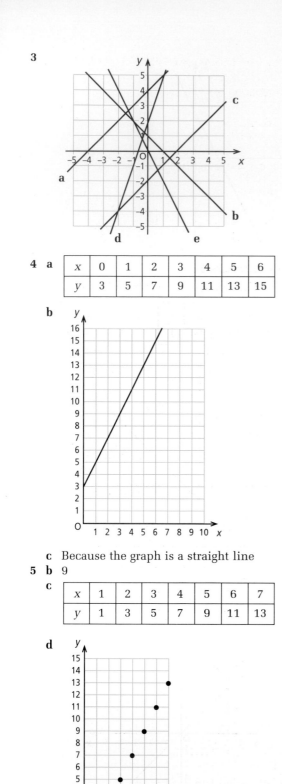

x	0	1	2	3	4	5	6
y	3	5	7	9	11	13	15

b

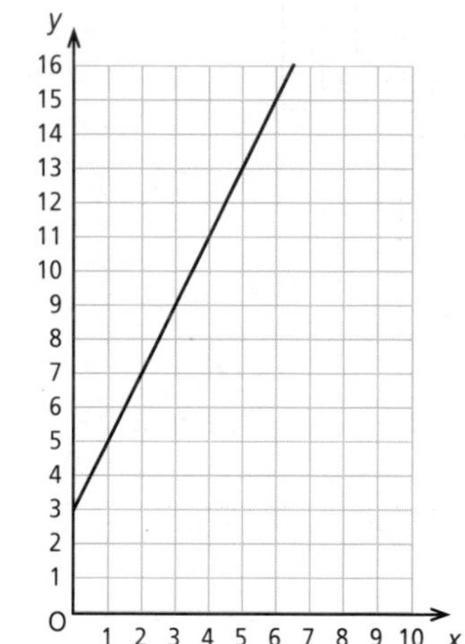

c Because the graph is a straight line

5 b 9

c

x	1	2	3	4	5	6	7
y	1	3	5	7	9	11	13

d

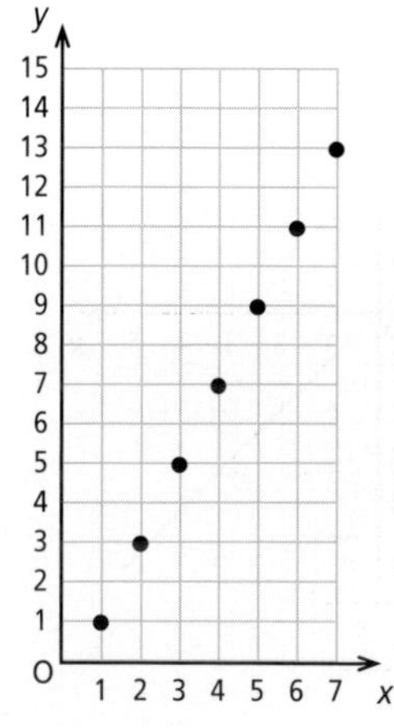

e Because the graph is a straight line

f There are only whole numbers of coins

6 a

x	0	1	2	3	4	5
y	12	11	10	9	8	7

b

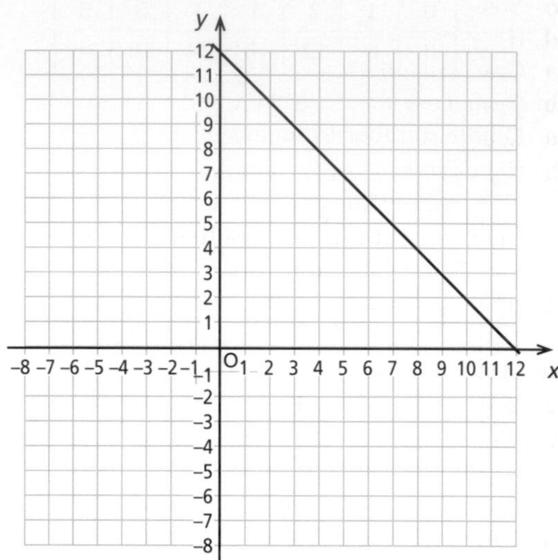

c Parts between points are 'valid'

Page 36 Exercise 2

1 a 0.4 b 0.2 c 0.1 d 0.17
e Not defined f 0

2 a, c, d

Page 37 Exercise 3

1 a 3 b 3 c −0.2 d −6
e 2 f −0.5 g 3 h 0

2 a (i) A(− 1, −5) (ii) B(2, 4)
b 3
c (i) 1 (ii) −4 (iii) 0.5
(iv) −0.25 (v) 1.5 (vi) 0

3 b (i) 0.67, 0.67 (ii) −1, −1 (iii) 3.5, 3.5
c Both lines have the same gradient
d Parallel lines have the same gradient

4 (i)

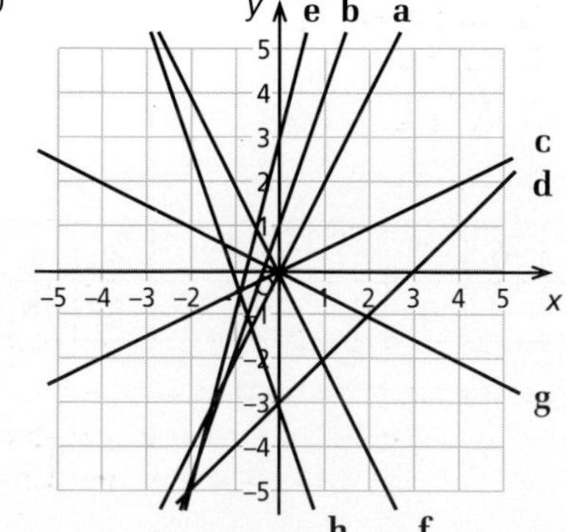

(ii) **a** 2 **b** 3 **c** 0.5 **d** 1
e 4 **f** −2 **g** −0.5 **h** −3

5 **a** 10 **b** 25 **c** −13 **d** a

6 **a** and **f**, **b** and **e**, **c** and **h**, **d** and **g**

7 **a** A(−5, 5), B(−2, 3), C(4, −1)
b (i) AB −0.67 (ii) BC −0.67
c Yes
d (i) Yes (ii) No

8 **a** Gradient = 0.5
b Gradient AC = 0.25, gradient CB = 0.2

9 **a** Gradient AB = 1.3, gradient BC = 1.2
b (i) Gradient DB = −0.25, gradiont BE = 0.17
(ii) Gradient FB = −3, gradient BE = −3, FBG is straight

10 **a** (i) Not parallel (ii) Not parallel

Page 41 Exercise 4

1 **a** 2, 5 **b** 3, −2 **c** 1, −2
d −3, 1 **e** −1, 5 **f** 5, 100
g −1, 0 **h** 0.67, −1 **i** 3, 0
j 0, 5 **k** −1, 4 **l** −2, 3
m −3, 6 **n** −7, 1

2 **a** (i) −2 (ii) 2 (iii) $y = 2x - 2$
b (i) 4 (ii) 0 (iii) $y = 4$
c (i) 1 (ii) $\frac{1}{4}$ (iii) $y = \frac{1}{4}x + 1$
d (i) 3 (ii) −1 (iii) $y = -x + 3$
e (i) −5 (ii) $-\frac{2}{3}$ (iii) $y = -\frac{2}{3}x - 5$

3 **a** $y = 2x + 8$ **b** $y = 2x$
c $y = 2x - 8$ **d** $y = 6$
e $y = -\frac{1}{2}x + 8$ **f** $y = -3$
g $y = -\frac{1}{2}x - 1$ **h** $y = -\frac{1}{2}x - 5$
i $x = 2$ **j** $x = -7$

4 **a** (**iv**), (**v**) and (**vi**)
b (**vii**) **c** (**iii**)
d (i) $-\frac{1}{3}$, 6, $y = -\frac{1}{3}x + 6$
(ii) −1, 5, $y = -x + 5$
(iii) undefined, none, $x = -4$
(iv) 4, −2, $y = 4x - 2$
(v) 1, 0, $y = x$
(vi) $\frac{1}{2}$, −1, $y = \frac{1}{2}x - 1$
(vii) 0, −3, $y = -3$
(viii) −1, −6, $y = -x - 6$

5 **a** $y = 2x + 5$ **b** $y = -4x$ **c** $y = 5\frac{1}{2}x - 1$
d $y = \frac{2}{3}x + 2$ **e** $y = 3$ **f** $y = -3x + 4$

6 Examples: $y = 4x$, $y = 4x + 1$, $y = 4x - 1$

7 **a** (0, 8) **b** −2 **c** $y = -2x + 3$

8 **a** $y = -x + 3$ **b** $y = -x - 4$ **c** $y = 1.5x + 5$
d $y = 1.5x - 1$

9 **a** $y = 0.75x + 4$, $y = 0.75x - 2$, $y = -0.75x + 4$, $y = -0.75x - 2$
b AB and DC, AD and BC
c $y = 1$, $x = 0$
d rhombus

10 **a** parallelogram
b $-\frac{2}{3}$ **c** SR
d PQ, $y = -\frac{2}{3}x + 2$; SR $y = -\frac{2}{3}x - 5$
e 0.5 **f** RQ **g** y-intercept

11 **a** (i) $y = -x + 5$ (ii) $y = -x - 5$
(iii) $y = x - 4$ (iv) $y = x + 4$
b QR, PS

Page 45 Exercise 5

1 **a** $y = 2x + 3$, 2, 3 **b** $y = 1.5x + 0.5$, 1.5, 0.5
c $y = x - 3$, 1, −3 **d** $y = -0.8x + 2$, 0.8, 2
e $y = x - 2.5$, 1, −2.5 **f** $y = -4x$, −4, 0
g $y = 2x + 7$, 2, 7 **h** $y = 2x - 5$, 2, −5
i $y = -2$, 0, −2 **j** $y = -0.5x + 6$, −0.5, 6

2 **a** $y = \frac{2}{3}x + 2$ **b** $y = -\frac{4}{5}x + 10$
c $x + 2y = 8$

3 **a** −2 **b** $y = -2x + 7$
c (i) $y = -x + 2$ (ii) $y = x - 4$
(iii) $y = -2x$ (iv) $y = -\frac{2}{3}x + 5$

4 **a** (1, 5), (3, 11) **b** (1, 2), (2, 7)
c (1, 4), (3, 2) **d** (2, 7), (3, 10)
e (1, 1), (2, 3) **f** (4, 5), (2, 2)

Page 46 Review

1 **a**

x	0	1	2	3	4	5
y	10	12	14	16	18	20

b/c

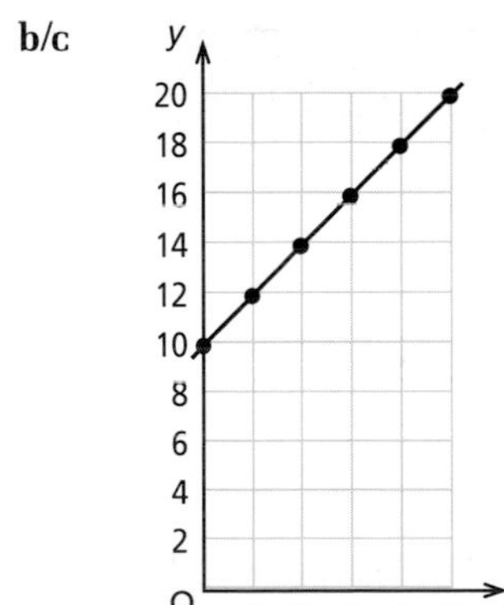

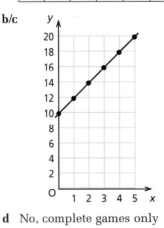

d No, complete games only

2 **a**

x	0	1	2
y	2	3	4

b

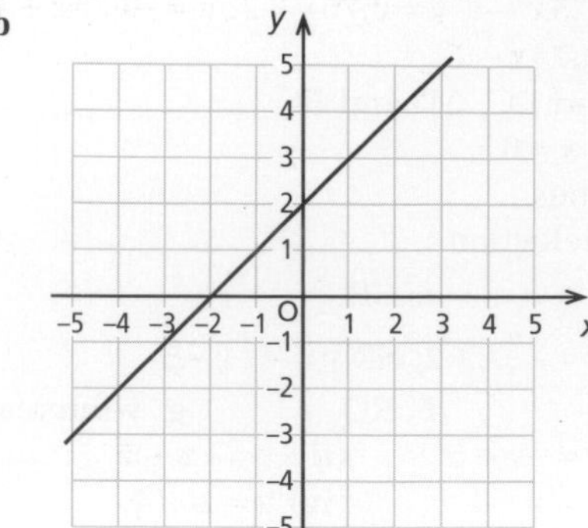

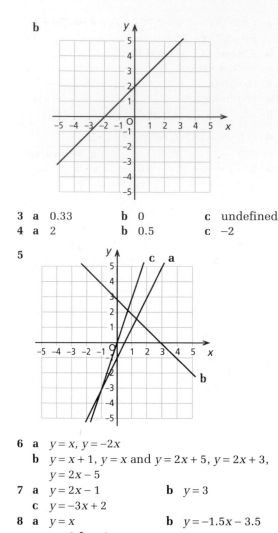

3 a 0.33 b 0 c undefined
4 a 2 b 0.5 c −2

5

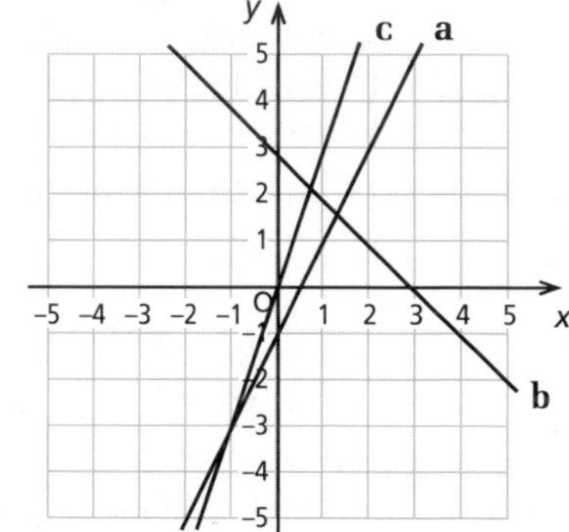

6 a $y = x$, $y = -2x$
b $y = x + 1$, $y = x$ and $y = 2x + 5$, $y = 2x + 3$, $y = 2x - 5$

7 a $y = 2x - 1$ b $y = 3$
c $y = -3x + 2$

8 a $y = x$ b $y = -1.5x - 3.5$
c $y = 0.5x - 2$

5 Algebraic Operations

Page 47 Starting Points

1 a $7y$ b $3x$ c a^2 d $6\ \text{m}^2$
e $15x$ f $5x$ g y^3

2 a −1 b −6 c −3 d −3
e −6 f −6 g 9 h −9
i 6 j 2 k −2 l $-\frac{1}{2}$

3 a $x = -3$ b $y = \frac{1}{2}$ c $x = -\frac{2}{3}$

Page 48 Exercise 1

1 a $2x + 2$ b $3y - 6$ c $5x + 5y$
d $30 - 6a$ e $4 - 2t$ f $3a - 3b$
g $20 - 10y$ h $6m - 18$ i $7n - 35$
j $11r - 11$ k $6 + 2y$ l $6 + 6t$
m $4a + 4b$ n $18 - 3c$ o $5d - 50$
p $10y - 30$ q $2c + 2d$ r $4e - 48$

2 a 4 times the cost of a sandwich plus 4 times the cost of a coffee
b 8 times the cost of a postcard plus 8 times the cost of a stamp
c 12 times the cost of the cola minus 12 times the discount

3 a (i) $3(x + 6)$ (ii) $3x + 18$
b (i) $4(x - 2)$ (ii) $4x - 8$
c (i) $6(10 - x)$ (ii) $60 - 6x$
d (i) $3(17 - y)$ (ii) $51 - 3y$

4 a $6x - 3$ b $30x + 20$ c $14 + 10x$
d $20 - 6y$ e $ab - 2a$ f $xy + 2y$
g $mn - 3m$ h $ab + ac$ i $ax - ay$
j $x^2 + 2x$ k $3y - y^2$ l $n^2 + 4n$
m $a^2 - ab$ n $b^2 - ab$ o $pq - p^2$
p $2a^2 + a$ q $3x^2 - 2x$ r $10y - 2y^2$
s $5t - t^2$ t $2w^2 - wy$ u $12c + 3c^2$
v $2x^2 - 6x$ w $3y^2 + 12y$ x $20m - 6m^2$

5 a $-2x - 6$ b $-3y + 6$ c $-25 + 5y$
d $-12 + 2x$ e $-x - y$ f $-x + y$
g $-4y - 4x$ h $-7a + 7b$ i $-x^2 - 2x$
j $-2p + p^2$ k $-l^2 - lm$ l $-8x + 6x^2$
m $-2a^2 + 3a$ n $-3t^2 + 4mt$

6 a $2 - 2x$ b $2 + y$ c $12 - 3y$
d $8 + 6x$ e $18 - 7x$ f $-1 + 2x$
g $6x - 15$ h $-2x + 5$ i $4x - 6$
j $2y - 4$ k $-x - 12$ l $9y - 4$

7 a $y^2 - 8y + 8$ b $x^2 - 3x + 14$
c $-x^2 + 15x - 32$

8 a $x - 2$ b $5y - 12$
c $x^2 - 3x + 2$ d $x^2 - x - 6$
e $x^2 - 2x - 3$ f $t^2 - 8t + 15$
g $m^2 - 2m - 15$ h $2x^2 + x - 3$
i $3x^2 - 17x + 10$

Page 50 Exercise 2

1 a $x^2 + 3x + 2$ b $x^2 + x - 2$
c $x^2 - x - 2$ d $x^2 - 3x + 2$
e $x^2 + 5x + 6$ f $x^2 - x - 6$
g $x^2 + x - 6$ h $x^2 - 5x + 6$
i $y^2 - 3y - 10$ j $t^2 - 6t + 9$
k $m^2 + 5m + 6$ l $k^2 + k - 2$
m $q^2 + 6q - 7$ n $r^2 + r - 12$
o $t^2 - 2t - 24$ p $15 - 8n + n^2$
q $4 + 3x - x^2$ r $3 + 4y + y^2$
s $x^2 + 6x + 5$ t $-y^2 + 14y - 48$
u $-c^2 + 22c - 121$

2 a $y^2 + 7y + 10\ \text{cm}^2$ b $x^2 + 18x + 45\ \text{cm}^2$
c $t^2 + 4t + 3\ \text{cm}^2$ d $x^2 + 8x + 16\ \text{cm}^2$

3 **a** $e^2 - 5e - 14$ **b** $x^2 - 4x + 4$
c $y^2 + 10y + 25$ **d** $m^2 - 7m + 12$
e $n^2 - 4n - 12$ **f** $r^2 - 2r + 1$
g $t^2 - 7t - 30$ **h** $w^2 + 16w + 64$
i $y^2 - 14y + 49$ **j** $x^2 + 4x - 5$
k $k^2 - 6k - 16$ **l** $n^2 + 2n - 8$
m $a^2 - 2a + 1$ **n** $y^2 + 5y - 6$
o $w^2 + 2w + 1$ **p** $t^2 + 4t - 21$
q $u^2 - 7u + 10$ **r** $x^2 - 10x - 11$
s $r^2 - 10r + 9$ **t** $b^2 - 4b + 4$

4 **a** $2x^2 + 7x - 4$ **b** $2x^2 + x - 3$
c $4x^2 - 1$ **d** $9x^2 - 6x + 1$
e $4y^2 + 4y + 1$ **f** $9m^2 - 1$
g $2n^2 - 15n + 7$ **h** $2k^2 - 9k - 5$
i $4c^2 + 10c - 6$

5 **a** $y^3 + y^2 - y - 1$ **b** $m^3 + 6m^2 + 7m - 6$
c $2x^3 + 7x^2 + 2x - 3$ **d** $3t^3 - 8t^2 + t + 6$
e $2x^3 - 7x^2 - 9x - 30$ **f** $6k^3 + 17k^2 - 18$

Page 52 Exercise 3

1 **a** 1, 2, 7, 14
b 1, 2, 3, 4, 6, 9, 12, 18, 36
c 1, 2, 4, 5, 10, 20, 25, 50, 100
d 1, 3, 9, 27, 81
e 1, 2, x, $2x$
f 1, 3, y, $3y$
g 1, a, b, ab
h 1, 2, 4, x, $2x$, $4x$
i 1, 2, 3, 6, x, $2x$, $3x$, $6x$
j 1, y, y^2
k 1, 2, x, $2x$, x^2, $2x^2$
l 1, 3, m, $3m$, m^2, $3m^2$
m 1, 3, 5, 15, w, $3w$, $5w$, $15w$
n 1, 7, x, $7x$, x^2, $7x^2$

2 **a** $3x$ **b** $5y$ **c** 3 **d** $7y$
e $3x$ **f** $2x$ **g** $2b$

3 **a** (i) 1, 2, 3, 4, 6, 12 (ii) 1, 3, 5, 15
b 1, 3

4 1, 2, x, $2x$

5 **a** 1, x **b** 1, 5 **c** 1, b **d** 1, y
e 1, 2, 4, n, $2n$, $4n$ **f** 1, b

6 **a** x **b** 3 **c** 6 **d** 5
e x **f** $2m$ **g** $3y$ **h** $2a$
i $7k$ **j** $2c$ **k** $3w$ **l** ab

Page 53 Exercise 4

1 **a** $3(x + 2)$ **b** $2(x - 1)$ **c** $2x(2y - 1)$
d $x(5x - 1)$ **e** $3(2a - 1)$ **f** $a(6 + 7a)$
g $5(2x - 3)$ **h** $y(y - 1)$

2 **a** $3(a - b)$ **b** $x(2x - 1)$ **c** $y(5 + y)$
d $a(3b + 2)$ **e** $3(3y - 5)$ **f** $x(x - 5)$
g $7(3m - 1)$ **h** $4x(1 + 2x)$ **i** $x(1 - 2x)$
j $7(c - 2)$ **k** $5k(k - 2)$ **l** $3m(1 + 3m)$
m $5a(b + 2)$ **n** $2b(3 - 4a)$ **o** $2r(2q + 3)$
p $3x(x - 3y)$ **q** $8(2 - xy)$ **r** $3y(5y - x)$
s $y(x - 5y)$ **t** $8a(b + 3a)$

3 **a** $2x(2x - 3)$ **b** $3a(b - 2a)$ **c** $6y(y - 2)$
d $8(1 - 2m)$ **e** $12n(n + 4)$ **f** $3ab(2 + 3b)$

4 **a** $x^2(x - 1)$ **b** $5x(x^2 - 2)$ **c** $ab(b + a)$
d $3(2a - 3b + 1)$ **e** $2(x^2 - 3x + 4)$
f $6ab(2b - 1)$

Page 54 Exercise 5

1 **a** $2^2 - x^2$ **b** $3^2 - y^2$ **c** $7^2 - (2x)^2$
d $1^2 - (4x)^2$ **e** $x^2 - 5^2$ **f** $(9x)^2 - 5^2$
g $(10x)^2 - (11y)^2$

2 **a** $(y - 3)(y + 3)$ **b** $(m - 2)(m + 2)$
c $(n - 1)(n + 1)$ **d** $(t - 4)(t + 4)$
e $(3 - x)(3 + x)$ **f** $(7 - t)(7 + t)$
g $(8 - y)(8 + y)$ **h** $(m - n)(m + n)$
i $(p - q)(p + q)$ **j** $(d - 9)(d + 9)$
k $(5 - e)(5 + e)$ **l** $(1 - x)(1 + x)$
m $(10 - y)(10 + y)$ **n** $(w - x)(w + x)$
o $(4 - f)(4 + f)$ **p** $(g - 1)(g + 1)$

3 **a** $(2x - 1)(2x + 1)$ **b** $(3y - 2)(3y + 2)$
c $(a - 2b)(a + 2b)$ **d** $(2p - q)(2p + q)$
e $(4 - 3r)(4 + 3r)$ **f** $(5 - 2x)(5 + 2x)$
g $(b - 3c)(b + 3c)$ **h** $(5w - x)(5w + x)$
i $(8y - 1)(8y + 1)$ **j** $(5x - 2)(5x + 2)$
k $(2a - 3b)(2a + 3b)$ **l** $(3x - y)(3x + y)$
m $(3t - 4)(3t + 4)$ **n** $(2k - 1)(2k + 1)$
o $(9a - 10b)(9a + 10b)$ **p** $(4e - f)(4e + f)$

4 **a** $6(y - 2)(y + 2)$ **b** $2(2 - m)(2 + m)$
c $3(1 - a)(1 + a)$ **d** $2(w - 3)(w + 3)$
e $5(2 - t)(2 + t)$ **f** $2(2y - 3)(2y + 3)$
g $3(1 - 2b)(1 + 2b)$ **h** $3(3x - 2)(3x + 2)$
i $7(a - 2)(a + 2)$ **j** $4(2k - 1)(2k + 1)$
k $5(3e - f)(3e + f)$ **l** $2(8x - 1)(8x + 1)$

Page 56 Exercise 6

1 **a** $(x + 1)(x + 1)$ **b** $(y + 2)(y + 1)$
c $(m + 2)(m + 2)$

2 **a** $(t + 2)(t - 1)$ **b** $(x + 4)(x - 3)$
c $(y + 5)(y - 2)$

3 **a** $(a - 2)(a + 1)$ **b** $(w - 4)(w + 2)$
c $(e - 3)(e + 1)$

4 **a** $(b - 2)(b - 2)$ **b** $(y - 3)(y - 2)$
c $(y - 3)(y - 1)$

5 **a** $(k - 6)(k + 1)$ **b** $(x + 5)(x + 3)$
c $(p - 5)(p + 1)$ **d** $(x - 9)(x - 2)$
e $(y - 5)(y + 3)$ **f** $(n + 8)(n - 1)$
g $(q - 2)(q - 7)$ **h** $(x + 2)(x + 6)$
i $(k - 3)(k - 3)$ **j** $(x - 4)(x + 1)$

k $(y+6)(y-5)$ **l** $(a-4)(a-5)$
m $(c+4)(c+4)$ **n** $(e-3)(e-5)$
o $(f+7)(f-3)$ **p** $(x-7)(x+1)$
q $(y-2)(y-8)$ **r** $(x+10)(x-1)$
s $(m-9)(m+1)$ **t** $(k+3)(k+6)$
u $(p+6)(p-3)$ **v** $(x+4)(x-2)$
w $(y-3)(y-8)$ **x** $(m-4)(m+3)$

6 a $(x-7)(x+6)$ **b** $(y-5)(y-8)$
c $(x+4)(x+8)$ **d** $(t+6)(t-4)$
e $(t-9)(t+3)$ **f** $(k-2)(k-10)$
g $(k+9)(k-2)$ **h** $(x-4)(x-10)$
i $(y-10)(y+3)$ **j** $(x+4)(x+7)$
k $(a-5)(a-5)$ **l** $(b+6)(b+6)$
m $(w-9)(w+5)$ **n** $(x+10)(x-6)$
o $(y-6)(y-8)$ **p** $(k-7)(k+5)$

Page 57 Exercise 7

1 a $(2x+1)(x+2)$ **b** $(2x-3)(x-3)$
c $(2x-3)(x+2)$ **d** $(2x+5)(x-1)$
e $(3x-4)(x+1)$ **f** $(3x+2)(x-3)$
g $(2x-7)(x-2)$ **h** $(2x-1)(2x+5)$
i $(3x-1)(x-4)$ **j** $(3y-2)(y+4)$
k $(3m+2)(m-2)$ **l** $(2k+3)(3k-1)$
m $(2p+1)(p+3)$ **n** $(5w-7)(w+1)$
o $(3c+1)(c+2)$ **p** $(2a+1)(a-5)$
q $(4x-1)(2x-3)$ **r** $(7b+13)(b-1)$
s $(3e-1)(e+7)$ **t** $(3t+5)(t-1)$
u $(2y-7)(y+4)$

2 a $(3x+2)(4x+5)$ **b** $3(2y+1)(2y+5)$
c $(3m-4)(3m+2)$ **d** $(2k-3)^2$
e $2(a+4)(5a-1)$ **f** $3(y-4)(2y-1)$

Page 57 Exercise 8

1 $3(x-2)(x+2)$ **2** $y(y+4)$
3 $2(x+4)^2$ **4** $5(m-3)(m+3)$
5 $3(x-2)(x-3)$ **6** $3(m-4)(m+4)$
7 $2(x+3)(x+4)$ **8** $7(x-2)(x+1)$
9 $3(2n-5)$ **10** $5(a-2b)(a+2b)$
11 $5(w-1)(w+1)$ **12** $4(a-3)(a+3)$
13 $(b-1)^2$ **14** $2(9-y)(9+y)$
15 $(6k-7)(6k+7)$ **16** $2m(m-2)(m+2)$
17 $5(u+2)(u+1)$ **18** $2(m-3n)(m+3n)$
19 $b^2(a-2)(a+2)$ **20** $2(10y-1)(10y+1)$
21 $3(1+9x^2)$ **22** $3c(c-1)(c+1)$
23 $2(x-9)(x+8)$ **24** $2(2a+5)(a-1)$

Page 58 Review

1 a $6x$ **b** $5x-x^2$ **c** $-x$
d $4x+5$ **e** $2x$

2 a m^2-1 **b** $x^2-3x-18$
c p^2-4p+4 **d** $2x^2+5x-3$
e $4t^2-14t+12$ **f** $9y^2-12y+4$

3 a $2(y-4)$ **b** $x(x+1)$
c $3m(5m-n)$

4 a $(e-f)(e+f)$ **b** $(4x-1)(4x+1)$
c $(9a-5b)(9a+5b)$

5 a $(x+3)(x+1)$ **b** $(y-2)(y-3)$
c $(2a-1)(a+3)$

6 a $2(1-3x)(1+3x)$ **b** $3(x-5)(x-1)$
c $y(y-1)(y+1)$

6 Circles

Page 59 Starting Points

1 a circumference **b** centre
c diameter **d** radius

2 a 10 cm **b** 9.2 m

3 a 44.0 cm **b** 62.8 cm

4 47.1 cm

5 a 78.5 cm^2 **b** 452 cm^2

6 314 cm^2

7 28.3 cm

8 3.92 m

Page 60 Exercise 1

1 a 11.0 cm **b** 12.0 cm **c** 28.5 cm

2 a 86.2 mm **b** 192 cm **c** 43.3 m

3 a 29.3 mm **b** 9.90 m **c** 56.7 cm

4 31.4 m

5 30.5 cm

6 90.3 cm

7 28.3 cm

8 54.5 cm

9 a **(i)** 2 m **(ii)** 300°
b 31.4 m

Page 62 Exercise 2

1 a 101 cm^2 **b** 2036 mm^2 **c** 6.93 m^2

2 a $\frac{110}{360}$ **b** $\frac{90}{360}$ or $\frac{1}{4}$ **c** $\frac{260}{360}$
d $\frac{174}{360}$

3 a 63.6 cm^2 **b** 24.5 cm^2 **c** 2680 mm^2

4 a **(i)** 270° **(ii)** 236 cm^2
b **(i)** 260° **(ii)** 32.8 cm^2
c **(i)** 240° **(ii)** 1310 mm^2
d **(i)** 330° **(ii)** 348 cm^2
e **(i)** 200° **(ii)** 7370 cm^2

5 a 12.6 cm^2 **b** 58.7 cm^2 **c** 2770 mm^2
d 2.68 m^2

6 452 cm^2

7 2570 cm^2

8 11.9 cm^2

9 a 39.1 cm^2 **b** 10.4 cm^2

Page 64 Exercise 3

1 **a** (i) 130° **(ii)** 11.3 cm
 b (i) 230° **(ii)** 128 cm^2
 c (i) 50° **(ii)** 3.40 cm^2
 d (i) 145° **(ii)** 7.91 cm^2

2 50.1°

3 **a** 70.3° **b** 8.96 m

4 **a** 280° **b** 4.13 m^2

Page 66 Exercise 4

1 $a° = 70°$, $b° = 70°$

2 $a° = 30°$, $b° = 120°$

3 $a° = 36°$, $b° = 72°$

4 $a° = 62°$, $b° = 124°$

5 $a° = 20°$, $b° = 140°$, $c° = 40°$, $d° = 70°$

6 $a° = 50°$, $b° = 50°$, $c° = 65°$

7 $a° = 58°$, $b° = 64°$, $c° = 122°$

8 $a° = 130°$, $b° = 65°$

9 $a° = 60°$, $b° = 15°$

10 Student's own results

Page 68 Exercise 5

1 **a** $a° = 90°$, $b° = 53°$, $x = 5$ cm, $y = 4$ cm, $z = 3$ cm
 b $a° = 27°$, $b° = 126°$, $c° = 54°$, $d° = 36°$, $x = 5$ cm, $y = 5$ cm
 c $y = 1$ cm, $z = 2.4$ cm

2 **a** 90° **b** 6 cm

3 **a** 6.7 cm **b** 6.2 cm **c** 8.1 cm **d** 32.0 cm

4 **a** 10 cm **b** 20.4 cm **c** 2.4 cm **d** 25 cm

5 **a** 4.6 cm **b** 10.6 cm

6 **a** 6.7 cm **b** 2.3 cm

7 **a** 3.25 m **b** 8.25 m

8 **a** 0.8 m **b** 3.67 m **c** 2.65 m

9 1.73 cm

Page 70 Exercise 6

1 Student's own investigation

2 **e** The angle in a semicircle = 90°

Page 71 Exercise 7

1 **a**

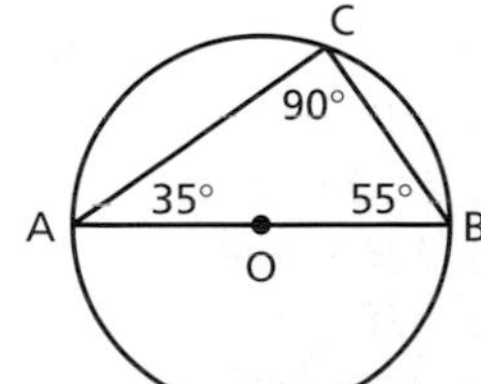

b

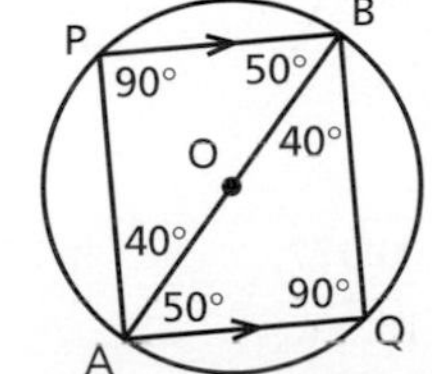

c

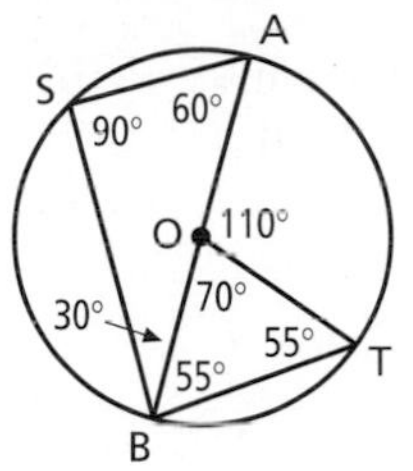

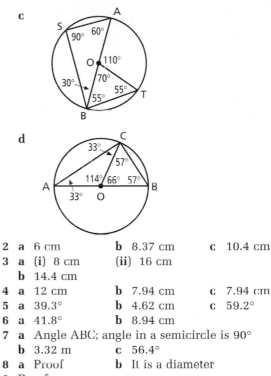

d

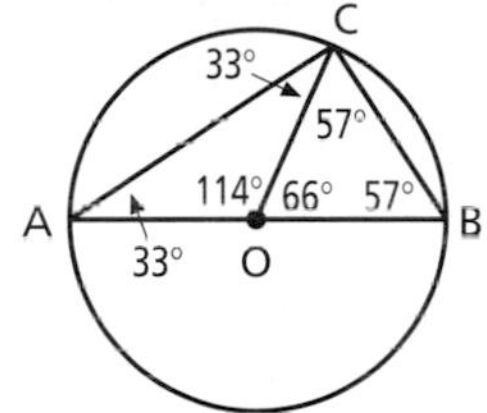

2 **a** 6 cm **b** 8.37 cm **c** 10.4 cm

3 **a** (i) 8 cm **(ii)** 16 cm
 b 14.4 cm

4 **a** 12 cm **b** 7.94 cm **c** 7.94 cm

5 **a** 39.3° **b** 4.62 cm **c** 59.2°

6 **a** 41.8° **b** 8.94 cm

7 **a** Angle ABC; angle in a semicircle is 90°
 b 3.32 m **c** 56.4°

8 **a** Proof **b** It is a diameter

9 Proofs

10 **a** Student's own drawing
 b Angle in a semicircle is a right angle
 c Move the paper further round the circle and do the same again. The intersection of the two diameters is the centre of the circle.

11 A square with sides 7.07 cm

Page 73 Exercise 8

1 **a** 26° **b** 52° **c** 18°

2 **a** 90° **b** 60° **c** 50°

3 **a** 70° **b** 40° **c** 20°

4

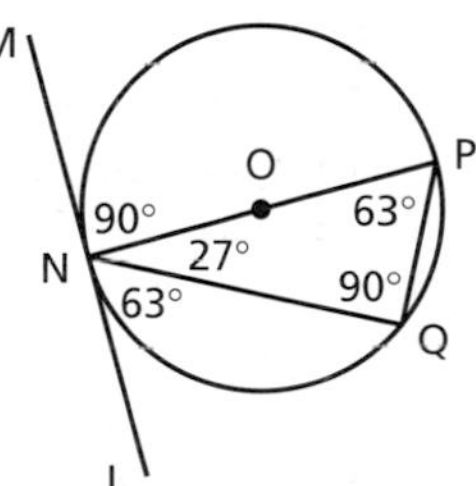

5 9.8 cm

6 **a** 33.7° **b** 56.3°

7 **a** 11.0 cm **b** 65° **c** 17.2 cm
 d 28.2 cm

8 **a** 61° **b** 11.4 cm

9 **a** 1.4 cm **b** 4.2 cm **c** 1.98 cm
 d 4.43 cm

10 a 30°
  b (i) 3 cm (ii) 6 cm (iii) 5.2 cm
  (iv) 10.4 cm (v) 3 cm
11 a 13.4 cm b 83.6°

Page 76 Review

1 a arc b sector c chord
  d tangent
2 4.61 m
3 22.5 cm
4 52.8 cm^2
5 6130 mm^2
6 a (i) 6 cm (ii) 12 cm
  b (i) 50° (ii) 80° (iii) 90°
7 a 6.26 cm b 47.3°
8

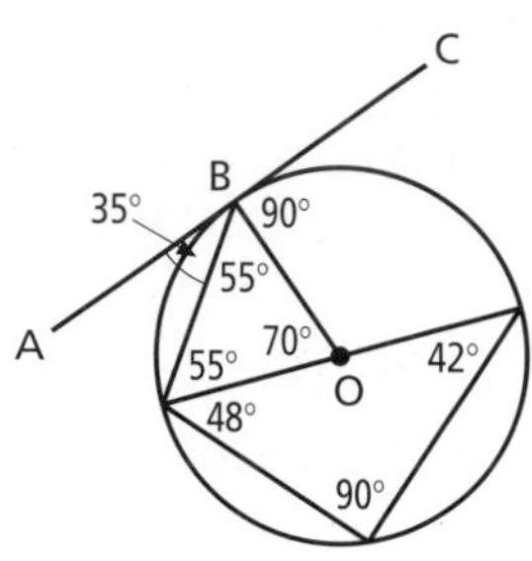

9 13.4 cm
10 $a° = 90°$, $b° = 66°$, $c° = 24°$
11 13.1 cm

7 Revising Unit 1

Page 78 Exercise 1

1 a £240 b £9 c £1.50
2 a £18.83 b £185.45 c £142.80
  d £15.10
3 £506.45
4 56.67%
5 £8261.25
6 £7130
7 £14 182.84
8 a £19 297.88 b After 4 years
9 a £408.24 b £514.26 c £599.84
10 £1203.31
11 Week 1 £185.50, Week 2 £134.80, Week 3 £265.55, Week 4 £120.35, Week 5 £173.55
12 13 500 bricks
13 £5.15
14 £99.81
15 £355.17
16 £824.51
17 £8912.71

Page 80 Exercise 2

1 a $113\,097.34 \text{ cm}^3$ b $91\,952.32 \text{ mm}^3$
  c 11.49 m^3
2 a 670.21 cm^3 b 339.29 cm^3
  c 0.905 cm^3
3 a 60 cm^3 b 285 cm^3
  c 27.52 cm^3
4 a 1357.17 cm^3 b 1847.26 mm^3
  c 2.26 m^3
5 1350 cm^3
6 250 cm^3
7 268.08 cm^3
8 100.53 cm^3 (ml)
9 $11\,309.7 \text{ mm}^2$
10 2094.4 m^3
11 a $53\,180 \text{ cm}^3$ b $15\,954 \text{ cm}^3$
12 8.685 litres
13 a $2.24 \times 10^{10} \text{ km}^3$ b $1.8 \times 10^{10} \text{ km}^3$
14 a 3.28 m^3
  b (i) 26.27 m^3 (ii) 8 times bigger

Page 83 Exercise 3

1 a

x	0	1	2
y	−1	1	3

b

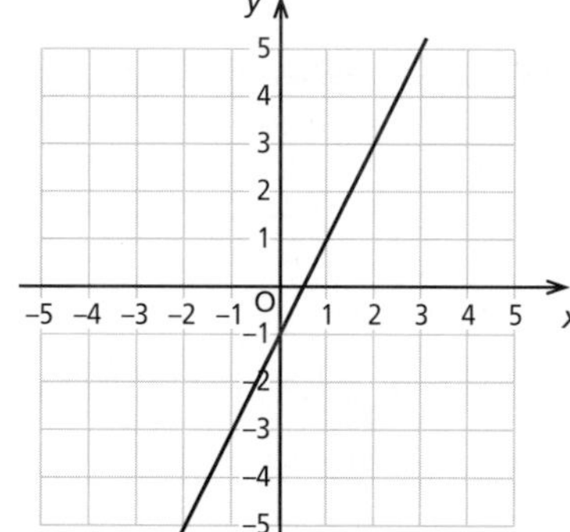

2

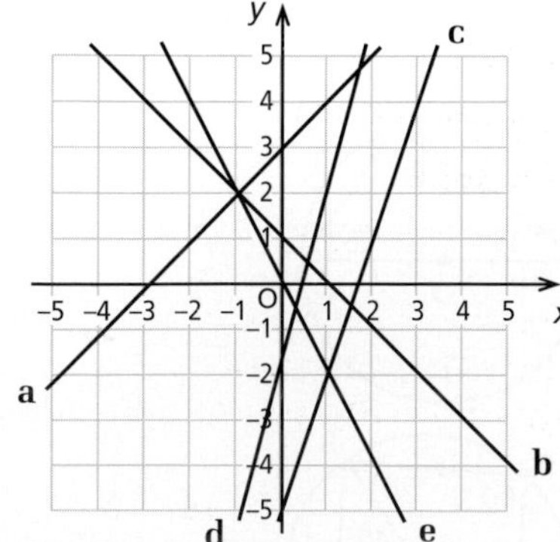

3 a 0.5 b 0.677 c 0.833
  d 0.692 e 0.4

4 **a** 2 **b** −1 **c** −1.5 **d** 2
e 0.6 **f** −1 **g** −1 **h** 0.6

5 **a** 3 **b** −0.5 **c** −3.5 **d** −0.667
e 1 **f** −0.1

6 **a** 2 **b** 1 **c** −4 **d** 0.3
e −1

7 **a** and **g**, **b** and **e**, **c** and **f**, **d** and **h**

8 **a** **(i)** 0.667 **(ii)** 0.857
b No
c PQ 0.5, QR 0.5, straight line

9 **a** −2 **b** 20 **c** 0
d 7.8 **e** 1000 **f** −12
g 3 **h** 15 **i** 0.1

10 **a** **(i)** 1 **(ii)** −2 **(iii)** $y = -2x + 1$
b **(i)** −4 **(ii)** 3 **(iii)** $y = 3x - 4$
c **(i)** 2 **(ii)** 0.2 **(iii)** $y = 0.2x + 2$
d **(i)** −2 **(ii)** −1.2 **(iii)** $y = -1.2x - 2$

11 **a** 2, 3 **b** −5, 1 **c** −2, 5
d 0.5, −0.4 **e** 1, −1 **f** −0.667, 0
g 0.3, 0.7 **h** 0.333, 0

12 **a** (3, 9) on the line, (1, 6) above, (2, 4) below
b (1, −5) below, (0, 0) and (−3, 12) on the line
c (2, −3) and (−1, 0) on the line, (0, 2) above
d (2, 3) below, (−1, −5) on the line, (0, 2) above
e (3, −3) below, (6, −2) and (0, 0) on the line
f (3, −1) on, (−8, 3) below, (0, 2) above

13 **a** **(i)** $y = 1.5x$ **(ii)** $y = 1.5x - 3.5$
(iii) $y = 1$ **(iv)** $y = -x - 3$
(v) $y = -0.889x + 1.44$
b **(i)** is parallel to **(ii)**

14 **a** 0.1
b **(i)** Gradient 0.07°, 0.1
(ii) Gradient 0.06°, 0.1
c 3.4

15 **a** **(i)** (1, 3) **(ii)** (9, 1)
(iii) (9, 5) **(iv)** (11, 8)
b **(i)** $y = 0.25x + 2.75$ **(ii)** $x = 9$
(iii) $y = 1.5x - 8.5$
c No, gradient = 0.333

Page 86 Exercise 4

1 **a** $3x + 6$ **b** $2y - 2$ **c** $5a - 5$
d $7p + 56$ **e** $10c - 10$ **f** $8x - 48$

2 **a** **(i)** $6(x + 3)$ **(ii)** $6x + 18$
b **(i)** $11(y - 7)$ **(ii)** $11y - 77$
c **(i)** $4(y - 13)$ **(ii)** $4y - 52$
d **(i)** $9(b + 8)$ **(ii)** $9b + 72$

3 **a** $6x + 15$ **b** $20y - 8$
c $24a - 32$ **d** $18p + 6q$
e $6d - 8e$ **f** $20x - 30y$
g $x^2 + 3x$ **h** $4y^2 + 2y$
i $5x^2 - 2xy$ **j** $a^2 + 2ab$
k $8c - 6c^2$ **l** $18x^2 + 6xy$
m $32a^2 - 8ab$ **n** $21x^2 + 28xy$
o $8ax - 6bx$ **p** $-12x - 4x^2$
q $-8c^2 + 8cd$ **r** $-8x^2 - 12xy$
s $-8x^2 + 6xy$ **t** $-12t^2 - 6t$
u $4fg - 2fh$ **v** $-8y^2 - 24y$
w $-x^2 + 3xy$

4 **a** $4a + 23$ **b** $6m$ **c** $-5a + 37$
d $-5d - 23$ **e** $4 - 2a$ **f** $20 - 4x$
g $3a + 61$ **h** $13 - 12p$ **i** $12 - y$
j $5x + 30$ **k** $x + 21$ **l** $2b + 7$

5 **a** $5x - 8$ **b** $x + 14$
c $8a + 2$ **d** $x^2 + 4x - 2$
e $4x^2 + 17x + 2$ **f** $10a^2 + 9a + 15$
g $2y^2 - y - 9$ **h** $8m^2 + 3m - 4$
i $12x^2 - 22x + 4$ **j** $5x^2 + 15x$
k $13b^2 - 34b$ **l** $-2x^2 + 50$

6 **a** $x^2 + 5x + 6$ **b** $x^2 + x - 2$
c $a^2 - 1$ **d** $x^2 + 6x - 7$
e $a^2 + 2a - 15$ **f** $p^2 + p - 6$
g $t^2 - 5t + 6$ **h** $r^2 + 9r + 20$
i $s^2 - 10s + 9$ **j** $k^2 - 2k - 3$
k $g^2 + 9g - 22$ **l** $j^2 - 12j + 35$

7 **a** $a^2 - 16$ **b** $x^2 - 2x + 1$
c $w^2 + 10w + 25$ **d** $y^2 - 25$
e $s^2 + s - 2$ **f** $x^2 + 6x + 9$
g $g^2 - 4g + 4$ **h** $k^2 + 5k - 14$
i $m^2 - 10m + 24$ **j** $p^2 - 1$
k $f^2 - 4f + 4$ **l** $x^2 - 10x + 25$

8 **a** **b**

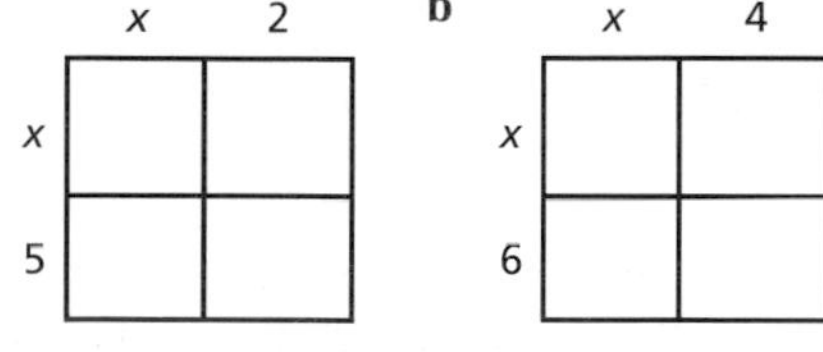

9 **a** $x^3 + 4x^2 + 9x + 10$
b $2k^3 + 9k^2 + 19k + 15$
c $6y^3 + 11y^2 + 6y + 1$

10 **a** $x^3 + 4x^2 + 7x + 6$
b $a^3 + 5a^2 + 3a - 4$
c $x^3 - 4x^2 + x + 2$
d $3px^2 - 24x^2 + px - 8x - 2p + 16$
e $2f^3 - 7f^2 - 13f - 4$
f $3x^3 - 17x^2 + 9x + 5$

11 **a** $3(t + 3)$ **b** $2(2g + 1)$
c $5(2a - 1)$ **d** $4p(1 - 2p)$

e $2(x+y)$ **f** $2(3a+b)$
g $3a(1+b)$ **h** $4(r-3s)$
i $3y(x+3)$ **j** $5n(3m+2)$
k $2c(c-3)$ **l** $3x(4x-y^2)$
m $x(11+3y)$ **n** $b(9a+b)$
o $4r(4r-s)$ **p** $8x(3xy-y^2)$

12 a $3(t+3)$ **b** $2(2g+1)$
c $5(2a-1)$ **d** $4p(1-2p)$
e $2(x+y)$ **f** $2(3a+b)$
g $3a(1+b)$ **h** $4(r-3s)$
i $3y(x+3)$ **j** $5n(3m+2)$
k $2c(c-3)$ **l** $3x(4x-y^2)$
m $x(11+3y)$ **n** $b(9a+b)$
o $4r(4r-s)$ **p** $8xy(3x-y)$
q $3t(2+3t^2)$ **r** $2x^2(2x-1)$
s $5(2x-3)(x+1)$ **t** $2(k-4k^2-3)$

13 a $(x-2)(x+2)$ **b** $(2x-1)(2x+1)$
c $(3y-5)(3y+5)$ **d** $(t-10)(t+10)$
e $(6-y)(6+y)$ **f** $(7a-b)(7a+b)$
g $(1-3a)(1+3a)$ **h** $(2p-5q)(2p+5q)$

14 a $3(x-1)(x+1)$ **b** $2(2p-1)(2p+1)$
c $2(3r-2s)(3r+2s)$ **d** $3(2x-3y)(2x+3y)$
e $2(6-k)(6+k)$ **f** $6(a-3b)(a+3b)$
g $2(1-2b)(1+2b)$ **h** $2(2c-5d)(2c+5d)$

15 a $(x+1)(x+2)$ **b** $(a+3)(a+2)$
c $(v+3)(v+4)$ **d** $(w-3)(w-1)$
e $(s-2)(s-6)$ **f** $(a-8)(a-2)$
g $(x-4)(x+3)$ **h** $(y+3)(y-2)$
i $(m-5)(m+3)$ **j** $(x+9)(x-2)$
k $(g-5)(g-4)$ **l** $(k-3)(k-7)$

16 a $3x(2-3y)$ **b** $(a-b)(a+b)$
c $7x(3x+y)$ **d** $2(w-1)(w+1)$
e $6(2a+b)$ **f** $x(x-10)$
g $5x(10-7x)$ **h** $3y(6y+1)$
i $5(2k-3)(2k+3)$ **j** $3a(4-5b)$
k $(11-x)(11+x)$ **l** $3(2x+y+5z)$
m $3(x-2)(x+2)$ **n** $5r(r+3s)$
o $7(x+7y)$ **p** $(w-10)(w-1)$
q $(p+4)(p+1)$ **r** $(2x-2)(x-2)$

17 a $(2x+1)(x+3)$ **b** $(3x+1)(3x-4)$
c $(5x+2)(2x+1)$ **d** $(5x+3)(x+2)$
e $(3x+2)(x+1)$ **f** $(2x-5)(4x-3)$
g $(4x-3)(x-3)$ **h** $(5x-2)(3x+1)$
i $(2x-3)(6x+5)$ **j** $(2x-3)(x-6)$
k $(3x-2)(3x-4)$ **l** $(2x+1)(2x+3)$

Page 89 Exercise 5

1 a 15.7 cm **b** 8.38 cm **c** 11.0 cm
d 126 mm **e** 5.93 cm **f** 188 cm
g 37.5 mm **h** 7.85 km

2 a 39.3 cm^2 **b** 0.785 cm^2 **c** 8.38 cm^2
d 98.3 cm^2 **e** 206 cm^2 **f** 29.9 cm^2
g 57.6 cm^2 **h** 1830 cm^2

3 a 4.4 m **b** 2.64 m^2

4 73.9 m

5 a 1.71 cm^2
b (i) 1.22 cm **(ii)** 8.55 cm
c 6.72 cm

6 1069 mm^2

7 a 55 cm **b** No, inner rim 62.8 cm

8 3927 m^2

9 a 68 cm **b** 173 cm **c** 4817 cm^2

10 a $a=30°$, $b=30°$
b $a=45°$, $b=90°$
c $a=114°$, $b=33°$
d $a=58°$, $b=64°$, $c=116°$, $d=32°$, $e=32°$
e $a=36°$, $b=36°$, $c=72°$
f $a=126°$, $b=27°$, $c=54°$

11 a 7.81 cm **b** 11.7 cm **c** 13.6 cm

12 a OC, OB, OA **b** AC, CB **c** PA
d AB **e** ∠ACB, ∠PAO

13 ∠OBE, ∠ABC, ∠ADC
b (i) 72° **(ii)** 36° **(iii)** 36°

14 ∠RQX = ∠QRY = 90°, QX = RY,
198 cm^2

15 Perimeter = 6.03 m, Area = 2.69 m^2

UNIT 2

8 Trigonometry

Page 93 Starting Points

1 a 13 cm b 14.0 cm
2 a 29.7° b 23.6° c 53.3°
3 a 7.39 m b 11.3 cm c 39.2 mm
4 a 4.9 cm^2 b 45 m^2 c 247 mm^2
5 a 6 b 5.4 c 3.5

Page 94 Exercise 1

1 a $\frac{1}{2}$ b $\frac{1}{2}$ c $\sqrt{3}$
2 a–c

$x°$	0°	30°	45°	60°	90°
$\sin x°$	0	$\frac{1}{2}$	$\frac{1}{\sqrt{2}}$	$\frac{\sqrt{3}}{2}$	1
$\cos x°$	1	$\frac{\sqrt{3}}{2}$	$\frac{1}{\sqrt{2}}$	$\frac{1}{2}$	0
$\tan x°$	0	$\frac{1}{\sqrt{3}}$	1	$\sqrt{3}$	not defined

d Error
3 See **2a–c**
4 $\cos 60° = \frac{x}{10}$
$x = \cos 60° \times 10$
$x = \frac{1}{2} \times 10$
$x = 5$
YZ = 5 cm
5 13 cm
6 $8\sqrt{3}$ cm
7 30°
8 a 12 cm b $12\sqrt{2}$ cm

Page 97 Exercise 2

1 a 0.8, −0.6, −1.3 b −0.8, −0.6, 1.3
c −0.2, 1, −0.2 d −0.4, −0.9, 0.4
e 0.7, 0.7, 1 f −0.8, 0.6, −1.3
2 Student's own diagram
3 a 0.819 b −0.940 c 0.249
d 0.643 e −2.14

Page 99 Exercise 3

1 a 77.1 cm^2 b 28.0 cm^2 c 36.2 cm^2
d 39.3 m^2 e 30.1 cm^2 f 1200 mm^2

Page 100 Exercise 4

1 a 56 cm^2 b 256 cm^2 c 23.4 cm^2
2 30.6 cm^2
3 156 m^2
4 1880 m^2
5 a 65°, 65°, 50° b 300 mm^2
6 97.4 cm^2
7 a 12 m^2 b 1.05 m^2 c 13.9 m^2
8 1077 m^2

Page 102 Exercise 5

1 7.05 cm
2 11.7 cm
3 26.9 mm

Page 103 Exercise 6

1 a $\frac{a}{\sin A} = \frac{b}{\sin B} = \frac{c}{\sin C}$
b $\frac{d}{\sin D} = \frac{e}{\sin E} = \frac{f}{\sin F}$
c $\frac{x}{\sin X} = \frac{y}{\sin Y} = \frac{z}{\sin Z}$
2 a $r = \frac{10 \times \sin 50°}{\sin 60°}$
$r = 8.8455$
PQ = 8.85 cm (to 3 s.f.)
b $\frac{d}{\sin D} = \frac{e}{\sin E} = \frac{f}{\sin F}$
$\frac{e}{\sin 65°} = \frac{6.4}{\sin 40°}$
$e = \frac{6.4 \times \sin 65°}{\sin 40°}$
$e = 9.0237$
DF = 9.02 cm (to 3 s.f.)
3 a 3.88 cm b 6.13 cm c 23.0 mm
d 3.13 cm
4 a 48.5 cm b 1.08 km c 14.1 m
5 80.1 m

Page 104 Exercise 7

1 a 25.7 m
b (i) 20° (ii) 10.4 m
2 a 5.76 m b 2.53 m c 5.60 m
3 a 2.62 km b 3.30 km c 8.72 km
4 a 13.3 km b 36.1 km
5 224 m

Page 106 Exercise 8

1 a 43.9° b 48.7° c 47.3°
d 24.2° e 41.4° f 30.3°
g 55.2° h 56.9°
2 a (i) 45.6° (ii) 82.4°
b (i) 45.1° (ii) 48.9°

Page 107 Exercise 9

1 46.1°
2 50.5°
3 68.0°
4 32.5°
5 124°

Page 108 Exercise 10

1 a 136.1°
b Angles of a triangle add up to 180°, and P + R > 180°, so this is unacceptable for a triangle
2 a (i) 82.6° (ii) 55.4°
b (i) 97.4° (ii) 40.6° (iii) Yes
3 a ∠P = 63.3°, ∠Q = 78.7°, q = 4.9 m or ∠P = 116.7°, ∠Q = 25.3°, q = 2.2 m
b ∠Q = 68.0°, ∠P = 62°, q = 8.8 cm or ∠Q = 112°, ∠P = 18°, q = 3.1 cm
c ∠Q = 33.7°, ∠P = 116.3°, q = 16.1 cm or ∠Q = 146.3°, ∠P = 3.7°, q = 1.2 cm

Page 110 Exercise 11

1 8.29 cm
2 1.80 m
3 26.3 mm

Page 112 Exercise 12

1 a $b^2 = a^2 + c^2 - 2ac \cos B$
b $r^2 = p^2 + q^2 - 2pq \cos R$
c $m^2 = l^2 + n^2 - 2ln \cos M$
2 7.41 cm
3 7.81 cm
4 a 7.82 cm b 20.3 mm c 11.2 cm
d 4.92 km e 8.98 m f 12.3 cm
g 63.9 cm h 153 km
5 a 67.5 m b 152.5 m
6 367 m
7 a 14.6 cm b 4.5 cm
8 a 44.6 m b 46.4 m
c The first golfer's
9 6630 km
10 61.5 cm
11 a 0.85 m b 0.60 m
12 48.4 km

Page 114 Exercise 13

1 a $\cos P = \dfrac{q^2 + r^2 - p^2}{2qr}$
b $\cos Y = \dfrac{x^2 + z^2 - y^2}{2xz}$
c $\cos C = \dfrac{a^2 + b^2 - c^2}{2ab}$
2 a 59.6° b 97.4° c 40.8° d 33.0°
e 61.0° f 143° g 109°
3 a 90°
b In a right-angled triangle $y^2 = x^2 + z^2$
4 a/b ∠A = 112°, ∠B = 39.4°, ∠C = 29.5°
c The largest side is opposite the largest angle and the smallest side is opposite the smallest angle
5 67.5°
6 95.1°

7 a 38.3° b 44.7°
8 104°, 57°, 92°, 107°
9 039°
10 4.8°

Page 117 Exercise 14

1 a 17.0 cm b 26.3 cm
c 66.4° or 113.6° d 60.9°
e 52.1 mm f 78.5° or 15.5°
2 a b = 81.4 mm, ∠A = 50.6°, ∠C = 42.4°
b ∠N = 69°, m = 31.8 cm, n = 47.1 cm
c ∠P = 73.7°, ∠Q = 54.8°, ∠R = 51.5°
d s = 2.7 cm, ∠T = 66.1°, ∠U = 41.9°,
e ∠D = 42.9°, ∠E = 31.1°, e = 12.9 cm
f ∠X = 49.5°, ∠W = 95.5°, w = 69.4 cm or ∠X = 130.5°, ∠W = 14.5°, w = 17.5 cm
3 8.2°
4 19.5 cm
5 4.1 m, 8.1 m, 12.2 m
6 a 69° b 36.8 km
7 a 80° b (i) 1.19 km (ii) 0.97 km
8 70°, 28.4°, 81.6°, 98.4°, 0.48 m

Page 119 Review

1 310 cm^2
2 a 23.3 cm^2, 25.0 cm^2
b Green by 1.7 cm^2
3 6.8 m
4 63.6° or 24.4°
5 58.2°
6 2.97 m
7 7.77 cm
8 58.9°

9 Simultaneous Linear Equations

Page 120 Starting Points

1 a (i) $5x$ (ii) 0 (iii) $-3y$
(iv) $2m$ (v) $-4k$
b (i) $6x$ (ii) $10x$ (iii) $-6y$
(iv) 0 (v) $-10y$
2 a 70 b 17
3 a $x = 3$ b $x = 4$ c $x = -2$
4 a −3, −1, 1, 3, 5, 7
b/c

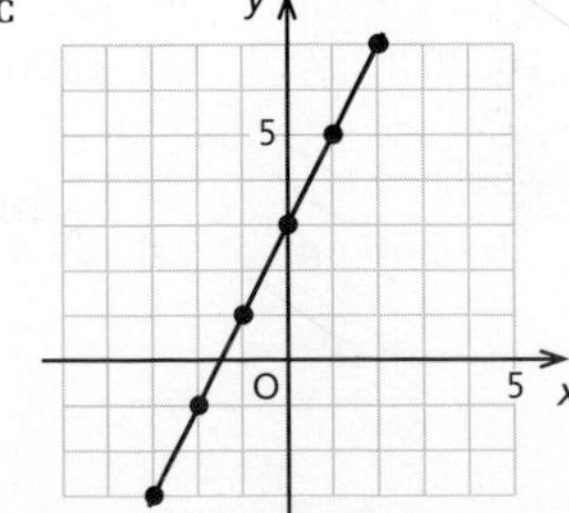

d (i) 2 (ii) (0, 3)

5 a–c

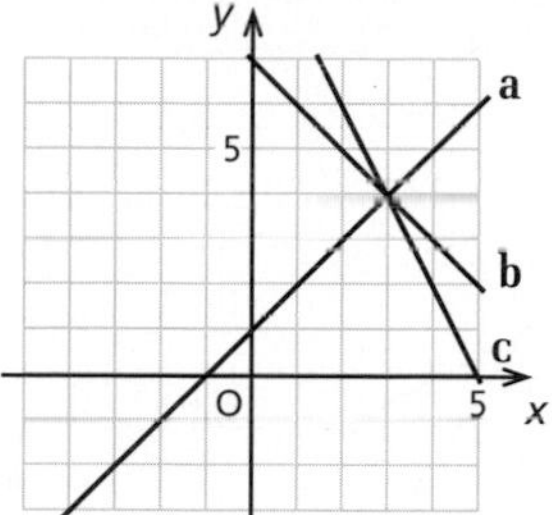

d (i)

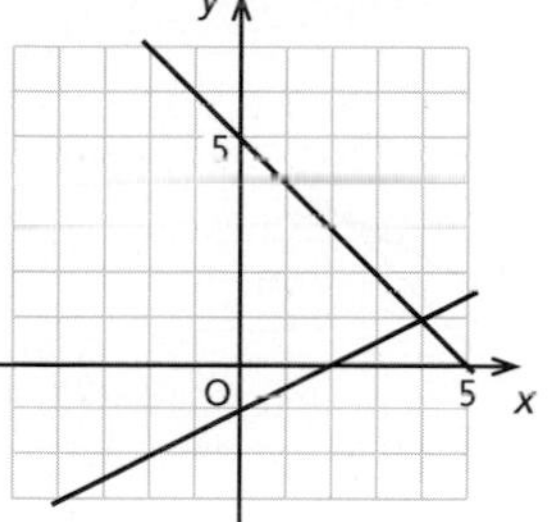

(ii) (4, 1)

6 a $C = 7x$ **b** $N = 30t$ **c** $K = 3a + 2c$

Page 121 Exercise 1

1 a (i)

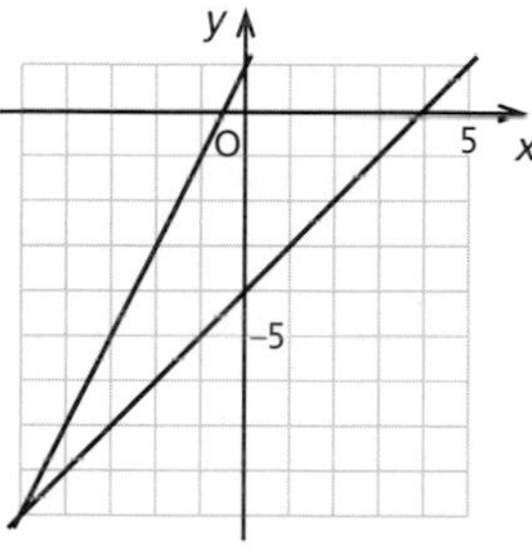

(ii) (−5, −9)

b (i)

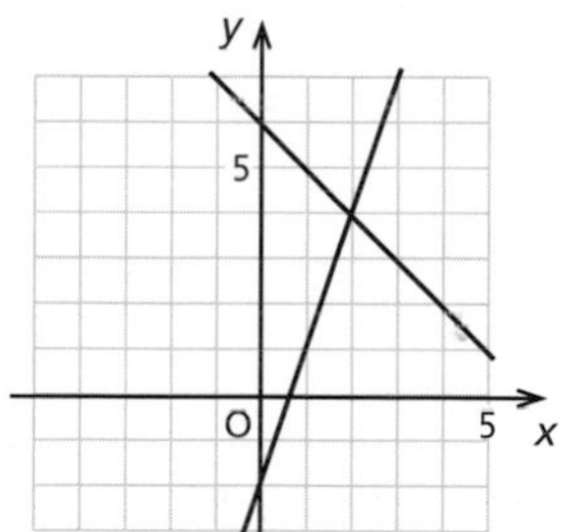

(ii) (2, 4)

c (i)

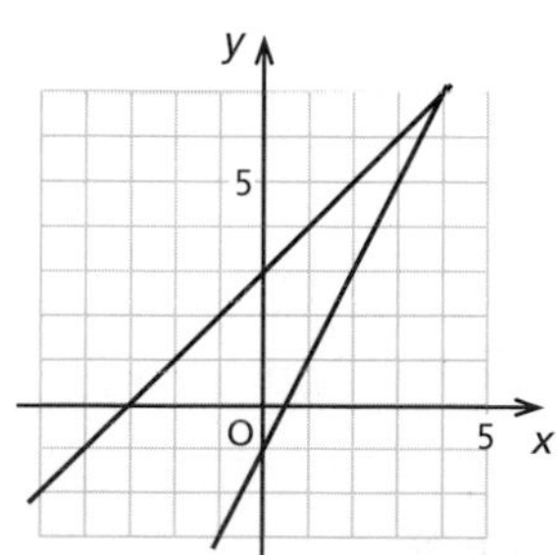

(ii) (4, 7)

2 a (i) (0, 4), (1, 3), (2, 2)
b (i) (0, 6), (1, 4), (2, 2)
c (i) (−5, 8), (0, 4), (5, 0)
d (i) (0, −8), (1, −7), (2, −6)

a–d (ii)

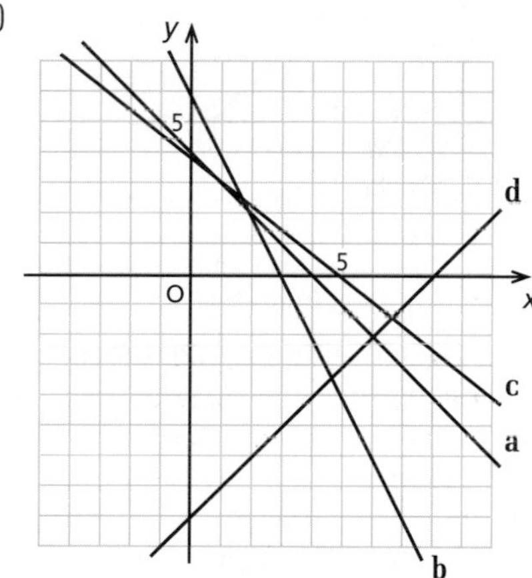

3 a (ii) (1,2) **b (ii)** (2, 1)
c (ii) (2, 3) **d (ii)** (2, −6)
e (ii) (1, 3) **f (ii)** (1, 2)
g (ii) (2, −2) **h (ii)** (6, 13)
i (ii) (3, −6) **j (ii)** (−2, 1)
k (ii) $(\frac{8}{3}, 8)$

4

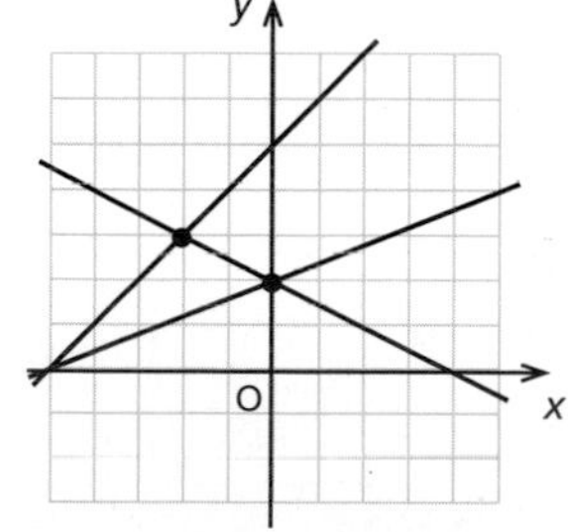

(−5, 0), (−2, 3), (0, 2)

5 (1, 1), (3, 7), (−3, 5)

Page 123 Exercise 2

1 a

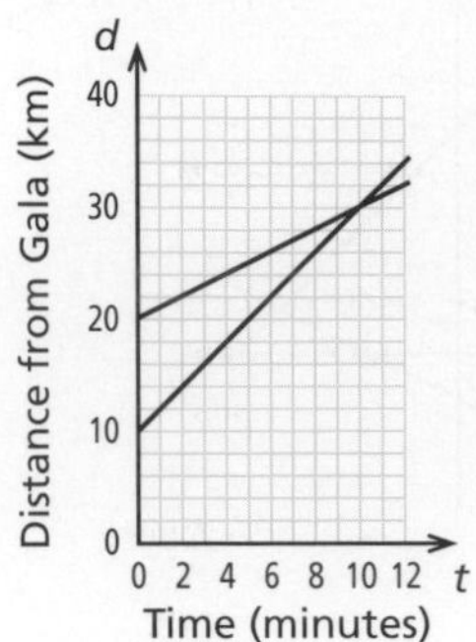

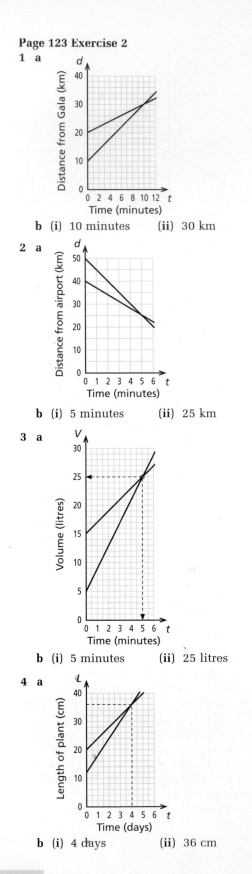

b (i) 10 minutes (ii) 30 km

2 a

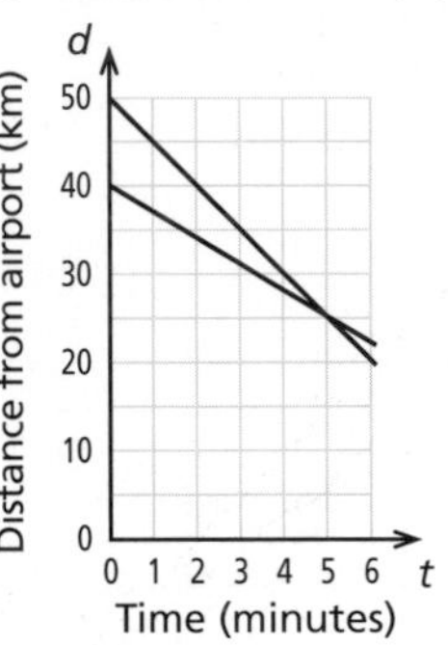

b (i) 5 minutes (ii) 25 km

3 a

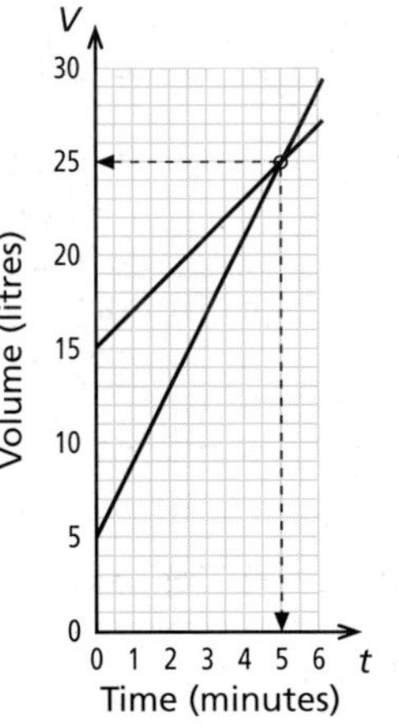

b (i) 5 minutes (ii) 25 litres

4 a

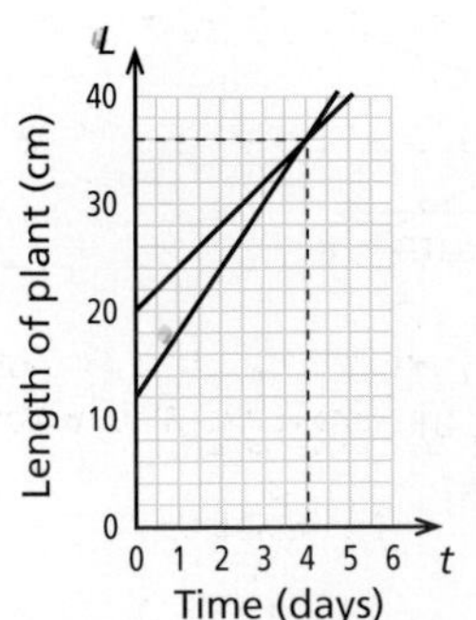

b (i) 4 days (ii) 36 cm

5 a

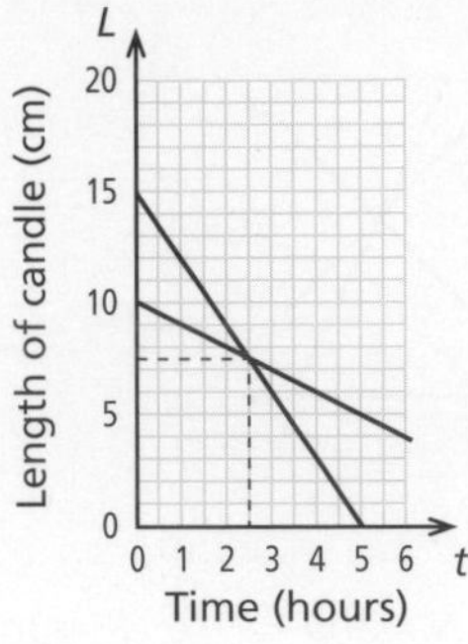

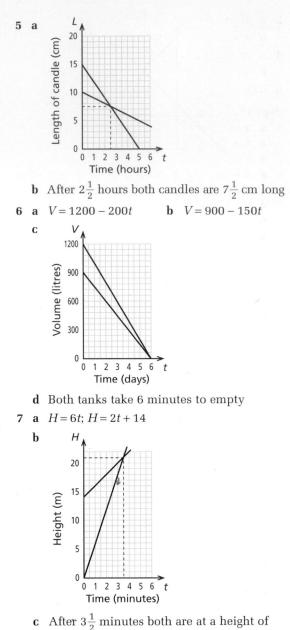

b After $2\frac{1}{2}$ hours both candles are $7\frac{1}{2}$ cm long

6 a $V = 1200 - 200t$ b $V = 900 - 150t$

c

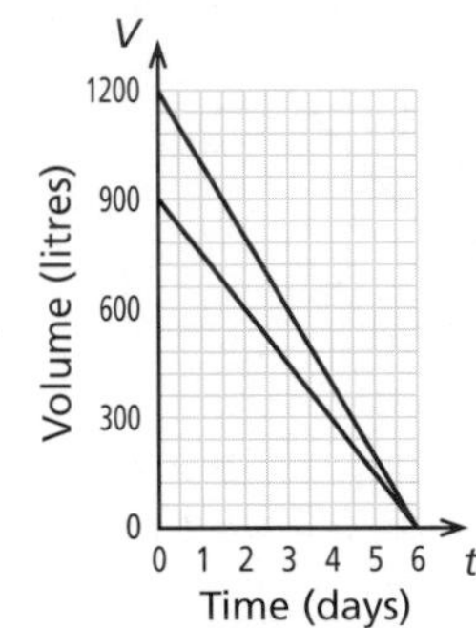

d Both tanks take 6 minutes to empty

7 a $H = 6t$; $H = 2t + 14$

b

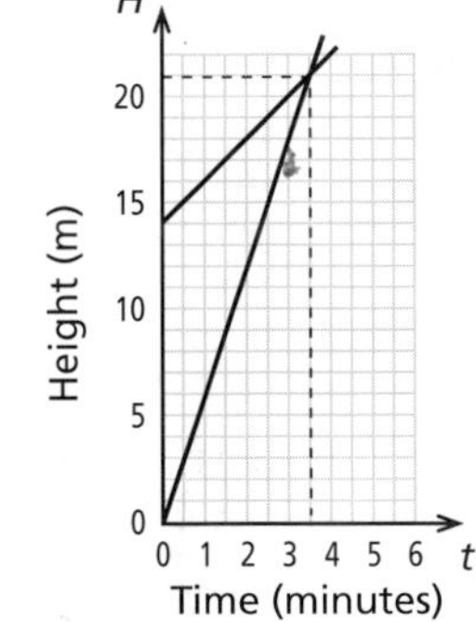

c After $3\frac{1}{2}$ minutes both are at a height of 21 metres

8 a $D = 22 - 5t$; $D = 15 - 3t$

b After $3\frac{1}{2}$ minutes both are $4\frac{1}{2}$ km from the airport

Page 125 Exercise 3

1 a $x + 2y = 10$ b (4, 3)

c (i) £4 (ii) £3 (iii) £33

2 a £x is the cost per km by Tube, £y is the cost per km by bus

b $2x + 6y = 6$

c £1.50 by Tube, £0.50 by bus

d £10

3 **a** $4x + 3y = 20$, $2x + 5y = 17$
b $x = \frac{7}{2}$, $y = 2$ **c** 23p
4 **a** $6x + 5y = 14$, $8x + 3y = 15$
b $x = \frac{3}{2}$, $y = 1$ **c** 60 units
5 £23

Page 127 Exercise 4

1 **a** $x = 2, y = 1$ **b** $x = 3, y = 6$
c $x = 10, y = 7$ **d** $x = -4, y = -7$
e $x = 1, y = 2$ **f** $x = 2, y = 9$
g $x = 5, y = 2$ **h** $x = -1, y = 7$
i $x = 6, y = 9$
2 **a** $x = 2, y = 7$ **b** $x = -7, y = 2$
c $x = 0, y = -3$ **d** $x = 3, y = 7$
e $x = -2, y = 1$ **f** $x = 2, y = 16$
3 **a** **(i)** $x = y + 3$ **(ii)** $x + y = 13$
b $x = 8$, $y = 5$; 8 km by road and 5 km cross country
4 **a** $x = y - 120$; $x + y = 300$
b **(i)** £90 **(ii)** £210
5 **a** $y = 3x$; $3x + 2y = 54$
b **(i)** 6 adults **(ii)** 18 children
6 **a** Jenny: x years; grandfather: y years; $y + 1 = 3x$; $y - x = 41$
b Jenny is 21 and grandfather is 62 years
7 **a** $20x + 5y = 180$; $x + y = 12$
b He won 8 and lost 4
8 **a** 48 **b** 26
9 **a** $2\frac{1}{2}$ hours on each type
b Motorway: 175 miles; A roads: 125 miles

Page 130 Exercise 5

1 **a** $x = 2, y = 1$ **b** $x = 3, y = 1$
c $x = 2, y = -2$ **d** $x = 2, y = 3$
e $x = 2, y = 1$ **f** $x = 7, y = -5$
g $x = 3, y = 1$ **h** $x = 2, y = 6$
i $x = 4, y = -1$ **j** $x = 5, y = 5$
k $x = 1, y = 2$ **l** $x = 1, y = -1$
m $x = -1, y = -4$ **n** $a = 7, b = 3$
o $m = 3, n = 1$ **p** $x = 7, y = 2$
q $p = \frac{1}{2}, q = 1$ **r** $x = 7, y = 5$
2 **a** $x = 3, y = \frac{3}{2}$ **b** $a = 1, b = 0$
c $x = 1, y = \frac{1}{2}$ **d** $m = \frac{3}{2}, n = 1$
e $d = 1, e = 1$ **f** $x = 0, y = -1$
g $x = \frac{1}{2}, y = -1$ **h** $x = -\frac{1}{2}, y = 2$
i $u = 1, v = -1$ **j** $x = 4, y = 0$
k $a = \frac{1}{2}, b = -1$ **l** $m = 4, n = \frac{3}{2}$
3 **a** $a = 7, b = 3$ **b** $x = 2, y = 1$
c $x = 3, y = \frac{1}{2}$ **d** $x = -2, y = -9$
e $d = 0, e = 2$ **f** $u = 2, v = -2$
g $x = 1, y = 1$ **h** $a = \frac{1}{2}, b = \frac{3}{2}$
i $w = \frac{1}{2}, y = \frac{1}{10}$
4 **a** $3h + 2c = 410$, $4h + 3c = 570$
b **(i)** 90p **(ii)** 70p
5 **a** $4a + 6b = 34$, $5a + 2b = 26$
b **(i)** 4 m **(ii)** 3 m
6 **a** 20p **b** 25p
7 390 minutes
8 **a** **(i)** 80 mm **(ii)** 15 mm
b 935 mm

Page 132 Review

1 **b** 280 km
c **(i)** $240 - 40t$
(ii)

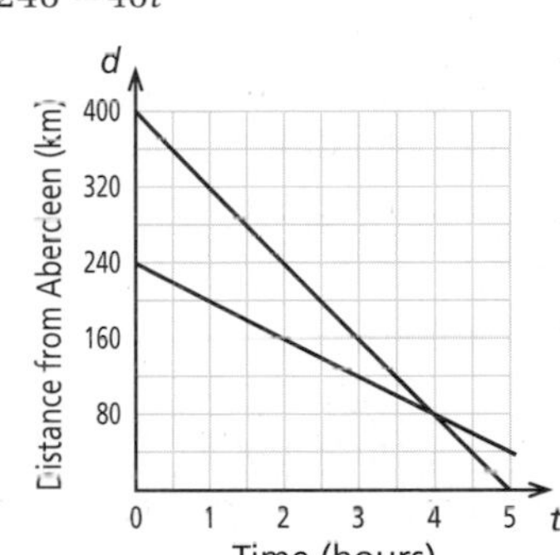

d After 4 hours both coaches were 80 km from Aberdeen
2 **a** $x = 3, y = 9$ **b** $x = 5, y = 2$
3 **a** x: cost of glass of wine; y: cost of coffee
b $4x + 4y = 18$ **c** $x = 3, y = 1.5$
d **(i)** £3 **(ii)** £1.50 **(iii)** £19.50
4 **a** $x = 3, y = 13$ **b** $x = 2, y = -1$
c **(i)** $x = 3, y = 0$ **(ii)** $x = 5, y = 2$
(iii) $a = 3, b = -2$

10 Graphs, Charts and Tables

Page 134 Starting Points

1 **a** Minto **b** 3 **c** 25 **d** $\frac{1}{5}$
2 **a** A–3 B–15 C–18 D–18 E–7 F–8 G–2 H–1
b Heights of bars: 3 15 18 18 7 8 2 1
c C and D
3 **a** 120 **b** 130
c Increasing
d **(i)** Heights of points: 20 10 30 40 40 100 120 **(ii)** Increase at weekends
4 **a** 40 min
b **(i)** 10 min **(ii)** 80 min
c 70 min
d 60

5 a Heights of points: 5 7 18 9 1
b 30 mph
c 10

6 a (i) 11.2 cm (ii) 7.1 cm
b 9 c 9.7 cm d 9.7 cm

7 a

1	1 6 7 8 9
2	2 2 6 6 8 9
3	0 3 5
4	5 7

b 36 min

8

10	1 3 8
11	0 1 5 8 8
12	0 1 2 2 6 7 7 9
13	1 1 2 6 7 8 9
14	1 1 2 6 9
15	4
16	5

$n = 30$ 10 | 1 represents 101

9 a

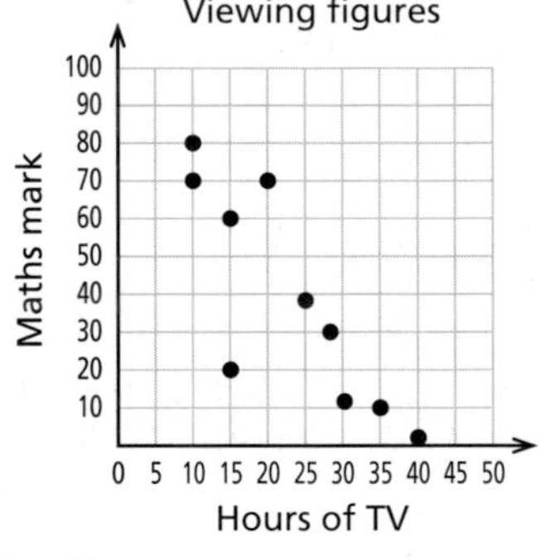

b Negative

10 a Negative b Approx. 180
c September

11 a/b

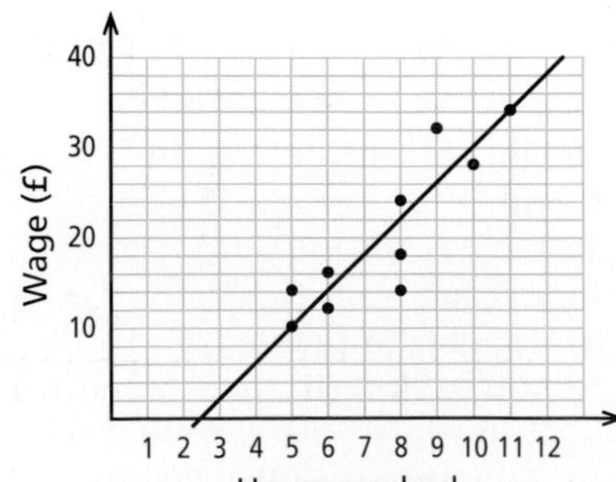

c (i) £18 (ii) 9 hours

12 a/b

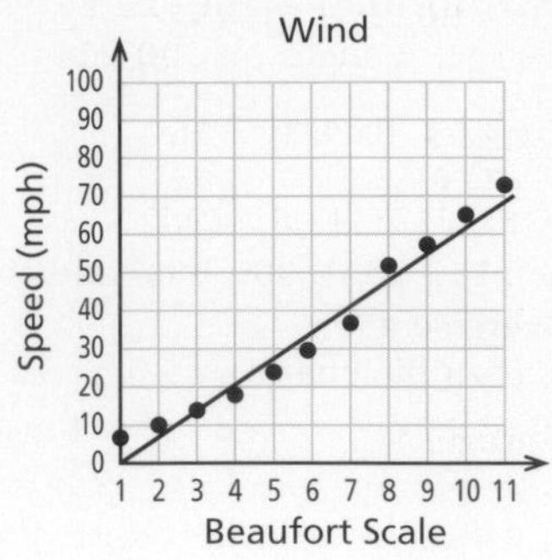

c (i) 7 (ii) 40 mph

Page 138 Exercise 1

1 a Total 300
b 0.4 + 0.2 + 0.15 + 0.1 + 0.05 + 0.1 = 1
c Probabilities should total 1
d 9 min

2 a (i) 0.47 (ii) 0.53
c 0.5

3 a Total 250; 0.16, 0.64, 0.2
b Pie chart should have angles of 58°, 230° and 72°
c 80, 320, 100

4 a Total 400; 0.23, 0.41, 0.195, 0.1, 0.065
b (i) $\frac{92}{400} = 0.23$ (ii) $\frac{256}{400} = 0.64$

5 a Total 300; 0.36, 0.42, 0.08, 0.14
b Pie chart should have angles of 130°, 151°, 29° and 50°
c (i) Total 232; 0.36, 0.42, 0.08, 0.14
(ii) Approximately the same

Page 140 Exercise 2

1 a 70°, 80°, 120°, 90° b $\frac{70}{360}, \frac{80}{360}, \frac{120}{360}, \frac{90}{360}$
c 111 d 28

2 a 45°, 100°, 155°, 60° b $\frac{45}{360}, \frac{100}{360}, \frac{155}{360}, \frac{60}{360}$
c (i) 431 (ii) 278
d 42

3 Youth 417, young adult 1806, middle-aged 1111, OAP 1667

Page 141 Exercise 3

1 a (i) 18° (ii) 54° (iii) 270°
b Pie chart with angles of 18°, 54° and 270°

2 a (i) 90 (ii) 18 (iii) 54 (iv) 36
b Pie chart with angles of 90°, 18°, 54° 36° and 162°

3 a $\frac{10}{60}, \frac{30}{60}, \frac{12}{60}, \frac{8}{60}$
b Pie chart with angles of 60°, 180°, 72° and 48°

4 a 0.4, 0.3, 0.1, 0.2
b Pie chart with angles of 144°, 108°, 36° and 72°

5 a (i) 40% (ii) 10% (iii) 20%
  b Pie chart with angles of 108°, 144°, 36° and 72°

6 a $\frac{18}{97}, \frac{59}{97}, \frac{12}{97}, \frac{8}{97}$
  b (i) 66.8°, 219°, 44.5°, 29.7°
    (iii) 67°, 219°, 45°, 30°, total adds to 361°
    (iv) to 1°

7 Student's own pie charts

Page 143 Exercise 4

1 a (i) 2 (ii) 24
  b (i) 49 (ii) 90

2 a 14, 52, 117, 143, 154, 156
  b Week 3 c 156 d Week 4

3 a 10, 30, 55, 85, 95, 100
  b 3 h c 85

4 a 7, 8, 9, 10, 11, 12; 50, 170, 200, 150, 100, 50; 50, 220, 420, 570, 670, 720
  b 720 c 10

5 a 140, 150, 160, 170, 180, 190; 8, 18, 24, 30, 14, 10; 8, 26, 50, 80, 94, 104
  b (i) 94 (ii) 0 c 104

Page 145 Exercise 5

1 a (i) 145 (ii) 40
  b (i) 120 (ii) 30

2 a 1, 4, 12, 24, 33, 38, 40
  b

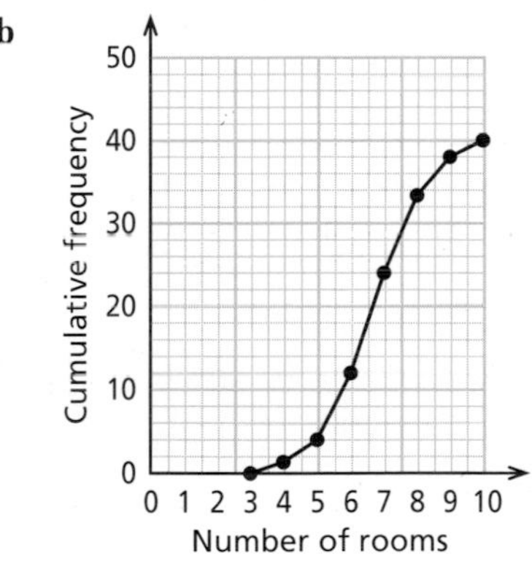

  c 16

3 a 4, 9, 17, 32, 45, 50; 4, 11, 19, 27, 35, 41, 45, 48, 50
  b

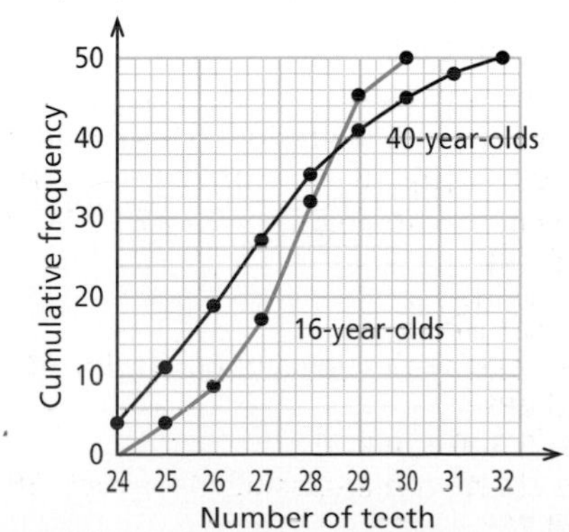

  c Yes. Two wisdom teeth grow late.

4 a 9, 32, 64, 89, 100
  b

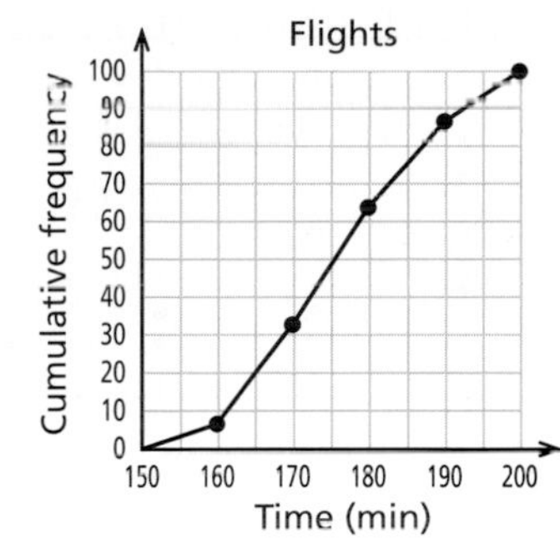

  c 20; no

Page 147 Exercise 6

1 a 4, 7, 11, 13, 18, 21, 22, 23, 25, 25, 26, 26, 26, 27, 29
  b (i) 29 (ii) 4 (iii) 23
  c Skewed to the left

2 a

  b (i) 6 (ii) 1 (iii) 3.5
  c Uniform distribution

3 a (i) 16 (ii) 9
  b 13
  c Symmetric distribution
  d Approximate contents 13

4 a

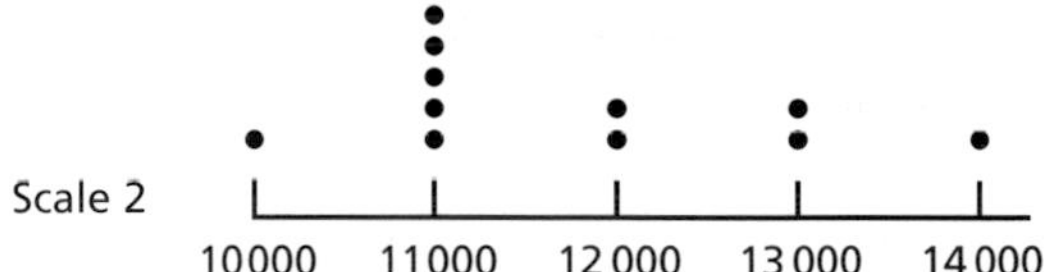

Scale 2

10000 11000 12 000 13 000 14 000

  b (i) and (ii) Skewed to the right
  c Cars from £11 000 upwards

5 a

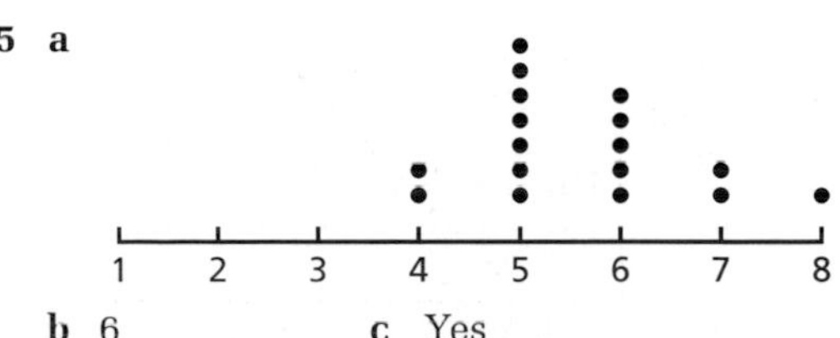

  b 6 c Yes

6 a (i)

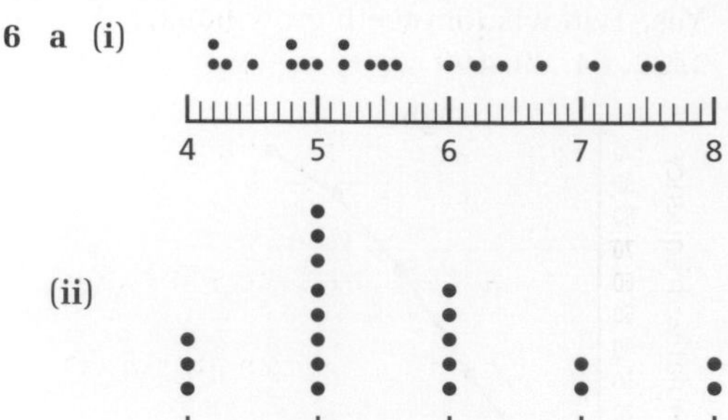

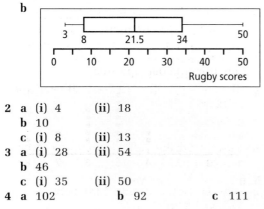

b Rates are mainly between 4% and 6%

Page 149 Challenge

a (i) 2 (ii) 3 (iii) 0

b (i) 2, 3, 0

(ii) Remainder gives how many numbers are creased

c 1

d (i) 5th below, 6th above

(ii) 5th below, 7th above

(iii) 6th below, 7th above

e (i) between 30 and 31, 61, between 91 and 92

(ii) 31, 62, 93

Page 151 Exercise 7

1 a 2, 7, 24, 45, 48,

b 18, 23, 25, 29, 37

c 23, 28.5, 35, 40.5, 61

d 98, 99.5, 116, 131, 147

2 a 4, 10, 17, 21, 25

b 17, 23, 28, 31, 56

c 72, 74, 83, 86, 89

d 7, 10, 16.5, 21.5, 25

Page 152 Exercise 8

1 a 3, 8, 21.5, 34, 50

b

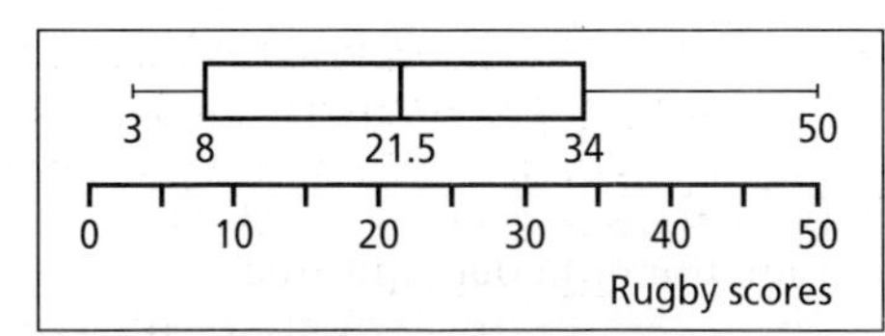

2 a (i) 4 (ii) 18

b 10

c (i) 8 (ii) 13

3 a (i) 28 (ii) 54

b 46

c (i) 35 (ii) 50

4 a 102 b 92 c 111

d

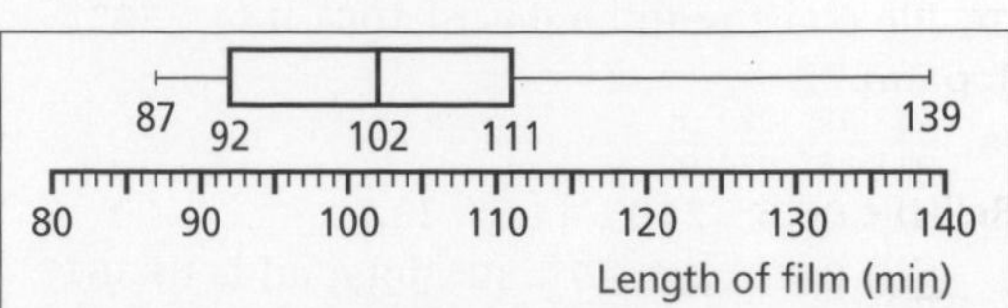

5 a 18, 24.5, 32, 42, 50

b

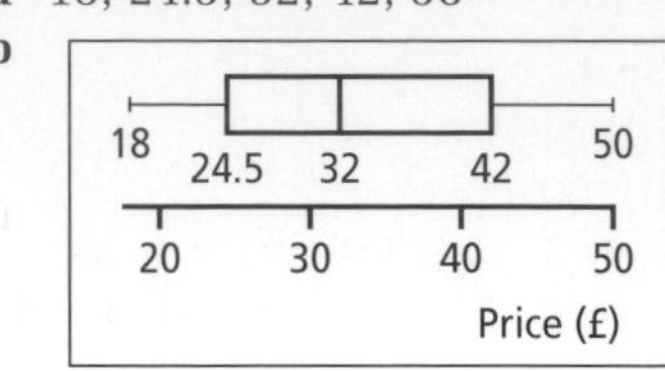

6 a 17.5, 13, 19.5

b

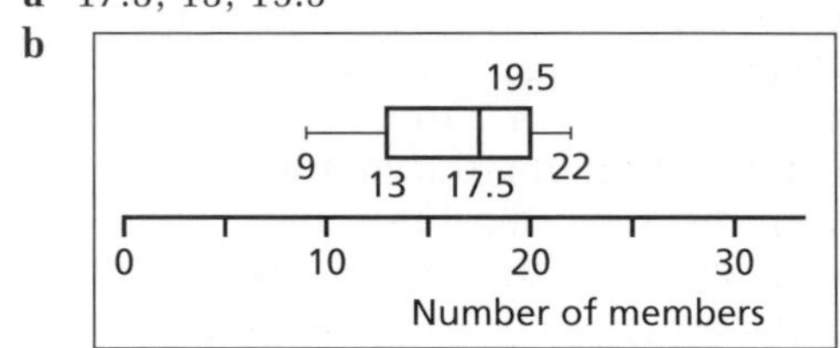

7 a 25, 25, 26, 28, 28, 30, 38, 38, 41, 41, 42, 43, 44, 45, 46, 50, 55, 56, 59, 60

b 25, 29, 41.5, 48, 60

c

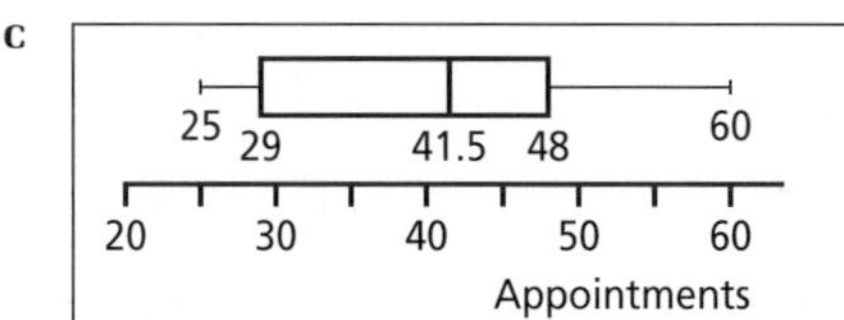

Page 155 Exercise 9

1 a 30, 55, 125, 190, 250

b 50, 85, 170, 255, 300

c

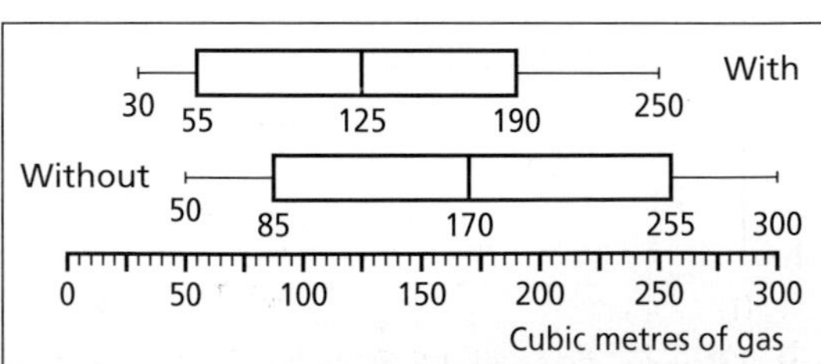

d (i) Yes (ii) Type of other gas appliances

2 a

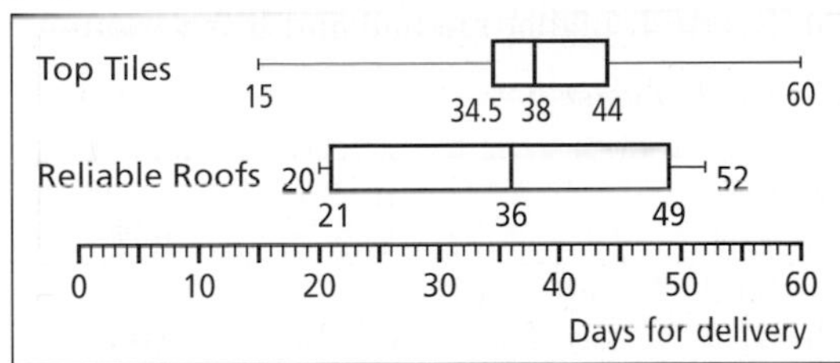

b 32, 45 c 14, 4.75

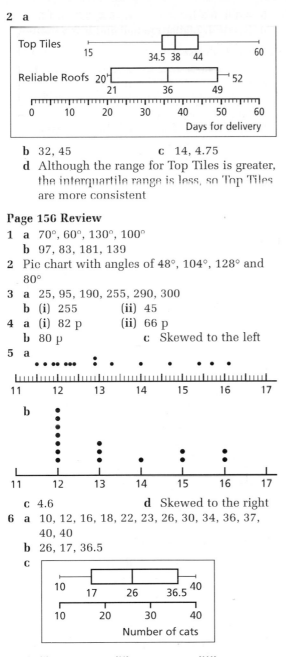

d Although the range for Top Tiles is greater, the interquartile range is less, so Top Tiles are more consistent

Page 156 Review

1 a 70°, 60°, 130°, 100°
b 97, 83, 181, 139

2 Pie chart with angles of 48°, 104°, 128° and 80°

3 a 25, 95, 190, 255, 290, 300
b (i) 255 (ii) 45

4 a (i) 82 p (ii) 66 p
b 80 p c Skewed to the left

5 a

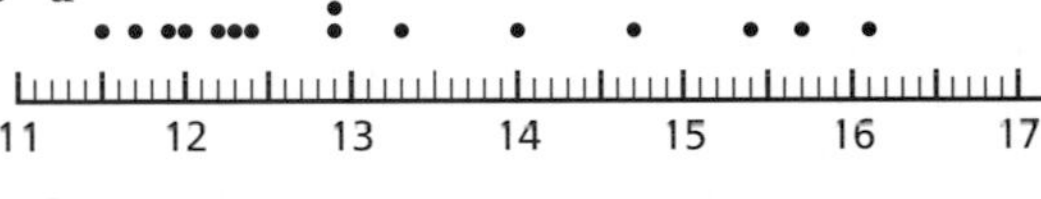

b

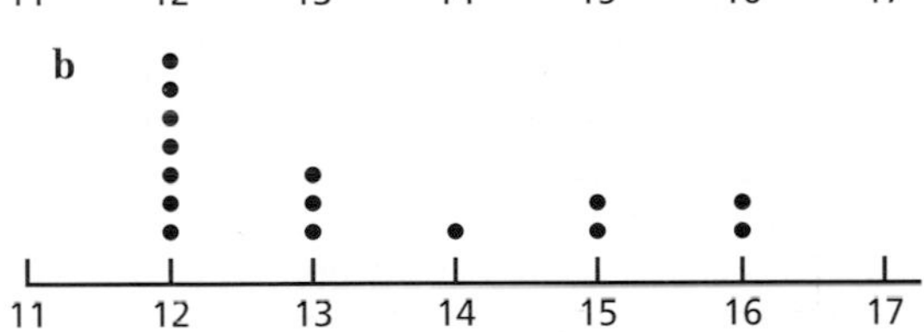

c 4.6 d Skewed to the right

6 a 10, 12, 16, 18, 22, 23, 26, 30, 34, 36, 37, 40, 40
b 26, 17, 36.5
c

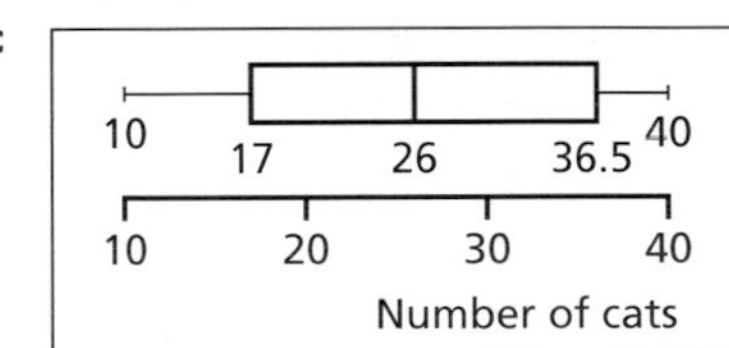

7 a (i) 33, 47 (ii) 57, 74 (iii) 11, 8
b French has a higher median, a smaller interquartile range but the range is greater.

11 Statistics

Page 158 Starting Points

1 a (i) 50 (ii) 42 (iii) 8
b 45.75 c 45
d Heights of bars: 1 2 1 4 3 1 2 1 1
e Claim is truthful

2 a (i) 4 (ii) 6 (iii) 6
b 19 c 40 cm

3 a and d

4 a 1: 3; 2: 4; 3: 7; 4: 5; 5: 3; 6: 2; 7: 1
b Heights of bars: 3 4 7 5 3 2 1

5 a 3, 5, 8, 4 b 20

6 a £100. It is the lowest and there are only two wages of £100
b £255. No, one person earns a high wage
c £170. Yes
d £700. Yes

7 a 12, 24, 35, 6; totals 18, 77
b (i) 77 (ii) 18 (iii) 4.3
c 5
d 4, halfway between 9th and 10th
e 3
f Yes
g Mean indicates he usually scores about 4 or 5

8 a 13, 13, 13.5, 13
b (i) 10.5, 14 (ii) 8.5, 13.5
c (i) 15 (ii) 11

9 a Negative b Zero
c Positive d Positive

10 a/c

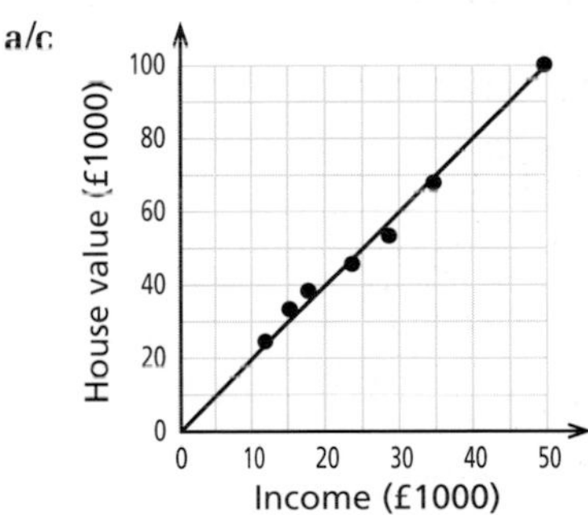

b Positive d £80 000

Page 162 Exercise 1

1 a (i) 9th (ii) between 17th and 18th
(iii) 26th
b (i) between 7th and 8th, between 14th and 15th, between 21st and 22nd
(ii) between 8th and 9th, 17th, between 25th and 26th
(iii) 6th, 12th, 18th

2 a (i) 8th (ii) between 15th and 16th
(iii) 23rd
b 3, 4, 6

3 a 25
b between 6th and 7th, 13th, between 19th and 20th
c 15.5, 25, 37

4 a between 11th and 12th, 23rd, between 34th and 35th
b 30, 37, 44 c 14

5 a

Number of customers

Stem	Leaf
1	2 3 3 5 7 9
2	0 0 1 3 3 4 6 6 6 7 7 7 8
3	0 0 1 3 5 5 5 5 7
4	1 3 4 4 4 6 7 8 8 9
5	0 0 0

$n = 41$ 1 | 2 represents 12 customers

b 30, 23, 44 **c** 21

Page 163 Exercise 2

1 a 3, 8, 16, 25, 33 **b** 33
c 5.5, 7, 7.5

2 a 6, 14, 24, 36, 42 **b** 42
c 6, 7, 8 **d** 2

3 a 20, 35, 40 **b** 20
c

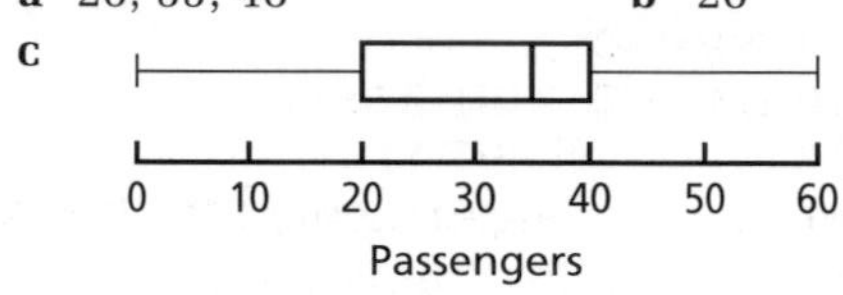

4 a 15
b (i) 10, 20 (ii) 10

Page 166 Exercise 3

1 a 172 **b** 167 **c** 177 **d** 10
e 5 **f** 20th out of 100

2 a (i) 7 (ii) 11
b 8, 16 **c** 8 **d** 4

3 a 64.5, 68.5
b Men 63.5, 66, 2.5, 1.25;
Women 65.5, 71.5, 6, 3
c Women live longer than men and their life expectancy varies more

4 a

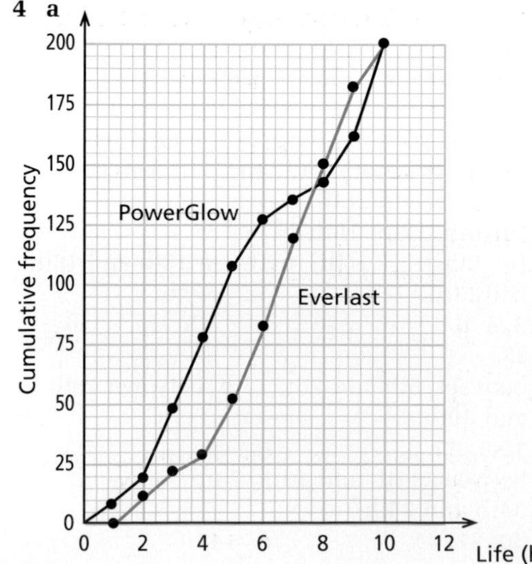

b 4.8 h, 6.3 h **c** 5.4, 2.7, 3, 1.5
d Everlast, higher median and less variation

Page 169 Exercise 4

1 b −3, −3, 2, 4; 9, 9, 4, 16; totals 40, 38
c 9.5 **d** 3.1

2 a (i) 5 (ii) −2, −1, −1, 2, 2; 4, 1, 1, 4, 4; totals 25, 14 (iii) 1.7
b (i) 7 (ii) 1.3 (iii) Boys (iv) No

Page 171 Exercise 5

1 a 74, 2.2
b (i) 90 (ii) 7.7 (iii) The athletes
(iv) The pulse rates of the athletes are less varied

2 a (i) 3.5 (ii) 2.9
b (i) 3.5, 0.9 (ii) No (iii) Yes

3 a (i) 93 (ii) 47 (iii) 31
b (i) 64 (ii) 37 (iii) 22.1
c The range

Page 172 Exercise 6

1 a (i) 3.4 (ii) 1.6
b Yes, on average their batteries last longer than the guarantee
c The standard deviation is acceptable

2 a (i) 20.2 (ii) 1.2
b The test is passed

3 a (i) 79.5 (ii) 5.9
b The standard deviation is above 5 so it needs adjusting

4 a (i) 36.3, 33.3 (ii) 6.8, 27.0
b Roadside Rescue. Although the mean is slightly greater the waiting time is more predictable.

5 a A **b** A

Page 175 Exercise 7

1 c $\frac{20-16}{10-6} = 1$ **d** 10
e $H = S + 10$ **f** 21

2 a −13 **b** 69 **c** $P = -13E + 69$
d 43 mpg **e** No

3 a/c

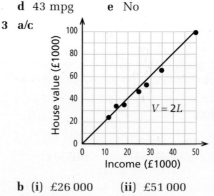

House value (£1000)
100
80
60
40
20
0
$V = 2L$
0 10 20 30 40 50
Income (£1000)

b (i) £26 000 (ii) £51 000
d $V = 2L$

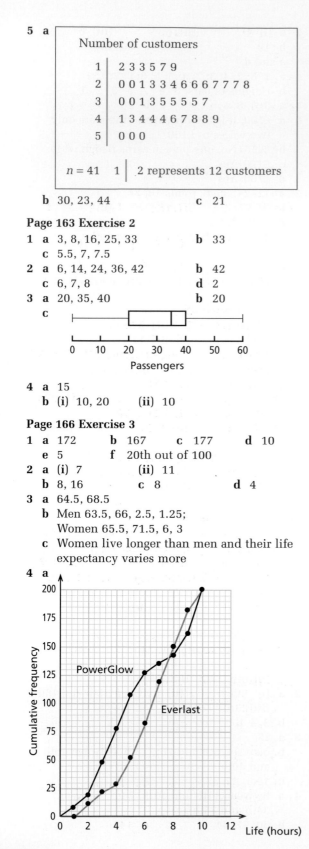

e £80 000

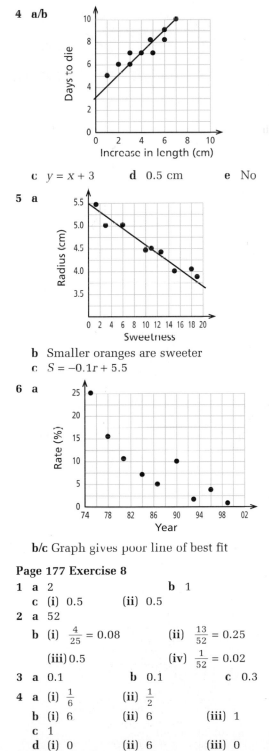

f No, a £6000 income is not enough to buy a house

4 a/b

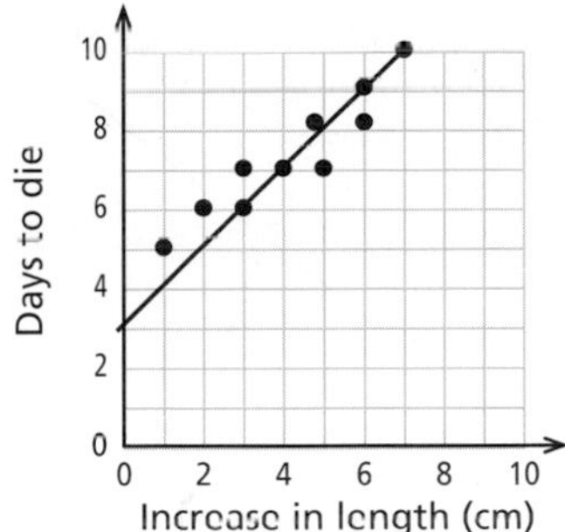

c $y = x + 3$ d 0.5 cm e No

5 a

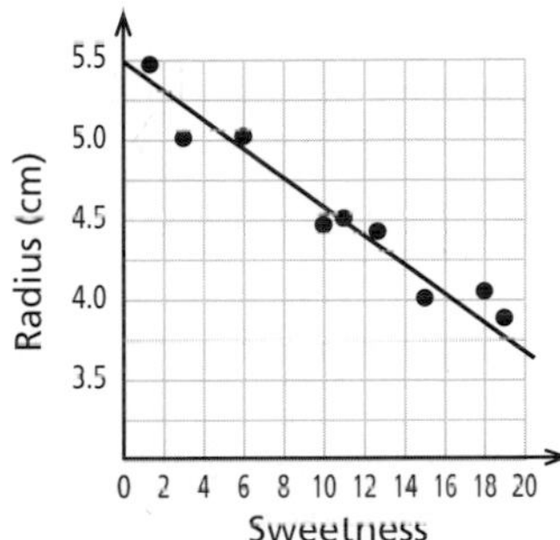

b Smaller oranges are sweeter

c $S = -0.1r + 5.5$

6 a

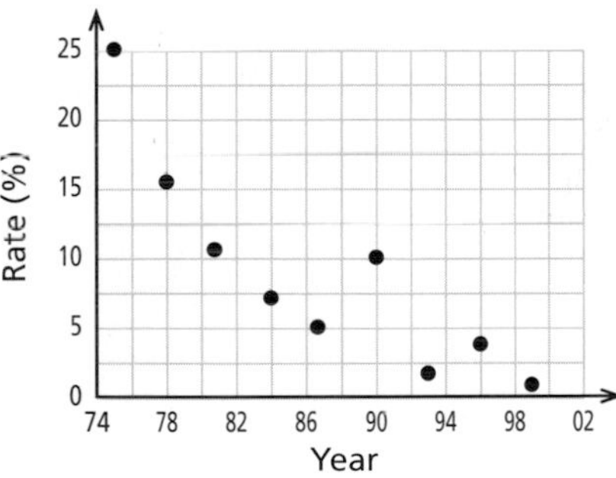

b/c Graph gives poor line of best fit

Page 177 Exercise 8

1 a 2 b 1

c (i) 0.5 (ii) 0.5

2 a 52

b (i) $\frac{4}{25} = 0.08$ (ii) $\frac{13}{52} = 0.25$

(iii) 0.5 (iv) $\frac{1}{52} = 0.02$

3 a 0.1 b 0.1 c 0.3

4 a (i) $\frac{1}{6}$ (ii) $\frac{1}{2}$

b (i) 6 (ii) 6 (iii) 1

c 1

d (i) 0 (ii) 6 (iii) 0

e 0

5 a 0.01 b 0.1

6 a $\frac{3}{9} = \frac{1}{3}$ b $\frac{6}{9} = \frac{2}{3}$

7 a $\frac{5}{26}$ b $\frac{21}{26}$

8 a (i) $\frac{25}{40} = 0.625$ (ii) $\frac{15}{40} = 0.375$

b (i), (ii) and (iii)

9 a (i) $\frac{5}{30} = 0.17$ (ii) $\frac{10}{30} = 0.33$

(iii) $\frac{15}{30} = 0.5$

b 24

10 a H1, H2, H3, H4, H5, H6; T1, T2, T3, T4, T5, T6

b (i) $\frac{1}{12}$ (ii) $\frac{3}{12} = \frac{1}{4}$ (iii) $\frac{5}{12}$

11 a (i) 0.3 (ii) 0.25

b (i)

Page 179 Exercise 9

1 a 0.24, 0.28, 0.2, 0.12, 0.16

b (i) 0.24 (ii) 0.44

c Pie chart with angles of 86°, 101°, 72°, 43° and 58°

2 a 0.27, 0.07, 0.32, 0.21, 0.13

b (i) 0.13 (ii) 0.27 (iii) 0.73

3 a 0.22, 0.08, 0.14, 0.24, 0.32

b (i) 0.22 (ii) 0.56

c 28

4 a 0.15, 0.18, 0.35, 0.11, 0.22

b (i) 0.15 (ii) 0.65 or 0.66

c 77, 88, 173, 54, 108

Page 181 Exercise 10

1 a 0.7, 0.6, 0.4 b Claire c 0.4

2 a 0.45, 0.2, 0.35; totals 100, 1

b (i) 0.45 (ii) 0.2 (iii) 0.35

3 a 0.5, 0.55, 0.4, 0.35, 0.36, 0.33, 0.31, 0.3

b 0.3

4 a 0.8, 0.75, 0.7, 0.65, 0.65

b 0.65

c Not quite, the lights are on red approx. two thirds of the time

Page 184 Review

1 a 38, 80, 106, 120, 130

b 130

c (i) 2 (ii) 1, 3

2 a (i) 30 (ii) 22 (iii) 38

b (i) 16 (ii) 8

3 a 1.4

b One standard deviation above average

4 a £66 400

b £9000

5 a

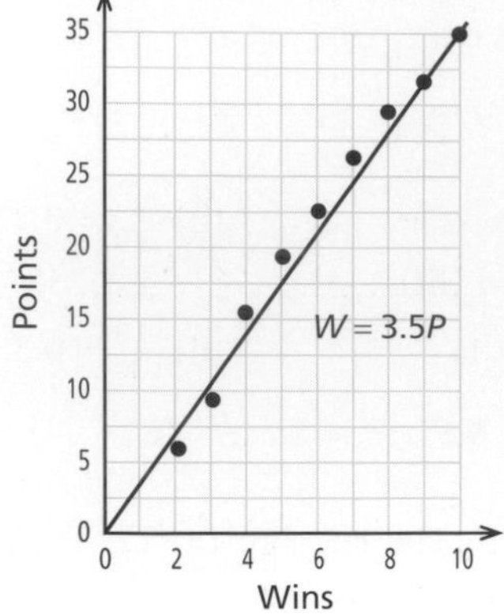

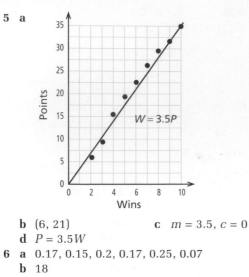

b (6, 21) **c** $m = 3.5, c = 0$

d $P = 3.5W$

6 a 0.17, 0.15, 0.2, 0.17, 0.25, 0.07

b 18

c 0.33, 0.17, 0.17, 0.06, 0.17, 0.11

d (i) 60 (ii) 18 (iii) 0.3

7 a (i) $\frac{1}{8}$ (ii) $\frac{3}{8}$ (iii) $\frac{1}{2}$

12 Revising Unit 2

Page 186 Exercise 1

1 a 23.1 cm **b** 18.9 cm **c** 10.3 cm

2 a 33.3° **b** 51.7° **c** 30.4°

3 a (i) 22.3 m^2 (ii) 27.8 m^2 (iii) 41.6 m^2

b (i) 7.11 m (ii) 13.5 m (iii) 13.0 m

4 a 53.1° **b** 132.8° **c** 70.8°

5 a (i) Cassinni (ii) 10.5 cm^2

b (i) 19.8 cm (ii) 20.8 cm

c XY by 1 cm

6 78.4°, 101.6°

7 a (i) 32.4° (ii) 50.8° (iii) 96.8°

b 41.8 m

8 a (i) 67.8 m (ii) 52.4 m

b 145 m

c 578 m^2

Page 188 Exercise 2

1 a $x = 2, y = 4$

b $x = 0.5, y = -2.5$

2 $x = 1, y = 3$

3 a $x = 3, y = 6$ **b** $x = 2, y = 6$

c $x = 3, y = 4$ **d** $x = 2, y = 5$

e $x = 3, y = 9$ **f** $x = 1, y = 2$

4 a $x = 8, y = 2$ **b** $x = 5, y = 2$

c $x = -3, y = 3$ **d** $x = 6, y = 1$

e $x = 1, y = 4$ **f** $x = 2, y = -1$

5 a (i) £12, £16 (ii) £24, £22

b (i) 5 (ii) £20

6 a (i) $V = 4m$ (ii) $V = 90 - 6m$

b

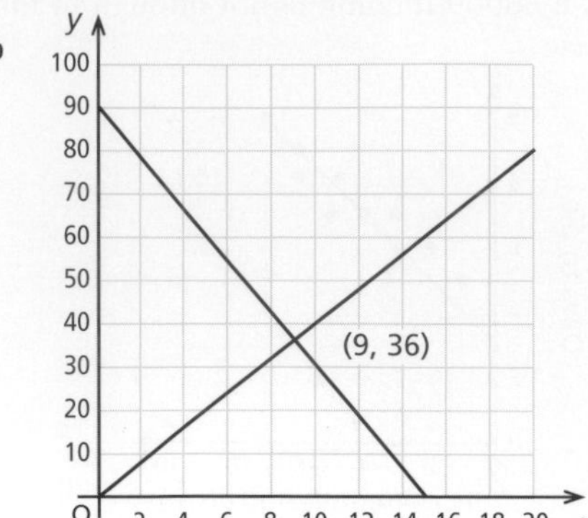

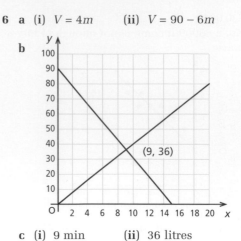

c (i) 9 min (ii) 36 litres

7 a $y = 3x, y - x = 22$ **b** 11 and 33 years

8 a $4x + 3y = 36, 2x + y = 16$

b (i) 6 g (ii) 4 g

9 a $20x + 50y = 142, 40x + 20y = 108$

b 1.6, 2.2

Page 190 Exercise 3

1 a $\frac{1}{12}, \frac{1}{4}, \frac{5}{12}, \frac{1}{6}$

b Pie chart with angles of 30°, 120°, 150° and 60°

2 a

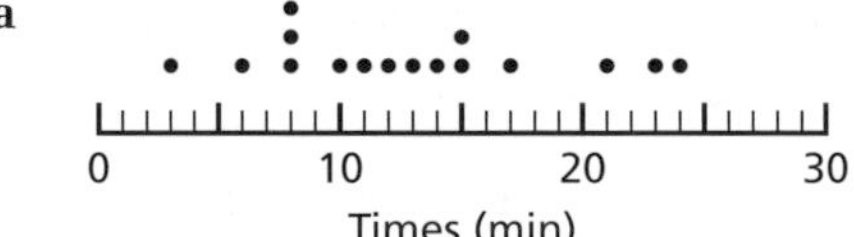

b 21 min

c

0	3 6 8 8 8
1	0 1 2 3 4 5 5 7
2	1 3 4

$n = 16$ 2 | 1 represents 21

d (i) 12.5 (ii) 8, 16

3 a (i) 3, 4, 6, 6, 5, 3, 6, 3

(ii) 3, 7, 13, 19, 24, 27, 33, 36

b (i) 9 (ii) 24

c (i) £50 (ii) £40 (iii) £75

d

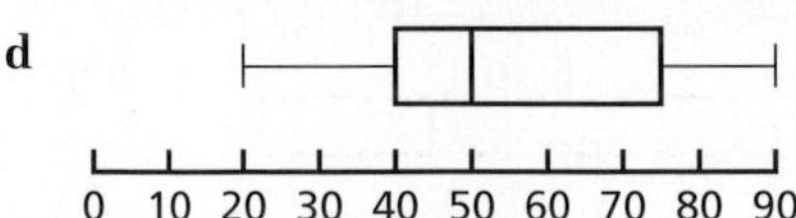

4 a 3, 8, 16, 28, 36, 40

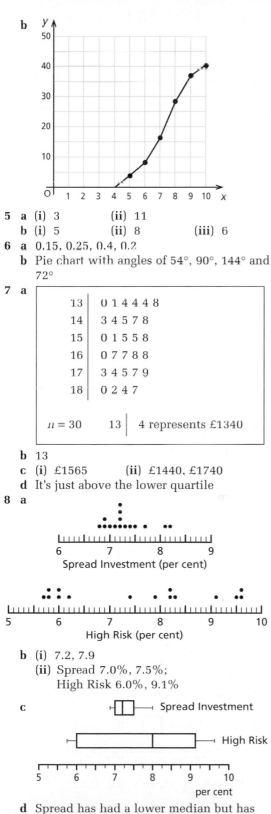

b

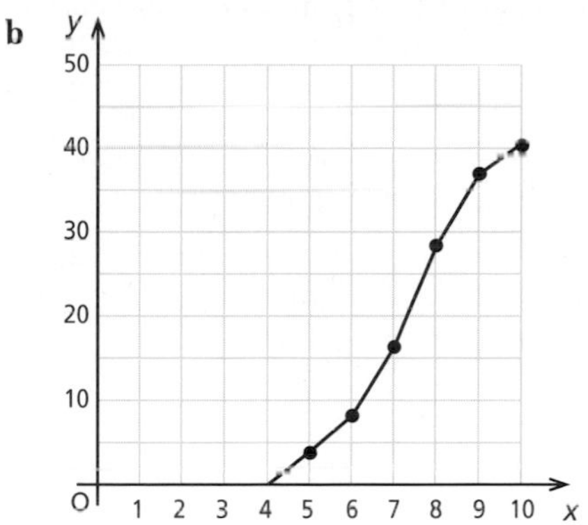

5 **a** (i) 3 (ii) 11
b (i) 5 (ii) 8 (iii) 6

6 **a** 0.15, 0.25, 0.4, 0.2
b Pie chart with angles of 54°, 90°, 144° and 72°

7 **a**

Stem	Leaf
13	0 1 4 4 4 8
14	3 4 5 7 8
15	0 1 5 5 8
16	0 7 7 8 8
17	3 4 5 7 9
18	0 2 4 7

$n = 30$ 13 | 4 represents £1340

b 13
c (i) £1565 (ii) £1440, £1740
d It's just above the lower quartile

8 **a**

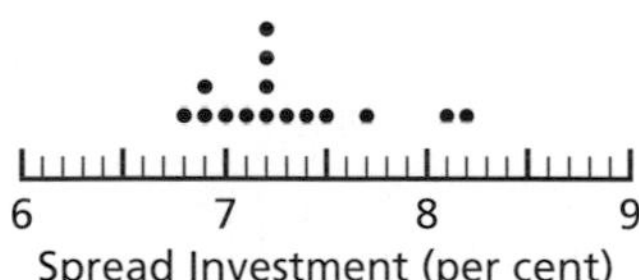

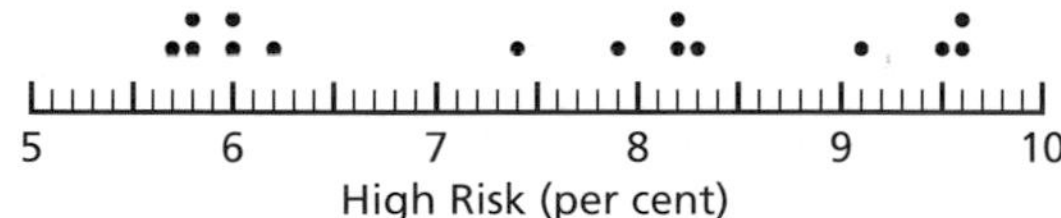

b (i) 7.2, 7.9
(ii) Spread 7.0%, 7.5%;
High Risk 6.0%, 9.1%

c

Spread Investment

High Risk

5 6 7 8 9 10
per cent

d Spread has had a lower median but has varied less than High Risk

9 **a** Marie 4, 7.5, 9, 11, 13;
Tony 6, 11, 14, 16, 20

b

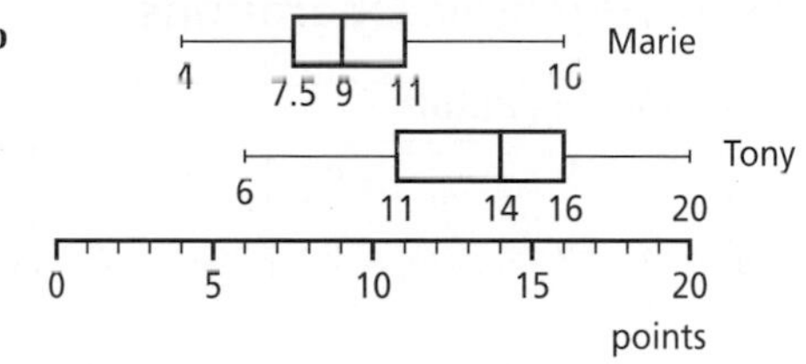

c Tony is a lot luckier than Marie

Page 194 Exercise 4

1 **a** 7, 19, 34, 50 **b** 15
c (i) 10, 20 (ii) 5

2 **a** (i) 4.9 (ii) 4.6 (iii) 5.25
b (i) 0.65 (ii) 0.325

3 **a** 7°C
b (i) −3, −1, 0, 2, 2; 9, 1, 0, 4, 4; totals 5, 18
(ii) 1.9 °C

4 **a** 6 **b** 34 **c** $C = 6t + 34$
d £52 **e** 3.5 h

5 **a** 0.05 **b** 0.25 **c** 0.3

6 **a** 0.375, 0.2, 0.15, 0.1, 0.175
b (i) 0.375 (ii) 0.175

7 **a** 38, 56, 102, 156, 192, 200
b £2000
c (i) 1000, 4000 (ii) 1500
d Above the median by £1000
e £2000

8 **a** (i) 0.045 (ii) 0.05
b Tania **c** 1

9 **a** (i) 0.003, 0.037, 0.132
(ii) 0.001, 0.023, 0.117
b (i) 0.003 (ii) 0.024
c A male driver is more likely to be killed or injured than a female driver

10 **a** (i) 72.4, 42.0 (ii) 161.4, 18.2
b The mean has dropped by over half and the catch is less consistent

11 **a**

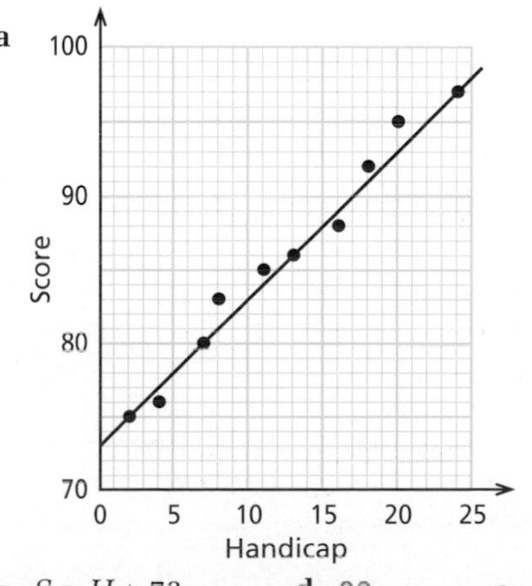

c $S = H + 73$ **d** 82 **e** 17

UNIT 3

13 More Algebraic Operations

Page 197 Starting Points

1 **a** $\frac{2}{3}$ **b** $\frac{3}{4}$ **c** $\frac{2}{5}$ **d** $\frac{3}{2}$

2 **a** $\frac{4}{8}$ **b** $\frac{6}{9}$ **c** $\frac{9}{12}$ **d** $\frac{6}{15}$
e $\frac{10}{14}$ **f** $\frac{6}{27}$

3 **a** 10 **b** 14 **c** 12 **d** 24
e 60 **f** 100

4 $\frac{3}{6}+\frac{4}{6}=\frac{3+4}{6}=\frac{7}{6}$

5 **a** $\frac{3}{4}$ **b** $\frac{1}{6}$ **c** $\frac{5}{8}$ **d** $\frac{3}{4}$

6 **a** 8 **b** 81 **c** 10 **d** 8 **e** 2

7 **a** $y \times y \times y \times y$ **b** $\frac{1}{a \times a \times a \times a \times a}$

8 **a** $6x - 9y$ **b** $x^2 - x$ **c** $x^2 - 1$
d $2x^2 - 3x^3$

Page 198 Exercise 1

1 **a** $\frac{3}{4}$ **b** $\frac{7}{10}$ **c** $\frac{3}{7}$ **d** $\frac{2}{3}$ **e** $\frac{5}{7}$

2 **a** x **b** 1 **c** $\frac{1}{a}$ **d** $\frac{1}{m}$
e y^3 **f** 1 **g** $\frac{1}{t^3}$ **h** $\frac{1}{d}$

3 **a** 2 **b** 2 **c** $2x$ **d** a
e $\frac{2t}{3}$

4 **a** $3y$ **b** $\frac{x}{4}$ **c** $\frac{4}{3x}$ **d** b
e ab

5 **a** xy **b** x^2y **c** $2x$ **d** 1
e xy **f** $\frac{y}{x}$ **g** $2a$ **h** $\frac{3}{2m}$
i b **j** df

6 **a** $x + 1$ **b** $\frac{1}{y-1}$ **c** $(y-1)^2$
d $\frac{1}{m-3}$ **e** $a - 2$ **f** $\frac{1}{(d-5)^2}$
g $\frac{1}{2y+3}$ **h** 1 **i** $2 - x$
j $(3a-2)^2$ **k** $\frac{1}{(6-2d)^2}$ **l** $x^2 - 1$
m $\frac{1}{(1+8y)^2}$ **n** $\frac{1}{(4-2y)^2}$ **o** $1 + 2a + a^2$

7 **a** $m - 1$ **b** $x + 3$ **c** $\frac{1}{4y+10}$
d $\frac{2a+3}{2a-1}$ **e** 1 **f** $\frac{5-y}{5+y}$
g $(1-2x)^2(1+3x)$ **h** $\frac{(4+2a)^2(4-2a)}{5+2a}$

Page 200 Exercise 2

1 **a** $\frac{3}{5}$ **b** $\frac{7}{12}$ **c** $\frac{1}{15}$ **d** $\frac{1}{6}$ **e** $\frac{29}{24}$

2 **a** $\frac{3}{a}$ **b** $\frac{5}{m}$ **c** $\frac{2b-a}{ab}$
d $\frac{5d-2c}{cd}$ **e** $\frac{3f+5e}{ef}$

3 **a** $\frac{4q+p}{pq}$ **b** $\frac{3k+p}{pk}$ **c** $\frac{3h-7b}{bh}$
d $\frac{8n-3m}{mn}$ **e** $\frac{g+3f}{fg}$

4 **a** $\frac{1}{y}$ **b** $\frac{5}{d^2}$ **c** $\frac{5}{3a}$
d $\frac{-8}{a}$ **e** $\frac{5}{6c}$

5 **a** $\frac{5}{6h}$ **b** $\frac{19}{12m}$ **c** $\frac{4b-3a}{6ab}$
d $\frac{9d+16c}{12cd}$ **e** $\frac{6f+35e}{15ef}$

6 **a** $\frac{3+t}{t^2}$ **b** $\frac{1-m}{m^2}$ **c** $\frac{2a-3}{a^2}$
d $\frac{2-2x}{x^2}$ **e** $\frac{9-3y}{3y^2}$

Page 200 Exercise 3

1 **a** $\frac{2}{5}$ **b** $\frac{3}{10}$ **c** $\frac{2}{9}$ **d** $\frac{1}{12}$ **e** $\frac{7}{54}$

2 **a** $\frac{a^2}{8}$ **b** $\frac{15}{y^2}$ **c** $\frac{1}{2}$ **d** $\frac{10}{9}$ **e** $\frac{7}{4b}$

3 **a** $\frac{1}{2}$ **b** $\frac{15}{8}$ **c** $\frac{5}{2}$ **d** $\frac{15}{7}$ **e** $\frac{8}{7}$

4 **a** 2 **b** $\frac{1}{5}$ **c** $\frac{y^2}{6}$ **d** $\frac{10}{9}$ **e** $\frac{5a^2}{9}$

5 **a** $\frac{m}{2}$ **b** $\frac{1}{c}$ **c** $6t$ **d** $\frac{c^2}{2}$ **e** $2a^2$

6 **a** $\frac{10}{9y}$ **b** $\frac{4}{3x}$ **c** $\frac{2b^2}{15}$
d $\frac{2uv^3}{3}$ **e** $8mn^2$

7 **a** $\frac{v^2}{12u}$ **b** $\frac{4}{a}$ **c** $10b$
d $(1+x)(1+y)$ **e** $\frac{a+2}{a-2}$

8 **a** $x \neq 1$ **b** $x \neq -2$ **c** $x \neq -\frac{3}{2}$

Page 202 Exercise 4

1 **a** **(i)** $y = x - 3$ **(ii)** $q = p + 7$
(iii) $b = a - c$ **(iv)** $e = d + f$
b **(i)** $b = 4a$ **(ii)** $d = \frac{8}{c}$
(iii) $D = ST$ **(iv)** $T = \frac{D}{S}$
c **(i)** $x = \frac{a-2}{3}$ **(ii)** $h = \frac{g+9}{4}$
(iii) $s = \frac{y+t}{4}$ **(iv)** $x = \frac{y-c}{m}$

d **(i)** $q = \frac{p}{3} - 2$ **(ii)** $q - \frac{m}{n} = 0$

(iii) $x = \frac{v}{u} - y$ **(iv)** $b = \frac{a}{c - d}$

2 $m = D - d$

3 $a = \frac{P}{2} - b$

4 **a** $f = T - 6k$ **b** $k = \frac{T - f}{6}$

5 **a** $l = \frac{V}{bh}$ **b** $b = \frac{V}{lh}$ **c** $h = \frac{V}{lb}$

6 $r = \frac{C}{2\pi}$

7 **a** $F = \frac{P}{1 + r}$ **b** $r = \frac{P}{F} - 1$

8 **a** $A = \frac{T - 7C}{12}$ **b** $C = \frac{T - 12A}{7}$

Page 204 Exercise 5

1 $A = L^2$

2 $T = \sqrt{\frac{C}{k}}$

3 $w = \sqrt{\frac{V}{h}}$

4 **a** $T = \sqrt{kL}$ **b** $L = \frac{T^2}{k}$

5 **a** **(i)** $u = v - at$ **(ii)** $t = \frac{v - u}{a}$

b **(i)** $u = \frac{s - 0.5at^2}{t}$ **(ii)** $a = \frac{s - ut}{0.5t^2}$

c **(i)** $a = \frac{v^2 - u^2}{2s}$ **(ii)** $u = \sqrt{\left(v^2 - 2as\right)}$

6 $r = \sqrt{\frac{A}{\pi}}$

7 **a** $h = \frac{V}{\pi r^2}$ **b** $r = \sqrt{\frac{V}{\pi h}}$

8 **a** $a^2 = L^2 - b^2$

b **(i)** $a = \sqrt{\left(L^2 - b^2\right)}$ **(ii)** $b = \sqrt{\left(L^2 - a^2\right)}$

9 **a** $P = \frac{C}{1 + \frac{r}{100}}$ **b** $r = 100\left(\frac{C}{P} - 1\right)$

10 **a** $\frac{1}{u} = \frac{1}{f} - \frac{1}{v}$ **b** $f = \frac{uv}{u + v}$

c $u = \frac{fv}{v - f}$

Page 205 Exercise 6

1 **(i)** **b, d, e, i**

(ii) **a** 4 **c** 5 **f** 9 **g** 3

h 4 **j** 6 **k** 4 **l** 10

2 **a** 24, 24; 20, 20; 90, 90

b 5, 7; 13, 17; 10, 14

c 3, 3; 2, 2; $\frac{3}{2}$, $\frac{3}{2}$

d 9, 3; 12, 8; 21, 9

Page 206 Exercise 7

1 **a** $2\sqrt{2}$ **b** $2\sqrt{3}$ **c** $2\sqrt{5}$ **d** 9

e $5\sqrt{2}$ **f** $3\sqrt{3}$ **g** $4\sqrt{3}$ **h** $6\sqrt{2}$

i $4\sqrt{2}$ **j** $5\sqrt{3}$

2 **a** $6\sqrt{3}$ **b** $12\sqrt{2}$ **c** $5\sqrt{6}$ **d** $3\sqrt{10}$

e 30 **f** $7\sqrt{10}$ **g** 70 **h** $4\sqrt{10}$

i 40 **j** 50

3 **a** $\frac{2}{3}$ **b** $\frac{2}{5}$ **c** $\frac{3}{4}$ **d** $\frac{3}{5}$

e $\sqrt{\left(\frac{3}{2}\right)}$ **f** $\frac{2\sqrt{3}}{7}$ **g** $\frac{5}{3\sqrt{2}}$ **h** $\frac{4}{5}$

i $\frac{2}{3}$ **j** $\frac{\sqrt{3}}{2}$

4 **a** 0.1 **b** 0.6 **c** $\frac{1}{5\sqrt{10}}$ **d** 0.5

e 0.04 **f** 0.7 **g** 0.08 **h** 0.003

i 0.05 **j** 0.9

5 $6\sqrt{2}$ cm

6 **a** $\frac{5\sqrt{2}}{3}$ cm **b** $\frac{4\sqrt{3}}{5}$ cm **c** $\frac{4\sqrt{5}}{9}$ cm

Page 207 Exercise 8

1 **a** 10 **b** 9 **c** 4 **d** 14 **e** 6

2 **a** 2 **b** 3 **c** $\frac{1}{2}$ **d** $\frac{1}{6}$ **e** 4

3 **a** $2\sqrt{6}$ **b** $2\sqrt{10}$ **c** $2\sqrt{5}$ **d** $6\sqrt{2}$

e $5\sqrt{3}$

4 **a** $\sqrt{3}$ **b** $\sqrt{6}$ **c** $2\sqrt{2}$ **d** $2\sqrt{3}$

e $\frac{1}{2\sqrt{5}}$

5 **a** $3\sqrt{11}$ **b** $12\sqrt{2}$ **c** $4\sqrt{7}$ **d** $\frac{1}{5\sqrt{2}}$

e $\frac{1}{3\sqrt{2}}$

Page 208 Exercise 9

1 **a** $\frac{\sqrt{2}}{2}$ **b** $\sqrt{2}$ **c** $\frac{3\sqrt{2}}{2}$ **d** $\frac{2\sqrt{3}}{3}$

e $\sqrt{3}$ **f** $3\sqrt{3}$ **g** $\frac{10\sqrt{3}}{3}$ **h** $\frac{\sqrt{5}}{5}$

i $\frac{3\sqrt{5}}{5}$ **j** $2\sqrt{5}$ **k** $\sqrt{7}$ **l** $\frac{10\sqrt{7}}{7}$

2 **a** $\frac{\sqrt{10}}{2}$ **b** $\frac{3\sqrt{6}}{2}$ **c** $\frac{2\sqrt{15}}{5}$ **d** $\frac{\sqrt{2}}{4}$

e $\frac{\sqrt{3}}{12}$ **f** $\frac{\sqrt{5}}{25}$

3 a $\frac{\sqrt{2}+2}{2}$ b $\frac{\sqrt{5}-5}{5}$ c $\frac{\sqrt{6}+2}{2}$

d $3(\sqrt{3}+1)$ e $\frac{3\sqrt{10}-10}{5}$

Page 209 Exercise 10

1 a -1 b 7 c 1 d -4

2 a $2-\sqrt{3}$ b $\sqrt{2}-1$ c $\frac{4+\sqrt{2}}{14}$

d $\frac{\sqrt{5}+1}{4}$ e $\frac{5-\sqrt{3}}{22}$ f $\frac{3(2+\sqrt{2})}{2}$

g $\frac{7(4-\sqrt{3})}{13}$ h $-(\sqrt{3}+2)$ i $-3(1+\sqrt{2})$

j $-2(1-\sqrt{8}) = 2(\sqrt{8}-1)$

Page 209 Exercise 11

1 a a^5 b a^9 c a^4 d m^{10} e t^3

2 a y^6 b $(0.1)^5$ c p^5 d $\left(\frac{1}{8}\right)^8$ e h^{20}

3 a 2^1 b 3^4 c 2^5 d 5^3 e 10^0

4 a a b a^4 c t^3 d m^6 e y^9

5 a $8y^5$ b $5a^6$ c $12t^7$ d $8m^6$ e $12y^6$

6 a $2c^7$ b $\frac{4t^3}{3}$ c $5a^3$ d $\frac{4m}{3}$ e $3c^3$

7 a a^9 b $24y^5$ c t^2 d a

Page 210 Exercise 12

1 a y^{-2} b a^{-3} c x^{-5} d $3y^{-4}$

e $10x^{-3}$ f $2a^{-5}$ g $\frac{y^{-4}}{6}$ h $\frac{m^{-6}}{2}$

i $\frac{3x^{-2}}{7}$ j $\frac{6y^{-3}}{5}$

2 a $\frac{1}{a^4}$ b $\frac{1}{b^2}$ c $\frac{1}{y^6}$ d $\frac{2}{m^4}$

e $\frac{7}{t^3}$ f $\frac{1}{5y^4}$ g $\frac{1}{4x^4}$ h $\frac{3}{2c^4}$

i $\frac{4}{3a^4}$ j $\frac{2}{7x^4}$

3 a x^6 b y^8 c t^{12} d g^{14}

e h^{-6} f a^{-15} g p^{-9} h q^{-20}

i k^6 j a^{20}

4 a $\frac{1}{a}$ b $\frac{1}{y^2}$ c $\frac{1}{a^3}$ d $\frac{1}{d}$

e $\frac{6}{t^2}$ f $\frac{8}{h}$ g $\frac{18}{m^5}$ h $\frac{6}{a^7}$

i $\frac{1}{a^4}$ j $\frac{1}{y}$ k $\frac{1}{2a}$ l $\frac{3}{2c^3}$

m 1 n 1 o 6 p 15

5 a a^{-2} b y^{-7} c x^{-1} d 1

e t^{-5} f y^{-7} g $3m^{-3}$ h $2x^{-8}$

i a^{-1} j c^{-3} k $\frac{t^{-5}}{5}$ l $\frac{3y^{-3}}{4}$

6 a $y^{-1}+2y^{-2}$ b $m^{-2}-5m^{-6}$

c $3t^{-2}+7t^{-4}$ d $8a^{-7}-10a^{-1}$

Page 211 Exercise 13

1 a 4 b 3 c 3 d 5 e 10

f 27 g 25 h 8 i 16 j 100

2 a $a^{\frac{2}{5}}$ b $3y^{\frac{3}{2}}$ c $6m$ d $8a^{\frac{7}{3}}$

3 a $a^{\frac{1}{4}}$ b $\frac{2x}{3}$ c $3b^{\frac{2}{3}}$ d $c^{\frac{4}{5}}$

e 1 f $\frac{1}{m}$ g $\frac{1}{y^{\frac{3}{2}}}$ h $\frac{6}{u^{\frac{4}{3}}}$

i $\frac{50}{k^{\frac{6}{5}}}$

4 a $\frac{3}{4a^{\frac{1}{2}}}$ b $\frac{1}{b^{\frac{2}{3}}}$ c $\frac{5}{c^{\frac{6}{5}}}$ d $\frac{9}{d^{\frac{1}{6}}}$

5 a $a^{-\frac{4}{5}}$ b $c^{-\frac{5}{3}}$ d $h^{-\frac{6}{5}}$ e $\frac{3k^{-2}}{4}$

e $m^{-\frac{1}{2}}$ f $4p^{-\frac{2}{5}}$ g $\frac{t^{-\frac{7}{3}}}{2}$ h $\frac{n^{-\frac{1}{3}}}{3}$

Page 213 Exercise 14

1 a a^6 b x^6 c 1 d 1

e $h^{\frac{3}{4}}$ f $k^{-\frac{2}{3}}$ g m^{-1} h n^6

i t j $u^{-\frac{3}{8}}$ k $9b^4$ l $8a^{12}$

m $3c^2$ n $2h^2$ o $\frac{u^{\frac{2}{3}}}{4}$ p x^3y^6

q $4a^4b^6$ r $\frac{1}{27p^9q^{12}}$ s $\frac{u^{\frac{2}{3}}v^{\frac{3}{2}}}{25}$ t $2ab^{\frac{1}{6}}$

u $9x^2y^4$ v $\frac{b^6}{a^2}$ w $\frac{1}{27mn^{\frac{3}{2}}}$

2 a 2 b 2 c 4 d 8

e 25 f $\frac{1}{5}$ g $\frac{1}{2}$ h $\frac{1}{3}$

i 8 j $\frac{1}{8}$ k $\frac{1}{27}$ l 1

3 a $a^{\frac{1}{2}}$ b $c^{\frac{1}{3}}$ c $y^{\frac{3}{2}}$ d $m^{\frac{2}{3}}$

e $a^{-\frac{1}{2}}$ f $h^{-\frac{3}{2}}$ g $t^{\frac{5}{4}}$ h $3x^2$

i $2y^3$ j $3a^{-\frac{3}{2}}$ k $5c^{-1}$ l $\frac{1}{4a^4}$

m $\frac{1}{5^{\frac{1}{2}}t^2}$ n $\frac{3}{y^2}$ o $\frac{1}{2^{\frac{1}{2}}x^{\frac{5}{2}}}$

4 a $\sqrt[3]{a}$ b $\sqrt[4]{w}$ c $\frac{1}{\sqrt{c}}$ d $\frac{1}{\sqrt[3]{h}}$
e $\frac{1}{\sqrt[5]{y}}$ f $2\sqrt{x}$ g $5\sqrt[3]{y}$ h $\frac{9}{\sqrt{a}}$
i $\frac{8}{\sqrt[3]{c}}$ j $\frac{1}{\sqrt{3a}}$

Page 214 Review

1 a $\frac{1}{4c}$ b $5y$ c $\frac{u^2}{w^2}$
d $(3-4a)^2$
2 a $\frac{5}{x}$ b $\frac{3b+4a}{ab}$ c $\frac{m^2+6}{2m}$
d $\frac{4v+10}{5uv}$ e $\frac{3x-8}{4x}$ f $\frac{2b-3a}{ab}$
g $\frac{-5}{2k}$ h $\frac{k^2-5}{5k}$ i $\frac{1}{6}$
j $\frac{6}{y}$ k $\frac{1}{12}$ l $\frac{9yq}{10}$
m $\frac{2}{5}$ n $\frac{8x}{27y}$ o $\frac{k^2}{y^2}$
p $\frac{4}{5yz}$
3 a $u = \frac{B-f}{2}$
b (i) $m = \frac{k}{5} + n$ (ii) $n = m - \frac{k}{5}$
4 a $2\sqrt{3}$ b $4\sqrt{2}$ c $2\sqrt{6}$
d $\frac{1}{5\sqrt{2}}$ e $\frac{3\sqrt{3}}{2\sqrt{2}}$
5 a $\sqrt{5}$ b $\frac{2\sqrt{3}}{9}$
6 a y^6 b a^3 c y^5 d $\frac{2}{m^2}$
e $6t^{\frac{1}{3}}$
7 a $8a^{-\frac{5}{4}}$ b $2y^{-\frac{3}{2}}$
8 a $2(4+\sqrt{5})$ b $3(\sqrt{7}-1)$
9 a x^{-6} b x

14 Quadratic Functions

Page 215 Starting Points

1 (ii) $y = 2x + 3$
2 a (i) 4 (ii) (0, 2)
b (i) −2 (ii) (0, 7)
c (i) 0.5 (ii) (0, −4)
3 a (i) 2 (ii) 5 (iii) 8
(iv) 11 (v) 14 (vi) 17
b 8, 11, 14, 17, 20
c

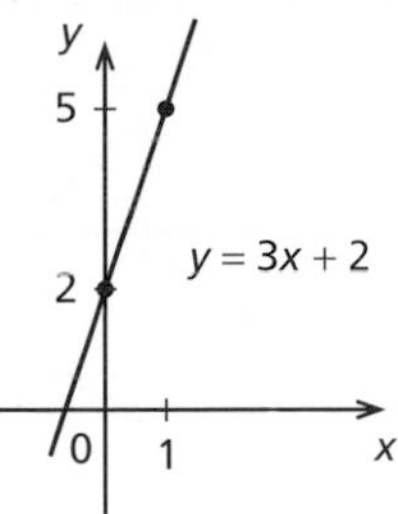

4 a 14 b 37.7 c 7
5 a $x = 6$ b $x = 4$ c ±2
6 a (i) $3x(1+4x)$ (ii) $4y(2-3x)$
b (i) $(a+b)(a-b)$ (ii) $(2a-3b)(2a+3b)$
c (i) $(x+3)(x+2)$ (ii) $(x-6)(x+2)$

Page 216 Exercise 1

1 a (i) 3 (ii) 6 (iii) 15
b (i) 0 (ii) 28 (iii) 42
c (i) 4 (ii) 8 (iii) 10
d (i) 3 (ii) 9 (iii) 12
e (i) 0 (ii) 1 (iii) 0.6
2 a (i) 0 (ii) 12.5
b 0, 2.5, 5, 7.5, 10, 12.5, 15
c

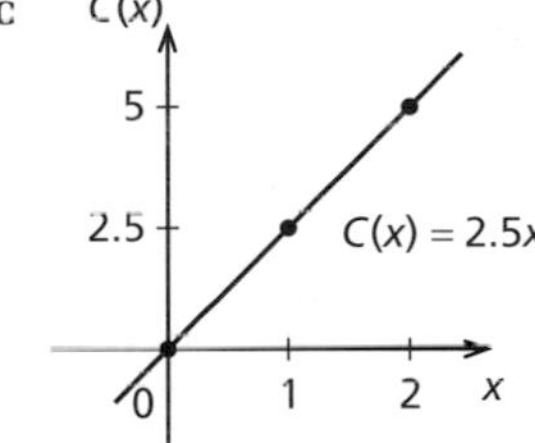

3 a (i) (0, 8) (ii) 5
b (i) (0, 4) (ii) 7
c (i) (0, −3) (ii) 2
d (i) (0, −2) (ii) 1
e (i) (0, 3) (ii) −2
f (i) (0, −1) (ii) −3
g (i) (0, −5) (ii) −1
h (i) (0, 0) (ii) −1
4 a

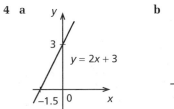

y
3
y = 2x + 3
−1.5
0
x

b

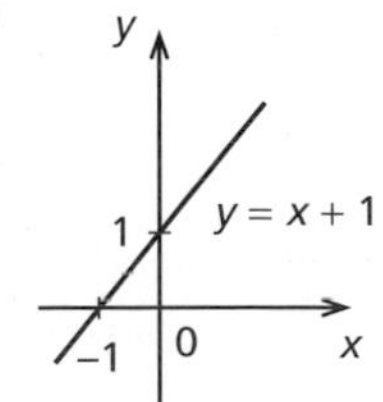

c

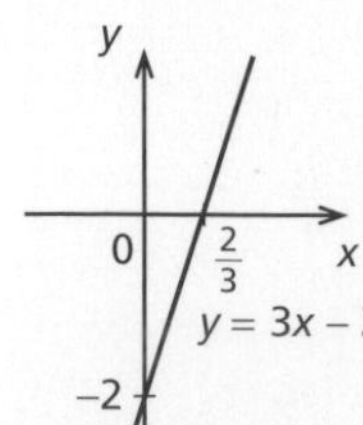

d

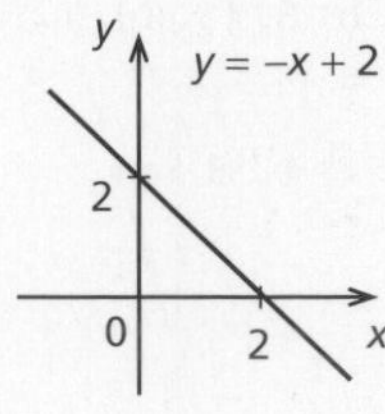

e

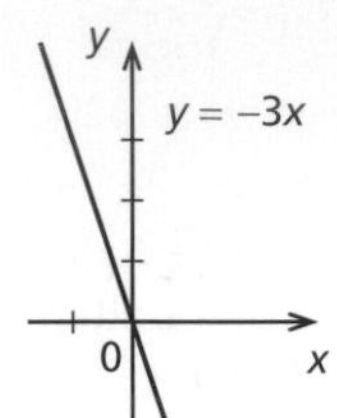

f

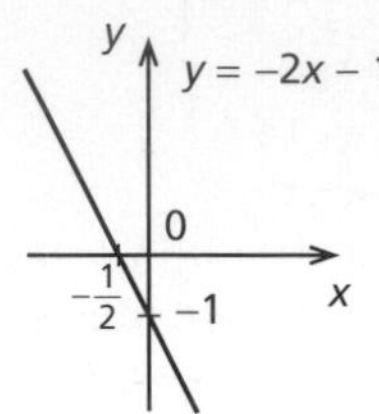

g

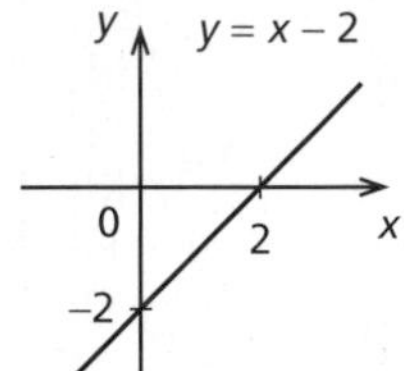

h

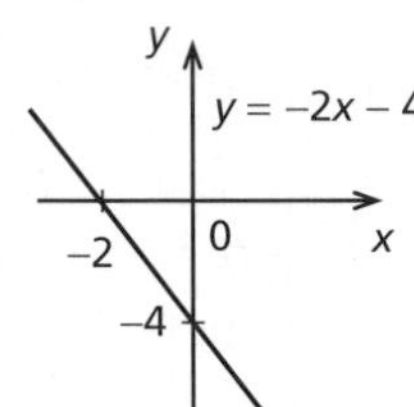

5 **a**

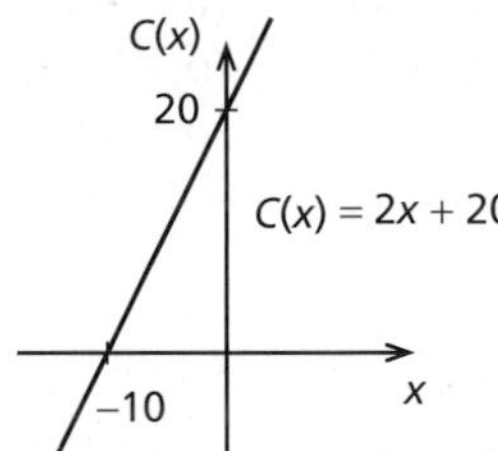

b (i) 30 (ii) 36
c (i) £32 (ii) £40
d 40 m

6 **b**

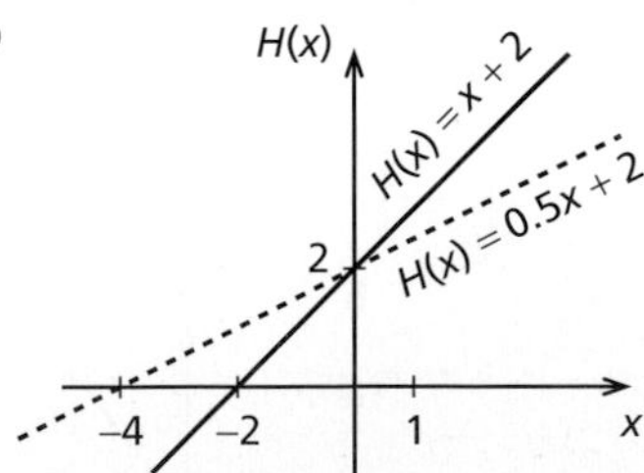

c The head gardener

7 **a** $V(x) = 20x + 12$ **b** £212 **c** £12

Page 218 Exercise 2

1 **b** 8, 2, 0, 2, 8, 18

c

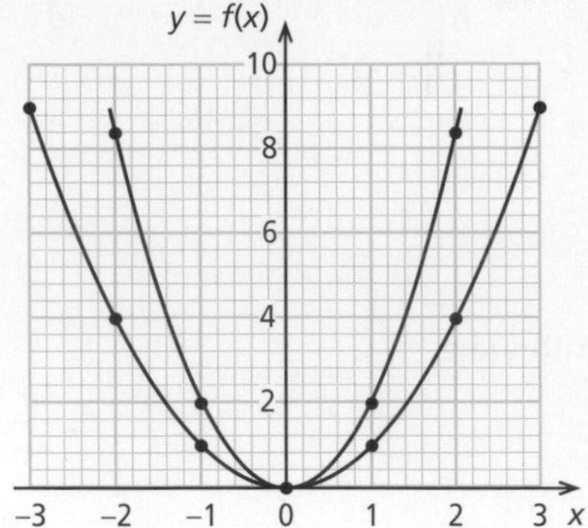

d (i) Same parabolic shape, same vertex, same axis of symmetry
(ii) Second graph has steeper sides than the first

2 **a** (i) 0, 3, 12, 27
(ii) Graph as table
(iii) Width = 6 (2 × coefficient of x^2)
b (i) 0, 5, 20, 45
(ii) Graph as table
(iii) Width = 10 (2 × coefficient of x^2)
c (i) –1, 0, –1, –4, –9
(ii) Graph as table
(iii) Width = 2 (2 × coefficient of x^2)
d (i) –2, 0, –2, –8, –18
(ii) Graph as table
(iii) Width = 4 (2 × coefficient of x^2)

3 **a** $f(x) = 4x^2$ **b** $f(x) = 8x^2$ **c** $f(x) = -4x^2$
d $f(x) = 5x^2$ **e** $f(x) = 10x^2$ **f** $f(x) = -2x^2$

4 **a** (0, 2) **b** *y* axis

5 **a** (i) Graph as table (ii) (0, 4) (iii) *y* axis
b (i) Graph as table (ii) (0, –1) (iii) *y* axis
c (i) Graph as table (ii) (0, –1) (iii) *y* axis
d (i) Graph as table (ii) (0, 3) (iii) *y* axis
e (i) Graph as table (ii) (0, –2) (iii) *y* axis

7 **a** $f(x) = 6x^2 + 1$ **b** $f(x) = 3x^2 - 2$
c $f(x) = x^2 - 14$ **d** $f(x) = -5x^2 - 2$
e $f(x) = -2x^2 + 8$ **f** $f(x) = -2x^2 + 10$

Page 221 Exercise 3

1 **a** (1, 0)

2 **a** (i)

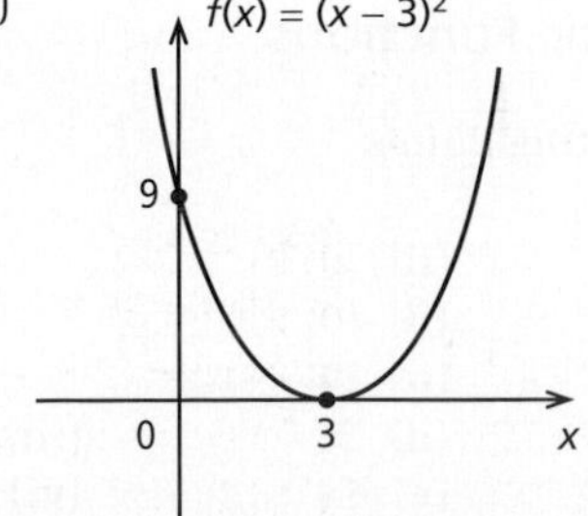

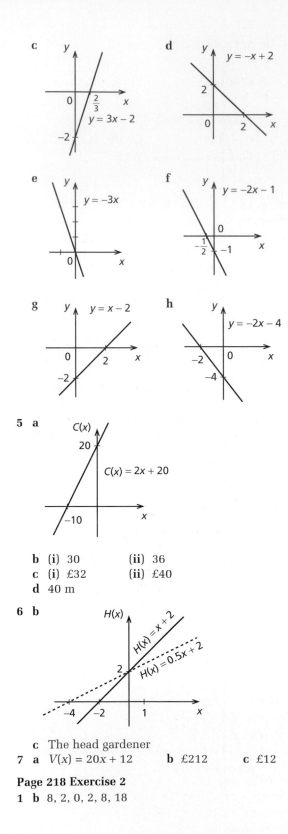

(ii) (3, 0) (iii) $x = 3$

b (i)

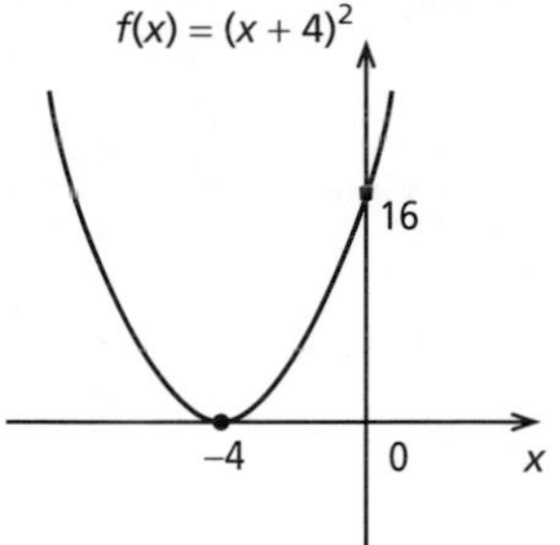

(ii) (4, 0) (iii) $x = -4$

c (i)

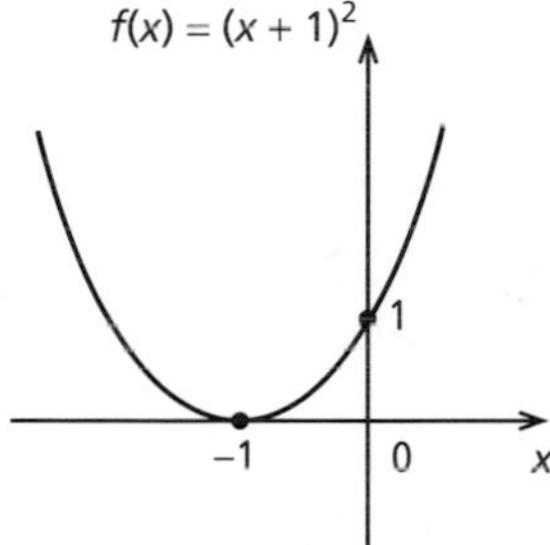

(ii) (–1, 0) (iii) $x = -1$

d (i)

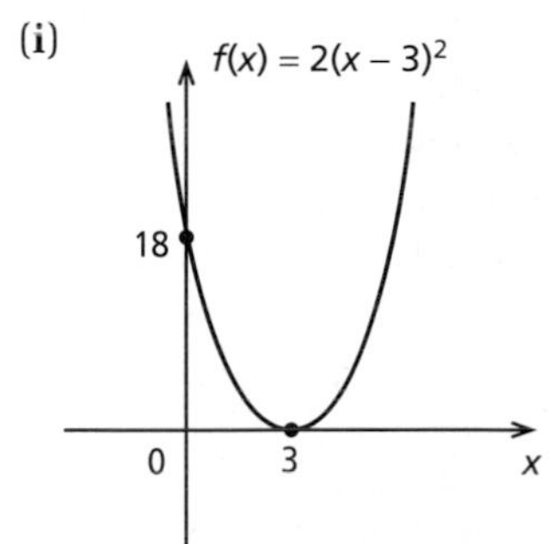

(ii) (3, 0) (iii) $x = 3$

e (i)

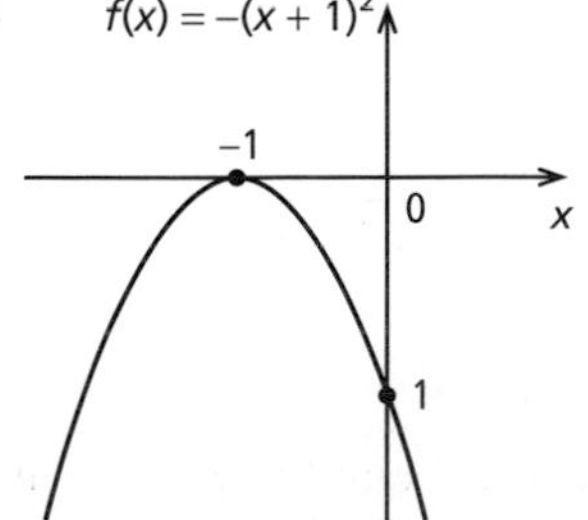

(ii) (–1, 0) (iii) $x = -1$

4 **a** $f(x) = 6(x - 2)^2$ **b** $f(x) = 4(x - 3)^2$
c $f(x) = 2(x + 4)^2$ **d** $f(x) = -2(x - 5)^2$
e $f(x) = -6(x + 3)^2$ **f** $f(x) = -3(x - 2)^2$

5 **a** (iv) **b** (ii) **c** (iii) **d** (i)

Page 223 Exercise 4

1 **a** $(1, \frac{1}{50})$ **b** 0.001 25 m
2 **a** (i) (2, 0) (ii) $x = 2$
b 3.24
c B(6, 3.24)
d 3.6 m
3 **a** (i) (0, 50) (ii) y axis
b 200 m
c 600 m
4 **a** (i) (14, 0) (ii) $x = 14$
b 49 m

Page 225 Exercise 5

1 **a** (i) $a = 1, b = 3, c = 2$ (ii) $x = 3$
(iii) (3, 2) minimum (iv) (0, 11)
b (i) $a = 1, b = 7, c = 5$ (ii) $x = 7$
(iii) (7, 5) minimum (iv) (0, 54)
c (i) $a = 1, b = -4, c = 2$ (ii) $x = -4$
(iii) (–4, 2) minimum (iv) (0, 18)
d (i) $a = 1, b = -6, c = 3$ (ii) $x = -6$
(iii) (–6, 3) minimum (iv) (0, 39)
e (i) $a = 1, b = 1, c = 9$ (ii) $x = 1$
(iii) (1, 9) minimum (iv) (0, 10)
f (i) $a = 1, b = -2, c = 1$ (ii) $x = -2$
(iii) (–2, 1) minimum (iv) (0, 5)
g (i) $a = -1, b = 1, c = -4$ (ii) $x = 1$
(iii) (1, –4) maximum (iv) (0, –5)
h (i) $a = -1, b = 2, c = -7$ (ii) $x = 2$
(iii) (2, –7) maximum (iv) (0, –11)
i (i) $a = -1, b = -2, c = -3$ (ii) $x = -2$
(iii) (–2, –3) maximum (iv) (0, –7)
j (i) $a = -1, b = -5, c = -2$ (ii) $x = -5$
(iii) (–5, –2) maximum (iv) (0, –27)
k (i) $a = -1, b = -1, c = -8$ (ii) $x = -1$
(iii) (–1, –8) maximum (iv) (0, –9)
l (i) $a = -1, b = 4, c = -10$ (ii) $x = 4$
(iii) (4, –10) maximum (iv) (0, –26)

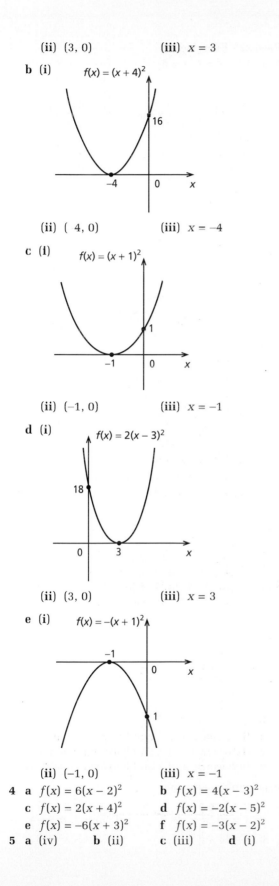

2 **a** (i) $a = 1, b = 2, c = 1$
(ii) $y = (x - 2)^2 + 1$
(iii) (0, 5)
b (i) $a = 1, b = -3, c = 1$
(ii) $y = (x + 3)^2 + 1$
(iii) (0, 10)
c (i) $a = -1, b = -2, c = -1$
(ii) $y = -(x + 2)^2 - 1$
(iii) (0, –5)
d (i) $a = 1, b = -2, c = 5$
(ii) $y = (x + 2)^2 + 5$
(iii) (0, 9)
e (i) $a = 1, b = 3, c = -2$
(ii) $y = (x - 3)^2 - 2$
(iii) (0, 7)
f (i) $a = -1, b = -2, c = 3$

(ii) $y = -(x + 2)^2 + 3$
(iii) (0, −1)

g (i) $a = -1, b = 4, c = 5$
(ii) $y = -(x - 4)^2 + 5$
(iii) (0, −11)

h (i) $a = 1, b = 3, c = -2$
(ii) $y = (x - 3)^2 - 2$
(iii) (0, 7)

Page 226 Exercise 6

1 a 8, 9, 8, 5, 0

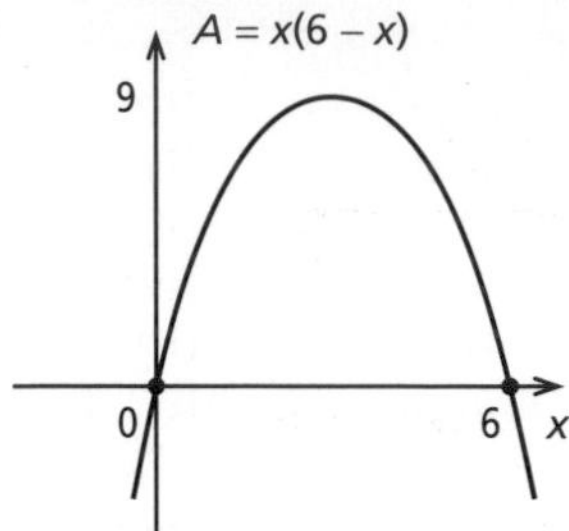

c (0, 0) and (6, 0) **d** 9 cm^2
e when $x = 3$ **f** $y = -(x - 3)^2 + 9$

2 a 75, 84, 96, 100

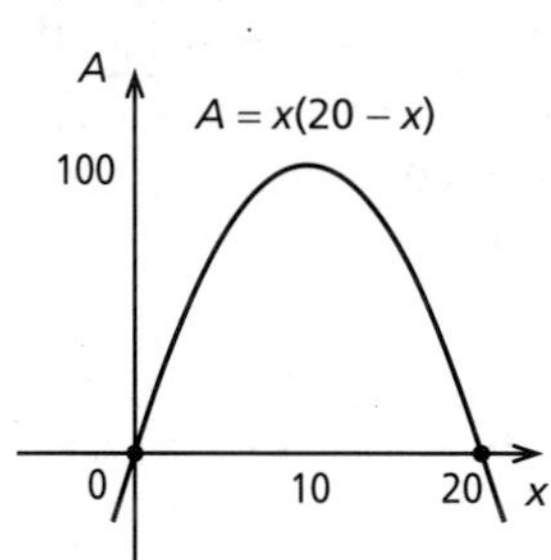

c (0, 0) and (20, 0) **d** $x = 10$
e 100 m^2 **f** $y = -(x - 10)^2 + 100$

3 a 16, 12, 0

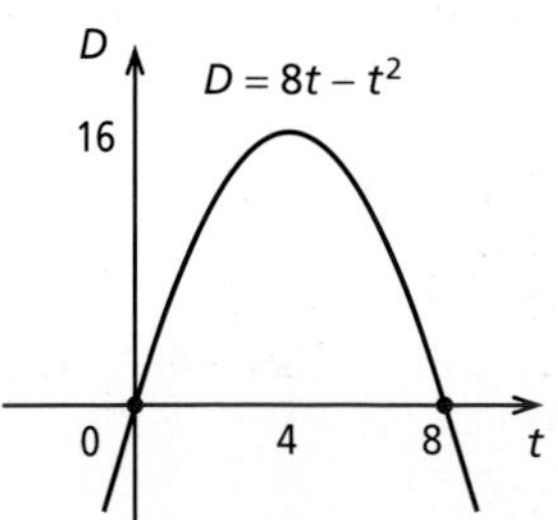

c 8 units of time **d** 4 units
e 16

4 a (i) (16, 7) (ii) $x = 16$
b 23 **c** (32, 23)

5 a (i) (25, 25) (ii) $x = 25$
b 40 **c** (50, 40)
d (i) 50 m (ii) 25 m

Page 227 Exercise 7

1 a (i) $x = 1, x = 5$ (ii) $x = 3$
(iii) (3, −4) (iv) (0, 5)
b (i) $x = 6, x = 2$ (ii) $x = 4$
(iii) (4, −4) (iv) (0, 12)
c (i) $x = 3, x = 5$ (ii) $x = 4$
(iii) (4, −1) (iv) (0, 15)
d (i) $x = 3, x = -1$ (ii) $x = 1$
(iii) (1, −4) (iv) (0, −3)
e (i) $x = 2, x = -4$ (ii) $x = -1$
(iii) (−1, −9) (iv) (0, −8)
f (i) $x = -3, x = -1$ (ii) $x = -2$
(iii) (−2, −1) (iv) (0, 3)

2 b

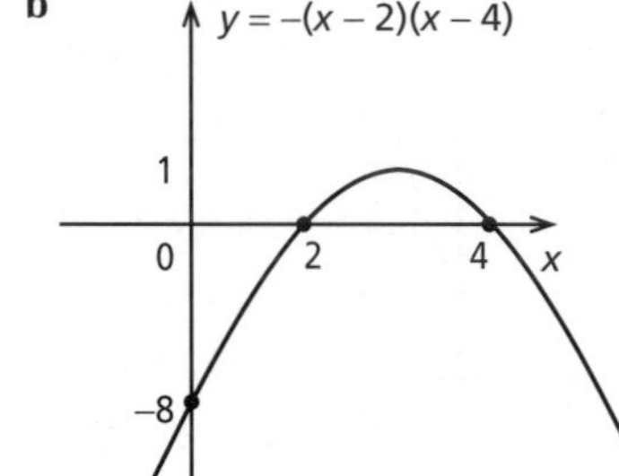

3 a $y = (x - 2)(x - 7)$ **b** $y = (x - 1)(x - 4)$
c $y = (x + 2)(x - 3)$ **d** $y = -(x - 2)(x - 4)$

4 a 8, 3, 0, −1, 0, 3, 8 **b** The same

Page 228 Exercise 8

1 a 0, 1 **b** −3, 1 **c** 0, 3 **d** −1, 2
e −3, 2 **f** −2, 1 **g** 1, 3 **h** −2, −1
i 2, 3

2 a 0 and 6 **b** 6 seconds
c at 3 seconds **d** 36 m

3 a 5 °C **b** 1 and 5
c −4 °C

4 a

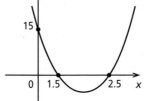

$y = 4x^2 - 16x + 15$ (graph: 15, 0, 1.5, 2.5, x)

b 2.5

5 a Between 2 and 3 and between −1 and −2
b Between 0 and 1 and between 3 and 4
c Between 1 and 2 and between −5 and −6

Page 229 Exercise 9

1 a $y = 1, y = -2$ **b** $x = 0, x = -1$
c $x = -1, x = -2$ **d** $m = 3, m = -4$
e $x = 0, x = 5$ **f** $x = \frac{1}{2}, x = -3$

g $a = -2$ twice h $x = \frac{1}{3}, x = -\frac{1}{2}$
i $c = 5, c = \frac{3}{2}$

2 a $x = -1$ twice b $y = -1, y = 2$
c $x = \pm 2$ d $k = 0, k = -2$
e $n = -3, n = 2$ f $x = -4, x = -1$
g $x = 2$ twice h $e = -3, e = 1$
i $x = 2, x = 3$ j $x = 4$ twice
k $x = 0, x = 3$ l $p = 0, p = 1$

3 a $x = 1, x = 2$ b $x = -2, x = 3$
c $x = -5, x = 1$ d $x = 0, x = 4$
e $x = 3$ twice f $x = -\frac{1}{2}, x = 0$

4 a $y = \pm 3$ b $y = -5, y = 2$
c $x = -4, x = 3$ d $m = -3, m = 4$
e $n = -6, n = 2$ f $y = -5, y = -4$
g $x = -4, x = 2$ h $y = -3, y = 4$
i $k = -3, k = 5$ j $a = -2, a = 6$
k $x = 0, x = 4$ l $m = -5, m = 6$

5 a $y = -\frac{1}{2}, y = -1$ b $y = -2, y = \frac{1}{3}$
c $x = \frac{3}{2}, x = -2$ d $m = \frac{3}{4}, m = 3$
e $n = -\frac{4}{3}, n = 1$ f $y = \frac{1}{2}, y = \frac{3}{2}$
g $x = \pm\frac{2}{3}$ h $y = -\frac{1}{3}, y = \frac{3}{2}$
i $k = -\frac{2}{3}, k = \frac{4}{3}$

6 a A(−2, 0), B(10, 0) b 12 cm
c 36 mm

Page 232 Exercise 10

1 a $x = -2, x = -1$ b $x = -2, x = 1$
c $x = 1, x = 3$ d $x = 1$ twice
e $x = -1, x = 3$ f $x = -2, x = 4$
g $x = -5, x = 1$ h $x = -3, x = -2$

2 a $x = -1.7, x = -0.3$ b $x = -3.8, x = 0.8$
c $x = 0.7, x = 2.8$ d $x = -0.1, x = 8.1$
e $x = -3.6, x = 0.6$ f $x = 0.9, x = -2.6$
g $x = 2.7, x = -0.7$ h $x = -0.4, x = 1.7$
i $x = 1.4, x = 0.4$ j $x = 1.9, x = -0.9$
k $x = 11.6, x = 0.4$ l $x = -6.2, x = 0.2$

3 a $x = 0.2, x = -5.2$ b $x = -\frac{1}{2}, x = 2$
c $x = -0.2, x = 2.2$ d $x = -0.6, x = 4.6$

4 $x = -5, x = 10$

5 $x = -1.75, x = 1$

6 a $x = -1, x = 12$ b $x = -0.4, x = 1.2$
c $x = -0.4, x = 12.4$ d $x = -0.9, x = 1.9$
e $x = 0.2, x = 4.8$

Page 233 Review

1 11

2 a $C(x) = 20 + 10x$

b

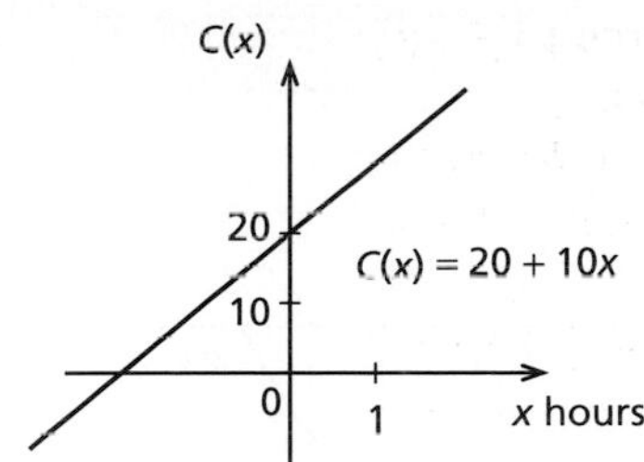

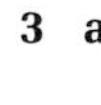

3 a

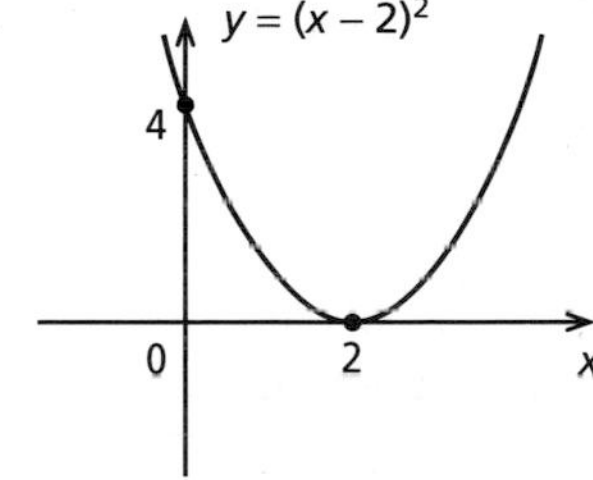

b (i) $x = 2$ (ii) (2, 0)
c minimum

4 a (i) (4, 2) (ii) $x = 4$ (iii) (0, 18)
b (i) (6, 1) (ii) $x = 6$ (iii) (0, 37)
c (i) (5, −3) (ii) $x = 5$ (iii) (0, −28)
d (i) (2, 1) (ii) $x = 2$ (iii) (0, 13)

5 a $y = (x - 2)^2 + 1$ b $y = 2(x - 3)^2 - 1$
c $y = -(x - 1)^2 + 5$ d $y = -(x + 3)^2 + 4$

6 a Maximum area = 200
b $A(x) = -2(x - 10)^2 + 200$

7 $x = -1, x = 4$

8 a $x = -2, x = 4$ b $x = -1, x = \frac{2}{3}$

9 a $x = 2.1, x = -1.6$ b $x = 1.2, x = -3.2$

15 Further Trigonometry

Page 234 Starting Points

1 a 0.5 b 0.707 c 1
d 0 e 0 f 2.75
g −0.985 h −0.342 i −0.839

2 a Error b Error

3 a 36.6° b 77.4° c 77.3° d 0°
e 51.1° f 67.0°

4 a 55.2° b 51.7° c 46.3°

5 a (i) −3 (ii) 21 (iii) −3 (iv) 0

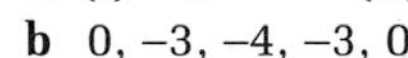

b 0, −3, −4, −3, 0

c

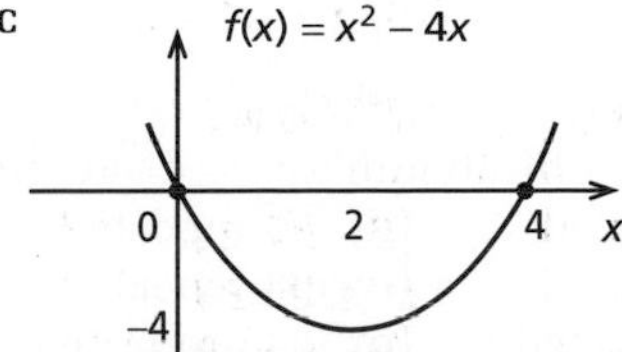

d 0 and 4
e (i) (2, −4) (ii) minimum

Page 235 Exercise 1

1 c

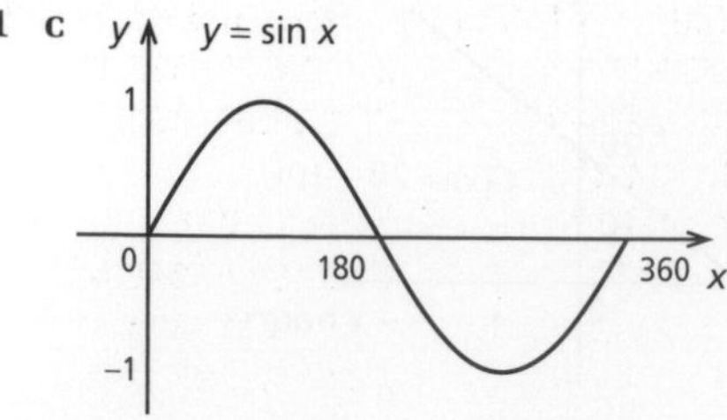

d (i) 1 **(ii)** –1 **(iii)** (90°, 1), (270°, –1)
(iv) 0, 180°, 360°

e (i) $0° < x < 180°$ **(ii)** $180° < x < 360°$

f The maximum value for sine of an angle is 1

2 a (450, 1) (630, –1) **b** 360°, 540°, 720°

3 b The same for each function 0°, 180°, 360°

c 360°

d (i) 1 **(ii)** 2 **(iii)** 3 **(iv)** a

4 Replace a on y axis by coefficient of sin x.

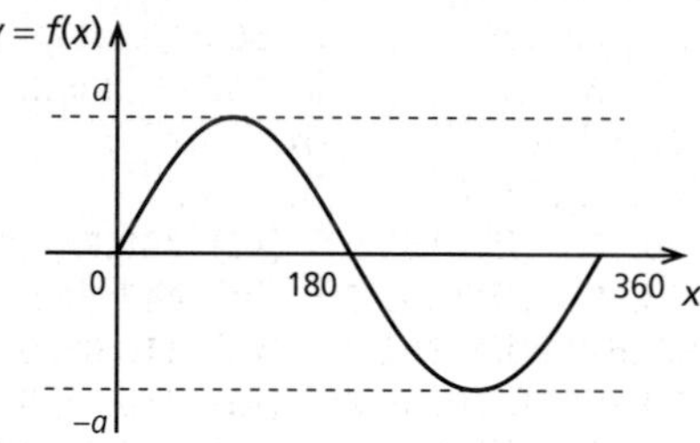

5 Replace a on y axis by coefficient of sin x.

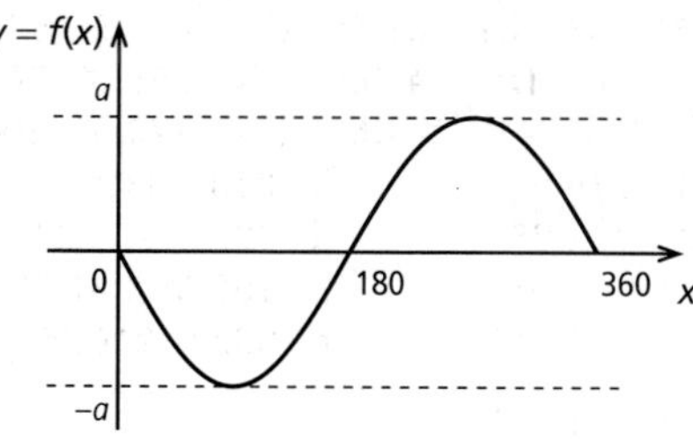

6 $y = -6 \sin x$

7 a 6.5 cm **b** –6.5 cm

c 0°, 180°, 360°

8 b 55 m **c** 55 m

9 a 11 m **b** 0°, 180°, 360°

c 11 m **d** $y = 11 \sin x$

Page 238 Exercise 2

1 a 20 mm **b** 30 mm **c** 10 mm

2 a (i) 23 repeated **(ii)** 54 repeated
(iii) 01 repeated **(iv)** 98 repeated

b (i) 023 repeated **(ii)** 543 repeated
(iii) 021 repeated **(iv)** 006 repeated

d 1234 ÷ 99 999

3 a 360° **b** 360°

4 b (i) 1 **(ii)** –1 **(iii)** 180°

c (i) 1; –1; 120° **(ii)** 1; –1; 720°

d (i) 90° **(ii)** 60°

7 a (i) 5 **(ii)** 3 **(iii)** $y = 5 \sin 3x$

b (i) 7 **(ii)** 2 **(iii)** $y = 7 \sin 2x$

c (i) 3 **(ii)** 4 **(iii)** $y = 3 \sin 4x$

d (i) 3 **(ii)** 5 **(iii)** $y = 3 \sin 5x$

8 a Reflection in x axis

b (i) $y = -4 \sin 20x$ **(ii)** $y = -8 \sin 3.6x$

10 c 27.7°

Page 241 Exercise 3

2 Example 1: **a (i)** 3 **(ii)** –3
b 45°, 135°, 225°, 315°
c 180°

Example 2: **a (i)** 3 **(ii)** –3
b 45°, 135°, 225°, 315°
c 180°

4 a (i) 6 **(ii)** 9 **(iii)** $y = 6 \cos 9x$

b (i) 2 **(ii)** 3 **(iii)** $y = 2 \cos 3x$

5 a (i) 4 **(ii)** 12 **(iii)** 9 **(iv)** 6

b 9 pm

6 a $y = 9 \cos 4x$ **b** $y = 12 \sin 45x$

c $y = -20 \sin \frac{1}{2}x$ **d** $y = -5 \cos 2x$

Page 243 Exercise 4

1 b (i) Value gets very large
(ii) Error
(iii) Dividing by zero gives 'error'

c 180°

2 b $a > 1$ the curve is steeper, when $0 < a < 1$, the curve is less steep

3 b Changes the period of the graph

4 a 9 **b** $b = 9$ **c** $a = 2$

5 a $y = 5 \tan 2x$

b $y = 4 \tan 3x$

6 a $a = 100$

b

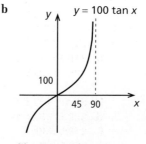

c (i) Remains 100 m
(ii) Gets larger
(iii) Increases

7

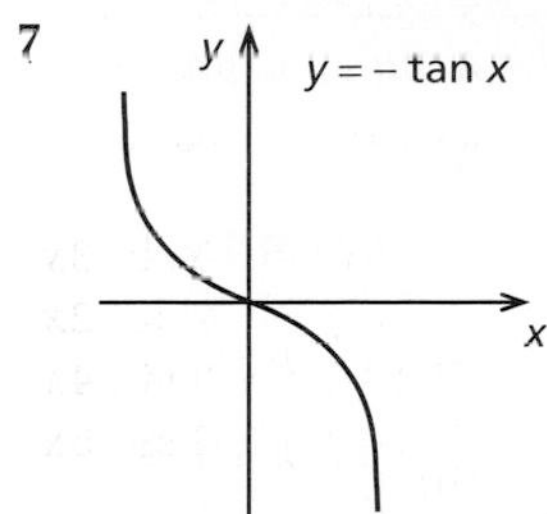

Page 245 Exercise 5

1 a $a = 1$, $b = 30°$ b $a = 4$, $b = 45°$
2 a (i) $a = 1$, $b = 10°$
(ii) $a = 2$, $b = 30°$
b (i) max (10°, 1), min (190°, –1)
(ii) max (30°, 2), min (210°, –2)
3 a 10 b 25
4 a Both the same b 90° c $y = \sin x$
5 b Both the same
6 b (i) $y = \cos (x - 40)$, $y = \cos (x + 320)$, $y = \sin (x - 310)$, $y = \sin (x + 50)$
(ii) $y = \cos (x - 340)$, $y = \cos (x + 20)$, $y = \sin (x - 250)$, $y = \sin (x + 110)$
7 a/b

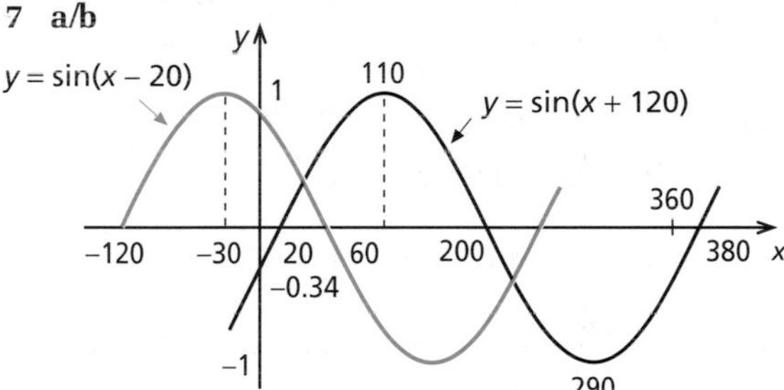

c when $x = 40°$, 220°

Page 249 Exercise 6

1 a (i) 53.1° (ii) 126.86° (iii) 413.1°, 486.9°
b (i) 13.7° (ii) 166.3° (iii) 373.7°, 526.3°
c (i) 65.5° (ii) 114.5° (iii) 425.5°, 474.5°
d (i) 10.3° (ii) 169.7° (iii) 370.3°, 529.7°
e (i) 13.1° (ii) 166.9° (iii) 373.1°, 526.9°
f (i) 46.9° (ii) 133.1° (iii) 406.9°, 493.1°
2 a 224.4°, 315.6° b 210.8°, 329.2°
c 231.4°, 308.6° d 224.3°, 315.7°
e 201.0°, 339.0°
3 a 30°, 150° b 53.1°, 126.9°
c 25.4°, 154.6° d 228.6°, 311.4°
e 189.6°, 350.4° f 210°, 330°
g 191.5°, 348.5° h 19.5°, 160.5°
i 218.7°, 321.3° j 231.1°, 308.9°
4 a 12.6 m b 60, 119.9
5 a (i) 45.6° (ii) 314.4° (iii) 405.6°, 674.4°
b (i) 63.3° (ii) 296.7° (iii) 423.3°, 656.7°
c (i) 44.1° (ii) 315.9° (iii) 404.1°, 675.9°
d (i) 35.8° (ii) 324.2° (iii) 395.8°, 684.2°
e (i) 45.8° (ii) 314.2° (iii) 405.8°, 674.2°
6 a 143.1°, 216.9° b 126.2°, 233.8°
c 100.6°, 259.4° d 126.9°, 233.1°
e 95.7°, 264.3°
7 a 70.5°, 289.5° b 60°, 300°
c 48.2°, 311.8° d 113.6°, 246.4°
e 115.4°, 244.6° f 123.7°, 236.3°
g 112.0°, 248.0° h 80.4°, 279.6°
8 a (i) 9.7 cm (ii) 5.9 cm
b 78.5 seconds, 281.5 seconds
9 a (i) 71.6° (ii) 251.6° (iii) 431.6°, 611.6°
b (i) 37.6° (ii) 217.6° (iii) 397.6°, 577.6°
c (i) 78.7° (ii) 258.7° (iii) 438.7°, 618.7°
d (i) 42.4° (ii) 222.4° (iii) 402.4°, 582.4°
e (i) 85.2° (ii) 265.2° (iii) 445.2°, 625.2°
10 a 116.6°, 296.6° b 150.7°, 330.7°
c 99.6°, 279.6° d 106.7°, 286.7°
e 149.1°, 329.1°
11 a 68.2°, 248.2° b 14.0°, 194.0°
c 82.6°, 262.6° d 66.0°, 246.0°
e 105.9°, 285.9° f 56.3°, 236.3°
g 158.2°, 338.2° h 156.8°, 336.8°
12 a (i) 2.15 km (ii) 2.87 km
b (i) 79.7°, 259.7° (ii) 79.7°
13 a (i) 26.7° (ii) 153.3° (iii) 386.7°, 513.3°
b (i) 82.0° (ii) 262.0° (iii) 442°, 622°
c (i) 58.6° (ii) 301.4° (iii) 418.6°, 661.4°
d (i) 50.2° (ii) 230.2° (iii) 410.2°, 590.2°
e (i) 68.4° (ii) 111.6° (iii) 428.4°, 47.6°
f (i) 134.4° (ii) 225.6° (iii) 494.4°, 585.6°
g (i) 210.4° (ii) 329.6° (iii) 570.4°, 689.6°
h (i) 101.5° (ii) 281.5° (iii) 461.5°, 641.5°
i (i) 198.0° (ii) 342.0° (iii) 558.0°, 702.0°
j (i) 113.5° (ii) 246.5° (iii) 473.5°, 606.5°
14 a 66.8°, 246.8° b 210°, 330°
c 48.2°, 311.8° d 63.4°, 243.4°
e 98.2°, 261.8° f 192.8°, 347.2°
g 113.6°, 246.4° h 36.9°, 216.9°

Page 252 Exercise 7

2 a $\sin^2 A = 1 - \cos^2$ b $\cos^2 A = 1 - \sin^2 A$
3 a 0.8 b 0.69 c 0.75
d 0.8 e –0.8
4 a $\cos x$ b 1 c $\sin x$
d $\cos^2 x - \sin^2 x$ e 1
5 a $\sin x$ b $\tan^2 x$ c $2 \tan^2 x$
6 a 45°, 225° b 26.6°, 206.6°
c 21.8°, 201.8° d 143.1°, 323.1°
e 31.0°, 211.0° f 166.0°, 346.0°
g 156.8°, 336.8° h 11.3°, 191.3°

Page 253 Review

3 a $y = 7 \sin 9x$ b $y = 3 \cos 4x$
4 See page 243 for tan curve

5 a 30°, 150° b 120°, 240°
c 199.5°, 340.5° d 48.2°, 311.8°
e 26.6°, 206.6° f No solution

7 $a = 6, b = 50$

8 a 1 b $\tan x$ c 2

9 a 21.8°, 201.8° b 161.6°, 341.6°

16 Revising Unit 3

Page 254 Exercise 1

1 a $\frac{3}{a}$ b $\frac{2}{y^2}$ c $\frac{3}{2x}$
d $\frac{2}{3m}$ e $\frac{5}{6m}$ f $\frac{1}{12t}$
g $\frac{19}{6y}$ h $\frac{2 + 3c}{c^2}$ i $\frac{8 + a^2}{4a}$
j $\frac{5 - 6c^2}{15c}$ k $\frac{2 + x}{2x^2}$ l $\frac{15y + 8}{10y^2}$

2 a c^5 b y^7 c m^4 d a^6
e $\frac{1}{m}$ f $(k + 3)^6$ g $(a - 3)^2$ h $\frac{1}{2t - 1}$
i $x - 1$ j $(n - 5)^5$

3 a $L = \frac{P}{4}$ b $y = x - 4$ c $C = 3B$
d $n = \frac{m - p}{6}$ e $u = \frac{8T - v}{2}$ f $B = \frac{A}{3} - C$

4 a 3 b $\frac{12}{c^2}$ c $\frac{2}{3}$ d $\frac{2}{5}$
e $\frac{8}{t}$ f $\frac{3w}{4}$ g $\frac{mn^2}{8}$ h $\frac{4v^3}{27}$

5 a $\sqrt{6}$ b 8 c 10 d 5
e 10 f 4

6 a $\frac{\sqrt{5}}{5}$ b $\frac{\sqrt{7}}{7}$ c $\frac{\sqrt{6}}{3}$ d $\sqrt{10}$
e $\frac{\sqrt{8}}{6}$

7 a a b y^{-2} c m^{-3} d 1
e t^{-7} f u^{-1} g w^{-1} h y^{-6}
i a^{-5} j c^{-4} k h^{-3} l $k^{\frac{4}{3}}$

8 a $2\sqrt{5}$ b $3\sqrt{3}$ c $4\sqrt{2}$ d $3\sqrt{5}$
e $2\sqrt{3}$ f $4\sqrt{5}$ g $7\sqrt{2}$ h $6\sqrt{3}$
i $4\sqrt{7}$ j $2\sqrt{2}$

9 a $6m$ b $\frac{9}{2t}$ c $\frac{5y}{2}$
d $\frac{10y + 4}{y^2}$

10 a x^{-2} b $2x^{-2}$ c $\frac{1}{2}x^{-2}$ d $\frac{3}{4}x^{-5}$
e $x^{-\frac{2}{3}}$ f $2x^{\frac{1}{4}}$ g $\frac{3}{4}x^{-\frac{1}{2}}$ h $x^{-\frac{1}{2}}$
i $3x^{-\frac{1}{2}}$ j $\frac{1}{5}x^{-\frac{1}{2}}$ k $\frac{7}{3}x^{-\frac{1}{2}}$ l $\frac{4}{5}x^{-\frac{1}{3}}$

11 a a b $c^{\frac{4}{3}}$ c $m^{\frac{3}{2}}$ d $h^{\frac{3}{5}}$
e $k^{\frac{5}{2}}$ f t g y^2 h x

12 a (i) $C = \frac{1}{3}B - A$ (ii) $B = 3(A + C)$
b (i) $V = \frac{T + R}{P}$ (ii) $T = PV - R$
c (i) $D = BC - 2A$ (ii) $C = \frac{2A + D}{B}$
d (i) $q = \frac{p}{3} - 2r$
(ii) $r = \frac{\frac{p}{3} - q}{2} = \frac{p - 3q}{6}$
e (i) $N = 4M + P$ (ii) $P = N - 4M$
f (i) $W = \frac{5(u + v)}{T}$ (ii) $u = \frac{WT}{5} - v$

13 a (i) 1 m^2 (ii) $\frac{4 + x^2}{x}$ m
b (i) $\frac{6}{y}$ m^2 (ii) $\frac{4y^3 + 54}{3y^2}$ m

14 a $\frac{10 + y^2}{4y}$ b $\frac{y^2 - 10}{4y}$

15 a $5x^{\frac{3}{2}} + 3x^{\frac{1}{2}} - 2x^{-\frac{1}{2}}$ b $4x^{\frac{5}{3}} - x^{\frac{2}{3}} + 5x^{-\frac{1}{3}}$

16 a $y = 4x - 1$ b $x = \frac{y + 1}{4}$

17 a $\sqrt{2} - 1$ b $\frac{3 + \sqrt{5}}{4}$
c $2(\sqrt{10} + 3)$ d $\frac{5 - \sqrt{7}}{2}$

18 a x^6 b x^6 c y^{12} d $a^{\frac{3}{2}}$
e $a^{\frac{3}{2}}$ f $m^{\frac{1}{6}}$ g $8c^3$ h $\frac{1}{9h^2}$
i $\frac{1}{4k}$ j $\frac{1}{2\sqrt{m}}$ k $2t^{\frac{2}{3}}$ l $\frac{64}{t}$

19 a $x^{-\frac{2}{3}}$ b $\frac{1}{2}x^{-1}$ c $\frac{1}{\sqrt{5}}x^{-2}$
d $\frac{2}{3\sqrt{6}}x^{-\frac{1}{2}}$ e $\frac{1}{4}x^{-\frac{3}{2}}$ f $\frac{2}{3}x^{-\frac{1}{2}}$

Page 257 Exercise 2

1 a $y = 3x^2$ b $y = -2x^2$ c $y = 5x^2$

2 a $y = (x - 5)^2 + 3$
b $y = (x - 4)^2 - 16$
c $y = -(x - 3)^2 + 11$
d $y = -(x + 4)^2 + 1$

3 a (i) (1, −5) (ii) minimum (iii) $x = 1$
b (i) (3, 4) (ii) maximum (iii) $x = 3$

ANSWERS

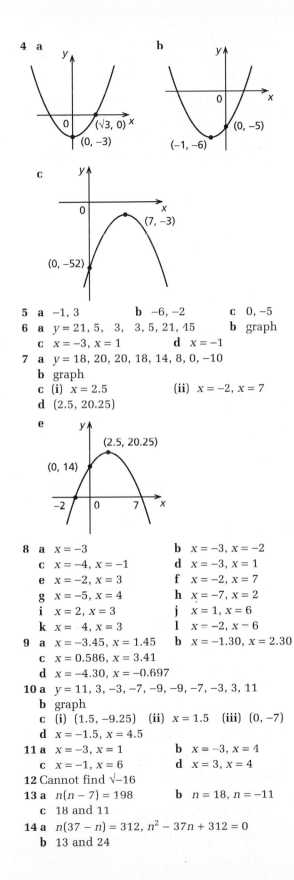

4 a

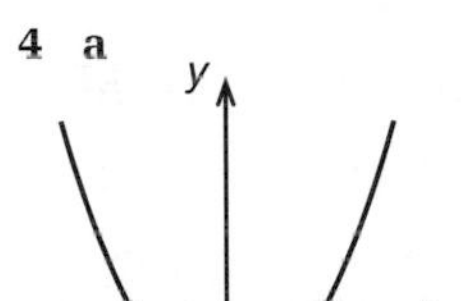

b

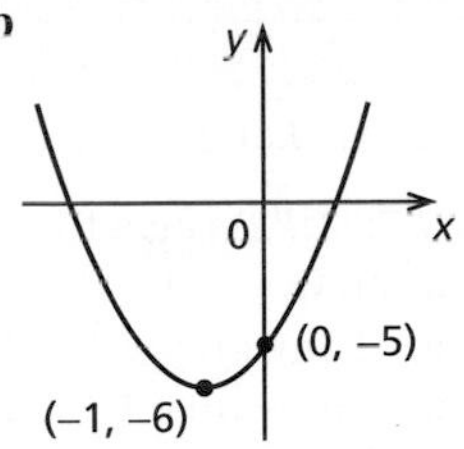

c

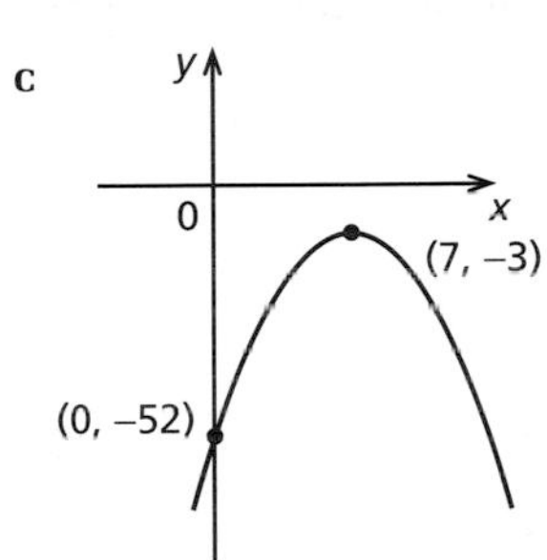

5 a −1, 3 **b** −6, −2 **c** 0, −5

6 a $y = 21, 5, -3, -3, 5, 21, 45$ **b** graph
c $x = -3, x = 1$ **d** $x = -1$

7 a $y = 18, 20, 20, 18, 14, 8, 0, -10$
b graph
c (i) $x = 2.5$ **(ii)** $x = -2, x = 7$
d (2.5, 20.25)
e

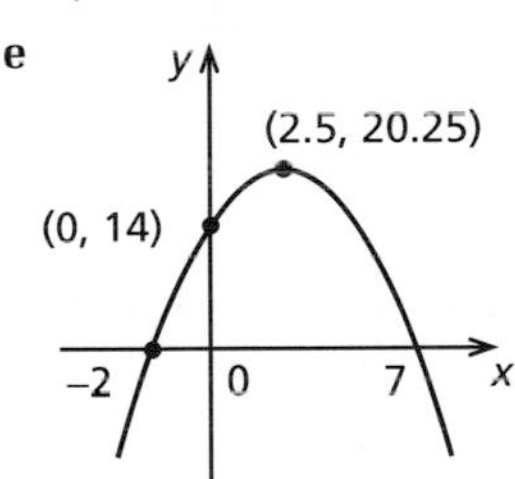

8 a $x = -3$ **b** $x = -3, x = -2$
c $x = -4, x = -1$ **d** $x = -3, x = 1$
e $x = -2, x = 3$ **f** $x = -2, x = 7$
g $x = -5, x = 4$ **h** $x = -7, x = 2$
i $x = 2, x = 3$ **j** $x = 1, x = 6$
k $x = -4, x = 3$ **l** $x = -2, x = 6$

9 a $x = -3.45, x = 1.45$ **b** $x = -1.30, x = 2.30$
c $x = 0.586, x = 3.41$
d $x = -4.30, x = -0.697$

10 a $y = 11, 3, -3, -7, -9, -9, -7, -3, 3, 11$
b graph
c (i) (1.5, −9.25) **(ii)** $x = 1.5$ **(iii)** (0, −7)
d $x = -1.5, x = 4.5$

11 a $x = -3, x = 1$ **b** $x = -3, x = 4$
c $x = -1, x = 6$ **d** $x = 3, x = 4$

12 Cannot find $\sqrt{-16}$

13 a $n(n - 7) = 198$ **b** $n = 18, n = -11$
c 18 and 11

14 a $n(37 - n) = 312, n^2 - 37n + 312 = 0$
b 13 and 24

15 a $x(x - 6) = 432$ **b** 24 m by 18 m

16 $x^2 - 8x - 560 = 0$, 28 m by 20 m

17 a (i) 1 m **(ii)** 8 m
b 8 m **c** 12.25 m

18 a $(2x + 1)(x + 3) = 0;\ x = -3, x = -0.5$
b $(2x + 3)(x + 2) = 0;\ x = -2, x = -1.5$
c $(2x + 1)(x - 5) = 0;\ x = 5, x = -0.5$
d $(2x - 5)(x - 2) = 0;\ x = 2, x = 2.5$
e $(3x + 1)(x + 3) = 0;\ x = -3, x = -\frac{1}{3}$
f $(3x - 2)(x - 2) = 0;\ x = 2, x = \frac{2}{3}$
g $(3x - 2)(x - 3) = 0;\ x = 3, x = \frac{2}{3}$
h $(5x + 2)(x - 2) = 0;\ x = 2, x = -\frac{2}{5}$

19 a $x = -2.28, x = -0.219$
b $x = 0.634, x = 2.37$
c $x = -1.22, x = 0.549$
d $x = -2.47, x = 0.135$

Page 260 Exercise 3

1 a $y = 2 \cos x°$ **b** $y = 3 \sin 2x°$
c $y = \tan 2x°$

2 a graph of $y = 3 \sin x°$, $0 \le x \le 360$
b 360° **c** $x = 0, 180, 360$

3 a

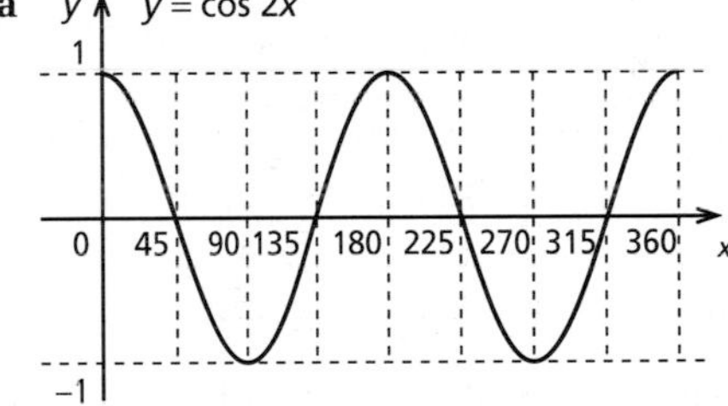

b 180°
c (i) 45°, 135°, 225°, 315° **(ii)** 90°, 270°

4 a $y = 4 \cos 3x°$ **b** $y = 5 \sin 9x°$
c $y = 4 \cos 2x°$ **d** $y = 3 \sin 4x°$

5 a 120° **b** 40° **c** 180° **d** 90°

6 a 36.9°, 143° **b** 78.5°, 282°
c 56.3°, 236° **d** 143°, 217°
e 194°, 346° **f** 113°, 293°

7 a 0°, 360° **b** 270°
c 120°, 240° **d** 78.7°, 259°
e 19.5°, 161° **f** 41.4°, 319°
g 127°, 233° **h** 222°, 318°

8 b (i) 180° **(ii)** 0°, 720°
c 720°

10 a $x = 0, 180, 360$ **b** $x = 90$ **c** $x = 60$
d $x = 300$ **e** $x = 210$ **f** $x = 30$

11 a $\tan^2 x°$ **b** $\tan x°$
c 1 **d** $\tan A°$

12 a 3 m **b** 90 m
c (i) 2.60 m **(ii)** 1.03 m below sea-level

13 a 10 m **b** 120 m **c** 240 m **d** $x > 240$

14 a 12 m **b** 80 m **c** 170 m **d** 2.08 m

UNIT 4

17 Calculations in a Social Context

Page 263 Starting Points

1 a (iii) b (iv) c (v) d (i) e (ii)
2 a £61.20 b £493.50
3 £180
4 a 30 min b 15 min c 45 min
5 £1321
6 £236.40
7 a 3 years b 5 years
8 £6696
9 £15.22

Page 264 Exercise 1

1 a £30 b £30 c £31.50
d £33.75 e £27.20 f £43.20
g £60 h £54 i £20.25
j £24.75
2 Friday night
3 a £300 b £299.20 c £169
d £239.25
4 £181.50
5 a £214.50 b £255.55 c £228.80

Page 266 Exercise 2

1 a £490 b £1225
2 £1624
3 a £1340 and £1439.50 b Elsie Duncan
c Elsie Duncan
4 £115.05, £87.18, £201.93, £232.49
5 a £20 b £97.50 c £148.50

Page 268 Exercise 3

1 a £4 c No d £12.20
f £139 − £21.22 = £117.78
2 a A £114, B £24, C £138, D £22.33, E £115.67
b A £157.50, B £17.50, C £175, D £28.57, E £146.43
3 a (i) £464.90 (ii) £86.03 (iii) £378.87
b (i) £458.54 (ii) £88.30 (iii) £370.24
4 a (i) £511.11 (ii) £1265.14
b £2066.12
5 b 39.5 h c 4.5 h
d (i) £292.10 (ii) £77.35 (iii) £214.75

Page 270 Exercise 4

1 a (i) £11 189 (ii) £2450.47
b (i) £15 600 (ii) £3465
c (i) £29 546 (ii) £7258.40
2 a £292.96, £47.12 b £360, £66.63
c £2951.75, £604.87
3 a £14 619.80 b £10 574.80
c £281.15 d £44.41
4 a (i) £22 425 (ii) £5277
(iii) £17 148
b (i) £3821.04 (ii) £318.42

Page 271 Exercise 5

1 a 405L b 399L c 561H d 711H
2 a Allowance £4520, married
b Allowance £2390, single
c Allowance £4180, married
d Allowance £4210, single
3 a (i) £5640 (ii) £19 702
b £4728.48
4 a £3420, £9362, £2340.50
b £6720, £15 404, £4621.20
c £8290, £26 710, £6410.40

Page 272 Exercise 6

1 a 1.1 b 1.05 c 1.035 d 1.01
e 1.005
2 a (i) £255.46 (ii) £716.43
b (i) £360.72 (ii) £1166.50
c (i) £23.87 (ii) £111.30
3 a £144.29 b £376.09 c £93.99
4 a £42.58 b £19.56 c £56.45
d £19.99 e £10.03 f £29.99
5 a 10% b 30% c 15% d 18%

Page 274 Exercise 7

1 a £321.51 b £22.51
2 a £171.92 b £6189.12 c £2189.12
3 a £147.84 b £14.79
4 With protection is £20.24 more per month
5 a (i) £150.43 (ii) £128.94
b £773.64 c £30
6 a £3450 b £170.02 c £34.50
7 a 60 months
b £16 126.20, £15 832.80
c (i) Loansafe (ii) £293.40
d Loansafe
8 a 5 b 14.9% c £101.52
d £771.25 e £7013.52 f £2934.60
g £5000 h 3% i £57.33
j £8000 over 36 months

Page 276 Exercise 8

1 a 1.67% b 1.67% c 29.8%
d 2.8% e £5 by £0.29 f Vantage
g (i) £6.75 (ii) £1.92
2 a 1.9% b 23.3% c £26.40
3 £3.44
4 a £4.06 b £248.73 c £12.44
5 a £351.89 b £5.74 c £357.63
d £10.73
6 a £165 b 1.72% c £2.84
d £167.84 e £5.04
7 £549.97

Page 278 Review

1 £45.13
2 £309.75
3 a £448.80 b £1353.00
4 a £166.50 b £16.88 c £183.38
d £33.57 e £149.81
5 a £12 740 b £2985 c £13 800
d £265.38 e 404L
6 a 619H b Allowance £7120, single
7 a (i) £2172.96 (ii) £6229.08
(iii) £8616 (iv) £273.11
b 14.8%
c £277.98
d (i) £5000 (ii) 36 months
8 a £198.06 b £4.36
c £202.42 d £6.07

18 Logic Diagrams

Page 280 Starting Points

1 a (i) Finetip pen (ii) 14.90
(iii) 2.61 (iv) 17.51
b 10.35, 1.81, 12.16 c £38.59
2 a 41.1 b 1.5 m × 0.8 m by 0.03 m^2
c 217 cm^3 d £1040
3 a Via Colmonell by 4 miles
b 22 minutes
4 a 124 miles b 136 miles

Page 282 Exercise 1

1 a (i) A1 (ii) C4 (iii) C1
b B3
c (i) B4 (ii) 62.80
d 133
2 a (i) A3 (ii) B2
b (i) C2 (ii) D1
c (i) C4 (ii) D3
3 a (i) D5 (ii) D6 (iii) E5
b (i) B3 (ii) B4 (iii) C3
c (i) D7 (ii) D8 (iii) E7
d (i) A3 (ii) A4 (iii) B3
4 b (i) 3 (ii) 2 (iii) 76.5
5 a C1 b B3 c A3 d D5
6 a (i) 0.6 (ii) 0.4 (iii) 0.3
b 2.4
7 a £5
b (i) 200 (ii) 40 (iii) Profit
c Select C6, type 180, press 'Tab'

Page 285 Exercise 2

1 a (i) label (ii) formula (iii) data
b (i) = 2*(A6 + B6) (ii) = 2*(A7 + B7)
2 a 32 b 29, 27, 18.6, 115
3 a 67
b (i) = B3 + C3 + D3 + E3 + F3
(ii) – B4 + C4 + D4 + E4 + F4
c = G2 + G3 + G4
4 a (i) = SUM(C2..C4) (ii) = SUM(E2..E4)
b (i) = SUM(B3..F3) (ii) = SUM(B4..F4)
5 a (i) = 2*PI()*A3 (ii) = 2*PI()*A4
(iii) = PI()*A2*A2 (iv) = PI()*A3*A3
b r = 1.78 cm
6 a (i) = B3/3 (ii) = B4/3
b (i) = B2 – C2 (ii) = B3 – C3
(iii) = B4 – C4
7 C4: = B4 – A4; D5: = C4*D4;
D6: = D5*0.08; D7: = D5 + D6

Page 289 Exercise 3

1 a (i) = A9 + 0.1 (ii) 1.8
b All cells contain 5
c = PI()*A2*A2*B2
d Precision 2
2 a = A1*2
b (i) = B1 – 2 (ii) C1/2
(iii) = D1*2 + 1
3 a = A5 + 1 b = A4*A4
c = SQRT(A5) d = A3^3
4 a (i) = A2^2 – 4*A2
(ii) = 3*A2^2 – 2*A2 + 1
b $x = 0$ or $x = 4$
5 a 1, 2, 3, …, 9
b (i) = A7*A7 (ii) 16
c all 7s
d (i) = B6*C6 (ii) 567
f (i) row 13 (ii) 12 cm
6 b 12 workers give minimum cost of £8000

Page 292 Exercise 4

1 a = B2 + C2 b = B6 + C6
c (i) = AVERAGE(C2..C6)
(ii) = AVERAGE(D2..D6)
2 a = 1.02*B2
b = (B14 – B2)/B2*100
c B3 – B2 d £2.24
3 a (i) 20.98% (ii) £8.74
b (i) 18.16% (ii) £22.69
c (i) 11.35% (ii) £113.51

Page 293 Exercise 5

1–3 Student's own spreadsheets and graphs
4 a $x = 2, y = 5$ b $x = 2, y = 1$
c $x = 4, y = -3$ d $x = -5, y = -4$

Page 295 Challenge

$x = -1.5$ or 4

Page 295 Exercise 6

1 a Tea, no sugar, milk
b Tea, no sugar, no milk

c Coffee, sugar, milk
d Coffee, no sugar, no milk
2 b 8 c 16
4 b 23
5 b 12, 13, 27, 20, 34, 13, 32, 33, 13
c (i) ACD (ii) ACBED
7 a 12
b (i) $\frac{1}{4}$ (ii) $\frac{1}{6}$ (iii) $\frac{1}{12}$
8 a $\frac{1}{4}$ b $\frac{1}{2}$
9 a (i) $\frac{7}{8}$ (ii) $\frac{3}{8}$ (iii) $\frac{1}{8}$

Page 298 Exercise 7

1 a (i) 6 vertices, 6 arcs (ii) Bathroom, 1, odd; Living room, 2, even; Hall, 4, even; Kitchen, 1, odd; Bedroom 2, 2, even; Bedroom 1, 2, even
b (i) 7 vertices, 7 arcs (ii) Bedroom 2, 1, odd; Bedroom 1, 1, odd; Outside, 1, odd; Hall, 5, odd; Living room, 2, even; Kitchen, 3, odd; Bathroom, 1, odd

2 a (i)

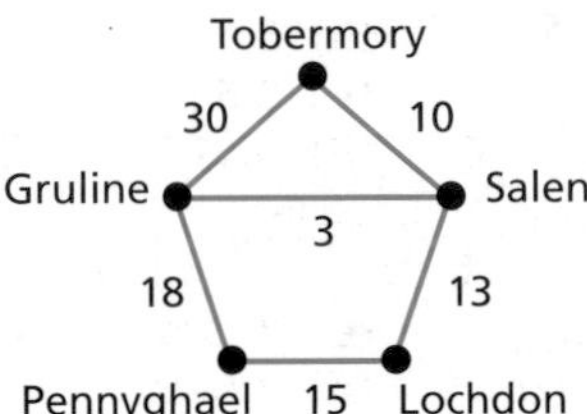

(ii)

Pennyghael 15 Lochdon
Tobermory
18 30 10 13
Gruline 3 Salen

(iii)

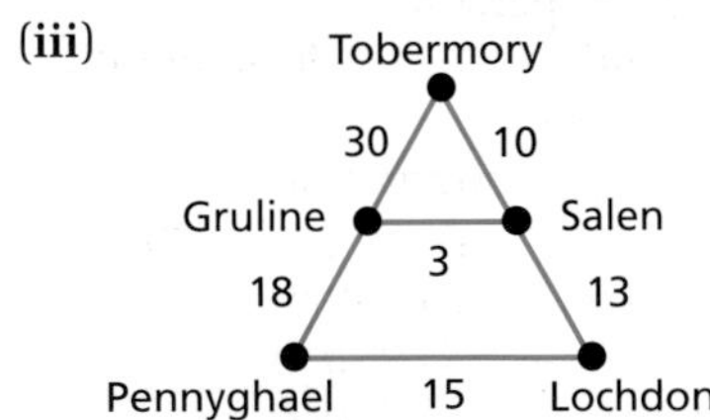

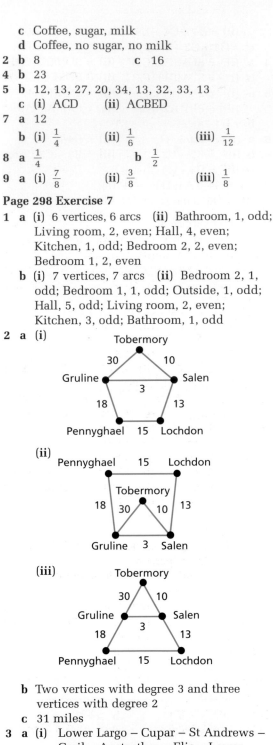

b Two vertices with degree 3 and three vertices with degree 2
c 31 miles

3 a (i) Lower Largo – Cupar – St Andrews – Crail – Anstruther – Elie – Lower Largo – St Andrews – Anstruther
(ii) 63 miles
b Elie, 2, even; Anstruther, 3, odd; Crail, 2, even
c Each 'passing through' uses up 2 arcs, an even number. Starting and stopping each use up only 1 arc. Starting and stopping at different vertices therefore requires an odd number of arcs

4 a (i)

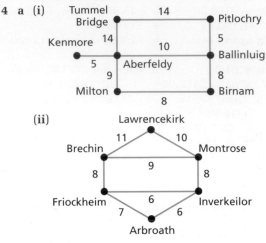

Tummel Bridge 14 Pitlochry
Kenmore 14 10 5
5 Aberfeldy Ballinluig
Milton 9 8 Birnam
8

(ii)

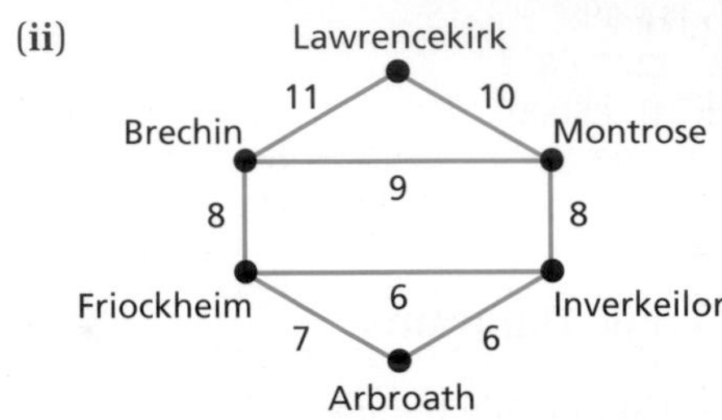

b Kenmore – Aberfeldy – Tummel Bridge – Pitlochry – Ballinluig – Aberfeldy – Milton – Birnam – Ballinluig
c Not possible. There are 4 odd vertices; at most 2 are needed for such a route to exist

6 a A, 2, even; B, 3, odd; C, 3, odd; D, 2, even; E, 4, even; F, 2, even. Possible route: B – A – F – E – B – C – E – D – C
b A, 2, even; B, 4, even; C, 4, even; D, 2, even; E, 3, odd; F, 2, even; G, 5, odd; H, 2, even; I, 4, even.
Possible route: G – H – I – G – B – I – A – B – C – G – F – E – D – C – E

7 a (i)

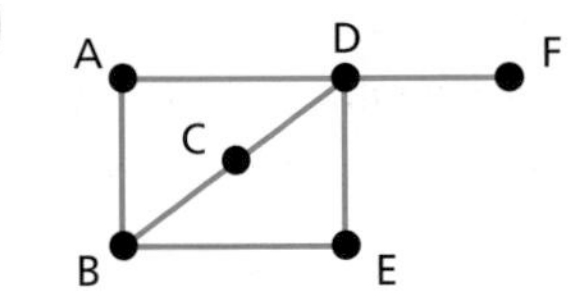

(ii)

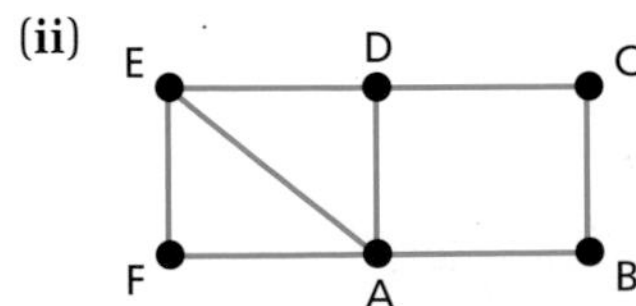

(iii)

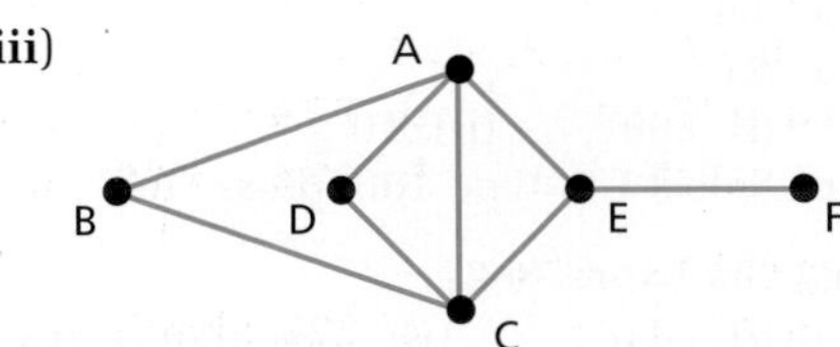

b (i) Impossible: 4 odd vertices
(ii) E – F – A – E – D – A – B – C – D
(iii) F – E – A – B – C – A – D – C – E

Page 301 Exercise 8

1 a (i) 4 (ii) 5
b (i) 15 min (ii) 5 min
c (i) 65 min (ii) 65 min

2 a (i) Let cement dry (ii) Pour cement
b 16.5 hours

3 a 2 hours b Set up furniture
c C, D and E d 15 hours

4 Critical path: start – A – E – D – F – I – J – finish, giving 32 days

5 Critical path: start – C – G – I – H – stop, giving 13 minutes

Page 303 Exercise 9

1 a £1200 b £100 c £800 d £250

2 a £900 b £500 c £1700 d £1000

3 a £10 b £120 c £168

4 a (i) 1850 m^2 (ii) 3180 m^2
(iii) 4420 m^2 (iv) 5970 m^2
b Minimum size 2800 pupils

5 a 1 min 19 s b 1 min 13 s

Page 306 Exercise 10

1 Equilateral; isosceles; scalene (from top down)

2 Male or female? Glasses or no glasses? Dark hair or light hair?

3 Student's own diagram (variety of answers)

4 a 10 b 20

Page 307 Review

1 a (i) = A2 + 0.1 (ii) = PI()*A2*A2
(iii) = A4 + 0.1 (iv) = PI()*A6*A6
b = PI()*A7*A7
c Precision 2
d Column A: 4, 4.1, 4.2, …

2 b Dimension for max area: $12\frac{1}{2}$ m × 25 m

3 Critical path: 0 + 12 + 3 + 6 + 2; minimum time is 23 days

4 a 8.29 °C b 8.89 °C
c 17.73 °C d 9.85 °C

19 Formulae

Page 308 Starting Points

1 a 8 b 4 c 16 d 38 e 3

2 −9, −7, −5, −3, −1, 1, 3

3 a 37.7 cm b 75.4 cm

4 a 4188.8 cm^3 b 150.8 cm^3 c 24 cm^3

Page 309 Exercise 1

1 a 50 km/h b 222.2 km/h

2 a (i) 133.3 m^2 (ii) 230 m^2 (iii) 420 m^2
b (i) 720 m^3 (ii) 8400 m^3 (iii) 4928 m^3

3 a (i) 9 km per litre (ii) 10.9 km per litre
b Simba

4 a (i) 26.07 (ii) 39.11 (iii) 1.00
b (i) 18.52 (ii) 11.11 (iii) 1.85
c (i) 31.05 (ii) 19.87 (iii) 13.66
d (i) 0.9 knot (ii) 1.7 km/h (iii) 1.1 mph
e 10% error

5 a (i) 2 m (ii) 1.5 m
b (i) 720 m^3 (ii) 900 m^3
c 1320 m^3

6 a (i) 77 °F (ii) 212 °F
b (i) 40 °F (ii) 50 °F (iii) 70 °F

7 a £20.58 b £1543.21 c £1.77
d £10.96 e £512.82 f £452.49

8 a 17.4 cm b 32.1 cm c 138.9 cm
d 52.6 cm

9 a £449.86 b £518.64 c £804.97

10 a (i) £182.64 (ii) £203.85 (iii) £533.39
b (i) £197.25 (ii) £220.16 (iii) £576.06

11 a 1000 watts b 60 watts c 3000 watts

Page 312 Exercise 2

1 a (i) 36 mm (ii) 299 mm
b (i) 5 (ii) 5
c (i) 20 g (ii) 2.5 g

2 a (i) 0.33 N (ii) 0.12 N (iii) 0.03 N
b The force decreases

3 a 16 b 21 c 24 d 25

4 a 4 mm b 13 mm c 14 mm

5 a (i) 7 cm (ii) 8.8 cm
b (i) 1 cm (ii) 5 cm
c (i) 7 cm (ii) 5.6 cm

6 a (i) 9 m (ii) 13.5 m (iii) 21 m
b (i) 6 m (ii) 54 m (iii) 73.5 m
c (i) 16.9 m (ii) 94.5 m

7 a 188
b (i) 942.5 cm
(ii) 2 of $2\pi r$ has cancelled with 70 of 70 cm/person

8 a 263.9 cm^2 b 88.0 mm^2
c 1913.2 mm^2

9 a (i) 26 ohms (ii) 9.5 ohms (iii) 9.3 ohms
b (i) 8 ohms (ii) 10 ohms (iii) 12 ohms

10 a (i) 14 m/s (ii) 18 m/s
b (i) 6 m/s (ii) 3 m/s
c (i) large (ii) large

11 a (i) 7.9 s (ii) 9.9 s (iii) 17.9 s
b longer

12 a 2617.99 cm^3 b No

13 a (i) 28 588.5 cm^3 (ii) 32 741.7 cm^3

Page 316 Exercise 3

1 a 1256.6 cm^2 b 137.6 cm^2
c 62.8 cm^2 d 125.7 cm^2

2 a $2\pi rh$ b 1885.0 cm^2

3 a $2\pi rh$ b 8.8 m^2

4 a $157.1\ m^2$ b $251.3\ m^2$ c $408.4\ m^2$
5 a 2.5 mm b $157.1\ mm^2$
c $\pi D(D - C)$

Page 317 Exercise 4

1 a 8 b 2.4 c 3 d 12
e 3 f 8
2 a 125 m/s
b (i) 24 (ii) 4
3 a 14 cm
b (i) 41 (ii) 2.2
4 a (i) 120 m (ii) 210 m
b (i) 23 m/s (ii) 18 m/s (iii) 0
5 a 12.96 b 21.57 c 777.8
d 0.0013
6 a 15.9 b 51.8 c 4
7 a (i) 21.7 cm (ii) 14.3 cm
b (i) 88.6°, 271.4° (ii) 88.2°, 271.8°
(iii) 90.7°, 269.3°

Page 319 Review

1 a 1.4% b 18%
2 a $90\ m^2$ b $62.5\ m^2$
3 a (i) $286.5\ cm^2$ (ii) $2.0\ cm^2$
b $5.09 \times 10^8\ m^2$
4 a 1 year
b (i) 11.9 years (ii) 1.9 years
5 a 55.3 m b 280.6 m

20 Statistical Assignment

Page 320 Starting Points

1 a 4 b 4 c 21 d 3.1
2 a 8, 20, 65, 86, 98, 100
c (i) £2.60 (ii) £2.20, £3.40
d £0.60

Page 322 Exercise 1

1 b $10 \le t < 20$ c 16 min
2 a $10 \le d < 20$ b 14 c 130
3 a $60 \le t < 80$ b £72 c 55
4 b 41–50 c 44
5 b $8 \le h < 9$ c 8.8

Page 323 Exercise 2

1 a 1, 3, 5, 7, 9; 48, 207, 200, 217, 108; totals 200, 780
b 780 ÷ 200 = 3.9 min
2 a 5.5, 15.5, 25.5, 35.5, 45.5; 22, 248, 714, 710, 546; total 2240
b 28 c 4 marks above the mean
3 a 37.5, 42.5, 47.5, 52.5, 57.5; 300, 1275, 1615, 1050, 460; totals 100, 4700
b 47 c $45 \le t < 50$
d 8 min longer than the mean

4 a 90, 110, 130, 150; 630, 1650, 2470, 1650; totals 150, 6400
b 52 c 123
d 4 above

Page 326 Exercise 3

1 b (i) 18 (ii) 25 (iii) 30
c 6
2 a Frequency: 5, 12, 6, 9, 12, 11, 5
b Cumulative frequency: 5, 17, 23, 32, 44, 55, 60
d (i) 204 (ii) 266 (iii) 301
e 48.5
3 a 25, 95, 190, 255, 290, 300
c (i) 95 (ii) 130
d (i) 13 (ii) 8 or 9, 17 or 18
e approx. 4 or 5
4 a 4, 15, 43, 90, 126, 145, 150
c 4.5

Page 331 Review

1 a 2, 7, 6, 8, 9, 14, 4; total 50
b 50
c $65 \le W < 70$
e 66 g
2 a 100
b (i) 44 (ii) 8
c (i) 31 (ii) 27, 35 (iii) 4
d 31.05

21 Revising Unit 4

Page 332 Exercise 1

1 £81
2 £310.38
3 a (i) £450 (ii) £1550
b (i) £394 (ii) £1156
4 a £154 b £52.80 c £206.80
d £51.70 e £155.10
5 a 715H
b Lower personal allowance between £6470 and £6479
6 a £21 178 b £5094.50
c £21 697.50 d £417.26
e 561H
7 a £24 105 b £18 909
c (i) £4538.16 (ii) £19 566.84
8 a £37 160 b £34 060
c (i) £8738 (ii) £28 422

Page 334 Exercise 2

1 a (i) 16.77% (ii) 23.87% (iii) 26.82%
b (i) 16% APR is equivalent to a monthly rate of between 1.2% and 1.3%
(ii) 20%, between 1.5% and 1.6%

(iii) 25%, between 1.8% and 1.9%
c (i) £89.41 (ii) £91.68 (iii) £95.14
d (i) £276.75 (ii) £497.97 (iii) £5673.60
e (i) £2172.96
(ii) £2186.64
f Between £172.96 and £186.64
g Between £373.28 and £400.64
2 a £182.90 b £2194.80 c £194.80
3 a (i) £3719 (ii) £133 884 (iii) £33 884
b £51 272
4 a (i) £256.65 (without), £282.30 (with)
(ii) £188.05 (without), £212.50 (with)
b 36 months
c £1769.80 (without), £2650 (with)
5 a (i) £615.96 (ii) £14 783.04
b £115.20 more
6 a £375.10 b £8.25 c £383.35
d £11.50

Page 337 Exercise 3

1 a (i) = A2 + 1 (ii) = A3 + 1
(iii) = A4 + 1
b (i) = 12/A2 (ii) = 12/A3
(iii) = 12/A4
c (i) = A2*B2 (ii) = A3*B3
(iii) = A4*B4
d (i) = 2*(A2 + B2) (ii) = 2*(A3 + B3)
(iii) = 2*(A4 + B4)
e Between a 3 by 4 and a 4 by 3 rectangle
f (i) Changed from 1 to 3
(ii) = A2 + 0.1
(iii) 3.40 × 3.53, 3.50 × 3.43
g (i) Changed from 3.00 to 3.40, formula = A2 + 0.01, fixed precision 3
(ii) 2 decimal places are not enough to differentiate between rectangles
(iii) √12 = 3.46 (2 d.p.), solution is a square
2 a = B2*C2 b = B2*E2*1.5
c = D2 + F2 d = SUM(G2..G4)
3 a 3.5
b (i) = AVERAGE(B2..K2)
(ii) = AVERAGE(B6..K6)
c = AVERAGE(B2..K8)
= AVERAGE(L2..L8)
d = 48*RAND () + 1 entered in six cells. Repeat if doubles appear.
4 a A3, = A2 + 1, filled down
b $x = 1$ and $y = 3$ approx.
c $x = 0.8$ and $y = 2.6$

Page 340 Exercise 4

1 a
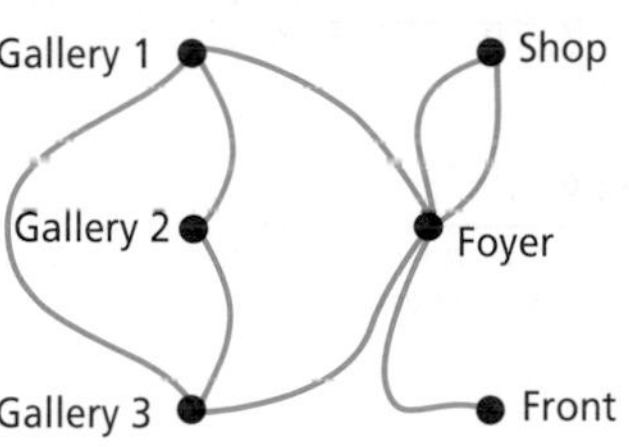

b
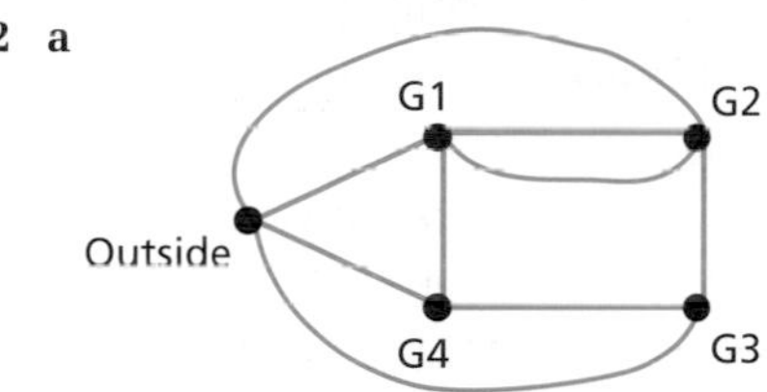

2 a
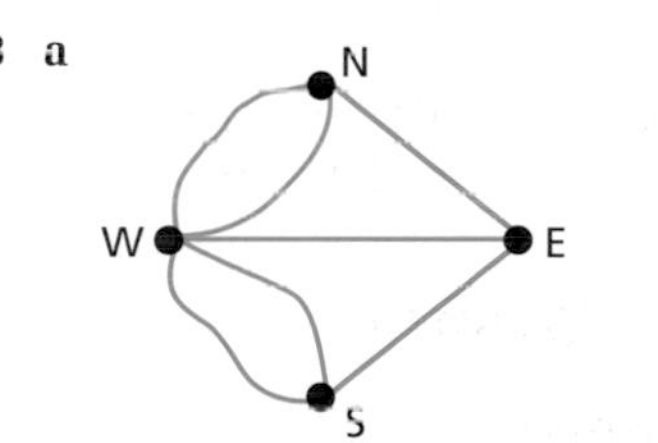

3 a
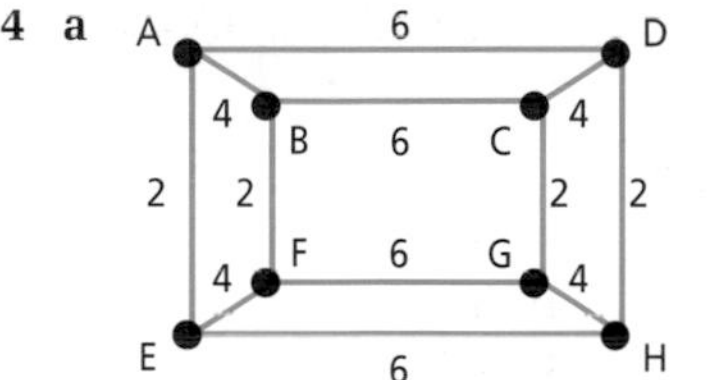

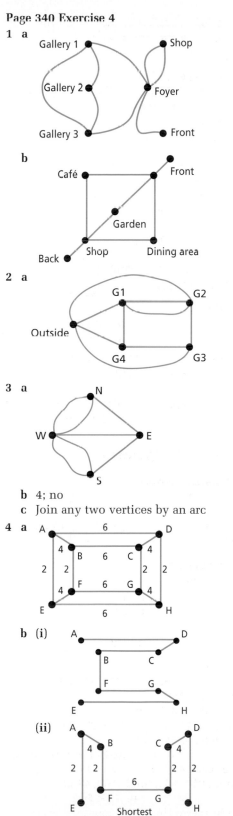

b 4; no
c Join any two vertices by an arc

4 a
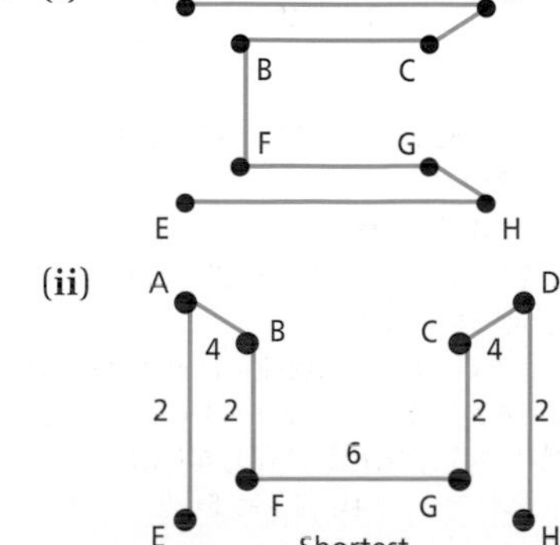

b (i)

A D B C F G E H

(ii)

A D B C 4 4 2 2 2 2 6 F G E H
Shortest

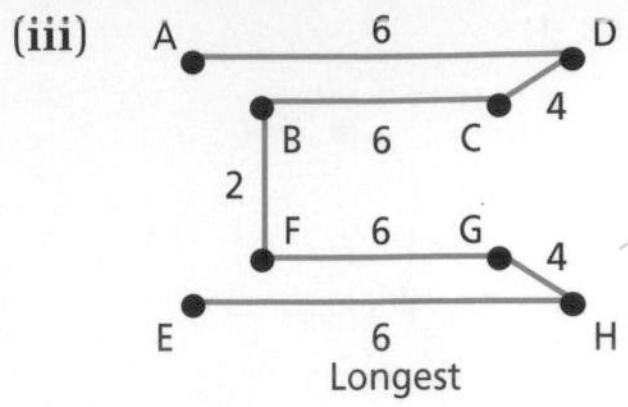

5 **a** (i) AGBFCED
(ii) AGBGFEDCEGA
b (i) BGAGFBCFECDE
(ii) BGFBCFECDE (omits A)

6

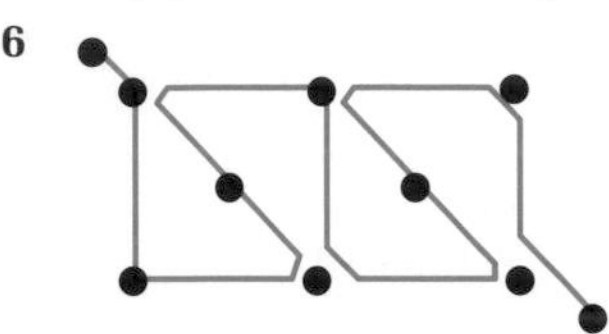

7 4 + (2 + 2 + 3) + (3 + 2) + 0 = 16 hours

Page 342 Exercise 5

1	**a** £12	**b** £128	**c** £196
2	**a** 75p	**b** £1.98	**c** £12.75
3	**a** £231.20	**b** £421	**c** £80
4	**a** £1280	**b** £2240	**c** £800
5	**a** 12		
	b (i) 13%	(ii) 43%	(iii) 80%

6 **a**

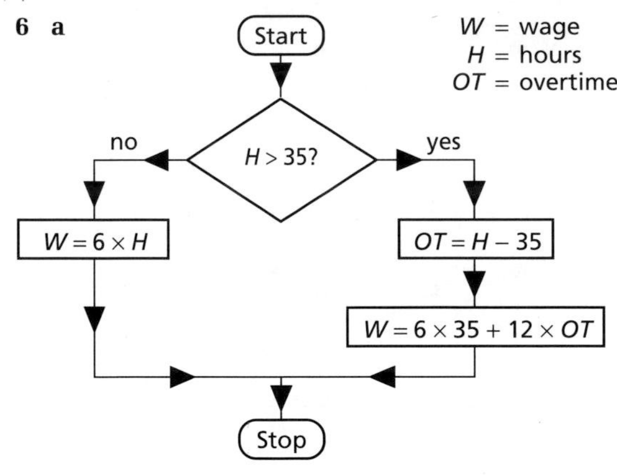

b (i) £180 (ii) £270

7

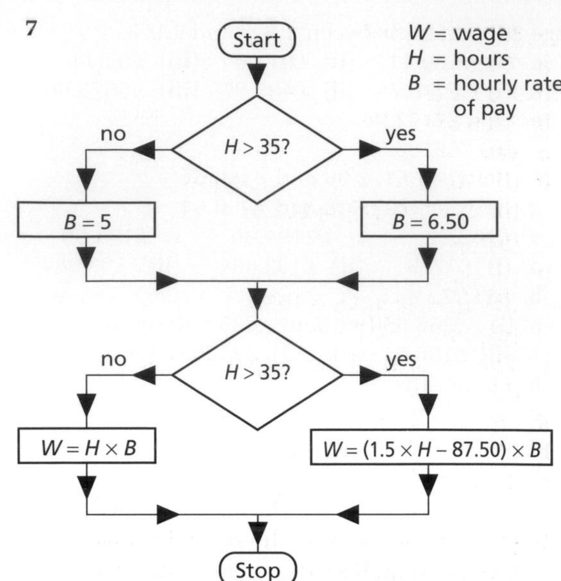

8

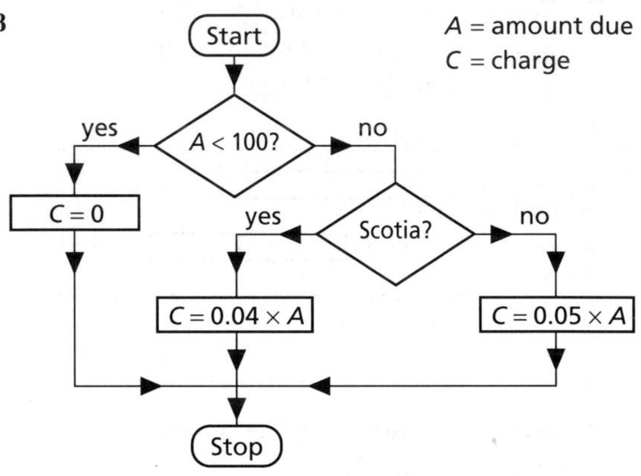

Page 345 Exercise 6

1 **a** 300 rpm **b** 583.3 rpm (1 d.p.)
2 **a** 16 cm **b** 56 cm **c** 400 m
3 **a** 6 m^2 **b** 12.6 m^2 **c** 5.44 m^2
4 **a** 7.3 cm **b** 4.67 cm
5 **a** 2 cm/s **b** 2.8 cm/s **c** 2.3 cm/s
6 **a** (i) 21.7 m^3 (ii) 8.98 m^3
b (i) 49.8 m^3 (ii) 18.2 m^3
7 **a** (i) 833 cm (ii) 941 cm
b 25 kg
8 **a** (i) 6 cm (ii) 9 cm (iii) 7.35 cm
b (i) 6 cm^2 (ii) 11.6 cm^2
(iii) 8.2 cm^2 (1 d.p.)

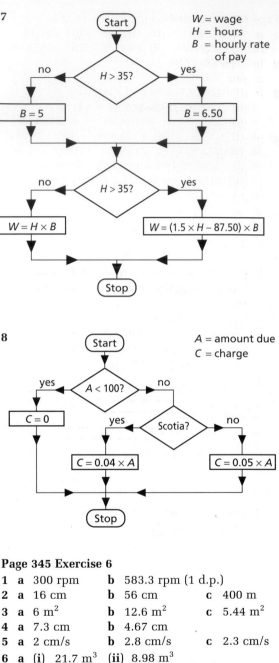

Page 347 Exercise 7

1 a $7 \leq L < 8$

c 7.6 hours

2 b 1006 ml

c yes

3 b (i) 101.5

(ii) $Q_1 = 100$, $Q_3 = 103.5$

(iii) 1.75

4 b (i) 100.5

(ii) $Q_1 = 99.8$, $Q_3 = 101.1$

(iii) 1.3

c The majority of the output fits the description

5 a 66

b 25, 35, 45, 55, 65, 75

c 55 km/h

6 a 66.4 cm

b 68.0 cm; on average, the second set were taller though the ranges in height were the same

7 a 8.31 cm, 8.38 cm

b Without: $Q_1 = 8.19$ cm, $Q_2 = 8.31$ cm, $Q_3 = 8.45$ cm; with: $Q_1 = 8.28$ cm, $Q_2 = 8.4$ cm, $Q_3 = 8.5$ cm

c

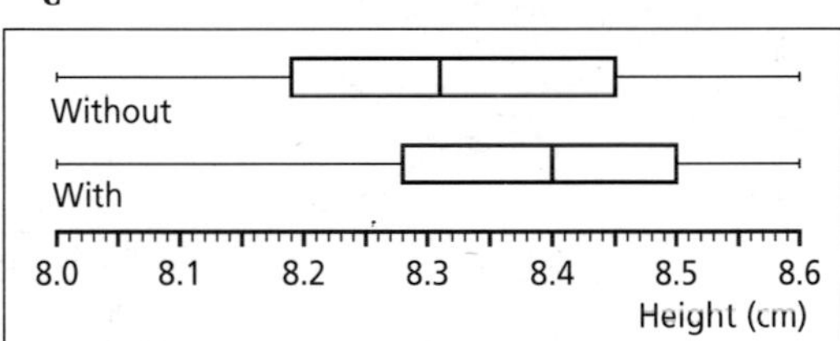

d The plants given fertiliser show an improved growth.